MCSA/MCSE

Self-Paced Training Kit

2

Second Edition

Microsoft

WINDOWS 2000
PROFESSIONAL

Exam 70-210

PUBLISHED BY
Microsoft Press
A Division of Microsoft Corporation
One Microsoft Way
Redmond, Washington 98052-6399

Library of Congress Cataloging-in-Publication Data
MCSE Training Kit--Microsoft Windows 2000 Professional / Microsoft Corporation.
      p. cm.
    Includes index.
    ISBN 1-57231-901-1
    ISBN 0-7356-1771-6 (Core Requirements, Second Edition)
    1. Electronic data processing personnel--Certification. 2. Microsoft software--Examinations--Study guides. 3. Microsoft Windows (Computer file) I. Microsoft Corporation.

    QA76.3 .M33454   2000
    005.4'4769--dc21   99-059499

Printed and bound in the United States of America.

2 3 4 5 6 7 8 9   QWT   7 6 5 4 3 2

Distributed in Canada by H.B. Fenn and Company Ltd.

A CIP catalogue record for this book is available from the British Library.

Microsoft Press books are available through booksellers and distributors worldwide. For further information about international editions, contact your local Microsoft Corporation office or contact Microsoft Press International directly at fax (425) 936-7329. Visit our Web site at www.microsoft.com/mspress. Send comments to *tkinput@microsoft.com.*

Acquisitions Editor: Jeff Madden
Project Editor: Michael Bolinger

Authors: Rick Wallace, Ethan Wilansky

SubAsy Part No. X08-78643
Body Part No. X08-73010

Contents

Part 2   Preparation for MCP Exam 70-210

About This Book

Welcome to the *MCSE Training Kit—Microsoft Windows 2000 Professional*. This book is organized in two parts. Part 1 is a self-paced training course designed to introduce you to the Windows 2000 family of products, and prepare you to install, configure, administer, and support Microsoft Windows 2000 Professional. Part 1 also prepares you for the related Microsoft Certified Professional exam 70-210: Installing, Configuring, and Administering Microsoft Windows 2000 Professional. Part 2 is designed to give you a focused, timesaving way to identify the information you need to know to pass the exam, and is accompanied by a realistic electronic assessment tool to help you become familiar with the types of questions that you will encounter on MCP exam 70-210. By reviewing the objectives and sample questions in Part 2, you can focus on the specific skills you need to improve before taking the exam.

Before You Begin Part 1

Part 1 introduces the various tools for administering and configuring Windows 2000 including the Microsoft Management Console, Task Scheduler, Control Panel, and the registry. You will learn about the network protocols and services that ship with Windows 2000. Part 1 concentrates on Transmission Control Protocol/Internet Protocol (TCP/IP), the network protocol of choice for Windows 2000. It also introduces you to the Domain Name System (DNS), which is an Internet and TCP/IP standard name service, and is required for Windows 2000 domains and directory services based on Active Directory technology.

Windows 2000 domains and Active Directory directory services are also introduced in this course, but both these features are available only with the Windows 2000 Server family of products. Active Directory directory services integrate the Internet concept of a namespace with Windows 2000 directory service. Active Directory directory services use DNS as its domain naming and location service so Windows 2000 domain names are also DNS names. In fact, the core unit of logical structure in Active Directory directory services is the domain.

Each chapter in Part 1 is divided into lessons. Most lessons include hands-on procedures that allow you to practice or demonstrate a particular concept or skill. Each lesson ends with a short summary and each chapter ends with a set of review questions to test your knowledge of the chapter material.

The "Getting Started" section of this chapter provides important setup instructions that describe the hardware and software requirements to complete the procedures in this course. It also provides information about the networking configuration necessary to complete some of the hands-on procedures. Read through this section thoroughly before you start the lessons.

Intended Audience

Anyone who wants to learn more about Windows 2000 Professional will find this book useful. This book was developed for information technology (IT) professionals who need to design, plan, implement, and support Windows 2000 Professional or who plan to take the related Microsoft Certified Professional exam 70-210, Installing, Configuring, and Administering Microsoft Windows 2000 Professional.

Note For more information on becoming a Microsoft Certified Systems Engineer, see the section, "The Microsoft Certified Professional Program," later in this chapter.

Prerequisites

This course requires that students meet the following prerequisite: A knowledge of the fundamentals of current networking technology is required.

Reference Materials

You might find the *Windows 2000 Professional Resource Kit* a useful reference for this training kit.

About the CD-ROM

The Supplemental Course Materials CD-ROM contains a variety of informational aids that may be used throughout this book. This includes an online version of the book, Internet Explorer 6.0, and an electronic assessment program for exam 70-210. For information regarding the contents of the CD-ROM, see the "Getting Started" and "Using the Electronic Assessment" sections, and the README.TXT file located in the root directory of the CD-ROM.

Features of This Book

Each chapter opens with a "Before You Begin" section, which prepares you for completing the chapter.

► The chapters are then broken into lessons. Whenever possible, lessons contain practices that give you an opportunity to use the skills being presented or explore the part of the application being described. All practices offer step-by-step procedures that are identified with a bullet symbol like the one to the left of this paragraph.

The "Review" section at the end of the chapter allows you to test what you have learned in the chapter's lessons. Appendix A, "Questions and Answers," contains all of Part 1's questions and corresponding answers.

Notes

Several types of notes appear throughout the lessons.

■ Notes marked **Tip** contain explanations of possible results or alternative methods.

Notes marked **Important** contain information that is essential to completing a task.

Notes marked **Note** contain supplemental information.

Notes marked **Caution** contain warnings about possible loss of data.

Conventions

The following conventions are used throughout Part 1.

Notational Conventions

Characters or commands that you type appear in **bold lowercase** type.

Italic in syntax statements indicates placeholders for variable information. *Italic* is also used for book titles.

Names of files and folders appear in Title Caps, except when you are to type them directly. Unless otherwise indicated, you can use all lowercase letters when you type a filename in a dialog box or at a command prompt.

Filename extensions appear in all lowercase.

Acronyms appear in all uppercase.

Monospace type represents code samples, examples of screen text, or entries that you might type at a command prompt or in initialization files.

Square brackets [ ] are used in syntax statements to enclose optional items. For example, [*filename*] in command syntax indicates that you can choose to type a filename with the command. Type only the information within the brackets, not the brackets themselves.

- Braces { } are used in syntax statements to enclose required items. Type only the information within the braces, not the braces themselves.

- Icons represent specific sections in the book as follows:

Icon	Represents
	A hands-on practice. You should perform the practice to give yourself an opportunity to use the skills being presented in the lesson.
	Chapter review questions. These questions at the end of each chapter allow you to test what you have learned in the lessons. You will find the answers to the review questions in Appendix A, "Questions and Answers."

Keyboard Conventions

- A plus sign (+) between two key names means that you must press those keys at the same time. For example, "Press Alt+Tab" means that you hold down Alt while you press Tab.

- A comma (,) between two or more key names means that you must press each of the keys consecutively, not together. For example, "Press Alt, F, X" means that you press and release each key in sequence. "Press Alt+W, L" means that you first press Alt and W together, and then release them and press L.

- You can choose menu commands with the keyboard. Press the Alt key to activate the menu bar, and then sequentially press the keys that correspond to the highlighted or underlined letter of the menu name and the command name. For some commands, you can also press a key combination listed on the menu.

- You can select or clear check boxes or option buttons in dialog boxes with the keyboard. Press the Alt key, and then press the key that corresponds to the underlined letter of the option name. Or you can press Tab until the option is highlighted, and then press the spacebar to select or clear the check box or option button.

- You can cancel the display of a dialog box by pressing the Esc key.

Chapter and Appendix Overview

This self-paced training course combines notes, hands-on procedures, and review questions to teach you how to install, configure, administer, and support Windows 2000 Professional. It is designed to be completed from beginning to end, but you can choose a customized track and complete only the sections that interest you. (See the next section, "Finding the Best Starting Point for You," for more information.) If you choose the customized track option, see the

"Before You Begin" section in each chapter. Any hands-on procedures that require preliminary work from preceding chapters refer to the appropriate chapters.

Part 1 is divided into the following chapters:

- The "About This Book" section contains a self-paced training overview and introduces the components of this training. Read this section thoroughly to get the greatest educational value from this self-paced training and to plan which lessons you will complete.

- Chapter 1, "Introduction to Windows 2000," presents an overview of the Windows 2000 operating system and the four products that make up this family. It introduces some of the new features and benefits of Windows 2000 and explains why Windows 2000 is easier to use and manage and provides greater compatibility, file management capabilities, and security than previous versions of Windows. This chapter also provides an introduction to workgroups and domains.

- Chapter 2, "Installing Windows 2000 Professional," presents a list of preinstallation tasks that you need to complete before you begin your installation, as well as the hardware requirements for installing Windows 2000 Professional. It then steps you through the process of installing from a CD-ROM, and as a hands-on exercise, has you install Windows 2000 Professional on your computer. Finally the chapter discusses installing Windows 2000 over the network and how to troubleshoot installation problems.

- Chapter 3, "Using Microsoft Management Console and Task Scheduler," presents two of the primary administrative tools available in Windows 2000: the Microsoft Management Console (the MMC) and Task Scheduler. It defines custom consoles, console trees, details panes, snap-ins, and extensions, and discusses the differences between Author mode and User mode. It also explains how you can use custom consoles for remote administration and troubleshooting. The hands-on portion has you use the MMC to create custom consoles, and then add a snap-in to an existing custom console. In the second hands-on practice, you configure Task Scheduler to launch a program, at a specified time.

- Chapter 4, "Using Windows Control Panel," presents some of the applications in Control Panel that you use to customize the hardware and software configuration for a computer. You use the System icon to configure hardware devices or services by creating and configuring hardware profiles. You also use it to configure performance options, environment variables, and startup and recovery settings. The hands-on practice allows you to change the paging file size and to add an environment variable. You use the Display icon to view or modify display properties. Windows 2000 supports a maximum of nine monitors. This chapter also includes a section on installing hardware, both Plug and Play hardware and non–Plug and Play hardware. It explains how to use the Add/Remove Hardware Wizard and how to manually install hardware.

- Chapter 5, "Using the Registry," introduces the registry, the hierarchical database where Windows 2000 stores system configuration information. This chapter also presents an overview of Registry Editor, a tool that allows you to view and modify the registry. The hands-on practice has you use Registry Editor to view information in the registry, use the Find Key command to search the registry, modify the registry by adding a value to it, and save a subtree as a file so that you can use an editor, like Notepad, to search the file.

- Chapter 6, "Managing Disks," presents an overview of Windows 2000 disk management. You can manage disks locally or on remote computers. You can create a custom console and add the Disk Management snap-in to it, or you can use the Disk Management snap-in included in the preconfigured Computer Management snap-in. The Disk Management snap-in provides shortcut menus to show you which tasks you can perform on the selected object, and it includes wizards to guide you through creating partitions and volumes and upgrading disks. The hands-on practice has you upgrade a basic disk to a dynamic disk, create a new volume, and mount a volume.

- Chapter 7, "Installing and Configuring Network Protocols," presents the skills and knowledge necessary to configure Transmission Control Protocol/Internet Protocol (TCP/IP) and to install other network protocols, including NWLink, NetBIOS Enhanced User Interface (NetBEUI), and Data Link Control (DLC). The chapter also discusses the process for configuring network bindings. The hands-on practices allow you to verify your computer's configuration and then configure your computer to use a static IP address. Next you configure your computer to use a DHCP server to automatically assign an IP address to your computer, and test the Automatic Private IP Addressing feature in Windows 2000. Finally, you install and configure NWLink, change the binding order, unbind a protocol, and then bind a protocol.

- Chapter 8, "Using the DNS Service," introduces Domain Name System (DNS), a distributed database that is used in TCP/IP networks to translate computer names to IP addresses. It also presents the skills and knowledge necessary to configure clients to use the DNS Service. In the hands-on practice, you configure a computer running Windows 2000 Professional to be a DNS client.

- Chapter 9, "Introducing Active Directory Directory Services," presents the Windows 2000 directory service, Active Directory directory services. A directory service uniquely identifies users and resources on a network. Active Directory directory services provide a single point of network management, allowing you to add, remove, and relocate users and resources easily. Active Directory directory services are available only with the Windows 2000 Server family of products.

- Chapter 10, "Setting Up and Managing User Accounts," introduces you to user accounts and how to plan your user accounts. It also presents the skills and knowledge necessary to create local user accounts and to set properties for them. In the hands-on practices, you create local user accounts. You then test the user accounts, modify some of the user account properties, and then test the modified user account properties.

- Chapter 11, "Setting Up and Managing Groups," introduces you to groups and to group user accounts to allow for easier assignment of permissions. It also presents the skills and knowledge necessary to implement local groups and built-in groups. In the hands-on practice, you create local groups, add members to the local groups when you create them, and add members to the groups after the groups have been created. You delete a member from one of the groups, and then you delete one of the local groups that you created.

- Chapter 12, "Setting Up and Configuring Network Printers," introduces you to the Windows 2000 printing terminology, as well as presenting the skills and knowledge necessary to set up and share network printers. This chapter also presents how to troubleshoot common printing problems that are associated with setting up network printers. In the hands-on practice, you use the Add Printer wizard to install and share a local printer. This chapter also introduces printer pools and setting priorities.

- Chapter 13, "Administering Network Printers," presents the four major types of tasks involved with administering network printers: managing printers, managing documents, troubleshooting printers, and performing tasks that require the Manage Printers permission. This chapter also explains how Microsoft Windows 2000 allows you to control printer usage and administration by assigning permissions. In the hands-on practices, you assign forms to paper trays, set up a separator page, and take ownership of a printer. You also print a document, set a notification for a document, change the priority for a document, and then cancel a document.

- Chapter 14, "Securing Resources with NTFS Permissions," introduces the NTFS folder and file permissions and explains how to assign them to user accounts and groups. It explains how moving or copying files and folders affects NTFS file and folder permissions. It also explains how to troubleshoot common resource access problems. In the hands-on practices, you plan and apply NTFS permissions for folders and files based on business scenarios, and then test them. You also observe the effects of taking ownership of a file, and determine the effects of permission and ownership when you copy or move files.

- Chapter 15, "Administering Shared Folders," explains how to share folders so that the folders and their contents are accessible over the network. This chapter also explains how sharing folders provides another way to secure file resources, one that can be used on FAT or FAT32 partitions. In the hands-on exercises, you share a folder, determine the current permissions for the shared folder and assign shared folder permissions to groups, and stop sharing a folder. In the optional hands-on exercises, you connect to a shared folder and test the combined effects of shared folder permissions and NTFS permissions.

- Chapter 16, "Auditing Resources and Events," introduces the Microsoft Windows 2000 Local Security Policy and Group Policy. One of the features controlled by Local Security Policy or Group Policy is auditing. Auditing is a tool for maintaining network security that allows you to track user activities and systemwide events. This chapter also introduces audit policies and what you need to consider before you set one up, as well as how to set up auditing on resources and how to maintain security logs. In the hands-on practices, you plan an audit policy for your computer, set up an audit policy by enabling auditing on certain events, view the security log file, and configure Event Viewer to overwrite events when the log file is filled.

- Chapter 17, "Configuring Group Policy and Local Security Policy," explains how to use the Windows 2000 Local Security Policy or Group Policy snap-in to improve the security on your computer. This chapter explains the Windows 2000 Account Policies and some of the available Security Options. In the first hands-on practice, you configure and test one of the Account Policies settings, Minimum Password Length. In the second hands-on practice, you configure and test three of the Security Policy settings.

- Chapter 18, "Managing Data Storage," introduces data storage management on NTFS-formatted volumes. Data management includes using compression, using disk quotas, increasing the security of files and folders on your computer by using the Encrypting File System (EFS), and defragmenting a disk. In the hands-on practice, you compress files and folders, display the compressed files and folders in a different color, uncompress a file, and test the effects that copying and moving files have on compression. You also configure default quota management settings to limit the amount of data users can store on a drive and configure a custom quota setting for a user account. You test the disk quota and then turn off quota management. Finally, you encrypt a file and then attempt to access it.

- Chapter 19, "Backing Up and Restoring Data," introduces the Windows Backup tool that allows you to back up and restore data. It explains the five types of backup—normal, copy, incremental, differential, and daily—and how these can be combined to meet your backup needs. In the hands-on practices, you use the Backup Wizard to back up some files to your hard disk, and you create a backup job to perform a backup operation later by using Task Scheduler. You then restore some of the files you backed up.

- Chapter 20, "Monitoring Access to Network Resources," prepares you to monitor network resources. You learn about the Shared Folders snap-in and how to use it to view and create shares. You also learn how to use the Shared Folders snap-in to view sessions and open files and how to use it to disconnect users from shared folders. In the hands-on practices, you use the Shared Folders snap-in to view the shared folders, to open files, and to disconnect all users from all open files. You also use the Shared Folders snap-in to create a new share and then stop sharing it.

- Chapter 21, "Configuring Remote Access," presents the new protocols for use with remote access, and it provides an understanding of the new options and interfaces in Windows 2000 to connect computers and configure protocols correctly to meet all your remote access requirements. In the hands-on practices, you use Network And Dial-up Connections to launch the Network Connection wizard to configure an inbound dial-up connection and allow Virtual Private Connections, and then to configure an outbound connection.

- Chapter 22, "The Windows 2000 Boot Process," introduces the Microsoft Windows 2000 boot process for Intel-based computers. It also introduces the Boot.ini file and explains how to create a Windows 2000 boot disk. In the hands-on practice, you create a Windows 2000 boot disk for Intel-based computers and then test it. In addition, you repair a boot problem by using a Windows 2000 boot disk and by using the Last Known Good Configuration option.

- Chapter 23, "Deploying Windows 2000," introduces Setup Manager and the system preparation tools. Setup Manager makes it easy to create the Unattend.txt files that are necessary for scripted installations, and the System Preparation tool helps you prepare master disk images for efficient mass installations. This chapter also explains remote installations, outlines how to install and configure remote installation servers, lists the client requirements for remote installations, and lists the steps to create boot floppies and a remote boot disk to help you efficiently deploy Windows 2000 Professional. Finally, this chapter explains how to upgrade previous versions of Windows to Windows 2000 and how to deploy service packs.

- Chapter 24, "Configuring Windows 2000 for Mobile Computers," introduces the new features in Microsoft Windows 2000 Professional that make mobile computing easier to do. The features discussed in this chapter include using offline folders and files, using Synchronization Manager, configuring and using power schemes, enabling Hibernate mode, and enabling Advanced Power Management.

- Chapter 25, "Implementing, Managing, and Troubleshooting Hardware Devices and Drivers," introduces Device Manager and explains how you use it to manage and troubleshoot devices. It also introduces the System Information snap-in and explains how it helps you manage your system. You learn how to use Device Manager, the System File Checker utility, and the Windows Signature Verification utility to configure, monitor, and troubleshoot driver signing. You also learn how to use Device Manager to upgrade your computer from a single processor to a multiprocessor system, and you learn how to use Performance Console as a tool to monitor system performance. Finally, you learn how to install, configure, and troubleshoot miscellaneous devices, including fax support, scanners, cameras, and mouse devices.

Following Part 2 you will find:

- Appendix A, "Questions and Answers," lists all of the practice questions and review questions from Part 1, showing the chapter and section where the question appears, and the suggested answer.

- Appendix B, "Creating Setup Boot Disks," outlines the steps to create the Windows 2000 Setup disks for computers that don't support booting from a CD-ROM drive.

- Appendix C, "Understanding the DHCP Service," provides an introduction to the DHCP service.

- Appendix D, "Managing Backup Tapes," provides an introduction to rotating and archiving backup tapes.

- The glossary provides definitions for many of the key words and concepts presented in the course. It also contains some additional basic networking terminology.

Finding the Best Starting Point for You

Because Part 1 is self-paced, you can skip some lessons and revisit them later. But note that you must complete the procedures in Chapter 2, "Installing Windows 2000 Professional," before you can perform procedures in the other chapters. Use the following table to find the best starting point for you:

If you	Follow this learning path
Are preparing to take the Microsoft Certified Professional exam 70-210, Installing, Configuring, and Administering Microsoft Windows 2000 Professional	Read the "Getting Started" section. Then work through Chapters 1–2. Work through the remaining chapters in any order.
Are reviewing information about specific topics from the exam	Use the "Where to Find Specific Skills in This Book" section that follows this table.

Where to Find Specific Skills in This Book

The following tables provide a list of the skills measured on certification exam 70-210, Installing, Configuring, and Administering Microsoft Windows 2000 Professional. The table provides the skill, and where in this book you will find the lesson relating to that skill. For sample questions to help gauge your readiness for exam 70-210, see Part 2, "Preparation for MCP Exam 70-210."

Note Exam skills are subject to change without prior notice and at the sole discretion of Microsoft.

Installing Windows 2000 Professional

Skill Being Measured	Location in Book
Perform an attended installation of Windows 2000 Professional	Chapter 2, Lessons 2 and 3
Perform an unattended installation of Windows 2000 Professional	Chapter 23, Lessons 1–3
Upgrade from a previous version of Windows to Windows 2000 Professional	Chapter 23, Lessons 1 and 4
Deploy service packs	Chapter 23, Lesson 5
Troubleshoot failed installations	Chapter 2, Lesson 4

Implementing and Conducting Administration of Resources

Skill Being Measured	Location in Book
Monitor, manage, and troubleshoot access to files and folders	Chapter 14, Lessons 1–6 Chapter 18, Lesson 1
Manage and troubleshoot access to shared folders	Chapter 15, Lessons 1, 3, and 4
Connect to local and network print devices	Chapter 12, Lesson 3 Chapter 13, Lessons 1–3
Configure and manage file systems	Chapter 2, Lesson 1

Implementing, Managing, and Troubleshooting Hardware Devices and Drivers

Skill Being Measured	Location in Book
Implement, manage, and troubleshoot disk devices	Chapter 4, Lessons 4 and 5 Chapter 6, Lessons 1 and 2 Chapter 18, Lesson 2 Chapter 25, Lesson 1
Implement, manage, and troubleshoot display devices	Chapter 4, Lessons 2, 4, and 5 Chapter 25, Lesson 1
Implement, manage, and troubleshoot mobile computer hardware	Chapter 24, Lesson 2
Implement, manage, and troubleshoot input and output devices	Chapter 25, Lessons 1 and 4
Update drivers	Chapter 25, Lesson 3
Monitor and configure multiple processing units	Chapter 25, Lesson 3
Install, configure, and troubleshoot network adapters	Chapter 7, Lessons 1–4 Chapter 25, Lesson 1

Monitoring and Optimizing System Performance and Reliability

Skill Being Measured	Location in Book
Manage and troubleshoot driver signing	Chapter 25, Lesson 2
Configure, manage, and troubleshoot Task Scheduler	Chapter 3, Lesson 3
Manage and troubleshoot the use and synchronization of offline files	Chapter 24, Lesson 1
Optimize and troubleshoot performance of the Windows 2000 Professional desktop	Chapter 4, Lesson 3 Chapter 7, Lesson 4 Chapter 18, Lesson 4 Chapter 25, Lesson 3
Manage hardware profiles	Chapter 3, Lesson 1 Chapter 4, Lesson 1 Chapter 25, Lessons 1, 3, and 4
Recover systems and user data	Chapter 22, Lessons 3 and 5

Configuring and Troubleshooting the Desktop Environment

Skill Being Measured	Location in Book
Configure and manage user profiles	Chapter 10, Lesson 4
Configure support for multiple languages or multiple locations	Chapter 4, Lesson 6
Manage applications by using Windows Installer packages	Chapter 1, Lesson 2
Configure and troubleshoot desktop settings	Chapter 4, Lesson 6
Configure and troubleshoot fax support	Chapter 25, Lesson 4
Configure and troubleshoot accessibility services	Chapter 4, Lesson 6

Implementing, Managing, and Troubleshooting Network Protocols and Services

Skill Being Measured	Location in Book
Configure and troubleshoot the TCP/IP protocol	Chapter 7, Lesson 1
Connect to computers by using dial-up networking	Chapter 21, Lessons 2 and 3
Connect to shared resources on a Microsoft network	Chapter 15, Lessons 1–4

Implementing, Monitoring, and Troubleshooting Security

Skill Being Measured	Location in Book
Encrypt data on a hard disk by using Encrypting File System (EFS)	Chapter 18, Lesson 3
Implement, configure, manage, and troubleshoot local security policy	Chapter 11, Lessons 1–2 Chapter 18, Lesson 3
Implement, configure, manage, and troubleshoot local user accounts	Chapter 10, Lessons 1–4 Chapter 11, Lessons 1 and 2
Implement, configure, manage, and troubleshoot local user authentication	Chapter 10, Lessons 1–4
Implement, configure, manage, and troubleshoot a security configuration	Chapter 16, Lesson 3 Chapter 17, Lessons 1 and 2 Chapter 18, Lesson 3

Getting Started

This self-paced training course contains hands-on procedures to help you learn about Windows 2000 Professional.

Hardware Requirements

Each computer must have the following minimum configuration. All hardware should be on the Microsoft Windows 2000 Professional Hardware Compatibility List.

- 133 MHz or higher Pentium-compatible CPU
- 64 MB RAM
- One or more hard disks with a minimum of 650 MB of free disk space (2 GB recommended)
- Network adapter card
- Video display adapter with VGA resolution or higher
- CD-ROM drive, 12X or faster recommended (Note: A CD-ROM drive is not required for installing Windows 2000 over a network.)
- Keyboard
- Microsoft Mouse or compatible pointing device

Software Requirements

Microsoft Windows 2000 Professional is required to complete the procedures in this course.

Setup Instructions

Complete installation instructions are provided in Lesson 2, "Installing Windows 2000 from a CD-ROM," of Chapter 2, "Installing Windows 2000 Professional."

About the eBook

The Supplemental Course Materials CD-ROM includes an online version of the book that you can view on screen using Microsoft Internet Explorer 5.01 or later. For installation information, see the README.TXT file included in the root directory of the Supplemental Course Materials CD-ROM.

Note You must have the CD inserted in your CD-ROM drive for the online version of the book to run properly.

Before You Begin Part 2

Part 2 will help you evaluate your readiness for the MCP Exam 70-210: Installing, Configuring, and Administering Microsoft Windows 2000 Professional. When you pass this exam, you earn core credit toward Microsoft Certified Systems Engineer (MCSE) certification. In addition, when you pass this exam, you achieve Microsoft Certified Professional status.

Note You can find a complete list of MCP exams and their related objectives on the Microsoft Certified Professional Web site at *http://www.microsoft.com/mcp/*.

The Components of Part 2

An electronic assessment program for Exam 70-210 is provided on the Supplemental Course Materials CD. This program is a practice certification test that helps you evaluate your skills. It provides instant scoring feedback so that you can determine areas in which additional study might be helpful before you take the certification exam. Although your score on the electronic assessment does not necessarily indicate what your score will be on the certification exam, it does give you the opportunity to answer questions that are similar to those on the actual certification exam.

Part 2 is organized by the exam's objectives. Each chapter of the book covers one of the seven primary groups of objectives on the actual exam, called the *Objective*

Domains. Each Objective Domain lists the tested skills you need to master in order to answer the exam questions. Because the certification exams focus on real-world skills, the "Tested Skills and Suggested Practices" sections emphasize the practical application of the exam objectives. Each Objective Domain includes a list of further readings to help you understand the objectives and increase your ability to perform the tasks or skills specified by the objectives.

Within each Objective Domain, you will find the related objectives that are covered on the exam. Each objective provides you with the following:

- Key terms you must know to understand the objective. Knowing these terms can help you answer the objective's questions correctly.

- Several sample exam questions with the correct answers. The answers are accompanied by explanations of each correct and incorrect answer. (These questions match the questions on the electronic assessment.)

Take the electronic assessment first to determine which exam objectives you need to study; then use the book to learn more about those particular objectives. You can also use the book to research the answers to specific sample test questions. Keep in mind that to pass the exam, you should understand not only the answer to the question, but also the concepts on which the correct answer is based.

MCP Exam Prerequisites

No exams or classes are required before you take the Installing, Configuring, and Administering Microsoft Windows 2000 Professional exam. However, in addition to the skills tested by the exam, you should have a working knowledge of the operation and support of hardware and software in standalone computers. This knowledge should include the following:

- Be able to use an operating system with a graphical user interface, such as Microsoft Windows 95, Microsoft Windows 98, Microsoft Windows NT 4.0, or Microsoft Windows 2000.

- Understand current networking technology.

- Successfully complete Part 1, "Self-Paced Training for Microsoft Windows 2000 Professional."

Note After you have determined that you are prepared for the exam, use the Get More MCP Information link provided on the home page of the electronic assessment tool for information on scheduling the exam. You can schedule exams up to six weeks in advance, or as late as one working day before the exam date.

Know the Products

Microsoft's certification program relies on exams that measure your ability to perform a specific job function or set of tasks. Microsoft develops the exams by analyzing the tasks performed by people who are currently working in the field. Therefore, the specific knowledge, skills, and abilities relating to the job are reflected in the certification exam.

Because the certification exams are based on real-world tasks, you need to gain hands-on experience with the applicable technology to master the exam. You should consider hands-on experience a prerequisite for passing an MCP exam. Many of the questions relate directly to Microsoft products or technology, so use opportunities at your organization or home to practice using the relevant tools.

Using the Electronic Assessment and Part 2

Although you can use the electronic assessment and Part 2 in a number of ways, you might start your studies by taking the electronic assessment as a pretest. After completing the exam, review your results for each Objective Domain and focus your study first on the Objective Domains on which you received the lowest scores. The electronic assessment allows you to print your results, and a printed report of how you fared can be useful when reviewing the exam material in this book.

After you have taken the electronic assessment, use Part 2 of the book to learn more about the Objective Domains that you find difficult and to find listings of appropriate study materials that might supplement your knowledge. By reviewing why the answers are correct or incorrect, you can determine whether you need to study the objective topics more.

You can also use Part 2 to focus on the exact objectives that you need to master. Each objective in the book contains several questions that help you determine whether you understand the information related to that particular skill. Part 2 is also designed to allow you to answer each question before turning the page to review the correct answer.

The best method to prepare for the MCP exam is to use Part 2 in conjunction with the electronic assessment and other study material. A thorough study of the material combined with substantial real-world experience is the best preparation for the MCP exam.

Understanding the Conventions for Part 2

Before you begin Part 2, you need to understand the terms and conventions used in the electronic assessment and book.

Question Numbering System

The electronic assessment tool and Part 2 of the book contain reference numbers for each question. Understanding the numbering format will help you use this part of the training kit more effectively. When Microsoft creates the exams, the questions are grouped by job skills called *objectives*. These objectives are then organized by sections known as *Objective Domains*. Each question can be identified by the Objective Domain and the objective it covers. The question numbers follow this format:

Test Number.Objective Domain.Objective.Question Number

For example, question number 70-210.02.01.003 means this is question three (003) for the first objective (01) in the second Objective Domain (02) of the Installing, Configuring, and Administering Microsoft Windows 2000 Professional exam (70-210). Each question is numbered based on its presentation in the printed book. You can use this numbering system to reference questions on the electronic assessment or in Part 2 of the book. Even though the questions in the book are organized by objective, questions in the electronic assessment and the actual certification exam are presented in random order.

Notational Conventions

The following conventions are used throughout Part 2 to differentiate various technical elements:

- Characters or commands that you type appear in **bold lowercase** type. Bold type is also used to identify key terms in the text that are defined in the glossary of the electronic assessment program.
- Variable information, URLs, and emphasized words are *italicized*. *Italic* is also used for book titles.
- Acronyms, filenames with extensions, and NetBIOS short names for domains appear in FULL CAPITALS.
- Folder names and interface elements, such as radio buttons and check box labels, are displayed in Initial Capitals.

Notes

Notes appear throughout the book.

- Notes marked **Caution** contain information you will want to know before continuing with the book's material.
- Notes marked **Note** contain supplemental information.
- Notes marked **Tip** contain helpful process hints.

Using the Electronic Assessment

The electronic assessment is designed to provide you with an experience that simulates that of the actual MCP exam. The electronic assessment questions are similar to those you will see on the certification exam. Furthermore, the electronic assessment format approximates the certification exam format and includes additional features to help you prepare for the real exam.

Each iteration of the electronic assessment consists of 50 questions covering all the objectives for the Installing, Configuring, and Administering Microsoft Windows 2000 Professional exam. (The actual certification exams generally consist of 50 to 70 questions.) Just as on a real certification exam, you see questions from the objectives in random order during the practice test. Similar to the certification exam, the electronic assessment allows you to mark questions and review them after you finish the test.

To increase its value as a study aid, you can take the electronic assessment multiple times. Each time, you are presented with a different set of questions in a revised order; however, some questions might be repeated.

If you have used one of the certification exam preparation tests available from Microsoft, the electronic assessment should look familiar. The difference is that the electronic assessment provides you with the opportunity to learn as you take the exam.

Installing and Running the Electronic Assessment Software

Before you begin using the electronic assessment, you need to install the software. You need a computer running Microsoft Windows 95 or Windows NT 4.0 with Service Pack 3 or later and Internet Explorer 5.01 or later with the following minimum configuration:

- A multimedia PC with a 75-MHz Pentium or higher processor
- Microsoft Internet Explorer 5.01 or later
- 16 MB RAM for Windows 95 or Windows 98, or

- 32 MB RAM for Windows NT, or
- 64 MB RAM for Windows 2000
- 17 MB of available hard disk space
- A double-speed CD-ROM drive or better
- A super VGA display with at least 256 colors
- A Microsoft Mouse or compatible pointing device (recommended)

▶   **To install the electronic assessment, perform these steps.**

1. Insert the Supplemental Course Materials compact disc into your CD-ROM drive.

   A starting menu will display automatically, with links to the resources included on the CD-ROM. Click the link to the exam you want to install.

2. Click Next.

   The License Agreement dialog box appears.

3. To continue with the installation of the electronic assessment engine, you must accept the license agreement by clicking Yes.

4. The Choose Destination Location dialog box appears showing a default installation directory.

   Either accept the default or change the installation directory if needed. Click Next to copy the files to your hard drive.

5. A Question dialog box appears asking whether you would like Setup to create a desktop shortcut for this program. If you click Yes, an icon will be placed on your desktop.

6. The Setup Complete dialog box appears. Select whether you want to view the README.TXT file after closing the Setup program, and then click Finish.

   The electronic assessment software is completely installed. If you chose to view the README.TXT file, it will launch in a new window. For optimal viewing, enable word wrap.

To start the electronic assessment, follow these steps.

1. From the Start menu, point to Programs, point to MCSE Readiness Review, and then click MCSE RR Exam 70-210.

   The electronic assessment program starts.

2. Click Start Test.

   Information about the electronic assessment program appears.

3. Click OK.

> **Note** The electronic assessment programs are designed to run one at a time and will not run simultaneously with other electronic assessment programs.

Taking the Electronic Assessment

The electronic assessment consists of 50 multiple-choice questions, and as in the certification exam, you can skip questions or mark them for later review. Each exam question contains a question number that you can use to refer back to Part 2 of the book.

Before you end the electronic assessment, you should make sure to answer all of the questions. When the exam is graded, unanswered questions are counted as incorrect and will lower your score. Similarly, on the actual certification exam, you should complete all questions or they will be counted as incorrect. No trick questions appear on the exam. The correct answer will always be among the list of choices. Some questions might have more than one correct answer, and this will be indicated in the question. A good strategy is to eliminate the most obvious incorrect answers first to make it easier for you to select the correct answers.

You have 75 minutes to complete the electronic assessment. During the exam, you will see a timer indicating the amount of time you have remaining. This will help you to gauge the amount of time you should use to answer each question and to complete the exam. The amount of time you are given on the actual certification exam varies with each exam. Generally, certification exams take approximately 90 minutes to complete.

Ending and Grading the Electronic Assessment

When you click the Score Test button, you have the opportunity to review the questions you marked or left incomplete. The electronic assessment is graded when you click the Score Test button, and the software presents your section scores and your total score.

> **Note** You can always end a test without grading your electronic assessment by clicking the Home button.

After your electronic assessment is graded, you can view the correct and incorrect answers by clicking the Review Questions button.

Interpreting the Electronic Assessment Results

The Score screen shows you the number of questions in each Objective Domain section, the number of questions you answered correctly, and a percentage grade for each section. You can use the Score screen to determine where to spend additional time studying. On the actual certification exam, the number of questions and passing score will depend on the exam you are taking. The electronic assessment records your score each time you grade an exam so that you can track your progress over time.

▶ **To view your progress and exam records, follow these steps.**

1. From the electronic assessment main menu, click View History.

   All of your attempt scores appear.

2. Click on a test attempt date/time to view your score for each objective domain.

   The section score for each attempt appears. You can review the section score information to determine which Objective Domains you should study further. You can also use the scores to determine your progress as you continue to study and prepare for the real exam.

Ordering More Questions

Self Test Software offers practice tests to help you prepare for a variety of MCP certification exams. These practice tests contain hundreds of additional questions and are similar to the electronic assessment. For a fee, you can order exam practice tests for this exam and other Microsoft certification exams. Click the Order More Questions link on the electronic assessment home page for more information.

Using Part 2 of This Book

You can use Part 2 of the book as a supplement to the electronic assessment or as a standalone study aid. If you decide to use the book as a standalone study aid, review the Table of Contents to find topics of interest or an appropriate starting point for you. To get the greatest benefit from the book, use the electronic assessment as a pretest to determine which Objective Domains to study. Or, if you would like to research specific questions while taking the electronic assessment, you can use the question number located on the question screen to reference the question number in the book.

One way to determine areas where additional study might be helpful is to carefully review your individual section scores from the electronic assessment and note objective areas where your score could be improved. The section scores correlate to the Objective Domains listed in the book.

Reviewing the Objectives

Each Objective Domain in the book contains an introduction and a list of practice skills. Each list of practice skills describes suggested tasks you can perform to help you understand the objectives. Some of the tasks suggest reading additional material, while others are hands-on practices using software or hardware. Pay particular attention to the hands-on suggestions, as the certification exam reflects real-world knowledge you can gain only by working with the technology. Increasing your real-world experience will improve your performance on the exam.

After you have determined the objectives you would like to study, you can use the Table of Contents to locate the objectives in Part 2 of the book. When reviewing a specific objective, you should make sure you understand the purpose of the objective and the skill or knowledge it is measuring on the certification exam. You can study each objective separately, but you might need to understand the concepts explained in other objectives.

Make sure you understand the key terms in each objective. You will need a thorough understanding of these terms to answer the objective's questions correctly. Key term definitions are located in the glossary of the electronic assessment on the Supplemental Course Materials compact disc.

Reviewing the Questions

Each objective contains three or more questions followed by the possible answers. After you review the question and select a probable answer, you can turn to the corresponding answer section to determine whether you answered the question correctly. (For information about the question numbering format, see "Question Numbering System," earlier in this introduction.)

Part 2 briefly discusses each possible answer and provides a specific reason why each answer is correct or incorrect. You should review the answer explanations to help you understand why the correct answer is the best answer among the choices given. You should understand not only the answer to the question, but the concepts that the correct answer is based on. If you feel you need more information about a topic or you do not understand the answer, use the "Further Readings" section to learn where you can find more information.

The answers to the questions in Part 2 and the electronic assessment are based on current industry specifications and standards. However, the information provided by the answers is subject to change as technology improves and changes.

The Microsoft Certified Professional Program

The Microsoft Certified Professional (MCP) program provides the best method to prove your command of current Microsoft products and technologies. Microsoft, an industry leader in certification, is on the forefront of testing methodology. Our exams and corresponding certifications are developed to validate your mastery of critical competencies as you design and develop, or implement and support, solutions with Microsoft products and technologies. Computer professionals who become Microsoft certified are recognized as experts and are sought after industry-wide.

The Microsoft Certified Professional program offers multiple certifications, based on specific areas of technical expertise, including:

- *Microsoft Certified Professional (MCP).* Demonstrated in-depth knowledge of at least one Microsoft operating system. Candidates may pass additional Microsoft certification exams to further qualify their skills with Microsoft BackOffice products, development tools, or desktop programs.

- *Microsoft Certified Professional + Internet.* MCPs with a specialty in the Internet are qualified to plan security, install and configure server products, manage server resources, extend servers to run scripts, monitor and analyze performance, and troubleshoot problems.

- *Microsoft Certified Professional + Site Building.* Demonstrated what it takes to plan, build, maintain, and manage Web sites using Microsoft technologies and products.

- *Microsoft Certified Systems Administrator (MCSA)* on Microsoft Windows 2000. Individuals who implement, manage, and troubleshoot existing network and system environments based on the Microsoft Windows 2000 and Windows .NET Server operating systems.

- *Microsoft Certified Systems Engineer (MCSE).* Qualified to effectively plan, implement, maintain, and support information systems in a wide range of computing environments with Microsoft Windows NT Server and the Microsoft BackOffice integrated family of server software.

- *Microsoft Certified Systems Engineer + Internet.* MCSEs with an advanced qualification to enhance, deploy, and manage sophisticated intranet and Internet solutions that include a browser, proxy server, host servers, database, and messaging and commerce components. In addition, an MCSE + Internet–certified professional is able to manage and analyze Web sites.

- *Microsoft Certified Database Administrator (MCDBA).* Individuals who derive physical database designs, develop logical data models, create physical databases, create data services by using Transact-SQL, manage and maintain databases, configure and manage security, monitor and optimize databases, and install and configure Microsoft SQL Server.

- *Microsoft Certified Solution Developer (MCSD).* Qualified to design and develop custom business solutions with Microsoft development tools, technologies, and platforms, including Microsoft Office and Microsoft BackOffice.

- *Microsoft Certified Trainer (MCT).* Instructionally and technically qualified to deliver Microsoft Official Curriculum through a Microsoft Certified Technical Education Center (CTEC).

Microsoft Certification Benefits

Microsoft certification, one of the most comprehensive certification programs available for assessing and maintaining software-related skills, is a valuable measure of an individual's knowledge and expertise. Microsoft certification is awarded to individuals who have successfully demonstrated their ability to perform specific tasks and implement solutions with Microsoft products. Not only does this provide an objective measure for employers to consider, it also provides guidance for what an individual should know to be proficient. And as with any skills-assessment and benchmarking measure, certification brings a variety of benefits to the individual and to employers and organizations.

Microsoft Certification Benefits for Individuals

As a Microsoft Certified Professional, you receive many benefits:

- Industry recognition of your knowledge and proficiency with Microsoft products and technologies.
- Access to technical and product information directly from Microsoft through a secured area of the MCP Web site.
- MSDN Online Certified Membership that helps you tap into the best technical resources, connect to the MCP community, and gain access to valuable resources and services. (Some MSDN Online benefits might be available only in English or might not be available in all countries.) See the MSDN Web site for a growing list of certified member benefits.
- Logos to enable you to identify your Microsoft Certified Professional status to colleagues or clients.
- Invitations to Microsoft conferences, technical training sessions, and special events.
- A Microsoft Certified Professional certificate.
- Subscription to *Microsoft Certified Professional Magazine* (North America only), a career and professional development magazine.

Additional benefits, depending on your certification and geography, include

- A complimentary one-year subscription to the *Microsoft TechNet Technical Plus*, providing valuable information on monthly CD-ROMs.
- A one-year subscription to the Microsoft Beta Evaluation program. This benefit provides you with up to 12 free monthly CD-ROMs containing beta software (English only) for many of Microsoft's newest software products.

Microsoft Certification Benefits for Employers and Organizations

Through certification, computer professionals can maximize the return on investment in Microsoft technology. Research shows that Microsoft certification provides organizations with

- Excellent return on training and certification investments by providing a standard method of determining training needs and measuring results.

- Increased customer satisfaction and decreased support costs through improved service, increased productivity, and greater technical self-sufficiency.

- A reliable benchmark for hiring, promoting, and career planning.

- Recognition and rewards for productive employees by validating their expertise.

- Retraining options for existing employees so they can work effectively with new technologies.

- Assurance of quality when outsourcing computer services.

Requirements for Becoming a Microsoft Certified Professional

The certification requirements differ for each certification and are specific to the products and job functions addressed by the certification.

To become a Microsoft Certified Professional, you must pass rigorous certification exams that provide a valid and reliable measure of technical proficiency and expertise. These exams are designed to test your expertise and ability to perform a role or task with a product, and are developed with the input of professionals in the industry. Questions in the exams reflect how Microsoft products are used in actual organizations, giving them real-world relevance.

Microsoft Certified Product Specialists are required to pass one operating system exam. Candidates can pass additional Microsoft certification exams to further qualify their skills with Microsoft BackOffice products, development tools, or desktop applications.

Microsoft Certified Professional + Internet specialists are required to pass the prescribed Microsoft Windows NT Server 4, TCP/IP, and Microsoft Internet Information System exam series.

Microsoft Certified Professionals with a specialty in site building are required to pass two exams covering Microsoft FrontPage, Microsoft Site Server, and Microsoft Visual InterDev technologies to provide a valid and reliable measure of technical proficiency and expertise.

Microsoft Certified Systems Engineers are required to pass a series of core Microsoft Windows operating system and networking exams, and BackOffice technology elective exams.

Microsoft Certified Systems Engineers + Internet specialists are required to pass seven operating system exams and two elective exams that provide a valid and reliable measure of technical proficiency and expertise.

Microsoft Certified Database Administrators are required to pass three core exams and one elective exam that provide a valid and reliable measure of technical proficiency and expertise.

Microsoft Certified Solution Developers are required to pass two core Microsoft Windows operating system technology exams and two BackOffice technology elective exams.

Microsoft Certified Trainers are required to meet instructional and technical requirements specific to each Microsoft Official Curriculum course they are certified to deliver. In the United States and Canada, call Microsoft at (800) 636-7544 for more information on becoming a Microsoft Certified Trainer, or visit *http://www.microsoft.com/traincert/mcp/*. Outside the United States and Canada, contact your local Microsoft subsidiary.

Technical Training for Computer Professionals

Technical training is available in a variety of ways, with instructor-led classes, online instruction, or self-paced training available at thousands of locations worldwide.

Self-Paced Training

For motivated learners who are ready for the challenge, self-paced instruction is the most flexible, cost-effective way to increase your knowledge and skills.

A full line of self-paced print and computer-based training materials is available direct from the source—Microsoft Press. Microsoft Official Curriculum courseware kits from Microsoft Press designed for advanced computer system professionals are available from Microsoft Press and the Microsoft Developer Division. Self-paced training kits from Microsoft Press feature print-based instructional materials, along with CD-ROM-based product software, multimedia presentations, lab exercises, and practice files. The Mastering Series provides in-depth, interactive training on CD-ROM for experienced developers. They're both great ways to prepare for Microsoft Certified Professional (MCP) exams.

Online Training

For a more flexible alternative to instructor-led classes, turn to online instruction. It's as near as the Internet and it's ready whenever you are. Learn at your own pace and on your own schedule in a virtual classroom, often with easy access to an online instructor. Without ever leaving your desk, you can gain the expertise you need. Online instruction covers a variety of Microsoft products and technologies. It includes options ranging from Microsoft Official Curriculum to choices available nowhere else. It's training on demand, with access to learning resources 24 hours a day. Online training is available through Microsoft Certified Technical Education Centers.

Microsoft Certified Technical Education Centers

Microsoft Certified Technical Education Centers (CTECs) are the best source for instructor-led training that can help you prepare to become a Microsoft Certified Professional. The Microsoft CTEC program is a worldwide network of qualified technical training organizations that provide authorized delivery of Microsoft Official Curriculum courses by Microsoft Certified Trainers to computer professionals.

For a listing of CTEC locations in the United States and Canada, visit *http://www.microsoft.com/traincert/CTEC/*.

Technical Support

Every effort has been made to ensure the accuracy of this book. If you have comments, questions, or ideas regarding this book, please send them to Microsoft Press using either of the following methods:

E-mail:
TKINPUT@MICROSOFT.COM

Postal Mail:
Microsoft Press
Attn: *MCSE Training Kit—Microsoft Windows 2000 Professional* Editor
One Microsoft Way
Redmond, WA 98052-6399

Microsoft Press provides corrections for books through the World Wide Web at the following address:

http://www.microsoft.com/mspress/support/

Please note that product support is not offered through the above mail addresses. For further information regarding Microsoft software support options, please connect to *http://www.microsoft.com/support/* or call Microsoft Support Network Sales at (800) 936-3500.

For information about ordering the full version of any Microsoft software, please call Microsoft Sales at (800) 426-9400 or visit *www.microsoft.com*.

PART 1

Self-Paced Training for Microsoft Windows 2000 Professional

C H A P T E R   1

Introduction to Windows 2000

About This Chapter

This book was written to prepare you to install, configure, and support Microsoft Windows 2000 Professional; therefore, this chapter helps you to understand Windows 2000 Professional and where it fits in the Windows 2000 family of products. It presents an overview of the Microsoft Windows 2000 operating system and the four products that make up this family. The Windows 2000 family of products consists of Windows 2000 Professional, Windows 2000 Server, Windows 2000 Advanced Server, and Windows 2000 Datacenter Server.

Before You Begin

You need no special preparation to complete this chapter.

Lesson 1: Overview of the Windows 2000 Platform

The Microsoft Windows 2000 family of operating systems builds on Microsoft Windows NT technology by adding many features and enhancements. This lesson introduces you to the family of Windows 2000 products. It explains some of the key differences between these products and the environment for which each product is designed.

After this lesson, you will be able to

- Identify the key features of Windows 2000, including features that are specific to Windows 2000 Professional and to Windows 2000 Server.

Estimated lesson time: 10 minutes

Overview of Windows 2000

Windows 2000 is a multipurpose operating system with integrated support for client/server and peer-to-peer networks. It incorporates technologies that reduce the total cost of ownership (TCO) and provides for scalability from a small network to a large enterprise network. *Total cost of ownership* is the total amount of money and time associated with purchasing computer hardware and software, and deploying, configuring, and maintaining the hardware and software. TCO includes hardware and software updates, training, maintenance and administration, and technical support. One other major factor in TCO is lost productivity. Lost productivity can occur because of many factors, including user errors, hardware problems, or software upgrades and retraining.

The Windows 2000 platform consists of the following four versions:

- **Windows 2000 Professional.** This product is a high-performance, secure-network client computer and corporate desktop operating system that includes the best features of Microsoft Windows 98, while significantly extending the manageability, reliability, security, and performance of Windows NT Workstation 4. This product is the main Microsoft desktop operating system for businesses of all sizes.

- **Windows 2000 Server.** This product is a file, print, and applications server, as well as a Web-server platform, that contains all of the features of Windows 2000 Professional plus many new server-specific functions. This product is ideal for small- to medium-sized enterprise application deployments, Web servers, workgroups, and branch offices.

- **Windows 2000 Advanced Server (formerly Windows NT Server 5 Enterprise Edition).** This product is a more powerful departmental and application server, and it also provides a rich network operating system (NOS) and

Internet services. This product is beyond the scope of this training kit; features unique to Advanced Server are not covered in this kit.

- **Windows 2000 Datacenter Server.** This new product is the most powerful and functional server operating system ever offered by Microsoft. It is optimized for large data warehouses, econometric analysis, large-scale simulations in science and engineering, and server consolidation projects. This product is outside the scope of this kit; features unique to Datacenter Server are not covered in this kit.

Table 1.1 describes the features and benefits of Windows 2000.

Table 1.1   Features and Benefits of Windows 2000

Feature	Benefit
Lower total cost of ownership	Reduces the cost of running and administering a network by providing automatic installation and upgrading of applications, and by simplifying the setup and configuration of client computers.
	Reduces the amount of calls to support by providing the familiar Microsoft Windows interface for users and administrators, including wizards, interactive help, and more.
	Reduces the need for administrators to travel to desktop computers to upgrade the operating system.
Security	Authenticates users before they gain access to resources or data on a computer or the network.
	Provides local and network security and auditing for files, folders, printers, and other resources.
Directory services (available only in Windows 2000 Server, Windows 2000 Advanced Server, and Windows Windows 2000 Datacenter)	Store information about network resources, such as user accounts, applications, print resources, and security information.
	Provide the services that permit users to gain access to resources throughout the entire Windows 2000 network and to locate users, computers, and other resources. Also enables administrators to manage and secure these resources.

(continued)

Feature	Benefit
	Store and manage services based on Active Directory technology. Active Directory directory services is the Windows 2000 directory service. The directory is the database that stores information about network resources, such as computers and printers, and the directory services make this information available to users and applications. Active Directory directory services also provide administrators with the capability to control access to resources.
Performance and scalability	Supports symmetric multiprocessing (SMP) on computers that are configured with multiple microprocessors. Also supports multitasking for system processes and programs.
	Windows 2000 Professional supports up to two microprocessors.
Networking and communication services	Provide built-in support for the most popular network protocols, including TCP/IP and network client utilities.
	Provide connectivity with Novell NetWare, UNIX, and AppleTalk.
	Provide Dial-Up Networking, which lets mobile users connect to a computer running Windows 2000.
	Windows 2000 Professional supports one inbound dial-up networking session. (The Windows 2000 Server products support 256 simultaneous inbound dial-up sessions.)
Internet integration	Integrates users' desktops with the Internet, thereby removing the distinction between the local computer and the Internet. Users can securely browse the network, intranet, and Internet for resources, as well as send and receive e-mail messages.
	Windows 2000 Professional provides a personal Web server, which enables users to host a personal Web site.
Integrated administration tools	Provide the means to create customized tools to manage local and remote computers with a single standard interface.
	Provide the means to incorporate third-party administrative tools into the standard interface.

(continued)

Feature	Benefit
Hardware support	Supports *universal serial bus (USB)*, an external bus standard that eliminates many constraints of earlier computer peripherals.
	Supports Plug and Play hardware, which Windows 2000 automatically detects, installs, and configures.

Lesson Summary

In this lesson, you learned that Windows 2000 consists of a family of four separate products: Windows 2000 Professional, Windows 2000 Server, Windows 2000 Advanced Server, and Windows 2000 Datacenter Server.

Lesson 2: Windows 2000 Professional

Windows 2000 Professional is easier to use and manage and provides greater compatibility, file management capabilities, and security than earlier versions of Windows. This lesson discusses how Windows 2000 Professional improves the capabilities of earlier versions of Windows in these areas: ease of use, simplified management, increased hardware support, enhanced file management, and enhanced security features.

After this lesson, you will be able to

- Identify features and enhancements in Windows 2000 Professional.

Estimated lesson time: 15 minutes

Ease of Use

Windows 2000 Professional includes changes to the look and functionality of the desktop, windows, and the Start menu, making it easier to use than previous versions of Windows. Besides these user interface enhancements, Windows 2000 Professional also contains features that improve support for mobile users and make printing easier and more flexible.

User Interface Enhancements

The enhancements and features that improve the Windows 2000 Professional user interface include the following:

- **Customized Start menu.** Personalized Menus can be activated to keep track of the programs you use and to update the Programs menu so that it presents only the programs that you use most often. Applications that you use less frequently are hidden from normal view, making the Start menu easier to use. For more information on customized Start menus, see Chapter 2, "Installing Windows 2000 Professional."

- **Log On and Shut Down dialog boxes.** The Log On and Shut Down dialog boxes are easier to use with fewer, better organized choices. For more information on the Log On and Shut Down dialog boxes, see Chapter 2, "Installing Windows 2000 Professional."

- **Task Scheduler.** The enhanced Task Scheduler allows users to schedule scripts and programs to run at specific times. For more information on Task Scheduler, see Chapter 3, "Using Microsoft Management Console and Task Scheduler."

Support for Mobile Users

Windows 2000 Professional supports the latest laptop technologies based on Advanced Power Management (APM) and Advanced Configuration and Power Interface (ACPI), which turns off power to the display and hard disks after a period of inactivity, and allows you to change or remove devices without turning off the computer. ACPI also lengthens battery life with power management and suspend or resume capabilities. For more information on APM and ACPI, see Chapter 24, "Configuring Windows 2000 for Mobile Computers."

Features in Windows 2000 Professional that provide support for mobile users include the following:

- **Network Connection Wizard.** Consolidates all of the processes for creating network connections. Users can now set up the following networking features from one wizard: dial-up connections to a private network or to the Internet, virtual private network (VPN) connections through the Internet to a private network, incoming calls, and direct connections to another computer. For more information on the Network Connection wizard, see Chapter 21, "Configuring Remote Access."

- **Virtual private network support.** Provides secure access to corporate networks from off-site locations by using a local Internet service provider (ISP) rather than using a long distance, dial-up connection. For more information on the VPN support, see Chapter 21, "Configuring Remote Access."

- **Offline Folders.** Allows you to copy documents that are stored on the network to your local computer, making it easier to access data when you aren't connected to the network. For more information on the Offline Folders, see Chapter 24, "Configuring Windows 2000 for Mobile Computers."

- **Synchronization Manager.** Compares items on the network to items that you opened or updated while working offline. Synchronization occurs when you log on, and any changes made offline to files and folders, Web pages, and e-mail messages are saved to the network. For more information on Synchronization Manager, see Chapter 24, "Configuring Windows 2000 for Mobile Computers."

Printing Support

Printing in Windows 2000 Professional has been improved to assist you in providing a more flexible network of printers. Windows 2000 Professional includes the following printing features and enhancements:

- **Internet Printing Protocol (IPP).** Allows users to send documents to any printer on a Microsoft Windows 2000 network that is connected to the Internet. Internet printing enables users to do the following:

  - Print to a Uniform Resource Locator (URL) over an intranet or the Internet.

  - View printer and job-related information in Hypertext Markup Language (HTML) format from any browser.

  - Download and install printer drivers over the Internet.

- **Add Printer wizard.** Simplifies the process of connecting to local and network printers from within a program. You no longer need to open the Printers system folder or specify driver models, printer languages, or ports when you add printers. For more information on the Add Printer wizard, see Chapter 12, "Setting Up and Configuring Network Printers."

- **Image Color Management (ICM) 2.** Allows you to send high-quality color documents to a printer or another computer with greater speed and reliability than ever before. ICM 2 is an operating system API that helps ensure that the colors you see on your monitor match those on your scanner and printer.

Simplified Management

The configuration management capabilities in Windows 2000 create a more consistent environment for the end user and help ensure that users have any data, applications, and operating system settings that they need.

Windows 2000 includes the following configuration management enhancements:

- **Add/Remove Programs wizard.** Simplifies the process of installing and removing programs. Users can install applications by pointing directly to a location on the corporate network or Internet. The user interface provides additional feedback and sort options to view installed or available applications by size, frequency of use, and time of last use.

- **Windows Installer service.** Manages application installation, modification, repairs, and removal. It provides a standard format for managing the components of a software package, and an API for managing applications and tools.

Troubleshooting Tools

Windows 2000 Professional includes diagnostic and troubleshooting tools that make it easier to support the operating system. Troubleshooting tools in Windows 2000 Professional include the following:

- **Compatibility tool.** Detects and warns the user about whether certain installed applications or components will cause an upgrade to fail, or whether the components won't work after an upgrade is complete. The compatibility tool can be run by using the /checkupgradeonly switch with the command to start Setup. This generates the Report System Compatibility screen that lists any items found that are incompatible with Windows 2000. For more information on the compatibility tool, see Chapter 2, "Installing Windows 2000 Professional."

- **Troubleshooters.** Included in Windows 2000 online Help as troubleshooting wizards that can be used to solve many common computer problems.

Increased Hardware Support

Microsoft Windows 2000 Professional now supports more than 7,000 hardware devices, such as infrared devices, scanners, digital cameras, and advanced multimedia devices that Windows NT Workstation 4 did not support. Enhancements to hardware support in Windows 2000 Professional include the following:

- **Add/Remove Hardware wizard.** Allows you to add, remove, troubleshoot, and upgrade computer peripherals. When a device isn't working properly, you can use the wizard to stop operation and safely remove the device.

- **Win32 Driver Model (WDM).** Provides a common model for device drivers across Windows 98 and Windows 2000. Drivers that are written to the WDM will work in both Windows 98 and Windows 2000.

- **Plug and Play support.** Enhances previous Plug and Play functionality and allows the following:

  - Automatic and dynamic reconfiguration of installed hardware
  - Loading of appropriate drivers
  - Registration for device notification events
  - Changeable and removable devices

- **Power options.** Prevent unnecessary power drains on your system by directing power to devices as they need it. The options available to you depend on your hardware. These options include the following:

  - **Standby.** Turns off your monitor and hard disks, and your computer uses less power.

  - **Hibernation.** Turns off your monitor and hard disk, saves everything in memory on disk, and turns off your computer. When you restart your computer, your desktop is restored exactly as you left it.

Note Microsoft Windows 2000 also supports DirectX 7, which provides low-level application APIs that give access to high-performance media acceleration on Microsoft Windows–based computers.

Symmetric Multiprocessing

Windows 2000 is a multiprocessing operating system capable of running on computers containing more than one processor. Windows 2000 Professional provides symmetric multiprocessing (SMP) system capabilities and supports two processors. It assumes that all of the processors are equal and that they all have access to the same physical memory. Therefore, Windows 2000 can run any thread on any available processor regardless of which process—user or executive—owns the thread.

The design of Windows 2000 also supports processor affinity, whereby a process or thread can specify that it is to run on a particular set of processors. As with earlier versions of Windows NT, Windows 2000 includes APIs that a process can use for processor affinity. These APIs must be defined in the application to make use of processor affinity.

Windows 2000 uses the same rules for scheduling on a multiprocessor system as it does on a single-processor system. Therefore, at any given time, the threads that are ready and have the highest priorities are actually running.

Asymmetric Multiprocessing

Asymmetric multiprocessing (ASMP) systems also exist, in which processors are different. They might address different physical memory spaces, or they might have other discrepancies. These operating systems run only certain processes on certain processors. For example, the kernel might always execute on a particular processor. Windows 2000 doesn't support ASMP.

Enhanced File Management

Windows 2000 Professional provides significant enhancements to file management capabilities. Features that enhance file management in Windows 2000 Professional include the following:

- **NTFS file system.** Supports file encryption and enables you to add disk space to an NTFS volume without having to restart the computer. It also supports distributed link tracking, and per-user disk quotas to monitor and limit disk space use. For more information on the NTFS file system, see Chapter 2, "Installing Windows 2000 Professional."

- **FAT32 file system.** Supports FAT32 file system for compatibility with Windows 95 OEM Service Release (OSR) 2 systems and later. FAT32 is an enhanced version of the FAT file system for use on disk volumes larger than 2 GB. For more information on the FAT32 file system, see Chapter 2, "Installing Windows 2000 Professional."

- **Disk Defragmenter utility.** Rearranges files, programs, and unused space on your computer's hard disk so that programs run faster and files open more quickly. For more information on Disk Defragmenter, see Chapter 18, "Managing Data Storage."

- **Backup utility.** Helps to protect data from accidental loss because of hardware or storage media failure. The Backup utility in Windows 2000 allows you to schedule backups to occur automatically. For more information on the Backup utility, see Chapter 19, "Backing Up and Restoring Data." You can back up data to a wide variety of storage media, such as the following:
  - Tape drives
  - External hard disks
  - Zip disks
  - Recordable CD-ROMs
  - Logical drives

- **Volume mount points.** Allow you to connect, or mount, a local drive at any empty folder on a local NTFS-formatted volume.

Enhanced Security Features

Windows 2000 Professional is the most secure Windows desktop operating system for either a stand-alone computer or any type of public or private network. Security features and enhancements in Windows 2000 Professional include the following:

- Kerberos 5. Supports single logon, allowing faster authentication and faster network response. Kerberos 5 is the primary security protocol for domains in Windows 2000.

- Encrypting File System (EFS). Strengthens security by encrypting files on your hard disk so that no one can access them without using the correct password.

- Internet Protocol Security (IPSec). Encrypts Transmission Control Protocol/ Internet Protocol (TCP/IP) traffic to secure communications within an intranet and provides the highest levels of security for VPN traffic across the Internet.

- Smart card support. Enables portability of credentials and other private information between computers at work, home, or on the road. This eliminates the need to transmit sensitive information, such as authentication tickets and private keys, over networks.

Lesson Summary

Windows 2000 Professional improves the capabilities of previous versions of Windows in five main areas: ease of use, simplified management, increased hardware support, enhanced file management, and enhanced security features.

Some of the ease-of-use improvements include enhancements to the user interface, such as a customized Start menu that presents only the programs that you use most often, and improved Log On and Shut Down dialog boxes. Windows 2000 Professional includes support for the latest laptop technologies based on APM and ACPI, and provides a Network Connection wizard and VPN support. It provides Offline Folders that allow you to copy documents stored on the network to your local computer for access when you are offline; and it provides Synchronization Manager—which compares items on the network to items that you opened or updated while working offline—and synchronizes them.

Printing in Windows 2000 Professional has also been improved. IPP allows users to print to a URL over an intranet or the Internet, view printer and job-related information in HTML format from any browser, and download and install printer drivers over the Internet. The Windows 2000 Add Printer wizard simplifies the process of connecting to local and network printers from within a program, and Image Color Management 2 allows you to send high-quality color documents to a printer or another computer with greater speed and reliability than ever before.

Windows 2000 also simplifies the process of setting up a computer. The Windows 2000 System Preparation tool allows you to create an image of a computer's hard disk so that you can use a third-party tool to duplicate the hard disk on similarly configured computers. The Setup Manager wizard guides you through the process of creating answer files for unattended installation scripts.

Microsoft Windows 2000 Professional now supports more than 7,000 hardware devices, such as infrared devices, scanners, digital cameras, and advanced multimedia devices. Other enhancements to hardware support include the following: an Add/Remove Hardware wizard that allows you to add, remove, troubleshoot, and upgrade computer peripherals; a Win32 Driver Model that allows device drivers written to the WDM to work in both Windows 98 and Windows 2000; enhanced Plug and Play support; power options that prevent unnecessary power drains on your system by directing power to devices as they need it; and support for DirectX 7. Windows 2000 Professional also supports symmetric multiprocessing, which means it is capable of running on computers containing more than one processor.

Windows 2000 Professional enhancements to file management capabilities include a disk defragmenter utility and an NTFS file system that supports file encryption, distributed link tracking, and per-user disk quotas to monitor and limit disk space use. A Backup utility allows you to back up data to a wide variety of storage media: tape drives, external hard disks, zip disks, recordable CD-ROMs, and logical drives.

Windows 2000 Professional is the most secure Windows desktop operating system for either a stand-alone computer or any type of public or private network. Security features and enhancements in Windows 2000 Professional include support for Kerberos 5; Encrypting File System, which strengthens security by encrypting files on your hard disk; and IPSec, which encrypts TCP/IP traffic and provides the highest levels of security for VPN traffic across the Internet.

Lesson 3: Windows 2000 Workgroups and Domains

Windows 2000 supports secure network environments in which users are able to share common resources, regardless of network size. The two types of networks that Windows 2000 supports are workgroups and domains.

After this lesson, you will be able to

- Identify the key characteristics of workgroups and domains.

Estimated lesson time: 10 minutes

Windows 2000 Workgroups

A Windows 2000 *workgroup* is a logical grouping of networked computers that share resources, such as files and printers. A workgroup is referred to as a *peer-to-peer network* because all computers in the workgroup can share resources as equals, or as peers, without a dedicated server. Each computer in the workgroup, running either Windows 2000 Professional or Windows 2000 Server, maintains a local security database, as shown in Figure 1.1. A *local security database* is a list of user accounts and resource security information for the computer the database is on. Therefore, the administration of user accounts and resource security in a workgroup is decentralized.

Figure 1.1   An example of a Windows 2000 workgroup

Because workgroups have decentralized administration and security

- A user must have a user account on *each* computer to which he or she wants to gain access.

- You must make any changes to user accounts, such as changing a user's password or adding a new user account, on *each* computer in the workgroup. If you forget to add a new user account to one of the computers in your workgroup, the new user won't be able to log on to that computer and will be unable to access resources on it.

A Windows 2000 workgroup provides the following advantages:

- It doesn't require a computer running Windows 2000 Server to hold centralized security information.

- It's simple to design and implement. A workgroup doesn't require the extensive planning and administration that a domain requires.

- It's convenient for a limited number of computers in close proximity. A workgroup becomes impractical in environments with more than 10 computers.

Note In a workgroup, a computer running Windows 2000 Server is called a *stand-alone server.*

Windows 2000 Domains

A Windows 2000 *domain* is a logical grouping of network computers that share a central directory database. (See Figure 1.2.) A *directory database* contains user accounts and security information for the domain. This directory database is known as the Directory and is the database portion of Active Directory directory services, which is the Windows 2000 directory service.

In a domain, the Directory resides on computers that are configured as domain controllers. A *domain controller* is a server that manages all security-related aspects of user/domain interactions. Security and administration are centralized.

Note You can designate only a computer running Windows 2000 Server, Windows 2000 Advanced Server, or Windows 2000 Datacenter as a domain controller. If all computers on the network are running Windows 2000 Professional, the only type of network available is a workgroup.

A domain doesn't refer to a single location or specific type of network configuration. The computers in a domain can share physical proximity on a small local area network (LAN) or can be located in different corners of the world, communicating over any number of physical connections, including dial-up lines,

Figure 1.2   A Windows 2000 domain

integrated Services Digital Network (ISDN) lines, fiber lines, Ethernet lines, token ring connections, frame relay connections, satellite connections, and leased lines.

The benefits of a domain are as follows:

- Provides centralized administration because all user information is stored centrally.

- Provides a single logon process for users to gain access to network resources, such as file, print, and application resources for which they have permissions. In other words, a user can log on to one computer and use resources on another computer in the network as long as he or she has appropriate privileges to the resource.

- Provides scalability so that you can create large networks.

A typical Windows 2000 domain has the following types of computers:

- **Domain controllers running Windows 2000 Server.** Each domain controller stores and maintains a copy of the Directory. In a domain, you create a user account once, which Windows 2000 records in the Directory. When a user logs on to a computer in the domain, a domain controller checks the Directory for the user name, password, and logon restrictions to authenticate the user. When a domain has multiple domain controllers, they periodically replicate their Directory information.

- **Member servers running Windows 2000 Server.** A member server is a server that isn't configured as a domain controller. A member server doesn't store Directory information and can't authenticate users. Member servers provide shared resources such as shared folders or printers.

- **Client computers running Windows 2000 Professional.** Client computers run a user's desktop environment and allow the user to gain access to resources in the domain.

Lesson Summary

In this lesson, you learned about Windows 2000 workgroups and domains. A Windows 2000 workgroup is a logical grouping of networked computers that share resources, such as files and printers. Workgroups are referred to as peer-to-peer networks because all computers in the workgroup can share resources as equals (peers), without a dedicated server. Security and administration aren't centralized in a workgroup because each computer maintains a list of user accounts and resource security information for that computer.

A Windows 2000 domain is a logical grouping of network computers that share a central directory database that contains user accounts and security information for the domain. This directory database is known as the Directory and is the database portion of Active Directory directory services, which is the Windows 2000 directory service. In a domain, security and administration are centralized because the Directory resides on domain controllers, which manage all security-related aspects of user/domain interactions. To create a domain, at least one computer must be running a Windows 2000 server product and must have Active Directory directory services installed on it.

Lesson 4: Logging On to Windows 2000

This lesson explains the Log On To Windows dialog box that you use to log on to Windows 2000. It also explains how Windows 2000 authenticates a user during the logon process to verify the identity of the user. This mandatory process ensures that only valid users can gain access to resources and data on a computer or the network.

After this lesson, you will be able to
- Identify the features of the Log On To Windows dialog box.
- Identify how Windows 2000 authenticates a user when the user logs on to a domain or logs on locally.

Estimated lesson time: 10 minutes

Logging On Locally to the Computer

To log on to a computer running Windows 2000, a user provides a user name and password. Windows 2000 authenticates the user during the logon process to verify the identity of the user. Only valid users can gain access to resources and data on a computer or the network. Windows 2000 authenticates users who either log on locally to the computer at which they are seated or log on to a domain.

A user can log on locally to either of the following:

- A computer that is a member of a workgroup.
- A computer that is a member of a domain but is not a domain controller. The user selects the computer name in the Log On To box in the Enter Password dialog box.

Note Domain controllers don't maintain a local security database. Therefore, local user accounts aren't available on domain controllers, and a user can't log on locally to a domain controller.

When a user starts a computer running Windows 2000 Professional, the user is prompted to enter a user name and a password in the Log On To Windows dialog box, as shown in Figure 1.3.

Notice that the Log On To Windows dialog box contains an Options button. This button is a toggle that displays or hides additional logon options. Table 1.2 describes the available options in the Log On To Windows dialog box.

Figure 1.3   The Log On To Windows dialog box

Table 1.2   Log On To Windows Dialog Box Options

Option	Description
User Name	A unique user logon name that is assigned by an administrator. To log on to a domain with the user name, the user account must reside in the Directory.
Password	The password that is assigned to the user account. Users must enter a password to prove their identity.
	Passwords are case sensitive. The password appears in the Password box as asterisks (*) to protect it from onlookers. To prevent unauthorized access to resources and data, users must keep passwords secret.
Log On Using Dial-up Connection	A check box that appears when you click the Options button. It permits a user to connect to a domain server by using dial-up networking. Dial-up networking allows a user to log on and perform work from a remote location.
Shutdown	A button that appears when you click the Options button. It closes all files, saves all operating system data, and prepares the computer so that a user can safely turn it off.
Options	A button that toggles on and off the Log On To drop-down list, the Log On Using Dial-up Connection check box option, and the Shutdown button. See Figure 1.4.

Figure 1.4 The Log On To Windows dialog box showing the Log On To drop-down list

Windows 2000 Authentication Process

To gain access to a computer running Windows 2000 or to any resource on that computer, a user must provide a user name and password.

How Windows 2000 authenticates a user varies, based on whether the user is logging on to a domain or logging on locally to a computer. (See Figure 1.5.)

Figure 1.5 Windows 2000 authentication process at Logon

When logging on locally, the steps in the authentication process are as follows:

1. The user logs on by providing logon information, such as *user name* and *password*, and Windows 2000 forwards this information to the security subsystem of that local computer.

2. Windows 2000 compares the logon information with the user information that is in the local security database.

   The security subsystem of the local computer contains the local security database that Windows 2000 uses to validate the logon information.

3. If the information matches and the user account is valid, Windows 2000 creates an access token for the user.

   An *access token* is the user's identification for that local computer, and it contains the user's security settings. These security settings allow the user to gain access to the appropriate resources and to perform specific system tasks.

Note In addition to the logon process, any time a user makes a connection to a computer, that computer authenticates the user and returns an access token. This authentication process is invisible to the user.

Lesson Summary

In this lesson, you learned that when a user starts a computer running Windows 2000 Professional, the Log On To Windows dialog box appears, and the user must enter a valid user name and password to log on. You also learned about the various options available in the Log On To Windows dialog box.

When a user logs on, he or she can log on to the local computer; or, if the computer is a member of a domain, the user can log on to the domain. The authentication process for logging on locally and logging on to a domain is similar. However, when a user logs on locally, the local computer performs the authentication; and when a user logs on to a domain, a domain controller must perform the authentication. If the user is logging on locally, the security subsystem of the local computer contains the local security database that Windows 2000 uses to validate the logon information. If the user is logging on to a domain, a domain controller contains a copy of the Directory that Windows 2000 uses to validate the logon information.

Lesson 5: The Windows Security Dialog Box

This lesson explains the options and functionality of the Windows Security dialog box.

After this lesson, you will be able to

- Identify the features of the Windows Security dialog box.

Estimated lesson time: 5 minutes

Using the Security Dialog Box

Windows 2000 gives you access to the Windows Security dialog box, which provides information such as the user account currently logged on and the domain or computer to which the user is logged on. This information is important for users with multiple user accounts, such as a user who has a regular user account as well as a user account with administrative privileges.

You access the Windows Security dialog box by pressing Ctrl+Alt+Delete. Figure 1.6 shows the Windows Security dialog box, and Table 1.3 describes the Windows Security dialog box options.

Figure 1.6   Windows Security dialog box

Table 1.3   The Windows Security Dialog Box Options

Option	Description
Lock Computer	Allows you to secure the computer without logging off. All programs remain running. You should lock your computer when you leave for a short period of time.
	The user who locks the computer can unlock it by typing a valid password in the Password box.
	An administrator can also unlock a locked computer, logging off the current user.
Log Off	Allows you to log off as the current user and close all running programs, but leaves Windows 2000 running.
Shut Down	Allows you to close all files, save all operating system data, and prepare the computer so that you can safely turn it off.
Change Password	Allows you to change your user account password. You must know the old password to create a new one.
	Administrators can also change your password.
Task Manager	Provides a list of the current programs that are running, a summary of overall CPU and memory use, and a quick view of how each program, program component, or system process is using the CPU and memory resources.
	You can also use Task Manager to switch between programs and to stop a program that isn't responding.
Cancel	Closes the Windows Security dialog box.

Lesson Summary

In this lesson, you learned that you access the Windows Security dialog box by pressing Ctrl+Alt+Delete, and that this dialog box provides information such as the user account currently logged on and the domain or computer to which the user is logged on. You also learned that you can use the Windows Security dialog box to lock your computer, to change your password, to log off your computer while leaving Windows 2000 running, to shut down your computer, and to access Task Manager.

Review

The following questions will help you determine whether you have learned enough to move on to the next chapter. If you have difficulty answering these questions, please go back and review the material in this chapter before beginning the next chapter. The answers for these questions are in Appendix A, "Questions and Answers."

1. What is the major difference between a workgroup and a domain?

2. What are Active Directory directory services, and what do they provide?

3. What information must a user provide when he or she logs on to a computer?

4. What happens when a user logs on locally to a computer?

5. How do you use the Windows Security dialog box?

CHAPTER 2

Installing Windows 2000 Professional

About This Chapter

This chapter prepares you to install Microsoft Windows 2000 Professional.

Before You Begin

To complete this chapter, you must have

- A computer that meets the minimum hardware requirements located in "About This Book."
- A Windows 2000 Professional CD-ROM.
- Four 3.5-inch floppy disks to create the Setup disks, if your computer isn't configured with an El Torito–compatible CD-ROM drive, which allows you to boot off your Windows 2000 Professional CD-ROM.

Lesson 1: Getting Started

When you install Windows 2000 Professional, the Windows 2000 Setup program asks you to provide information about how you want to install and configure the operating system. Good preparation helps you avoid problems during and after the installation.

After this lesson, you will be able to

- Complete preinstallation tasks, such as identifying the hardware requirements and the required installation information you need to install Microsoft Windows 2000 Professional.

Estimated lesson time: 30 minutes

Preinstallation Tasks

Before you start the installation, complete the following preinstallation tasks:

- Identify the hardware requirements to install Windows 2000 Professional, and make sure that your hardware meets these requirements.
- Determine whether your hardware is on the Hardware Compatibility List (HCL).
- Determine how you want to partition the hard disk on which you are going to install Windows 2000.
- Choose a file system for the installation partition.
- Identify whether your computer will join a domain or a workgroup.
- Complete a checklist of preinstallation tasks to help ensure a successful installation.

Hardware Requirements

You must know the minimum hardware requirements for installing and operating Windows 2000 Professional to determine whether your hardware meets these requirements. (See Figure 2.1 and Table 2.1.) Make sure that your hardware meets or exceeds these hardware requirements.

Figure 2.1   Minimum hardware requirements

Table 2.1   Windows 2000 Professional Hardware Requirements

Component	Requirements
CPU	Pentium compatible
Memory	64 MB minimum
Hard disk space	One or more hard disks with a minimum of about 650 MB (2 GB recommended) on the partition that will contain the system files
Networking	Network adapter card
Display	Video display adapter and monitor with Video Graphics Adapter (VGA) resolution or higher
Other drives	CD-ROM drive, 12X or faster recommended (not required for installing Windows 2000 over a network)
Accessories	Keyboard and mouse or other pointing device

Hardware Compatibility List

Before you install Windows 2000, verify that your hardware is on the Windows 2000 Hardware Compatibility List. Microsoft provides tested drivers for only those devices that are included on this list. Using hardware that isn't listed on the HCL might cause problems during and after installation. For a copy of the HCL, see the Hcl.txt file in the Support folder on the Windows 2000 Professional CD-ROM.

You will also find the most recent versions of the HCL for released operating systems on the Internet at the Microsoft Web site (http://www.microsoft.com).

Note Microsoft supports only those devices that are listed on the HCL. If you have hardware that isn't on this list, contact the hardware manufacturer to determine whether a manufacturer-supported Windows 2000 driver exists for the component.

Disk Partitions

The Windows 2000 Setup program examines the hard disk to determine its existing configuration. Setup then allows you to install Windows 2000 on an existing partition or to create a new partition on which to install Windows 2000.

Creating a New Partition or Using an Existing Partition

The Setup program gives you flexibility in how you configure the hard disk prior to installing the Windows 2000 operating system. Depending on the state of the hard disk, you can choose one of the following options during the installation:

- If the hard disk is unpartitioned, you must create and size the Windows 2000 partition.
- If the hard disk has partitions and has enough unpartitioned disk space, you can create the Windows 2000 partition by using the unpartitioned space.
- If the hard disk has an existing partition that is large enough, you can install Windows 2000 on that partition. Installing on an existing partition will overwrite any existing data.
- If the hard disk has an existing partition, you can delete it to create more unpartitioned disk space to use to create the Windows 2000 partition.

Configuring the Remaining Free Hard Disk Space

Although you can use Setup to create other partitions, you should create and size only the partition on which you will install Windows 2000. After you install Windows 2000, use the Disk Management administrative tool to partition any remaining unpartitioned space on the hard disk.

Sizing the Installation Partition

Microsoft recommends that you install Windows 2000 on a 2 GB or larger partition. Although Windows 2000 requires a minimum of about 650 MB of disk space for installation, using a larger partition for installation provides flexibility in the future. Then, if required, you can install updates to Windows 2000, operating system tools, or other files that are required by Windows 2000.

File Systems

After you create the installation partition, Setup prompts you to select the file system with which to format the partition. Windows 2000 supports three file systems: Windows 2000 file system (NTFS), file allocation table (FAT), and FAT32. Figure 2.2 summarizes some of the features of these file systems.

Figure 2.2   Summary of file systems features

NTFS

Use NTFS when the partition on which Windows 2000 will reside requires any of the following features:

- **File- and folder-level security.** NTFS allows you to control access to files and folders. For additional information, see Chapter 14, "Securing Resources with NTFS Permissions."

- **Disk compression.** NTFS compresses files to store more data on the partition. For additional information, see Chapter 18, "Managing Data Storage."

- **Disk quotas.** NTFS allows you to control disk use on a per-user basis. For additional information, see Chapter 18, "Managing Data Storage."

- **Encryption.** NTFS allows you to encrypt file data on the physical hard disk. For additional information, see Chapter 18, "Managing Data Storage."

NTFS in Windows 2000 also supports remote storage, dynamic volumes, and the mounting of volumes to folders. Windows 2000 and Windows NT are the only operating systems that can access data on a local hard disk that is formatted with NTFS.

FAT and FAT32

FAT and FAT32 allow access by, and compatibility with, other operating systems. To dual boot Windows 2000 and another operating system, format the system partition with either FAT or FAT32.

Setup determines whether to format the hard disk with FAT or FAT32 based on the size of the installation partition.

Partition size	Format
Smaller than 2 GB	Setup formats the partition as FAT
Larger than 2 GB	Setup formats the partition as FAT32

FAT and FAT32 don't offer many of the features that NTFS supports—for example, file-level security. Therefore, in most situations, you should format the hard disk with NTFS. The only reason to use FAT or FAT32 is for dual booting. If you're setting up a computer for dual booting, you would have to format only the system partition as FAT or FAT32. For example, if drive C is the system partition, you could format drive C as FAT or FAT32 and format drive D as NTFS.

Licensing

In addition to the license that is required to install and run Windows 2000 Server and the license that is required to install and run an operating system on each client computer, each client connection to the server must also be licensed.

Client Access License

A Client Access License (CAL) gives client computers the right to connect to computers running Windows 2000 Server so that the client computers can connect to network services, shared folders, and print resources. When Windows 2000 Server is installed, the network administrator must choose a CAL mode: Per Seat or Per Server.

The following services do not require Client Access Licenses:

- Anonymous or authenticated access to Windows 2000 Server with Microsoft Internet Information Services (IIS) version 4 or a Web-server application that provides Hypertext Transfer Protocol (HTTP) sharing of Hypertext Markup Language (HTML) files.
- Telnet and File Transfer Protocol (FTP) connections.

Note If your company uses Microsoft BackOffice products, you must also have licenses for them. A Windows 2000 license doesn't cover BackOffice products.

Per Seat Licensing

The Per Seat licensing mode requires a separate CAL for each client computer that is used to access Windows 2000 Server for basic network services. After a client computer has a CAL, it can be used to access any computer running Windows 2000 Server on the enterprise network. Per Seat licensing is often more economical for large networks where client computers are used to connect to more than one server.

Per Server Licensing

With Per Server licensing, CALs are assigned to a particular server. Each CAL allows one connection per client computer to the server for basic network services. You must have at least as many CALs that are dedicated to the server as the maximum number of client computers that will be used to concurrently connect to that server at any time.

Per Server licensing is preferable for small companies that have only one computer running Windows 2000 Server. It is also useful for Internet or remote-access servers where client computers might not be licensed as Windows 2000 network client computers. In this situation, Per Server licensing allows you to specify a maximum number of concurrent server connections and reject any additional logon attempts.

Domain or Workgroup Membership

During installation, you must choose the type of network security group that you want the computer to join: a domain or a workgroup. (See Figure 2.3.)

Joining a Domain

During installation, you can add the computer on which you are installing Windows 2000 Professional to an existing domain. Adding a computer to a domain is referred to as *joining a domain*.

Joining a domain during installation requires the following:

- **A domain name.** Ask the domain administrator for the Domain Name System (DNS) name for the domain that you want to join. An example of a DNS-compatible domain name is microsoft.com, where *microsoft* is the name of your organization's DNS identity.

Joining a domain requires:

- A domain name
- A computer account
- An available domain controller and a DNS server

Joining a workgroup requires:

- A new or an existing workgroup name

Figure 2.3   Domain or workgroup membership

- **A computer account.** Before a computer can join a domain, it must have a computer account in the domain. You can ask a domain administrator to create the computer account before installation, or, if you have administrative privileges for the domain, you can create the computer account during installation. If you create the computer account during installation, Setup prompts you for a name and password of a user account with authority to add domain computer accounts.

- **An available domain controller and a server running the DNS Service (called the *DNS server*).** At least one domain controller in the domain that you are joining and one DNS server must be online when you install a computer in the domain.

Note You can join a domain during installation or after installation.

Joining a Workgroup

During installation, you can add the computer on which you are installing Windows 2000 Professional to an existing workgroup. Adding a computer to a workgroup is referred to as *joining a workgroup.*

Note When you install Windows 2000 Server and join a workgroup, the computer is added as a stand-alone server. A computer running Windows 2000 Server that isn't a member of a domain is called a *stand-alone server.*

When you join a workgroup during installation, you must assign a workgroup name to your computer. The workgroup name that you assign can be the name of an existing workgroup or the name of a new workgroup that you create during installation.

Preinstallation Checklist

The following is a preinstallation checklist that you can use to make sure you have all the necessary information available before you begin the installation process.

Task	Done
Verify that your components meet the minimum hardware requirements.	❏
Verify that all of your hardware is listed on the HCL.	❏
Verify that the hard disk on which you will install Windows 2000 has a minimum of 650 MB of free disk space, and preferably 2 GB.	❏
Select the file system for the Windows 2000 partition. Unless you need to dual boot operating systems, format all partitions with NTFS.	❏
Determine the name of the domain or workgroup that you will join. If you join a domain, be sure that you write down the DNS name for the domain. Also, determine the name of the computer before installation.	❏
Create a computer account in the domain that you are joining. You can create a computer account during the installation if you have administrative privileges in the domain.	❏
Create a password for the Administrator account.	❏

Lesson Summary

This lesson identified the preinstallation tasks you must understand and complete before you install Windows 2000. The first task is to identify the hardware requirements for installing Windows 2000 Professional and to ensure that your hardware meets these requirements. You learned about the Windows 2000 hardware compatibility list and that your hardware should be on the HCL so that it's compatible with Windows 2000.

After you have determined that your hardware is on the HCL, you must decide how you want to partition the hard disk on which you are going to install Windows 2000. You must also determine whether you are going to format the partition as NTFS so that you can have better security and a richer feature set, or as FAT or FAT32 so that other operating systems can access the data on the installation partition.

In addition, you learned about Client Access Licenses (CALs) and that a CAL gives client computers—for example, a computer running Windows 2000 Professional—the right to connect to computers running Windows 2000 Server. You learned that you must select Per Seat or Per Server licensing on the server. With Per Seat licensing mode, a separate CAL is required for each client computer that accesses a Windows 2000 Server. When a client computer has a CAL, it can be used to access any computer running Windows 2000 Server on the enterprise network. With Per Server licensing, CALs are assigned to a particular server. Each CAL allows one connection per client computer to the server, and you must have at least as many CALs that are dedicated to the server as the maximum number of client computers that will be used to concurrently connect to that server at any time.

You also learned that during installation, your computer must join a domain or a workgroup. If your computer is the first one installed on the network, or if for some other reason no domain is available for your computer to join, you can have the computer join a workgroup and then have the computer join a domain after the installation. This lesson also provided a checklist of preinstallation tasks that you can complete to help ensure a successful installation of Windows 2000.

Lesson 2: Installing Windows 2000 from a CD-ROM

This lesson teaches you about the four-stage process of installing Windows 2000 Professional from a CD-ROM. These four stages are as follows:

- Run the Setup program.
- Run the Setup wizard.
- Install Windows networking.
- Complete the Setup program.

After you learn about these four stages, you will install Windows 2000 on your computer.

After this lesson, you will be able to

- Install Windows 2000 Professional from a CD-ROM.

Estimated lesson time: 90 minutes

The Windows 2000 Setup Program

Installing Windows 2000 is a four-stage process (see Figure 2.4). You begin by running the Setup program that prepares the hard disk and copies files. Setup then runs a wizard that provides informational pages, which you use to complete the rest of the installation. The four stages of the installation process are described as follows:

Figure 2.4 Windows 2000 installation steps

Installing Windows 2000 from a CD-ROM to a clean hard disk consists of these four stages:

1. Run the Setup program.

   The Setup program prepares the hard disk for later stages of the installation and copies the necessary files to run the Setup wizard. This is the text mode portion of setup.

2. Run the Setup wizard.

   The Setup wizard requests setup information about the computer, which includes names, passwords, regional settings, and so on. This is the graphics mode portion of setup.

3. Install Windows networking.

   After gathering information about the computer, the Setup wizard prompts you for networking information and then installs the networking components so that the computer can communicate with other computers on the network.

4. Complete the Setup program.

   To complete the installation, Setup copies files to the hard disk, registers components, and configures the computer. The system restarts after installation is complete.

Running the Setup Program

To start Setup, use the Setup boot disks. Insert the disk labeled Setup Boot Disk (Disk 1) into drive A, and then turn on, or restart, the computer. If your computer supports booting from a CD-ROM drive, you can also start the installation by using the Windows 2000 CD-ROM.

The following steps describe running the Setup program on a clean disk drive. (See Figure 2.5.)

1. After the computer starts, a minimal version of Windows 2000 is copied into memory. This version of Windows 2000 starts the Setup program.

2. Setup starts the text-based version of the Setup program. This version of Setup prompts you to read and accept a licensing agreement.

3. Setup prompts you to select the partition on which to install Windows 2000. You can select an existing partition or create a new partition by using unpartitioned space on the hard disk. You can even delete a partition, if necessary, to reconfigure the hard disk's partitions.

4. After you create the installation partition, Setup prompts you to select a file system for the new partition. Then Setup formats the partition with the selected file system.

5. After formatting the Windows 2000 partition, Setup copies files to the hard disk and saves configuration information.

6. Setup restarts the computer and then starts the Windows 2000 Setup wizard. By default, the Windows 2000 operating system files are installed in the C:\Winnt folder.

Note For instructions on how to create the Windows 2000 Setup boot disks, see Appendix B, "Creating Setup Boot Disks."

Figure 2.5   Steps in the Setup program

Running the Setup Wizard

The graphical user interface (GUI)–based Windows 2000 Setup wizard leads you through the next stage of the installation process. It gathers information about you, your organization, and your computer.

After installing Windows 2000 security features and installing and configuring devices, the Windows 2000 Setup wizard asks you to provide the following information:

- **Regional settings.** Customize language, locale, and keyboard settings. You can configure Windows 2000 to use multiple languages and regional settings.

- **Name and organization.** Enter the name of the person and the organization to which this copy of Windows 2000 Professional is licensed.

- **Your Product Key.** Enter the 25-character Product Key that is on the sticker affixed to the back of your CD case.

- **Computer name.** Enter a computer name of up to 15 characters. The computer name must be different from other computer, workgroup, or domain names on the network. The Windows 2000 Setup wizard displays a default name, using the organization name that you entered earlier in the setup process.

- **Password for the Administrator account.** Specify a password for the Administrator user account, which the Windows 2000 Setup wizard creates during installation. The Administrator account provides administrative privileges that are required to manage the computer.

- **Modem dialing information.** Select the country or region where the computer is located. Often this is already completed, based on the selected regional setting. You also must enter the area (or city) for the computer's location as well as the number for obtaining an outside line, if relevant. Finally, select whether your phone system is tone dialing or pulse dialing.

Note You won't be prompted to enter modem dialing information during installation if a modem isn't attached to the computer on which you are installing Windows 2000 Professional.

- **Date and time settings.** If necessary, set the current date and time and select the correct time zone for your computer's location. These settings will most likely already be set correctly. You can also select whether to have Windows 2000 automatically adjust the computer's clock setting for daylight saving changes.

After you complete this stage in the installation, the Windows 2000 Setup wizard starts to install the Windows networking components.

Installing Windows Networking Components

After gathering information about your computer, the Windows 2000 Setup program automatically installs the network software.

The following list describes the steps in which Windows 2000 Professional installs networking components:

1. **Detect network adapter cards.** The Windows 2000 Setup wizard detects and configures any network adapter cards that are installed on the computer.

2. **Install networking components.** Windows 2000 installs (copies) files that allow your computer to connect to other computers, networks, and the Internet. Then the Setup program prompts you to choose whether to use typical settings or customized settings to configure the following networking components:

   - **Client for Microsoft Networks.** This component allows your computer to gain access to network resources.

- **File and Printer Sharing for Microsoft Networks.** This component allows other computers to gain access to file and print resources on your computer.

- **TCP/IP.** This protocol is the default networking protocol that allows your computer to communicate over local area networks (LANs) and wide area networks (WANs).

You can install other clients, services, and network protocols (such as NetBIOS Enhanced User Interface [NetBEUI], AppleTalk, and NWLink IPX/SPX/NetBIOS–compatible transport) any time after you install Windows 2000.

3. **Join a workgroup or domain.** If you create a computer account in the domain for your computer during the installation, the Windows 2000 Setup wizard prompts you for the name and password.

4. **Install components.** The Windows 2000 Setup wizard installs and configures the Windows networking components that you selected.

Completing the Installation

After installing the networking components, the Windows 2000 Professional Setup wizard copies additional files to configure Windows 2000 Professional. Then the Setup program automatically starts the fourth step in the installation process to perform a set of final tasks. (See Figure 2.6.)

Figure 2.6   The final steps in completing the installation

The following list describes the tasks that Setup performs to complete the installation stage:

1. **Installs Start-menu items.** The Setup program sets up shortcuts that will appear on the Start menu.

2. **Registers components.** Setup applies the configuration settings that you specified in the Windows 2000 Setup wizard.

3. **Saves the configuration.** Setup saves your configuration settings to the local hard disk. The next time that you start Windows 2000, the computer will use this configuration automatically.

4. **Removes temporary files.** To save hard disk space, Setup deletes any files that it installed for use only during installation.

5. **Restarts the computer.** After completing the preceding steps, Setup restarts the computer. This finishes the installation of Windows 2000 Professional on a client or stand-alone system from a CD-ROM.

Practice: Installing Windows 2000 from a CD-ROM

In this practice, you will install Windows 2000 Professional from a CD-ROM.

▶ **To begin the text-mode installation phase of Windows 2000 Professional setup**

1. Insert the Windows 2000 Professional CD-ROM into the CD-ROM drive.

   Note If your computer is configured with an El Torito–compatible CD-ROM drive, you can install Windows 2000 without using the Setup disks. You can run the Setup program by restarting the computer with the CD-ROM inserted into the CD-ROM drive and then skip to step 4 in this practice. If you need to create the Setup disks, see Appendix B, "Creating Setup Boot Disks."

2. Insert the disk labeled Setup Boot Disk into drive A, and then turn on, or restart, the computer.

3. When prompted, insert Setup Disk 2 into drive A and proceed as directed for Setup Disks 3 and 4.

4. If you're installing the Evaluation Software version of Windows 2000, Setup displays the Setup Notification message on the Windows 2000 Professional Setup screen; read it and then press Enter to continue. If you're installing the retail version, the Welcome To Setup screen appears.

   Setup displays the Welcome To Setup screen. Notice that, in addition to the initial installation of Windows 2000, you can use Windows 2000 Setup to repair a damaged Windows 2000 installation.

   Note Notice at this point that if you want to quit Setup for any reason, you can press F3 to exit.

5. Read the Welcome To Setup screen and press Enter to continue.

   Setup displays the Windows 2000 Licensing Agreement screen.

6. Read the licensing agreement, and then press F8 to agree with the licensing terms.

Setup prompts you to select an area of free space or an existing partition on which to install Windows 2000. This stage of Setup provides a way for you to create and delete partitions on your hard disk.

7. Press Enter to select the default C: partition.

Note If you already have an operating system installed on the C partition, you can choose another partition. For the rest of the course, remember to replace C:\ with the appropriate location for your Windows 2000 Professional installation.

If you have a version of Windows 2000 Professional already installed and you want to replace it with a fresh install, press Esc. When prompted, select the appropriate partition to install Windows 2000, press Enter, and follow the directions on the screen.

Setup displays a list of file system choices.

8. Ensure that the Format The Partition Using The NTFS File System option is highlighted and press Enter.

Note If you decide to format the partition with the FAT file system, Windows 2000 provides the Convert command, which you can use to convert a partition to NTFS without having to reformat the partition and lose all the information contained on the partition.

Setup formats the hard disk, examines it, and then copies files to the Windows 2000 installation folders. This might take several minutes. It then initializes Windows 2000.

Note If the partition is already formatted, Setup displays a Caution message indicating that formatting this drive will delete all files on it. If you see this message, and this is the partition where you want to install Windows 2000 Professional, ensure that this partition option is selected and press Enter to format the drive.

---

9. When Setup prompts you to restart the computer, remove all the disks from the disk drives, and then press Enter.

Important If your computer supports booting from the CD-ROM drive and you don't remove the Windows 2000 Professional CD-ROM before Setup restarts the computer, the computer might reboot from the Windows 2000 Professional CD-ROM. This will cause Setup to start again from the beginning. If this happens, remove the CD-ROM and then restart the computer.

The computer restarts, and a message box appears prompting you to insert the CD-ROM labeled Windows 2000 Professional into your CD-ROM drive.

▶ **To begin the graphics-mode installation phase of Windows 2000 Professional Setup**

1. Insert the CD-ROM labeled Windows 2000 Professional into your CD-ROM drive, and then click OK.

   The Windows 2000 Professional Setup wizard appears.

2. If necessary, click Next to continue.

   Setup detects and installs devices. This might take several minutes. Setup configures NTFS folder and file permissions for the operating system files, detects the hardware devices in the computer, and then installs and configures device drivers to support the detected hardware. This process will take several minutes.

   Setup then prompts you to customize Windows 2000 for different regions and languages.

3. Select the appropriate system locale, user locale, and keyboard layout, or ensure that they are correct for your language and location, and then click Next to continue.

Note You can modify regional settings after you install Windows 2000 by using Regional Settings in Control Panel. For more information, see Chapter 4, "Using Windows Control Panel."

Setup displays the Personalize Your Software page, prompting you for your name and organization name. Setup uses your organization name to generate the default computer name. Many applications that you install later will use this information for product registration and document identification.

4. In the Name box, type your name; in the Organization box, type the name of your organization. Click Next.

   Setup displays the Your Product Key page, prompting you for the 25-character Product Key that appears on the sticker affixed to your CD case.

5. Type the 25-character Product Key that appears on the back of your CD case in the five Product Key boxes, and then click Next.

   Setup displays the Computer Name And Administrator Password page.

6. Type **Pro1** in the Computer Name box.

   Note that Windows 2000 displays the computer name in all capital letters, no matter how you type it in.

> **Important** If your computer is on a network, check with the network adminis-
> trator before assigning a name to your computer. Throughout the rest of this
> self-paced training kit, the practice sections will refer to Pro1. If you don't
> name your computer Pro1, everywhere the materials reference Pro1 you will
> have to substitute the name of your computer.

7. In the Administrator Password box and in the Confirm Password box, type
   password, and then click Next.

> **Important** For the practice sections in this self-paced training kit, you will use
> *password* for the Administrator account. You should always use a complex
> password for the Administrator account (one that others cannot easily guess).
> Microsoft recommends mixing uppercase and lowercase letters, numbers, and
> symbols (for example, Lp6*g9).

If a modem is connected to the computer to which you are installing Windows
2000 Professional, Setup displays the Modem Dialing Information page;
otherwise, Setup displays the Date And Time Settings page. If your computer
doesn't have a modem, go to step 12.

8. Ensure that the correct country and region is selected.

9. Type in the correct area code or city code.

10. If you dial a number to get an outside line, type in the correct number.

11. Ensure that the correct phone system is selected, and then click Next.

    Setup displays the Date And Time Settings page.

12. On the Date And Time Settings page, confirm that the Date & Time setting
    and the Time Zone setting are correct for your location.

13. Select the Automatically Adjust Clock For Daylight Saving Changes check
    box if you want Windows 2000 to automatically change the time on your
    computer for daylight saving time changes, and then click Next.

> **Note** If you have configured your computer for dual booting with another
> operating system that can also adjust your clock for daylight saving time
> changes, enable this feature for only one operating system. Enable this feature
> on the operating system you use most frequently so that the daylight saving
> adjustment will occur only once.

Setup displays the Network Settings page and automatically installs network
software so that you can connect to other networks and to the Internet. This

will take a few moments. After the files are copied, the Setup program prompts you to choose whether to use typical or custom settings for configuring network components.

14. Ensure that the Typical Settings option is selected, and click Next.

    Setup displays the Workgroup Or Computer Domain page.

15. Select the option No, This Computer Is Not On A Network, Or Is On A Network Without A Domain. Ensure that WORKGROUP appears in the Workgroup Or Computer Domain box, and click Next.

    Setup displays the Installing Components page, displaying the status as Setup copies files to install and configure Windows 2000 components. This process will take several minutes.

    Setup then displays the Performing Final Tasks page and displays the status as Setup installs Start-menu items, registers components, saves settings, and removes any temporary files. This process will also take several minutes.

    The Completing The Windows 2000 Setup Wizard page appears.

16. Remove the CD-ROM from the CD-ROM drive, and then click Finish to continue setting up Windows 2000 Professional.

Important If your computer supports booting from the CD-ROM drive and you don't remove the Windows 2000 Professional CD-ROM before Setup restarts the computer, the computer might reboot from the Windows 2000 Professional CD-ROM. This will cause Setup to start again from the beginning. If this happens, remove the CD-ROM and then restart the computer.

The computer restarts, and the Welcome To The Network Identification Wizard appears.

▶ **To configure your network**

1. To use the Welcome To The Network Identification Wizard, click Next.

    The Users Of This Computer page appears.

2. Select Users Must Enter A User Name And Password To Use This Computer, and then click Next.

    The Completing The Network Identification Wizard page appears.

3. Click Finish.

▶ **To log on as Administrator**

1. In the Log On To Windows dialog box, ensure that it says Administrator in the User Name box, and in the Password box, type **password.**

2. Click OK.

Note If the Found New Hardware wizard appears, read the information displayed, and then click Finish.

The Getting Started With Windows 2000 dialog box appears.

3. Clear the Show This Screen At Startup check box, and then click Exit to close the Getting Started With Windows 2000 dialog box.

Lesson Summary

In this lesson, you learned that installing Windows 2000 Professional is a four-stage process. You learned the tasks that are completed during each of these four stages, and then you installed Windows 2000 Professional from a CD-ROM. During installation, you formatted your installation partition as NTFS and had the computer join the default workgroup.

Lesson 3: Installing Windows 2000 over the Network

In addition to installing from a CD-ROM, you can install Windows 2000 over the network. This lesson demonstrates the similarities and differences between installing from a CD-ROM and installing over the network. The major difference is the location of the source files needed to install Windows 2000. This lesson also lists the requirements for a network installation.

After this lesson, you will be able to

- Identify the steps for completing a network installation of Windows 2000.

Estimated lesson time: 10 minutes

Preparing for a Network Installation

In a network installation, the Windows 2000 installation files reside in a shared location on a network file server, which is called a *distribution server*. From the computer on which you want to install Windows 2000 (the target computer), you connect to the distribution server and then run the Setup program.

The basic environment requirement for a network installation is shown in Figure 2.7. The pre-Setup requirements for a network installation are explained in more detail in the list that follows.

Requirements for a network installation:

- Distribution server
- FAT partition on the target computer
- Network client

Figure 2.7   A network installation's basic environment

- **Locate a distribution server.** The distribution server contains the installation files from the i386 folder on the Windows 2000 Professional CD-ROM. These files must reside in a common network location in a shared folder. This shared folder allows computers on the network to gain access to the installation files. Contact a network administrator to obtain the path to the installation files on the distribution server.

Note Once you have created or located a distribution server, you can use the over-the-network installation method to install Windows 2000 concurrently on multiple computers.

- **Create a FAT partition on the target computer.** The target computer requires a formatted partition on which to copy the installation files. Create a 650-MB (2-GB or larger recommended) partition and format it with the FAT file system.
- **Install a network client.** A network client is software that allows the target computer to connect to the distribution server. On a computer without an operating system, you must boot from a client disk that includes a network client that enables the target computer to connect to the distribution server.

Creating a Distribution Server

A distribution server stores the distribution folder structure. The distribution folder structure contains the files necessary to install Windows 2000 Professional over the network. If you have a lot of computers on which to install Windows 2000 or if you will be doing multiple Windows 2000 installations simultaneously, create more than one set of distribution folders. Having distribution folders set up on several computers will make the file copy portion of Windows 2000 Setup faster. Even if you have several different types of hardware configurations on which to install Windows 2000, you create one set of distribution folders and use them with different answer files to install to all the different hardware types.

Note If you are installing Windows 2000 on a computer running Windows 95, Windows 98, Windows NT, or an earlier version of Windows 2000, the Winnt32.exe program allows you to specify up to eight locations for the distribution folders.

To create a distribution server, follow these steps:

1. Log on to the server as administrator or connect to the server on which you want to create a distribution file structure.
2. Create a folder on the server named W2000P.

Note The name W2000P is for a distribution folder structure containing the source files for Windows 2000 Professional. You can use W2000S for Windows 2000 Server and W2000AS for Windows 2000 Advanced Server. If you're creating distribution folder structures on more than one server, you can name them W2000P1, W2000P2, W2000P3, W2000P4, and so on.

3. Copy the contents of the i386 folder from the Windows 2000 Professional CD-ROM to the folder you created on the distribution server.

4. In the W2000P folder you created, create an OEM subfolder.

Note The OEM subfolder is used to hold applications, drivers, or utilities you want Setup to copy to the target computer.

If Setup finds the OEM folder in the root of the distribution folder, it copies all of the files found in this directory to the temporary directory created during the text portion of Setup.

Note The OEMFILESPATH key in the answer file allows you to create the OEM subfolder outside of the distribution folder.

Performing an Installation over the Network

The Windows 2000 Setup program copies the installation files to the target computer. After copying the installation files, Setup restarts the target computer. From this point on, you install Windows 2000 in the same way that you install from a CD-ROM.

The following steps describe the process for installing Windows 2000 over the network (see Figure 2.8):

1. On the target computer, boot from the network client.

2. Connect to the distribution server. After you start the network client on the target computer, connect to the shared folder on the distribution server that contains the Windows 2000 Professional installation files.

3. Run Winnt.exe or Winnt32.exe to start the Setup program. Use Winnt.exe for installation if you are using Windows 3.x on the target system, and use Winnt32.exe for installation if you are using Windows 95, 98, NT 4 (or NT 3.51), or 2000 on the target system. Winnt.exe and Winnt32.exe reside in the shared folder on the distribution server. When you run Winnt.exe from the shared folder, it does the following:

   - Creates the Win_nt.~ls temporary folder on the target computer.
   - Copies the Windows 2000 installation files from the shared folder on the distribution server to the Win_nt.~ls folder on the target computer.

4. Install Windows 2000. Setup restarts the target computer and begins installing Windows 2000.

Figure 2.8   Installing Windows 2000 over the network

Modifying the Setup Process

You can modify a server-based installation by changing how Winnt.exe runs the setup process. Table 2.2 describes the switches that you can use with Winnt.exe to control the setup process.

Table 2.2   Available Switches for Winnt.exe

Switch	Description
/a	Enables accessibility options.
/e[:*command*]	Specifies a command to be executed at the end of Setup's GUI mode.
/r[:*folder*]	Specifies an optional folder to be installed. The folder is retained after installation.
/rx[:*folder*]	Specifies an optional folder to be copied. Setup deletes the folder after installation.
/s[:*sourcepath*]	Specifies the source location of Windows 2000 files. The location must be a full path of the form x:\ [path] or \\server\share\ [path]. The default is the current folder.
/t[:*tempdrive*]	Specifies a drive to contain temporary setup files. If not specified, Setup attempts to locate a drive for you.
/u[:*answer file*]	Performs an unattended setup using an answer file. The answer file provides answers to some or all of the prompts that you normally respond to during Setup. (Requires /s.)
/udf:*id*[,*UDF_file*]	Establishes an identifier (ID) that Setup uses to specify how a Uniqueness Database File (UDF) modifies an answer file. This switch overrides answer-file values, and the identifier determines the values in the UDB file that are used. If you don't specify a UDB file, Setup prompts for the disk containing the $Unique$.udb file.

Modifying the Setup Process Using Winnt32.exe

You can modify a server-based installation by changing how Winnt32.exe runs the setup process. Table 2.3 describes the switches that you can use with Winnt32.exe to control the setup process.

Table 2.3   Available Switches for Winnt32.exe

Switch	Description
/checkupgradeonly	Checks the computer for upgrade compatibility with Windows 2000; for upgrade installations, it creates a report.
/copydir:*folder_name*	Creates an additional folder within the *systemroot* folder (the folder that contains the Windows 2000 system files). For example, if your source folder contains a folder called My_drivers, type **/copydir:My_drivers** to copy the My_drivers folder to your system folder. You can use the /copydir switch to create as many additional folders as you like.
/copysource:*folder_name*	Creates an additional folder within the *systemroot* folder. Setup deletes files created with /copysource after installation completes.
/cmd: *command_line*	Executes a command before the final phase of Setup.
/cmdcons	Adds a Recovery Console option to the operating system selection screen.
/debug[*level*] [:*file_name*]	Creates a debug log at the specified level. By default, it creates C:\Winnt32.log at level 2 (the warning level).
/m:*folder_name*	Forces Setup to copy replacement files from another location and to look in that location first. If files are present, this switch tells Setup to use those files instead of files from the default location.
/makelocalsource	Forces Setup to copy all installation files to the local hard disk. Use this switch when installing Windows 2000 from a CD-ROM if you want to access installation files when the CD-ROM drive isn't available later in the installation.
/noreboot	Forces Setup to not restart the computer following the file copy phase, which enables a command to be entered by the user prior to completing setup.
/s:*source_path*	Specifies the source location of Windows 2000 installation files. To simultaneously copy files from multiple paths, use a separate /s switch for each source path.
/syspart:*drive_letter*	Copies Setup startup files to a hard disk and marks the drive as active. You can then install the drive on another computer. When you start that computer, Setup starts at the next phase. Use of /syspart requires use of the /tempdrive switch.
/tempdrive:*drive_letter*	Places temporary files on the specified drive and installs Windows 2000 on that drive.

Switch	Description
/unattend [number] [:*answer_file*]	Performs an unattended installation. The answer file provides your custom specifications to Setup. If you don't specify an answer file, all user settings are taken from the previous installation.
	You can specify the number of seconds between the time that Setup finishes copying the files and when it restarts. You can specify the number of seconds only on a computer running Windows 2000 that is upgrading to a later version of Windows 2000.
/udf:id[,*udf_file*]	Indicates an identifier (ID) that Setup uses to specify how a Uniqueness Database File (UDF) modifies an answer file. The .UDF file overrides values in the answer file, and the identifier determines which values in the .UDF file are used. For example, /udf:RAS_user, Our_company.udf overrides settings that are specified for the RAS_user identifier in the Our_company.udf file. If you don't specify a .UDF file, Setup prompts the user to insert a disk that contains the $Unique$.udb file.

Lesson Summary

In this lesson, you learned that the main difference between an over-the-network installation and an installation from a CD-ROM is the location of the source files. Once you connect to the shared folder containing the source files and start Winnt.exe or Winnt32.exe, the installation proceeds like an installation from a CD-ROM. Several switches are available for Winnt.exe and for Winnt32.exe to modify the installation process.

Lesson 4: Troubleshooting Windows 2000 Setup

Your installation of Windows 2000 should complete without any problems. However, this lesson covers some common issues that you might encounter during installation.

After this lesson, you will be able to

- Troubleshoot problems encountered during the setup of Windows 2000.

Estimated lesson time: 5 minutes

Resolving Common Problems

Table 2.4 lists some common installation problems and offers solutions to resolve them.

Table 2.4   Troubleshooting Tips

Problem	Solution
Media errors	If you are installing from a CD-ROM, use a different CD-ROM. To request a replacement CD-ROM, contact Microsoft or your vendor.
Nonsupported CD-ROM drive	Replace the CD-ROM drive with one that is supported, or if that isn't possible, try another method of installing, such as installing over the network, and then after you have completed the installation, you can add the adapter card driver for the CD-ROM drive if it is available.
Insufficient disk space	Use the Setup program to create a partition by using existing free space on the hard disk; or, delete and create partitions as needed to create a partition that is large enough for installation; or, reformat an existing partition to create more space.
Failure of dependency service to start	In the Windows 2000 Setup wizard, return to the Network Settings dialog box and verify that you installed the correct protocol and network adapter. Verify that the network adapter has the proper configuration settings, such as transceiver type, and that the local computer name is unique on the network.
Inability to connect to the domain controller	Verify that the server running the DNS Service and the domain controller are both running and online. If you can't locate a domain controller, install in a workgroup and then join the domain after installation.
	Verify that the domain name is correct.
	Verify that the network adapter card and protocol settings are set correctly.

Problem	Solution
	If you are reinstalling Windows 2000 and using the same computer name, delete and then recreate the computer account.
Failure of Windows 2000 to install or start	Verify that Windows 2000 is detecting all of the hardware and that all of the hardware is on the HCL.

Setup Logs

During setup, Windows 2000 generates a number of log files. These logs contain information about the installation process that can help you resolve any problems that occur after the Setup program completes. Two of the logs are especially useful for troubleshooting: the action log and the error log.

Using the Action Log

The action log provides a description of the actions that Setup performs. These actions are recorded in chronological order, and they include such actions as copying files and creating registry entries. The action log also includes any entries that are written to the error log. The action log is stored in the file Setupact.log.

Using the Error Log

The error log contains a description of any errors that occur during setup, along with an indication of the severity of each error. If errors occur, the log viewer shows the user the error log at the end of setup. The error log is stored in the file Setuperr.log.

Additional Logs

A number of additional logs are created during setup. These logs include the following:

- *windir*\comsetup.log. Outlines installation for Optional Component Manager and Com+ components.
- *windir*\mmdet.log. As a detection log for multimedia devices, details port ranges for each device.
- *windir*\setupapi.log. Logs an entry each time a line from an .INF file is implemented. If for some reason an error occurs, it will log information here to indicate the failure.
- *windir*\debug\NetSetup.log. Logs activity for joining a domain or workgroup.

Lesson Summary

In this lesson, you learned some common problems that you might encounter when installing Windows 2000. For example, bad media can cause installation problems, in which case you will have to get a new CD-ROM to be able to install. You might also encounter problems with your installation if your hardware isn't on the HCL. If your CD-ROM drive isn't on the HCL, you can swap it out for a supported drive or install over the network and add the driver to support the CD-ROM drive if it's available.

If you failed to complete your preinstallation tasks and none of the partitions have enough room to install Windows 2000, you can create a new partition from unused space on the hard disk if the space is available; you can delete some existing partitions so that you can create one large enough to install Windows 2000; or you can format an existing partition to provide enough space to install Windows 2000.

You also learned some tips to try in case you can't connect to the domain controller. If you can't connect to the domain controller, you can complete the installation by joining the computer to a workgroup. After you have completed the installation and determined what is preventing you from connecting to the domain controller, you can join the computer to the domain.

Review

The following questions will help you determine whether you have learned enough to move on to the next chapter. If you have difficulty answering these questions, please go back and review the material in this chapter before beginning the next chapter. See Appendix A, "Questions and Answers," for the answers for these questions.

1. Your company has decided to install Windows 2000 Professional on all new computers that are purchased for desktop users. What should you do before you purchase new computers to ensure that Windows 2000 can be installed and run without difficulty?

2. You are attempting to install Windows 2000 Professional from a CD-ROM; however, you have discovered that your computer doesn't support booting from the CD-ROM drive. How can you install Windows 2000?

3. You are installing Windows 2000 Professional on a computer that will be a client in an existing Windows 2000 domain. You want to add the computer to the domain during installation. What information do you need, and what computers must be available on the network, before you run the Setup program?

4. You are using a CD-ROM to install Windows 2000 Professional on a computer that was previously running another operating system. How should you configure the hard disk to simplify the installation process?

5. You are installing Windows 2000 Professional over the network. Before you install to a client computer, what must you do?

C H A P T E R   3

Using Microsoft Management Console and Task Scheduler

About This Chapter

The primary administrative tools that you use to manage Microsoft Windows 2000 are the Microsoft Management Console (MMC), Task Scheduler, and Control Panel. This chapter presents an overview of the MMC and Task Scheduler. Chapter 4, "Using Windows Control Panel," discusses Control Panel.

Before You Begin

To complete this chapter, you must have

- A computer that meets the minimum hardware requirements located in "About This Book."
- The Windows 2000 Professional software installed on the computer.

Lesson 1: Introducing the Microsoft Management Console

This lesson introduces the MMC and defines consoles, console trees, details panes, snap-ins, and extensions. The lesson also covers the differences between Author mode and User mode. This lesson discusses the .MSC file extension assigned to the consoles you create and the My Administrative Tools folder where the consoles you create are stored as files. The My Administrative Tools folder is accessible from the Programs menu and offers easy access to the consoles that you create.

After this lesson, you will be able to

- Describe the function and components of the Microsoft Management Console, including snap-ins, console options, and modes.

Estimated lesson time: 20 minutes

Microsoft Management Consoles

One of the primary administrative tools that you use to manage Windows 2000 is the Microsoft Management Console. The MMC provides a standardized method to create, save, and open administrative tools, which are called *consoles*. The MMC doesn't provide management functions itself, but it's the program that hosts management applications, called *snap-ins,* which you use to perform one or more administrative tasks. The MMC is also a great troubleshooting tool.

The MMC allows you to do the following:

- **Administer tasks and troubleshoot problems.** You can perform most of your administrative tasks and troubleshoot many problems by using only the MMC. Being able to use one interface saves time instead of having to use numerous interfaces.

- **Centralize administration.** You can use consoles to perform the majority of your administrative tasks from one computer.

- **Administer tasks and troubleshoot problems remotely.** You can use most snap-ins for remote administration and troubleshooting. Not all snap-ins are available for you to use on remote computers, so Windows 2000 prompts you with a dialog box when you can use the snap-in remotely.

Note Third-party vendors can design their administrative tools as snap-ins for use in the MMC.

Consoles contain one or more snap-ins. They are saved as files that have the .MSC extension. All the settings for the snap-ins contained in the console are saved and are restored when the file is opened, even if the console file is opened on a different computer or network.

You configure consoles to hold snap-ins to perform specific tasks. Console options determine how a console operates. By using console options, you can create consoles for other administrators to use from their own computers to perform specific tasks.

Console Tree and Details Pane

Every console has a console tree. A *console tree* displays the hierarchical organization of the snap-ins that are contained within that console. As you can see in Figure 3.1, this console contains the Disk Defragmenter snap-in and the Device Manager On Local Computer snap-in.

Figure 3.1   The MMC window

The console tree organizes snap-ins that are a part of a console. This allows you to easily locate a specific snap-in. Items that you add to the console tree appear under the console root. The *details pane* lists the contents of the active snap-in.

Every console contains an Action menu and a View menu. The choices on these menus vary, depending on the current selection in the console tree.

Administrative Tools

By default, Windows 2000 saves custom console files (with an .MSC extension) in the Administrative Tools folder. Assuming that your Windows 2000 Professional operating system is on drive C and that you are logged on as Administrator, the path to these files would be C:\Documents and Settings\Administrator\ Start Menu\Programs\Administrative Tools. The folder structure below C:\Documents and Settings doesn't exist until the first time a user logs on.

Even after the folder structure is created for a new user who logs on for the first time, the Administrative Tools folder might not appear on the Programs menu if its display is turned off, which it is by default when Windows 2000 Professional is first installed. (To turn on its display without using MMC, click Start, point to Settings, click Taskbar & Start Menu, and select the Display Administrative Tools check box on the Advanced tab of the Taskbar And Start Menu Properties dialog box.) However, when you run MMC and save a custom console, Windows 2000 turns on the display of the Administrative Tools folder for each user.

Note In Windows 2000 Server, the private folder containing the consoles you create are in the My Administrative Tools folder. There is an Administrative Tools folder, but it holds some preconfigured consoles for use with the MMC.

Snap-Ins

Snap-ins are applications that are designed to work in the MMC. You use snap-ins to perform administrative tasks. Two types of snap-ins exist: stand-alone snap-ins and extension snap-ins.

Stand-Alone Snap-Ins

Stand-alone snap-ins are usually referred to simply as snap-ins. Use stand-alone snap-ins to perform Windows 2000 administrative tasks. Each snap-in provides one function or a related set of functions. Windows 2000 Server comes with standard snap-ins. Windows 2000 Professional includes a smaller set of standard snap-ins.

Extension Snap-Ins

Extension snap-ins are usually referred to as *extensions*. They are snap-ins that provide additional administrative functionality to another snap-in. The following are characteristics of extensions:

- Extensions are designed to work with one or more stand-alone snap-ins, based on the function of the stand-alone snap-in.

- When you add an extension, Windows 2000 displays only extensions that are compatible with the stand-alone snap-in. Windows 2000 places the extensions in the appropriate location within the stand-alone snap-in.

- When you add a snap-in to a console, MMC adds all available extensions by default. You can remove any extension from the snap-in.

- You can add an extension to multiple snap-ins.

Figure 3.2 demonstrates the concept of snap-ins and extensions. A toolbox holds a drill. You can use a drill with its standard drill bit. You can perform additional functions with different drill bits. The same is true for snap-ins and extensions.

- **Snap-ins are administrative tools.**
- **Extensions provide additional functionality to snap-ins.**
  - Extensions are preassigned to snap-ins.
  - Multiple snap-ins may use the same extensions.

Figure 3.2   Snap-ins and extensions

Console Options

Some stand-alone snap-ins can use extensions that provide additional functionality, for example, Computer Management. However, some snap-ins, like Event Viewer, can act as a snap-in or an extension.

Use console options to determine how each console operates by selecting the appropriate *console mode*. The console mode determines the console functionality for the person who is using a saved console. The two available console modes are *Author mode* and *User mode*.

Author Mode

When you save a console in Author mode, you enable full access to all MMC functionality, which includes modifying the console. Save the console using Author mode to allow those using it to do the following:

- Add or remove snap-ins
- Create new windows
- View all portions of the console tree
- Save consoles

Note By default, all new consoles are saved in Author mode.

User Mode

Usually, if you plan to distribute a console to other administrators, you should save the console in User mode. When you set a console to User mode, users can't add snap-ins to, remove snap-ins from, or save the console. Three types of User modes exist, which allow different levels of access and functionality. Table 3.1 describes when to use each User mode.

Table 3.1   Console User Modes

Use	When
Full Access	Grants users full access to all window management commands and to the console tree provided. Prevents users from adding or removing snap-ins or changing console properties.
Limited Access, Multiple Windows	You don't want to allow users to open new windows or gain access to a portion of the console tree. You do want to allow users to view multiple windows in the console.
Limited Access, Single Window	You don't want to allow users to open new windows or gain access to a portion of the console tree. You do want to allow users to view only one window in the console.

Lesson Summary

In this lesson, you learned that one of the primary administrative tools that you use to manage Windows 2000 is the Microsoft Management Console. The MMC provides a standardized method to create, save, and open administrative tools, which are called consoles. Consoles hold one or more applications called snap-ins, which you use to perform administrative tasks and troubleshoot problems locally and on remote computers. By default, Windows 2000 saves custom console files (with an .MSC extension) in the Administrative Tools folder of the user who created it.

You learned that every console has a console tree. The console tree displays the hierarchical organization of the snap-ins that are contained within that console. This allows you to easily locate a specific snap-in. The details pane lists the contents of the active snap-in. You also learned about the two types of snap-ins: stand-alone snap-ins and extension snap-ins. A stand-alone snap-in is usually referred to simply as a snap-in and provides one function or a related set of functions. An extension snap-in is usually referred to as an extension, and it provides additional administrative functionality to a snap-in. An extension is designed to work with one or more stand-alone snap-ins, based on the function of the stand-alone snap-in.

Finally, in this lesson you learned about console options. You use console options to determine how each console operates by selecting the appropriate console mode. The two available console modes are Author mode and User mode. When you save a console in Author mode, you enable full access to all MMC functionality, which includes modifying the console. You save the console using Author mode to allow those using it to add or remove snap-ins, create new windows, view all portions of the console tree, and save consoles. Usually, if you plan to distribute a console to other administrators, save the console in User mode. When you set a console to User mode, users can't add snap-ins to, remove snap-ins from, or save the console.

Lesson 2: Using Consoles

This lesson explains how you can create, use, and modify consoles. This lesson also explains how you can use consoles for remote administration.

After this lesson, you will be able to

- Create and use consoles.
- Create custom consoles for remote administration.

Estimated lesson time: 40 minutes

Creating Consoles

You can create your own custom consoles by combining multiple preconfigured snap-ins with third-party snap-ins, which are provided by independent software vendors (ISVs) that perform related tasks. You can then do the following:

- Save the custom consoles to be able to use them again.
- Distribute the custom consoles to other administrators.
- Use the custom consoles from any computer to centralize and unify administrative tasks.

Creating custom consoles allows you to meet your administrative requirements by combining snap-ins that you use to perform common administrative tasks. By creating a custom console, you don't have to switch between different programs because all of the snap-ins that you need to perform your job are located in the custom console. You start MMC with an empty console open as follows:

1. Click the Start button.
2. Click Run.
3. Type **mmc** in the Open box, and then click OK.

   A console window titled Console1 opens; it contains a window titled Console Root. This is an empty console that is ready for you to customize. Use the Console menu to create, open, save, and customize a console. The following table describes when to use the different commands on the Console menu.

Command	Purpose
New	To create a new custom console
Open	To use a saved console
Save or Save As	To use the console later
Add/Remove Snap-In	To add or remove one or more snap-ins and their associated extensions to or from a console
Options	To configure the console mode and create a custom console

4. Close the MMC window.

Using Consoles for Remote Administration

When you create custom consoles, you can set up a snap-in for remote administration. Remote administration allows you to perform administrative tasks from any location. For example, you can use a computer running Windows 2000 Professional to perform administrative tasks on a computer running Windows 2000 Server. You can't use all snap-ins for remote administration; the design of each snap-in dictates whether you can use it for remote administration.

To perform remote administration

- You can use snap-ins from computers running either Windows 2000 Professional or Windows 2000 Server.

- You must use specific snap-ins that are designed for remote administration. If the snap-in is available for remote administration, Windows 2000 prompts you to choose the target computer to administer.

Practice: Creating a Customized Microsoft Management Console

In this practice, you will create a customized console. You will use this console to confirm the last time that your computer was started. You will also add a snap-in with extensions.

▶ **To create a customized console**

1. Click the Start button, and then click Run.

2. In the Open box, type **mmc** and then click OK.

   MMC starts and displays an empty console.

3. Maximize the Console1 window by clicking its Maximize button.

4. Maximize the Console Root window by clicking its Maximize button.

5. To view the currently configured options, click Options on the Console menu.

   Notice that the default console mode is Author mode. Remember that Author mode grants users full access to all MMC functionality.

6. In the Console Mode box, make sure that Author Mode is selected, and then click OK.

7. On the Console menu, click Add/Remove Snap-In.

   MMC displays the Add/Remove Snap-In dialog box.

8. Click Add.

   MMC displays the Add Standalone Snap-In dialog box, as shown in Figure 3.3.

Figure 3.3   The Add Standalone Snap-In dialog box

Notice the available snap-ins. MMC allows you to add one or more snap-ins to a console, enabling you to create your own customized management tools.

9. Select Computer Management and then click Add.

   The Computer Management dialog box displays.

10. Ensure that Local Computer: (The Computer This Console Is Running On) is selected, and then click Finish.

    Notice that Computer Management (Local) appears in the Add/Remove Snap-In dialog box.

11. Click Close to close the Add Standalone Snap-In dialog box.

12. Click OK to close the Add/Remove Snap-In dialog box.

13. On the Console menu, click Save As.

    MMC displays the Save As dialog box.

14. In the File Name box, type **All Events** and then click Save.

    The name of your console appears on the MMC title bar.

    Now you will confirm that the console was saved in the Administrative Tools folder by closing and then reopening the console.

▶   **To confirm the location of a customized console**

1. On the Console menu, click Exit.

   You have now created and saved a customized console named All Events.

2. Click the Start button, click Run, type **mmc**, and then click OK.

3. On the Console menu, click Open.

   MMC displays the Open dialog box. Notice that the console you created (All Events.Msc) is in the Administrative Tools folder.

4. Click the All Events file and then click Open.

   Windows 2000 opens the All Events console that you saved previously.

► **To add the Event Viewer snap-in to a console**

1. On the Console menu, click Add/Remove Snap-In.

   MMC displays the Add/Remove Snap-In dialog box with the Standalone tab showing. Notice that Computer Management is the only loaded snap-in. You will add a snap-in to the console root.

2. In the Add/Remove Snap-In dialog box, click Add.

   MMC displays the Add Standalone Snap-In dialog box.

3. In the Add Standalone Snap-In dialog box, select Event Viewer, and then click Add.

   MMC displays the Select Computer dialog box, allowing you to specify which computer you want to administer.

   Notice that you can add Event Viewer for the local computer on which you are working, or if your local computer is part of a network, you can also add Event Viewer for a remote computer.

   To add Event Viewer for a remote computer, you select the Another Computer option, and then click Browse. In the Select Computer dialog box, you click the remote computer for which you would like to add Event Viewer, and then click OK.

   In this case, you will add Event Viewer for your computer, the local computer.

4. In the Select Computer dialog box, make sure that Local Computer is selected, and then click Finish.

5. In the Add Standalone Snap-In dialog box, click Close; and in the Add/Remove Snap-In dialog box, click OK.

   Event Viewer (Local) now appears in the console tree along with Computer Management (Local).

Tip   To see the entire folder name, drag the border between the console and details panes to the right.

► **To determine the last time that the computer was started**

1. In the console tree of the All Events console, expand the Event Viewer (Local) folder, and then click System.

   MMC displays the most recent system events in the details pane.

2. In the details pane, double-click the most recent Information event listed as Eventlog in the Source column. If the Description box doesn't say "The Event Log Service Was Started," click the up arrow until you find this description.

The Event log service starts as part of your system startup. The date and time represents the approximate time that your system was started. Make a note of the date and time.

3. To close the Event Properties dialog box, click OK.

4. On the Console menu, click Exit to close the All Events console.

A Microsoft Management Console dialog box appears, asking whether you want to save the console settings to All Events.

5. Click No.

▶ **To remove extensions from a snap-in**

1. Click the Start button, and then click Run.

2. In the Open box, type **mmc**, if necessary, and then click OK.

MMC displays an empty console.

3. Maximize the Console1 and Console Root windows, if necessary.

4. On the Console menu, click Add/Remove Snap-In.

MMC displays the Add/Remove Snap-In dialog box with the Standalone tab showing. You will add a snap-in to the console root.

5. Click Add.

All snap-ins that are listed here are stand-alone snap-ins.

6. In the Add Standalone Snap-In dialog box, in the Available Standalone Snap-Ins box, click Computer Management, and then click Add.

MMC displays the Computer Management dialog box, allowing you to specify which computer you want to administer. In this procedure, you will add the Computer Management snap-in for your own computer.

7. Verify that Local Computer is selected, and then click Finish.

8. Click Close.

Computer Management appears in the list of snap-ins that have been added.

9. In the Add/Remove Snap-In dialog box, click OK.

MMC displays the Computer Management snap-in in the console tree below Console Root. Console Root acts as a container for several categories of administrative functions.

10. Expand Computer Management and review the available functions, and then expand System Tools.

Note Do not use any of the tools at this point.

Notice that several extensions are available, including Event Viewer, System Information, and Device Manager. You can restrict the functionality of a snap-in by removing extensions.

11. On the Console menu, click Add/Remove Snap-In.

    The MMC displays the Add/Remove Snap-In dialog box with the Standalone tab active.

12. Click Computer Management (Local), and then click the Extensions tab.

    The MMC displays a list of available extensions for the Computer Management snap-in.

    What option determines which extensions MMC displays in the Available Extensions list in this dialog box?

13. Clear the Add All Extensions check box, and then in the Available Extensions box, clear the Device Manager Extension check box and the System Information Extension check box.

14. Click OK.

15. Expand Computer Management and then expand System Tools to confirm that Device Manager and System Information have been removed.

Note Do not use any of the tools at this point.

---

16. Close the console.

    MMC displays a message, prompting for confirmation to save console settings.

17. Click No.

Lesson Summary

In this lesson, you learned how to create custom consoles to perform a unique set of administrative tasks. Once you create customized consoles, you can access them by using the Run command on the Start menu. In the practice portion of this lesson, you created two customized consoles. The first console contained the Computer Management snap-in and then you added the Event Viewer snap-in to it. You used the Event Viewer snap-in to determine the last time your computer was started. The second custom console you created contained the Computer Management snap-in. After you created the second customized console, you learned how to restrict the functionality of a console by removing two of the extensions normally available with the Computer Management snap-in. Finally, in this lesson, you learned how to create custom consoles for remote administration.

Lesson 3: Using Task Scheduler

You use Task Scheduler to schedule programs and batch files to run once, at regular intervals, or at specific times. You can also use Task Scheduler to schedule any script, program, or document to start at a specified time and interval or when certain operating system events occur. You can use Task Scheduler to complete many administrative tasks for you.

After this lesson, you will be able to

- Use Task Scheduler to schedule tasks.

Estimated lesson time: 25 minutes

Introduction to Task Scheduler

Windows 2000 saves scheduled tasks in the Scheduled Tasks folder, which is in Control Panel in My Computer. In addition, you can access Scheduled Tasks on another computer by browsing that computer's resources using My Network Places. This allows you to move tasks from one computer to another. For example, you can create task files for maintenance and then add them to a user's computer as needed.

Use Task Scheduler to

- Run maintenance utilities at specific intervals.
- Run programs when less demand exists for computer resources.

Options

Use the Scheduled Task wizard to schedule tasks. You access the wizard in the Scheduled Tasks folder by double-clicking Add Scheduled Task. Table 3.2 describes the options that you can configure in the Scheduled Task wizard.

Table 3.2   Scheduled Task Wizard Options

Option	Description
Application	The applications to schedule. Select the applications to schedule from a list of applications that are registered with Windows 2000, or click Browse to specify any program or batch file.
Task Name	A descriptive name for the task.
Frequency	The number of times Windows 2000 will perform the task. You can select among several options to have the task performed daily, weekly, monthly, one time only, when the computer starts, or when you log on.

Option	Description
Time And Date	The start time and start date for the task to occur. If applicable, you can enter the days on which to repeat the task.
Name And Password	A user name and password. You can enter your user name and password or another user name and password to have the application run under the security settings for that user account.
	If the user account that you used to log on doesn't have the rights that are required by the scheduled task, you can use another user account that does have the required rights. For example, you can run a scheduled backup by using a user account that has the required rights to back up data but doesn't have other administrative privileges.
Advanced Properties	A check box that you can select if you want the wizard to display the Advanced Properties dialog box so that you can configure additional properties after you click Finish.

Advanced Properties

In addition to the options that are available in the Scheduled Task wizard, you can set several other options for tasks. You can change options that you set with the Scheduled Task wizard or set additional advanced options by configuring advanced properties for the task.

Table 3.3 describes the tabs in the Advanced Properties dialog box for the scheduled task.

Table 3.3 Scheduled Task Wizard Advanced Options

Tab	Description
Task	Changes the scheduled task or changes the user account that is used to run the task. You can also turn the task on and off.
Schedule	Sets and displays multiple schedules for the same task. You can set the date, time, and number of repeat occurrences for the task. For example, you can set up a task to run every Friday at 10:00 P.M.
Settings	Set options that affect when a task starts or stops, such as how long a backup can take, whether the computer can be in use, or whether the computer can be running on batteries when it runs the task.
Security	Changes the list of users and groups that have permission to perform the task, or changes the permissions for a specific user or group.

Practice: Using Task Scheduler

In this practice, you will schedule WordPad to start at a predetermined time. You can use this as a reminder to review address information. You will also configure Task Scheduler options.

▶ **To schedule a task to start automatically**

1. Double-click My Computer, double-click Control Panel, and then double-click Scheduled Tasks.

   Windows 2000 opens the Scheduled Tasks window. Because no tasks are currently scheduled, only the Add Scheduled Task icon appears.

2. Double-click Add Scheduled Task.

   The Scheduled Task wizard appears.

3. Click Next.

   Windows 2000 displays a list of currently installed programs. To schedule a program that isn't registered with Windows 2000, click the Browse button to locate the program.

4. Click Browse.

   The Select Program To Schedule dialog box appears.

5. Double-click Program Files, and then double-click Windows NT.

6. Double-click Accessories, and then double-click WordPad.

7. In the Name box, type **Launch WordPad,** as shown in Figure 3.4.

   The Name box allows you to enter a description that is more intuitive than the program name. Windows 2000 displays this name in the Scheduled Tasks folder when you finish the wizard.

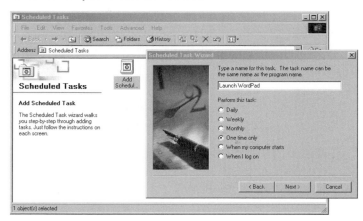

Figure 3.4   Using the Scheduled Task wizard

8. Click One Time Only, and then click Next.

9. In the Start Time box, set the time to four minutes after the current system time and make a note of this time.

   To confirm the current system time, look at the taskbar. Don't change the entry in the Start Date box.

10. Click Next.

    The wizard requires you to enter the name and password of a user account. When Task Scheduler runs the scheduled task, the program receives all of the rights and permissions of the user account that you enter here. The program is also bound by any restrictions on the user account. Notice that your user name, Pro1\ Administrator, is already filled in as the default. (If your computer name isn't Pro1, Pro1 will be replaced by your computer's name.) You must type the correct password for the user account in both password boxes before you can continue.

    You will schedule the console to run with your administrative privileges.

11. In both the Enter The Password box and the Confirm Password box, type **password.**

12. Click Next.

    Don't select the check box to open the Advanced Properties dialog box for this task. You will review these properties in the next procedure.

13. Click Finish.

    Notice that the wizard added the task to the list of scheduled tasks.

14. To confirm that you scheduled the task successfully, wait for the time that you configured in step 9. WordPad will start.

15. Close WordPad.

▶   **To configure advanced Task Scheduler options**

1. In the Scheduled Tasks window, double-click Launch WordPad.

   Windows 2000 displays the Launch WordPad dialog box. Notice the tabs and review the options on the tabs. These are the same options that are available if you select the check box for setting advanced options on the last page of the Scheduled Task wizard. Don't change any of the settings.

2. Click the Settings tab.

   Review the options that are available on the Settings tab.

3. Select the Delete The Task If It Is Not Scheduled To Run Again check box.

4. Click the Schedule tab, and then set the start time for two minutes after the current system time.

   Make a note of this time.

5. Click OK.

   To confirm that you scheduled the task successfully, wait for the time that you set in step 4 of this procedure. WordPad will start.

6. Close WordPad.

   Notice that the scheduled event is no longer in the Scheduled Tasks folder. The option to automatically delete a task after it finishes is useful for cleaning up after tasks that need to run only once.

7. Close the Scheduled Tasks window.

8. Log off Windows 2000.

Lesson Summary

In this lesson, you learned that you can use Task Scheduler to schedule programs and batch files to run once, at regular intervals, at specific times, or when certain operating system events occur. Windows 2000 saves scheduled tasks in the Scheduled Tasks folder, which is in Control Panel in My Computer. Once you have scheduled a task to run, you can modify any of the options or advanced features for the task, including the program to be run.

In addition, you learned that you can access Scheduled Tasks on another computer by browsing that computer's resources using My Network Places. This allows you to move tasks from one computer to another. For example, you can create task files for maintenance and then add them to a user's computer as needed. In the practice portion of this lesson, you used the Scheduled Task wizard to schedule WordPad to launch at a specified time.

Review

These questions will help you determine whether you have learned enough to move on to the next chapter. If you can't answer these questions, please go back and review the material in this chapter before beginning the next chapter. The answers for these questions are in Appendix A, "Questions and Answers."

1. When and why would you use an extension?

2. You need to create a custom console for an administrator who needs to use only the Computer Management and Active Directory Users And Computers snap-ins. The administrator

   a. Must not be able to add any additional snap-ins.

   b. Needs full access to all snap-ins.

   c. Must be able to navigate between snap-ins.

   Which console mode would you use to configure the custom console?

3. What do you need to do to remotely administer a computer running Windows 2000 Server from a computer running Windows 2000 Professional?

4. You need to schedule a maintenance utility to automatically run once a week on your computer, which is running Windows 2000 Professional. How do you accomplish this?

C H A P T E R   4

Using Windows Control Panel

About This Chapter

Microsoft Windows 2000 stores configuration information in two locations: the registry and the directory services based on Active Directory technology. Modifications to the registry or Active Directory directory services change the configuration of the Windows 2000 environment. You use the following tools to modify the registry or Active Directory directory services:

- Microsoft Management Console
- Control Panel
- Registry Editor

Control Panel, the subject of this chapter, contains applications that you use to customize selected aspects of the hardware and software configuration for a computer. For more information about Microsoft Management Console, see Chapter 3, "Using Microsoft Management Console and Task Scheduler." For more information on using Registry Editor, see Chapter 5, "Using the Registry."

Before You Begin

To complete this chapter, you must have

- A computer that meets the minimum hardware requirements located in "About This Book."
- The Windows 2000 Professional software installed on the computer.

Lesson 1: Configuring Hardware Settings

You use Control Panel to configure hardware settings, manage user-specific settings, and manage settings that apply to the computer regardless of which user is currently logged on. This lesson introduces the Control Panel programs that you use to configure hardware devices or services. You configure hardware settings by creating and configuring hardware profiles.

After this lesson, you will be able to
- Manage hardware profiles.

Estimated lesson time: 10 minutes

Understanding Hardware Profiles

A *hardware profile* stores configuration settings for a set of devices and services. Windows 2000 can store different hardware profiles to meet the user's different needs. For example, a portable computer can use different hardware configurations depending on whether it is docked or undocked. A portable-computer user can create a hardware profile for each state (docked and undocked) and choose the appropriate profile when starting Windows 2000.

Creating or Modifying a Hardware Profile

To create or modify a hardware profile in Control Panel, double-click the System icon, and then click the Hardware tab in the System Properties dialog box. Click Hardware Profiles to view the Available Hardware Profiles list. (See Figure 4.1.)

Figure 4.1   The Available Hardware Profiles list

Tip To open the System Properties dialog box from the desktop, right-click My Computer, and then click Properties.

Windows 2000 creates an initial profile during installation, which is listed as Profile 1 (Current). You can create a new profile with the same configuration as another profile. To create a new profile, in the Hardware Profiles dialog box, in the Available Hardware Profiles list, select the profile that you want to copy, and then click Copy.

The order of the profiles in the Available Hardware Profiles list determines the default order at startup. The first profile in the list becomes the default profile. To change the order of the profiles, use the arrow buttons to the right of the list box.

Activating a Hardware Profile

If two or more profiles are available in the Available Hardware Profiles list, Windows 2000 prompts the user to make a selection during startup. You can set the time that the computer waits before starting the default configuration. To adjust this time delay, click the Select The First Profile Listed If I Don't Select A Profile In option and then specify the number of seconds in the Seconds box within the Hardware Profiles Selection group. You can configure Windows 2000 to start the default profile by setting the number of seconds to 0. To override the default during startup, press the Spacebar during the system prompt.

When using hardware profiles, be careful not to disable one of the boot devices with the Devices program in Control Panel. If you disable a required boot device, Windows 2000 might not start. You should make a copy of the default profile and then make changes to the new profile. This way, you can use the default profile again if a problem occurs.

Viewing Hardware Profile Properties

To view the properties for a hardware profile, in the Available Hardware Profiles list, select a profile, and then click Properties. This displays the Properties dialog box for the profile.

If Windows 2000 identifies your computer as a portable unit, the This Is A Portable Computer check box is selected. If Windows 2000 determines that your portable computer is docked, it automatically selects the appropriate option. You can't change this docked option setting after Windows 2000 selects it.

Lesson Summary

In this lesson, you learned to use the System icon in Control Panel to configure hardware devices or services by creating and configuring hardware profiles. A hardware profile stores configuration settings for a set of devices and services.

During installation, Windows 2000 automatically creates an initial profile, but you can create additional profiles. To create a new profile, in the Hardware Profiles dialog box, in the Available Hardware Profiles list, you select the profile that you want to copy and then click Copy. To view the properties for a hardware profile, in the Available Hardware Profiles list, you select a profile and then click Properties. This displays the Properties dialog box for the profile.

You also learned that the order of the profiles in the Available Hardware Profiles list determines the default order at startup. The first profile in the list becomes the default profile. To change the order of the profiles, you use the arrow buttons. If two or more profiles are in the Available Hardware Profiles list, Windows 2000 prompts you to make a selection during startup.

Lesson 2: Configuring the Display

Users with permission to load and unload device drivers can also install and test video drivers. Windows 2000 can change video resolutions dynamically without restarting the system.

After this lesson, you will be able to

- Use Control Panel to configure the display.

Estimated lesson time: 25 minutes

Setting Display Properties

To view or modify the display properties, in Control Panel, double-click the Display icon, and then click the Settings tab. (See Figure 4.2.) Alternatively, you can also right-click your desktop and select Properties from the shortcut menu. Configurable display options include the number of colors, video resolution, font size, and refresh frequency.

Figure 4.2   The Settings tab of the Display Properties dialog box

Table 4.1 describes the options available on the Settings tab for configuring the display settings.

Table 4.1   Settings Tab Options for Configuring the Display

Option	Description
Colors	Lists color depths for the display adapter
Screen Area	Allows you to set the resolution for the display adapter
Troubleshoot	Opens the Display Troubleshooter to aid in diagnosing display problems
Advanced	Opens the Properties dialog box for the display adapter, as described next

To open the Properties dialog box for the display adapter, click Advanced. Table 4.2 describes the display adapter options.

Table 4.2   Display Adapter Advanced Options

Tab	Option group	Description
General	Display	Provides the Small Font, Large Font, and Other options.
		The Other option lets you choose any custom font size you want.
	Compatibility	Lets you choose what Windows 2000 should do when you change display settings. After you change the color settings, you must choose one of the following options:
		▪ Restart The Computer Before Applying The New Display Settings.
		▪ Apply The New Display Settings Without Restarting.
		▪ Ask Me Before Applying The New Display Settings.
Adapter	Adapter Type	Provides the manufacturer and model number of the installed adapter. The Properties button tells you additional information including device status, resource settings, and whether there are any conflicting devices.
	Adapter Information	Provides additional information about the display adapter, such as video chip type, digital-to-analog converter (DAC) type, memory size, and BIOS.
	List All Modes	Displays all compatible modes for your display adapter and lets you select resolution, color depth, and refresh frequency in one step.

(continued)

Tab	Option group	Description
Monitor	Monitor Type	Provides the manufacturer and model number of the monitor currently installed. The Properties button provides additional information and gives access to the Display Troubleshooter to help in resolving problems with this device.
	Monitor Settings	Lets you configure the refresh rate frequency. This option applies only to high-resolution drivers. Don't select a refresh rate/screen resolution combination that is unsupported by the monitor. If you are unsure, refer to your monitor documentation, or select the lowest refresh rate option.
Troubleshooting	Hardware Acceleration	Lets you progressively decrease your display hardware's acceleration features to help you isolate and eliminate display problems.
Color Management		Lets you choose the color profile for your monitor.

Using Multiple Displays

Windows 2000 adds support for multiple display configurations. Multiple displays allow you to extend your desktop across more than one monitor, as shown in Figure 4.3. Windows 2000 supports extending your display across a maximum of 9 monitors.

- Use of multiple displays extends the desktop across a maximum of 10 monitors.
- Multiple displays must use Peripheral Component Interconnect (PCI) or Accelerated Graphics Port (AGP) devices.
- Hardware requirements for primary (main) and secondary displays differ.

Figure 4.3   Multiple displays

Important You must use Peripheral Component Interconnect (PCI) or Accelerated Graphics Port (AGP) devices when configuring multiple displays.

If one of the display adapters is built into the motherboard, note these additional considerations:

- The motherboard adapter always becomes the secondary adapter. It must be multiple-display compatible.
- You must set up Windows 2000 before installing another adapter. Windows 2000 Setup will disable the motherboard adapter if it detects another adapter. Some systems completely disable the onboard adapter upon detecting an add-in adapter. If you are unable to override this detection in the basic input/output system (BIOS), you can't use the motherboard adapter with multiple displays.

Typically, the system BIOS selects the primary display based on PCI slot order. However, on some computers, the BIOS allows the user to select the primary display device.

You can't stop the primary display. This consideration is important for laptop computers with docking stations. For example, some docking stations contain a display adapter; these often disable, or turn off, a laptop's built-in display. Multiple display support will not function on these configurations unless you attach multiple adapters to the docking station.

Configuring Multiple Displays

You must configure each display in a multiple display environment.

Do the following to configure your display in a multiple display environment:

1. In Control Panel, double-click Display.
2. In the Display Properties dialog box, click the Settings tab.
3. Click the monitor number for the primary display device.
4. Select the display adapter for the primary display, and then select the color depth and resolution.
5. Click the monitor number for the secondary display device.
6. Select the display adapter for the secondary display, and then select the Extend My Windows Desktop Onto This Monitor check box.
7. Select the color depth and resolution for the secondary display.
8. Repeat steps 5–7 for each additional display.

Windows 2000 uses the virtual desktop concept to determine the relationship of each display. The virtual desktop uses coordinates to track the position of each individual display desktop.

The coordinates of the upper-left corner of the primary display always remain 0,0. Windows 2000 sets secondary display coordinates so that all the displays adjoin each other on the virtual desktop. This allows the system to maintain the illusion of a single, large desktop, where users can cross from one monitor to another without losing track of the mouse.

To change the display positions on the virtual desktop, on the Settings tab, click Identify, and drag the display representations to the desired position. The positions of the icons dictate the coordinates and the relative positions of the displays to one another.

Troubleshooting Multiple Displays

If you encounter problems with multiple displays, use the troubleshooting guidelines in Table 4.3 to help resolve those problems.

Table 4.3   Troubleshooting Tips for Multiple Displays

Problem	Solution
You can't see any output on the secondary displays.	Activate the device in the Display Properties dialog box.
	Confirm that you chose the correct video driver.
	Restart the computer to confirm that the secondary display is initialized. If not, check the status of the video adapter in Device Manager.
	Switch the order of the adapters in the slots. (The primary adapter must qualify as a secondary adapter.)
The Extend My Windows Desktop Onto This Monitor check box is unavailable.	Select the secondary display rather than the primary one in the Display Properties dialog box.
	Confirm that the secondary display adapter is supported.
	Confirm that Windows 2000 can detect the secondary display.
An application fails to display on the secondary display.	Run the application on the primary display.
	Run the application in full-screen mode (Microsoft MS-DOS) or maximized (Microsoft Windows).
	Disable the secondary display to determine whether the problem is specific to multiple display support.

Lesson Summary

In this lesson, you learned that users with permission to load and unload device drivers can also install and test video drivers. With Windows 2000, you can change video resolutions dynamically without restarting the system.

You also learned that you use the Display icon in Control Panel to view or modify display properties, such as the number of colors, video resolution, font size, and refresh frequency. And you learned that Windows 2000 supports multiple displays, with up to a maximum of 10 additional monitors, and that you must configure each display. This lesson concluded with a section on troubleshooting multiple displays.

Lesson 3: Configuring Operating System Settings

You use certain Control Panel programs to configure operating system settings. The System Properties dialog box allows you to configure the following:

- Performance options
- Registry size
- Environment variables
- Startup and recovery settings

The Control Panel programs that you use to configure the operating system settings affect the operating system environment regardless of the user who is logged on to the computer.

After this lesson, you will be able to
- Use Control Panel to configure the operating system.

Estimated lesson time: 30 minutes

Performance Options

The first Control Panel program that allows you to configure operating system settings is accessed through System Properties. To view operating system performance configuration options, double-click the System icon in Control Panel, click the Advanced tab in the System Properties dialog box, and then click Performance Options. The Performance Options dialog box is shown in Figure 4.4.

Figure 4.4   The Performance Options dialog box

The options in this dialog box allow you to adjust the *application response,* which is the priority of foreground applications versus background applications, and virtual memory.

Application Response

Windows 2000 uses the Application Response settings to distribute microprocessor resources between running programs. If you select Applications, more resources are assigned to the foreground application (the active program that is responding to user input), but if you select Background Services, an equal amount of resources are assigned to all programs.

Virtual Memory

The Windows 2000 memory model is based on a flat, linear, 32-bit address space. Windows 2000 uses a *virtual memory management system* to manage memory. This system provides several advantages, including the following:

- The ability to run more applications concurrently than would normally be possible using the amount of physical memory installed in the computer.

- The protection of memory resources. Virtual memory management helps prevent situations where one process interferes with the memory space for another process.

Physical memory refers to the RAM hardware chips inside your computer. *Virtual memory* refers to the way that an operating system makes this physical memory available to an application.

Windows 2000 represents each memory byte, both physical and virtual, with a unique address. The amount of physical RAM installed in the computer limits the number of physical addresses that are available. However, the number of virtual addresses is limited only by the number of bits in the virtual address. Windows 2000, which uses a 32-bit virtual address scheme, has 4 GB of virtual addresses available for use.

Virtual Memory Manager (VMM) manages memory. VMM has two specific roles:

- VMM maintains a memory-mapping table. This table tracks the list of virtual addresses that belong to each process and where the actual data referenced by these virtual addresses resides. (See Figure 4.5.) When a thread requests access to memory, it requests a virtual address space. VMM uses the virtual address requested by the thread to locate the corresponding physical address. It then transfers the data requested by the thread.

- VMM moves memory contents to and from the hard disk when required. This process is referred to as *paging*.

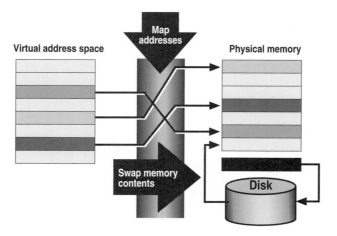

Figure 4.5   Virtual Memory Manager

Virtual Address Space

A *virtual address* is the address space that an application uses to reference memory. When a process is launched in Windows 2000, VMM presents the process with 4 GB of virtual address space. (See Figure 4.6.)

Figure 4.6   Virtual address space

This 4 GB of virtual address space is divided as follows:

- The upper 2 GB is reserved for the system or for kernel-mode threads only. The lower portion of this upper 2 GB area is mapped directly by the hardware. Access to this lower portion is extremely fast.

- The lower 2 GB is available to both user-mode threads: for example, applications and kernel-mode threads. VMM can move it to disk if required. Windows

2000 divides the upper portion into a paged and a nonpaged pool. Addresses in the paged pool can be swapped out to disk, but those in the nonpaged pool must remain in physical memory. The size of each page is 4 KB.

Paging

The process of moving data in and out of physical memory is called *paging*. When physical memory becomes full and a thread needs access to code or data not currently in physical memory, VMM moves some pages from physical memory to a storage area on disk called a *pagefile*. (See Figure 4.7.) VMM loads the code or data requested by the thread into the area of physical memory that is released by VMM.

Figure 4.7 Paging

The virtual address space assigned to a process is divided up into either valid pages or invalid pages. *Valid pages* are those pages that are located in physical memory and are available to the process. *Invalid pages* are those pages that don't exist in physical memory. They aren't available to the process or stored on disk.

When a thread requests access to an invalid page, the microprocessor issues a *page fault*. VMM intercepts, or traps, the page fault, locates the required page, and then loads it from disk into a free page frame in physical memory. Conversely, to free up physical memory, VMM takes the contents of certain pages and transfers them to disk.

VMM performs three tasks as part of the paging process:

- It determines which pages to remove from physical memory when memory is full. VMM keeps track of the pages currently in memory for each process. This group of pages is referred to as a process's working set. VMM uses a local first-in, first-out replacement policy to decide which pages to move out of physical memory. The data that has been in physical memory for the longest is the first to be removed. When a thread generates a page fault, VMM examines the working set for the thread's process and then moves to disk the page that has resided in physical memory for the longest.

- It brings pages from disk into physical memory—a process called *fetching*. VMM also uses a method known as demand paging with clustering. *Demand paging with clustering* means that when a page fault is triggered, VMM loads the needed page into memory, plus some of the pages that surround it. This helps to reduce the number of page faults that are generated.

- It determines where to place pages retrieved from disk. If physical memory isn't full, VMM loads the data into the first free page. If physical memory is full, VMM determines which page or pages to move to disk to make room in physical memory for the pages retrieved from disk.

Paging File Size

When you install Windows 2000, Setup creates a virtual-memory paging file, Pagefile.sys, on the partition where you installed Windows 2000. The minimum paging file size is 2 MB. The default or recommended paging file size for Windows 2000 Professional is equal to 1.5 times the total amount of RAM. Typically, you can leave the size of the paging file set to the default value. In some circumstances, such as when you run a large number of applications simultaneously, you might want to use a larger paging file or multiple paging files.

To configure the paging file, click Change in the Performance Options dialog box. The Virtual Memory dialog box identifies the drives on which the paging files reside and allows you to modify the paging file size for the selected drive. (See Figure 4.8.)

Paging files never decrease below the initial size that was set during installation. Unused space in the paging file remains available to the internal Windows 2000 Virtual Memory Manager.

If you set the size of the initial paging file significantly below the recommended size, Windows 2000 may display the Windows - Virtual Memory Minimum Too Low message box sometime after you log on following the change. (See Figure 4.9.) The message indicates that Windows is increasing the size of your virtual memory paging file. While this occurs, any programs you are running may run more slowly or they may pause because any memory requests by those applications may be denied. Only users with administrative rights can use the System program to increase the paging file size.

Figure 4.8 Configuring the paging file

Figure 4.9 A warning that the virtual memory minimum is set too low

As needed, a paging file grows from its initial size to the maximum configured size. When the paging file reaches the maximum size, system performance might degrade if you place additional demands on the system by running more applications.

When you restart a computer running Windows 2000, the system resizes all paging files to the initial size.

Registry Size

At the bottom of the Virtual Memory dialog box shown in Figure 4.8, the Maximum Registry Size option allows you to specify the maximum size of the registry. This setting doesn't reserve the space for the registry, so the registry might not be able to grow to the maximum size you have set. This setting simply limits the size to which the registry can grow. For more information on the registry, see Chapter 5, "Using the Registry."

Enhancing Performance

You can enhance your system's performance in several ways. First, if your computer has multiple hard disks, you can create a paging file for each disk. Distributing information across multiple paging files improves performance because the hard disk controller can read from and write to multiple hard disks simultaneously. When attempting to write to the paging file, VMM tries to write the page data to the paging file on the disk that is the least busy.

Second, you can enhance your system's performance by moving the paging file off the drive that contains the Windows 2000 *systemroot* folder (by default, the Winnt folder). Moving the paging file off the drive containing the boot partition avoids competition between the various reading and writing requests. If you place a paging file on the Windows 2000 system partition to facilitate recovery, which is discussed in the "Startup and Recovery Settings" section later in this chapter, you can still increase performance by creating multiple paging files. Because the VMM alternates write operations between paging files, the paging file on the boot partition is accessed less frequently.

Third, you can enhance your system's performance by setting the initial size of the paging file to the value displayed in the Virtual Memory dialog box's Maximum Size box. This eliminates the time required to enlarge the file from the initial size to the maximum size.

Note When applying new settings, be sure to click Set before clicking OK.

Environment Variables

Environment variables define the system and user environment information, and they contain information such as a drive, path, or filename. Environment variables provide information that Windows 2000 uses to control various applications. For example, the TEMP environment variable specifies where an application places its temporary files.

Click Environment Variables on the Advanced tab of the System Properties dialog box to display the system and user environment variables that are currently in effect. (See Figure 4.10.)

System Environment Variables

The *system environment variables* apply to the entire system. Consequently, these variables affect all system users. During installation, Setup configures the default system environment variables, including the path to the Windows 2000 files. Only an administrator can add, modify, or remove a system environment variable.

Figure 4.10   Setting environment variables

User Environment Variables

The *user environment variables* differ for each user of a particular computer. The user environment variables include any user-defined settings (such as a desktop pattern) and any variables defined by applications (such as the path to the location of the application files). Users can add, modify, or remove their user environment variables in the System Properties dialog box.

How Windows 2000 Sets Environment Variables

Windows 2000 sets environment variables in the following order:

1. By default, Windows 2000 searches the Autoexec.bat file, if it exists, and sets any environment variables.

2. Windows 2000 sets the system environment variables. If any system environment variables conflict with environment variables set from the search of the Autoexec.bat file, the system environment variables override them.

3. Windows 2000 sets the user environment variables. If any user environment variables conflict with environment variables set from the search of the Autoexec.bat file or from the system environment variables, the user environment variables override them.

For example, if you add the line SET TMP=C:\ in Autoexec.bat, and a TMP=X:\TEMP user variable is set, the user environment variable setting (X:\TEMP) overrides the prior setting C:\.

Note You can prevent Windows 2000 from searching the Autoexec.bat file by editing the registry and setting the value of the ParseAutoexec entry to 0. The ParseAutoexec entry is located in the registry under the following subkey:

\HKEY_CURRENT_USER\SOFTWARE\Microsoft\Windows NT\CurrentVersion\Winlogon

Startup and Recovery Settings

The System Properties dialog box also controls the startup and recovery settings for a computer. In addition to using Control Panel to access the System icon, you can right-click My Computer, click Properties, click the Advanced tab of the System Properties dialog box, and then click Startup And Recovery.

The Startup And Recovery dialog box contains two groups of information, as shown in Figure 4.11. The System Startup options control the behavior of the boot loader menu. The System Failure options control the actions that Windows 2000 performs in the event of a system failure that stops the computer. A *system failure* is a severe error that causes Windows 2000 to stop all processes. System failures are also known as *fatal system errors* or *blue screen errors*.

Figure 4.11   Startup and recovery settings

System Startup

When you first turn on the computer, the system displays a boot menu, which lists the available operating systems if more than one operating system is installed on the computer. By default, the system chooses one of the operating systems and displays a countdown timer. If you don't choose another operating system, the system starts the preselected operating system when the countdown timer reaches zero or when you press Enter. Modify the options under System Startup to determine which operating system is preselected, how long the countdown timer runs, and whether to display the boot menu.

System Failure

Table 4.4 describes the four System Failure options that Windows 2000 provides to assist the user in the event of a system failure.

Important You must be logged on as a member of the Administrators group to set the system failure options.

Table 4.4 Recovery Options

Option	Additional information
Write An Event To The System Log	Select this check box to have Windows 2000 write an event to the system log when a system stops unexpectedly.
Send An Administrative Alert	Select this check box to send an administrative alert to administrators when the system stops unexpectedly.
Automatically Reboot	Select this check box to have Windows 2000 reboot whenever the system stops unexpectedly.
Write Debugging Information	Select the first option in this group to specify which information Windows 2000 should write to the dump file, Memory.dmp. The following four choices are available:
	None. Nothing is written to the dump file.
	Small Memory Dump. The minimum amount of information will be dumped. The paging file space required is 2 MB. The small dump directory stores a history of these dumps and can be set. By default, the small dump directory is %SystemRoot%\Minidump.
	Kernel Memory Dump. Only kernel memory is written to the dump file. Depending on the amount of RAM on your computer, you must have from 50 to 800 MB available in the paging file.
	Complete Memory Dump. The entire contents of system memory is recorded when the system stops unexpectedly. You must have a paging file on the boot partition large enough to hold all the RAM on your system plus 1 MB.

Note Windows 2000 always writes to the same dump file, Memory.dmp. After a system crash, you should rename the dump file so that it won't be overwritten.

The following requirements must be met for the Write Debugging Information options to work:

- A paging file must be on the boot partition (the partition that contains the *systemroot* folder).

- The paging file must be at least 1 MB larger than the amount of physical RAM in your computer.

- You must have enough disk space to write the file in the location you specify. To overwrite an existing file, select the Overwrite Any Existing File check box in the Startup And Recovery dialog box.

Practice: Using Control Panel to Change Operating System Settings

In this practice, you will use the Advanced tab of the System Properties dialog box to change some of the system settings. First you will change the length of time for the boot delay. Then you will change the paging file size, and finally, you will add and test a new system environment variable.

Exercise 1: Decreasing the Boot Delay

In this exercise, you will decrease the boot delay by changing the number of seconds before the default operating system loads.

Note If your computer has Windows 2000 Professional as its sole operating system, then skip Exercise 1 and go on to Exercise 2. If you would like to change the boot delay setting in Exercise 1 for practice, bear in mind that it will have no effect on your computer.

▶ **To decrease the boot delay**

1. Log on as Administrator.

2. In Control Panel, double-click the System icon.

   The System Properties dialog box appears.

3. On the Advanced tab, click Startup And Recovery.

   The Startup And Recovery dialog box appears. Notice that the list of operating systems will be displayed for 30 seconds by default.

4. In the Display List Of Operating Systems For box, for the number of seconds, type **0** and then click OK.

   You are returned to the System Properties dialog box.

5. Click OK to close the System Properties dialog box.

6. Close Control Panel.

7. Restart your computer.

   Notice that the boot loader menu doesn't appear.

8. Log on as Administrator.

9. Return to the Startup And Recovery dialog box, change the boot delay setting to 15 seconds, and then click OK. Leave the System Properties dialog box open.

Exercise 2: Changing the Paging File Size

In this exercise, you will use the System Properties dialog box to change the size of the Windows 2000 paging file.

▶ **To change the paging file size**

1. On the Advanced tab, click Performance Options.

   The Performance Options dialog box appears.

2. Click Change.

   The Virtual Memory dialog box appears.

3. In the Drive box, click the drive that contains your paging file, if necessary.

4. In the Initial Size (MB) box, increase the value by 10, and then click Set.

5. Click OK to close the Virtual Memory dialog box.

6. Click OK to close the Performance Options dialog box.

Exercise 3: Adding a System Environment Variable

In this exercise, you will use the System Properties dialog box to add a new system environment variable. You will then test the new variable by using it at the command prompt.

▶ **To add a system environment variable**

1. In the System Properties dialog box, click the Advanced tab and click Environment Variables.

   The Environment Variables dialog box appears.

2. Under System Variables, click New.

   The New System Variable dialog box appears.

3. Type **Pro2000dir** in the Variable Name box.

4. In the Variable Value box, type the path to the Winnt folder on your computer, for example, C:\Winnt.

   If you aren't sure of the path to Winnt, use Windows Explorer to locate it.

5. Click OK.

   You are returned to the Environment Variables dialog box.

6. Click OK to close the Environment Variables dialog box, and then click OK to close the System Properties dialog box.

7. Close Control Panel.

▶ **To test the new variable**

1. From the Start menu, point to Programs, point to Accessories, and then click Command Prompt.

2. At the command prompt, type **set | more** and then press Enter.

   The list of current environment variables is displayed.

3. Press Spacebar to display the remaining environment variables.

4. If necessary, type **c:** and then press Enter to switch to the drive on which you installed Windows 2000. (Adjust the drive letter if necessary.)

5. Type **cd** and then press Enter if you aren't already in the root folder.

6. Type **cd %Pro2000dir%** and then press Enter.

   You should now be in the Winnt folder.

7. Type **exit** and press Enter to close the Command Prompt window.

Lesson Summary

In this lesson, you learned that you use the System Properties dialog box to configure performance options, registry size, environment variables, and startup and recovery settings. Performance options, which you access from the Advanced tab, allow you to adjust the application response, which is the priority of foreground applications versus background applications, and virtual memory. Environment variables, which you also access from the Advanced tab of the System Properties dialog box, define the system and user environment information, and they contain information such as a drive, path, or filename. Environment variables provide information that Windows 2000 uses to control various applications.

Windows 2000 sets the environment by first searching the Autoexec.bat file, if it exists, and setting any environment variables. Next the system environment variables are set. If any conflicts exist with the environment variables set from the search of the Autoexec.bat file, the system environment variables override them. Finally the user environment variables are set. If any conflicts exist with environment variables set from the search of the Autoexec.bat file or from the system environment variables, the user environment variables override them.

You can access startup and recovery settings also from the Advanced tab of the System Properties dialog box. The System Startup options control the behavior of the boot loader menu. You modify the options under System Startup to determine which operating system is preselected, how long the countdown timer runs, and whether the boot menu is displayed. The System Failure options control the actions that Windows 2000 performs in the event of a system failure, which are also known as fatal system errors or blue screen errors.

The Control Panel programs that you use to configure the operating system settings affect the operating system environment regardless of the user who is logged on to the computer.

Lesson 4: Installing Hardware Automatically

Windows 2000 supports both Plug and Play and non-Plug and Play hardware. This lesson introduces you to the automatic hardware installation features of Windows 2000.

After this lesson, you will be able to

- Describe how to install hardware automatically.

Estimated lesson time: 15 minutes

Installing Plug and Play Hardware

With most Plug and Play hardware, you simply connect the device to the computer, and Windows 2000 automatically configures the new settings. However, you might occasionally need to initiate automatic installation for some Plug and Play hardware. You do this with the Add/Remove Hardware wizard.

Installing Non-Plug and Play Hardware

For non-Plug and Play hardware, Windows 2000 often identifies the hardware and automatically installs and configures it. For non-Plug and Play hardware that Windows 2000 doesn't identify, install, and configure, you initiate the automatic installation of the hardware with the Add/Remove Hardware wizard.

For automatic hardware installations, you can do the following:

1. Initiate automatic hardware installation by starting the Add/Remove Hardware wizard.

   Windows 2000 queries the hardware about the hardware resources that it requires and the settings for those resources. A hardware resource allows a hardware device to communicate directly with the operating system. Windows 2000 can resolve conflicts between Plug and Play hardware for hardware resources.

2. Confirm the automatic hardware installation.

   Once Windows 2000 finishes the installation, verify correct installation and configure the hardware.

Using the Add/Remove Hardware Wizard

You use the Add/Remove Hardware wizard to initiate automatic hardware installation and to troubleshoot devices. You also use the wizard for undetected hardware devices—both Plug and Play devices and non-Plug and Play devices.

You can do the following to start the Add/Remove Hardware wizard:

1. In Control Panel, double-click Add/Remove Hardware.
2. Click Next to close the welcome page.
3. Select Add/Troubleshoot A Device, and then click Next.

   Windows searches for new devices.

After the Add/Remove Hardware Wizard starts, it searches for any new Plug and Play hardware and then installs any it finds. If the wizard can't find a new device, it displays the Choose A Hardware Device page, shown in Figure 4.12. If no new hardware devices are discovered, Windows 2000 prompts you to select one of the installed devices to troubleshoot it.

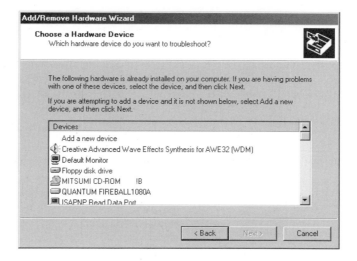

Figure 4.12   Troubleshooting with the Add/Remove Hardware wizard

Confirming Hardware Installation

After installing hardware, confirm the installation by using Device Manager.

You can do the following to start Device Manager:

1. Double-click the System icon in Control Panel.
2. Click the Hardware tab, and then click Device Manager.

   This allows you to view the installed hardware, as shown in Figure 4.13.

Windows 2000 uses icons in the right pane of the Computer Management window to identify each installed hardware device. If Windows 2000 doesn't have an icon for the device type, it displays a question mark.

Figure 4.13   The Device Manager window showing devices listed by type

Expand the device tree to locate the newly installed hardware device. The device icon indicates whether the hardware device is operating properly. You can use the information in Table 4.5 to determine the hardware status.

Table 4.5   Device Manager Hardware Status

Icon	Hardware status
Normal icon	Hardware is operating properly.
Stop sign on icon	Windows 2000 disabled the hardware device because of hardware conflicts. To correct this, right-click the device icon, and then click Properties. Set the hardware resources manually according to what is available on the system.
Exclamation point on icon	The hardware device is incorrectly configured or its drivers are missing.

Lesson Summary

In this lesson, you learned that Windows 2000 supports both Plug and Play and non-Plug and Play hardware. With most Plug and Play hardware, you connect the device to the computer, and Windows 2000 automatically configures the new settings. For non-Plug and Play hardware, Windows 2000 often identifies the hardware and automatically installs and configures it. For the occasional Plug and Play hardware device and for any non-Plug and Play hardware that Windows 2000 doesn't identify, install, and configure, you initiate automatic hardware installation with the Add/Remove Hardware Wizard.

Lesson 5: Installing Hardware Manually

Occasionally, Windows 2000 fails to automatically detect a hardware device. When this occurs, you must manually install the hardware device. You might also have to manually install a hardware device if the device requires a specific hardware resource. You manually install these devices to ensure that they have the necessary resources.

To manually install hardware, you need to do the following:

- Determine which hardware resource the hardware device requires.
- Determine the available hardware resources.
- Change hardware resource assignments.

After this lesson, you will be able to

- Install hardware manually.

Estimated lesson time: 10 minutes

Determining Which Hardware Resources Are Required

When installing new hardware, you need to know which resources the hardware can use. You can reference the product documentation to determine the resources that a hardware device requires. Table 4.6 describes the resources that hardware devices use to communicate with an operating system.

Table 4.6   Hardware Device Resources

Resource	Description
Interrupts	Hardware devices use interrupts to send messages. The microprocessor knows this as an interrupt request (IRQ). The microprocessor uses this information to determine which device needs its attention and the type of attention that it needs. Windows 2000 provides 16 IRQs, numbered 0–15, which are assigned to devices; for example, Windows 2000 assigns IRQ 1 to the keyboard.
Input/output (I/O) ports	I/O ports are a section of memory that a hardware device uses to communicate with the operating system. When a microprocessor receives an IRQ, the operating system checks the I/O port address to retrieve additional information about what the hardware device wants it to do. An I/O port is represented as a hexadecimal number.

(continued)

Resource	Description
Direct memory access (DMA)	DMAs are channels that allow a hardware device, such as a floppy disk drive, to access memory directly, without interrupting the microprocessor. DMA channels speed up access to memory. Windows 2000 has eight DMA channels, numbered 0–7.
Memory	Many hardware devices, such as a network adapter card (NAC), use onboard memory or reserve system memory. This reserved memory is unavailable for use by other devices or Windows 2000.

Determining Available Hardware Resources

After you determine which resources a hardware device requires, you can look for an available resource. Device Manager provides a list of all hardware resources and their availability, as shown in Figure 4.14.

Figure 4.14   The Device Manager window showing resources listed by connection

You can do the following to view the hardware resources lists

1. From the System Properties dialog box, click the Hardware tab, and then click Device Manager.

2. On the View menu, click Resources By Connection.

   Device Manager displays the resources that are currently in use (for example, IRQs).

3. To view a list of resources for another type of hardware resource, on the View menu, click the type of hardware resource that you want to see.

Once you know which hardware resources are available, you can install the hardware manually with the Add/Remove Hardware wizard.

Note If you select a hardware resource during manual installation, you might need to configure the hardware device so that it can use the resource. For example, for a network adapter to use IRQ 5, you might have to set a jumper on the adapter and configure Windows 2000 so that it recognizes that the adapter now uses IRQ 5.

Changing Hardware Resource Assignments

You might need to change hardware resource assignments. For example, a hardware device might require a specific resource presently in use by another device. You might also encounter two hardware devices requesting the same hardware resource, resulting in a conflict.

To change a resource setting, use the Resources tab in the device's Properties dialog box. You can do the following to access the Resources tab:

1. From the Hardware tab of the System Properties dialog box, click Device Manager.

2. Expand the device list, right-click the specific device, and then click Properties.

3. In the Properties dialog box for the device, click the Resources tab.

Tip When you change a hardware resource, print the content of Device Manager. This will provide you with a record of the hardware configuration. If you encounter problems, you can use the printout to verify the hardware resource assignments.

From this point, follow the same procedures that you used to choose a hardware resource during a manual installation.

Note Changing the resource assignments for non-Plug and Play devices in Device Manager doesn't change the resources used by that device. You use Device Manager only to set device configuration for the operating system. To change the resources used by a non-Plug and Play device, consult the device documentation to see whether switches or jumpers must be configured on the device.

Lesson Summary

In this lesson, you learned about installing hardware manually. If Windows 2000 fails to automatically detect a hardware device, or if a hardware device requires a specific hardware resource, you might have to manually install these devices. When you manually install hardware, you must determine any resources required by that hardware device. Hardware resources include interrupts, I/O ports, and memory. You can reference the product documentation to determine any resources that a device requires. You also must determine which hardware resources are available. The Device Manager snap-in provides a list of all hardware resources and their availability.

You also learned that you might need to change hardware resource assignments. For example, a hardware device might require a specific resource presently in use by another device. You saw that to change a hardware resource, you also use Device Manager. To view or change the hardware resources used by a device, in the Device Manager snap-in, you expand the relevant device category in the right pane, right-click the specific device, and then click Properties. In the Device Properties dialog box, you click the Resources tab to view the current resources being used, and you click Change Setting to make changes to the resources in use.

Lesson 6: Configuring and Troubleshooting the Desktop Environment

Windows 2000 provides great flexibility in configuring the desktop. You can configure you computer for multiple languages and multiple locations. This is especially important for employees of international companies that do business with customers in more than one country or who live in a country where more than one language is spoken. Windows 2000 also provides Accessibility options that allow you to make Windows 2000 easier to use. All of the Desktop settings available through Control Panel are as easy to configure as those that will be discussed in detail in this lesson.

After this lesson, you will be able to

- Configure and troubleshoot multiple language settings.
- Configure and troubleshoot multiple locale settings.
- Configure and troubleshoot accessibility options.
- Configure and troubleshoot desktop settings.

Estimated lesson time: 25 minutes

Configuring Language and Location Settings

Through the Regional Options program in Control Panel, Windows 2000 gives you the ability to configure your computer for multiple languages and multiple locations. You can select multiple languages on the General tab of the Regional Options dialog box by clicking the check box in front of each language that you want your computer to support. If you select more than one language, your computer now supports multiple languages. Regional Options also allow you to configure your computer to use multiple locations or locales. The General tab shows you the current locale setting, and the Input Locale tab allows you to add additional locales.

There are additional tabs in the Regional Options dialog box that allow you to configure the rest of the items that vary from language to language. The Numbers tab allows you to configure the appearance of numbers, including the following: the decimal symbol; the number of places after a decimal; the digital grouping symbol, such as the comma in 1,246; and the measurement symbol. There are also a Currency tab, a Time tab, and a Date tab that allow you to configure the way money, the time, and the date are displayed.

If there are any problems with the way your multiple languages or locales support are working, you may want to double-check your settings. You can also try uninstalling the multiple language support or multiple locales support. Make sure that everything is working correctly with only one language or locale, and then reconfigure and reinstall the multiple language or multiple locale support.

Practice: Using Control Panel to Configure a Computer for Multiple Languages and Multiple Locations

In this practice, you use the Regional Options program in Control Panel to configure multiple languages and multiple locations.

▶ **To configure multiple languages**

1. Log on as Administrator.

2. In Control Panel, double-click the Regional Options icon.

   The Regional Options dialog box appears.

3. On the General tab, scroll through the items in the box labeled Your System Is Configured To Read And Write Documents In Multiple Languages to determine the current default language and some of the available languages.

   Note If you want to have your system use multiple languages, click the check box in front of each language you want to support.

   ---

4. Click Advanced.

   The Advanced Regional Options dialog box appears.

5. Click to select 1147 (IBM EBCDIC – France (20297 + Euro)), and then click OK.

6. When prompted, insert the Windows 2000 Professional CD-ROM into your CD-ROM drive.

   When the files have finished copying, your system is configured for multiple languages.

   Note If configuring for multiple languages is all you were going to do, you would click OK to close the Regional Options dialog box. Leave the Regional Options dialog box open for the next procedure.

▶ **To configure multiple locales**

1. On the General tab, note the default locale in the Your Locale (Location) box, and scroll through some of the choices.

   Note Do not change your default locale.

   ---

2. Click the Input Locales tab.

Note The Installed Input Locales box shows which locales are currently installed on your computer and the current keyboard layout. For example, if you are in the United States, you will probably see the following:
EN English Language   **US**

3. Click Properties.

   The Input Locale Properties dialog box appears.

4. Click the down arrow for the Keyboard Layout/IME drop-down list to view the other keyboard layout options you could select.

Note Be careful not to change your keyboard layout.

5. Click Cancel.

   The Regional Options dialog box is again active.

6. Click Add.

   The Add Input Locale dialog box appears.

Note This is the dialog box that allows you to configure for multiple locales.

7. Click Cancel.

8. Close the Regional Options dialog box and the Control Panel window.

Configuring and Troubleshooting Accessibility Options

Windows 2000 provides you with the ability to configure accessibility options through the Accessibility Options program in Control Panel. The five areas that you can configure in Accessibility Options are controlled by these tabs: Keyboard, Sound, Display, Mouse, and General.

Configuring Keyboard Options

The Keyboard tab allows you to configure StickyKeys. Turning on StickyKeys allows you to press a multiple key combination, such as Ctrl+Alt+Delete, one key at a time. This is useful for people who have difficulty pushing more than one key at a time. This is a check box selection, so it is either on or off.

The Keyboard tab also allows you to configure FilterKeys. Turning on FilterKeys causes the keyboard to ignore brief or repeated keystrokes. This option also allows you to configure the keyboard repeat rate, or the rate at which a key continuously held down repeats the keystroke. This is a check box selection, so it too is either on or off.

The Keyboard tab allows you to configure ToggleKeys. Turning on ToggleKeys causes the computer to make a high-pitched sound each time the Caps Lock, Num Lock, or Scroll Lock keys are switched on. Turning on ToggleKeys also causes the computer to make a low-pitched sound each time these three keys are turned off.

Configuring Sound Options

The Sound tab allows you to configure Windows 2000 to use SoundSentry. SoundSentry causes Windows 2000 to generate visual warnings when your computer makes a sound. The Sound tab also allows you to configure ShowSounds, which causes Windows 2000 programs to display captions for the speech and sounds they make. These two features are toggled on or off by selecting the respective check boxes.

Configuring Display Options

The Display tab provides a check box that allows you to configure Windows 2000 to use color and fonts designed for easy reading.

Configuring Mouse Options

The Mouse tab provides a check box that allows you to configure Windows 2000 to allow you to control the pointer with the numeric keypad.

Configuring General Tab Options

The General tab allows you to configure Automatic Reset, which turns off all the accessibility features, except the SerialKeys devices, after the computer has been idle for a specified amount of time. The General tab also allows you to activate the SerialKeys devices feature, which configures Windows 2000 to support an alternative input device (also called an augmentative communication device) connected to your computer's serial port.

Other options on the General tab include the Notification feature and the Administrative options. The Notification feature allows you to configure Windows 2000 to display a warning message when a feature is activated and to make a sound when turning a feature on or off. The Administrative Options provide two check boxes that allow you to configure Windows 2000 to apply all configured accessibility options to this user at logon and to apply all configured accessibility options to all new users.

Configuring and Troubleshooting Additional Desktop Settings

There are many configurable desktop settings in Windows 2000 that are configured through Control Panel programs. Some of these programs include Fax Services, Internet Options, and Phone And Modem Options. To configure any of the settings these programs control, double-click the appropriate icon, click the appropriate tab, and provide the requested information.

Lesson Summary

In this lesson you learned how to use the Regional Options program in Control Panel to configure Windows 2000 Professional for multiple languages and multiple locales. You also learned how to change your keyboard layout and how to configure currency, date, and time settings.

You also learned how to use the Accessibility Options program in Control Panel to make Windows 2000 Professional easier to use. All of the configurable settings for the desktop that are set through Control Panel are easy to configure and troubleshoot. To configure or troubleshoot them, simply double-click the appropriate icon and provide the appropriate information.

Review

Here are some questions to help you determine whether you have learned enough to move on to the next chapter. If you have difficulty answering these questions, please go back and review the material in this chapter before beginning the next chapter. The answers for these questions are in Appendix A, "Questions and Answers."

1. What should you do if you can't see any output on the secondary display?

2. You have configured recovery options on a computer running Windows 2000 Professional to write debugging information to a file if a system failure occurs. You notice, however, that the file isn't being created. What could be causing this problem?

3. How can you optimize virtual memory performance?

4. You installed a new network interface card (NIC) in your computer, but it doesn't seem to be working. Describe how you would troubleshoot this problem.

CHAPTER 5

Using the Registry

About This Chapter

The Microsoft Windows 2000 operating system stores system configuration information in a hierarchical database called the registry. This chapter presents an overview of the registry and introduces Registry Editor, which is a tool that allows you to view and modify the registry.

Before You Begin

To complete this chapter, you must have

- A computer that meets the minimum hardware requirements located in "About This Book."
- Windows 2000 Professional installed on the computer.

Lesson 1: Understanding the Registry

Microsoft Windows 2000 stores hardware and software settings centrally in a hierarchical database called the *registry*. The registry replaces many of the .INI, .SYS, and .COM configuration files used in earlier versions of Microsoft Windows. The registry controls the Windows 2000 operating system by providing the appropriate initialization information to start applications and load components, such as device drivers and network protocols.

After this lesson, you will be able to

- Identify the purpose of the registry.
- Define the hierarchical structure of the registry.

Estimated lesson time: 30 minutes

Purpose of the Registry

The registry contains a variety of different types of data, including the following:

- The hardware installed on the computer, including the central processing unit (CPU), bus type, pointing device or mouse, and keyboard.
- Installed device drivers.
- Installed applications.
- Installed network protocols.
- Network adapter card settings. Examples include the IRQ number, memory base address, I/O port base address, I/O channel ready, and transceiver type.

The registry structure provides a secure set of records. The data in the registry is read, updated, or modified by many of the Windows 2000 components. The components that access and store data in the registry include those shown in Figure 5.1 and explained in Table 5.1.

Figure 5.1   The Registry Editor

Table 5.1   Components That Use the Registry

Component	Description
Windows NT kernel	During startup, the Windows 2000 kernel (Ntoskrnl.exe) reads information from the registry, including the device drivers to load and the order in which they should be loaded. The kernel writes information about itself to the registry, such as the version number.
Device drivers	Device drivers receive configuration parameters from the registry. They also write information to the registry. A device driver informs the registry of which system resources it is using, such as hardware interrupts or DMA channels. Device drivers also report discovered configuration data.
User profiles	Windows 2000 creates and maintains user work environment settings in a user profile. When a user logs on, the system caches the profile in the registry. Windows 2000 first writes user configuration changes to the registry and then to the user profile.
Setup programs	During setup of a hardware device or application, a Setup program can add new configuration data to the registry. It can also query the registry to determine whether required components have been installed.

(continued)

Component	Description
Hardware profiles	Computers with two or more hardware configurations use hardware profiles. When Windows 2000 starts, the user selects a hardware profile and Windows 2000 configures the system accordingly.
Ntdetect.com	During system startup, on Intel-based computers, Ntdetect.com performs hardware detection. This dynamic hardware configuration data is stored in the registry.
	Reduced-instruction-set-computing (RISC)–based computers extract the data from the computer firmware.

The Hierarchical Structure of the Registry

The registry is organized in a hierarchical structure similar to the hierarchical structure of folders and files on a disk. Figure 5.2 shows the hierarchical structure of the registry as displayed by one of the registry editing tools included with Windows 2000.

Figure 5.2   The Registry Editor displaying the hierarchical structure of the registry

Table 5.2 describes the components that make up the hierarchical structure of the registry.

Table 5.2   Components That Make Up the Registry

Component	Description
Subtree	A *subtree* (or subtree key) is analogous to the root folder of a disk. The Windows 2000 registry has two subtrees: HKEY_LOCAL_MACHINE and HKEY_USERS. However, to make the information in the registry easier to find and view, five predefined subtrees appear in the editor: HKEY_LOCAL_MACHINE HKEY_USERS HKEY_CURRENT_USER HKEY_CLASSES_ROOT HKEY_CURRENT_CONFIG
Keys	*Keys* are analogous to folders and subfolders. Keys correspond to hardware or software objects and groups of objects. Subkeys are keys within higher-level keys.
Entries	Keys contain one or more entries. An *entry* has three parts: name, data type, and value (or configuration parameter).
Hive	A *hive* is a discrete body of keys, subkeys, and entries. Each hive has a corresponding registry file and .LOG file located in *systemroot*\System32\Config. Windows 2000 uses the .LOG file to record changes and ensure the integrity of the registry.
Data types	Each entry's value is expressed as one of these data types: ■ REG_DWORD. One value; must be a string of 1–8 hexadecimal digits. ■ REG_SZ. One value; Windows 2000 interprets it as a string to store. ■ REG_EXPAND_SZ. Similar to REG_SZ, except the text can contain a replaceable variable; for example, in the string systemroot\Ntvdm.exe, Windows 2000 replaces the systemroot environmental variable with the path to the Windows 2000 System32 folder. ■ REG_BINARY. Only one value; it must be a string of hexadecimal digits; Windows 2000 interprets each pair as a byte value. ■ REG_MULTI_SZ. Multiple values allowed; Windows 2000 interprets each string as a component of MULTI_SZ separate entries. ■ REG_FULL_RESOURCE_DESCRIPTOR. Stores a resource list for hardware components or drivers. You can't add or modify an entry with this data type.

Registry Subtrees

Understanding the purpose of each subtree can help you to locate specific keys and values in the registry. The following five subtrees or subtree keys are displayed in Registry Editor (see Figure 5.3).

- **HKEY_LOCAL_MACHINE.** Contains all configuration data for the local computer, including hardware and operating system data such as bus type, system memory, device drivers, and startup control data. Applications, device drivers, and the operating system use this data to set the computer configuration. The data in this subtree remains constant regardless of the user.

- **HKEY_USERS.** Contains the system default settings (system default profile) data used to control individual user identities and environments, such as desktop settings, windows environment or interface settings, and custom software settings.

- **HKEY_CURRENT_USER.** Contains data about the current user. Retrieves a copy of each user account used to log on to the computer and stores it in the *systemroot*\Documents And Settings*username* key.

- **HKEY_CLASSES_ROOT.** Contains software configuration data: object linking and embedding (OLE) and file-class association data. This subtree points to the Classes subkey under HKEY_LOCAL_MACHINE\ SOFTWARE.

- **HKEY_CURRENT_CONFIG.** Contains data on the active hardware profile extracted from the SOFTWARE and SYSTEM hives. This information is used to configure settings such as the device drivers to load and the display resolution to use.

Figure 5.3   Registry subtrees

The HKEY_LOCAL_MACHINE Subtree

The HKEY_LOCAL_MACHINE key provides a good example of the subtrees in the registry for two reasons:

- The structure of all subtrees is similar.

- HKEY_LOCAL_MACHINE contains information specific to the local computer and is always the same, regardless of the user who is logged on.

The HKEY_LOCAL_MACHINE root key has five subkeys, which are explained in Table 5.3.

Table 5.3   HKEY_LOCAL_MACHINE Subkeys

Subkey	Description
HARDWARE	The type and state of physical devices attached to the computer. This subkey is volatile, meaning that Windows 2000 builds it from information gathered during startup. Because the values for this subkey are volatile, this subkey doesn't map to a file on the disk. Applications query this subkey to determine the type and state of physical devices attached to the computer.
SAM	The Directory database for the computer. The SAM hive maps to the SAM and Sam.log files in the *systemroot*\System32\Config folder. Applications that query SAM must use the appropriate APIs.
SECURITY	The security information for the local computer. The SECURITY hive maps to the Security and Security.log files in the *systemroot*\System32\Config folder. Applications can't modify the keys contained in the SECURITY subkey. Instead, applications must query security information by using the security APIs.
SOFTWARE	Information about the local computer software that is independent of per-user configuration information. This hive maps to the Software, Software.log, and Software.sav files in the *systemroot*\System32\Config folder. It also contains file associations and OLE information.
SYSTEM	Information about system devices and services. When you install or configure device drivers or services, they add or modify information under this hive. The SYSTEM hive maps to the System, System.log, and System.sav files in the *systemroot*\System32\Config folder. The registry keeps a backup of the data in the SYSTEM hive in the System.alt file.

Lesson Summary

In this lesson, you learned that the Microsoft Windows 2000 operating system stores hardware and software settings in the registry. The registry is a hierarchical database and replaces many of the .INI, .SYS, and .COM configuration files used in earlier versions of Microsoft Windows. The registry contains a variety of different types of data, including the hardware installed on the computer, as well as the installed device drivers, applications, and network protocols. The registry also provides the appropriate initialization information to start applications and load components, such as device drivers and network protocols.

You also learned that the registry structure provides a secure set of records, and the data in the registry can be read, updated, or modified by many of the Windows 2000 components. A number of components make up the hierarchical structure of the registry. First, subtrees (or subtree keys) are analogous to the root folder of a disk. The Windows 2000 registry has two subtrees: HKEY_LOCAL_MACHINE and HKEY_USERS. However, to make the information in the registry easier to find and view, the following five predefined subtrees appear in the editor: HKEY_LOCAL_MACHINE, HKEY_USERS, HKEY_CURRENT_USER, HKEY_CLASSES_ROOT, and HKEY_CURRENT_CONFIG. The other components of the registry include keys, entries, hives, and data types.

Lesson 2: Using Registry Editor

Most Windows 2000 users never need to access the registry. However, management of the registry is an important part of the system administrator's job and includes viewing, editing, backing up, and restoring the registry. You use Registry Editor to view and change the registry configuration.

After this lesson, you will be able to

- Edit the registry with Registry Editor.

Estimated lesson time: 40 minutes

Regedt32.exe

Setup installs Registry Editor (Regedt32.exe) in the *systemroot*\System32 folder during installation. However, because most users don't need to use Registry Editor, it doesn't appear on the Start menu. You start Registry Editor by clicking Run on the Start menu.

Note Setup also installs a second Registry Editor (Regedit.exe). Regedit.exe doesn't have a security menu or a read-only mode and doesn't support REG_EXPAND_SZ or REG_MULTI_SZ, so it is not the recommended Registry Editor for Windows 2000.

Although Registry Editor allows you to perform manual edits on the registry, it is intended for troubleshooting and problem resolution. You should make most configuration changes through either Control Panel or Administrative Tools. However, some configuration settings can be made only directly through the registry.

Caution Using Registry Editor incorrectly can cause serious, system-wide problems that could require reinstallation of Windows 2000. When using Registry Editor to view data, save a backup copy of the registry file before viewing, and click Read Only Mode on the Options menu to prevent accidental updating or deleting of configuration data.

Registry Editor saves data automatically as you make entries or corrections. New registry data takes effect immediately. You can find some of the most useful Registry Editor commands on the Registry menu and the View menu in Registry Editor. Table 5.4 describes the commands on these menus.

Table 5.4   Registry Editor Commands

Command	Menu	Description
Save Key	Registry	Saves part of the registry in binary format. It saves the currently selected key and all subkeys. You can then use this file with the Restore command to reload a set of values after testing a change.
Restore	Registry	Loads the data in the selected file under the currently selected key. If the selected key was saved in the data file, Registry Editor will overwrite the key with the values in the file.
Save Subtree As	Registry	Saves the selected key and all subkeys in a text file. You can then use a text editor to search for a specific value or key that was added or modified. Note that you can't convert this text file back to registry data.
Select Computer	Registry	Opens the registry on a remote computer. Windows 2000 Server restricts remote access to the Administrators group, but Windows 2000 Professional allows remote access by any valid user account. To modify remote access permissions for either operating system, create this registry key: HKEY_LOCAL_MACHINE\SYSTEM\ CurrentControlSet\Control\SecurePipeServers \winreg, of type REG_DWORD, with a value of 1. Permissions on this key define who can have remote access to the registry.
Find Key	View	Searches the registry for a specific key. Key names appear in the left pane of Registry Editor. The search begins at the currently selected key and parses all descendant keys for the specified key name. The search is local to the subtree in which the search begins. For example, a search for a key in the HKEY_LOCAL_MACHINE subtree doesn't include keys under HKEY_CURRENT_USER.

Practice: Using Registry Editor

In this practice, you will use Registry Editor to view the information in the registry. You will determine information such as the BIOS, the processor on your computer, and the version of the operating system. You use Registry Editor's Find Key command to search the registry for a specific word with key names. You modify the registry by adding a value to it, and you save a subtree as a file so that you can use an editor, like Notepad, to search the file.

Exercise 1: Exploring the Registry

In this exercise, you will use Registry Editor to view information in the registry.

▶ **To view information in the registry**

1. Ensure that you are logged on as Administrator.

2. Start Registry Editor (Regedt32.exe).

3. On the Options menu, click Read Only Mode to place a check mark to the left of the option.

4. On the View menu, ensure that Tree And Data is selected.

5. Maximize the Registry Editor window, and then maximize the window titled HKEY_LOCAL_MACHINE On Local Machine.

6. Double-click the HARDWARE\DESCRIPTION\System subkey to expand it, and then answer the following questions:

   What is the basic input/output system (BIOS) version of your computer and its date?

   What is the computer type of your local machine according to the Identifier entry?

7. Expand the SOFTWARE\Microsoft\Windows NT\CurrentVersion subkey, and then fill in the following information.

Software configuration	Value and string
Current build number	
Current version	
Registered organization	
Registered owner	

Exercise 2: Using the Find Key

In this exercise, you will use Registry Editor's Find Key command to search the registry to find a specific word in the key names in the registry.

▶ **To use the find key**

1. Click the HKEY_LOCAL_MACHINE subkey to ensure that the entire subtree is searched.

2. On the View menu, click Find Key.

   The Find dialog box appears.

3. In the Find What box, type **serial**

4. Click Find Next and wait for the first matching entry to appear.

5. Continue clicking Find Next until a Warning dialog box appears, indicating that Registry Editor can't find the desired key.

   Notice that this key appears in multiple locations in the registry.

6. Click OK to close the Warning dialog box.

7. Click Cancel to close the Find dialog box.

Exercise 3: Modifying the Registry

In this exercise, you will add a value to the registry.

▶ **To add a value to the registry**

1. On the Options menu, click Read Only Mode.

   This will disable Read Only Mode, which was enabled in Exercise 1.

2. On the Window menu, click HKEY_CURRENT_USER On Local Machine.

   The HKEY_CURRENT_USER window appears in Registry Editor.

3. In the left pane of the Registry Editor window, click Environment.

   The values in the Environment key appear in the right pane of the Registry Editor window.

4. On the Edit menu, click Add Value.

Note If Add Value is unavailable, make sure Read Only Mode is not selected on the Options menu. If you are having problems deselecting Read Only Mode, exit Registry Editor and then restart it.

The Add Value dialog box appears.

5. In the Value Name box, type **test**

6. In the Data Type list, click REG_EXPAND_SZ, and then click OK.

   The String Editor dialog box appears.

7. In the String box, type **%windir%\system32** and then click OK.

   test:REG_EXPAND_SZ : %windir%\system32 should appear in the right pane of the Registry Editor window.

8. Minimize the Registry Editor window.

► **To verify the new registry value**

1. Right-click My Computer, and then click Properties.

   The System Properties dialog box appears.

2. Click the Advanced tab, and then click Environment Variables.

   The Environment Variables dialog box appears.

3. Close the Environment Variables dialog box, and then close the System Properties dialog box.

Exercise 4: Saving a Subtree as a File

In this exercise, you will save a subtree as a file. Saving a subtree as a file allows you to use Notepad or some other editor to search the file. The file can also be stored or printed as a record of the contents of the subtree and might come in handy for troubleshooting a problem, should something accidentally get changed in the registry.

► **To save a subtree as a file**

1. Restore the Registry Editor window.

2. On the Window menu, click HKEY_LOCAL_MACHINE On Local Machine.

3. Click HKEY_LOCAL_MACHINE\ SOFTWARE.

4. On the Registry menu, click Save Subtree As.

   The Save As dialog box appears.

5. In the Save In box, click Desktop.

6. In the File Name box, type **Software.txt** and then click Save.

   Note You might experience a long delay while Registry Editor saves the subtree.
   ---

7. Exit Registry Editor.

8. On your desktop, double-click Software.

   Notepad opens the Software file.

9. On the Edit menu, click Find.

   The Find dialog box appears.

10. In the Find What box, type **CurrentBuildNumber** and then click Find Next.

11. Click Cancel to close the Find dialog box.

12. Scroll down (if necessary) to see the data for CurrentBuildNumber.

13. Close Notepad.

Lesson Summary

In this lesson, you learned that you use Registry Editor (Regedt32.exe) to view and change the registry configuration. However, Registry Editor is primarily intended for troubleshooting. For most configuration changes, you should use either Control Panel or Administrative Tools, not Registry Editor. You also learned that some configuration settings can be made only directly through the registry, and for these you use Registry Editor.

You learned that you find some of the most useful Registry Editor commands on the Registry menu and the View menu. These commands include Find Key, which allows you to search the registry for a specific key. The Save Key command allows you to save part of the registry in binary format. The Save Subtree As command allows you to save the selected key and all subkeys in a text file, and the Select Computer command allows you to open the registry on a remote computer.

Review

The following questions will help you determine whether you have learned enough to move on to the next chapter. If you have difficulty answering these questions, please go back and review the material in this chapter before beginning the next chapter. See Appendix A, "Questions and Answers," for the answers to these questions.

1. What is the registry and what does it do?

2. What is a hive?

3. What is the recommended editor for viewing and modifying the registry?

4. What option should you enable when you are viewing the contents of the registry? Why?

CHAPTER 6

Managing Disks

About This Chapter

This chapter presents an overview of Microsoft Windows 2000 disk management. You can create a custom MMC and add the Disk Management snap-in to it. The Disk Management snap-in is also included in the preconfigured Computer Management MMC on the Administrative Tools menu. The Disk Management snap-in provides shortcut menus to show you which tasks you can perform on the selected object, and it includes wizards to guide you through creating partitions and volumes and upgrading disks.

Before You Begin

To complete this chapter, you must have

- A computer that meets the minimum hardware requirements located in "About This Book."
- Windows 2000 Professional installed on the computer.

Lesson 1: Introduction to Disk Management

In this lesson, you will learn about disk management concepts. For example, if you have free space on your hard disk, you need to partition and format it so that you can store data on that part of the disk. In addition, if you have more than one hard disk, each disk will also have to be partitioned and formatted so that you can store data on it.

After this lesson, you will be able to

■ Describe disk management concepts.

Estimated lesson time: 25 minutes

Tasks in Setting Up a Hard Disk

Whether you are setting up the remaining free space on a hard disk on which you installed Windows 2000 or setting up a new hard disk, you need to be aware of the tasks that are involved. Before you can store data on a new hard disk, you must perform the following tasks to prepare the disk:

1. Initialize the disk with a storage type. Initialization defines the fundamental structure of a hard disk.

   Windows 2000 supports basic storage and dynamic storage.

2. Create partitions on a basic disk or create volumes on a dynamic disk.

3. Format the disk. After you create a partition or volume, you must format it with a specific file system—NTFS file system, FAT, or FAT32.

   The file system that you choose affects disk operations. This includes how you control user access to data, how data is stored, hard disk capacity, and which operating systems can gain access to the data on the hard disk.

Before you can decide how to perform the tasks of setting up a hard disk, you must understand the storage types, partition types, and volume types available in Windows 2000.

Storage Types

Windows 2000 supports the following two types of disk storage: basic storage and dynamic storage. A physical disk must be either basic or dynamic; you can't use both storage types on one disk. You can, however, use both types of disk storage in a multidisk system.

Basic Storage

The traditional industry standard is *basic storage*. It dictates the division of a hard disk into partitions (see Figure 6.1). A *partition* is a portion of the disk that functions as a physically separate unit of storage. Windows 2000 recognizes primary and extended partitions. A disk that is initialized for basic storage is called a *basic disk*. A basic disk can contain primary partitions, extended partitions, and logical drives. New disks added to a computer running Windows 2000 are basic disks.

Figure 6.1   Basic and dynamic storage types

Because basic storage is the traditional industry standard, all versions of Microsoft Windows, MS-DOS, Windows NT, and Windows 2000 support basic storage. For Windows 2000, basic storage is the default, so all disks are basic disks until you convert them to dynamic storage.

Dynamic Storage

Only Windows 2000 supports *dynamic storage,* which is a standard that creates a single partition that includes the entire disk. A disk that you initialize for dynamic storage is a *dynamic disk.*

You divide dynamic disks into *volumes,* which can consist of a portion, or portions, of one or more physical disks. On a dynamic disk, you can create simple volumes, spanned volumes, and striped volumes, as described later in this chapter. You create a dynamic disk by upgrading a basic disk.

Dynamic storage doesn't have the restrictions of basic storage; for example, you can size and resize a dynamic disk without restarting Windows 2000.

Note Removable storage devices contain primary partitions only. You can't create extended partitions, logical drives, or dynamic volumes on removable storage devices. You can't mark a primary partition on a removable storage device as active.

Partition Types (Basic Disks)

You can divide a basic disk into primary and extended partitions. *Partitions* function as physically separate storage units. This allows you to separate different types of information, such as user data on one partition and applications on another. A basic disk can contain up to four primary partitions, or up to three primary partitions and one extended partition, for a maximum of four partitions. Only one partition can be an extended partition, as shown in Figure 6.2.

Figure 6.2   Partition types

Primary Partitions

Windows 2000 can use the parts of a disk called *primary partitions* to start the computer. Only a primary partition can be marked as the active partition. The active partition is where the hardware looks for the boot files to start the operating system. Only one partition on a single hard disk can be active at a time. Multiple primary partitions allow you to isolate different operating systems or types of data.

To dual boot Windows 2000 with Microsoft Windows 95 or MS-DOS, the active partition must be formatted as FAT because Windows 95 can't read a partition formatted as FAT32 or NTFS. To dual boot with Microsoft Windows 95 OSR2 (a later release of Windows 95 that contained enhancements to Windows 95, such as the ability to read partitions formatted with FAT32) or Windows 98, the active partition must be formatted as FAT or FAT32.

Extended Partitions

An *extended partition* is created from free space. There can be only one extended partition on a hard disk, so you should include all remaining free space in the extended partition. Unlike primary partitions, you don't format extended partitions or assign drive letters to them. You divide extended partitions into segments. Each segment is a logical drive. You assign a drive letter to each logical drive and format it with a file system.

Note The Windows 2000 *system partition* is the active partition that contains the hardware-specific files required to load the operating system. The Windows 2000 *boot partition* is the primary partition or logical drive where the operating system files are installed. The boot partition and the system partition can be the same partition. However, the system partition must be on the active partition, typically drive C, while the boot partition could be on another primary partition or on an extended partition.

Volume Types (Dynamic Disks)

You can convert basic disks to dynamic storage and then create Windows 2000 volumes. Consider which volume type best suits your needs for efficient use of disk space and performance.

- A *simple volume* contains disk space from a single disk and is not fault tolerant.

- A *spanned volume* includes disk space from multiple disks (up to 32). Windows 2000 writes data to a spanned volume on the first disk, completely filling the space, and continues in this manner through each disk that you include in the spanned volume. A spanned volume is not fault tolerant. If any disk in a spanned volume fails, the data in the entire volume is lost.

- A *striped volume* combines areas of free space from multiple hard disks, up to 32, into one logical volume. In a striped volume, Windows 2000 optimizes performance by adding data to all disks at the same rate. If a disk in a striped volume fails, the data in the entire volume is lost.

Note The Windows 2000 Server products provide fault tolerance on dynamic disks. *Fault tolerance* is the ability of a computer or operating system to respond to a catastrophic event without loss of data. The Windows 2000 Server products provide mirrored volumes and RAID-5 volumes that are fault tolerant. Windows 2000 Professional does not provide fault tolerance.

Creating multiple partitions or volumes on a single hard disk allows you to efficiently organize data for tasks such as backing up. For example, partition one-third of a hard disk for the operating system, one-third for applications, and one-third for data. Then, when you back up your data, you can back up the entire partition instead of just a specific folder.

File Systems

Windows 2000 supports the NTFS, FAT, and FAT32 file systems. Use NTFS when you require a partition to have file- and folder-level security, disk compression, disk quotas, or encryption. Only Windows 2000 and Windows NT can access data on a local hard disk that is formatted as NTFS. If you plan to promote a server to a domain controller, format the installation partition with NTFS.

FAT and FAT32 allow access by, and compatibility with, other operating systems. To dual boot Windows 2000 and another operating system, format the system partition with either FAT or FAT32. FAT and FAT32 don't offer many of the features that NTFS supports, for example, file-level security. Therefore, in most situations, you should format the hard disk with NTFS. The only reason to use FAT or FAT32 is for dual booting.

Note For a review of file systems, see Chapter 2, "Installing Windows 2000 Professional."

If you have a volume that is formatted with FAT or FAT32, Windows 2000 provides the Convert command to allow you to convert it from FAT or FAT32 to NTFS without having to reformat your volume. To do this you enter the following command in a Command Prompt window:

```
Convert volume /FS:NTFS /V
```

Note that *volume* is replaced by the drive letter followed by a colon. The /V indicates the command should be run in verbose mode. For example, if you wanted to convert drive C from FAT to NTFS you would type the following command:

```
Convert C: /FS:NTFS /V
```

The Disk Management Snap-In

Use the Disk Management snap-in to configure and manage your network storage space. The Disk Management snap-in can display your storage system in either a graphical view or a list view. You can modify the display to suit your preferences by using the commands on the View menu.

Lesson Summary

In this lesson, you learned that before you can store data on a new hard disk, you must use the Disk Management snap-in to initialize the disk with a storage type. Windows 2000 supports basic storage and dynamic storage. A basic disk can contain primary partitions, extended partitions, and logical drives. All versions of Microsoft Windows, MS-DOS, and Windows 2000 support basic storage. For Windows 2000, basic storage is the default, so all disks are basic disks until you convert them to dynamic storage.

You also learned that dynamic storage creates a single partition that includes the entire disk. You divide dynamic disks into volumes, which can consist of a portion, or portions, of one or more physical disks. A dynamic disk can contain simple volumes, spanned volumes, and striped volumes. Dynamic storage doesn't have the restrictions of basic storage; for example, you can size and resize a dynamic disk without restarting Windows 2000.

Then you learned that after you create partitions on a basic disk or create volumes on a dynamic disk, you must format the partition or volume with a specific file system such as NTFS, FAT, or FAT32. The file system that you choose affects disk operations. This includes how you control user access to data, how data is stored, how much hard disk capacity you have, and which operating systems can gain access to the data on the hard disk. You use the Disk Management snap-in to configure and manage your network storage space.

Lesson 2: Common Disk Management Tasks

The Disk Management snap-in provides a central location for disk information and management tasks, such as creating and deleting partitions and volumes. With the proper permissions, you can manage disks locally and on remote computers. In addition to monitoring disk information, some of the other disk management tasks that you might need to perform include adding and removing hard disks and changing the disk storage type.

This lesson introduces the following disk management tasks:

- Working with simple volumes
- Working with spanned volumes
- Working with striped volumes
- Adding disks
- Changing storage types
- Viewing and updating information
- Managing disks on a remote computer

After this lesson, you will be able to

- Identify common disk management tasks.
- Create and configure a dynamic disk.

Estimated lesson time: 50 minutes

Working with Simple Volumes

A simple volume contains disk space from a single disk. You can extend a simple volume to include unallocated space on the same disk.

You can create a simple volume and format it with NTFS, FAT, or FAT32 (see Figure 6.3). You can extend a simple volume only if it is formatted with NTFS.

You can create a simple volume by following these steps:

1. Select Disk Management in the Storage section of the Computer Management snap-in.
2. On the dynamic disk where you want to create the volume, right-click the unallocated space, and then click Create Volume.

   This launches the Create Volume wizard.
3. In the Create Volume wizard, click Next.
4. Click Simple Volume, and then follow the instructions on your screen.

Figure 6.3   Creating a simple volume

To extend an NTFS simple volume, right-click the simple volume that you want to extend, click Extend Volume, and then follow the instructions on your screen. When you extend a simple volume to another disk, it becomes a spanned volume.

Working with Spanned Volumes

A spanned volume consists of disk space from multiple disks; spanned volumes enable you to use the total available free space on multiple disks more effectively. You can create spanned volumes only on dynamic disks, and you need at least two dynamic disks to create a spanned volume. Spanned volumes can't be part of a striped volume and are not fault tolerant. Figure 6.4 introduces some of the important concepts for combining free space to create spanned volumes, to extend spanned volumes, and to delete spanned volumes.

- **Combining free space**
  - Spanned volumes combine space from 2 – 32 disks
  - Data is written to one disk until full
- **Extending and deleting**
  - Only NTFS-spanned volumes can be extended
  - Deleting any part of a spanned volume deletes the entire volume

Figure 6.4   Creating, extending, and deleting spanned volumes

Combining Free Space to Create a Spanned Volume

You create spanned volumes by combining various-sized areas of free space from 2 to 32 disks into one large logical volume. The areas of free space that comprise a spanned volume can be different sizes. Windows 2000 organizes spanned volumes so that data is stored in the space on one disk until it is full, and then, starting at the beginning of the next disk, data is stored in the space on the second disk. Windows 2000 continues this process in the same way on each subsequent disk up to a maximum of 32 disks.

By deleting smaller volumes and combining them into one spanned volume, you can free drive letters for other uses and create a large volume for file system use.

Extending and Deleting Spanned Volumes

You can extend existing spanned volumes formatted with NTFS by adding free space. Disk Management formats the new area without affecting any existing files on the original volume. You can't extend volumes formatted with FAT or FAT32.

You can extend spanned volumes on dynamic disks onto a maximum of 32 dynamic disks. After a volume is extended onto multiple disks (spanned), it can't be part of a striped volume. After a spanned volume is extended, no portion of it can be deleted without deleting the entire spanned volume. You can't extend a system volume or a boot volume.

Working with Striped Volumes

Striped volumes offer the best performance of all the Windows 2000 disk management strategies. In a striped volume, data is written evenly across all physical disks in 64-KB units, as shown in Figure 6.5. Because all the hard disks that belong to the striped volume perform the same functions as a single hard disk, Windows 2000 can issue and process concurrent I/O commands simultaneously on all hard disks. In this way, striped volumes can increase the speed of system I/O.

You create striped volumes by combining areas of free space from multiple disks (from 2 to 32) into one logical volume. With a striped volume, Windows 2000 writes data to multiple disks, similar to spanned volumes. However, on a striped volume, Windows 2000 writes files across all disks so that data is added to all disks at the same rate. Like spanned volumes, striped volumes don't provide fault tolerance. If a disk in a striped volume fails, the data in the entire volume is lost.

You need at least two dynamic disks to create a striped volume. You can create a striped volume onto a maximum of 32 disks. You can't extend striped volumes.

You can create a striped volume by doing the following:

1. In Disk Management, on the dynamic disk where you want to create the striped volume, right-click the unallocated space, and then click Create Volume. This launches the Create Volume wizard.

2. In the Create Volume wizard, click Next, click Striped Volume, and then follow the instructions on your screen.

Figure 6.5   Benefits of working with striped volumes

Adding Disks

When you install new disks in a computer running Windows 2000, they are added as basic storage.

Adding New Disks

To add a new disk, install or attach the new physical disk (or disks), and then click Rescan Disks on the Action menu of the Disk Management snap-in, as shown in Figure 6.6. You must use Rescan Disks every time you remove or add disks to a computer.

You shouldn't need to restart the computer when you add a new disk to your computer. However, you might need to restart the computer if Disk Management doesn't detect the new disk after you run Rescan Disks.

Figure 6.6   Adding disks using the Disk Management snap-in

Adding Disks That You Removed from Another Computer

If you want to uninstall or remove a disk from one computer and then install the disk in a different computer, the process is different. You can add a disk that has been removed from another computer by doing the following:

1. Remove the disk from the original computer and install the disk in the new computer.

2. Open Disk Management.

   Disk Management displays the new disk labeled as Foreign.

3. Right-click the new disk, and then click Import Foreign Disk. A wizard provides on-screen instructions.

Adding Multiple Disks That You Removed from Another Computer

If you want to uninstall or remove multiple disks from one computer and then install the disks in a different computer, the process is much the same as doing so for a single disk.

You can add multiple inherited disks by following these steps:

1. Remove the disks from the original computer and install them in the new computer.

2. Open Disk Management.

3. Right-click any of the new disks, and then click Add Disk. The disks appear as a group.

4. To specify the disks from the group that you want to add, click Select Disk. However, if you don't have any dynamic disks installed, all of the disks are added regardless of the disks that you select.

When you move a dynamic disk to your computer from another computer running Windows 2000, you can see and use any existing volumes on that disk. However, if a volume on a foreign disk extends to multiple disks and you don't move all the disks for that volume, Disk Management will not show the portion of the volume that resides on the foreign disk.

Changing Storage Type

You can upgrade a disk from basic storage to dynamic storage at any time, with no loss of data. When you upgrade a basic disk to a dynamic disk, any existing partitions on the basic disk become simple volumes. Any existing striped or spanned volume sets created with Windows NT 4 become dynamic striped or spanned volumes, respectively.

Any disks to be upgraded must contain at least 1 MB of unallocated space for the upgrade to succeed. Before you upgrade disks, close any programs that are running on those disks.

Table 6.1 shows the results of converting a disk from basic storage to dynamic storage.

Table 6.1   Basic Disk and Dynamic Disk Organization

Basic disk organization	Dynamic disk organization
System partition	Simple volume
Boot partition	Simple volume
Primary partition	Simple volume
Extended partition	Simple volume for each logical drive and any remaining unallocated space
Logical drive	Simple volume
Volume set	Spanned volume
Stripe set	Striped volume

Important Always back up the data on a disk before converting the storage type.

Upgrading Basic Disks to Dynamic Disks

To upgrade a basic disk to a dynamic disk, in the Disk Management snap-in, right-click the basic disk that you want to upgrade, and then click Upgrade To Dynamic Disk. A wizard provides on-screen instructions. The upgrade process requires that you restart your computer.

After you upgrade a basic disk to a dynamic disk, you can create volumes with improved capabilities on the disk. After you upgrade a disk to dynamic storage, it can't contain partitions or logical drives. Only Windows 2000 can access dynamic disks.

Reverting to a Basic Disk from a Dynamic Disk

You must remove all volumes from the dynamic disk before you can change it back to a basic disk. To change a dynamic disk back to a basic disk, right-click the dynamic disk that you want to change back to a basic disk, and then click Revert To Basic Disk.

Caution Converting a dynamic disk to a basic disk causes all data to be lost.

Viewing and Updating Information

The Properties dialog box for a selected disk or volume provides a concise view of all of the pertinent properties.

Disk Properties

To view disk properties in Disk Management, right-click the name of a disk in the Graphical View window (don't click one of its volumes), and then click Properties. Table 6.2 describes the information displayed in the Properties dialog box for a disk.

Table 6.2   The Properties Dialog Box for a Disk

Category	Description
Disk	The number for the disk in the system, for example, Disk 0, Disk 1, Disk 2, and so on
Type	The type of storage (basic, dynamic, or removable)
Status	The current status of the disk (online, offline, foreign, or unknown)
Capacity	The total capacity for the disk
Unallocated Space	The amount of available free space
Device Type	The type of devices—Integrated Device Electronics (IDE), Small Computer System Interface (SCSI), or Enhanced IDE (EIDE)—as well as the IDE channel (primary or secondary) on which the disk resides
Hardware Vendor	The hardware vendor for the disk and the disk type
Adapter Name	The type of controller to which the disk is attached
Volumes Contained On This Disk	The volumes that exist on the disk and their total capacity

Volume Properties

To view volume properties in Disk Management, right-click a volume in the Graphical View window or in the Volume List window, and then click Properties. Table 6.3 describes the tabs in the Properties dialog box for a volume.

Table 6.3   Properties Dialog Box for a Volume

Tab	Description
General	Lists the volume label, type, file system, and used and free space. Click Disk Cleanup to delete unnecessary files. NTFS volumes list two options: Compress Drive To Save Disk Space, and Allow Indexing Service To Index This Disk For Fast File Searching.
Tools	Provides a single location from which you can perform volume error-checking, backup, and defragmentation tasks.
Hardware	Checks properties of and troubleshoots the physical disks installed on the system.
Sharing	Sets network-shared volume parameters and permissions.
Security	Sets NTFS access permissions. This tab is available only for NTFS version 4 and 5 volumes. (Windows 2000 uses NTFS version 5.0.)
Quota	Sets user quotas for NTFS 5 volumes.

Refresh and Rescan

When you are working with Disk Management, you might need to update the information in the display. The two commands for updating the display are Refresh and Rescan.

Refresh updates drive letter, file system, volume, and removable media information, and determines whether unreadable volumes are now readable. To update drive letter, file system, and volume information, click Action and then click Refresh.

Rescan Disks updates hardware information. When Disk Management rescans disks, it scans all attached disks for disk configuration changes. It also updates information on removable media, CD-ROM drives, basic volumes, file systems, and drive letters. Rescanning disks can take several minutes, depending on the number of hardware devices installed. To update disk information, click Action, and then click Rescan Disks.

Managing Disks on a Remote Computer

As a member of the Administrators group or the Server Operators group, you can manage disks on a computer running Windows 2000 that is a member of the domain or a trusted domain from any other computer running Windows 2000 on the network.

Note To have a domain requires that at least one computer running one of the Windows 2000 Server products be configured as a domain controller on your network.

If you are in a workgroup, you can also manage disks on a remote computer running Windows 2000 Professional, if you have the same account with the exact same password set up on both the local and remote computers. The passwords must match or the service will fail and you will not be able to manage disks on a remote computer. In a workgroup, each computer has its own local security database.

To manage one computer from another computer—*remote management*—create a custom console that is focused on the remote computer.

You can create a custom console to manage disks on a remote computer by doing the following:

1. Click Start, click Run, type **mmc** and then click OK.
2. On the Console menu, click Add/Remove Snap-In.
3. Click Add.
4. Click Disk Management, and then click Add.
5. In the Choose Computer dialog box shown in Figure 6.7, click Another Computer, and then type the name of the computer.
6. Click Finish.

Figure 6.7   Creating a custom console to manage disks on a remote computer

Practice: Working with Dynamic Storage

After completing this practice, you will be able to

- Upgrade a basic disk to a dynamic disk.
- Create a new volume.
- Mount a simple volume.

Before working on this practice, you should have completed this chapter so that you are familiar with disk management and the Disk Management snap-in.

Exercise 1: Upgrading a Disk

In this exercise, you will use Disk Management to upgrade a basic disk to a dynamic disk.

▶ **To upgrade a basic disk**

1. Ensure that you are logged on as Administrator.

2. Right-click My Computer, and then click Manage.

   The Computer Management window appears.

3. In the console tree, if necessary, double-click Storage to expand it, and then click Disk Management.

   Notice that Disk 0's storage type is Basic.

Note If the Upgrade Disk wizard starts automatically, click Cancel. This might occur if your computer contains a disk configured for basic storage that doesn't contain the Windows 2000 boot partition.

---

4. In the lower-right pane of the Computer Management window, right-click Disk 0, and then click Upgrade To Dynamic Disk.

   The Upgrade To Dynamic Disk dialog box appears.

5. Ensure that Disk 0 is the only disk selected for upgrade, and then click OK.

   The Disks To Upgrade dialog box appears.

6. Click Upgrade.

   A Disk Management dialog box appears, warning that after this upgrade, you will not be able to boot previous versions of Windows from any volumes on this disk.

Caution If you are dual booting with another operating system, for example, Windows 95 or Windows 98 loaded on drive C, these operating systems will no longer run. Only Windows 2000 can access a dynamic drive.

---

7. Click Yes.

   An Upgrade Disks dialog box appears notifying you that file systems on any of the disks to be upgraded will be force dismounted.

8. Click Yes.

   A Confirm message box appears notifying you that a reboot will take place to complete the upgrade process.

9. Click OK.

   Your computer restarts.

▶   **To confirm the upgrade**

1. Log on as Administrator.

> **Note** If the System Settings Change dialog box appears, prompting you to restart your computer, click Yes. After the computer restarts and you log on as Administrator, if you see this same System Settings Change message box again prompting you to restart your computer, click No. Restarting the computer again is not necessary.

2. Right-click My Computer, and then click Manage.

   The Computer Management window appears.

3. In the console tree, if necessary, double-click Storage to expand it, and then click Disk Management.

> **Note** If your computer has more than one disk, the Upgrade Disk wizard might appear. If it does, click Cancel to close it.

   Notice that the storage type of Disk 0 is Dynamic.

4. Minimize the Computer Management window.

Exercise 2: Extending a Volume

In this exercise, you will use Disk Management to create a new simple volume. You then mount the new volume onto an existing folder on another volume. If drive C is formatted as NTFS, you create a folder named Mount under the root folder of drive C. If drive C isn't formatted as NTFS, you create the folder named Mount on the volume that is formatted as NTFS and contains the Windows 2000 files.

▶   **To create a folder for mounting the new volume**

1. Right-click My Computer.

2. Click Explore.

3. Click Local Disk C if it is formatted as NTFS; otherwise, click the disk that is formatted as NTFS and contains your Windows 2000 files.

4. On the File menu, click New, and then click Folder.

5. Type **Mount** and then press Enter.

▶   **To create a new simple volume**

1. Restore the Computer Management window.

2. Right-click the remaining unallocated space on Disk 0 in the lower-right pane, and then click Create Volume.

   The Create Volume wizard appears.

3. Click Next.

   The Select Volume Type page appears.

   Notice that Simple Volume is the only available option.

4. Click Next.

   The Select Disks page appears. The value in the For Selected Disks box represents the remaining free space on Drive 0.

5. Set the volume size to an appropriate size based on the amount of space available (25 MB is plenty), and then click Next.

   The Assign Drive Letter Or Path page appears.

6. Click Mount This Volume At An Empty Folder That Supports Drive Paths, and then type **x:\mount** where *x* is the letter of the drive containing the Mount folder.

7. Click Next.

   The Format Volume page appears.

8. Ensure that Format This Volume As Follows is selected and that File System To Use is set to NTFS.

9. Type **Mounted Vol** in the Volume Label box.

10. Click Perform A Quick Format, and then click Next.

11. Read the information on the Completing The Create Volume Wizard page, and then click Finish.

    The new volume is created, formatted, and mounted on the C:\Mount folder; or if C is not formatted as NTFS, it is mounted where you created the Mount folder.

12. Leave the Computer Management window open.

► **To examine the new volume**

1. Open Microsoft Windows Explorer.

2. Click Local Disk (C:) (if necessary) to display the Local Disk (C:) window.

   Important If you mounted your volume on a drive other than drive C, click that drive instead.

   ---

3. Right-click Mount, and then click Properties.

   The Mount Properties dialog box appears.

   Notice that *x*:\Mount (where *x* is the drive on which you mounted the volume) is a mounted volume.

4. Click OK.

5. Create a new text document in the *x*:\Mount folder.

6. Close Windows Explorer.

7. Open a command prompt.

8. Change the working directory to the root directory of drive C (if necessary) or to the root directory of the drive where you mounted your volume, type **dir** and then press Enter.

   How much free space does the Dir command report?

   Why is there a difference between the free space reported for drive C and the free space reported for C:\Mount? (If you mounted your volume on a drive other than drive C, replace C with the appropriate drive letter.)

9. Close the command prompt.

10. Close the Computer Management window.

Lesson Summary

In this lesson, you learned that the Disk Management snap-in provides a central location for disk information and management tasks, such as creating and deleting partitions and volumes. With the proper permissions, you can manage disks locally and on remote computers. In addition to monitoring disk information, some of the other disk management tasks that you might need to perform include adding and removing hard disks and changing the disk storage type.

This lesson also introduced you to the following disk management tasks: working with simple volumes, spanned volumes, and striped volumes. And it introduced you to adding disks, changing the storage type, viewing and updating information, and managing disks on a remote computer.

Review

The following questions will help you determine whether you have learned enough to move on to the next chapter. If you have difficulty answering these questions, please go back and review the material in this chapter before beginning the next chapter. See Appendix A, "Questions and Answers," for the answers to these questions.

1. You install a new 10-GB disk drive that you want to divide into five equal 2-GB sections. What are your options?

2. You are trying to create a striped volume on your Windows NT Server to improve performance. You confirm that you have enough unallocated disk space on two disks in your computer, but when you right-click an area of unallocated space on a disk, your only option is to create a partition. What is the problem and how would you resolve it?

3. You add a new disk to your computer and attempt to extend an existing volume to include the unallocated space on the new disk, but the option to extend the volume isn't available. What is the problem and how would you resolve it?

4. You dual boot your computer with Windows 98 and Windows 2000 Professional. You upgrade a second drive—which you are using to archive files—from basic storage to dynamic storage. The next time you try to access your archived files from Windows 98, you are unable to read the files. Why?

C H A P T E R   7

Installing and Configuring Network Protocols

About This Chapter

A *protocol* is a set of rules and conventions for sending information over a network. Microsoft Windows 2000 relies on TCP/IP for logon, file and print services, replication of information between one domain controller and another, and other common functions.

This chapter presents the skills and knowledge necessary to configure TCP/IP and to install other network protocols, including NWLink, NetBIOS Enhanced User Interface (NetBEUI), and Data Link Control (DLC). The chapter also discusses the process for configuring *network bindings,* which are links that enable communication between network adapter cards, protocols, and services.

Before You Begin

To complete this chapter, you must have

- A computer that meets the minimum hardware requirements located in "About This Book."
- Windows 2000 Professional installed on the computer.

Lesson 1: TCP/IP

TCP/IP provides communication across networks of computers with various hardware architectures and operating systems. Microsoft's implementation of TCP/IP enables enterprise networking and connectivity on computers running Windows 2000.

After this lesson, you will be able to

- Describe the TCP/IP protocol suite and the TCP/IP utilities that ship with Windows 2000.
- Configure TCP/IP.

Estimated lesson time: 65 minutes

Understanding the TCP/IP Protocol Suite

TCP/IP is an industry-standard suite of protocols that enables enterprise networking and connectivity on Windows 2000–based computers. Adding TCP/IP to a Windows 2000 configuration offers the following advantages:

- A routable networking protocol supported by most operating systems. Most large networks rely on TCP/IP.
- A technology for connecting dissimilar systems. You can use many standard connectivity utilities to access and transfer data between dissimilar systems. Windows 2000 includes several of these standard utilities.
- A robust, scaleable, cross-platform client/server framework. TCP/IP supports the Microsoft Windows Sockets (winsock) interface, which is ideal for developing client/server applications for WinSock-compliant stacks.
- A method of gaining access to Internet resources.

The TCP/IP suite of protocols provides a set of standards for how computers communicate and how networks are interconnected. The TCP/IP suite of protocols map to a four-layer conceptual model: network interface, Internet, transport, and application. These layers can be seen in Figure 7.1.

The Network Interface Layer

At the base of the model is the network interface layer. This layer puts frames on the wire and pulls frames off the wire.

Figure 7.1 The TCP/IP suite of protocols within four layers

The Internet Layer

Internet layer protocols encapsulate packets into Internet datagrams and run all the necessary routing algorithms. The four Internet layer protocols are Internet Protocol (IP), Address Resolution Protocol (ARP), Internet Control Message Protocol (ICMP), and Internet Group Management Protocol (IGMP). Table 7.1 describes these four Internet layer protocols.

Table 7.1   Protocols Included in the Internet Layer

Protocol	Description
IP	Provides connectionless packet delivery for all other protocols in the suite. Doesn't guarantee packet arrival or correct packet sequence.
ARP	Provides IP address mapping to the media access control (MAC) sublayer address to acquire the physical MAC control address of the destination. IP broadcasts a special ARP inquiry packet containing the IP address of the destination system. The system that owns the IP address replies by sending its physical address to the requester. The MAC sublayer communicates directly with the network adapter card and is responsible for delivering error-free data between two computers on a network.
ICMP	Provides special communication between hosts, allowing them to share status and error information. Higher-level protocols use this information to recover from transmission problems. Network administrators use this information to detect network trouble. The ping utility uses ICMP packets to determine whether a particular IP device on a network is functional.

(continued)

Protocol	Description
IGMP	Provides multicasting, which is a limited form of broadcasting, to communicate and manage information between all member devices in a multicast group. IGMP informs neighboring multicast routers of the host group memberships present on a particular network. Windows 2000 supports multicast capabilities that allow developers to create multicast programs, such as Windows 2000 Server NetShow Services.

The Transport Layer

Transport layer protocols provide communication sessions between computers. The desired method of data delivery determines the transport protocol. The two transport layer protocols are Transmission Control Protocol (TCP) and User Datagram Protocol (UDP). Table 7.2 describes the two protocols included in the transport layer.

Table 7.2   Protocols Included in the Transport Layer

Protocol	Description
TCP	Provides connection-oriented, reliable communications for applications that typically transfer large amounts of data at one time or that require an acknowledgment for data received. TCP guarantees the delivery of packets, ensures proper sequencing of the data, and provides a checksum feature that validates both the packet header and its data for accuracy.
UDP	Provides connectionless communications and doesn't guarantee that packets will be delivered. Applications that use UDP typically transfer small amounts of data at one time. Reliable delivery is the responsibility of the application.

The Application Layer

At the top of the model is the application layer, in which applications gain access to the network. Many standard TCP/IP utilities and services reside in the application layer, such as FTP, Telnet, Simple Network Management Protocol (SNMP), Domain Name System (DNS), and so on.

TCP/IP provides two interfaces for network applications to use the services of the TCP/IP protocol stack: Winsock and the NetBIOS over TCP/IP (NetBT) interface. Table 7.3 describes the two interfaces, which network applications use for TCP/IP services.

Table 7.3   Interfaces Through Which Applications Use TCP/IP Services

Interface	Description
Winsock	Serves as the standard interface between socket-based applications and TCP/IP protocols.
NetBT	Serves as the standard interface for NetBIOS services, including name, datagram, and session services. It also provides a standard interface between NetBIOS-based applications and TCP/IP protocols.

Configuring TCP/IP to Use a Static IP Address

By default, client computers running Windows 2000, Windows 95, or Windows 98 obtain TCP/IP configuration information automatically from the Dynamic Host Configuration Protocol (DHCP) Service. However, even in a DHCP-enabled environment, you should assign a static IP address to selected network computers. For example, the computer running the DHCP Service can't be a DHCP client, so it must have a static IP address. If the DHCP Service isn't available, you must also configure TCP/IP to use a static IP address. For each network adapter card that uses TCP/IP in a computer, you can configure an IP address, subnet mask, and default gateway, as shown in Figure 7.2.

Figure 7.2   Configuring a static TCP/IP address

Table 7.4 describes the options used in configuring a static TCP/IP address.

Table 7.4   Options for Configuring a Static TCP/IP Address

Option	Description
IP address	A logical 32-bit address that identifies a TCP/IP host. Each network adapter card in a computer running TCP/IP requires a unique IP address, such as 192.168.1.108. Each address has two parts: a network ID, which identifies all hosts on the same physical network, and a host ID, which identifies a host on the network. In this example, the network ID is 192.168.1, and the host ID is 108.

(continued)

Option	Description
Subnet mask	A network in a multiple-network environment that uses IP addresses derived from a single network ID. Subnets divide a large network into multiple physical networks connected with routers. A subnet mask blocks out part of the IP address so that TCP/IP can distinguish the network ID from the host ID. When TCP/IP hosts try to communicate, the subnet mask determines whether the destination host is on a local or remote network. To communicate on a network, computers must have the same subnet mask.
Default gateway	The intermediate device on a local network that stores network IDs of other networks in the enterprise or Internet. To communicate with a host on another network, configure an IP address for the default gateway. TCP/IP sends packets for remote networks to the default gateway (if no other route is configured), which forwards the packets to other gateways until the packet is delivered to a gateway connected to the specified destination.

You can follow these steps to configure TCP/IP to use a static IP address:

1. Right-click My Network Places, and then click Properties.

2. In the Network And Dial-Up Connections window, right-click Local Area Connection, and then click Properties.

3. In the Local Area Connection Properties dialog box, click Internet Protocol (TCP/IP), verify that the check box to its left is selected, and then click Properties.

4. In the Internet Protocol (TCP/IP) Properties dialog box, on the General tab, click Use The Following IP Address, type the TCP/IP configuration parameters, and then click OK.

5. Click OK to close the Local Area Connection Properties dialog box and then close the Network And Dial-Up Connections window.

Caution IP communications can fail if duplicate IP addresses exist on a network. Therefore, you should always check with the network administrator to obtain a valid static IP address.

Configuring TCP/IP to Obtain an IP Address Automatically

If a server running the DHCP Service is available on the network, it can automatically assign TCP/IP configuration information to the DHCP client, as shown in Figure 7.3. Then you can configure any clients running Windows 2000, Windows 95, and Windows 98 to obtain TCP/IP configuration information automatically from the DHCP Service. Using DHCP to configure TCP/IP automatically on client computers can simplify administration and ensure correct configuration information.

Note Windows 2000 Professional doesn't include the DHCP Service. Only the Windows 2000 Server products provide the DHCP Service.

Figure 7.3 A server running the DHCP Service assigns TCP/IP addresses

Note Windows 2000 also includes an Automatic Private IP Addressing feature that provides DHCP clients with limited network functionality if a DHCP server is unavailable during startup.

You can use the DHCP Service to provide clients with TCP/IP configuration information automatically. However, you must configure a computer as a DHCP client before it can interact with the DHCP Service.

You can configure a DHCP client by doing the following:

1. Right-click My Network Places, and then click Properties.
2. In the Network And Dial-Up Connections window, right-click Local Area Connection, and then click Properties.
3. In the Local Area Connection Properties dialog box, click Internet Protocol (TCP/IP), verify that the check box to its left is selected, and then click Properties.
4. In the Internet Protocol (TCP/IP) Properties dialog box, on the General tab, click Obtain An IP Address Automatically.
5. Click OK to close the Local Area Connection Properties dialog box, and then close the Network And Dial-Up Connections window.

Using Automatic Private IP Addressing

The Windows 2000 implementation of TCP/IP supports a new mechanism for automatic address assignment of IP addresses for simple LAN-based network configurations. This addressing mechanism is an extension of dynamic IP address assignment for LAN adapters, enabling configuration of IP addresses without using static IP address assignment or installing the DHCP Service.

For the Automatic Private IP Addressing feature to function properly on a computer running Windows 2000, you must configure a network LAN adapter for TCP/IP and click Obtain An IP Address Automatically in the Internet Protocol (TCP/IP) Properties dialog box.

The process for the Automatic Private IP Addressing feature, as shown in Figure 7.4, is explained in the following steps:

1. Windows 2000 TCP/IP attempts to find a DHCP server on the attached network to obtain a dynamically assigned IP address.

2. In the absence of a DHCP server during startup—for example, the server is down for maintenance or repairs—the client cannot obtain an IP address.

3. Automatic Private IP Addressing generates an IP address in the form of 169.254.*x.y* (where *x.y* is the client's unique identifier) and a subnet mask of 255.255.0.0.

Figure 7.4   The Automatic Private IP Addressing feature

Note The Internet Assigned Numbers Authority (IANA) has reserved 169.254.0.0–169.254.255.255 for Automatic Private IP Addressing. As a result, Automatic Private IP Addressing provides an address that is guaranteed not to conflict with routable addresses.

After the computer generates the address, it broadcasts to this address and then assigns the address to itself, if no other computer responds. The computer continues to use this address until it detects and receives configuration information from a DHCP server. This allows two computers to be plugged in to a LAN hub to restart without any IP address configuration and to be able to use TCP/IP for local network access.

Note Windows 98 also supports Automatic Private IP Addressing.

Automatic Private IP Addressing can assign a TCP/IP address to DHCP clients automatically. However, Automatic Private IP Addressing doesn't generate all the information that typically is provided by DHCP, such as the address of a default gateway.

Consequently, computers enabled with Automatic Private IP Addressing can communicate only with computers on the same subnet that also have addresses of the form 169.254.*x.y*.

Disabling Automatic Private IP Addressing

By default, the Automatic Private IP Addressing feature is enabled. However, you can disable this feature by adding the IPAutoconfigurationEnabled value to the HKEY_LOCAL_MACHINE\SYSTEM\CurrentControlSet\Services\Tcpip\ Parameters\Interfaces\Adapter subkey of the registry and setting its value to 0.

Note This subkey includes the globally unique identifier (GUID) for the computer's LAN adapter. For more information about GUIDs, see Chapter 9, "Introducing Active Directory Directory Services." For more information about the registry, see Chapter 5, "Using the Registry."

The IPAutoconfigurationEnabled entry takes a REG_DWORD data type. To disable Automatic Private IP Addressing, specify a value of 0 for the entry. Specify a value of 1 to enable Automatic Private IP Addressing, the default state when this value is omitted from the registry.

Using TCP/IP Utilities

Windows 2000 includes the utilities diagrammed in Figure 7.5 that you can use to troubleshoot TCP/IP and test connectivity.

Utilities for troubleshooting TCP/IP

Utilities for testing TCP/IP connectivity

Figure 7.5   TCP/IP utilities included with Windows 2000

Troubleshooting TCP/IP

Windows 2000 offers several utilities to assist you in troubleshooting TCP/IP. Table 7.5 describes the Windows 2000 utilities that you can use to trouble-shoot TCP/IP.

Table 7.5   Utilities Used to Troubleshoot TCP/IP

Option	Description
Ping	Verifies configurations and tests connections
ARP	Displays locally resolved IP addresses as physical addresses
Ipconfig	Displays the current TCP/IP configuration
Nbtstat	Displays statistics and connections using NetBIOS over TCP/IP
Netstat	Displays TCP/IP protocol statistics and connections
Route	Displays or modifies the local routing table
Hostname	Returns the local computer's host name for authentication by the Remote Copy Protocol (RCP), remote shell (RSH), and remote execution (REXEC) utilities.
Tracert	Checks the route to a remote system

These troubleshooting utilities are all executed from within the Command Prompt window. For information on how to use all of these commands, except Hostname and Tracert, open the Command Prompt window, type the command followed by **/?** and then press Enter. For example, for information on the Ping command, open the Command Prompt window, type **Ping /?** and then press Enter.

To use the Hostname utility, open the Command Prompt window, type Hostname, and then press Enter. Hostname will return the name of the local computer.

For information on how to use the Tracert command, open a Command Prompt window, type **Tracert** and then press Enter.

Testing TCP/IP Connectivity

Windows 2000 also provides utilities for testing TCP/IP connectivity. Table 7.6 describes these Windows 2000 utilities.

Table 7.6   Utilities Used to Test TCP/IP Connectivity

Option	Description
FTP	Provides bidirectional file transfer between a computer running Windows 2000 and any TCP/IP host running FTP. Windows 2000 Server ships with the ability to serve as an FTP client or server.
Trivial File Transfer Protocol (TFTP)	Provides bidirectional file transfer between a computer running Windows 2000 and a TCP/IP host running TFTP.
Telnet	Provides terminal emulation to a TCP/IP host running Telnet. Windows 2000 Server ships with the ability to serve as a Telnet client.
Remote Copy Protocol (RCP)	Copies files between a client and a host that support RCP; for example, a computer running Windows 2000 and a UNIX host.
Remote shell (RSH)	Runs commands on a UNIX host.
Remote execution (REXEC)	Runs a process on a remote computer.
Finger	Retrieves system information from a remote computer that supports TCP/IP and the finger utility.

Testing a TCP/IP Configuration

After configuring TCP/IP and restarting the computer, you should use the ipconfig and ping command-prompt utilities to test the configuration and connections to other TCP/IP hosts and networks. Such testing helps to ensure that TCP/IP is functioning properly.

Using Ipconfig

You use the ipconfig utility to verify the TCP/IP configuration parameters on a host. This helps to determine whether the configuration is initialized, or whether a duplicate IP address exists. Use the ipconfig command with the /all switch to verify configuration information.

Tip Type **ipconfig /all | more** to prevent the ipconfig output from scrolling off the screen; to scroll down and view additional output, press the Spacebar.

The result of the ipconfig /all command is as follows:

- If a configuration has initialized, the ipconfig utility displays the IP address and subnet mask, and, if it is assigned, the default gateway.

- If a duplicate IP address exists, the ipconfig utility indicates that the IP address is configured; however, the subnet mask is 0.0.0.0.

- If the computer is unable to obtain an IP address from a server running the DHCP Service on the network, the ipconfig utility displays the IP address as the address provided by Automatic Private IP Addressing.

Using Ping

After you have verified the TCP/IP configuration, use the ping utility to test connectivity. The *ping utility* is a diagnostic tool that you can use to test TCP/IP configurations and diagnose connection failures. Use the ping utility to determine whether a particular TCP/IP host is available and functional. To test connectivity, use the Ping command with the following syntax:

```
ping IP_address
```

Using Ipconfig and Ping

Figure 7.6 outlines the steps for verifying a computer's configuration and for testing router connections.

Figure 7.6   Using ipconfig and ping

The following list explains the steps outlined in Figure 7.6:

1. Use the ipconfig command to verify that the TCP/IP configuration has been initialized.

2. Use the ping command with the loopback address (ping 127.0.0.1) to verify that TCP/IP is correctly installed and bound to your network adapter card.

3. Use the ping command with the IP address of the computer to verify that your computer is not a duplicate of another IP address on the network.

4. Use the ping command with the IP address of the default gateway to verify that the default gateway is operational and that your computer can communicate with the local network.

5. Use the ping command with the IP address of a remote host to verify that the computer can communicate through a router.

Note Typically, if you ping the remote host (step 5) and the ping command is successful, steps 1 through 4 are successful by default. If the ping command isn't successful, ping the IP address of another remote host before completing the entire diagnostic process because the current host might be turned off.

By default, the following message appears four times in response to a successful ping command:

```
Reply from IP_address
```

Practice: Installing and Configuring TCP/IP

In this practice, you will use two TCP/IP utilities to verify your computer's configuration. Then you will configure your computer to use a static IP address and verify your computer's new configuration. Next you will configure your computer to use a DHCP server to automatically assign an IP address to your computer, whether or not a DHCP server is available on your network. Finally you will test the Automatic Private IP Addressing feature in Windows 2000 by disabling the DHCP server, if one exists on your network.

To complete this practice, you need

- TCP/IP as the only installed protocol.

- Optional: A server running the DHCP Service to provide IP addresses. If you are working on a computer that isn't part of a network and a server isn't running the DHCP service, you won't be able to do certain procedures in this practice.

In the following table, record the IP address, subnet mask, and default gateway that your network administrator provides for you to use during this practice. Also, ask your network administrator whether you can use another computer to test your computer's connectivity, and record the IP address of that computer as well. If you are not on a network, you can use the suggested values.

Variable value	Suggested value	Your value
Static IP address	192.168.1.201	
Subnet mask	255.255.255.0	
Default gateway (if required)	None	
Computer to test connectivity	N/A	

Exercise 1: Verifying a Computer's TCP/IP Configuration

In this exercise, you will use two TCP/IP utilities, ipconfig and ping, to verify your computer's configuration.

Note As you complete the exercises in this practice, you will use the Command Prompt and Network Connections windows frequently. For the sake of efficiency, you will open the windows one time and then minimize and restore them as necessary.

▶ **To verify a computer's configuration**

1. Open the Command Prompt window.

2. At the command prompt, type **ipconfig /all | more** and then press Enter.

    The Windows 2000 IP Configuration utility displays the TCP/IP configuration of the physical and logical adapters configured on your computer.

3. Press Spacebar as necessary to display the heading Local Area Connection. Use the information displayed in this section to complete as much of the following table as possible. Press Spacebar to display additional information, as necessary, and to return to the command prompt.

Setting	Value
Host name	
Description	
Physical address	
DHCP enabled	
Autoconfiguration enabled	
IP address	
Subnet mask	
Default gateway	
DNS servers	

4. Press Spacebar as necessary to scroll through the configuration information and return to the command prompt.

5. To verify that the TCP/IP is working and configured for your adapter, type **ping 127.0.0.1** and then press Enter.

A response similar to the following indicates a successful ping:

```
Pinging 127.0.0.1 with 32 bytes of data:

Reply from 127.0.0.1: bytes=32 time<10ms TTL=128
Reply from 127.0.0.1: bytes=32 time<10ms TTL=128
Reply from 127.0.0.1: bytes=32 time<10ms TTL=128
Reply from 127.0.0.1: bytes=32 time<10ms TTL=128

Ping statistics for 127.0.0.1:
    Packets: Sent = 4, Received = 4, Lost = 0 <0% loss>,
Approximate round trip times in milliseconds:

    Minimum = 0ms, Maximum = 0ms, Average = 0ms
```

6. Minimize the Command Prompt window.

Exercise 2: Configuring TCP/IP to Use a Static IP Address

In this exercise, you will configure TCP/IP to use a static IP address.

▶ **To configure TCP/IP to use a static IP address**

1. Right-click My Network Places, and then click Properties.

   The Network And Dial-Up Connections window appears.

2. Right-click Local Area Connection, and then click Properties.

   The Local Area Connection Properties dialog box appears, displaying the network adapter in use and the network components used in this connection.

3. Click Internet Protocol (TCP/IP), and then verify that the check box to the left of the entry is selected.

4. Click Properties.

   The Internet Protocol (TCP/IP) Properties dialog box appears.

5. Click Use The Following IP Address.

6. In the IP Address box, the Subnet Mask box, and the Default Gateway box (if required), type the values that you entered in the table at the top of page 166, or the suggested values listed in the table.

Important Be careful when manually entering IP configuration settings, especially numeric addresses. The most frequent cause of TCP/IP connection problems is incorrectly entered IP address information.

---

7. Click OK.

   You are returned to the Local Area Connection Properties dialog box.

8. Click OK to close the Local Area Connection Properties dialog box.

9. Minimize the Network And Dial-Up Connections window.

▶ **To test the static TCP/IP configuration**

1. Restore the Command Prompt.

2. At the command prompt, type **ipconfig /all | more** and then press Enter.

   The Windows 2000 IP Configuration utility displays the physical and logical adapters configured on your computer.

3. Press Spacebar as needed to scroll through the configuration information and locate the local area connection information.

4. Record the current TCP/IP configuration settings for your local area connection in the following table.

Setting	Value
IP address	
Subnet mask	
Default gateway	

5. Press Spacebar as necessary to scroll through the configuration information and return to the command prompt.

6. To verify that the IP address is working and configured for your adapter, type **ping 127.0.0.1** and then press Enter.

   What happens?

7. If you have a computer that you are using to test connectivity, type **ping** *ip_address* (where *ip_address* is the IP address of the computer you are using to test connectivity), and then press Enter. If you don't have a computer to test connectivity, skip to step 8.

   What happens?

8. Minimize the command prompt.

Exercise 3: Configuring TCP/IP to Automatically Obtain an IP Address

In this exercise, you will configure TCP/IP to automatically obtain an IP address. Then you will test the configuration to verify that the DHCP Service has provided the appropriate IP addressing information. Be sure to perform the first part of this exercise even if you have no DHCP Service server because you will also use these settings in Exercise 4.

▶ **To configure TCP/IP to automatically obtain an IP address**

1. Restore the Network And Dial-Up Connections window, right-click Local Area Connection, and then click Properties.

   The Local Area Connection dialog box appears.

2. Click Internet Protocol (TCP/IP), and then verify that the check box to the left of the entry is selected.

3. Click Properties.

   The Internet Protocol (TCP/IP) Properties dialog box appears.

4. Click Obtain An IP Address Automatically.

   Which IP address settings will the DHCP Service configure for your computer?

5. Click OK to close the Internet Protocol (TCP/IP) Properties dialog box.

6. Click OK to close the Local Area Connection Properties dialog box.

7. Minimize the Network And Dial-Up Connections window.

▶ **To test the TCP/IP configuration**

Note If a server isn't available running the DHCP Service to provide an IP address, skip this procedure and continue with Exercise 4.

1. Restore the command prompt, type **ipconfig /release** and then press Enter.

2. At the command prompt, type **ipconfig /renew** and then press Enter.

3. At the command prompt, type **ipconfig | more** and then press Enter.

4. Pressing Spacebar as necessary, record the current TCP/IP configuration settings for your local area connection in the following table.

Setting	Value
IP address	
Subnet mask	
Default gateway	

5. To test that TCP/IP is working and bound to your adapter, type **ping 127.0.0.1** and then press Enter.

The internal loopback test displays four replies if TCP/IP is bound to the adapter.

Exercise 4: Obtaining an IP Address By Using Automatic Private IP Addressing

In this exercise, if you have a server running the DHCP Service, you will need to disable it on that server so that a DHCP server will not be available to provide an IP address for your computer. Without a DHCP server available to provide an IP address, the Windows 2000 Automatic Private IP Addressing feature will provide unique IP addresses for your computer. If the DHCP Service can't be disabled, you can simply disconnect the server network adapter cable. However, your computer's network adapter cable must remain connected.

▶ **To obtain an IP address by using Automatic Private IP Addressing**

1. At the command prompt, type **ipconfig /release** and then press Enter.

2. At the command prompt, type **ipconfig /renew** and then press Enter.

   There will be a pause while Windows 2000 attempts to locate a DHCP server on the network.

   What message appears, and what does it indicate?

▶ **To test the TCP/IP configuration**

1. At the command prompt, type **ipconfig | more** and then press Enter.

2. Pressing Spacebar as necessary, record the current TCP/IP settings for your local area connection in the following table.

Setting	Value
IP address	
Subnet mask	
Default gateway	

   Is this the same IP address assigned to your computer in Exercise 3? Why or why not?

3. Press Spacebar to finish scrolling through the configuration information, as necessary.

4. To verify that TCP/IP is working and bound to your adapter, type **ping 127.0.0.1** and then press Enter.

   The internal loopback test displays four replies if TCP/IP is bound to the adapter.

5. If you have a computer to test TCP/IP connectivity with your computer, type **ping** *ip_address* (where *ip_address* is the IP address of the computer that you are using to test connectivity), and then press Enter. If you don't have a computer to test connectivity, skip this step and proceed to Exercise 5.

   Were you successful? Why or why not?

Exercise 5: Obtaining an IP Address by Using DHCP

In this exercise, enable the DHCP Service running on the computer that is acting as a DHCP server (or reconnect your network cable if you disconnected it in Exercise 4). Your computer will obtain IP addressing information from the DHCP server.

Note If a server isn't available running the DHCP Service to provide an IP address, skip this exercise.

▶ **To obtain an IP address by using DHCP**

1. At the command prompt, type **ipconfig /release** and then press Enter.
2. At the command prompt, type **ipconfig /renew** and then press Enter.

   After a short wait, a message indicates the adapter's local area connection.

3. At the command prompt, type **ipconfig /all | more** and then press Enter.
4. Verify that the DHCP server has assigned an IP address to your computer.
5. Close the Command Prompt window.

Lesson Summary

In this lesson, you learned that Microsoft's implementation of TCP/IP enables enterprise networking and connectivity on computers running Windows 2000. It provides a robust, scaleable, cross-platform client/server framework that is supported by most large networks, including the Internet. You learned that the TCP/IP suite of protocols map to a four-layer conceptual model: network interface, Internet, transport, and application.

By default, client computers running Windows 2000 obtain TCP/IP configuration information automatically from the Dynamic Host Configuration Protocol (DHCP) Service. However, even in a DHCP-enabled environment, some computers, such as the computer running the DHCP Service, require a static IP address. For each network adapter card that uses TCP/IP in a computer, you can configure an IP address, subnet mask, and default gateway.

You also learned that Windows 2000 includes utilities that you can use to troubleshoot TCP/IP and test connectivity. Ping and ipconfig are two of the common troubleshooting utilities, and FTP and telnet are two of the connectivity utilities.

Finally, in this lesson you learned that the Windows 2000 implementation of TCP/IP supports automatic private IP addressing. Automatic private IP addressing is a new mechanism for automatic address assignment of IP addresses for simple LAN-based network configurations. It is an extension of dynamic IP address assignment for LAN adapters and enables configuration of IP addresses without using static IP address assignments or installing the DHCP Service. By default, the Automatic Private IP Addressing feature is enabled. However, you can disable this feature by adding IPAutoconfigurationEnabled to the registry.

Lesson 2: NWLink

This lesson discusses the NWLink IPX/SPX/NetBIOS-compatible transport protocol (usually referred to as NWLink), Microsoft's implementation of Novell's NetWare Internetwork Packet Exchange/Sequenced Packet Exchange (IPX/SPX) protocol. NWLink is most commonly used in environments where clients running Microsoft operating systems are used to access resources on NetWare servers, or where clients running NetWare are used to access resources on computers running Microsoft operating systems.

After this lesson, you will be able to
- Install and configure NWLink.

Estimated lesson time: 30 minutes

Understanding NWLink Features

NWLink allows computers running Windows 2000 to communicate with other network devices that are using IPX/SPX. You can also use NWLink in small network environments that use only clients running Windows 2000 and other Microsoft operating systems.

NWLink supports the networking APIs that provide the interprocess communications (IPC) services described in Table 7.7.

Table 7.7   Networking APIs Supported by NWLink

Networking API	Description
Winsock	Supports existing NetWare applications written to comply with the NetWare IPX/SPX Sockets interface
NetBIOS over IPX	Implemented as NWLink NetBIOS; supports communication between a NetWare client running NetBIOS and a computer running Windows 2000 and NWLink NetBIOS

NWLink also provides NetWare clients with access to applications designed for Windows 2000 Server, such as Microsoft SQL Server and Microsoft SNA Server. To provide NetWare client access to file and print resources on a computer running Windows 2000 Server, you should install File and Print Services for NetWare (FPNW).

In summary, the 32-bit Windows 2000 implementation of NWLink provides the following features:

- Supports communications with NetWare networks
- Supports sockets and NetBIOS over IPX
- Provides NetWare clients with access to Windows 2000 servers

Installing NWLink

The procedure for installing NWLink is the same process that you use to install any network protocol in Windows 2000:

1. Right-click My Network Places, and then click Properties.
2. In the Network And Dial-Up Connections window, right-click Local Area Connection, and then click Properties.

   The Local Area Connection Properties dialog box appears, displaying the network adapter in use and the network components configured for this adapter.

3. Click Install.
4. In the Select Network Component Type dialog box, click Protocol, and then click Add.
5. In the Select Network Protocol dialog box, in the Network Protocol list, click NWLink IPX/SPX/NetBIOS Compatible Transport Protocol (see Figure 7.7), and then click OK.

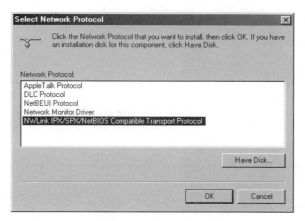

Figure 7.7   The Select Network Protocol dialog box

Configuring NWLink

NWLink configuration involves three components: frame type, network number, and internal network number. By default, Windows 2000 detects a frame type and a network number automatically when you install NWLink. Windows 2000 also provides a generic internal network number. However, you must manually specify an internal network number if you plan to run FPNW or IPX routing, as shown in Figure 7.8.

Note Each network adapter card bound to NWLink in a computer requires a frame type and network number.

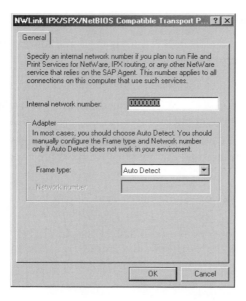

Figure 7.8   Configuring NWLink

Frame Type

A *frame type* defines the way that the network adapter card formats data. To ensure proper communication between a computer running Windows 2000 and a NetWare server, you must configure the NWLink frame type to match the frame type on the NetWare server.

Note   A connection between two computers that use different frame types is possible if the NetWare server is acting as a router. However, this is inefficient and could result in a slow connection.

Table 7.8 lists the topologies and frame types supported by NWLink.

Table 7.8   Topologies and Frame Types Supported by NWLink

Topology	Frame type
Ethernet	Ethernet II, 802.3, 802.2, and Sub Network Access Protocol (SNAP), which defaults to 802.2
Token Ring	802.5 and SNAP
Fiber Distributed Data Interface (FDDI)	802.2 and SNAP

Note   On Ethernet networks, the standard frame type for NetWare 2.2 and NetWare 3.11 is 802.3. For NetWare 3.12 and later, the default is 802.2.

When you install NWLink, Windows 2000 automatically determines which IPX frame type is in use on the network and sets the NWLink frame type accordingly. If Windows 2000 detects frame types in addition to 802.2 during NWLink installation, the frame type for NWLink defaults to 802.2.

Network Number

Each frame type configured on a network adapter card requires a *network number,* which must be unique for each network segment. All computers on a segment using the same frame type *must* use the same network number to communicate with one another.

Note On a computer running Windows 2000, type **ipxroute config** at a command prompt to display the network number, frame type, and device in use.

Although Windows 2000 automatically detects a network number during NWLink installation by default, you can also manually specify a network number by using Registry Editor.

Setting a network number in the registry for a given frame type requires entering two corresponding entries, NetworkNumber and PktType, in this subkey of the registry: HKEY_LOCAL_MACHINE\SYSTEM\CurrentControlSet\Services\ Nwlnkipx\Parameters\Adapters*Adapter.*

- NetworkNumber specifies the network number (in hexadecimal) for the adapter. If the value for this entry is 0, NWLink gets the network number from the network while it is running. Network numbers are 4 bytes (eight hexadecimal characters). The NetworkNumber entry takes the data type REG_MULTI_SZ.

- PktType specifies the packet form to use. The PktType entry takes a data type REG_MULTI_SZ. Table 7.9 lists the values for the PktType entry and the packet forms supported by NWLink.

Table 7.9   Packet Types or Forms Supported by NWLink

Value	Packet form
0	Ethernet_II
1	Ethernet_802.3
2	802.2
3	SNAP
4	ArcNet
FF (default)	Auto-detect

Note If an adapter uses multiple packet types, you can specify the network number for each packet type by adding corresponding values in the NetworkNumber entry.

Internal Network Number

An *internal network number* uniquely identifies a computer on the network for internal routing. This eight-digit hexadecimal number, or virtual network number, is set to 00000000 by default.

The internal network number identifies a virtual network segment inside the computer. That is, the internal network number identifies another (virtual) segment on the network. So, if an internal network number is configured for a computer running Windows 2000, a NetWare server or a router adds an extra hop in its route to the computer.

You must manually assign a unique, nonzero internal network number in the following situations:

- FPNW is installed, and there are multiple frame types on a single adapter.
- FPNW is installed, and NWLink is bound to multiple adapters in the computer.
- An application is using the NetWare Service Advertising Protocol (SAP). SQL Server and SNA Server are examples of applications that can use SAP.

Note If a computer has multiple network adapter cards bound to NWLink, and if you want each one to use a different frame type, configure each network adapter card to use the Manual Frame Type Detection option. You must also specify a frame type, network number, and internal network number for each network adapter card.

Practice: Installing and Configuring NWLink

In this practice, you will install and configure the NWLink IPX/SPX/NetBIOS Compatible Transport Protocol.

Note You can install any of the available protocols in Windows 2000 by using this procedure.

▶ **To install and configure NWLink**

1. Restore the Network And Dial-Up Connections window.
2. Right-click Local Area Connection, and then click Properties.

The Local Area Connection Properties dialog box appears, displaying the network adapter card in use and the network components used in this connection.

3. Click Install.

The Select Network Component Type dialog box appears.

4. Click Protocol, and then click Add.

The Select Network Protocol dialog box appears.

What protocols can you install?

5. Select NWLink IPX/SPX/NetBIOS Compatible Transport Protocol, and then click OK.

Notice that the NWLink IPX/SPX/NetBIOS Compatible Transport Protocol is listed in the Components list in the Local Area Connection Properties dialog box that appears.

6. Select NWLink IPX/SPX/NetBIOS Compatible Transport Protocol, and then click Properties.

Which type of frame detection is selected by default?

7. Click OK to close the NWLink IPX/SPX/NetBIOS Compatible Transport Protocol Properties dialog box.

8. Click OK to close the Local Area Connection Properties dialog box.

Lesson Summary

In this lesson, you learned that NWLink is Microsoft's implementation of Novell's NetWare IPX/SPX protocol. NWLink is most commonly used in environments where clients running Microsoft operating systems are used to access resources on NetWare servers, or where clients running NetWare are used to access resources on computers running Microsoft operating systems. NWLink supports Winsock and NetBIOS over IPX networking APIs. Winsock supports existing NetWare applications written to comply with the NetWare IPX/SPX Sockets. NetBIOS over IPX is implemented as NWLink NetBIOS and supports communication between a NetWare client running NetBIOS and a computer running Windows 2000 and NWLink NetBIOS.

Lesson 3: Other Protocols Supported by Windows 2000

Windows 2000 also supports other protocols, including NetBEUI, DLC, AppleTalk protocol, and the Network Monitor Driver 2.

After this lesson, you will be able to

- Explain the capabilities and limitations of NetBEUI.
- Explain the capabilities and limitations of DLC.
- Describe other protocols supported by Windows NT.

Estimated lesson time: 20 minutes

NetBEUI

NetBEUI is a protocol developed for LANs with 20–200 computers. However, while NetBEUI is a small, fast, and efficient protocol, it isn't routable and therefore is unsuitable for use in a WAN environment.

NetBEUI Capabilities

NetBEUI provides compatibility with existing LANs that use the NetBEUI protocol. NetBEUI provides computers running Windows 2000 with the following capabilities:

- Connection-oriented and connectionless communication between computers
- Self-configuration and self-tuning
- Error protection
- Small memory overhead

NetBEUI Limitations

NetBEUI also has a number of limitations. NetBEUI is

- Designed for department-sized LANs.
- Nonroutable. Because of this limitation, you must connect computers running Windows 2000 and NetBEUI by using bridges instead of routers.
- Broadcast-based. NetBEUI protocol relies on broadcasts for many of its functions, such as name registration and discovery, which creates more broadcast traffic than other protocols.

DLC

As shown in Figure 7.9, DLC is a special-purpose, nonroutable protocol that enables computers running Windows 2000 to communicate with the following:

- Other computers running the DLC protocol stack, such as IBM mainframes
- Network peripherals that use a network adapter card to connect directly to the network, such as a Hewlett-Packard LaserJet 4Si print device, which can connect directly to the network by using an HP JetDirect network adapter

Connectivity to IBM mainframes, AS400s, LAN print devices

Print device   Mainframe   AS 400

Figure 7.9 DLC connectivity

Note You must install the DLC protocol on the print server for the print device. Computers sending print jobs to the print server don't require DLC.

DLC isn't designed to be a primary protocol for use between personal computers and should be installed only on computers performing the previously mentioned tasks.

AppleTalk Protocol

The AppleTalk protocol allows computers running Windows 2000 Server and Apple Macintosh clients to share files and printers.

Note For the AppleTalk protocol to function properly, a computer running Windows 2000 Server configured with Windows 2000 Services for Macintosh must be available on the network.

Network Monitor Driver 2

The Network Monitor driver on a Windows 2000–based computer collects and displays statistics about activity detected by the network card in the computer. You can view these statistics on a computer that is running Network Monitor Agent Service. You can also use Microsoft Systems Management Server (SMS) and Network Monitor to collect statistics from computers that are running Network Monitor Agent.

Lesson Summary

In this lesson, you learned that Windows 2000 supports protocols besides TCP/IP and NWLink. These other protocols include NetBEUI, DLC, AppleTalk, and the Network Monitor driver 2. NetBEUI is a protocol developed for LANs with 20–200 computers. It is a small, fast, and efficient protocol, but it isn't routable and therefore is unsuitable for use in a WAN environment. NetBEUI provides compatibility with existing LANs that use the NetBEUI protocol. DLC is a special-purpose, nonroutable protocol that enables computers running Windows 2000 to communicate with other computers running the DLC protocol stack, such as IBM mainframes. DLC is also used to communicate with network peripherals that use a network adapter card to connect directly to the network, such as a Hewlett-Packard LaserJet 4Si print device.

Lesson 4: Network Bindings

Network bindings enable communication between network adapter card drivers, protocols, and services. Figure 7.10 shows an example of network bindings. In Figure 7.10, the workstation service is bound to each of three protocols, and each protocol is bound to at least one network adapter card. This lesson describes the function of bindings in a network and the process for configuring them.

The Windows 2000 network architecture uses a series of interdependent layers. The bottom layer of the network architecture ends at the network adapter card, which places information on the cable, allowing information to flow between computers.

After this lesson, you will be able to
- Explain how to configure network bindings.

Estimated lesson time: 20 minutes

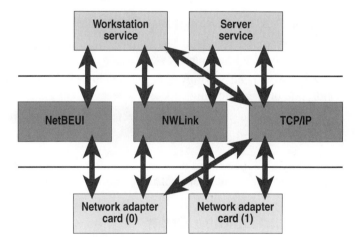

Figure 7.10   Network bindings

Binding Between Architectural Levels

Binding is the process of linking network components on different levels to enable communication between those components. A network component can be bound to one or more network components above or below it. The services that each component provides can be shared by all other components that are bound to it. For example, in Figure 7.10, TCP/IP is bound to both the Workstation service and the Server service.

Combining Network Bindings

Many combinations of network bindings are possible. In the example shown in Figure 7.10, all three protocols are bound to the Workstation service, but only the routable protocols, NWLink and TCP/IP, are bound to the Server service. It is possible to select which protocols are bound to the network adapter cards. Network adapter card (0) is bound to all three protocols, while network adapter card (1) is bound only to the routable protocols. To control which components are bound together, you must be a member of the Administrators group.

When adding network software, Windows 2000 automatically binds all dependent network components accordingly. Network Driver Interface Specification (NDIS) 5 provides the capability to bind multiple protocols to multiple network adapter card drivers.

Configuring Network Bindings

You can configure your network bindings by using My Network Places.

You can configure network bindings by following these steps:

1. Right-click My Network Places, and then click Properties.
2. In the Network And Dial-Up Connections window, click Advanced, and then click Advanced Settings.
3. In the Advanced Settings dialog box, under Client For Microsoft Networks, do one of the following:
   - To bind the protocol to the selected adapter, click to select the adapter.
   - To unbind the protocol from the selected adapter, click to clear the adapter.

Note Only an experienced network administrator who is familiar with the requirements of the network software should attempt to change binding settings.

Specifying Binding Order

You can also specify binding order to optimize network performance. For example, a computer running Windows 2000 Workstation has NetBEUI, NWLink IPX/SPX, and TCP/IP installed. However, most of the servers to which this computer connects are running only TCP/IP. Verify that the Workstation binding to TCP/IP is listed *before* the Workstation bindings for the other protocols. In this way, when a user attempts to make a connection to a server, the Workstation service first attempts to use TCP/IP to establish the connection.

You can follow these steps to specify binding order:

1. Right-click My Network Places, and then click Properties.
2. In the Network And Dial-Up Connections window, click Advanced, and then click Advanced Settings.

3. In the Advanced Settings dialog box, under Client For Microsoft Networks, click the protocol for which you want to change the binding order.

4. Use the arrow buttons to change the binding order for protocols that are bound to a specific adapter:

   - To move the protocol higher in the binding order, click the Up Arrow button.
   - To move the protocol lower in the binding order, click the Down Arrow button.

Practice: Working with Network Bindings

In this practice, you will change the binding order of the protocols bound to your network adapter card. Next you will unbind a protocol from your network adapter card and then bind a protocol to your network adapter card. Finally you will uninstall a network protocol.

After completing this practice, you will be able to

- Change the binding order of protocols.
- Bind and unbind a protocol.
- Remove a protocol.

Exercise 1: Changing the Binding Order of a Protocol

In this exercise, you will change the binding order of the protocols bound to your network adapter card.

▶ **To change the protocol binding order**

1. Right-click My Network Places and click Properties.

2. Maximize the Network And Dial-Up Connections window, and on the Advanced menu, click Advanced Settings.

   The Advanced Settings dialog box appears.

   What is the order of the protocols listed under Client For Microsoft Networks in the Bindings For Local Area Connection list?

3. Under Client For Microsoft Networks, click NWLink IPX/SPX/NetBIOS Compatible Transport Protocol.

4. Click the downward-pointing arrow.

   Notice that the order of the protocols listed under Client For Microsoft Networks has changed. NWLink IPX/SPX/NetBIOS Compatible Transport Protocol should now be listed below Internet Protocol (TCP/IP). If it's not, click the downward-pointing arrow again to move it below Internet Protocol (TCP/IP).

5. Leave the Advanced Settings dialog box open.

Exercise 2: Unbinding a Protocol

In this exercise, you will unbind TCP/IP from your network adapter card, which will leave NWLink as the only protocol available to access other computers.

▶ **To unbind TCP/IP**

1. In the Advanced Settings dialog box, under Client For Microsoft Networks in the Bindings For Local Area Connection list, unbind Internet Protocol (TCP/IP) by clearing the check box to the left of the entry.

   TCP/IP is now unbound from your network adapter card.

2. Click OK to close the Advanced Settings dialog box.

Exercise 3: Uninstalling NWLink

In this exercise, you will uninstall the NWLink IPX/SPX/NetBIOS Compatible Transport Protocol.

▶ **To remove NWLink**

1. In the Network And Dial-Up Connections window, right-click Local Area Connection, and then click Properties.

   The Local Area Connection Properties dialog box appears, displaying the adapter in use and the network components configured for this connection.

2. Click NWLink IPX/SPX/NetBIOS Compatible Transport Protocol, and then click Uninstall.

   The Uninstall NWLink IPX/SPX/NetBIOS Compatible Transport Protocol dialog box appears.

3. Click Yes to continue.

   Notice that NWLink IPX/SPX/NetBIOS Compatible Transport Protocol is no longer listed as an installed protocol.

4. Click Close.

Exercise 4: Binding a Protocol

In this exercise, TCP/IP is the only protocol installed, so you will bind TCP/IP to your network adapter card.

▶ **To bind TCP/IP**

1. On the Advanced menu of the Network And Dial-Up Connections window, click Advanced Settings.

   The Advanced Settings dialog box appears.

2. Under Client For Microsoft Networks, select Internet Protocol (TCP/IP) by clicking the check box to the left of the option.

3. Click OK.

   TCP/IP is now bound to your network adapter card.

4. Close the Network And Dial-Up Connections window.

Lesson Summary

In this lesson, you learned that binding is the process of linking network components on different levels to enable communication between them. A network component can be bound to one or more network components above or below it, which allows the services that each component provides to be shared by all other components that are bound to it. When you install network software, Windows 2000 automatically binds all dependent network components accordingly. NDIS 5 provides the capability to bind multiple protocols to multiple network adapter card drivers, and you can optimize network performance by specifying the binding order.

Review

The following questions will help you determine whether you have learned enough to move on to the next chapter. If you have difficulty answering these questions, please go back and review the material in this chapter before beginning the next chapter. See Appendix A, "Questions and Answers," for the answers to these questions.

1. Your computer running Windows 2000 Client for Microsoft Networks was configured manually for TCP/IP. You can connect to any host on your own subnet, but you can't connect to or even ping any host on a remote subnet. What is the likely cause of the problem and how would you fix it?

2. Your computer running Windows 2000 Professional can communicate with some, but not all, of the NetWare servers on your network. Some of the NetWare servers are running frame type 802.2 and some are running 802.3. What is the likely cause of the problem?

3. What are the limitations of the NetBEUI protocol?

4. What is the primary function of the DLC protocol?

5. What is the significance of the binding order of network protocols?

C H A P T E R   8

Using the DNS Service

About This Chapter

Domain Name System (DNS) is a distributed database that is used in TCP/IP networks to translate computer names to IP addresses. This chapter presents an introduction to DNS and name resolution. It also provides the skills and knowledge necessary to configure clients to use the DNS Service.

Note The DNS Service is not available in Microsoft Windows 2000 Professional. You must have a computer running one of the Windows 2000 Server products to use Microsoft's DNS Service.

Before You Begin

To complete this chapter, you must have

- A computer that meets the minimum hardware requirements located in "About This Book."
- Windows 2000 Professional installed on the computer.
- TCP/IP installed as the only protocol.

Lesson 1: Understanding DNS

DNS is most commonly associated with the Internet. However, private networks use DNS extensively to resolve computer names and to locate computers within their local networks and the Internet. DNS provides the following benefits:

- DNS names are user-friendly, which means that they are easier to remember than IP addresses.

- DNS names remain more constant than IP addresses. An IP address for a server can change, but the server name remains the same.

- DNS allows users to connect to local servers by using the same naming convention as the Internet.

> **Note** For more information on DNS, see RFC 1034 and RFC 1035. A Request for Comment (RFC) is a published document on a standard, protocol, or other information pertaining to the operation of the Internet. To read the text of these RFCs, use your Web browser to search for "RFC 1034" and "RFC 1035."

After this lesson, you will be able to

- Explain the function of DNS and its components.

Estimated lesson time: 15 minutes

Domain Name Space

The *domain name space* is the naming scheme that provides the hierarchical structure for the DNS database. Each node represents a partition of the DNS database. These nodes are referred to as *domains*.

The DNS database is indexed by name; therefore, each domain must have a name. As you add domains to the hierarchy, the name of the parent domain is appended to its child domain (called a *subdomain*). Consequently, a domain's name identifies its position in the hierarchy. For example, in Figure 8.1, the domain name

sales.microsoft.com

identifies the sales domain as a subdomain of the microsoft.com domain and microsoft as a subdomain of the com domain. The hierarchical structure of the domain name space consists of a root domain, top-level domains, second-level domains, and host names.

> **Note** The term domain, in the context of DNS, is not related to domain as used in Microsoft Windows 2000's directory services based on Active Directory technology. A Windows 2000 domain is a grouping of computers and devices that are administered as a unit.

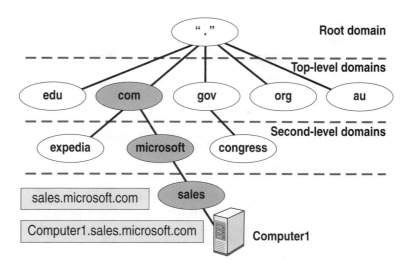

Figure 8.1   The hierarchical structure of a domain name space

Root Domain

The *root domain* is at the top of the hierarchy and is represented as a period (.). The Internet root domain is managed by several organizations, including Network Solutions, Inc.

Top-Level Domains

Top-level domains are two- or three-character name codes. Top-level domains are arranged by organization type or geographic location. Table 8.1 provides some examples of top-level domain names.

Table 8.1   Top-Level Domains

Top-level domain	Description
gov	Government organizations
com	Commercial organizations
edu	Educational institutions
org	Noncommercial organizations
au	Country code of Australia

Top-level domains can contain second-level domains and host names.

Second-Level Domains

Organizations, such as Network Solutions, Inc., assign and register *second-level domains* to individuals and organizations for the Internet. A second-level name has two name parts: a top-level name and a unique second-level name. Table 8.2 provides some examples of second-level domains.

Table 8.2   Second-Level Domains

Second-level domain	Description
Ed.gov	United States Department of Education
Microsoft.com	Microsoft Corporation
Stanford.edu	Stanford University
W3.org	World Wide Web Consortium
Pm.gov.au	Prime Minister of Australia

Host Names

Host names refer to specific computers on the Internet or a private network. For example, in Figure 8.1, Computer1 is a host name. A host name is the leftmost portion of a *fully qualified domain name (FQDN),* which describes the exact position of a host within the domain hierarchy. In Figure 8.1, Computer1.sales.microsoft.com. (including the end period, which represents the root domain) is an FQDN.

DNS uses a host's FQDN to resolve a name to an IP address.

Note The host name doesn't have to be the same as the computer name. By default, TCP/IP setup uses the computer name for the host name, replacing illegal characters, such as the underscore (_), with a hyphen (-). For the accepted domain naming conventions, see RFC 1035.

Domain Naming Guidelines

When you create a domain name space, consider the following domain guidelines and standard naming conventions:

- Limit the number of domain levels. Typically, DNS host entries should be three or four levels down the DNS hierarchy and no more than five levels down the hierarchy. Increasing the number of levels increases the administrative taskload.

- Use unique names. Each subdomain must have a unique name within its parent domain to ensure that the name is unique throughout the DNS name space.

- Use simple names. Simple and precise domain names are easier for users to remember and enable users to search intuitively and locate Web sites or other computers on the Internet or an intranet.

- Avoid lengthy domain names. Domain names can be up to 63 characters, including the periods. The total length of an FQDN can't exceed 255 characters. Case-sensitive naming is not supported.

- Use standard DNS characters and Unicode characters.

- Windows 2000 supports the following standard DNS characters: A–Z, a–z, 0–9, and the hyphen (-), as defined in RFC 1035.

- The DNS Service also supports the Unicode character set. The Unicode character set includes additional characters not found in the American Standard Code for Information Interchange (ASCII) character set, which are required for languages such as French, German, and Spanish.

Note Use Unicode characters only if all servers running the DNS Service in your environment support Unicode. For more information on the Unicode character set, read RFC 2044 by searching for "RFC 2044" with your Web browser.

Zones

A zone represents a discrete portion of the domain name space. Zones provide a way to partition the domain name space into manageable sections.

- Multiple zones in a domain name space are used to distribute administrative tasks to different groups. For example, Figure 8.2 depicts the microsoft.com domain name space divided into two zones. The two zones allow one administrator to manage the microsoft and sales domains and another administrator to manage the development domain.

- A zone must encompass a contiguous domain name space. For example, in Figure 8.2, you couldn't create a zone that consists of only the sales.microsoft.com and development.microsoft.com domains, because these two domains are not contiguous.

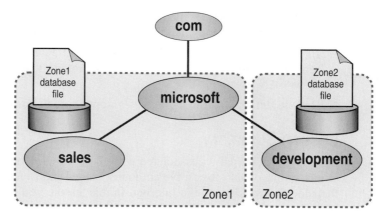

Figure 8.2   A domain name space divided into zones

The name-to-IP address mappings for a zone are stored in the zone database file. Each zone is anchored to a specific domain, which is referred to as the zone's root domain. The zone database file doesn't necessarily contain information for all subdomains of the zone's root domain, only those subdomains within the zone.

In Figure 8.2, the root domain for Zone1 is microsoft.com, and its zone file contains the name-to-IP address mappings for the microsoft and sales domains. The root domain for Zone2 is development, and its zone file contains the name-to-IP address mappings for the development domain only. The zone file for Zone1 doesn't contain the name-to-IP address mappings for the development domain, although development is a subdomain of the microsoft domain.

Name Servers

A DNS *name server* stores the zone database file. Name servers can store data for one zone or multiple zones. A name server is said to have authority for the domain name space that the zone encompasses.

One name server contains the master zone database file, referred to as the *primary zone database file,* for the specified zone. As a result, there must be at least one name server for a zone. Changes to a zone, such as adding domains or hosts, are performed on the server that contains the primary zone database file.

Multiple name servers act as a backup to the name server containing the primary zone database file. Multiple name servers provide the following advantages:

- Perform zone transfers. The additional name servers obtain a copy of the zone database file from the name server that contains the primary database zone file. This is called a *zone transfer*. These name servers periodically query the name server containing the primary zone database file for updated zone data.

- Provide redundancy. If the name server containing the primary zone database file fails, the additional name servers can provide service.

- Improve access speed for remote locations. If a number of clients are in remote locations, use additional name servers to reduce query traffic across slow WAN links.

- Reduce the load on the name server containing the primary zone database file.

Lesson Summary

DNS is most commonly associated with the Internet. However, many private networks also use DNS to resolve computer names and to locate computers within their local networks and the Internet. In this lesson, you learned that some of the benefits that DNS provides include providing user-friendly DNS names that are less likely to change than IP addresses, and allowing users to connect to local servers by using the same naming convention as the Internet.

You also learned that the domain name space is the naming scheme that provides the hierarchical structure for the DNS database. The DNS database is indexed by name, so each domain (node) must have a name. The hierarchical structure of the domain name space consists of a root domain, top-level domains, second-level domains, and host names. Host names refer to specific computers on the Internet or a private network. A host name is the leftmost portion of a fully qualified domain name (FQDN), which describes the exact position of a host within the domain hierarchy.

Finally, you learned about the following naming guidelines for domains: limit the number of domain levels, use unique names, and use simple names. Zones provide a way to divide the domain name space into smaller sections that represent a discrete portion of the domain name space. You also learned that a DNS name server stores the zone database file, that the zone database file is replicated, and how to configure these zone transfers.

Lesson 2: Understanding Name Resolution

Name resolution is the process of resolving names to IP addresses. Name resolution is similar to looking up a name in a telephone book, where the name is associated with a telephone number. For example, when you connect to the Microsoft Web site, you use the name www.microsoft.com. DNS resolves www.microsoft.com to its associated IP address. The mapping of names to IP addresses is stored in the DNS distributed database.

DNS name servers resolve forward and reverse lookup queries. A forward lookup query resolves a name to an IP address. A reverse lookup query resolves an IP address to a name. A name server can resolve a query only for a zone for which it has authority. If a name server can't resolve the query, it passes the query to other name servers that can resolve the query. The name server caches the query results to reduce the DNS traffic on the network.

After this lesson, you will be able to

- Explain the name resolution process.

Estimated lesson time: 5 minutes

Forward Lookup Query

The DNS Service uses a client/server model for name resolution. To resolve a *forward lookup query*, which resolves a name to an IP address, a client passes a query to a local name server. The local name server either resolves the query or queries another name server for resolution.

Figure 8.3 represents a client querying the name server for an IP address of www.microsoft.com. The numbers in the figure depict the following activities:

1. The client passes a forward lookup query for www.microsoft.com to its local name server.
2. The local name server checks its zone database file to determine whether it contains the name-to-IP address mapping for the client query. The local name server doesn't have authority for the microsoft.com domain, so it passes the query to one of the DNS root servers, requesting resolution of the host name. The root name server sends back a referral to the com name servers.
3. The local name server sends a request to a com name server, which responds with a referral to the Microsoft name servers.
4. The local name server sends a request to the Microsoft name server. The Microsoft name server receives the request. Because the Microsoft name server has authority for that portion of the domain name space, it returns the IP address for www.microsoft.com to the local name server.

5. The name server sends the IP address for www.microsoft.com to the client.

6. The name resolution is complete, and the client can access www.microsoft.com.

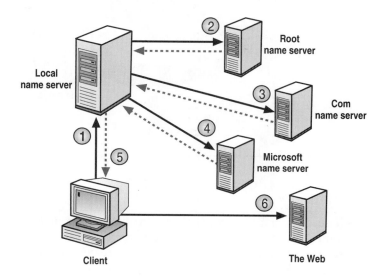

Figure 8.3   Resolving a forward lookup query

Name Server Caching

When a name server is processing a query, it might be required to send out several queries to find the answer. With each query, the name server discovers other name servers that have authority for a portion of the domain name space. The name server caches these query results to reduce network traffic.

When a name server receives a query result, the following actions take place (see Figure 8.4):

1. The name server caches the query result for a specified amount of time; this is referred to as Time to Live (TTL).

Note The zone that provided the query results specifies the TTL. The default value is 60 minutes.

---

2. Once the name server caches the query result, TTL starts counting down from its original value.

3. When TTL expires, the name server deletes the query result from its cache.

Caching query results enables the name server to resolve other queries to the same portion of the domain name space quickly.

Figure 8.4   Caching query results

Note Shorter TTL values help ensure that data about the domain name space is more current across the network. Shorter TTL values *do* increase the load on name servers, however. A longer TTL value decreases the time required to resolve information. However, if a change does occur, the client will not receive the updated information until the TTL expires and a new query to that portion of the domain name space is resolved.

Reverse Lookup Query

A *reverse lookup query* maps an IP address to a name. Troubleshooting tools, such as the nslookup command-line utility, use reverse lookup queries to report back host names. Additionally, certain applications implement security based on the ability to connect to names, not IP addresses.

Because the DNS distributed database is indexed by name and not by IP address, a reverse lookup query would require an exhaustive search of every domain name. To solve this problem, a special second-level domain called *in-addr.arpa* was created.

The in-addr.arpa domain follows the same hierarchical naming scheme as the rest of the domain name space; however, it is based on IP addresses, not domain names:

- Subdomains are named after the numbers in the dotted-decimal representation of IP addresses.
- The order of the IP address octets is reversed.
- Companies administer subdomains of the in-addr.arpa domain based on their assigned IP addresses and subnet mask.

For example, Figure 8.5 shows a dotted-decimal representation of the IP address 169.254.16.200. A company that has an assigned IP address range of 169.254.16.0 to 169.254.16.255 with a subnet mask of 255.255.255.0 will have authority over the 16.254.169.in-addr.arpa domain.

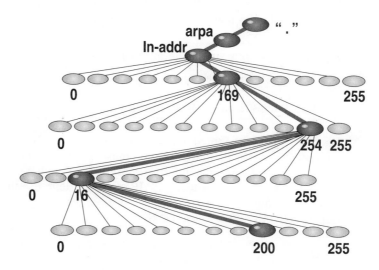

Figure 8.5   The in-addr.arpa domain

Lesson Summary

In this lesson, you learned that name resolution is the process of resolving names to IP addresses and that the mapping of names to IP addresses is stored in the DNS distributed database. You learned that DNS name servers resolve forward lookup queries and what happens when a client queries the name server for an IP address. You also learned about name server caching and that the name server caches the query results to reduce the DNS traffic on the network.

You also learned that in addition to forward lookup queries, DNS name servers resolve reverse lookup queries. A reverse lookup query resolves an IP address to a name. Because the DNS distributed database is indexed by name and not by IP address, a special second-level domain called in-addr.arpa was created. The in-addr.arpa domain follows the same hierarchical naming scheme as the rest of the domain name space; however, it is based on IP addresses instead of domain names.

Lesson 3: Configuring a DNS Client

If a computer on your network is running Windows 2000 Server and has the DNS Service installed and configured on it, you need to know how to configure your computer that is running Windows 2000 Professional as a DNS client. In this lesson, you will learn how to configure DNS clients.

After this lesson, you will be able to

- Configure a DNS client.

Estimated lesson time: 10 minutes

Since DNS is a distributed database that is used in TCP/IP networks to translate computer names to IP addresses, you must first install TCP/IP on a client running Windows 2000 Professional before configuring the client to use the DNS Service. Once you have installed TCP/IP on your client, use the Network And Dial-Up Connections window to access the Properties dialog box for your client's TCP/IP to configure it to use DNS.

If you are configuring a local area connection in the Network And Dial-Up Connections window, right-click Local Area Connection, and click Properties. On the General tab, click TCP/IP and then click Properties (see Figure 8.6). For all other types of connections, on the Networking tab in the connection's Properties dialog box, click TCP/IP and then click Properties.

Figure 8.6   The Internet Protocol (TCP/IP) Properties dialog box

You must select one of the two following options:

- **Obtain DNS Server Address Automatically.** If you select this option, you must have a DHCP Server available on your network to provide the IP address of a DNS Server. For more information on DHCP, see Appendix C, "Understanding the DHCP Service."

- **Use The Following DNS Server Addresses.** If you select this option, you must type in the IP addresses of the DNS Servers you want this client to use.

Preconfiguration Considerations

If your client is connected to a network that has a DNS server, you can check the following options on the server that has the DNS service installed:

- Ensure a static IP address has been assigned to the DNS server.
- Ensure the appropriate IP address of the DNS server and DNS domain name are assigned. Click Advanced in the Internet Protocol (TCP/IP) Properties dialog box to configure the advanced TCP/IP settings. On the DNS tab, check the assigned DNS address and domain name.

Practice: Configuring a DNS Client

After completing this practice, you will be able to configure your computers running Windows 2000 Professional as DNS clients.

▶ **To configure a client to use the DNS Service**

1. Right-click My Network Places, and then click Properties.
2. Right-click Local Area Connection, and then click Properties.
3. Select Internet Protocol (TCP/IP), and then click Properties.
4. In the Internet Protocol (TCP/IP) Properties dialog box, select Use The Following DNS Server Addresses.
5. In the Preferred DNS Server box, type the IP address of the primary name server for this client.

Note If you are on a network, ask your network administrator for the IP address of a DNS server you can use and type that address in the Preferred DNS Server box. If you aren't on a network or if you do not have a DNS Server on your network, you can type 192.168.1.203 as the Preferred DNS Server IP address.

---

6. If a second name server is available for this client, in the Alternate DNS Server box, type the IP address of the second name server for this client.

Note If you are on a network, ask your network administrator for the IP address of a second DNS server you can use and type that address in the Alternate DNS Server box. If you are not on a network or if you don't have a DNS Server on your network, you can type 192.168.1.205 as the Alternate DNS Server IP address.

A client will attempt to send its query requests to the preferred name server. If that name server isn't responding, the client will send the query request to the alternate name server.

Tip If you're going to configure several computers running Windows 2000 Professional as DNS clients, configure some of the clients to use the alternate name server as the preferred name server. This reduces the load on the primary server.

7. Click OK to close the Internet Protocol (TCP/IP) Properties dialog box.
8. Click OK to close the Local Connection Properties dialog box, and then close the Network And Dial-Up Connections window.

Lesson Summary

In this lesson, you learned that you must first install TCP/IP on a client running Windows 2000 before you can configure the client to use the DNS Service. Once you have installed TCP/IP on your client, you use the Network And Dial-Up Connections window to access the Internet Protocol (TCP/IP) Properties dialog box for your client to configure it to use DNS. In configuring your client, you must select whether to have the client obtain the address of the DNS server automatically by having it provided by a DHCP server, or whether you want to manually type in the address of a DNS server. In the practice, you configured your computer to be a DNS client.

Review

The following questions will help you determine whether you have learned enough to move on to the next chapter. If you have difficulty answering these questions, please go back and review the material in this chapter before beginning the next chapter. See Appendix A, "Questions and Answers," for the answers to these questions.

1. What is the function of the following DNS components?

   Domain name space

   Zones

   Name servers

2. Why would you want to have multiple name servers?

3. What is the difference between a forward lookup query and a reverse lookup query?

4. When would you configure your connection to obtain a DNS server address automatically?

C H A P T E R   9

Introducing Active Directory Directory Services

About This Chapter

You use a directory service to uniquely identify users and resources on a network. Directory services based on Active Directory technology in Microsoft Windows 2000 is a significant enhancement over the directory services provided in previous versions of Windows. Active Directory directory services provide a single point of network management, allowing you to add, remove, and relocate users and resources easily. This chapter introduces you to Active Directory directory services, a feature available with the Windows 2000 Server products.

Note Active Directory directory services are not available in Windows 2000 Professional. You must have a computer running one of the Windows 2000 Server products configured as a domain controller to use Microsoft's Active Directory directory services.

Before You Begin

To complete this chapter, you must have

- A computer that meets the minimum hardware requirements located in "About This Book."

- Windows 2000 Professional installed on the computer.

Lesson 1: Understanding Active Directory Directory Services

Before you implement Active Directory directory services, you should understand the overall purpose of a directory service and the role that Active Directory directory services plays in a Windows 2000 network. In addition, you should know about the key features of Active Directory directory services, which have been designed to provide flexibility and ease of administration.

After this lesson, you will be able to

- Explain the purpose and function of Active Directory directory services.

Estimated lesson time: 10 minutes

What Are Active Directory Directory Services?

Active Directory directory services make up the directory service included in the Windows 2000 Server products. A *directory service* is a network service that identifies all resources on a network and makes them accessible to users and applications.

Active Directory directory services include the *Directory,* which stores information about network resources, as well as all the services that make the information available and useful. The resources stored in the Directory, such as user data, printers, servers, databases, groups, computers, and security policies, are known as objects.

Simplified Administration

Active Directory directory services organize resources hierarchically in domains. A *domain* is a logical grouping of servers and other network resources under a single domain name. The domain is the basic unit of replication and security in a Windows 2000 network.

Each domain includes one or more domain controllers. A *domain controller* is a computer running Windows 2000 Server that stores a complete replica of the domain directory. To simplify administration, all domain controllers in the domain are peers. You can make changes to any domain controller, and the updates are replicated to all other domain controllers in the domain.

Active Directory directory services further simplify administration by providing a single point of administration for all objects on the network. Since Active Directory directory services provide a single point of logon for all network resources, an administrator can log on to one computer and administer objects on any computer in the network.

Scalability

In Active Directory directory services, the Directory stores information by organizing itself into sections that permit storage for a huge number of objects. As a result, the Directory can expand as an organization grows, allowing you to scale from a small installation with a few hundred objects to a huge installation with millions of objects.

Note You can distribute Directory information across several computers in a network.

Open Standards Support

Active Directory directory services integrate the Internet concept of a namespace with the Windows 2000 directory services. This allows you to unify and manage the multiple namespaces that now exist in the heterogeneous software and hardware environments of corporate networks. Active Directory directory services use DNS for its name system and can exchange information with any application or directory that uses Lightweight Directory Access Protocol (LDAP) or HTTP.

Important Active Directory directory services also share information with other directory services that support LDAP version 2 and version 3, such as Novell Directory Services (NDS).

Domain Name System

Because Active Directory directory services use DNS as their domain naming and location service, Windows 2000 domain names are also DNS names. Windows 2000 Server uses Dynamic DNS (DDNS), which enables clients with dynamically assigned addresses to register directly with a server running the DNS Service and update the DNS table dynamically. DDNS eliminates the need for other Internet naming services, such as Windows Internet Name Service (WINS), in a homogeneous environment.

Important For Active Directory directory services and associated client software to function correctly, you must have installed and configured the DNS Service.

Support for LDAP and HTTP

Active Directory directory services further embrace Internet standards by directly supporting LDAP and HTTP. LDAP is an Internet standard for accessing directory services, which was developed as a simpler alternative to the Directory Access Protocol (DAP). For more information about LDAP, use your Web browser to search for RFC 1777 and retrieve the text of this Request for Comment document. Active Directory directory services support both LDAP version 2 and version 3. HTTP is the standard protocol for displaying pages on the World Wide Web. You can display every object in Active Directory directory services as an HTML page in a Web browser. Thus, users receive the benefit of the familiar Web browsing model when querying and viewing objects in Active Directory directory services.

Note Active Directory directory services use LDAP to exchange information between directories and applications.

Support for Standard Name Formats

Active Directory directory services support several common name formats. Consequently, users and applications can access Active Directory directory services by using the format with which they are most familiar. Table 9.1 describes some standard name formats supported by Active Directory directory services.

Table 9.1   Active Directory Standard Name Formats

Format	Description
RFC 822	RFC 822 names are in the form *somename@domain* and are familiar to most users as Internet e-mail addresses.
HTTP URL	HTTP URLs are familiar to users with Web browsers and take the form http://*domain/path-to-page*.
UNC	Active Directory directory services support UNC used in Windows 2000 Server–based networks to refer to shared volumes, printers, and files. An example is \\microsoft.com\xl\budget.xls.
LDAP URL	An LDAP URL specifies the server on which the Active Directory directory services reside and the attributed name of the object. Active Directory directory services support a draft to RFC 1779 and use the attributes in the following example: LDAP://someserver.microsoft.com/CN=FirstnameLastname,OU=sys, OU=product,OU=division,DC=devel CN represents CommonName OU represents OrganizationalUnitName DC represents DomainComponentName

Lesson Summary

Active Directory directory services are the directory services included in the Microsoft Windows 2000 Server products. Active Directory directory services are not included in Windows 2000 Professional, but if your Windows 2000 Professional clients are in a Windows 2000 domain, the features and benefits provided by Active Directory directory services are also available on the clients.

A directory service is a network service that identifies all resources on a network and makes them accessible to users and applications. Active Directory directory services include the Directory, which stores information about network resources, such as user data, printers, servers, databases, groups, computers, and security policies. The Directory can scale from a small installation with a few hundred objects to a huge installation with millions of objects.

Active Directory directory services use DNS as their domain naming and location service. Therefore, Windows 2000 domain names are also DNS names. Windows 2000 Server uses DDNS, so clients with dynamically assigned addresses can register directly with a server running the DNS Service and dynamically update the DNS table. In a homogeneous environment, DDNS eliminates the need for other Internet naming services, such as WINS.

Lesson 2: Active Directory Structure and Replication

Active Directory directory services provide a method for designing a directory structure that meets your organization's needs. As a result, before installing Active Directory directory services, examine your organization's business structure and operations. Active Directory directory services completely separate the logical structure of the domain hierarchy from the physical structure.

Many companies have a centralized structure. Typically, these companies have strong IT departments that define and implement the network structure down to the smallest detail. Other organizations, especially large enterprises, are decentralized. These companies have multiple businesses, each of which is quite focused. They need decentralized approaches to managing their business relationships and networks.

After this lesson, you will be able to

- Explain Active Directory structure and replication.

Estimated lesson time: 15 minutes

Logical Structure

In Active Directory directory services, you organize resources in a logical structure. Grouping resources logically enables you to find a resource by its name rather than by its physical location. Since you group resources logically, Active Directory directory services make the network's physical structure transparent to users.

Object

An *object* is a distinct, named set of attributes that represents a network resource. Object *attributes* are characteristics of objects in the Directory. For example, the attributes of a user account might include the user's first and last names, department, and e-mail address (see Figure 9.1).

In Active Directory directory services, you can organize objects in *classes*, which are logical groupings of objects. For example, an object class might be user accounts, groups, computers, domains, or organizational units.

Note Some objects, known as *containers,* can contain other objects. For example, a domain is a container object.

Figure 9.1   Active Directory objects and attributes

Organizational Units

An *organizational unit (OU)* is a container that you use to organize objects within a domain into logical administrative groups. An OU can contain objects such as user accounts, groups, computers, printers, applications, file shares, and other OUs (see Figure 9.2).

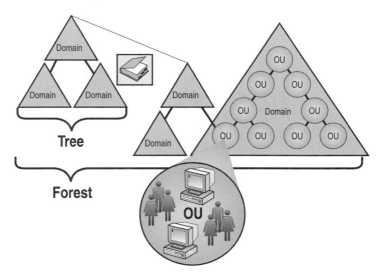

Figure 9.2   Resources organized in a logical hierarchical structure

The OU hierarchy within a domain is independent of the OU hierarchy structure of other domains—each domain can implement its own OU hierarchy. The depth of the OU hierarchy is unrestricted. However, a shallow hierarchy performs better than a deep one, so you should not create an OU hierarchy any deeper than necessary.

Note You can delegate administrative tasks by assigning permissions to OUs.

Domain

The core unit of logical structure in Active Directory directory services is the *domain*. Grouping objects into one or more domains allows your network to reflect your company's organization. Domains share these characteristics:

- All network objects exist within a domain, and each domain stores information only about the objects that it contains. Theoretically, a domain directory can contain up to 10 million objects, but 1 million objects per domain is more practical.

- A domain is a security boundary. Access to domain objects is controlled by *access control lists (ACLs)*. ACLs contain the permissions associated with objects that control which users can gain access to an object and which type of access users can gain to the objects. In Windows 2000, objects include files, folders, shares, printers, and Active Directory objects. All security policies and settings—such as administrative rights, security policies, and ACLs—do not cross from one domain to another. The domain administrator has absolute rights to set policies only within that domain.

Tree

A *tree* is a grouping or hierarchical arrangement of one or more Windows 2000 domains that share a contiguous namespace:

- Following DNS standards, the domain name of a child domain is the relative name of that child domain appended with the name of the parent domain.

- All domains within a single tree share a common *schema,* which is a formal definition of all object types that you can store in an Active Directory deployment.

- All domains within a single tree share a common *global catalog,* which is the central repository of information about objects in a tree.

Forest

A *forest* is a grouping or hierarchical arrangement of one or more domain trees that form a disjointed namespace. As such, forests have the following characteristics:

- All trees in a forest share a common schema.

- Trees in a forest have different naming structures, according to their domains.

- All domains in a forest share a common global catalog.

- Domains in a forest operate independently, but the forest enables communication across the entire organization.

Sites

The physical structure of Active Directory directory services is based on sites. A *site* is a combination of one or more IP subnets, which should be connected by a high-speed link. Typically, a site has the same boundaries as a LAN. When you group subnets on your network, you should combine only those subnets that have fast, cheap, and reliable network connections with one another. Fast network connections are at least 512 kilobits per second (Kbps). An available bandwidth of 128 Kbps and higher is sufficient.

With Active Directory directory services, sites are not part of the namespace. When you browse the logical namespace, you see computers and users grouped into domains and OUs, not sites. Sites contain only computer objects and connection objects used to configure replication between sites.

Note A single domain can span multiple geographical sites, and a single site can include user accounts and computers belonging to multiple domains.

Replication Within a Site

Active Directory directory services also include a replication feature. Replication ensures that changes to a domain controller are reflected in all domain controllers within a domain. To understand replication, you must understand domain controllers. A domain controller is a computer running Windows 2000 Server that stores a replica of the domain directory. A domain can contain one or more domain controllers.

The following list describes the functions of domain controllers:

- Each domain controller stores a complete copy of all Active Directory information for that domain, manages changes to that information, and replicates those changes to other domain controllers in the same domain.

- Domain controllers in a domain automatically replicate all objects in the domain to each other. When you perform an action that causes an update to Active Directory directory services, you are actually making the change at one of the domain controllers. The domain controller then replicates the change to all other domain controllers within the domain. You can control replication of traffic between domain controllers in the network by specifying how often replication occurs and the amount of data that Windows 2000 replicates at one time.

- Domain controllers immediately replicate certain important updates, such as a user account being disabled.

- Active Directory directory services use multimaster replication, in which no one domain controller is the master domain controller. Instead, all domain controllers within a domain are peers, and each domain controller contains a copy of the Directory database that can be written to. Domain controllers can hold different information for short periods of time until all domain controllers have synchronized changes to Active Directory directory services.

- Domain controllers affect fault tolerance. Having more than one domain controller in a domain provides fault tolerance. If one domain controller is offline, another domain controller can provide all required functions, such as recording changes to Active Directory directory services.

- Domain controllers manage all aspects of user domain interaction, such as locating Active Directory objects and validating user logon attempts.

Within a site, Active Directory directory services automatically generate a ring topology for replication among domain controllers in the same domain. The topology defines the path for directory updates to flow from one domain controller to another until all domain controllers receive the directory updates (see Figure 9.3).

Figure 9.3   Replication topology among domain controllers (DC)

The ring structure ensures that at least two replication paths flow from one domain controller to another; if one domain controller is down temporarily, replication still continues to all other domain controllers.

Active Directory directory services periodically analyze the replication topology within a site to ensure that it is still efficient. If you add or remove a domain controller from the network or a site, Active Directory directory services reconfigure the topology to reflect the change.

Lesson Summary

In this lesson you learned that Active Directory directory services offer you a method for designing a directory structure to meet the needs of your organization's business structure and operations. Active Directory directory services completely separate the logical structure of the domain hierarchy from the physical structure. Grouping resources logically enables you to find a resource by its name rather than by its physical location. Since you group resources logically, Active Directory directory services make the network's physical structure transparent to users.

You learned that the core unit of logical structure in Active Directory directory services is the domain. All network objects exist within a domain, and each domain stores information only about the objects that it contains. An OU is a container that you use to organize objects within a domain into logical administrative groups, and an OU can contain objects such as user accounts, groups, computers, printers, applications, file shares, and other OUs. A tree is a grouping or hierarchical arrangement of one or more Windows 2000 domains that share a contiguous namespace. A forest is a grouping or hierarchical arrangement of one or more trees that form a disjointed namespace.

You also learned that the physical structure of Active Directory directory services is based on sites. A site is a combination of one or more IP subnets, connected by a high-speed link. Active Directory directory services also include replication to ensure that changes to a domain controller are reflected in all domain controllers within a domain. Within a site, Active Directory directory services automatically generate a ring topology for replication among domain controllers in the same domain. The ring structure ensures that at least two replication paths exist from one domain controller to another; if one domain controller is down temporarily, replication still continues to all other domain controllers. If you add or remove a domain controller from the network or a site, Active Directory directory services reconfigure the topology to reflect the change.

Lesson 3: Understanding Active Directory Concepts

Several new concepts are introduced with Active Directory directory services. You should understand their meaning as applied to Active Directory directory services.

After this lesson, you will be able to

- Explain concepts associated with Active Directory directory services.

Estimated lesson time: 15 minutes

Schema

The *schema* contains a formal definition of the contents and structure of Active Directory directory services, including all attributes, classes, and class properties, as shown in Figure 9.4. For each object class, the schema defines which attributes an instance of the class must have, which additional attributes it can have, and which object class can be a parent of the current object class.

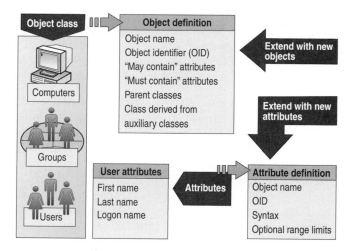

Figure 9.4   The schema defines the contents and structure of Active Directory directory services

Installing Active Directory directory services on the first computer in a network creates the domain and the schema. The default schema contains definitions of commonly used objects and properties (such as user accounts, computers, printers, groups, and so on). The default schema also contains definitions of objects and properties that Active Directory directory services use internally to function.

The Active Directory schema is extensible, which means that you can define new directory object types and attributes and new attributes for existing objects. You can extend the schema by using the Active Directory Schema snap-in or the Active Directory Services Interface (ADSI).

The schema is implemented and stored within Active Directory directory services itself (in the global catalog), and it can be updated dynamically. As a result, an application can extend the schema with new attributes and classes and then can use the extensions immediately.

Note Write access to the schema is limited to members of the Administrators group, by default.

Global Catalog

The *global catalog* is the central repository of information about objects in a tree or forest, as shown in Figure 9.5. Active Directory directory services automatically generate the contents of the global catalog from the domains that make up the Directory through the normal replication process.

Figure 9.5 The global catalog

The global catalog is a service and a physical storage location that contains a replica of selected attributes for every object in Active Directory directory services. By default, the attributes stored in the global catalog are those most frequently used in search operations (such as a user's first and last names, logon name, and so forth), and those necessary to locate a full replica of the object. As a result, you can use the global catalog to locate objects anywhere in the network without replication of all domain information between domain controllers.

Note You use the Active Directory Schema snap-in to define which attributes are included in the global catalog replication process.

When you install Active Directory directory services on the first domain controller in a new forest, that domain controller is, by default, a global catalog server. A *global catalog server* is a domain controller that stores a copy of the global catalog. The configuration of the initial global catalog server should have the capacity to support several hundred thousand to one million objects, with the potential for growth beyond those numbers.

You can designate additional domain controllers as global catalog servers by using the Active Directory Sites and Services snap-in. When considering which domain controllers to designate as global catalog servers, base your decision on the ability of your network structure to handle replication and query traffic. The more global catalog servers that you have, the greater the replication traffic. However, the availability of additional servers can provide quicker responses to user inquiries. Microsoft recommends that every major site in your enterprise have a global catalog server.

Namespace

Active Directory directory services, like all directory services, primarily comprise a namespace. A *namespace* is any bounded area in which a name can be resolved. *Name resolution* is the process of translating a name into some object or information that the name represents. The Active Directory namespace is based on the DNS naming scheme, which allows for interoperability with Internet technologies. An example namespace is shown in Figure 9.6.

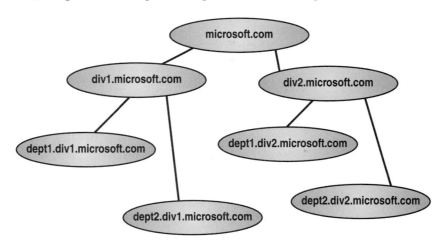

Figure 9.6   Namespace diagram

Using a common namespace allows you to unify and manage multiple hardware and software environments in your network. There are two types of namespaces:

- **Contiguous namespace.** The name of the child object in an object hierarchy always contains the name of the parent domain. A tree is a contiguous namespace.
- **Disjointed namespace.** The names of a parent object and of a child of the same parent object are not directly related to one another. A forest is a disjointed namespace.

Naming Conventions

Every object in Active Directory directory services is identified by a name. Active Directory directory services use a variety of naming conventions: distinguished names, relative distinguished names, globally unique identifiers, and user principal names.

Distinguished Name

Every object in Active Directory directory services has a *distinguished name (DN),* which uniquely identifies an object and contains sufficient information for a client to retrieve the object from the Directory. The DN includes the name of the domain that holds the object, as well as the complete path through the container hierarchy to the object.

For example, the following DN identifies the Firstname Lastname user object in the microsoft.com domain (where *Firstname* and *Lastname* represent the actual first and last names of a user account):

/DC=COM/DC=microsoft/OU=dev/CN=Users/CN=Firstname Lastname

Table 9.2 describes the attributes in the example.

Table 9.2   Distinguished Name Attributes

Attribute	Description
DC	DomainComponentName
OU	OrganizationalUnitName
CN	CommonName

DNs must be unique. Active Directory directory services do not allow duplicate DNs.

Relative Distinguished Name

Active Directory directory services support querying by attributes, so you can locate an object even if the exact DN is unknown or has changed. The *relative distinguished name (RDN)* of an object is the part of the name that is an attribute of the object itself. In the preceding example, the RDN of the Firstname Lastname user object is *Firstname Lastname.* The RDN of the parent object is *Users.*

You can have duplicate RDNs for Active Directory objects, but you can't have two objects with the same RDN in the same OU. For example, if a user account is named Jane Doe, you can't have another user account called Jane Doe in the same OU. However, objects with duplicate RDN names can exist in separate OUs because they have different DNs (see Figure 9.7).

Figure 9.7   Distinguished names and relative distinguished names

Globally Unique Identifier

A *globally unique identifier (GUID)* is a 128-bit number that is guaranteed to be unique. GUIDs are assigned to objects when the objects are created. The GUID never changes, even if you move or rename the object. Applications can store the GUID of an object and use the GUID to retrieve that object regardless of its current DN.

User Principal Name

User accounts have a "friendly" name, the *user principal name (UPN)*. The UPN is composed of a shorthand name for the user account and the DNS name of the tree where the user account object resides. For example, user *Firstname Lastname* (substitute the first and last names of an actual user) in the microsoft.com tree might have a UPN of FirstnameL@microsoft.com (using the full first name and the first letter of the last name).

Lesson Summary

In this lesson, you learned that the schema contains a formal definition of the contents and structure of Active Directory directory services, including all attributes, classes, and class properties. For each object class, the schema defines which attributes an instance of the class must have, which additional attributes it can have, and which object class can be a parent of the current object class. Installing Active Directory directory services on the first domain controller in a network creates a default schema. The Active Directory schema is extensible.

You also learned that the global catalog is a service and a physical storage location that contains a replica of selected attributes for every object in Active Directory directory services. Active Directory directory services automatically generate the contents of the global catalog from the domains that make up the Directory through the normal replication process. By default, the attributes stored in the global catalog are those most frequently used in search operations (such as a user's first and last names, logon name, and so forth) and those necessary to locate a full replica of the object. As a result, you can use the global catalog to locate objects anywhere in the network without replication of all domain information between domain controllers.

Finally, you learned about contiguous namespaces and disjointed namespaces. In a contiguous namespace, the name of the child object in an object hierarchy always contains the name of the parent domain. A tree is an example of a contiguous namespace. In a disjointed namespace, the names of a parent object and of a child of the same parent object aren't directly related to one another. A forest is an example of a disjointed namespace.

Review

The following questions will help you determine whether you have learned enough to move on to the next chapter. If you have difficulty answering these questions, please go back and review the material in this chapter before beginning the next chapter. See Appendix A, "Questions and Answers," for the answers to these questions.

1. What are four major features of Active Directory directory services?

2. What are sites and domains, and how are they different?

3. What is the schema, and how can you extend it?

4. Which Windows 2000 products provide Active Directory directory services?

C H A P T E R   1 0

Setting Up and Managing User Accounts

About This Chapter

This chapter introduces you to user accounts and to how to plan them. It also presents the skills and knowledge necessary to create local user accounts and to set properties for them.

Before You Begin

To complete this chapter, you must have

- A computer that meets the minimum hardware requirements located in "About This Book."
- Windows 2000 Professional installed on the computer.

Lesson 1: Understanding User Accounts

Microsoft Windows 2000 provides three different types of user accounts: local user accounts, domain user accounts, and built-in user accounts. A *local user account* allows a user to log on to a specific computer to gain access to resources on that computer. A *domain user account* allows a user to log on to the domain to gain access to network resources. A *built-in user account* allows a user to perform administrative tasks or to gain access to local or network resources.

After this lesson, you will be able to

- Describe the role and purpose of user accounts.

Estimated lesson time: 10 minutes

Local User Accounts

Local user accounts allow users to log on at and gain access to resources only on the computer where you create the local user account. When you create a local user account, Windows 2000 creates the account *only* in that computer's security database, which is called the *local security database,* as shown in Figure 10.1. Windows 2000 doesn't replicate local user account information to any other computer. After the local user account exists, the computer uses its local security database to authenticate the local user account, which allows the user to log on to that computer.

Local user accounts

- Provide access to resources on the local computer
- Are created only on computers that are not in a domain
- Are created in the local security database

Figure 10.1 Characteristics of local user accounts

If you have a workgroup that consists of five computers running Windows 2000 Professional and you create a local user account—for example, User1 on Computer1—you can log on to Computer1 only with the User1 account. If you need to be able to log on to all five of the computers in the workgroup as User1, you must create a local user account, User1, on each of the five computers. Furthermore, if you decide to change the password for User1, you must change the password for User1 on each of the five computers because each of these computers maintains its own local security database.

Note Do not create local user accounts on computers running Windows 2000 that are part of a domain because the domain doesn't recognize local user accounts. Therefore, the user is unable to gain access to resources in the domain and the domain administrator is unable to administer the local user account properties or assign access permissions for domain resources.

Domain User Accounts

Domain user accounts allow users to log on to the domain and gain access to resources anywhere on the network. The user provides his or her password and user name during the logon process. By using this information, Windows 2000 authenticates the user and then builds an access token that contains information about the user and security settings. The access token identifies the user to computers running Windows 2000 on which the user tries to gain access to resources. Windows 2000 provides the access token for the duration of the logon session.

Note You can have domain user accounts only if you have a domain. You can have a domain only if you have at least one computer running one of the Windows 2000 Server products that is configured as a domain controller, which has the directory services based on Active Directory techology installed.

You create a domain user account in the copy of the Active Directory database (the Directory) on a domain controller, as shown in Figure 10.2. The domain controller replicates the new user account information to all domain controllers in the domain. After Windows 2000 replicates the new user account information, all of the domain controllers in the domain tree can authenticate the user during the logon process.

Domain user accounts

- Provide access to network resources
- Provide the access token for authentication
- Are created in Active Directory directory services on a domain controller

Figure 10.2 Characteristics of domain user accounts

Built-In User Accounts

Windows 2000 automatically creates accounts called *built-in accounts*. Two commonly used built-in accounts are Administrator and Guest.

Administrator

Use the built-in Administrator account to manage the overall computer. If your computer is part of a domain, use the built-in Administrator account to manage the domain configuration. Tasks done using the Administrator account include creating and modifying user accounts and groups, managing security policies, creating printers, and assigning permissions and rights to user accounts to gain access to resources.

If you are the administrator, you should create a user account that you use to perform nonadministrative tasks. Log on by using the Administrator account only when you perform administrative tasks.

Note You can't delete the Administrator account. As a best practice, you should always rename the built-in Administrator account to provide a greater degree of security. Use a name that doesn't identify it as the Administrator account. This makes it difficult for unauthorized users to break into the Administrator account because they don't know which user account it is.

Guest

Use the built-in Guest account to give occasional users the ability to log on and gain access to resources. For example, an employee who needs access to resources for a short time can use the Guest account.

Note The Guest account is disabled by default. Enable the Guest account only in low-security networks and always assign it a password. You can rename the Guest account, but you can't delete it.

Lesson Summary

In this lesson, you learned that Microsoft Windows 2000 provides local user accounts and built-in user accounts. With a local user account, a user logs on to a specific computer to gain access to resources on that computer. With built-in user accounts, you can perform administrative tasks or gain access to resources.

When you create a local user account, Windows 2000 creates the account only in that computer's security database, which is called the local security database. If you need to have access to multiple computers in your workgroup, you must create an account on each of the computers in the workgroup. You don't create built-in user accounts; Windows 2000 automatically creates them.

You also learned that if your computer is part of a domain, Windows 2000 provides domain user accounts. With a domain user account, a user can log on to the domain to gain access to network resources. And built-in user accounts exist that are domain user accounts and are used to perform administrative tasks or gain access to network resources. When you create a domain user account, Windows 2000 creates the account in the copy of the Active Directory database (the Directory) on a domain controller. The domain controller then replicates the new user account information to all domain controllers in the domain, simplifying user account administration.

Lesson 2: Planning New User Accounts

You can streamline the process of creating user accounts by planning and organizing the information for the user accounts. You should plan the following areas:

- Naming conventions for user accounts
- Requirements for passwords

After this lesson, you will be able to

- Plan a strategy for creating new user accounts.

Estimated lesson time: 5 minutes

Naming Conventions

The naming convention establishes how users are identified in the domain. A consistent naming convention will help you and your users remember user logon names and locate them in lists. Table 10.1 summarizes some points you might want to consider in determining a naming convention for your organization.

Table 10.1   Naming Convention Considerations

Consideration	Explanation
User logon names must be unique	Local user account names must be unique on the computer where you create the local user account. User logon names for domain user accounts must be unique to the Directory.
Use 20 characters maximum	User logon names can contain up to 20 uppercase or lowercase characters; the field accepts more than 20 characters, but Windows 2000 recognizes only the first 20.
Avoid invalid characters	The following characters are invalid: " / \ [ ] : ;	= , + * ? < >
User logon names are not case sensitive	You can use a combination of special and alphanumeric characters to help uniquely identify user accounts. User logon names are *not* case sensitive, but Windows 2000 preserves the case.
Accommodate employees with duplicate names	If two users were named John Doe, you could use the first name and the last initial, and then add additional letters from the last name to differentiate the duplicate names. In this example, one user account logon name could be Johnd and the other Johndo. Another possibility would be to number each user logon name—for example, Johnd1 and Johnd2.

Consideration	Explanation
Identify the type of employee	In some organizations, it is useful to identify temporary employees by their user account. To identify temporary employees, you can use a T and a dash in front of the user's logon name—for example, T-Johnd. Alternatively, use parentheses in the name—for example, John Doe (Temp).

Password Requirements

To protect access to the computer, every user account should have a password. Consider the following guidelines for passwords:

- Always assign a password for the Administrator account to prevent unauthorized access to the account.

- Determine whether the Administrator or the users will control passwords. You can assign unique passwords for the user accounts and prevent users from changing them, or you can allow users to enter their own passwords the first time they log on. In most cases, users should control their passwords.

- Use passwords that are hard to guess. For example, avoid using passwords with an obvious association, such as a family member's name.

- Passwords can be up to 127 characters; a minimum length of eight characters is recommended.

- Use both uppercase and lowercase letters, numerals, and valid nonalphanumeric characters.

Lesson Summary

In this lesson, you learned that in planning user accounts, you should determine naming conventions for user accounts and requirements for passwords. You learned that domain user accounts can be up to 20 characters long and must be unique within the OU where you create the domain user account. Local user account names can also be up to 20 characters long and must be unique on the computer where you create the local user account. Making these decisions before you start creating user accounts will reduce the amount of time it takes to create the needed user accounts and will simplify managing these accounts.

Lesson 3: Creating User Accounts

Use the Computer Management snap-in to create a new local user account. When you create a local user account, it is always created in the local security database of that computer.

After this lesson, you will be able to

- Create a local user account.

Estimated lesson time: 10 minutes

The Computer Management Snap-In

The Computer Management snap-in (illustrated in Figure 10.3) is the tool you use to create local user accounts.

Figure 10.3   The Computer Management snap-in

You can create local user accounts by doing the following:

1. Click the Start button, point to Programs, point to Administrative Tools, and then click Computer Management.
2. In the Computer Management window, in the console pane, click Local Users And Groups.
3. In the details pane, right-click Users, and then click New User.
4. Fill in the appropriate fields in the New User dialog box (see Figure 10.4), and then click Create.

Table 10.2 describes the local user account options shown in Figure 10.4.

Figure 10.4   The New User dialog box

Table 10.2   Local User Account Options

Option	Description
User Name	The user's logon name. This field is required.
Full Name	The user's full name. This includes the user's first and last names but can also include the middle name or initial.
Description	An optional field that allows you to type descriptive text about the user account or the user.
Password	The password that is used to authenticate the user. For greater security, *always* assign a password. Notice that you don't see the password. It is represented as asterisks when you type the password, regardless of the length of the password.
Confirm Password	Confirm the password by typing it a second time to make sure that you typed the password correctly. This is required if you assign a password.
User Must Change Password At Next Logon	Select this check box if you want the user to change his or her password the first time that he or she logs on. This ensures that the user is the only person who knows the password. By default, this check box is selected.

(continued)

Option	Description
User Cannot Change Password	Select this check box if you have more than one person using the same user account (such as Guest) or to maintain control over user account passwords. This allows only administrators to control passwords. When the User Must Change Password At Next Logon check box is selected, the User Cannot Change Password check box isn't available.
Password Never Expires	Select this check box if you never want the password to change—for example, for a user account that will be used by a program or a Windows 2000 service. The User Must Change Password At Next Logon check box box overrides the Password Never Expires check box. When the User Must Change Password At Next Logon check box is selected, the Password Never Expires check box isn't available.
Account Is Disabled	Select this check box to prevent use of this user account—for example, for a new employee who hasn't started yet.

Note Always require new users to change their passwords the first time they log on. This will force them to use passwords that only they know.

Tip For added security on networks, create random initial passwords for all new user accounts by using a combination of letters and numbers. Creating a random initial password will help keep the user account secure.

Practice: Creating Local User Accounts

In this practice, you will create the user accounts shown in the following table. Then you will test the logon procedure with one of the users you created.

User name	Full name	Password	Change password
User1	User One	(blank)	Must
User2	User Two	(blank)	(blank)
User3	User Three	User3	Must
User4	User Four	User4	(blank)

The following procedure outlines the steps that are required to create the first user account by using the Computer Management snap-in. After you have created the first user account, follow the same steps to create the remaining user accounts and use the information in the table to set them up.

▶   **To create a local user account**

1. Log on as Administrator.
2. Click the Start button, point to Programs, point to Administrative Tools, and then click Computer Management.

   Windows 2000 displays the Computer Management snap-in.
3. Expand Local Users And Groups.
4. Right-click Users, and then click New User.

   Windows 2000 displays the New User dialog box.
5. Type **User1** in the User Name box.
6. Type **User One** in the Full Name box.
7. In the Password box and the Confirm Password box, type the password or leave these boxes blank if you aren't assigning a password.

   If you enter a password, notice that the password is displayed as asterisks as you type. This prevents onlookers from viewing the password as it is entered.

   In high-security environments, assign initial passwords to user accounts and then require users to change their password the next time that they log on. This prevents a user account from existing without a password, and once the user logs on and changes his or her password, only the user knows the password.
8. Specify whether or not the user can change his or her password.
9. After you have selected the appropriate password options, click Create.

   The New User dialog box clears and remains displayed so that you can create another user account.
10. Complete steps 5–9 for the remaining user accounts.
11. When you finishing creating users, click Close to close the New User dialog box.
12. Close the Computer Management window.

▶   **To test a local user account**

1. Log off as Administrator.
2. Log on as User1 with no password.

   A Logon Message box appears informing you that you are required to change your password at first logon.
3. Click OK.
4. When prompted to change User1's password, leave the Old Password box empty, type **password** in the Password and Confirm New Password boxes, and then click OK.

   A Change Password dialog box appears.
5. Click OK.

Lesson Summary

In this lesson, you learned how to use the Computer Management snap-in to create a new local user account. When you create a local user account, it is only created in the local security database of that computer. You can configure options for the accounts you create, including a user name, a full name, and a description. You can also configure password options such as whether users must change their passwords at the next logon, whether users can ever change their passwords, and whether the passwords expire. In the practice portion of this lesson, you created four local user accounts.

Lesson 4: Setting Properties for User Accounts

A set of default properties is associated with each local user account that you create. After you create a local user account, you can configure these account properties. A user's Properties dialog box has three tabs that contain information about each user account: the General tab, the Member Of tab, and the Profile tab.

After this lesson, you will be able to

- Set properties for user accounts.

Estimated lesson time: 15 minutes

The General Tab in a User Account's Properties

The General tab in the Properties dialog box for a user account (see Figure 10.5) allows you to set or edit all the fields from the New User dialog box, except for User Name, Password, and Confirm Password. It also provides one additional check box: Account Is Locked Out.

Figure 10.5   The General tab of a user's Properties dialog box

You can't select the Account Is Locked Out check box because it is unavailable when the account is active and not locked out of the system. The system locks out a user if he or she exceeds the limit set on the number of failed logon attempts. This is a security feature to make it more difficult for an unauthorized user to break into the system. If an account has been locked out by the system, the Account Is Locked Out check box becomes available and an administrator can clear the check box to allow the user access to the system.

The Member Of Tab in a User Account's Properties

The Member Of tab in the Properties dialog box for a user account allows you to add the user account to or remove the user account from a group. For information on groups, see Chapter 11, "Setting Up and Managing Groups."

The Profile Tab in a User Account's Properties

The Profile tab in the Properties dialog box for a user account allows you to set a path for the user profile, logon script, and home folder (see Figure 10.6).

Figure 10.6   The Profile tab of a user's Properties dialog box

User Profile

A *user profile* is a collection of folders and data that stores the user's current desktop environment and application settings, as well as personal data. A user profile also contains all of the network connections that are established when a user logs on to a computer, such as Start-menu items and mapped drives to network servers. User profiles maintain consistency for users in their desktop environments by providing each user the same desktop environment that he or she had the last time that he or she logged on to the computer.

Windows 2000 creates a user profile the first time that a user logs on at a computer. After the user logs on for the first time, Windows 2000 stores the user profile on that computer. This user profile is also known as a *local user profile*.

User profiles operate in the following manner:

- When a user logs on to a client computer running Windows 2000, the user always receives his or her individual desktop settings and connections, regardless of how many users share the same client computer.

- The first time that a user logs on to a client computer running Windows 2000, Windows 2000 creates a default user profile for the user and stores it in the boot partition root\Documents and Settings*user_logon_name* folder (typically C:\Documents and Settings*user_logon_name*), where *user_logon_name* is the name the user enters when logging on to the system.

- A user profile contains the My Documents folder, which provides a place for users to store personal files. My Documents is the default location for the File Open and Save As commands. By default, Windows 2000 creates a My Documents icon on the user's desktop. This makes it easier for users to locate their personal documents.

- A user can change his or her user profile by changing desktop settings. For example, a user makes a new network connection or adds a file to My Documents. Then, when the user logs off, Windows 2000 incorporates the changes into the user profile. The next time the user logs on, the new network connection and the file are present.

Note You should have users store their documents in My Documents rather than in home directories. Home directories are covered later in this chapter. Windows 2000 automatically sets up My Documents, and it is the default location for storing data for Microsoft applications.

By opening the System program in Control Panel and clicking the User Profiles tab, an administrator can easily copy, delete, or change the type of a user profile. Changing the type for user profiles allows an administrator to change it from a local user profile, which sets up the user's desktop environment on a specific computer, to a roaming user profile. A *roaming user profile* is especially helpful in a domain environment, because it follows the user around, setting up the same desktop environment for the user no matter what computer the user logs on to in the domain.

There is a third type of user profile, the mandatory user profile, which is a read-only roaming user profile. When the user logs off, Windows 2000 does not save any changes made during the session, so the next time the user logs on the profile is exactly the same as the last time the user logged on. You can create a mandatory user profile for a specific user or to be used with a group of users.

> **Note** A hidden file called Ntuser.dat contains the section of the Windows 2000 system settings that applies to the individual user account and contains the user environment settings. Create a user account that you can use to create user profiles. Log on as the user you created, and configure all the desktop environment settings you want. Log on as administrator and locate the Ntuser.dat file in C:\Documents and Settings\user_logon_name. You make the profile a mandatory roaming user profile by changing its name to Ntuser.man. You can then copy this file to apply the mandatory user profile to any other user or group.

Logon Script

A logon script is a file you can create and assign to a user account to configure the user's working environment. For example, a login script can be used to establish network connections or start applications. Each time a user logs on, the assigned logon script is run.

Home Folder

In addition to the My Documents folder, Windows 2000 provides you with the means to create another location for users to store their personal documents. This additional location is the user's home folder. You can store a home folder on a client computer or in a shared folder on a file server. In fact, you can locate all users' home folders in a central location on a network server.

Storing all home folders on a file server provides the following advantages:

- Users can gain access to their home folders from any client computer on the network.
- The backing up and administration of user documents is centralized.
- The home folders are accessible from a client computer running any Microsoft operating system (including MS-DOS, Windows 95, Windows 98, and Windows 2000).

> **Note** Store home folders on an NTFS file system volume so that you can use NTFS permissions to secure user documents. If you store home folders on a FAT volume, you can restrict home folder access only by using shared folder permissions.

To create a home folder on a network file server, you must perform the following three tasks:

1. Create and share a folder in which to store all home folders on a network server. The home folder for each user will reside in this shared folder.
2. For the shared folder, remove the default Full Control permission from the Everyone group and assign Full Control to the Users group. This ensures that only users with domain user accounts can gain access to the shared folder.

3. Provide the path to the user's home folder in the shared home directory folder on the Profile tab of the Properties dialog box for the user account. Since the home folder is on a network server, click Connect and specify a drive letter to use to connect. In the To box, you would specify a UNC name—for example, *server_name**shared_folder_name**user_logon_name*. Type the *username* variable as the user's logon name to automatically name each user's home folder the user logon name (for example, type **\\server_name\Users\ %username%**).

If you use the *username* variable to name a folder on an NTFS volume, the user is assigned the NTFS Full Control permission, and all other permissions are removed for the folder, including those for the Administrator account.

You can set User Account Properties by doing the following:

1. On the Administrative Tools menu, click Computer Management.

2. Right-click the appropriate local user account, and then click Properties.

3. Click the appropriate tab for the properties that you want to enter or change, and then enter values for each property.

Practice: Modifying User Account Properties

In this practice, you will modify user account properties. Then you will test them.

Exercise 1: Testing Account Properties

In this exercise, you will again test the User Must Change Password At Next Logon property that you configured when you created users in the previous Practice. You will then set the User Cannot Change Password Account property on User1 and the Account Is Disabled property on User2, and then test these account properties.

▶ **To test User Must Change Password At Next Logon Property**

1. If a user is currently logged on to your computer, log that user off.

2. Log on to the system as User3. Remember to use this user's password: User3.

   Windows 2000 displays a Logon Message dialog box indicating that you are required to change your password at first logon.

3. Click OK.

   Windows 2000 displays a Change Password dialog box. Notice that the password you just typed is in the Old Password box.

4. Type **password** in both the New Password box and in the Confirm New Password box.

5. Click OK.

Windows 2000 displays a Change Password dialog box indicating that your password has been changed.

6. Click OK.

Exercise 2: Setting User Account Properties

In this exercise, you will set and then test the User Cannot Change Password property.

▶ **To set the User Cannot Change Password Property**

1. Log off as User3.

2. Log on as Administrator.

3. Start Computer Management from the Administrative Tools menu.

4. Expand Local Users And Groups, and then click Users.

   Windows 2000 displays the users in the details pane.

5. Right-click User1 and then click Properties.

   The User1 Properties dialog box appears.

6. Select User Cannot Change Password.

   The User Cannot Change Password check box should contain a check mark, indicating that it is selected. Notice that the User Must Change Password At Next Logon check box is now unavailable.

7. Click OK to close the User1 Properties dialog box.

8. Right-click User2, and then select Properties.

   The User2 Properties dialog box appears.

9. Select Account Is Disabled.

   The Account Is Disabled check box should contain a check mark, indicating that it is selected.

10. Click OK to close the User2 Properties dialog box, close Computer Management, and then log off the computer.

▶ **To test User Account Properties**

1. Log on as User1 with a password of password.

2. Press Ctrl+Alt+Delete.

   Windows 2000 displays the Windows Security dialog box.

3. Click Change Password.

   The Change Password dialog box appears.

4. Type **password** in the Old Password box, and then type **User1** in the New Password and the Confirm New Password boxes.

5. Click OK.

   A Change Password dialog box appears indicating that you do not have permission to change your password.

6. Click OK.

7. Click Cancel to close the Change Password dialog box.

8. Log off as User1 and then log on as User2 with no password.

   A Logon Message dialog box appears, indicating that your account has been disabled.

9. Click OK to close the Logon Message dialog box.

Lesson Summary

In this lesson, you learned that a set of default properties is associated with each local user account that you create. These properties include whether users can change their own password, whether users are required to change their password at the next logon, and whether the account is disabled. The Computer Management snap-in allows you to easily configure or modify these account properties.

In the practice portion of this lesson, you were able to configure account properties, including prohibiting users from changing their passwords and disabling a user account. Finally, you tested these properties to verify that they worked as expected.

Review

The following questions will help you determine whether you have learned enough to move on to the next chapter. If you have difficulty answering these questions, please go back and review the material in this chapter before beginning the next chapter. See Appendix A, "Questions and Answers," for the answers to these questions.

1. Where does Windows 2000 create local user accounts?

2. What different capabilities do domain user accounts and local user accounts provide to users?

3. What should you consider when you plan new user accounts?

4. What information is required to create a local user account?

5. What are built-in accounts and what are they used for?

C H A P T E R   1 1

Setting Up and Managing Groups

About This Chapter

This chapter introduces you to groups and explains how to group user accounts to allow for easier assignment of permissions. It also presents the skills and knowledge necessary to implement local groups and built-in groups.

Before You Begin

To complete this chapter, you must have

- A computer that meets the minimum hardware requirements located in "About This Book."
- Microsoft Windows 2000 Professional installed on the computer.

Lesson 1: Implementing Local Groups

In this lesson, you will learn what groups are and how you can use them to simplify user account administration.

After this lesson, you will be able to

- Describe the key features of groups.
- Describe local groups.
- Create and delete local groups.
- Add members to local groups.
- Remove members from local groups.

Estimated lesson time: 30 minutes

Understanding Groups

A *group* is a collection of user accounts. Groups simplify administration by allowing you to assign permissions and rights to a group of users rather than having to assign permissions to each individual user account (see Figure 11.1).

- Groups are collections of user accounts.
- Members receive permissions given to groups.
- Users can be members of multiple groups.
- Groups can be members of other groups.

Figure 11.1   Groups simplify administration.

Permissions control what users can do with a resource, such as a folder, file, or printer. When you assign permissions, you give users the capability to gain access to a resource, and you define the type of access that they have. For example, if several users need to read the same file, you would add their user accounts to a group. Then you would give the group permission to read the file. Rights allow users to perform system tasks, such as changing the time on a computer, backing up or restoring files, or logging on locally.

When adding members to a group, remember that users can be members of multiple groups. A group contains a list of members, with references to the actual user account. Therefore, users can be members of more than one group.

Understanding Local Groups

A local group is a collection of user accounts on a computer. Use local groups to assign permissions to resources residing on the computer on which the local group is created. Windows 2000 creates local groups in the local security database.

Preparing to Use Local Groups

Guidelines for using local groups include the following:

- Use local groups on computers that don't belong to a domain.

  You can use local groups only on the computer where you create the local groups. Although local groups are available on member servers and domain computers running Windows 2000 Professional, don't use local groups on computers that are part of a domain. Using local groups on domain computers prevents you from centralizing group administration. Local groups don't appear in directory services based on Active Directory technology, and you have to administer local groups separately for each computer.

- You can assign permissions to local groups for access to only the resources on the computer where you create the local groups.

Note You can't create local groups on domain controllers because domain controllers cannot have a security database that is independent of the database in Active Directory directory services.

Membership rules for local groups include the following:

- Local groups can contain local user accounts from the computer where you create the local groups.
- Local groups can't be a member of any other group.

Creating Local Groups

Use the Computer Management snap-in to create local groups, as shown in Figure 11.2. You create local groups in the Groups folder.

Figure 11.2   The Computer Management snap-in

You can create a local group by doing the following:

1. In Computer Management, expand Local Users And Groups and click the Groups folder.
2. Right-click Groups, and then click New Group.

   Table 11.1 describes the options presented in the New Group dialog box.

3. Enter the appropriate information and then click Create.

Table 11.1   New Local Group Options

Option	Description
Group Name	A unique name for the local group. This is the only required entry. Use any character except for the backslash (\). The name can contain up to 256 characters; however, very long names might not display in some windows.
Description	A description of the group.
Add	Adds a user to the list of members.
Remove	Removes a user from the list of members.
Create	Creates the group.
Close	Closes the New Group dialog box.

You can add members to a local group when you create the group by using the Add button, but you can also add users to a local group after you create it.

Deleting Local Groups

Use the Computer Management snap-in to delete local groups. Each group that you create has a unique, nonreusable identifier. Windows 2000 uses this value to identify the group and the permissions that are assigned to it. When you delete a group, Windows 2000 doesn't use the identifier again, even if you create a new group with the same name as the group that you deleted. Therefore, you cannot restore access to resources by recreating the group.

When you delete a group, you delete only the group and remove the permissions and rights that are associated with it. Deleting a group doesn't delete the user accounts that are members of the group. To delete a group, right-click the group, and then click Delete.

Adding Members to a Group

To add members to a group that has already been created, start the Computer Management snap-in and expand Local Users And Groups. Click Groups, and then in the details pane, right-click the appropriate group and click Properties. In the Properties dialog box, click Add. The Select Users Or Groups dialog box appears, as shown in Figure 11.3.

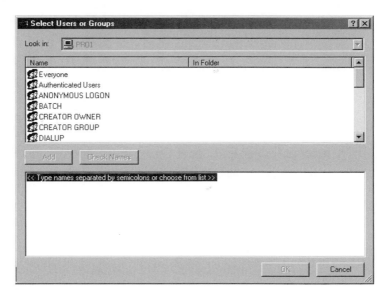

Figure 11.3   The Select Users Or Groups dialog box

In the Look In list, ensure that the computer on which you created the group is selected. In the Name box, select the user account that you want to add to the group, and then click Add.

Note If you want to add multiple user accounts, you can repeat the process of selecting them one at a time and then click Add, or you can hold down the Shift or Ctrl key to select multiple user accounts at once. The Shift key allows you to select a consecutive range of accounts, while the Ctrl key allows you to pick some accounts and skip others. Click Add once you have selected all the accounts that you want to add.

Clicking Add lists the accounts you have selected. Once you review the accounts to make sure that they are the accounts you want to add to the group, click OK to add the members.

Note You can also add a user account to a group by using the Member Of tab in the Properties dialog box for that user account. Use this method to quickly add the same user account to multiple groups.

Practice: Creating and Managing Local Groups

In this practice, you will create two local groups. You will add members to the local groups when you create them, and then add an additional member to one of the groups after they have been created. You delete a member from one of the groups, and then you delete one of the local groups that you created.

Note This practice requires user accounts that you create when you complete the practice in Chapter 10, "Setting Up and Managing User Accounts." If you didn't set up the user accounts as described in Chapter 10, go back and do the practice in that chapter to set up the user accounts you will work with in this practice.

Exercise 1: Creating Local Groups and Adding and Removing Members

In this exercise, you will create two local groups, Sales and Testing. You add members to both groups when you create them. You add a member to an existing group by adding an additional member to the Testing group, and then you remove a member from the Testing group.

▶ **To create a local group**

1. Log on to your computer as Administrator.
2. Click the Start button, point to Programs, point to Administrative Tools, and then click Computer Management.
3. Expand Local Users And Groups, and then click Groups.

In the details pane, Computer Management displays a list of current and built-in local groups.

4. To create a new group, right-click Groups, and then click New Group.

   Computer Management displays the New Group dialog box.

5. Type **Sales** in the Group Name box, and type **Access to Customer Files** in the Description box.

6. Click Add.

   The Select Users Or Groups dialog box appears.

7. Hold the Ctrl key down and select User1 and User3.

8. Click Add.

   PRO1\User1 and PRO1\User3 should be listed in the box below the Add button.

Note If you didn't name your computer PRO1, then PRO1 will be replaced by the name of your computer.

---

9. Click OK.

   In the New Group dialog box, notice that User1 and User3 are listed in the Members box.

10. Click Create.

    Windows 2000 creates the group and adds it to the list of users and groups. Note the New Group dialog box is still open and might block your view of the list of users and groups.

11. Repeat steps 5–10 to create a group named Testing. Type **Access to Trouble-shooting Tips File** in the Description box, and make User2 and User4 members of the Testing group.

12. When you have created both the Sales and the Testing groups, click Close to close the New Group dialog box.

    Notice that the Sales and Testing groups are listed in the details pane.

► **To add members to and remove members from a local group**

1. In the details pane of Computer Management, double-click Testing.

   The Testing Properties dialog box displays the properties of the group. Notice that User2 and User4 are listed in the Members box.

2. To add a member to the group, click Add.

   The Select Users Or Groups dialog box appears.

3. In the Name box, select User3, click Add, and then click OK.

   The Testing Properties dialog box displays User2, User3, and User4 listed in the Members box.

4. Select User4 and then click Remove.

   Notice that User4 is no longer listed in the Members box. User4 still exists as a local user account, but it is no longer a member of the Testing group.

5. Click OK.

Exercise 2: Deleting a Local Group

In this exercise, you will delete the Testing local group.

▶ **To delete a local group**

1. Right-click Testing in the Computer Management details pane, and then click Delete.

   A Local Users And Groups dialog box appears, asking whether you are sure that you want to delete the group.

2. Click Yes.

   Notice that Testing is no longer listed in the Computer Management window. The members of the group were not deleted. User2 and User3 are still local user accounts on PRO1.

3. Close Computer Management.

Lesson Summary

In this lesson, you learned that a group is a collection of user accounts. Groups simplify administration by allowing you to assign permissions and rights to a group of users rather than having to assign permissions to each individual user account.

When naming a group, you make the name intuitive. You also learned that you use the Computer Management snap-in to create groups, to add members to a group, to remove members from a group, and to delete groups. In the practice portion of this lesson, you created two local groups and added members to the groups as you created the local groups. You then added an additional member to one of the local groups. You deleted a member from one of the local groups, and then you deleted one of the local groups.

Lesson 2: Implementing Built-In Local Groups

Windows 2000 has two categories of built-in groups: local and system. Built-in groups have a predetermined set of user rights or group membership. Windows 2000 creates these groups for you so you don't have to create groups and assign rights and permissions for commonly used functions.

After this lesson, you will be able to

- Describe the Microsoft Windows 2000 built-in groups.

Estimated lesson time: 10 minutes

Built-In Local Groups

All stand-alone servers, member servers, and computers running Windows 2000 Professional have built-in local groups. *Built-in local groups* give rights to perform system tasks on a single computer, such as backing up and restoring files, changing the system time, and administering system resources. Windows 2000 places the built-in local groups into the Groups folder in Computer Management.

Table 11.2 describes the capabilities that members of the most commonly used built-in local groups have. Except where noted, there are no initial members in these groups.

Table 11.2   Built-In Local Groups

Local group	Description
Administrators	Members can perform all administrative tasks on the computer. By default, the built-in Administrator user account for the computer is a member.
	When a member server or a computer running Client for Microsoft Networks joins a domain, Windows 2000 adds the Domain Admins group to the local Administrators group.
Backup Operators	Members can use Windows Backup to back up and restore the computer.
Guests	Members can perform only tasks for which you have specifically granted rights and can gain access only to resources for which you have assigned permissions; members can't make permanent changes to their desktop environment. By default, the built-in Guest account for the computer is a member.
	When a member server or a computer running Client for Microsoft Networks joins a domain, Windows 2000 adds the Domain Guests group to the local Guests group.

(continued)

Local group	Description
Power Users	Members can create and modify local user accounts on the computer and share resources.
Replicator	Supports file replication in a domain.
Users	Members can perform only tasks for which you have specifically granted rights and can gain access only to resources for which you have assigned permissions. By default, Windows 2000 adds local user accounts that you create on the computer to the Users group. When a member server or a computer running Windows 2000 Professional joins a domain, Windows 2000 adds the Domain Users group to the local Users group.

Built-In System Groups

Built-in system groups exist on all computers running Windows 2000. *System groups* don't have specific memberships that you can modify, but they can represent different users at different times, depending on how a user gains access to a computer or resource. You don't see system groups when you administer groups, but they are available for use when you assign rights and permissions to resources. Windows 2000 bases system group membership on how the computer is accessed, not on who uses the computer. Table 11.3 describes the most commonly used built-in system groups.

Table 11.3   Commonly Used Built-In System Groups

System group	Description
Everyone	Includes all users who access the computer. Be careful if you assign permissions to the Everyone group and enable the Guest account. Windows 2000 will authenticate a user who does not have a valid user account as Guest. The user automatically gets all rights and permissions that you have assigned to the Everyone group.
Authenticated Users	Includes all users with a valid user account on the computer (or if your computer is part of a domain, it includes all users in Active Directory directory services). Use the Authenticated Users group instead of the Everyone group to prevent anonymous access to a resource.
Creator Owner	Includes the user account for the user who created or took ownership of a resource. If a member of the Administrators group creates a resource, the Administrators group is owner of the resource.
Network	Includes any user with a current connection from another computer on the network to a shared resource on the computer.

System group	Description
Interactive	Includes the user account for the user who is logged on at the computer. Members of the Interactive group gain access to resources on the computer at which they are physically located. They log on and gain access to resources by "interacting" with the computer.
Anonymous Logon	Includes any user account that Windows 2000 didn't authenticate.
Dialup	Includes any user who currently has a dial-up connection.

Lesson Summary

In this lesson, you learned that Windows 2000 has two categories of built-in groups: local and system. You also learned that built-in groups have a predetermined set of user rights or group membership. Windows 2000 creates these groups for you so you don't have to create groups and assign rights and permissions for commonly used functions.

Review

The following questions will help you determine whether you have learned enough to move on to the next chapter. If you have difficulty answering these questions, please go back and review the material in this chapter before beginning the next chapter. See Appendix A, "Questions and Answers," for the answers to these questions.

1. Why should you use groups?

2. How do you create a local group?

3. Are there any consequences to deleting a group?

4. What's the difference between built-in local groups and local groups?

C H A P T E R   1 2

Setting Up and Configuring Network Printers

About This Chapter

This chapter introduces you to setting up and configuring network printers so that users can print over the network. You will also learn how to troubleshoot common printing problems that are associated with setting up network printers.

Before You Begin

To complete this chapter, you must have

- A computer that meets the minimum hardware requirements located in "About This Book."
- Microsoft Windows 2000 Professional installed on the computer.

Note You do *not* need a printer to complete the exercises in this chapter.

Lesson 1: Introducing Windows 2000 Printing

With Windows 2000 printing, you can share printing resources across an entire network and administer printing from a central location. You can easily set up printing on client computers running Windows 2000, Windows NT 4, Windows 98, and Windows 95.

After this lesson, you will be able to

- Define Microsoft Windows 2000 printing terms.

Estimated lesson time: 15 minutes

Terminology

Before you set up printing, become familiar with Windows 2000 printing terminology to understand how the different components fit together, as shown in Figure 12.1.

Figure 12.1   Printing terminology

If you are new to Windows 2000, you might find some of the printing terminology to be different from what you expected. The following list defines a few Windows 2000 printing terms:

- **Printer.** A *printer* is the software interface between the operating system and the print device. The printer defines where a document will go to reach the print device (that is, to a local port, a port for a network connection, or a file), when it will go, and how various other aspects of the printing process will be handled.

When users make connections to printers, they use printer names, which point to one or more print devices.

- **Print device.** A *print device* is the hardware device that produces printed documents.

  Windows 2000 supports the following print devices:

  - *Local print devices,* which are connected to a physical port on the print server.

  - *Network-interface print devices,* which are connected to a print server through the network instead of a physical port. Network-interface print devices require their own network interface cards and have their own network address, or they are attached to an external network adapter.

- **Printer port.** A *printer port* is the software interface through which a computer communicates with a print device by means of a locally attached interface.

  Windows 2000 supports these interfaces: line printer (LPT), COM, USB, and network-attached devices such as the HP JetDirect and Intel NetPort.

- **Print server.** A *print server* is the computer on which the printers that are associated with local and network-interface print devices reside. The print server receives and processes documents from client computers. You set up and share network printers on print servers.

- **Printer driver.** A *printer driver* is one or more files containing information that Windows 2000 requires to convert print commands into a specific printer language, such as PostScript. This conversion makes it possible for a print device to print a document. A printer driver is specific to each print device model.

Requirements for Network Printing

The requirements for setting up printing on a Windows 2000 network include the following:

- At least one computer to operate as the print server. If the print server will manage many heavily used printers, Microsoft recommends a dedicated print server. The computer can run either of the following:

  - Windows 2000 Server, which can handle a large number of connections and supports Macintosh and UNIX computers and NetWare clients.

  - Windows 2000 Professional, which is limited to 10 concurrent connections from other computers for file and print services. It doesn't support Macintosh computers or NetWare clients, but it does support UNIX computers.

- Sufficient RAM to process documents.

  If a print server manages a large number of printers or many large documents, the server might require additional RAM beyond what Windows 2000 requires for other tasks. If a print server doesn't have sufficient RAM for its workload, printing performance deteriorates.

- Sufficient disk space on the print server to ensure that Windows 2000 can store documents that are sent to the print server until the print server sends the documents to the print device.

  This is critical when documents are large or likely to accumulate. For example, if 10 users send large documents to print at the same time, the print server must have enough disk space to hold all of the documents until the print server sends them to the print device. If there isn't enough space to hold all of the documents, users will get error messages and be unable to print.

Guidelines for a Network Printing Environment

Before you set up network printing, develop a network-wide printing strategy to meet users' printing needs without unnecessary duplication of resources or delays in printing. Table 12.1 provides some guidelines for developing a network printing strategy.

Table 12.1   Network Printing Environment Guidelines

Guideline	Explanation
Determine user's printing requirements	Determine the number of users who print and the printing workload. For example, 10 people in a billing department who print invoices continually will have a larger printing workload and might require more printers, print devices, and possibly, more print servers than 10 software developers who do all their work online.
Determine company's printing requirements	Determine the printing needs of your company. This includes the number and types of print devices that are required. In addition, consider the type of workload that each print device will handle. Don't use a personal print device for network printing.
Determine the number of print servers required	Determine the number of print servers that your network requires to handle the number and types of printers that your network will have.
Determine where to locate print devices	Determine where to put the print devices so that it's easy for users to pick up their printed documents.

Lesson Summary

In this lesson, your learned that in Windows 2000 terminology, a printer is the software interface between the operating system and the print device. The print device is the hardware device that produces printed documents. Windows 2000 supports local print devices, which are connected to a physical port on the print server, and network-interface print devices, which are connected to a print server through the network instead of through a physical port.

You also learned that a print server is a computer running either Windows 2000 Professional or Windows 2000 Server on which the printers reside. The print server receives and processes documents from client computers. You set up and share network printers on print servers. A printer driver is one or more files containing information that Windows 2000 requires to convert print commands into a specific printer language, such as PostScript. This conversion makes it possible for a print device to print a document. A printer driver is specific to each print device model.

Finally, you learned that the requirements for setting up printing on a Windows 2000 network include at least one computer to operate as the print server. If the print server will manage many heavily used printers, Microsoft recommends that you use a dedicated print server. A print server running Windows 2000 Professional is limited to 10 concurrent connections from other computers for file and print services, and it doesn't support Macintosh computers or NetWare clients but does support UNIX computers.

Lesson 2: Setting Up Network Printers

Setting up and sharing a network printer makes it possible for multiple users to print to it. You can set up a printer for a local print device that is connected directly to the print server, or you can set up a printer for a network-interface print device that is connected to the print server over the network. In larger organizations, most printers point to network-interface print devices.

After this lesson, you will be able to

- Identify the requirements for setting up a network printer and network printing resources.
- Add and share a new printer for a local print device or a network-interface print device.
- Set up client computers.

Estimated lesson time: 30 minutes

Adding and Sharing a Printer for a Local Print Device

The steps for adding a printer for a local print device or for a network-interface print device are similar. First, you add the printer for a local print device, as follows.

1. Log on as Administrator on the print server.
2. Click Start, point to Settings, and then click Printers.

   You add and share a printer by using the Add Printer wizard in the Printers folder.
3. Double-click Add Printer to launch the Add Printer wizard.

   The Add Printer wizard starts with the Welcome To The Add Printer Wizard page displayed.
4. Click Next and the Add Printer wizard displays the Local Or Network Printer page (see Figure 12.2).

The Add Printer wizard guides you through the steps to add a printer for a print device that is connected to the print server. The number of local print devices that you can connect to a print server through physical ports depends on your hardware configuration.

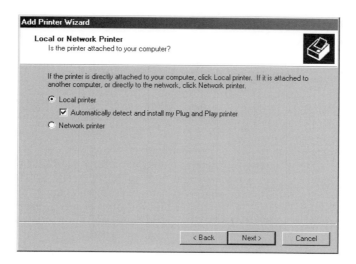

Figure 12.2   The Local Or Network Printer page

Table 12.2 describes the Add Printer wizard options for adding a printer for a local print device.

Table 12.2   The Add Printer Wizard Options for a Local Print Device

Option	Description
Local Printer	The designation that you are adding a printer to the computer at which you are sitting, which is the print server.
	The Automatically Detect And Install My Plug And Play Printer check box allows you to specify whether you want Windows 2000 to automatically detect and install a Plug and Play printer.
Use The Following Port	The port on the print server to which you attached the print device.
	You can also create a new port. Creating a port allows you to print to nonstandard hardware ports, such as a network-interface connection.
Manufacturers	The correct printer driver for the local print device. Select the manufacturer of your print device.
Printers	Select the printer model for your print device. If your print device isn't in the list, you must provide a printer driver from the manufacturer or select a model that is similar enough that the print device can use it.

(continued)

Option	Description
Printer Name	A name that will identify the printer to the users. Use a name that is intuitive and descriptive of the print device. Some applications might not support more than 31 characters in the server and printer name combinations.
	If your computer running Windows 2000 Professional is part of a domain, this name also appears in the result of an Active Directory search.
Default Printer	The default printer for all Windows-based applications. Select the Yes option button for the Do You Want Your Windows-Based Programs To Use This Printer As The Default Printer? option so that users don't have to set a printer for each application. The first time that you add a printer to the print server, this option doesn't appear because the printer is automatically selected as the default printer.
Share As	A share name that users (with the appropriate permission) can use to make a connection to the printer over the network. This name appears when users browse for a printer or supply a path to a printer.
	Ensure that the share name is compatible with the naming conventions for all client computers on the network. By default, the share name is the printer name truncated to an 8.3 character filename. If you use a share name that is longer than an 8.3 character filename, some client computers might not be able to connect.
Location	Information about the print device's location. Provide information that helps users determine whether the print device fits their needs.
Comment	Users can search Active Directory directory services for the information that you enter here or in the Location box. Because of this search capability, you should standardize the type of information that you enter so that users can compare printers in search results.
Do You Want To Print A Test Page?	Verification that you have installed the printer correctly. Select the Yes option button to print a test page.

Adding and Sharing a Printer for a Network-Interface Print Device

In larger companies, most print devices are network-interface print devices. These print devices offer several advantages. You don't need to locate print devices with the print server. In addition, network connections transfer data more quickly than printer cable connections.

You add a printer for a network-interface print device by using the Add Printer wizard. The main differences between adding a printer for a local print device and adding a printer for a network-interface print device is that for a typical net-work-interface print device, you provide additional port and network protocol information.

The default network protocol for Windows 2000 is TCP/IP, which many network-interface print devices use. For TCP/IP, you provide additional port information in the Add Standard TCP/IP Printer Port wizard.

Figure 12.3 shows the Select The Printer Port page of the Add Printer wizard, and Table 12.3 describes the options on the Select The Printer Port page that per-tain to adding a network-interface print device.

Figure 12.3   The Select The Printer Port page of the Add Printer wizard

Table 12.3   Select The Printer Port Page Options That Affect Adding a Network-Interface Print Device

Option	Description
Create A New Port	This selection starts the process of creating a new port for the print server to which the network-interface print device is connected. In this case, the new port points to the network connection of the print device.
Type	This selection determines the network protocol to use for the connection. If you select Standard TCP/IP Port, it will start the Add Standard TCP/IP Printer Port wizard.

Figure 12.4 shows the Add Port page of the Add Standard TCP/IP Printer Port wizard, and Table 12.4 describes the options on the Add Port page of the Add Standard TCP/IP Printer Port wizard.

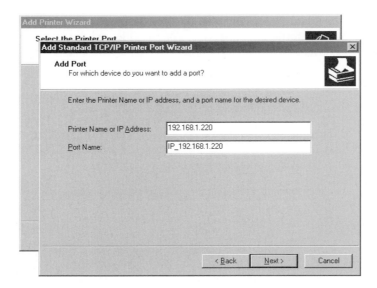

Figure 12.4   The Add Port page of the Add Standard TCP/IP Printer Port wizard

Table 12.4   Select The Printer Port Page Options That Affect Adding a Network-Interface Print Device

Option	Description
Printer Name Or IP Address	The network location of the print device. You must enter either the IP address or a DNS name of the network-interface print device.
	If you provide an IP address, Windows 2000 automatically supplies a suggested port name for the print device in the form IP_*IPaddress*.
	If Windows 2000 can't connect to and identify the network-interface print device, you must supply additional information about the type of print device. To enable automatic identification, make sure that the print device is powered on and connected to the network.
Port Name	The name that Windows 2000 assigns to the port that you created and defined. You can enter a different name.
	After you create the port, Windows 2000 displays it on the Select The Printer Port page of the Add Printer wizard. You don't have to redefine the port if you point additional printers to the same print device.

Note If your print device uses a network protocol other than TCP/IP, you must install the network protocol before you can add a printer for this device. After you install the protocol, you can add additional ports that use the protocol. The tasks and setup information that are required to configure a printer port depend on the network protocol.

Setting Up Client Computers

After you add and share a printer, you need to set up client computers so that users can print. Although the tasks to set up client computers vary depending on which operating systems are running on the client computers, all client computers require that a printer driver be installed.

The following summarizes the installation of printer drivers according to the computer's operating system:

- Windows 2000 automatically downloads the printer drivers for client computers running Windows 2000, Windows NT version 4 and earlier, Windows 98, or Windows 95.

- Client computers running other Microsoft operating systems require installation of printer drivers.

- Client computers running non-Microsoft operating systems require installation of both printer drivers and the print service on the print server.

Client Computers Running Windows 2000, Windows NT, Windows 98, or Windows 95

Users of client computers running Windows 2000, Windows NT, Windows 98, and Windows 95 need to make a connection only to the shared printer. The client computer automatically downloads the appropriate printer driver, as long as a copy of it resides on the print server.

If your client computer is running Windows 2000 and you want to make a connection to the shared printer, on the client computer, start the Add Printer wizard. On the Local Or Network Printer page (see Figure 12.2), select Network Printer, and then click Next. The Locate Your Printer page appears (see Figure 12.5).

Figure 12.5   The Locate Your Printer page

If you aren't sure what the name of the shared printer is, you can browse for it by leaving the Name box blank and clicking Next. The Browse For Printer page appears (see Figure 12.6).

Figure 12.6   The Browse For Printer page

Once you have located the shared printer and selected it, click Next and you will be asked whether it should be the default printer. If you want it to be the default printer, click Yes; otherwise, click No and then click Next. The Completing The Add Printer Wizard page appears. Check over the information and then click Finish. You have successfully made a connection from your client computer to the shared printer.

Client Computers Running Other Microsoft Operating Systems

For client computers running other Microsoft operating systems (such as Windows 3.*x* or MS-DOS) to print to a shared Windows 2000–based printer, you must manually install a printer driver on the client computer. You can get the appropriate printer driver for a Windows-based client computer from the installation disks for that client computer or from the printer manufacturer.

Client Computers Running Non-Microsoft Operating Systems

To enable users of client computers running non-Microsoft operating systems to print, the print server must have additional services installed on it. Table 12.5 lists services that are required for Macintosh and UNIX client computers or computers running a NetWare client.

Table 12.5   Services Required for Client Computers Running Non-Microsoft Operating Systems

Client computer	Required services
Macintosh	Services for Macintosh are included only with Windows 2000 Server, not Windows 2000 Professional.
UNIX	TCP/IP Printing, which is also called Line Printer Daemon (LPD) Service, is included with Windows 2000 Server but is not installed by default.
NetWare	File and Print Services for NetWare (FPNW), an optional add-on service for Windows 2000 Server, isn't included with Windows 2000 Server or Windows 2000 Professional.

Practice: Installing a Network Printer

In this practice, you will use the Add Printer wizard to install and share a local printer. By sharing the printer, it becomes available to other users on the network. You will also take the printer offline and then print a document. Printing a document with the printer offline loads the document into the print queue.

Exercise 1: Adding and Sharing a Printer

In this exercise, you will use the Add Printer wizard to add a local printer to your computer and share it.

▶ **To add a local printer**

1. Log on as Administrator.

2. Click the Start button, point to Settings, and then click Printers.

   Windows 2000 displays the Printers window. If you added a fax modem, a Fax icon appears in the Printers system folder.

3. Double-click Add Printer.

4. In the Add Printer Wizard, click Next.

   The Add Printer wizard prompts you for the location of the printer. Because you are creating the printer on the computer at which you are sitting and not on a different computer, this printer is referred to as a local printer.

5. Click Local Printer, ensure that the Automatically Detect And Install My Plug And Play Printer check box is not selected, and then click Next.

   Which port types are available depends on the installed network protocols. For this exercise, assume that the print device that you are adding is directly attached to your computer and using the LPT1 port.

Note If the print device is connected to a port that is not listed, click Other, and then enter the port type.

---

6. Verify that the Use The Following Port option is selected, and then under Use The Following Port, select LPT1.

7. Click Next.

   The wizard prompts you for the printer manufacturer and model. You will add an HP LaserJet 5Si printer.

Tip The list of printers is sorted in alphabetical order. If you can't find a printer name, make sure that you are looking in the correct location.

---

8. Under Manufacturers, click HP; under Printers, click HP LaserJet 5Si; and then click Next.

   The wizard displays the Name Your Printer page. In the Printer Name box, Windows 2000 automatically defaults to the printer name HP LaserJet 5Si. For this exercise, do not change this name.

9. If other printers are already installed, the wizard will also ask whether you want to make this the default printer. If the wizard displays the message, Do You Want Your Windows-Based Programs To Use This Printer As The Default Printer?, click Yes.

10. To accept the default printer name, click Next.

    The Printer Sharing page appears, prompting you for printer sharing information.

▶ **To share a printer**

1. In the Add Printer Wizard, on the Printer Sharing page, select the Share As option.

   Notice that you can assign a shared printer name, even though you already supplied a printer name. The shared printer name is used to identify a printer on the network and must conform to a naming convention. This shared name is different from the printer name that you entered previously. The printer name is a description that will appear with the printer's icon in the Printers system folder and in Active Directory directory services.

2. In the Share As box, type **Printer1** and then click Next.

   The Location And Comment page appears.

   Note If your computer running Windows 2000 Professional is part of a domain, Windows 2000 displays the values that you enter for Location and Comment when a user searches Active Directory directory services for a printer. Entering this information is optional, but it can help users locate the printer more easily.
   ---

3. In the Location box, type **Third Floor East** and in the Comment box, type **Mail Room**, and click Next.

   The Print Test Page page appears, prompting you whether you want to print a test page.

4. Click No and then click Next.

   The wizard displays the Completing The Add Printer Wizard page and provides a summary of your installation choices.

   Note As you review the summary, you might notice an error in the information you entered. To modify these settings, click Back.
   ---

5. Confirm the summary of your installation choices, and then click Finish.

   Windows 2000 will either copy files from the *systemroot* folder or display the Files Needed dialog box, prompting you for the location of the Windows 2000 Professional distribution files. If the Files Needed dialog box appears, continue with step 6; otherwise, Windows 2000 creates the shared printer and displays an icon for the HP LaserJet 5Si printer in the Printers window. In this case, you can skip steps 6–8.

6. Insert the Windows 2000 Professional CD-ROM, and wait for about 10 seconds.

7. If Windows displays the Windows 2000 CD-ROM window, close it.

8. Click OK to close the Insert Disk dialog box.

Windows 2000 copies the printer files and creates the shared printer. An icon for the HP LaserJet 5Si printer appears in the Printers window.

Notice that Windows 2000 displays an open hand under the printer icon. This indicates that the printer is shared. Notice also the check mark just above the printer, which indicates that the printer is the default printer.

Exercise 2: Taking a Printer Offline and Printing a Test Document

In this exercise, you will take the printer that you created offline. Taking a printer offline causes documents that you send to this printer to be held on the computer while the print device is not available. Doing this will eliminate error messages about unavailable print devices in later exercises. Windows 2000 will display such error messages when it attempts to send documents to a print device that isn't connected to the computer.

▶ **To take a printer offline**

1. In the Printers window, click the HP LaserJet 5Si icon.

2. On the File menu, click Use Printer Offline.

   Notice that Windows 2000 changes the icon to reflect that the printer is not available, and that the Status of the printer states Use Printer Offline.

▶ **To print a test document**

1. In the Printers window, double-click the HP LaserJet 5Si icon.

   Notice that the list of documents to be sent to the print device is empty.

2. Click the Start button, point to Programs, point to Accessories, and then click Notepad.

3. In Notepad, type any text that you want.

4. Arrange Notepad and the HP LaserJet 5Si window so that you can see the contents of each.

5. In Notepad, on the File menu, click Print.

   The Print dialog box appears, allowing you to select the printer and print options.

   Note Many programs running under Windows 2000 use the same Print dialog box.

   The Print dialog box displays the location and comment information that you entered when you created the printer, and it shows that the printer is currently offline. You can also use this dialog box to search Active Directory directory services for a printer.

   Notice that HP LaserJet 5Si is selected as the printer.

6. Click Print.

Notepad briefly displays a message, stating that the document is printing on your computer. On a fast computer, you might not be able to see this message.

In the HP LaserJet 5Si window, you will see the document waiting to be sent to the print device. Windows 2000 holds the document because you took the printer offline. Otherwise, Windows 2000 would have sent the document to the print device.

7. Close Notepad and click No when prompted to save changes to your document.

8. Because we don't want to print the document sitting in the print queue, select the document in the HP LaserJet 5Si window, and select Cancel All Documents from the Printer menu.

A Printers dialog box appears asking if you are sure you want to cancel all the documents.

9. Click Yes.

The document is removed from the HP LaserJet 5Si window.

10. Close the HP LaserJet 5Si and Printers windows.

Lesson Summary

In this lesson, you learned that to set up and share a printer for a local print device or for a network-interface print device, you use the Add Printer wizard in the Printers folder. Sharing a local printer makes it possible for multiple users on the network to print to it.

You also learned that users of client computers running Windows 2000, Windows NT, Windows 98, or Windows 95 need to make a connection only to the shared printer to be able to print. The client computer automatically downloads the appropriate printer driver, as long as a copy of it exists on the print server. For client computers running other Microsoft operating systems (such as Windows 3.x or MS-DOS) to print to a shared Windows 2000–based printer, you must manually install a printer driver on the client computer. You can get the appropriate printer driver for a Windows-based client computer from the installation disks for that client computer or from the printer manufacturer. To enable users of client computers running non-Microsoft operating systems to print, the print server must have additional services installed on it.

Lesson 3: Connecting to Network Printers

After you have set up the print server with all required printer drivers for the shared printers, users on client computers running Windows 2000, Windows NT, Windows 98, and Windows 95 can easily make a connection and start printing. For most Windows-based client computers, if the appropriate printer drivers are on the print server, the client computer automatically downloads the printer when the user makes a connection to the printer.

When you add and share a printer, by default, all users can make a connection to that printer and print documents. The method that is used to make a connection to a printer depends on the client computer. Client computers running Windows 2000, Windows NT, Windows 98, or Windows 95 can use the Add Printer Wizard, although the Add Printer Wizard in Windows 2000 provides more features than in the earlier versions. Client computers running Windows 2000 can also use a Web browser to make a connection to the printer.

After this lesson, you will be able to

- Make a connection to a network printer by using the Add Printer Wizard or a Web browser.

Estimated lesson time: 10 minutes

Using the Add Printer Wizard

The Add Printer Wizard is one method that client computers running Windows 2000, Windows NT, Windows 98, or Windows 95 can use to connect to a printer. This is the same wizard that you use to add and share a printer. The options that are available in the Add Printer Wizard that allow you to locate and connect to a printer vary depending on the operating system that the client computer is running (see Figure 12.7).

Client Computers Running Windows 2000

By using the Add Printer Wizard on client computers running Windows 2000, you can make a connection to a printer by using the following methods:

- Use the UNC name.

  You can use the UNC name (*print_server**printer_name*) to make connections by selecting Type The Printer Name Or Click Next To Browse For A Printer on the Locate Your Printer page of the Add Printer Wizard. If you know the UNC name, this can be a quick method to use.

- Browse the network.

  You can also browse the network for the printer by selecting Type The Printer Name Or Click Next To Browse For A Printer on the Locate Your Printer page of the Add Printer Wizard, leaving the Name box blank, and clicking Next.

- Use the URL name.

  You can also connect to a printer on the Internet or your intranet by selecting Connect To A Printer On The Internet Or On Your Intranet on the Locate Your Printer page of the Add Printer Wizard.

- Search Active Directory directory services.

  If your computer running Windows 2000 Professional is a member of a domain, you can find the printer by using Active Directory directory services' search capabilities. You can search either the entire Directory or just a portion of it. You can also narrow the search by providing features of the printer, such as color printing.

Figure 12.7   Using the Add Printer Wizard to locate and connect to a network printer

Client Computers Running Windows NT 4, Windows 98, or Windows 95

On client computers running Windows NT 4, Windows 98, or Windows 95, the Add Printer Wizard allows you only to enter a UNC name or to browse Network Neighborhood to locate the printer.

Note You can also make a connection to a printer by using the Run command on the Start menu. Type the UNC name of the printer in the Open box, and click OK.

Client Computers Running Other Microsoft Operating Systems

Users at client computers running Windows 3.*x* and Windows for Workgroups use Print Manager instead of the Add Printer Wizard to make a connection to a printer.

Users at any Windows-based client computer can make a connection to a network printer by using the following command:

```
net use lptx: \\server_name\share_name
```

where *x* is the number of the printer port.

The Net Use command is also the only method that is available for making a connection to a network printer from client computers running MS-DOS or OS/2 with Microsoft LAN Manager client software installed.

Using a Web Browser

If you're using a client computer running Windows 2000, you can make a connection to a printer through your corporate intranet. You can type a URL in your Web browser, and you don't have to use the Add Printer Wizard. After you make a connection, Windows 2000 automatically copies the correct printer drivers to the client computer.

A Web designer can customize this Web page, such as displaying a floor plan that shows the location of print devices to which users can connect. There are two ways to make a connection to a printer by using a Web browser:

- http://*server_name*/printers

  This Web page lists all of the shared printers on the print server that you have permission to use. The page contains information about the printers, including the printer name, status of print jobs, location, model, and any comments that were entered when the printer was installed. This information helps you select the correct printer for your needs. You must have permission to use the printer.

- http://server_name/printer_share_name

  You provide the intranet path for a specific printer. You must have permission to use the printer.

Downloading Printer Drivers

When users at client computers running Windows 2000, Windows NT, Windows 98, or Windows 95 make the first connection to a printer on the print server, the client computer automatically downloads the printer driver. The print server must have a copy of the printer driver.

Thereafter, client computers running Windows 2000 and Windows NT verify that they have the current printer driver each time that they print. If not, they download the new printer driver. For these client computers, you need to update printer drivers only on the print server. Client computers running Windows 98 or Windows 95 don't check for updated printer drivers. You must manually install updated printer drivers.

Lesson Summary

In this lesson, you learned that client computers running Windows 2000, Windows NT, Windows 98, or Windows 95 can use the Add Printer Wizard to connect to a printer. On client computers running Windows 2000, you can make a connection to a printer by using Active Directory directory services' search capabilities, or you can select Connect To The Printer Using A Network Name on the Locate Your Printers page of the Add Printer Wizard. If you know the UNC name, you can use it, or you can browse the network for the printer.

On client computers running Windows NT 4, Windows 98, or Windows 95, the Add Printer Wizard only allows you to enter a UNC name or to browse Network Neighborhood to locate the printer. Users at client computers running Windows 3.x and Windows for Workgroups use Print Manager to make a connection to a printer.

You also learned that users at any Windows-based client computer can make a connection to a network printer by using the Net Use command. The Net Use command is also the only method that is available for making a connection to a network printer from client computers running MS-DOS or OS/2 with Microsoft LAN Manager client software installed.

Lesson 4: Configuring Network Printers

After you have set up and shared network printers, user and company printing needs might require you to configure printer settings so that your printing resources fit these needs better.

Three common configuration changes you can make are as follows:

- You can share an existing nonshared printer if your printing load increases.

- You can create a printer pool so that the printer automatically distributes print jobs to the first available print device. Then users don't have to search for an available printer.

- You can set priorities between printers so that critical documents always print before noncritical documents.

After this lesson, you will be able to

- Share an existing printer.
- Create a printer pool.
- Set priorities between printers.

Estimated lesson time: 15 minutes

Sharing an Existing Printer

If the printing demands on your network increase and your network has an existing, nonshared printer for a print device, you can share it so that users can print to the print device.

When you share a printer

- You need to assign the printer a share name, which appears in My Network Places. Use an intuitive name to help users when they are browsing for a printer.

- You can add printer drivers for all versions of Windows NT, for Windows 95 and Windows 98, and for Windows 2000 and Windows NT running on different hardware platforms.

Use the Sharing tab, in the Properties dialog box for the printer, to share an existing printer (see Figure 12.8).

Figure 12.8 The Sharing Tab in the Properties dialog box for a printer

You can access the Sharing tab in a printer's Properties dialog box as follows:

1. In the Printers folder, click the icon for the printer that you want to share.
2. On the File menu, click Properties.
3. In the Properties dialog box for the printer, click the Sharing tab.

After you have shared the printer, Windows 2000 puts an open hand under the printer icon, indicating that the printer is shared.

Setting Up a Printer Pool

A *printer pool* is one printer that is connected to multiple print devices through multiple ports on a print server. The print devices can be local or network-interface print devices. Print devices should be identical; however, you can use print devices that are not identical but that use the same printer driver. (See Figure 12.9.)

When you create a printer pool, users can print documents without having to find out which print device is available—the printer checks for an available port.

Note When you set up a printer pool, place the print devices in the same physical area so that users can easily locate their documents.

- One printer with multiple identical print devices
- Local or network-interface print devices
- Document goes to first available print device

Figure 12.9   A printer pool

A printer pool has the following advantages:

- In a network with a high volume of printing, it decreases the time that documents wait on the print server.
- It simplifies administration because you can administer multiple print devices from a single printer.

Before you create a printer pool, make sure that you connect the print devices to the print server.

You can create a printer pool by doing the following:

1. In the Properties dialog box for the printer, click the Ports tab.
2. Select the Enable Printer Pooling check box.
3. Select the check box for each port to which a print device that you want to add to the pool is connected, and then click OK.

Setting Priorities Between Printers

Setting priorities between printers makes it possible to set priorities between groups of documents that all print on the same print device. Multiple printers point to the same print device, which allows users to send critical documents to a high-priority printer and noncritical documents to a lower-priority printer. The critical documents always print first. Consider the following two methods to set priorities between printers:

- Point two or more printers to the same print device—that is, the same port. The port can be either a physical port on the print server or a port that points to a network-interface print device.

- Set a different priority for each printer that is connected to the print device, and then have different groups of users print to different printers, or have users send different types of documents to different printers.

For an example, see Figure 12.10. User1 sends documents to a printer with the lowest priority of 1, while User2 sends documents to a printer with the highest priority of 99. In this example, User2's documents always print before User1's.

Figure 12.10   A Printer pool with different priorities set

You can set the priority for a printer as follows:

1. In the Properties dialog box for the printer, click the Advanced tab.
2. In the Priority box, select the appropriate priority, and then click OK.

    Windows 2000 sets the priority for the printer.

Lesson Summary

In this lesson, you learned that to share an existing printer, you use the Sharing tab in the Properties dialog box for the printer and select Shared As. After you have shared the printer, Windows 2000 puts an open hand under the printer icon, indicating that the printer is shared.

You also learned that a printer pool is one printer that is connected to multiple print devices through multiple ports on a print server. The print devices in a printer pool should be identical; however, you can use print devices that aren't identical if all the print devices use the same printer driver. A printer pool can decrease the time that documents wait on the print server, and it simplifies administration because you can administer multiple print devices from a single printer. To create a printer pool, in the Properties dialog box for the printer, use the Ports tab to select the Enable Printer Pooling check box.

Setting priorities between printers makes it possible to set priorities between groups of documents that all print on the same print device. Multiple printers point to the same print device, which allows users to send critical documents to a high-priority printer and noncritical documents to a lower-priority printer. The critical documents always print first.

Lesson 5: Troubleshooting Network Printers

During setup and configuration of a printer, problems can sometimes occur. This lesson introduces you to a few common problems that you might encounter and provides some suggested solutions.

After this lesson, you will be able to

- Troubleshoot network printing problems.

Estimated lesson time: 5 minutes

Common Troubleshooting Scenarios

Table 12.6 lists some of the common setup and configuration problems that you might encounter. It also lists some probable causes of the problems and some possible solutions.

Table 12.6   Common Printer Problems and Possible Solutions

Problem	Probable cause	Possible solution
Test page doesn't print. You have confirmed that the print device is connected and turned on.	The selected port is not correct.	Configure the printer for the correct port. For a printer that uses a network-interface print device, make sure that the network address is correct.
Test page or documents print incorrectly, as garbled text.	The installed printer driver is not correct.	Reinstall the printer with the correct printer driver.
Users report an error message that asks them to install a printer driver when they print to a print server running Windows 2000.	Printer drivers for the client computers are not installed on the print server.	On the print server, add the appropriate printer drivers for the client computers. Use the client computer's operating system CD-ROM or a printer driver from the vendor.
Documents from one client computer don't print, but documents from other client computers do.	The client computer is connected to the wrong printer.	On the client computer, remove the printer and then add the correct printer.
Documents print correctly on some print devices in a printer pool but not all of them.	The print devices in the printer pool are not identical.	Verify that all print devices in the printer pool are identical or that they use the same printer driver. Remove inappropriate devices.
Documents don't print in the right priority.	The printing priorities between printers are set incorrectly.	Adjust the printing priorities for the printers associated with the print device.

Lesson Summary

Troubleshooting is something you learn through experience. Certain problems can be solved based on the troubleshooting scenarios in this lesson or because you have encountered the problem before. However, in many cases you simply have to eliminate the possible causes one at a time until the problem is resolved.

Review

The following questions will help you determine whether you have learned enough to move on to the next chapter. If you have difficulty answering these questions, please go back and review the material in this chapter before beginning the next chapter. See Appendix A, "Questions and Answers," for the answers to these questions.

1. What's the difference between a printer and a print device?

2. A print server can connect to two different types of print devices. What are these two types of print devices, and what are the differences?

3. You have added and shared a printer. What must you do to set up client computers running Windows 2000 so that users can print, and why?

4. What advantages does connecting to a printer by using http://*server_name*/ printers provide for users?

5. Why would you connect multiple printers to one print device?

6. Why would you create a printer pool?

C H A P T E R   1 3

Administering Network Printers

About This Chapter

In this chapter, you will learn about setting up and administering network printers. You will learn how to manage printers and documents and how to troubleshoot common printing problems.

Before You Begin

To complete this chapter, you must have

- A computer that meets the minimum hardware requirements located in "About This Book."
- Microsoft Windows 2000 Professional installed on the computer.

Note You do *not* need a printer to complete the exercises in this chapter.

Lesson 1: Understanding Printer Administration

After your printing network is set up, you will be responsible for administering it. You can administer network printers at the print server or remotely over the network. In this lesson, you will learn about the four major types of tasks that are involved with administering network printers: managing printers, managing documents, troubleshooting printers, and performing tasks that require the Manage Printers permission. In this lesson, you will also learn that before you can administer printers, you must know how to access them and control access to them.

After this lesson, you will be able to

- Identify the tasks and requirements for administering a printer.
- Gain access to printers for administration.
- Assign printer permissions to user accounts and groups.

Estimated lesson time: 20 minutes

Managing Printers

One of the most important aspects of printer administration is managing printers. Managing printers includes the following tasks:

- Assigning forms to paper trays
- Setting a separator page
- Pausing, resuming, and canceling documents on a printer
- Redirecting documents
- Taking ownership of a printer

Managing Documents

A second major aspect of printer administration is managing documents. Managing documents includes the following tasks:

- Pausing and resuming a document
- Setting notification, priority, and printing time
- Deleting a document

Troubleshooting Printers

A third major aspect of printer administration is troubleshooting printers. Troubleshooting printers means identifying and resolving all printer problems. The types of problems you need to troubleshoot include the following:

- Handling printers that are off or offline
- Handling printers that are out of paper, ink, or toner
- Helping users who can't print or who can't print correctly
- Helping users who can't access a printer

Performing Tasks That Require the Manage Printers Permission

The following tasks involved with administering printers require the Manage Printers permission:

- Adding and removing printers
- Sharing printers
- Taking ownership of a printer
- Changing printer properties or permissions

By default, members of the Administrators and Power Users groups have the Manage Printers permission for all printers.

Accessing Printers

You can gain access to printers for administration by using the Printers window (shown in Figure 13.1), which you open by selecting the Start button, pointing to Settings, and clicking the Printers system folder. You can perform all administrative tasks by gaining access to the printer from the Printers window, as follows:

1. Click the Start button, point to Settings, and then click Printers.
2. In the Printers window, select the appropriate printer icon.
3. On the File menu
    - Click Open to open the printer's window to perform print document tasks.
    - Click Properties to open the Properties dialog box to change printer permissions or to edit Active Directory information about the printer.

Figure 13.1   Accessing printers using the Printers window

Setting Printer Permissions to Control Access

Windows 2000 allows you to control printer use and administration by assigning permissions. By using printer permissions, you can control who can use a printer. You can also assign printer permissions to control who can administer a printer and the level of administration, which can include managing printers and managing documents.

For security reasons, you might need to limit user access to certain printers. You can also use printer permissions to delegate responsibilities for specific printers to users who are not administrators. Windows 2000 provides three levels of printer permissions: Print, Manage Documents, and Manage Printers. Table 13.1 lists the capabilities of each level of permission.

Table 13.1   Printing Capabilities of Windows 2000 Printer Permissions

	Permissions		
Capabilities	**Print**	**Manage Documents**	**Manage Printers**
Print documents	✓	✓	✓
Pause, resume, restart, and cancel the user's own document	✓	✓	✓
Connect to a printer	✓	✓	✓
Control job settings for all documents		✓	✓

Capabilities	Print	Permissions Manage Documents	Manage Printers
Pause, resume, restart, and cancel all other users' documents		✓	✓
Cancel all documents			✓
Share a printer			✓
Change printer properties			✓
Delete a printer			✓
Change printer permissions			✓

You can allow or deny printer permissions. Denied permissions always override allowed permissions. For example, if you select the Deny check box next to Manage Documents for the Everyone group, no one can manage documents, even if you granted this permission to another user account or group. This is because all user accounts are members of the Everyone group.

Assigning Printer Permissions

By default, Windows 2000 assigns the Print permission for each printer to the built-in Everyone group, allowing all users to send documents to the printer. You can also assign printer permissions to users or groups, as follows:

1. Open the Properties dialog box for the printer, click the Security tab, and then click Add.
2. In the Select Users, Computers, Or Groups dialog box, select the appropriate user account or group, and then click Add. Repeat this step for all users or groups that you are adding.
3. Click OK.
4. On the Security tab, shown in Figure 13.2, select a user account or group, and then do one of the following:

   - Click the permissions in the bottom part of the dialog box that you want to assign.
   - Click Advanced, assign additional printer permissions that don't fit into the predefined permissions on the Security tab, and then click OK.

   The bottom part of the dialog box shows the permissions granted to the user or group selected in the upper part.

5. Click OK to close the Properties dialog box.

Figure 13.2   Assigning printer permissions

Modifying Printer Permissions

You can change the default printer permissions that Windows 2000 assigned, or that you previously assigned for any user or group, as follows:

1. Open the Printers window.

2. Right-click the printer and choose Properties.

3. On the Security tab of the Properties dialog box for the printer, select the appropriate user account or group, and then do one of the following:

   ■ Click the permissions that you want to change for the user or group.

   ■ Click Advanced to modify additional printer permissions that don't fit into the predefined permissions on the Security tab.

4. Click OK.

Lesson Summary

In this lesson, you learned that administering printers involves four major types of tasks: managing printers, managing documents, troubleshooting printers, and performing tasks that require the Manage Printers permission. You gain access to printers for administration by selecting the Start button, pointing to settings, and selecting the Printers system folder.

You also learned that Windows 2000 allows you to control printer use and administration by assigning permissions. You might need to limit access to certain printers—for example, a printer used to print checks. You can also use printer permissions to delegate responsibilities for specific printers to users who are not administrators.

Lesson 2: Managing Printers

Managing printers includes assigning forms to paper trays and setting a separator page. In addition, you can pause, resume, and cancel a document if a problem occurs on a print device. If a print device is faulty or you add print devices to your network, you might need to redirect documents to a different printer. In addition, you might need to change who has administrative responsibility for printers, which involves changing ownership.

After this lesson, you will be able to

- Assign forms to paper trays.
- Set a separator page.
- Pause, resume, and cancel documents on a printer.
- Redirect documents to a different printer.
- Take ownership of a printer.

Estimated lesson time: 30 minutes

Assigning Forms to Paper Trays

If a print device has multiple trays that regularly hold different paper sizes, you can assign a form to a specific tray. A *form* defines a paper size. Users can then select the paper size from within their application. When the user prints, Windows 2000 automatically routes the print job to the paper tray that holds the correct form. Examples of forms include the following: Legal, A4, Envelope #10, and Letter Small.

You can assign a form to a paper tray as follows:

1. Right-click the icon of the appropriate printing device, and then click Properties.
2. In the Properties dialog box for the printer, click the Device Settings tab.
3. In the drop-down list box next to each paper tray, click the form for the tray's paper type, as shown in Figure 13.3.
4. Click OK.

After you have set up a paper tray, users specify the paper size from within applications. Windows 2000 knows in which paper tray the form is located.

Figure 13.3   Setting forms for a printer

Setting a Separator Page

A *separator page* is a file that contains print device commands. Separator pages have two functions:

- To identify and separate printed documents.

- To switch print devices between print modes. Some print devices can switch between print modes that take advantage of different device features. You can use separator pages to specify the correct page description language. For example, you can specify PostScript or Printer Control Language (PCL) for a print device that can switch between different print modes but cannot automatically detect which language a print job uses.

Windows 2000 includes four separator page files. They are located in the *systemroot*\System32 folder. Table 13.2 lists the filename and describes the function for each of the included separator page files.

Table 13.2   Separator Page Files

Filename	Function
Sysprint.sep	Prints a page before each document. Compatible with PostScript print devices.
Pcl.sep	Switches the print mode to PCL for HP-series print devices and prints a page before each document.
Pscript.sep	Switches the print mode to PostScript for HP-series print devices but doesn't print a page before each document.
Sysprtj.sep	A version of Sysprint.sep that uses Japanese characters.

Once you have decided to use a separator page and have chosen an appropriate one, you use the Advanced tab in the printer's Properties dialog box to have the separator page printed at the beginning of each print job.

You can set up a separator page as follows:

1. On the Advanced tab in the Properties dialog box for the printer, click Separator Page.
2. In the Separator Page box, type the name of the separator page file. You can also browse for the file.
3. Click OK, and then click OK again.

Pausing, Resuming, and Canceling Documents

Pausing and resuming a printer or canceling all documents on a printer might be necessary if a printing problem occurs.

To pause or cancel all documents, right-click a printing device in the Printers folder, and then click the appropriate command. To resume printing, right-click the printer, and click Pause Printer to deselect it.

Table 13.3 describes the tasks that you might perform when you manage printers, how to perform the tasks, and examples of situations in which you might perform these tasks.

Table 13.3   Managing Printers Tasks

Task	Action	Example
To pause printing	Click Pause Printing. A check mark appears next to the Pause Printing command, which indicates that the printer is paused.	Pause the printer if a problem occurs with the printer or print device until you fix the problem.
To resume printing	Click Pause Printing. The check mark next to the Pause Printing command disappears, which indicates that the printer is active.	Resume printing after you fix a problem with a printer or print device

Task	Action	Example
To cancel all documents	Click Cancel All Documents. All documents are deleted from the printer.	Cancel all documents when you need to clear a print queue after old documents that no longer need to print have accumulated.

Note You can also pause a printer by taking the printer offline. When you take a printer offline, documents stay in the print queue, even when the print server is shut down and then restarted. To take a printer offline, open the printer's window and on the Printer menu, click Use Printer Offline.

Redirecting Documents to a Different Printer

You can redirect documents to a different printer. For example, if a printer is connected to a faulty print device, redirect the documents so that users don't need to resubmit them. You can redirect all print jobs for a printer, but you can't redirect specific documents. The new printer must use the same printer driver as the current printer.

You can redirect documents to a different printer as follows:

1. Open the Printers window, right-click the printer, and then click Properties.
2. In the Properties dialog box, click the Ports tab.
3. Click Add Port.
4. In the Available Port Types list, click Local Port, and then click the New Port button.
5. In the Port Name dialog box, in the Enter A Port Name box, type the UNC name for the printer to which you are redirecting documents (for example, \\prntsrv6\HPLaser5), as shown in Figure 13.4.
6. Click OK to close the Port Name dialog box.
7. Click Close to close the Printer Ports dialog box.
8. Click Close to close the printer's Properties dialog box.

If another print device is available for the current print server, you can continue to use the same printer and configure the printer to use the other print device. To configure a printer to use another local or network print device that uses the same printer driver, select the appropriate port on the print server and cancel the selection of the current port.

Figure 13.4   Redirecting documents to another printer

Taking Ownership of a Printer

Sometimes, the owner of a printer can no longer manage that printer and you will need to take ownership. Taking ownership of a printer enables you to change administrative responsibility for a printer. By default, the user who installed the printer owns it. If that user can no longer administer the printer, you should take ownership of it—for example, if the current owner leaves the company.

The following users can take ownership of a printer:

- A user or a member of a group who has the Manage Printers permission for the printer.

- Members of the Administrators and Power Users groups. By default, these groups have the Manage Printers permission, which allows them to take ownership.

You can take ownership of a printer as follows:

1. In the Properties dialog box for the printer, click the Security tab, and then click Advanced.

2. In the Access Control Settings dialog box, click the Owner tab, and then click your user account under Change Owner To, as shown in Figure 13.5.

Note If you are a member of the Administrators group and you want the Administrators group to take ownership of the printer, click the Administrators group.

---

3. Click OK, and then click Close.

Figure 13.5   Taking ownership of a printer

Practice: Performing Printer Management

In this practice, you will perform three tasks that are part of managing printers. In the first exercise, you will assign forms to paper trays. In the second exercise, you will set up a separator page. In the third exercise, you will learn how to take ownership of a printer.

Exercise 1: Assigning Forms to Paper Trays

In this exercise, you will assign a paper type (form) to a paper tray so that when users print to a specified form, the print job is automatically routed to and adjusted for the correct tray.

▶ **To assign forms to paper trays**

1. Click Start, point to Settings, and select Printers.

2. Right-click the icon for your printer, and then click Properties.

3. In the Properties dialog box, click the Device Settings tab.

   Notice that there are multiple selections under Form To Tray Assignment. Some of the selections are labeled Not Available because they depend on options that aren't installed.

4. Click Lower Paper Tray, and then select Legal.

   Whenever a user prints on legal size paper, Windows 2000 will instruct the printer to use paper from the lower paper tray.

5. Click Apply and leave the Properties dialog box open for the next exercise.

Exercise 2: Setting Up Separator Pages

In this exercise, you will set up a separator page to print between documents. This separator page includes the user's name and the date and time that the document was printed.

▶ **To set up a separator page**

1. Click the Advanced tab of the Properties dialog box.

2. Click Separator Page.

   The Separator Page dialog box appears.

3. In the Separator Page dialog box, click Browse.

   Windows 2000 displays another Separator Page dialog box.

4. Select Sysprint.sep, and then click Open.

   The selected separator page file's path appears in the first Separator Page dialog box.

5. Click OK.

   Windows 2000 will now print a separator page between print jobs.

6. Leave the Properties dialog box open for the next exercise.

Exercise 3: Taking Ownership of a Printer

In this exercise, you will practice taking ownership of a printer.

▶ **To take ownership of a printer**

1. Click the Security tab of the Properties dialog box.

2. On the Security tab, click Advanced, and then click the Owner tab.

   Who currently owns the printer?

3. To take ownership of the printer, select another user in the Name box.

4. If you actually wanted to take ownership, you would click Apply now, but click Cancel instead to leave the ownership unchanged.

5. Click OK to close the Properties dialog box, close the Printers window, and then log off Windows 2000.

Lesson Summary

In this lesson, you learned that managing printers includes assigning forms to paper trays; setting a separator page; pausing, resuming, and canceling documents on a printer; redirecting documents to a different printer; and taking ownership of a printer. In the practice portion, you assigned a form to a paper tray and set up a separator page. In addition, you learned how to change who has administrative responsibility for printers, which involves changing ownership.

Lesson 3: Managing Documents

In addition to managing printers, Windows 2000 allows you to manage documents. Managing documents includes pausing, resuming, restarting, and canceling a document if a printing problem occurs. In addition, you can set someone to notify when a print job is finished, set the priority to allow a critical document to print before other documents, and set a specific time for a document to print.

After this lesson, you will be able to

- Pause, resume, restart, and cancel the printing of a document.
- Set a notification, priority, and printing time.
- Delete a document from the print queue.

Estimated lesson time: 20 minutes

Pausing, Restarting, and Canceling a Document

If a printing problem occurs with a specific document, you can pause and resume printing of the document. Additionally, you can restart or cancel a document. You must have the Manage Documents permission for the appropriate printer to perform these actions. Because the creator of a document has the default permissions to manage that document, users can perform any of these actions on their own documents.

To manage a document, right-click the printing device for the document and click Open. Select the appropriate document(s), click the Document menu, and then click the appropriate command to pause, resume, restart from the beginning, or cancel a document, as shown in Figure 13.6.

Figure 13.6   Managing documents

Table 13.4 describes the tasks that you might perform when you manage individual documents, how to perform the tasks, and examples of situations in which you might perform these tasks.

Table 13.4   Managing Document Tasks

Task	Action	Example
To pause printing a document	Select the documents for which you want to pause printing, and then click Pause. (The status changes to Paused.)	Pause printing of a document when a problem occurs with the document.
To resume printing a document	Select the documents for which you want to resume printing, and then click Resume. (The status changes to Printing.)	Resume printing of the document after you fix the problem with the paused document.
To restart printing a document	Select the documents for which you want to restart printing, and then click Restart. Restart causes printing to start from the beginning of the document.	Restart printing of a partially printed document after you fix a problem with the document or the print device.
To cancel printing a document	Select the documents for which you want to cancel printing, and then click Cancel. You can also cancel a document by pressing the Delete key.	When a document has the wrong printer settings or is no longer needed, delete it before it prints.

Setting Notification, Priority, and Printing Time

You can control print jobs by setting the notification, priority, and printing time. To perform these document management tasks, you must have the Manage Documents permission for the appropriate printer.

You set the notification, priority, and printing time for a document on the General tab of the Properties dialog box for the document, as shown in Figure 13.7. To open the Properties dialog box for one or more documents, first select the documents in the printer's window, click the Document menu, and then click Properties.

Table 13.5 describes the tasks that you might perform when you control print jobs, how to perform the tasks, and examples of situations in which you might perform these tasks.

Figure 13.7   Setting notification, priority, and printing time for a document

Table 13.5   Setting a Notification, Changing Priority, and Scheduling Print Times

Task	Action	Example
Set a notification	In the Notify box, type the logon name of the user who should receive the notification. By default, Windows 2000 enters the name of the user who printed the document.	Change the print notification when someone other than the user who printed the document needs to retrieve it.
Change a document priority	Move the Priority slider to the priority that you want. The highest priority is 99 and the lowest is 1.	Change a priority so that a critical document prints before other documents.
Schedule print times	To restrict print times, click Only From in the Schedule section, and then set the hours between which you want the document to print.	Set the print time for a large document so that it will print during off hours, such as late at night.

Practice: Managing Documents

In this practice, you will manage documents by printing a document, setting a notification for a document, changing the priority for a document, and then canceling a document.

▶ **To verify that a printer is offline**

1. Log on as Administrator.
2. Click the Start button, point to Settings, and then click Printers.
3. In the Printers window, click the printer's icon.

4. Do one of the following to verify that the printer is offline:

   ▪ On the File menu, verify that Use Printer Offline is selected.

   ▪ Right-click the printer icon and verify that Use Printer Offline is selected.

   ▪ If the Printers window is displayed in Web view, verify that Use Printer Offline is displayed in the left portion of the folder window.

5. On the File menu (or by right-clicking the printer's icon), verify that Set As Default Printer is selected.

   The printer's icon will display a check mark to show that it is the default. If necessary, press F5 to update the display.

6. Minimize the Printers window.

Note Keep the printer offline to prevent it from trying to communicate with a nonexistent print device. This will eliminate error messages in later exercises when documents are spooled.

▶ **To print a document**

1. Insert the Windows 2000 Professional CD-ROM in the CD-ROM drive.

2. When the Microsoft Windows 2000 CD dialog box appears, click Browse This CD.

3. Double-click Readme.doc.

   WordPad starts and displays the Readme.doc file.

4. Click File and click Print.

   The Print dialog box appears. Notice that the file will be printed on the HP Laserjet 5SI printer.

5. Click Print, and then close WordPad.

▶ **To set a notification**

1. Restore the Printers window.

2. Double-click HP LaserJet 5Si.

3. In the printer's window, select README.doc, and then click Properties on the Document menu.

   Windows 2000 displays the README.doc Document Properties dialog box with the General tab active.

   Which user is specified in the Notify box? Why?

Note To change the person to be notified, you would type in the name of the user in the Notify box and click apply.

▶ **To increase the priority of a document**

1. In the README.doc Document Properties dialog box, on the General tab, notice the default priority.

   What is the current priority? Is it the lowest or highest priority?

2. In the Priority box, move the slider to the right to increase the priority of the document, and then click OK.

   Nothing changes visibly in the HP LaserJet 5Si - Use Printer Offline window.

3. On the Printer menu, click Use Printer Offline to remove the check mark, and then immediately click Use Printer Offline again.

Note If Windows 2000 displays a Printers Folder dialog box with an error message informing you that the printer port is unavailable, finish the following procedure, and then, in the dialog box, click Cancel.

---

4. Check the status of README.doc to confirm that Windows 2000 has started to print this document.

▶ **To cancel printing of a document**

1. Select README.doc in the document list in the printer's window.

2. On the Document menu, click Cancel.

   Notice that the Status column changes to Deleting. Then README.doc is removed from the document list.

Tip You can also cancel a document by pressing the Delete key.

---

3. Close the printer's window, and then close the Printers window.

Lesson Summary

In this lesson, you learned that managing documents includes pausing, resuming, restarting, and canceling a document; setting who is notified when a print job is finished; setting the document priority to allow a critical document to print before other documents; and setting a specific time for a document to print. You must have the Manage Documents permission for the appropriate printer to perform these actions. The creator of a document has the default permissions to manage that document, so users can perform any of these actions on their own documents.

Lesson 4: Administering Printers Using a Web Browser

Windows 2000 enables you to manage printers from any computer running a Web browser, regardless of whether the computer is running Windows 2000 or has the correct printer driver installed. All management tasks that you perform with Windows 2000 management tools are the same when you use a Web browser. The difference in administering with a Web browser is the interface, which is a Web-based interface. To gain access to a printer by using a Web browser, the print server on which the printer resides must have IIS installed.

After this lesson, you will be able to

- Describe the advantages of administering printers using a Web browser.
- Describe how to administer printers using a Web browser.

Estimated lesson time: 5 minutes

Understanding Web Servers

A *Web server* is a computer that responds to requests from a user's browser. Shortcuts or links to a resource on a Web server from a user's computer are known as *Web folders* or *HTTP folders*. For a Web server to provide Web folders, the Web server must support one of the following protocols or extensions: the Web Extension Client (WEC) protocol, FrontPage extensions, or the Web Distributed Authoring and Versioning (WebDAV) protocol and IIS.

Using a Web Browser to Manage Printers

The following are the advantages of using a Web browser to manage printers:

- It allows you to administer printers from any computer running a Web browser, regardless of whether the computer is running Windows 2000 or has the correct printer driver installed.
- It allows you to customize the interface. For example, you can create your own Web page containing a floor plan with the locations of the printers and the links to the printers.
- It provides a summary page listing the status of all printers on a print server.
- It can report real-time print device data, such as whether the print device is in power-saving mode, if the printer driver makes such information available. This information isn't available from the Printers window.

Accessing Printers Using a Web Browser

If you want to gain access to all printers on a print server by using a Web browser, open the Web browser, and then in the Address box, type

```
http://print_server_name/printers
```

If you want to gain access to a specific printer by using a Web browser, open the Web browser, and then in the Address box, type

```
http://server_name/printer_share_name
```

Lesson Summary

This lesson showed you one benefit of using a Web browser to administer printers: it allows you to administer printers from any computer running a Web browser, regardless of whether the computer is running Windows 2000 or has the correct printer driver installed.

Lesson 5: Troubleshooting Common Printing Problems

In this lesson, you will learn about some common printing problems and how to troubleshoot them.

After this lesson, you will be able to

- Describe how to troubleshoot some common printing problems.

Estimated lesson time: 5 minutes

Examining the Problem

When you detect a printing problem, always verify that the print device is plugged in, that it is on, and that it is connected to the print server. For a network-interface print device, verify that a network connection exists between the print device and the print server.

To determine the cause of a problem, first try printing from a different program to verify that the problem is with the printer and not with the program. If the problem is with the printer, ask the following questions:

- Can other users print normally? If so, the problem is most likely caused by insufficient permissions, lack of a network connection, or client computer complications.

- Does the print server use the correct printer driver for the print device?

- Is the print server operational, and is enough disk space available for spooling?

- Does the client computer have the correct printer driver?

Reviewing Common Printing Problems

Certain printing problems are common to most network printing environments. Table 13.6 describes some of these common printing problems, as well as some possible causes and solutions.

Table 13.6   Common Printing Problems, Causes, and Solutions

Problem	Possible cause	Solution
A user receives an Access Denied message when trying to configure a printer from an application (for example, earlier versions of Microsoft Excel).	The user doesn't have the appropriate permission to change printer configurations.	Change the user's permission, or configure the printer for the user.
The document doesn't print completely or comes out garbled.	The printer driver is incorrect.	Install the correct printer driver.
The hard disk starts thrashing and the document doesn't reach the print server.	Hard disk space is insufficient for spooling.	Create more free space on the hard disk.

Lesson Summary

In this lesson, you learned about a few basic issues to check when you have a printing problem. You were also given a list of some common printing problems and some suggested causes and solutions. In many cases, you will find that in troubleshooting a problem, you must investigate the problem as thoroughly as you can and then begin trying logical solutions until you discover one that works.

Review

The following questions will help you determine whether you have learned enough to move on to the next chapter. If you have difficulty answering these questions, please go back and review the material in this chapter before beginning the next chapter. See Appendix A, "Questions and Answers," for the answers to these questions.

1. For which printer permission does a user need to change the priority on another user's document?

2. In an environment where many users print to the same print device, how can you help reduce the likelihood of users picking up the wrong documents?

3. Can you redirect a single document?

4. A user needs to print a large document. How can the user print the job after hours, without being present while the document prints?

5. What are the advantages of using a Web browser to administer printing?

C H A P T E R   1 4

Securing Resources with NTFS Permissions

About This Chapter

This chapter introduces you to Microsoft Windows 2000's New Technology File System (NTFS) folder and file permissions. You will learn how to assign NTFS folder and file permissions to user accounts and groups, and you will see how moving or copying files and folders affects NTFS file and folder permissions. You will also learn how to troubleshoot common resource access problems.

Before You Begin

To complete this chapter, you must have

- A computer that meets the minimum hardware requirements located in "About This Book."
- Microsoft Windows 2000 Professional installed on the computer.

Lesson 1: Understanding NTFS Permissions

You use NTFS permissions to specify which users and groups can gain access to files and folders and what they can do with the contents of the file or folder. NTFS permissions are available only on NTFS volumes. NTFS permissions are *not* available on volumes that are formatted with FAT or FAT32 file systems. NTFS security is effective whether a user gains access to the file or folder at the computer or over the network. The permissions you assign for folders are different from the permissions you assign for files.

After this lesson, you will be able to

- Define the standard NTFS folder and file permissions.

Estimated lesson time: 5 minutes

NTFS Folder Permissions

You assign folder permissions to control the access that users have to folders and to the files and subfolders that are contained within the folder.

Table 14.1 lists the standard NTFS folder permissions that you can assign and the type of access that each permission provides.

Table 14.1   NTFS Folder Permissions

NTFS folder permission	Allows the user to
Read	See files and subfolders in the folder and view folder ownership, permissions, and attributes (such as Read-Only, Hidden, Archive, and System).
Write	Create new files and subfolders within the folder, change folder attributes, and view folder ownership and permissions.
List Folder Contents	See the names of files and subfolders in the folder.
Read & Execute	Move through folders to reach other files and folders, even if the users don't have permission for those folders, and perform actions permitted by the Read permission and the List Folder Contents permission.
Modify	Delete the folder, plus perform actions permitted by the Write permission and the Read & Execute permission.
Full Control	Change permissions, take ownership, and delete subfolders and files, plus perform actions permitted by all other NTFS folder permissions.

You can deny permission to a user account or group. To deny all access to a user account or group for a folder, deny the Full Control permission.

NTFS File Permissions

You assign file permissions to control the access that users have to files. Table 14.2 lists the standard NTFS file permissions that you can assign and the type of access that each permission provides.

Table 14.2   NTFS File Permissions

NTFS file permission	Allows the user to
Read	Read the file, and view file attributes, ownership, and permissions.
Write	Overwrite the file, change file attributes, and view file ownership and permissions.
Read & Execute	Run applications, plus perform the actions permitted by the Read permission.
Modify	Modify and delete the file, plus perform the actions permitted by the Write permission and the Read & Execute permission.
Full Control	Change permissions and take ownership, plus perform the actions permitted by all other NTFS file permissions.

Lesson Summary

In this lesson, you learned that you use NTFS permissions to specify which users and groups can gain access to files and folders, and what these permissions allow users to do with the contents of the files or folders. NTFS permissions are available only on NTFS volumes. NTFS security is effective whether a user gains access to the file or folder at the computer or over the network. The folder permissions are Read, Write, List Folder Contents, Read & Execute, Modify, and Full Control. The file permissions are similar to the folder permissions. The file permissions are Read, Write, Read & Execute, Modify, and Full Control.

Lesson 2: Applying NTFS Permissions

Administrators, the owners of files or folders, and users with Full Control permission can assign NTFS permissions to users and groups to control access to files and folders.

After this lesson, you will be able to

- Describe the result when you combine user account and group permissions.
- Describe the result when folder permissions are different from those of the files in the folder.

Estimated lesson time: 5 minutes

Access Control List

NTFS stores an *access control list (ACL)* with every file and folder on an NTFS volume. The ACL contains a list of all user accounts and groups that have been granted access for the file or folder, as well as the type of access that they have been granted. When a user attempts to gain access to a resource, the ACL must contain an entry, called an *access control entry (ACE),* for the user account or a group to which the user belongs. The entry must allow the type of access that is requested (for example, Read access) for the user to gain access. If no ACE exists in the ACL, the user can't gain access to the resource.

Multiple NTFS Permissions

You can assign multiple permissions to a user account and to each group in which the user is a member. To assign permissions, you must understand the rules and priorities regarding how NTFS assigns and combines multiple permissions and NTFS permission inheritance.

Cumulative Permissions

A user's *effective permissions* for a resource are the sum of the NTFS permissions that you assign to the individual user account and to all of the groups to which the user belongs. If a user has Read permission for a folder and is a member of a group with Write permission for the same folder, the user has both Read and Write permission for that folder.

Overriding Folder Permissions with File Permissions

NTFS file permissions take priority over NTFS folder permissions. A user with access to a file will be able to gain access to the file even if he or she doesn't have access to the folder containing the file. A user can gain access to the files for which he or she has permissions by using the full *universal naming convention (UNC)* or local path to open the file from its respective application, even though the folder in which it resides will be invisible if the user has no corresponding folder permission. In other words, if you don't have permission to access the folder containing the file you want to access, you will have to know the full path to the file to access it. Without permission to access the folder, you can't see the folder, so you can't browse for the file you want to access.

Overriding Other Permissions with Deny

You can deny permission to a user account or group for a specific file, although this is not the recommended way to control access to resources. Denying a permission overrides all instances where that permission is allowed. Even if a user has permission to gain access to the file or folder as a member of a group, denying permission to the user blocks any other permission that the user might have (see Figure 14.1).

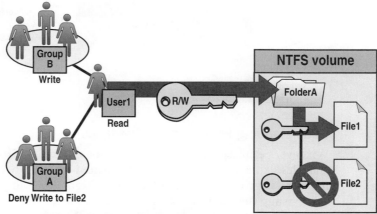

- NTFS permissions are cumulative.
- File permissions override folder permissions.
- Deny overrides other permissions.

Figure 14.1 Multiple NTFS permissions

In Figure 14.1, User1 has Read permission for FolderA and is a member of Group A and Group B. Group B has Write permission for FolderA. Group A has been denied Write permission for File2.

The user can read and write to File1. The user can also read File2, but she cannot write to File2 because she is a member of Group A, which has been denied Write permission for File 2.

NTFS Permissions Inheritance

By default, permissions that you assign to the parent folder are inherited by and propagated to the subfolders and files that are contained in the parent folder. However, you can prevent permissions inheritance, as shown in Figure 14.2.

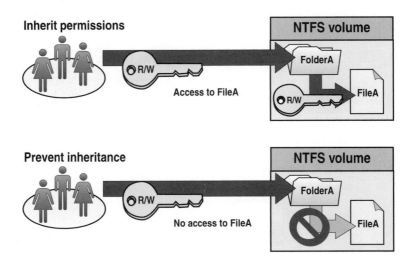

Figure 14.2   Inheritance

Understanding Permissions Inheritance

Whatever permissions you assign to the parent folder also apply to subfolders and files that are contained within the parent folder. When you assign NTFS permissions to give access to a folder, you assign permissions for the folder and for any existing files and subfolders, as well as for any new files and subfolders that are created in the folder.

Preventing Permissions Inheritance

You can prevent permissions that are assigned to a parent folder from being inherited by subfolders and files that are contained within the folder. That is, the subfolders and files will not inherit permissions that have been assigned to the parent folder containing them.

The folder for which you prevent permissions inheritance becomes the new parent folder, and permissions that are assigned to this folder will be inherited by the subfolders and files that are contained within it.

Lesson Summary

This lesson showed you that administrators, the owners of files or folders, and users with Full Control permission can assign NTFS permissions to users and groups to control access to files and folders. NTFS stores an ACL with every file and folder on an NTFS volume. The ACL contains a list of all user accounts and groups that have been granted access to the file or folder, as well as the type of access that they have been granted. A user attempting to gain access to a resource must have permission for the type of access that is requested for the user to gain access.

You also learned that you can assign multiple permissions to a user account by assigning permissions to his or her individual user account and to each group of which the user is a member. Rules and priorities control how NTFS assigns and combines multiple permissions; for example, NTFS file permissions take priority over NTFS folder permissions. A user's effective permissions for a resource are based on the NTFS permissions that you assign to the individual user account and to all of the groups to which the user belongs.

Lesson 3: Assigning NTFS Permissions

You should follow certain guidelines for assigning NTFS permissions. Assign permissions according to group and user needs, which includes allowing or preventing permissions inheritance from parent folders to subfolders and files that are contained in the parent folder.

After this lesson, you will be able to

- Assign NTFS folder and file permissions to user accounts and groups.

Estimated lesson time: 60 minutes

Planning NTFS Permissions

If you take the time to plan your NTFS permissions and follow a few guidelines, you will find that NTFS permissions are easy to manage. Use the following guidelines when you assign NTFS permissions:

- To simplify administration, group files into application, data, and home folders. Centralize home and public folders on a volume that is separate from applications and the operating system. Doing so provides the following benefits:

  - You assign permissions only to folders, not to individual files.

  - Backup is less complex because you don't need to back up application files, and all home and public folders are in one location.

- Allow users only the level of access that they require. If a user only needs to read a file, assign the Read permission to his or her user account for the file. This reduces the possibility of users accidentally modifying or deleting important documents and application files.

- Create groups according to the access that the group members require for resources, and then assign the appropriate permissions to the group. Assign permissions to individual user accounts only when necessary.

- When you assign permissions for working with data or application folders, assign the Read & Execute permission to the Users group and the Administrators group. This prevents application files from being accidentally deleted or damaged by users or viruses.

- When you assign permissions for public data folders, assign the Read & Execute permission and the Write permission to the Users group and the Full Control permission to the CREATOR OWNER user. By default, the user who creates a file is also the owner of the file. After you create a file, you can grant another user permission to take ownership of the file. The person who takes ownership would then become the owner of the file. If you assign the Read & Execute permission and the Write permission to the Users group and the Full

Control permission to the CREATOR OWNER user, users have the ability to read and modify documents that other users create and the ability to read, modify, and delete the files and folders that they create.

- Deny permissions only when it is essential to deny specific access to a specific user account or group.

- Encourage users to assign permissions to the files and folders that they create and educate users about how to do so.

Setting NTFS Permissions

By default, when you format a volume with NTFS, the Full Control permission is assigned to the Everyone group. You should change this default permission and assign other appropriate NTFS permissions to control the access that users have to resources.

Assigning or Modifying Permissions

Administrators, users with the Full Control permission, and the owners of files and folders (CREATOR OWNER) can assign permissions to user accounts and groups.

To assign or modify NTFS permissions for a file or a folder, on the Security tab of the Properties dialog box for the file or folder, configure the options that are shown in Figure 14.3 and described in Table 14.3.

Figure 14.3   The Security tab of the Properties dialog box for a folder

Table 14.3   Security Tab Options

Option	Description
Name	Select the user account or group for which you want to change permissions or that you want to remove from the list.
Permissions	Select the Allow check box to allow a permission.
	Select the Deny check box to deny a permission.
Add	Opens the Select Users, Computers, Or Groups dialog box, which you use to select user accounts and groups to add to the Name list.
Remove	Remove the selected user account or group and the associated permissions for the file or folder.
Advanced	Opens the Access Control Settings for the selected folder so that you can grant or deny additional permissions.

Preventing Permissions Inheritance

By default, subfolders and files inherit permissions that you assign to their parent folder. This is indicated on the Security tab in the Properties dialog box by a check mark in the Allow Inheritable Permissions From Parent To Propagate To This Object check box. To prevent a subfolder or file from inheriting permissions from a parent folder, clear the Allow Inheritable Permissions From Parent To Propagate To This Object check box. If you clear this check box, you are prompted to select one of the options that are described in Table 14.4.

Table 14.4   Preventing Permissions Inheritance Options

Option	Description
Copy	Copy the permissions from the parent folder to the current folder and then deny subsequent permissions inheritance from the parent folder.
Remove	Remove the permissions that are inherited from the parent folder and retain only the permissions that you explicitly assign to the file or folder.
Cancel	Cancel the dialog box and restore the check mark in the Allow Inheritable Permissions From Parent To Propagate To This Object check box.

Practice: Planning and Assigning NTFS Permissions

In this practice, you will plan NTFS permissions for folders and files based on a business scenario. Then you will apply NTFS permissions for folders and files on your computer, based on a second scenario. Finally, you will test the NTFS permissions that you set up to make sure that they are working properly.

Before beginning the exercises that follow, create the users and groups listed in the following table:

Group	User account
Managers	User81 (No password) Do not make them change password at the next logon. Member of Managers group
Accounting	User82 (No password) Do not make them change password at the next logon. Member of Accounting group
	User83 (No Password) Do not make them change password at the next logon. Member of Managers group and Accounting group
	User84 (No Password) Do not make them change password at the next logon. Not a member of the Accounting group or the Managers group.

Create the following folders:

- C:\Public
- C:\Public\Library
- C:\Public\Manuals
- C:\Public\Library\Misc

Exercise 1: Planning NTFS Permissions

In this exercise, you will plan how to assign NTFS permissions to folders and files on a computer running Windows 2000 Professional, based on the scenario that is described in the next section.

Scenario

The default NTFS folder and file permissions are Full Control for the Everyone group. Figure 14.4 shows the folder and file structure used for this practice. You need to review the following security criteria and record the changes that you should make to the NTFS folder and file permissions to meet the security criteria.

Figure 14.4   The folder and file structure for practice

To plan NTFS permissions, you must determine the following:

- Which groups to create and which built-in groups to use.
- Which permissions users will require to gain access to folders and files.
- Whether to clear the Allow Inheritable Permissions From Parent To Propagate To This Object check box for the folder or file for which you are assigning permissions.

Keep the following general guidelines in mind:

- NTFS permissions that are assigned to a folder are inherited by all of the folders and files that it contains. To assign permissions for all of the folders and files in the Apps folder, you need only assign NTFS permissions to the Apps folder.
- To assign more restrictive permissions to a folder or file that is inheriting permissions, you must either *deny* the unwanted permissions or block inheritance by clearing the Allow Inheritable Permissions From Parent To Propagate To This Object check box.

The decisions that you make are based on the following criteria:

- In addition to the default built-in groups, the following groups have been created:
  - Accounting
  - Managers
  - Executives
- Administrators require the Full Control permission for all folders and files.
- All users will run programs in the WordProcessing folder, but they should not be able to modify the files in the WordProcessing folder.
- Only members of the Accounting, Managers, and Executives groups should be able to read documents in the Spreadsheet and Database application folders by running the associated spreadsheet and database applications, but they should not be able to modify the files in those folders.
- All users should be able to read and create files in the Public folder.
- All users should be prevented from modifying files in the Public\Library folder.
- Only User81 should be able to modify and delete files in the Public\Manuals folder.

  When you apply custom permissions to a folder or file, which default permission entry should you remove?

Complete the following table to plan and record your permissions:

Path	User account or group	NTFS permissions	Block inheritance (yes/no)
Apps			
Apps\WordProcessing			
Apps\Spreadsheet			
Apps\Database			
Public			
Public\Library			
Public\Manuals			

Exercise 2: Assigning NTFS Permissions for the Public Folder

In this exercise, you will assign NTFS permissions for the Public folder based on the scenario that is described next.

Scenario

The permissions that you assign are based on the following criteria:

- All users should be able to read documents and files in the Public folder.
- All users should be able to create documents in the Public folder.
- All users should be able to modify the contents, properties, and permissions of the documents that they create in the Public folder.

▶ **To remove permissions from the Everyone group**

1. Log on as Administrator.
2. Right-click My Computer, and then click Explore.
3. Expand Local Disk (C:), right-click the Public folder, and then click Properties.

Windows 2000 displays the Public Properties dialog box with the General tab active.

4. Click the Security tab to display the permissions for the Public folder.

Windows 2000 displays the Public Properties dialog box with the Security tab active.

What are the existing folder permissions?

Notice that the current allowed permissions can't be modified.

5. Under Name, select the Everyone group, and then click Remove.

What do you see?

6. Click OK to close the message box.

7. Clear the Allow Inheritable Permissions From Parent To Propagate To This Object check box to block permissions from being inherited.

Windows 2000 displays the Security dialog box, prompting you to copy the currently inherited permissions to the folder or remove all permissions for the folder except those that you explicitly specify.

8. Click Remove.

What are the existing folder permissions?

▶ **To assign permissions to the Users group for the Public folder**

1. In the Public Properties dialog box, click Add.

Windows 2000 displays the Select Users, Computers, Or Groups dialog box.

2. Ensure that the Look In box at the top of the dialog box has your computer, PRO1, selected.

The Look In box allows you to select the computer, workgroup, or domain from which to select user accounts, groups, or computers when you assign permissions. You should specify your workgroup or domain to select from the user accounts and groups that you created.

3. In the Name box, click Users and then click Add.

The dialog box displays PRO1\Users in the box under the Name box at the bottom of the dialog box.

4. Click OK to return to the Public Properties dialog box.

What are the existing allowed folder permissions?

5. Make sure that Users is selected, and then next to Write, select the Allow check box.

6. Click Apply to save your changes.

▶   **To assign permissions to the CREATOR OWNER group for the Public folder**

1. In the Public Properties dialog box, click Add.

    Windows 2000 displays the Select Users, Computers, Or Groups dialog box.

2. In the Look In box at the top of the dialog box, ensure that your computer is selected.

3. In the Name list, select CREATOR OWNER, and then click Add.

    CREATOR OWNER appears in the box under the Name box at the bottom of the dialog box.

4. Click OK to return to the Public Properties dialog box.

5. Make sure that CREATOR OWNER is selected, next to Full Control, select the Allow check box, and then click Apply to save your changes.

6. Click Advanced to display the additional permissions.

    Windows 2000 displays the Access Control Settings For Public dialog box.

7. Under Permission Entries, select CREATOR OWNER, if necessary.

    Which permissions are assigned to CREATOR OWNER, and where do these permissions apply?

    The user who creates the new file or folder receives the permissions that are assigned to CREATOR OWNER for the parent folder.

8. Click OK to close the Access Control Settings For Public dialog box.

9. Click OK to close the Public Properties dialog box.

10. Close Windows Explorer.

▶   **To test the folder permissions that you assigned for the Public folder**

1. Log on as User81, and then start Windows Explorer.

2. Expand the Public folder.

3. In the Public folder, attempt to create a text file named User81.

    Were you successful? Why or why not?

4. Attempt to perform the following tasks for the file that you just created, and then record those tasks that you are able to complete.

- Open the file
- Modify the file
- Delete the file

The tasks that you can complete are opening, modifying, and deleting the file because CREATOR OWNER has been assigned the NTFS Full Control permission for the Public folder.

5. Close all applications, and then log off Windows 2000.

Exercise 3: Assigning NTFS Permissions

In this exercise, you will assign NTFS permissions to the Public, Library, Manuals, and Misc folders based on the scenario that is described in the following section.

Scenario

Assign the appropriate permissions to folders as listed in the following table:

Folder name	User account or group	Permissions
Public	Users group Administrators group	Read & Execute Full Control
Public\Library	Users group Administrators group Managers group	Read & Execute Full Control Modify
Public\Library\Misc	Users group Administrators group User82	Read & Execute Full Control Modify
Public\Manuals	Users group Administrators group Accounting group	Read & Execute Full Control Modify

▶ **To assign NTFS permissions for a folder**

1. Log on as Administrator, and then start Windows Explorer.

2. Expand the folder that contains the folder or folders to which you want to assign permissions.

3. Right-click the folder for which you are modifying permissions, and then click Properties.

   Windows 2000 displays the Properties dialog box for the folder with the General tab active.

4. In the Properties dialog box for the folder, click the Security tab.

5. On the Security tab, if you need to modify the inherited permissions for a user, account, or group, clear the Allow Inheritable Permissions From Parent

To Propagate To This Object check box, and then when prompted to copy or remove inherited permissions, click Copy.

6. To add permissions to user accounts or groups for the folder, click Add.

Windows 2000 displays the Select Users, Computers, Or Groups dialog box.

7. Make sure that your computer name appears in the Look In box at the top of the dialog box.

8. In the Name box, select the name of the appropriate user account or group, based on the preceding scenario, and then click Add.

Windows 2000 displays the user account or group under Name at the bottom of the dialog box.

9. Repeat step 8 for each user account or group that is listed for the folder in the preceding scenario.

10. Click OK to return to the Properties dialog box for the folder.

11. If the Properties dialog box for the folder contains user accounts and groups that are not listed in the preceding scenario, with the exception of the CREATOR OWNER group, select the user account or group, and then click Remove.

12. For all user accounts and groups that are listed for the folder in the preceding scenario, under Name, select the user account or group, and then under Permissions, select the Allow check box or the Deny check box next to the appropriate permissions that are listed for the folder in the preceding scenario.

13. Click OK to apply your changes and close the Properties dialog box for the folder.

14. Repeat this procedure for each folder for which you are assigning permissions as specified in the preceding scenario.

15. Log off Windows.

Exercise 4: Testing NTFS Permissions

In this exercise, you will log on using various user accounts and test NTFS permissions.

▶ **To test permissions for the Misc folder while logged on as User81**

1. Log on as User81, and then start Windows Explorer.

2. In Windows Explorer, expand the Public\Library\Misc folder.

3. Attempt to create a file in the Misc folder.

Were you successful? Why or why not?

4. Close Windows Explorer and log off Windows 2000.

▶ **To test permissions for the Misc folder while logged on as User82**

1. Log on as User82, and then start Windows Explorer.

2. Expand the Public\Library\Misc folder.

3. Attempt to create a file in the Misc folder.

   Were you successful? Why or why not?

4. Close Windows Explorer and log off Windows 2000.

▶ **To test permissions for the Manuals folder while logged on as Administrator**

1. Log on as Administrator, and then start Windows Explorer.

2. Expand the Public\Manuals folder.

3. Attempt to create a file in the Manuals folder.

   Were you successful? Why or why not?

4. Close Windows Explorer, and then log off Windows 2000.

▶ **To test permissions for the Manuals folder while logged on as User81**

1. Log on as User81, and then start Windows Explorer.

2. Expand the Public\Manuals folder.

3. Attempt to create a file in the Manuals folder.

   Were you successful? Why or why not?

4. Close Windows Explorer, and then log off Windows 2000.

▶ **To test permissions for the Manuals folder while logged on as User82**

1. Log on as User82, and then start Windows Explorer.

2. Expand the Public\Manuals folder.

3. Attempt to create a file in the Manuals folder.

   Were you successful? Why or why not?

4. Close all applications, and then log off Windows 2000.

Lesson Summary

In this lesson, you learned that by default, when you format a volume with NTFS, the Full Control permission is assigned to the Everyone group. You should change this default permission and assign other appropriate NTFS permissions to control the access that users have to resources. To assign or modify NTFS permissions for a file or a folder, you use the Security tab of the Properties dialog box for the file or folder.

You also learned that by default, subfolders and files inherit permissions that you assign to their parent folder. You can disable this feature so that subfolders and files don't inherit the permissions assigned to their parents. In the practice exercises, you created some folders, assigned NTFS permissions, and then tested the permissions you had set up to determine whether you set them up correctly.

Lesson 4: Assigning Special Access Permissions

The standard NTFS permissions generally provide all of the access control that you need to secure your resources. However, sometimes the standard NTFS permissions don't provide the specific level of access that you might want to assign to users. To create a specific level of access, you can assign NTFS special access permissions.

After this lesson, you will be able to

- Give users the ability to change permissions on files or folders.
- Give users the ability to take ownership of files and folders.

Estimated lesson time: 5 minutes

Using Special Access Permissions

There are 13 special access permissions. Two of them, shown in Figure 14.5, are particularly useful for controlling access to resources: Change Permissions and Take Ownership.

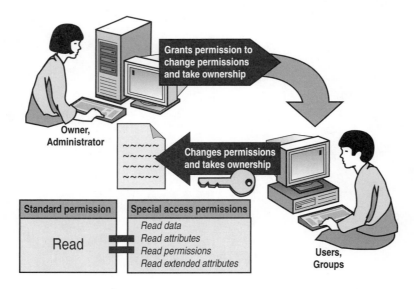

Figure 14.5   The Change Permissions and Take Ownership special access permissions

When you assign special access permissions to folders, you can choose where to apply the permissions down the tree to subfolders and files.

Changing Permissions

You can give other administrators and users the ability to change permissions for a file or folder without giving them the Full Control permission over the file or folder. In this way, the administrator or user can't delete or write to the file or folder but can assign permissions to the file or folder.

To give administrators the ability to change permissions, assign Change Permissions to the Administrators group for the file or folder.

Taking Ownership

You can transfer ownership of files and folders from one user account or group to another user account or group. You can give someone the ability to take ownership and, as an administrator, you can take ownership of a file or folder.

The following rules apply for taking ownership of a file or folder:

- The current owner or any user with Full Control permission can assign the Full Control standard permission or the Take Ownership special access permission to another user account or group, allowing the user account or a member of the group to take ownership.

- An administrator can take ownership of a folder or file, regardless of assigned permissions. If an administrator takes ownership, the Administrators group becomes the owner and any member of the Administrators group can change the permissions for the file or folder and assign the Take Ownership permission to another user account or group.

  For example, if an employee leaves the company, an administrator can take ownership of the employee's files, assign the Take Ownership permission to another employee, and then that employee can take ownership of the former employee's files.

Note You cannot *assign* anyone ownership of a file or folder. The owner of a file, an administrator, or anyone with Full Control permission can assign Take Ownership permission to a user account or group, allowing them to take ownership. To become the owner of a file or folder, a user or group member with Take Ownership permission must explicitly take ownership of the file or folder, as explained later in this chapter.

Setting Special Access Permissions

You assign special access permissions to enable users to change permissions and take ownership of files and folders, as follows:

1. In the Access Control Settings dialog box for a file or folder, on the Permissions tab, select the user account or group for which you want to apply NTFS special access permissions.

2. Click View/Edit to open the Permissions Entry dialog box (see Figure 14.6).

Figure 14.6   The Permissions Entry dialog box

The options in the Permissions Entry dialog box are described in Table 14.5.

Table 14.5   Options in the Permissions Entry Dialog Box

Option	Description
Name	The user account or group name. To select a different user account or group, click Change.
Apply Onto	The level of the folder hierarchy at which the special NTFS permissions are inherited. The default is This Folder, Subfolders And Files.
Permissions	The special access permissions. To allow the Change Permissions permission or Take Ownership permission, select the Allow check box.
Apply These Permissions To Objects And/Or Containers Within This Container Only	Specify whether subfolders and files within a folder inherit the special access permissions from the folder. Select this check box to propagate the special access permissions to files and subfolders. Clear this check box to prevent permissions inheritance.
Clear All	Click this button to clear all selected permissions.

Note In the Access Control Settings dialog box, on the Permissions tab, you can view the permissions that are applied to the file or folder, the owner, and where the permissions apply. When special access permissions have been assigned, Windows 2000 displays Special under Permissions.

Taking Ownership of a File or Folder

To take ownership of a file or folder, the user or a group member with Take Ownership permission must explicitly take ownership of the file or folder, as follows:

1. In the Access Control Settings dialog box, on the Owner tab, in the Change Owner To list, select your name.

2. Select the Replace Owner On Subcontainers And Objects check box to take ownership of all subfolders and files that are contained within the folder.

Lesson Summary

In this lesson, you learned that there are 13 special access permissions, and two of them are especially useful: Change Permissions and Take Ownership. You can give administrators and other users the ability to change permissions for a file or folder without giving them the Full Control permission over the file or folder. This prevents the administrator or user from deleting or writing to the file or folder, but it allows them to assign permissions to the file or folder.

You also learned that you can transfer ownership of files and folders from one user account or group to another user account or group. The current owner or any user with Full Control permission can assign the Full Control standard permission or the Take Ownership special access permission to another user account or group, allowing the user account or a member of the group to take ownership. An administrator can take ownership of a folder or file, regardless of assigned permissions. When an administrator takes ownership of a file or folder, the Administrators group becomes the owner, and any member of the Administrators group can change the permissions for the file or folder and assign the Take Ownership permission to another user account or group.

Lesson 5: Copying and Moving Files and Folders

When you copy or move files and folders, the permissions you set on the files or folders might change. Specific rules control how and when permissions change. You must understand how and when permissions change during a copy or move, as explained in this lesson.

After this lesson, you will be able to

- Describe the effect on NTFS file and folder permissions when files and folders are copied.
- Describe the effect on NTFS file and folder permissions when files and folders are moved.

Estimated lesson time: 5 minutes

Copying Files and Folders

When you copy files or folders from one folder to another folder, or from one volume to another volume, permissions change, as shown in Figure 14.7.

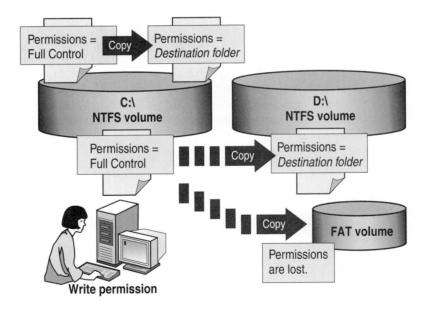

Figure 14.7   Copying files or folders between folders or volumes

When you copy a file within a single NTFS volume or between NTFS volumes:

- Windows 2000 treats it as a new file. As a new file, it takes on the permissions of the destination folder.

- You must have Write permission for the destination folder to copy files and folders.

- You become the CREATOR OWNER.

Note When you copy files or folders to FAT volumes, the folders and files lose their NTFS permissions because FAT volumes don't support NTFS permissions.

Moving Files and Folders

When you move a file or folder, permissions might or might not change, depending on where you move the file or folder. (See Figure 14.8.)

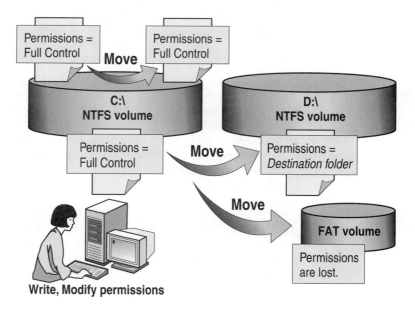

Figure 14.8 Moving files or folders between folders or volumes

Moving Within a Single NTFS Volume

When you move a file or folder within a single NTFS volume

- The file or folder retains the original permissions.

- You must have the Write permission for the destination folder to move files and folders into it.

- You must have the Modify permission for the source file or folder. The Modify permission is required to move a file or folder because Windows 2000 deletes the file or folder from the source folder after it is copied to the destination folder.

- The owner of the file or folder does not change.

Moving Between NTFS Volumes

When you move a file or folder between NTFS volumes

- The file or folder inherits the permissions of the destination folder.

- You must have the Write permission for the destination folder to move files and folders into it.

- You must have the Modify permission for the source file or folder. The Modify permission is required to move a file or folder because Windows 2000 deletes the file or folder from the source folder *after* it is copied to the destination folder.

- You become the CREATOR OWNER.

Note When you move files or folders to FAT volumes, the folders and files lose their NTFS permissions because FAT volumes don't support NTFS permissions.

Lesson Summary

In this lesson, you learned that when you copy or move files and folders, the permissions you set on the files or folders might change. Rules control how and when permissions change. For example, when you copy files or folders from one folder to another folder, or from one volume to another volume, permissions change. Windows 2000 treats the file or folder as a new file or folder, and therefore, it takes on the permissions of the destination folder.

You also learned that you must have Write permission for the destination folder to copy files and folders. When you copy a file, you become the CREATOR OWNER of the file. When you move a file or folder within a single NTFS volume, the file or folder retains the original permissions. However, when you move a file or folder between NTFS volumes, the file or folder inherits the permissions of the destination folder.

Lesson 6: Solving Permissions Problems

When you assign or modify NTFS permissions to files and folders, problems might arise. Troubleshooting these problems is important to keep resources available to users.

After this lesson, you will be able to

- Troubleshoot resource access problems.

Estimated lesson time: 20 minutes

Troubleshooting Permissions Problems

Table 14.6 describes some common permissions problems that you might encounter and provides solutions that you can use to try to resolve these problems.

Table 14.6   Permissions Problems and Troubleshooting Solutions

Problem	Solution
A user can't gain access to a file or folder.	If the file or folder was copied, or if it was moved to another NTFS volume, the permissions might have changed.
	Check the permissions that are assigned to the user account and to groups of which the user is a member. The user might not have permission or might be denied access either individually or as a member of a group.
You add a user account to a group to give that user access to a file or folder, but the user still can't gain access.	For access permissions to be updated to include the new group to which you have added the user account, the user must either log off and then log on again, or close all network connections to the computer on which the file or folder resides and then make new connections.
A user with Full Control permission to a folder deletes a file in the folder, although that user doesn't have permission to delete the file itself. You want to stop the user from being able to delete more files.	You have to clear the special access permission—the Delete Subfolders And Files check box—on the folder to prevent users with Full Control of the folder from being able to delete files in the folder.

Note Windows 2000 supports POSIX applications that are designed to run on UNIX. On UNIX systems, Full Control permission allows you to delete files in a folder. In Windows 2000, the Full Control permission includes the Delete Subfolders And Files special access permission, allowing you the same ability to delete files in that folder regardless of the permissions that you have for the files in the folder.

Avoiding Permissions Problems

The following list provides best practices for implementing NTFS permissions. These guidelines will help you avoid permission problems.

- Assign the most restrictive NTFS permissions that still enable users and groups to accomplish necessary tasks.

- Assign all permissions at the folder level, not at the file level. Group files in a separate folder for which you want to restrict user access, and then assign that folder restricted access.

- For all application-executable files, assign Read & Execute and Change Permissions to the Administrators group, and assign Read & Execute to the Users group. Damage to application files is usually a result of accidents and viruses. By assigning Read & Execute to Users and Read & Execute and Change Permissions to Administrators, you can prevent users or viruses from modifying or deleting executable files. To update files, members of the Administrators group can assign Full Control to their user account to make changes and then reassign Read & Execute and Change Permissions to their user account.

- Assign Full Control to the CREATOR OWNER group for public data folders so that users can delete and modify files and folders that they create. Doing so gives the user who creates the file or folder (CREATOR OWNER) full access to only the files or folders that he or she creates in the public data folder.

- For public folders, assign Full Control to the CREATOR OWNER group and Read and Write to the Everyone group. This gives users full access to the files that they create, but members of the Everyone group can only read files in the folder and add files to the folder.

- Use long, descriptive names if the resource will be accessed only at the computer. If a folder will eventually be shared, use folder and filenames that are accessible by all client computers.

- Allow permissions rather than denying permissions. If you don't want a user or group to gain access to a particular folder or file, don't assign permissions. Denying permissions should be an exception, not a common practice.

Practice: Managing NTFS Permissions

In this practice, you will observe the effects of taking ownership of a file. Then you will determine the effects of permission and ownership when you copy or move files. Finally, you will determine what happens when a user, having the Full Control permission to a folder, has been denied all access to a file in that folder, and the user attempts to delete the file.

To successfully complete this practice, you must have completed "Practice: Planning and Assigning NTFS Permissions," in Lesson 3 of this chapter.

Exercise 1: Taking Ownership of a File

In this exercise, you will observe the effects of taking ownership of a file. To do this, you must determine permissions for a file, assign the Take Ownership permission to a user account, and then take ownership as that user.

► **To determine the permissions for a file**

1. Log on as Administrator, and then start Windows Explorer.
2. In the Public folder, create a text file named Owner.
3. Right-click Owner.txt, and then click Properties.

   Microsoft Windows 2000 displays the Owner Properties dialog box with the General tab active.

4. Click the Security tab to display the permissions for the Owner.txt file.

   What are the current allowed permissions for Owner.txt?

5. Click Advanced.

   Windows 2000 displays the Access Control Settings For Owner dialog box with the Permissions tab active.

6. Click the Owner tab.

   Who is the current owner of the Owner.txt file?

► **To assign permission to a user to take ownership**

1. In the Access Control Settings For Owner dialog box, click the Permissions tab.
2. Click Add.

   Windows 2000 displays the Select User, Computer, Or Group dialog box.

3. In the Look In box at the top of the dialog box, ensure that your computer is selected.
4. Under Name, click User84, and then click OK.

   Windows 2000 displays the Permission Entry For Owner dialog box.

   Notice that all of the permission entries for User84 are blank.

5. Under Permissions, select the Allow check box next to Take Ownership.
6. Click OK.

   The Access Control Settings For Owner dialog box with the Permissions tab displayed is once again active.

7. Click OK to return to the Owner Properties dialog box.

8. Click OK to apply your changes and close the Owner Properties dialog box.

9. Close all applications, and then log off Windows 2000.

▶ **To take ownership of a file**

1. Log on as User84, and then start Windows Explorer.

2. Click the Public folder.

3. Right-click Owner.txt, and then click Properties.

   Windows 2000 displays the Owner Properties dialog box with the General tab active.

4. Click the Security tab to display the permissions for Owner.txt.

   Windows 2000 displays the Security message box, indicating that you can view only the current security information on Owner.txt.

5. Click OK.

   Windows 2000 displays the Owner Properties dialog box with the Security tab active.

6. Click Advanced to display the Access Control Settings For Owner dialog box, and then click the Owner tab.

   Who is the current owner of Owner.txt?

7. In the Change Owner To box, select User84, and then click Apply.

   Who is the current owner of Owner.txt?

8. Click Cancel to close the Access Control Settings For Owner dialog box.

   The Owner Properties dialog box with the Security tab displayed is once again active.

9. Click OK to close the Owner Properties dialog box.

▶ **To test permissions for a file as the owner**

1. While you are logged on as User84, assign User84 the Full Control permission for the Owner.txt file, and click Apply.

2. Clear the Allow Inheritable Permissions From Parent To Propagate To This Object check box.

3. In the Security dialog box, click Remove.

4. Click OK to close the Owner Properties dialog box.

5. Delete the Owner.txt file.

Exercise 2: Copying and Moving Folders

In this exercise, you will see the effects of permissions and ownership when you copy and move folders.

▶ **To create a folder while logged on as a user**

1. While you are logged on as User84, in Windows Explorer, in drive C, create a folder named Temp1.

   What are the permissions that are assigned to the folder?

   Who is the owner? Why?

2. Close all applications, and then log off Windows 2000.

▶ **To create a folder while logged on as Administrator**

1. Log on as Administrator, and then start Windows Explorer.

2. In drive C, create the following two folders: Temp2 and Temp3.

   What are the permissions for the folders that you just created?

   Who is the owner of the Temp2 and Temp3 folders? Why?

3. Remove the Everyone group, and then assign the following permissions to the Temp2 and Temp3 folders. You will have to clear the Allow Inheritable Permissions From Parent To Propagate To This Object check box. To select a group, select the group name in the Name list and then click Add.

Folder	Assign these permissions
Temp2	Administrators: Full Control Users: Read & Execute
Temp3	Backup Operators: Read & Execute Users: Full Control

▶ **To copy a folder to another folder within a Windows 2000 NTFS volume**

1. In Windows Explorer, copy C:\Temp2 to C:\Temp1 by selecting C:\Temp2, holding down the Ctrl key, and then dragging C:\Temp2 to C:\Temp1.

   Since this is a copy, C:\Temp2 and C:\Temp1\Temp2 should both exist.

2. Select C:\Temp1\Temp2, and then compare the permissions and ownership with C:\Temp2.

Who is the owner of C:\Temp1\Temp2 and what are the permissions? Why?

3. Close all applications, and then log off Windows 2000.

▶ **To move a folder within the same NTFS volume**

1. Log on as User84.
2. In Windows Explorer, select C:\Temp3, and then move it to C:\Temp1.

   What happens to the permissions and ownership for C:\Temp1\Temp3? Why?

3. Close all windows and log off.

Exercise 3: Deleting a File with All Permissions Denied

In this exercise, you will grant a user Full Control permission to a folder but deny all permissions to a file in the folder. You will then observe what happens when the user attempts to delete that file.

▶ **To assign the Full Control permission for a folder**

1. Log on as Administrator, and then start Windows Explorer.
2. Expand drive C, and then create a folder named Fullaccess.
3. Verify that the Everyone group has the Full Control permission for the Fullaccess folder.

▶ **To create a file and deny access to it**

1. In the Fullaccess folder, create a text file named Noaccess.txt.
2. Deny the Everyone group the Full Control permission for the Noaccess.txt file.

   Windows 2000 displays the Security dialog box with the following message:

   ```
   You have denied everyone access to NoAccess.txt. No one will be able
   to access NoAccess.txt and only the owner will be able to change
   permissions.

   Do you wish to continue?
   ```

3. Click Yes to apply your changes and close the Security dialog box.

▶ **To view the result of the Full Control permission for a folder**

1. In Windows Explorer, double-click Noaccess.txt in the Fullaccess folder to open the file.

Were you successful? Why or why not?

2. Click the Start button, point to Programs, point to Accessories, and then click Command Prompt.

3. Change to C:\Fullaccess.

4. Delete Noaccess.txt.

Were you successful? Why or why not?

How would you prevent users with Full Control permission for a folder from deleting a file in that folder for which they have been denied the Full Control permission?

5. Close all windows and log off Windows 2000.

Lesson Summary

When you assign or modify NTFS permissions for files and folders, problems might arise. Troubleshooting these problems is important to keep resources available to users. In this lesson, you learned some common permissions problems and some possible solutions to resolve these problems. In the practice exercises for this lesson, you determined the permissions for a file, assigned the Take Ownership permission to a user account, and then took ownership as that user. You also observed the effects of permissions and ownership when you copy and move folders. Finally, in these exercises you practiced assigning permissions to a folder and a file, and then you observed the results when a user has Full Control permission to a folder and has been denied all permissions to a file in that folder.

Review

The following questions will help you determine whether you have learned enough to move on to the next chapter. If you have difficulty answering these questions, please go back and review the material in this chapter before beginning the next chapter. See Appendix A, "Questions and Answers," for the answers to these questions.

1. What is the default permission when a volume is formatted with NTFS? Who has access to the volume?

2. If a user has Write permission for a folder and is also a member of a group with Read permission for the folder, what are the user's effective permissions for the folder?

3. If you assign the Modify permission to a user account for a folder and the Read permission for a file, and then you copy the file to that folder, what permission does the user have for the file?

4. What happens to permissions that are assigned to a file when the file is moved from one folder to another folder on the same NTFS volume? What happens when the file is moved to a folder on another NTFS volume?

5. If an employee leaves the company, what must you do to transfer ownership of his or her files and folders to another employee?

6. What three details should you check when a user cannot gain access to a resource?

C H A P T E R   1 5

Administering Shared Folders

About This Chapter

In Chapter 14, "Securing Resources with NTFS Permissions," you learned about Microsoft Windows 2000 File System (NTFS) permissions. You use NTFS permissions to specify which users and groups can gain access to files and folders, and what these permissions allow users to do with the contents of the file or folder. NTFS permissions are available only on NTFS volumes. NTFS security is effective whether a user gains access to the file or folder at the computer or over the network.

In this chapter, you will learn how to make folders accessible over the network. You can access a computer's folders and their contents only by physically sitting at the computer and logging on to it or by accessing a shared folder on a remote computer. Sharing folders is the only way to make folders and their contents available over the network. Shared folders also provide another way to secure file resources, one that can be used on FAT or FAT32 partitions. In this chapter, you will also learn how to share file resources, secure them with permissions, and provide access to them.

Before You Begin

To complete this chapter, you must have

- A computer that meets the minimum hardware requirements located in "About This Book."
- Microsoft Windows 2000 Professional installed on the computer.

Lesson 1: Understanding Shared Folders

You use *shared folders* to provide network users with access to file resources. When a folder is shared, users can connect to the folder over the network and gain access to the files that it contains. However, to gain access to the files, users must have permissions to access the shared folders.

After this lesson, you will be able to

- Use shared folders to provide access to network resources.
- Describe how permissions affect access to shared folders.

Estimated lesson time: 15 minutes

Shared Folder Permissions

A shared folder can contain applications, data, or a user's personal data, called a *home folder.* Each type of data requires different shared folder permissions.

The following are characteristics of shared folder permissions:

- Shared folder permissions apply to folders, not individual files. Since you can apply shared folder permissions only to the entire shared folder, and not to individual files or subfolders in the shared folder, shared folder permissions provide less detailed security than NTFS permissions.
- Shared folder permissions don't restrict access to users who gain access to the folder at the computer where the folder is stored. They apply only to users who connect to the folder over the network.
- Shared folder permissions are the only way to secure network resources on a FAT volume. NTFS permissions aren't available on FAT volumes.
- The default shared folder permission is Full Control, and it is assigned to the Everyone group when you share the folder.

Note A shared folder appears in Windows Explorer as an icon of a hand holding the shared folder. (Figure 15.1 shows the sharing icon.)

To control how users gain access to a shared folder, you assign shared folder permissions.

Table 15.1 explains what each of the shared folder permissions allows a user to do. The permissions are presented from most restrictive to least restrictive.

Figure 15.1   Shared folders in Windows Explorer

Table 15.1   Shared Folder Permissions

Shared folder permission	Allows the user to
Read	Display folder names, filenames, file data, and attributes; run program files; and change folders within the shared folder.
Change	Create folders, add files to folders, change data in files, append data to files, change file attributes, delete folders and files, plus, it allows the user to perform actions permitted by the Read permission.
Full Control	Change file permissions, take ownership of files, and perform all tasks permitted by the Change permission.

You can allow or deny shared folder permissions. Generally, it is best to allow permissions and to assign permissions to a group rather than to individual users. You deny permissions only when it is necessary to override permissions that are otherwise applied. In most cases, you should deny permissions only when it is necessary to deny permission to a specific user who belongs to a group to which you have given the permission. If you deny a shared folder permission to a user, the user won't have that permission. For example, to deny *all* access to a shared folder, deny the Full Control permission.

How Shared Folder Permissions Are Applied

Applying shared permissions to user accounts and groups affects access to a shared folder. Denying permission takes precedence over the permissions that you allow. The following list describes the effects of applying permissions.

- Multiple Permissions Combine. A user can be a member of multiple groups, each with different permissions that provide different levels of access to a shared folder. When you assign permission to a user for a shared folder, and that user is a member of a group to which you assigned a different permission, the user's effective permissions are the combination of the user and group permissions. For example, if a user has Read permission and is a member of a group with Change permission, the user's effective permission is Change, which includes Read.

- Denying Permissions Overrides Other Permissions. Denied permissions take precedence over any permissions that you otherwise allow for user accounts and groups. If you deny a shared folder permission to a user, the user won't have that permission, even if you allow the permission for a group of which the user is a member.

- NTFS Permissions Are Required on NTFS Volumes. Shared folder permissions are sufficient to gain access to files and folders on a FAT volume but not on an NTFS volume. On a FAT volume, users can gain access to a shared folder for which they have permissions, as well as all of the folder's contents. When users gain access to a shared folder on an NTFS volume, they need the shared folder permission and also the appropriate NTFS permissions for each file and folder to which they gain access.

- Copied or Moved Shared Folders Are No Longer Shared. When you copy a shared folder, the original shared folder is still shared, but the copy is not shared. When you move a shared folder, it is no longer shared.

Guidelines for Shared Folder Permissions

The following list provides some general guidelines for managing your shared folders and assigning shared folder permissions:

- Determine which groups need access to each resource and the level of access that they require. Document the groups and their permissions for each resource.

- Assign permissions to groups instead of user accounts to simplify access administration.

- Assign to a resource the most restrictive permissions that still allow users to perform required tasks. For example, if users need only to read information in a folder, and they will never delete or create files, assign the Read permission.

- Organize resources so that folders with the same security requirements are located within a folder. For example, if users require Read permission for several application folders, store the application folders within the same folder. Then share this folder instead of sharing each individual application folder.

- Use intuitive share names so that users can easily recognize and locate resources. For example, for the Application folder, use Apps for the share name. You should also use share names that all client operating systems can use.

Although Windows 2000 allows for very long share names, try to keep share names short, about 12 characters. Shorter names are easier to remember and type. Products such as MS-DOS, Windows 3.*x*, and Windows for Workgroups require an 8.3-character share name.

Microsoft Windows 2000 provides 8.3-character equivalent names, but the resulting names might not be intuitive to users. For example, a Windows 2000 folder named Accountants Database would appear as Account~1 on client computers running MS-DOS, Windows 3.*x*, and Windows for Workgroups.

Practice: Applied Permissions

In the following practice, User101 has been assigned permissions to gain access to resources as an individual and as a member of a group, as shown in Figure 15.2. Determine which effective permissions User101 has in each situation:

1. User101 is a member of Group1, Group2, and Group3. Group1 has Read permission and Group3 has Full Control permission for FolderA. Group2 has no permissions assigned for FolderA. What are User101's effective permissions for FolderA?

2. User101 is also a member of the Sales group, which has the Read permission for FolderB. User101 has been denied the shared folder permission Full Control for FolderB as an individual user. What are User101's effective permissions for FolderB?

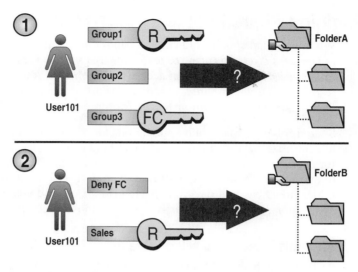

Figure 15.2   Applied permissions

Lesson Summary

In this lesson, you learned that you can make a folder and its contents available to other users over the network by sharing the folder. Using shared folder permissions is the only way to secure file resources on FAT volumes. Shared folder permissions apply to folders, not individual files. Shared folder permissions don't restrict access to users who gain access to the folder at the computer where the folder is stored. Shared folder permissions apply only to users who connect to the folder over the network.

You also learned about the three shared folder permissions: Read, Change, and Full Control. The Read permission allows users to display folder names, filenames, file data, and attributes. The Read permission also allows users to run program files and to change folders within the shared folder. The Change permission allows users to create folders, add files to folders, change data in files, append data to files, change file attributes, and delete folders and files, plus it allows the user to perform actions permitted by the Read permission. The Full Control permission allows users to change file permissions, take ownership of files, and perform all tasks permitted by the Change permission. The default shared folder permission is Full Control, and it is assigned to the Everyone group when you share the folder.

Lesson 2: Planning Shared Folders

When you plan shared folders, you can reduce administrative overhead and ease user access. You can organize resources that will be shared and put them into folders according to common access requirements. You can also determine which resources you want shared, organize resources according to function and use, and decide how you will administer the resources.

Shared folders can contain applications and data. Use shared application folders to centralize administration. Use shared data folders to provide a central location for users to store and gain access to common files. If all data files are centralized in one shared folder, users will find them easily. You will be able to back up data folders more easily if data folders are centralized, and you will be able to upgrade application software more easily if applications are centralized.

After this lesson, you will be able to

- Plan which shared folder permissions to assign to user accounts and groups for application and data folders.

Estimated lesson time: 5 minutes

Application Folders

Shared *application folders* are used for applications that are installed on a network server and can be used from client computers. The main advantage of shared applications is that you don't need to install and maintain most components of the applications on each computer. While program files for applications can be stored on a server, configuration information for most network applications is often stored on each client computer. The exact way in which you share application folders will vary depending on the application and your particular network environment and company organization.

When you share application folders, consider the points in Figure 15.3. These points are explained in more detail as follows:

- Create one shared folder for applications and organize all of your applications under this folder. When you combine all applications under one shared folder, you designate one location for installing and upgrading software.

- Assign the Administrators group the Full Control permission for the applications folder so that they can manage the application software and control user permissions.

- Remove the Full Control permission from the Everyone group and assign the Read permission to the Users group. This provides more security because the Users group includes only user accounts that you created, whereas the Everyone group includes anyone who has access to network resources, including the Guest account.

- Assign the Change permission to groups that are responsible for upgrading and troubleshooting applications.

- Create a separate shared folder outside your application folder hierarchy for any application for which you need to assign different permissions. Then assign the appropriate permissions to that folder.

Apps

- Create a shared folder for applications.

- Assign Full Control to Administrators.

- Remove Full Control from Everyone and assign Read to Users.

- Assign Change to groups that upgrade and troubleshoot.

App1

- Create a separate shared folder for each set of permissions.

Figure 15.3   Creating and sharing application folders

Data Folders

Users on a network use *data folders* to exchange public and working data. Working data folders are used by members of a team who need access to shared files. Public data folders are used by larger groups of users who all need access to common data.

When you use data folders, create and share common data folders on a volume that is separate from the operating system and applications. Data files should be backed up frequently, and with data folders on a separate volume, you can conveniently back them up. If the operating system requires reinstallation, the volume containing the data folder remains intact.

Public Data

When you share a common public data folder, do the following:

- Use centralized data folders so that data can be easily backed up.

- Assign the Change permission to the Users group for the common data folder (see Figure 15.4). This will provide users with a central, publicly accessible location for storing data files that they want to share with other users. Users will be able to gain access to the folder and read, create, or change files in it.

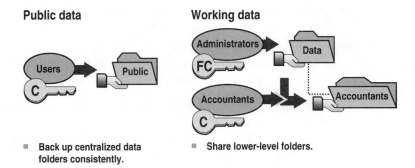

Public data

Working data

■ Back up centralized data folders consistently.

■ Share lower-level folders.

Figure 15.4   Public data and working data shared folders

Working Data

When you share a data folder for working files, do the following:

- Assign the Full Control permission to the Administrators group for a central data folder so that administrators can perform maintenance.

- Share lower-level data folders below the central folder with the Change permission for the appropriate groups when you need to restrict access to those folders.

For an example, see Figure 15.4. To protect data in the Accountants folder, which is a subfolder of the Data folder, share the Accountants folder and assign the Change permission only to the Accountants group so that only members of the Accountants group can gain access to the Accountants folder.

Lesson Summary

In this lesson, you learned that you use shared application folders to centralize administration and make it easier to upgrade application software. When you use shared application folders, you should assign the Administrators group the Full Control permission for the applications folder so that members of this group can manage the application software and control user permissions. You should also remove the Full Control permission from the Everyone group and assign Read permission to the Users group. This provides more security because the Users group includes only user accounts that you created, whereas the Everyone group includes anyone who has access to network resources, including the Guest account.

You also learned that you use shared data folders to provide a central location for users to store and gain access to common files. When you use data folders, create and share common data folders on a volume that is separate from the operating system and applications. Data files should be backed up frequently, and with data folders on a separate volume, you can conveniently back them up.

Lesson 3: Sharing Folders

You can share resources with others by sharing folders containing those resources. To share a folder, you must be a member of one of several groups, depending on the role of the computer where the shared folder resides. When you share a folder, you can control access to the folder by limiting the number of users who can simultaneously gain access to it, and you can also control access to the folder and its contents by assigning permissions to selected users and groups. Once you have shared a folder, users must connect to the shared folder and must have the appropriate permissions to gain access to it. After you have shared a folder, you might want to modify it. You can stop sharing it, change its share name, and change user and group permissions to gain access to it.

After this lesson, you will be able to

- Create and modify shared folders.
- Make a connection to a shared folder.

Estimated lesson time: 20 minutes

Requirements for Sharing Folders

In Windows 2000 Professional, members of the built-in Administrators and Power Users groups are able to share folders. Which groups can share folders and on which machines they can share them depends on whether it is a workgroup or a domain and the type of computer on which the shared folders reside:

- In a Windows 2000 domain, the Administrators and Server Operators groups can share folders residing on any machines in the domain. The Power Users group is a local group and can share folders residing only on the stand-alone server or computer running Windows 2000 Professional where the group is located.

- In a Windows 2000 workgroup, the Administrators and Power Users groups can share folders on the Windows 2000 Server stand-alone server or the computer running Windows 2000 Professional on which the group exists.

Note If the folder to be shared resides on an NTFS volume, users must also have at least the Read permission for that folder to be able to share it.

Administrative Shared Folders

Windows 2000 automatically shares folders for administrative purposes. These shares are appended with a dollar sign ($), which hides the shared folder from users who browse the computer. The root of each volume, the system root folder, and the location of the printer drivers are all hidden shared folders that you can gain access to across the network.

Table 15.2 describes the purpose of the administrative shared folders that Windows 2000 automatically provides.

Table 15.2   Windows 2000 Administrative Shared Folders

Share	Purpose
C$, D$, E$, and so on	The root of each volume on a hard disk is automatically shared, and the share name is the drive letter appended with a dollar sign ($). When you connect to this folder, you have access to the entire volume. You use the administrative shares to remotely connect to the computer to perform administrative tasks. Windows 2000 assigns the Full Control permission to the Administrators group.
	Windows 2000 also automatically shares CD-ROM drives and creates the share name by appending the dollar sign to the CD-ROM drive letter.
Admin$	The system root folder, which is C:\Winnt by default, is shared as Admin$. Administrators can gain access to this shared folder to administer Windows 2000 without knowing in which folder it is installed. Only members of the Administrators group have access to this share. Windows 2000 assigns the Full Control permission to the Administrators group.
Print$	When you install the first shared printer, the *systemroot*\System32\Spool\Drivers folder is shared as Print$. This folder provides access to printer driver files for clients. Only members of the Administrators, Server Operators, and Print Operators groups have the Full Control permission. The Everyone group has the Read permission.

Hidden shared folders aren't limited to those that the system automatically creates. You can share additional folders and append a dollar sign to the end of the share name. Then only users who know the folder name can gain access to it if they also possess the proper permissions to it.

Sharing a Folder

When you share a folder, you can give it a share name, provide comments to describe the folder and its content, limit the number of users who have access to the folder, assign permissions, and share the same folder multiple times.

You can share a folder as follows:

1. Log on with a user account that is a member of a group that is able to share folders.
2. Right-click the folder that you want to share, and then click Properties.
3. On the Sharing tab of the Properties dialog box, configure the options shown in Figure 15.5 and described in Table 15.3.

Figure 15.5 The Sharing tab of a folder's Properties dialog box

Table 15.3 Sharing Tab Options

Option	Description
Share Name	The name that users from remote locations use to make a connection to the shared folder. You must enter a share name.
Comment	An optional description for the share name. The comment appears in addition to the share name when users at client computers browse the server for shared folders. This comment can be used to identify contents of the shared folder.
User Limit	The number of users who can concurrently connect to the shared folder. If you click Maximum Allowed as the user limit, Windows 2000 Professional supports up to 10 connections. Windows 2000 Server can support an unlimited number of connections, but the number of Client Access Licenses (CALs) that you purchased limits the connections.
Permissions	The shared folder permissions that apply *only* when the folder is accessed over the network. By default, the Everyone group is assigned Full Control for all new shared folders.
Caching	The settings to configure offline access to this shared folder.

Caching

To make shared folders available offline, copies of the files are stored in a reserved portion of disk space on your computer called a *cache*. Since the cache is on your hard disk, the computer can access this cache regardless of whether it is connected to the network. By default, the cache size is set to 10 percent of the available disk space. You can change the size of the cache on the Offline Files tab of the Folder Options dialog box. You can also see how much space the cache is using by opening the Offline Files folder and clicking Properties on the File menu.

Note Shared network files are stored in the root folder of your hard disk. If you want to change the location of the cache, the Offline Files Mover (Cachemov.exe) is available in the Windows 2000 Professional Resource Kit to change the cache location.

When you share a folder, you can allow others to make the shared folder available offline by clicking Caching in the folder's Properties dialog box. In the Caching Settings dialog box (see Figure 15.6), the Allow Caching Of Files In This Shared Folder check box allows you to turn caching on and off.

Figure 15.6   The Caching Settings dialog box

The Caching Settings dialog box contains three caching options:

- Manual Caching For Documents. The files that someone using your shared folder specifically (or manually) identifies are the only ones available offline. This caching option is recommended for a shared network folder containing files that are to be accessed and modified by several people. This option is the default.

- Automatic Caching For Documents. Makes every file that someone opens from your shared folder available to him or her offline. Files that aren't opened are not available offline.

- Automatic Caching For Programs. Provides offline access to shared folders containing files that are read, referenced, or run, but that are not changed in the process. This setting reduces network traffic because offline files are opened directly without accessing the network versions in any way, and generally start and run faster than the network versions.

Note For more information on caching and Offline Folders, see Chapter 24, "Configuring Windows 2000 for Mobile Computers."

Assigning Shared Folder Permissions

After you share a folder, the next step is to specify which users have access to the shared folder by assigning shared folder permissions to selected user accounts and groups.

You can assign permissions to user accounts and groups for a shared folder, as follows:

1. On the Sharing tab of the Properties dialog box of the shared folder, click Permissions.

2. In the Permissions dialog box, ensure that the Everyone group is selected and then click Remove.

3. In the Permissions dialog box, click Add (see Figure 15.7).

Figure 15.7   Setting permissions for a shared folder

4. In the Select Users, Computers, Or Groups dialog box, click the user accounts and groups to which you want to assign permissions.

5. Click Add to add the user account or group to the shared folder. Repeat this step for all user accounts and groups to which you want to assign permissions.

6. Click OK.

7. In the Permissions dialog box for the shared folder, click the user account or group, and then, under Permissions, select the Allow check box or the Deny check box for the appropriate permissions for the user account or group.

Modifying Shared Folders

You can modify shared folders, stop sharing a folder, modify the share name, and modify shared folder permissions.

You can modify a shared folder as follows:

1. Click the Sharing tab in the Properties dialog box of the shared folder.

2. To complete the appropriate task, use the steps in Table 15.4.

Table 15.4   Steps to Modify a Shared Folder

To	Do this
Stop sharing a folder	Click Do Not Share This Folder.
Modify the share name	Click Do Not Share This Folder to stop sharing the folder; click Apply to apply the change; click Share This Folder, and then enter the new share name in the Share Name box.
Modify shared folder permissions	Click Permissions. In the Permissions dialog box, click Add or Remove. In the Select Users, Computers, Or Groups dialog box, click the user account or group whose permissions you want to modify.
Share folder multiple times	Click New Share to share a folder with an additional shared folder name. Do so to consolidate multiple shared folders into one while allowing users to continue to use the same shared folder name that they used before you consolidated the folders.
Remove a share name	Click Remove Share. This option appears only after the folder has been shared more than once.

Note If you stop sharing a folder while a user has a file open, the user might lose data. If you click Do Not Share This Folder and a user has a connection to the shared folder, Windows 2000 displays a dialog box notifying you that a user has a connection to the shared folder.

Connecting to a Shared Folder

You can gain access to a shared folder on another computer by using the Map Network Drive wizard, the Run command, or My Network Places. If you want to connect to a shared folder by using the Map Network Drive wizard, you can do the following:

1. Right-click the My Network Places icon on your desktop, and then click Map Network Drive.

2. In the Map Network Drive wizard, shown in Figure 15.8, click Folder, and then type a UNC path to the folder (for example, *computer_name*\ *sharedfolder_name*).

3. Enter a drive letter for the shared folder in the Drive list box.

4. Select the Reconnect At Logon check box if you want to reconnect to the shared folder each time that you log on.

5. Click the link labeled Connect Using A Different User Name to connect to a shared folder with a different user account, and then enter the user name and password in the Connect As dialog box.

You can connect to a shared folder by using the Run command, as follows:

1. Click the Start button, click Run, and then type *computer_name* in the Open box.

   Windows 2000 displays shared folders for the computer.

2. Double-click the shared folder to which you want to connect.

You can connect to a shared folder by using My Network Places, as follows:

1. Double-click the My Network Places icon.

2. Locate the computer on which the shared folder is located.

3. Double-click the shared folder to which you want to connect.

Figure 15.8   The Map Network Drive wizard

Lesson Summary

In this lesson, you learned that you can share resources with others by sharing folders containing those resources. To share a folder, you must be a member of one of several groups, depending on the role of the computer where the shared folder resides. You can control access to a shared folder by limiting the number of users who can simultaneously gain access to it, and you can also control access to the folder and its contents by assigning permissions to selected users and groups. To access a shared folder, users must connect to it and must have the appropriate permissions. You can modify a shared folder, stop sharing it, change its share name, and change user and group permissions to gain access to it.

Lesson 4: Combining Shared Folder Permissions and NTFS Permissions

You share folders to provide network users with access to resources. If you are using a FAT volume, the shared folder permissions are the only resource available to provide security for the folders you have shared and the folders and files they contain. If you are using an NTFS volume, you can assign NTFS permissions to individual users and groups to better control access to the files and subfolders in the shared folders. When you combine shared folder permissions and NTFS permissions, the more restrictive permission is always the overriding permission.

After this lesson, you will be able to

- Combine shared folder permissions and NTFS permissions.

Estimated lesson time: 45 minutes

Strategies for Combining Shared Folder Permissions and NTFS Permissions

One strategy for providing access to resources on an NTFS volume is to share folders with the default shared folder permissions and then control access by assigning NTFS permissions. When you share a folder on an NTFS volume, both shared folder permissions and NTFS permissions combine to secure file resources.

Shared folder permissions provide limited security for resources. You gain the greatest flexibility by using NTFS permissions to control access to shared folders. Also, NTFS permissions apply whether the resource is accessed locally or over the network.

When you use shared folder permissions on an NTFS volume, the following rules apply:

- You can apply NTFS permissions to files and subfolders in the shared folder. You can apply different NTFS permissions to each file and subfolder that a shared folder contains.

- In addition to shared folder permissions, users must have NTFS permissions for the files and subfolders that shared folders contain to gain access to those files and subfolders. This is in contrast to FAT volumes where permissions for a shared folder are the only permissions protecting files and subfolders in the shared folder.

- When you combine shared folder permissions and NTFS permissions, the more restrictive permission is always the overriding permission.

In Figure 15.9, the Everyone group has the shared folder Full Control permission for the Public folder and the NTFS Read permission for FileA. The Everyone group's effective permission for FileA is Read because Read is the more restrictive permission. The effective permission for FileB is Full Control because both the shared folder permission and the NTFS permission allow this level of access.

- NTFS permissions are required on NTFS volumes.
- Apply NTFS permissions to files and subfolders.
- The most restrictive permission is the effective permission.

Figure 15.9   Combining shared folder permissions and NTFS permissions

Practice: Managing Shared Folders

In this practice, you will determine users' effective permissions, plan shared folders, plan permissions, share a folder, assign shared folder permissions, connect to a shared folder, stop sharing a folder, and test the combined effects of shared folder permissions and NTFS permissions.

Important To complete the optional exercises (5 and 8), you must have two networked computers. One computer must be running Windows 2000 Professional and the other must be running one of the following Windows 2000 products: Windows 2000 Professional, Windows 2000 Server, or Windows 2000 Advanced Server. Both computers should have the Administrator user account using *password* for the Administrator account password.

Exercise 1: Combining Permissions

Figure 15.10 shows examples of shared folders on NTFS volumes. These shared folders contain subfolders that have also been assigned NTFS permissions. Determine a user's effective permissions for each example.

Figure 15.10   Combined permissions

1. In the first example, the Data folder is shared. The Sales group has the shared folder Read permission for the Data folder and the NTFS Full Control permission for the Sales subfolder.

   What are the Sales group's effective permissions for the Sales subfolder when they gain access to the Sales subfolder by making a connection to the Data shared folder?

2. In the second example, the Users folder contains user home folders. Each user home folder contains data that is accessible only to the user for whom the folder is named. The Users folder has been shared, and the Users group has the shared folder Full Control permission for the Users folder. User1 and User2 have the NTFS Full Control permission for *only* their home folder and no NTFS permissions for other folders. These users are all members of the Users group.

   What permissions does User1 have when he or she accesses the User1 subfolder by making a connection to the Users shared folder? What are User1's permissions for the User2 subfolder?

Exercise 2: Planning Shared Folders

In this exercise, you will plan how to share resources on servers in the main office of a manufacturing company. Record your decisions in the table at the end of this exercise.

Figure 15.11 illustrates a partial folder structure for the servers at the manufacturing company.

Figure 15.11   A partial folder structure for the servers at a manufacturing company

You need to make resources on these servers available to network users. To do this, determine which folders to share and which permissions to assign to groups, including the appropriate built-in groups.

Base your planning decisions on the following criteria:

- Members of the Managers group need to read and revise documents in the Management Guidelines folder. Nobody else should have access to this folder.
- Administrators need complete access to all shared folders, except for Management Guidelines.
- The customer service department requires its own network location to store working files. All customer service representatives are members of the Customer Service group.
- All employees need a network location to share information with each other.

- All employees need to use the spreadsheet, database, and word processing software.

- Only members of the Managers group should have access to the project management software.

- Members of the CustomerDBFull group need to read and update the customer database.

- Members of the CustomerDBRead group need to read only the customer database.

- Each user needs a private network location to store files. This location must be accessible only by that user.

- Share names must be accessible from Windows 2000, Windows NT, Windows 98, Windows 95, and non-Windows-NT-based platforms.

Record your answers in the following table.

Folder name and location	Shared name	Groups and permissions
Example:		
Management Guidelines	MgmtGd	Managers: Full Control

Exercise 3: Sharing Folders

In this exercise, you will share a folder.

▶ **To share a folder**

1. Log on as Administrator.

2. Start Windows Explorer, create a C:\MktApps folder, right-click MktApps, and then click Properties.

3. In the MktApps Properties dialog box, click the Sharing tab.

   Notice that the folder is currently not shared.

4. Click Share This Folder.

   Notice that Share Name defaults to the name of the folder. If you want the share name to be different from the folder's name, change it here.

5. In the Comment box, type **Shared Marketing Applications** and then click OK.

Notice that Windows Explorer changes the appearance of the Apps folder by placing a hand under it to indicate that it is a shared folder.

Exercise 4: Assigning Shared Folder Permissions

In this exercise, you will determine the current permissions for a shared folder and assign shared folder permissions to groups in your domain.

▶ **To determine the current permissions for the MktApps shared folder**

1. In Windows Explorer, right-click C:\MktApps, and then click Properties.

2. In the MktApps Properties dialog box, click the Sharing tab, and then click Permissions.

   Windows 2000 displays the Permissions For MktApps dialog box.

   Notice that the default permissions for the MktApps shared folder is for the Everyone group to have Full Control permissions.

▶ **To remove permissions for a group**

1. Verify that Everyone is selected.

2. Click Remove.

▶ **To assign Full Control to the Administrators group**

1. Click Add.

   Windows 2000 displays the Select Users, Computers, Or Groups dialog box.

2. Ensure that your computer name, PRO1, is displayed in the Look In box. In the Name box, click Administrators, and then click Add.

3. Click OK.

   Windows 2000 adds Administrators to the list of names with permissions.

   Which type of access does Windows 2000 assign to Administrators by default?

4. In the Permissions box, under Allow, click the Full Control check box.

   Why did Windows Explorer also select the Change permission for you?

5. Click OK to close the Permissions For MktApps dialog box.

6. Click OK to close the MktApps Properties dialog box.

7. Close Windows Explorer.

Exercise 5 (Optional): Connecting to a Shared Folder

In this exercise, you will use two methods to connect to a shared folder.

Important To complete Exercise 5, you must have two networked computers. One computer must be running Windows 2000 Professional, and the other must be running either Windows 2000 Professional, Windows 2000 Server, or Windows 2000 Advanced Server. Both computers should have the Administrator user account using *password* for the Administrator account password.

▶ **To connect to a network drive by using the Run command**

1. Log on as Administrator on your second computer.

2. Click the Start button, and then click Run.

3. In the Open box, type **\\PRO1**. (If you didn't use PRO1 as the name of your computer, use the appropriate name here and in the following steps.) Click OK.

   Windows 2000 displays the PRO1 window. Notice that only the folders that are shared appear to network users.

4. Double-click MktApps to confirm that you can gain access to its contents.

   MktApps contains no files or folders for you to access, but the system opens the folder and displays the contents of MktApps.

5. Close the MktApps On PRO1 window.

▶ **To connect a network drive to a shared folder by using the Map Network Drive command**

1. Right-click My Network Places, and then click Map Network Drive.

2. In the Map Network Drive wizard, in the Folder box, type **\\PRO1\MktApps** (if you didn't use PRO1 as the name of your computer, use the appropriate name here).

3. In the Drive box, select P.

4. Clear the Reconnect At Logon check box.

   You will gain access to this shared folder only in this exercise. Disabling the option to reconnect will ensure that Windows 2000 won't automatically attempt to reconnect to this shared folder later.

5. To complete the connection, click Finish.

   Windows 2000 displays the MktApps On 'PRO1' (P:) window.

   How does Windows Explorer indicate that this drive points to a remote shared folder?

6. Close the MktApps On 'PRO1' (P:) window.

▶ **To disconnect from a network drive by using Windows Explorer**

1. Start Windows Explorer.

2. Right-click MktApps On 'Pro1' (P:), and then click Disconnect.

   Windows 2000 removes MktApps On 'PRO1' (P:) from the Windows Explorer window.

3. Close Windows Explorer.

Exercise 6: Stopping Folder Sharing

In this exercise, you will stop sharing a shared folder.

▶ **To stop sharing a folder**

1. Log on as Administrator on the PRO1 computer (or the computer running Windows 2000 Professional with the name you specified), and then start Windows Explorer.

2. Right-click C:\MktApps, and then click Properties.

3. In the MktApps Properties dialog box, click the Sharing tab.

4. Click Do Not Share This Folder, and then click OK.

   Notice that Windows 2000 no longer displays the hand that identifies a shared folder under the Apps folder. You might need to refresh the screen; if so, press F5.

5. Close Windows Explorer.

Exercise 7: Assigning NTFS Permissions and Sharing Folders

In this exercise, you will assign NTFS permissions to the MktApps, Public, and Manuals folders. Then you will share the MktApps, Manuals, and Public folders.

▶ **To assign NTFS permissions**

Use Windows Explorer to create the necessary folders and to assign the NTFS permissions that are listed in the table that follows. For each folder, do not allow inherited permissions to propagate to the object and remove any previously existing NTFS permissions.

Path	Group or user account	NTFS permissions
C:\MktApps	Administrators	Full Control
	Users	Read & Execute
C:\MktApps\Manuals	Administrators	Full Control
	Users	Read & Execute
C:\MktApps\Public	Administrators	Full Control
	Users	Full Control

▶ **To share folders and assign shared folder permissions**

Share the appropriate application folders and assign permissions to network user accounts based on the information in the table that follows. Remove all other shared folder permissions.

Path and shared folder name	Group or user account	Shared folder permissions
C:\MktApps shared as MktApps	Administrators	Full Control
	Users	Full Control

Exercise 8 (Optional): Testing NTFS and Shared Folder Permissions

In this exercise, you will use different user accounts to test the permissions that you assigned in Exercise 1. To answer the questions in this exercise, refer to the tables in Exercise 7.

Important To complete Exercise 8, you must have two networked computers. One computer must be running Windows 2000 Professional, and the other must be running either Windows 2000 Professional, Windows 2000 Server, or Windows 2000 Advanced Server. Both computers should have the Administrator user account using *password* for the Administrator account password.

▶ **To test permissions for the Manuals folder when a user logs on locally**

1. Log on as User1 with a password of *password* on the PRO1 computer (or the computer running Windows 2000 Professional with the name you specified).

2. In Windows Explorer, expand C:\MktApps\Manuals.

3. In the Manuals folder, attempt to create a file.

   Were you successful? Why or why not?

4. Close Windows Explorer and log off.

▶ **To test permissions for the Manuals folder when a user makes a connection over the network**

1. Log on as Administrator with a password of *password* on your second computer.

2. Create a user account, User1, with a password of *password* and clear the User Must Change Password At Next Logon check box, if necessary.

Note In a workgroup, no centralized database of user accounts exists. Therefore, you must create the same user account with the same password on each computer in the workgroup. This applies to the Administrator account as well.

---

3. Log off and then log on as User1 at your second computer.

4. Click the Start button, and then click Run.

5. In the Open box, type **\\PRO1\MktApps** and then click OK.

6. In the MktApps On PRO1 window, double-click Manuals.

7. In the Manuals window, attempt to create a file.

   Were you successful? Why or why not?

8. Close all windows and log off.

▶ **To test permissions for the Manuals folder when a user logs on over the network as Administrator**

1. Log on as Administrator with a password of *password* at your second computer, not PRO1.

2. Make a connection to the shared folder C:\MktApps on PRO1.

3. In the MktApps On PRO1 window, double-click Manuals.

4. In the Manuals window, attempt to create a file.

   Were you successful? Why or why not?

5. Close all windows and log off.

▶ **To test permissions for the Public folder when a user makes a connection over the network**

1. Log on as User1 with a password of *password* on your second computer.

2. Click the Start button, and then click Run.

3. In the Open box, type **\\PRO1\MktApps** and then click OK.

4. In the MktApps On PRO1 window, double-click Public.

5. In the Public window, attempt to create a file.

   Were you successful? Why or why not?

6. Close all windows and log off.

Lesson Summary

In this lesson, you learned that you share folders to provide network users with access to resources. On a FAT volume, the shared folder permissions are all that is available to provide security for the folders you have shared and for the folders and files they contain. On an NTFS volume, you can assign NTFS permissions to individual users and groups to better control access to the files and subfolders in the shared folders. When you combine shared folder permissions and NTFS permissions, the more restrictive permission is always the overriding permission.

In the practice portion of this lesson, you created and shared folders, stopped sharing a folder, created folders, applied NTFS permissions, and then shared the folders. If you have a second computer, you were able to test how the shared folder permissions and NTFS permissions combined to provide access to resources.

Review

The following questions will help you determine whether you have learned enough to move on to the next chapter. If you have difficulty answering these questions, please go back and review the material in this chapter before beginning the next chapter. See Appendix A, "Questions and Answers," for the answers to these questions.

1. When a folder is shared on a FAT volume, what does a user with the Full Control shared folder permissions for the folder have access to?

2. What are the shared folder permissions?

3. By default, what are the permissions that are assigned to a shared folder?

4. When a folder is shared on an NTFS volume, what does a user with the Full Control shared folder permissions for the folder have access to?

5. When you share a public folder, why should you use centralized data folders?

6. What is the best way to secure files and folders that you share on NTFS partitions?

C H A P T E R   1 6

Auditing Resources and Events

About This Chapter

In this chapter, you will learn about the Microsoft Windows 2000 Local Security Policy. One of the features controlled by Local Security Policy is auditing. *Auditing* is a tool for maintaining network security that allows you to track user activities and systemwide events. In addition, you will learn about audit policies and what you need to consider before you set one up. You will also learn how to set up auditing on resources and how to maintain security logs.

Before You Begin

To complete this chapter, you must have

- A computer that meets the minimum hardware requirements located in "About This Book."
- Microsoft Windows 2000 Professional installed on the computer.

Lesson 1: Understanding Auditing

Auditing allows you to track both user activities and Windows 2000 activities, which are called *events,* on a computer. Through auditing, you can specify that Windows 2000 writes a record of an event to the security log. The *security log* maintains a record of valid and invalid logon attempts and events related to creating, opening, or deleting files or other objects. An audit entry in the security log contains the following information:

- The action that was performed
- The user who performed the action
- The success or failure of the event and when the event occurred

After this lesson, you will be able to

- Describe the purpose of auditing.

Estimated lesson time: 5 minutes

Using an Audit Policy

An *audit policy* defines the types of security events that Windows 2000 records in the security log on each computer. The security log allows you to track the events that you specify.

Windows 2000 writes events to the security log on the computer where the event occurs. For example, any time someone tries to log on and the logon attempt fails, Windows 2000 writes an event to the security log on the computer.

You can set up an audit policy for a computer to do the following:

- Track the success and failure of events, such as logon attempts by users, an attempt by a particular user to read a specific file, changes to a user account or to group memberships, and changes to your security settings.
- Eliminate or minimize the risk of unauthorized use of resources.

Using Event Viewer to View Security Logs

You use Event Viewer to view events that Windows 2000 has recorded in the security log. You can also archive log files to track trends over time—for example, to determine the use of printers or files or to verify attempts at unauthorized use of resources.

Lesson Summary

In this lesson, you learned about Windows 2000 auditing, which helps you ensure that your network is secure by tracking user activities and systemwide events. Auditing allows you to have Windows 2000 write a record of these events to the security log. To specify which events to record, you set up an audit policy. You use Event Viewer to view the security log. Each audit entry in the security log contains the action that was performed, the user who performed the action, and the success or failure of the action. You can also archive log files to track trends over time.

Lesson 2: Planning an Audit Policy

When you plan an audit policy, you need to determine what you want to audit and the computers on which to configure auditing.

After this lesson, you will be able to

- Plan an audit strategy and determine which events to audit.

Estimated lesson time: 5 minutes

Audit Policy Guidelines

When you plan an audit policy, you must determine the computers on which to set up auditing. Auditing is turned off by default. As you are determining which computers to audit, you must also plan what to audit on each computer. Windows 2000 records audited events on each computer separately.

The types of events that you can audit include the following:

- Accessing files and folders
- Logging on and off
- Shutting down and restarting a computer running Windows 2000
- Changing user accounts and groups
- Attempting to make changes to objects in directory services based on Active Directory technology (only if your Windows 2000 computer is part of a domain)

After you have determined the types of events to audit, you must also determine whether to audit the success of events, the failure of events, or both. Tracking successful events can tell you how often Windows 2000 or users gain access to specific files, printers, or other objects. You can use this information for resource planning.

Tracking failed events can alert you to possible security breaches. For example, if you notice a lot of failed logon attempts by a certain user account, especially if these attempts are occurring outside normal business hours, you can assume that an unauthorized person is attempting to break in to your system.

Other guidelines in determining your audit policy include the following:

- Determine whether you need to track trends of system use. If so, plan to archive event logs. Archiving these logs will allow you to view how use changes over time and will allow you to plan to increase system resources before they become a problem.

- Review security logs frequently. You should set a schedule and regularly review security logs because configuring auditing alone doesn't alert you to security breaches.

- Define an audit policy that is useful and manageable. Always audit sensitive and confidential data. Audit only those events that will provide you with meaningful information about your network environment. This will minimize use of the computer's resources and make essential information easier to locate. Auditing too many types of events can create excess overhead for Windows 2000.

- Audit resource access by using the Everyone group instead of the Users group. This will ensure that you audit anyone who can connect to the network, not just the users for whom you create user accounts in the domain.

Lesson Summary

In this lesson, you learned that in planning an audit policy, you must determine the computers on which to set up auditing and what to audit on each computer. The types of events that you can audit include the following: accessing files and folders, logging on and off, shutting down and restarting a computer running Windows 2000 Professional, and changing user accounts and groups.

You also learned that you can audit the success of events, the failure of events, or both. You track successful events to determine how often Windows 2000 or users gain access to specific files or printers. You can use this information for resource planning. You track failed events to look for possible security breaches. You can also archive the logs to track trends of system use.

Lesson 3: Implementing an Audit Policy

Auditing is a powerful tool for tracking events that occur on computers in your organization. To implement auditing, you need to consider auditing requirements and set the audit policy. After you set an audit policy on a computer, you can implement auditing on files, folders, and printers.

After this lesson, you will be able to

- Set up auditing on files and folders.
- Set up auditing on printers.

Estimated lesson time: 25 minutes

Configuring Auditing

For computers running Windows 2000 Professional, you set up an audit policy for each individual computer.

Auditing Requirements

The requirements to set up and administer auditing are as follows:

- You must have the Manage Auditing And Security Log user right for the computer where you want to configure an audit policy or review an audit log. By default, Windows 2000 grants these rights to the Administrators group.
- The files and folders to be audited must be on Microsoft Windows 2000 File System (NTFS) volumes.

Setting Up Auditing

Setting up auditing is a two-part process:

1. Set the audit policy. The audit policy enables auditing of objects but doesn't activate auditing of specific objects.
2. Enable auditing of specific resources. You specify the specific events to audit for files, folders, printers, and Active Directory objects. Windows 2000 then tracks and logs the specified events.

Setting an Audit Policy

The first step in implementing an audit policy is selecting the types of events that Windows 2000 audits. For each event that you can audit, the configuration settings indicate whether to track successful or failed attempts. You set audit policies in the Local Security Settings window, which you open by selecting Local Security Policy on the Administrative Tools menu.

Table 16.1 describes the types of events that Windows 2000 can audit.

Table 16.1   Types of Events Audited by Windows 2000

Event	Description
Account Logon Events	A domain controller received a request to validate a user account. (This is applicable only if your computer running Windows 2000 Professional joins a Windows 2000 domain.)
Account Management	An administrator created, changed, or deleted a user account or group. A user account was renamed, disabled, or enabled, or a password was set or changed.
Directory Service Access	A user gained access to an Active Directory object. You must configure specific Active Directory objects for auditing to log this type of event. (Active Directory directory services are available only if your computer running Windows 2000 Professional joins a Windows 2000 domain.)
Logon Events	A user logged on or logged off, or a user made or canceled a network connection to the computer.
Object Access	A user gained access to a file, folder, or printer. You must configure specific files, folders, or printers for auditing. Object access is auditing a user's access to files, folders, and printers.
Policy Change	A change was made to the user security options, user rights, or audit policies.
Privilege Use	A user exercised a right, such as changing the system time. (This doesn't include rights that are related to logging on and logging off.)
Process Tracking	A program performed an action. This information is generally useful only for programmers who want to track details of program execution.
System Events	A user restarted or shut down the computer, or an event occurred that affects Windows 2000 security or the security log. (For example, the audit log is full and Windows 2000 starts discarding entries.)

To set an audit policy on a computer that is running Windows 2000 Professional, use the Local Security Settings window, as follows:

1. Click Start, point to Programs, point to Administrative Tools, and then click Local Security Policy.

2. In the Local Security Settings window's console tree, double-click Local Policies, and then click Audit Policy.

   The console displays the current audit policy settings in the details pane, as shown in Figure 16.1.

Figure 16.1   Events that Windows 2000 can audit

3. Select the type of event to audit, and then, on the Action menu, click Security.

   The Local Security Policy Setting dialog box appears for the selected event. Figure 16.2 shows the Local Security Policy Setting dialog box for Audit Logon Events, and Table 16.2 defines the fields available in the Local Security Policy Setting dialog box.

4. Select the Success check box, the Failure check box, or both.

5. Click OK.

6. Restart your computer.

Figure 16.2   The Local Security Policy Setting dialog box for Audit Logon Events

Table 16.2   Local Security Policy Setting Dialog Box Fields

Field	Description
Effective Policy Setting	Indicates whether or not auditing is turned on.
	No auditing indicates it is not auditing this event.
	Failure indicates it is auditing failed attempts.
	Success indicates it is auditing successful attempts.
	Success, Failure indicates it is auditing all attempts.
Local Policy Setting	A check mark in the Success check box indicates that auditing is in effect for successful attempts.
	A check mark in the Failure check box indicates that auditing is in effect for failed attempts.

Once you have set the audit policy, remember that the changes that you make to your computer's audit policy don't take effect until you restart your computer.

Auditing Access to Files and Folders

If security breaches are an issue for your organization, you can set up auditing for files and folders on NTFS partitions. To audit user access to files and folders, you must first set your audit policy to audit object access, which includes files and folders.

Once you have set your audit policy to audit object access, you enable auditing for specific files and folders and specify which types of access, by which users or groups, to audit.

You can enable auditing for specific files and folders as follows:

1. On the Security tab in the Properties dialog box for a file or folder, click Advanced.
2. On the Auditing tab, click Add, select the users for whom you want to audit file and folder access, and then click OK.
3. In the Audit Entry dialog box, select the Successful check box or the Failed check box for the events that you want to audit. For a list of the events, see Figure 16.3.

   Table 16.3 describes when to audit these events.
4. Click OK to return to the Access Control Settings dialog box.

   By default, any auditing changes that you make to a parent folder also apply to all child folders and all files in the parent and child folders.
5. To prevent changes that are made to a parent folder from applying to the currently selected file or folder, clear the Allow Inheritable Auditing Entries From Parent To Propagate To This Object check box.
6. Click OK.

Figure 16.3   Events that can be audited for files and folders

Table 16.3   User Events and What Triggers Them

Event	User activity that triggers the event
Traverse Folder/Execute File	Running a program or gaining access to a folder to change directories
List Folder/Read Data	Displaying the contents of a file or folder
Read Attributes Read Extended Attributes	Displaying the attributes of a file or folder
Create Files/Write Data	Changing the contents of a file or creating new files in a folder
Create Folders/Append Data	Creating folders in the folder
Write Attributes Write Extended Attributes	Changing attributes of a file or folder
Delete Subfolders And Files	Deleting a file or subfolder in a folder
Delete	Deleting a file or folder
Read Permissions	Viewing permissions or the file owner for a file or folder
Change Permissions	Changing permissions for a file or folder
Take Ownership	Taking ownership of a file or folder

Auditing Access to Printers

Audit access to printers to track access to sensitive printers. To audit access to printers, set your audit policy to audit object access, which includes printers. Then enable auditing for specific printers and specify which types of access to audit and which users will have access. After you select the printer, you use the same steps that you use to set up auditing on files and folders. You set up auditing on a printer, as follows:

1. In the Properties dialog box for the printer, click the Security tab, and then click Advanced.

2. On the Auditing tab, click Add, select the appropriate users or groups for whom you want to audit printer access, and then click OK.

3. In the Apply Onto box in the Auditing Entry dialog box, select where the auditing setting applies.

4. Under Access, select the Successful check box or the Failed check box for the events that you want to audit. (See Figure 16.4.)

5. Click OK in the appropriate dialog boxes to exit.

Figure 16.4   Printer events that can be audited

Table 16.4 describes audit events for printers and explains which action triggers the event to occur.

Table 16.4   Printer Events and What Triggers Them

Event	User activity that triggers the event
Print	Printing a file
Manage Printers	Changing printer settings, pausing a printer, sharing a printer, or removing a printer
Manage Documents	Changing job settings; pausing, restarting, moving, or deleting documents; sharing a printer; or changing printer properties
Read Permissions	Viewing printer permissions
Change Permissions	Changing printer permissions
Take Ownership	Taking printer ownership

Lesson Summary

In this lesson, you learned that the first step in implementing an audit policy is selecting the types of events that Windows 2000 audits. You can select the events to audit for files and folders, and you can select the events you want to audit for printers. For each event that you can audit, the configuration settings indicate whether to track successful attempts, failed attempts, or both. You use the Local Security Settings window to set audit policies, and then you restart your computer to enable auditing.

You also learned that you can set up auditing for access to files, folders, and printers on NTFS partitions. To do so, you must first set your audit policy to audit object access, which includes files, folders, and printers. Once you have set your audit policy to audit object access, you enable auditing for specific files, folders, and printers and specify which types of access, by which users or groups, to audit.

Lesson 4: Using Event Viewer

You use Event Viewer to perform a variety of tasks, including viewing the audit logs that are generated as a result of setting the audit policy and auditing events. You can also use Event Viewer to view the contents of security log files and find specific events within log files.

After this lesson, you will be able to

- View a log.
- Locate events in a log.
- Archive security logs.
- Configure the size of audit logs.

Estimated lesson time: 45 minutes

Understanding Windows 2000 Logs

You use Event Viewer to view information contained in Windows 2000 logs. By default, Event Viewer has three logs available to view. These logs are described in Table 16.5.

Table 16.5   Logs Maintained by Windows 2000

Log	Description
Application log	Contains errors, warnings, or information that programs, such as a database program or an e-mail program, generate. The program developer presets which events to record.
Security log	Contains information about the success or failure of audited events. The events that Windows 2000 records are a result of your audit policy.
System log	Contains errors, warnings, and information that Windows 2000 generates. Windows 2000 presets which events to record.

Note If additional services are installed, they might add their own event log.

Viewing Security Logs

The security log contains information about events that are monitored by an audit policy, such as failed and successful logon attempts. You can view the security log, as follows:

1. Click the Start button, point to Programs, point to Administrative Tools, and then click Event Viewer.
2. In the console tree, select Security Log.

In the details pane, Event Viewer displays a list of log entries and summary information for each item, as shown in Figure 16.5.

Successful events appear with a key icon, and unsuccessful events appear with a lock icon. Other important information includes the date and time that the event occurred, the category of the event, and the user who generated the event.

The category indicates the type of event, such as object access, account management, directory service access, or logon events.

3. To view additional information for any event, select the event, and then click Properties on the Action menu.

Windows 2000 records events in the security log on the computer at which the event occurred. You can view these events from any computer as long as you have administrative privileges for the computer where the events occurred. To view the security log on a remote computer, start the MMC and create a custom console; point Event Viewer to a remote computer when you add this snap-in to a console.

Figure 16.5   Event Viewer displaying a sample security log

Locating Events

When you first start Event Viewer, it automatically displays all events that are recorded in the selected log. To change what appears in the log, you can locate selected events by using the Filter command. You can also search for specific events by using the Find command.

To filter or find events, start Event Viewer, and then click Filter or click Find on the View menu. (See Figure 16.6.)

Figure 16.6   Using Event Viewer to filter or find events in a log

Table 16.6 describes the options for filtering and finding events.

Table 16.6   Options for Filtering and Finding Events

Option	Description
From and To	The date range for which to view events (Filter tab only).
Event Types	The types of events to view.
Event Source	The software or component driver that logged the event.
Category	The type of event, such as a logon or logoff attempt or a system event.
Event ID	An event number to identify the event. This number helps product support representatives track events.
Computer	A computer name.
User	A user logon name.
Description	The text that is in the description of the event (Find dialog box only).
Search Direction	The direction (up or down) in which to search the log (Find dialog box only).

Managing Audit Logs

You can track trends in Windows 2000 by archiving event logs and comparing logs from different periods. Viewing trends helps you determine resource use and plan for growth. You can also use logs to determine a pattern if unauthorized use of resources is a concern. Windows 2000 allows you to control the size of the logs and to specify the action that Windows 2000 takes when a log becomes full.

You can configure the properties of each individual audit log. To configure the settings for logs, select the log in Event Viewer, and then display the Properties dialog box for the log.

Use the Properties dialog box for each type of audit log to control the following:

- The size of each log, which can be from 64 KB to 4,194,240 KB (4 GB). The default size is 512 KB.

- The action that Windows 2000 takes when the log fills up, by clicking one of the options described in Table 16.7.

Table 16.7   Options for Handling Full Audit Log Files

Option	Description
Overwrite Events As Needed	You might lose information if the log becomes full before you archive it. However, this setting requires no maintenance.
Overwrite Events Older Than X Days	You might lose information if the log becomes full before you archive it, but Windows 2000 will only lose information that is at least x days old. Enter the number of days for this option.
Do Not Overwrite Events (Clear Log Manually)	This option requires you to clear the log manually. When the log becomes full, Windows 2000 will stop. However, no security log entries are overwritten.

Archiving Logs

Archiving security logs allows you to maintain a history of security-related events. Many companies have policies on keeping archive logs for a specified period to track security-related information over time.

If you want to archive, clear, or view an archived log, select the log you want to configure in Event Viewer, click the Action menu, and then click one of the options described in Table 16.8.

Table 16.8   Options to Archive, Clear, or View a Log File

To	Do this
Archive the log	Click Save Log File As, and then type a filename.
Clear the log	Click Clear All Events to clear the log. Windows 2000 creates a security log entry, stating that the log was cleared.
View an archived log	Click New Log View to add another view of the selected log.

Practice: Auditing Resources and Events

In this practice, you will plan an audit policy for your computer. Then you will set up an audit policy by enabling auditing on certain events. You will also set up auditing of a file and a printer. Then you will view the security log file and configure Event Viewer to overwrite events when the log file is filled.

Exercise 1: Planning an Audit Policy

In this exercise, you will plan an audit policy for your computer. You need to determine the following:

- Which types of events to audit
- Whether to audit the success or failure of an event, or both

Use the following criteria to make your decisions:

- Record unsuccessful attempts to gain access to the computer.
- Record unauthorized access to the files that make up the Customer database.
- For billing purposes, track color printer use.
- Track whenever someone tries to tamper with the computer's hardware.
- Keep a record of actions that an administrator performs to track unauthorized changes.
- Track backup procedures to prevent data theft.
- Track unauthorized access to sensitive Active Directory objects.

Record your decisions to audit successful events, failed events, or both for the actions listed in the following table:

Action to audit	Successful	Failed
Account Logon Events	❏	❏
Account Management	❏	❏
Directory Service Access	❏	❏

(continued)

Action to audit	Successful	Failed
Logon Events	❏	❏
Object Access	❏	❏
Policy Change	❏	❏
Privilege Use	❏	❏
Process Tracking	❏	❏
System Events	❏	❏

Exercise 2: Setting Up an Audit Policy

In this exercise, you will enable auditing for selected events.

▶ **To set up an audit policy**

1. Log on to your computer as Administrator.

2. Click Start, point to Programs, point to Administrative Tools, and then click Local Security Policy.

3. In the Local Security Settings window's console tree, double-click Local Policies, and then click Audit Policy.

4. To set the audit policy, in the details pane, double-click each type of event, and then select either the Success check box or the Failure check box for the Audit These Attempts setting, as listed in the following table.

Event	Audit Successful Attempts	Audit Failed Attempts
Account Logon Events	☐	☐
Account Management	☐	☐
Directory Service Access	☐	☐
Logon Events	☐	☑
Object Access	☑	☑
Policy Change	☐	☐
Privilege Use	☑	☐
Process Tracking	☐	☐
System Events	☑	☑

5. Close the Local Security Settings window.

6. Restart your computer.

Exercise 3: Setting Up Auditing of Files

In this exercise, you will set up auditing for a file.

▶ **To set up auditing of files**

1. Log on as Administrator.

2. In Windows Explorer, create a text file named Audit in the root folder of your system disk (for example, C:\Audit).

3. Right-click the Audit.txt file, and then click Properties.

4. In the Properties dialog box, click the Security tab, and then click Advanced.

5. In the Access Control Settings dialog box, click the Auditing tab.

6. Click Add.

7. In the Select User, Computer, Or Group dialog box, double-click Everyone in the list of user accounts and groups.

8. In the Audit Entry For Audit dialog box, select the Successful check box and the Failed check box for each of the following events:

   - Create Files/Write Data

   - Delete

   - Change Permissions

   - Take Ownership

9. Click OK.

   Windows 2000 displays the Everyone group in the Access Control Settings For Audit dialog box.

10. Click OK to apply your changes.

▶ **To change file permissions**

1. In the Properties dialog box, change the NTFS permissions for the file to only the Read permission for Everyone. Remove any other permissions and prevent inheritable permissions to propagate from the parent.

2. Click OK to close the Properties dialog box, and then close Windows Explorer.

Exercise 4: Setting Up Auditing of a Printer

In this exercise, you will set up auditing of a printer.

▶ **To set up auditing of a printer**

1. Click the Start button, point to Settings, and then click Printers.

2. In the Printers window, right-click HP LaserJet 5Si (the procedures for installing this printer are in Chapter 12, "Setting Up and Configuring Network Printers"), and then click Properties.

3. Click the Security tab, and then click Advanced.

4. In the Access Control Settings For HP LaserJet 5Si dialog box, click the Auditing tab, and then click Add.

5. In the Select User, Computer, Or Group dialog box, double-click Everyone in the list box.

6. In the Audit Entry For HP LaserJet 5Si dialog box, select the Successful check box for all types of access.

7. Click OK.

   Windows 2000 displays the Everyone group in the Access Control Settings For HP LaserJet 5Si dialog box.

8. Click OK to apply your changes.

9. Click OK to close the HP LaserJet 5Si Properties dialog box.

10. Close the Printers window.

Exercise 5: Viewing the Security Log

In this exercise, you will view the security log for your computer. Then you will use Event Viewer to filter events and to search for potential security breaches.

▶ **To view the security log for your computer**

1. Click the Start menu, click Programs, click Administrative Tools, and then click Event Viewer.

2. In the console tree, click each of the three logs and view the contents. As you scroll through the logs, double-click a couple of events to view a description.

Exercise 6: Managing the Security Log

In this exercise, you will configure Event Viewer to overwrite events when the Security log gets full. You will also increase the size of the Security log to 2048 KB.

▶ **To control the size and contents of a log file**

1. Verify that in the console tree, Security Log is selected.

2. On the Action menu, click Properties.

3. In the Security Log Properties dialog box, click Overwrite Events As Needed.

4. In the Maximum Log Size box, change the maximum log size to 2048 (KB), and click OK.

   Windows 2000 will now allow the log to grow to 2048 KB and will then overwrite older events with new events as necessary.

5. Close Event Viewer.

Lesson Summary

In this lesson, you learned that Windows 2000 Professional has the following three logs by default: the Application log, the Security log, and the System log. You use Event Viewer to view the contents of the Windows 2000 logs. You can use the Filter and Find commands in Event Viewer to easily locate specific events or types of events. You can manage the Windows 2000 logs by archiving them to allow you to track trends over time and by controlling the size of the log files. The practice portion of this exercise gave you hands-on experience with these tasks.

Review

The following questions will help you determine whether you have learned enough to move on to the next chapter. If you have difficulty answering these questions, please go back and review the material in this chapter before beginning the next chapter. See Appendix A, "Questions and Answers," for the answers to these questions.

1. What two tasks must you perform to audit access to a file?

2. Who can set up auditing for a computer?

3. When you view a security log, how do you determine whether an event failed or succeeded?

4. If you click the Do Not Overwrite Events option in the Properties dialog box for an audit log, what happens when the log file becomes full?

C H A P T E R   1 7

Configuring Group Policy and Local Security Policy

About This Chapter

In this chapter, you will learn how to use the Microsoft Windows 2000 Group Policy and Local Security Policy snap-ins to improve the security on your computer. In Chapter 16, you learned about auditing one of the features that can be controlled either by creating a custom console for Group Policy or by using Local Security Policy. In this chapter, you will learn about configuring the two Account Policies: Password Policy and Account Lockout Policy. And you will learn how to configure some of the available security options.

Before You Begin

To complete this chapter, you must have

- A computer that meets the minimum hardware requirements located in "About This Book."
- Microsoft Windows 2000 Professional software installed on the computer.

Lesson 1: Configuring Account Policies

In Chapter 10, "Setting Up and Managing User Accounts," you learned about assigning user account passwords and how to unlock an account that was locked by the system. In this lesson, you will learn how to improve the security of your users' passwords and how to control when the system locks out a user account.

After this lesson, you will be able to

- Configure Account Policies

Estimated lesson time: 35 minutes

Configuring Password Policy

Password Policy allows you to improve security on your computer by controlling how passwords are created and managed. You can specify the maximum length of time a password can be used before the user must change it. Changing passwords decreases the chances of an unauthorized person breaking into your computer. If a hacker has discovered a user account and password combination for your computer, forcing users to change their passwords regularly will cause the user account and password combination to fail and lock the hacker out of the system.

Other settings are available in Password Policy that you can use to improve your computer's security. For example, you can specify a minimum password length. The longer the password, the more difficult it is to discover. Another example is to maintain a history of the passwords used. This prevents a user from having two passwords and alternating between them.

You can configure Password Policy on a computer running Windows 2000 Professional by using Group Policy or Local Security Policy. You use Group Policy to configure Password Policy as follows:

1. Use MMC to create a custom console, add the Group Policy snap-in, and save it with the name Group Policy. (For more information on using MMC to create custom consoles, see Chapter 3, "Using Microsoft Management Console and Task Scheduler.")

2. Expand Local Computer Policy, under Computer Configuration expand Windows Settings, expand Security Settings, expand Account Policies, and then click on Password Policy.

3. Select the setting you want to configure, and then, on the Action menu, click Security.

The console displays the current Password Policy settings in the details pane, as shown in Figure 17.1.

Figure 17.1   Current Password Policy settings using Group Policy

Table 17.1 explains the settings available in Password Policy.

Table 17.1   Password Policy Settings

Setting	Description
Enforce Password History	The value you enter in this setting indicates the number of passwords to be kept in a password history.
	A value of 0 indicates that no password history is being kept. This is the default.
	You can set the value from 0 to 24, indicating the number of passwords to be kept in password history. This value indicates the number of new passwords that a user must access before he or she can reuse an old password.
Maximum Password Age	The value you enter in this setting is the number of days a user can access a password before he or she is required to change it.
	A value of 0 indicates that the password will not expire.
	The default value is 42 days. You can set the range of values from 0 to 999 days.
Minimum Password Age	The value you enter in this setting is the number of days a user must keep a password before he or she can change it.
	A value of 0 indicates that the password can be changed immediately. This is the default. If you are enforcing password history, you should not set this value to 0.

(continued)

Setting	Description
	You can set the range of values from 0 to 999 days. This value indicates how long the user must wait before changing his or her password again. Use this value to prevent a user who was forced by the system to change his or her password from immediately changing it back to the old password.
	The minimum password age must be less than the maximum password age.
Minimum Password Length	The value you enter in this setting is the minimum number of characters required in a password. The value can range from 0 up to 14 characters inclusive.
	A value of 0 indicates that no password is required. This is the default value.
Passwords Must Meet Complexity Requirements	The options are Enabled or Disabled. The default is Disabled.
	If enabled, all passwords must meet or exceed the specified minimum password length; must comply with the password history settings; must contain capitals, numerals or punctuation; and cannot contain the user's account or full name.
Store Password Using Reversible Encryption For All Users In The Domain	The options are Enabled or Disabled. The default is Disabled. This enables Windows 2000 to store a reversibly encrypted password for all users in the domain—for example to be used with the Challenge Handshake Authentication Protocol (CHAP). This option is only applicable if your computer running Windows 2000 Professional is in a domain.

The Local Security Policy Setting dialog box appears for the selected policy. Figure 17.2 shows the Local Security Policy Setting dialog box for the Maximum Password Age policy.

By carefully planning and configuring your Password Policy options, you can improve the security of your computer by decreasing the chances of an unauthorized user gaining access to it.

Configuring Account Lockout Policy

The Account Lockout Policy settings also allow you to improve the security on your computer. If no account lockout policy is in place, an unauthorized user can repeatedly try to break into your computer. If, however, you have set an account lockout policy, the system will lock out the user account under the conditions you specify in Account Lockout Policy.

Figure 17.2   The Local Security Policy Setting dialog box
for the Maximum Password Age policy

You access Account Lockout Policy using either the Group Policy snap-in or
the Local Security Settings window, just as you did to configure Password Policy.
The Group Policy console displaying the current Account Lockout Policy settings in the details pane is shown in Figure 17.3.

Figure 17.3   Current Account Lockout Policy settings using Group Policy

Table 17.2 explains the settings available in Account Lockout Policy.

Table 17.2 Account Lockout Policy Settings

Setting	Description
Account Lockout Duration	This value indicates the number of minutes that the account is locked out. A value of 0 indicates that the user account is locked out indefinitely until the Administrator unlocks the user account. You can set the value from 0 to 99999 minutes. (The maximum value of 99999 minutes is approximately 69.4 days.)
Account Lockout Threshold	The value you enter in this setting is the number of invalid logon attempts it takes before the user account is locked out from logging on to the computer.
	A value of 0 indicates that the account will not be locked out, no matter how many invalid logon attempts are made.
	You can set the range of values from 0 to 999 attempts.
Reset Account Lockout Counter After	The value you enter in this setting is the number of minutes to wait before resetting the account lockout counter.
	You can set the range of values from 1 to 99999 minutes.

Practice: Configuring Account Policies

In this practice, you will configure the account policies for your computer and then test your Account Policy to make sure it is correctly configured.

Exercise 1: Configuring Minimum Password Length

In this exercise, you will configure a Password Policy setting, Minimum Password Length, for your computer. Then you will test the password length you configured to confirm that it was set.

▶ **To configure the Minimum Password Length setting**

1. Log on to your computer as Administrator.

2. Use MMC to create a custom console containing the Group Policy snap-in.

3. In the Group Policy console, expand Local Group Policy, expand Computer Configuration, expand Windows Settings, expand Security Settings, and then expand Account Policies.

4. Click Password Policy in the console tree.

5. In the details pane, right-click Minimum Password Length and then click Security.

6. Type **6** in the Characters box, and then click OK.

7. Close the Local Computer Policy custom console, and save the custom console as Group Policy.

▶ **To test the Minimum Password Length setting**

1. Press Ctrl+Alt+Delete, and in the Windows Security dialog box, click Change Password.

2. In the Old Password box, type **password** and type **water** in the New Password and Confirm New Password boxes.

3. Click OK.

   A Change Password message box appears indicating that your new password must be at least six characters long. So the Minimum Password Length setting in Password Policy is working.

4. Click OK, and then click Cancel.

5. Click Cancel to close the Windows Security dialog box.

Exercise 2: Configuring and Testing Additional Account Policies Settings

In this exercise, you will configure and test additional Account Policies settings.

▶ **To configure Account Policies settings**

1. Use the Group Policy console to configure the following Account Policies settings:

   - A user should have at least 5 different passwords before he or she accesses a previously used password.

   - After changing a password, a user must wait 24 hours before changing it again.

   - A user should change his or her password every three weeks.

   Which settings did you use for each of the three listed items?

2. Close the Group Policy console and save the settings.

▶ **To test Account Policies settings**

1. Log on as User4 with a password of *User4*.

   Note If you get a Logon Message dialog box indicating that your password will expire in a specified number of days and asking whether you want to change it now, click No.

   ---

2. Change your password to *waters*.

   Were you successful? Why or why not?

3. Change your password to *papers*.

   Were you successful? Why or why not?

4. Close all windows and log off.

Exercise 3: Configuring Account Lockout Policy

In this exercise, you will configure the Account Lockout Policy settings, and then you will test them to make sure they're set up correctly.

▶ **To configure the Account Lockout Policy settings**

1. Log on to your computer as Administrator.
2. Click Start, point to Programs, point to Administrative Tools, and then click Group Policy.
3. In the Group Policy console tree, if necessary, double-click Local Computer Policy, then Computer Configuration, then Windows Settings, then Security Settings, and then Account Policies.
4. Click Account Lockout Policy.
5. Use Account Lockout Policy settings to do the following:

   ▪ Lock out a user account after four failed logon attempts.

   ▪ Lock out user accounts until the administrator unlocks the user account.

   Which Account Lockout Policy settings did you use for each of the two conditions?

6. Close the Group Policy console, save changed settings, and log off as Administrator.

▶ **To test the Account Lockout Policy settings**

1. Try to log on as User4 with a password of *papers*. Try this four times.
2. Try to log on as User4 with a password of *papers*.

   A message box appears, indicating that the account is locked out.

3. Click OK and then log on as Administrator.

Lesson Summary

In this lesson, you learned that the Windows 2000 Local Security Settings window allows you to improve the security on your computer by making it more difficult for an unauthorized user to gain access. Using the Password Policy settings is one method you can use to improve the security on your computer. Setting Password Policy allows you to manage the passwords used on your computer. For example, Password Policy includes settings that allow you to force users to change their passwords regularly and to control the minimum length of a password.

You also learned about another method of improving security on your computer: using Account Lockout Policy. If no Account Lockout Policy settings are in place, an unauthorized user can repeatedly try to break into your computer. Using Account Lockout Policy, you can determine the number of invalid logon attempts it takes before a user account is locked out of the computer. Account Lockout Policy also allows you to determine how long the account will be locked out; you can even set Account Lockout Policy to require that an administrator manually unlock the user account. In the practice portion of the lesson, you set and tested various account settings.

Lesson 2: Configuring Security Options

The Security Options node lives under the Local Policies node. Close to 40 additional security options are available here that allow you to increase the effective security on your computer. In this lesson, you will learn about a few of these available options.

After this lesson, you will be able to

- Configure Security Options.

Estimated lesson time: 15 minutes

Shutting Down the Computer Without Logging On

By default, Windows 2000 Professional doesn't require a user to be logged on to the computer to shut it down. Security Options allow you to disable this feature and force users to log on to the computer before it can be shut down. You access Security Options using the Group Policy snap-in, just as you did to configure the Account Policies settings. Once you open the Group Policy snap-in, expand Local Computer Policy, expand Computer Configuration, expand Windows Settings, expand Security Settings, expand Local Policies, and then select Security Options.

Figure 17.4 shows the Local Security Policy Setting dialog box for the Allow System To Be Shut Down Without Having To Log On option. This option is either enabled, which is the default, or disabled.

Figure 17.4   Setting the Allow System To Be Shut Down Without Having To Log On option

Clear Virtual Memory Pagefile When System Shuts Down

By default, Windows 2000 Professional doesn't clear the virtual memory pagefile when the system is shut down. In some organizations, this is considered a breach of security because the data in the pagefile might be accessible to users who aren't authorized to that information. To enable this feature and clear the pagefile each time the system is shut down, open the Group Policy snap-in, expand Local Computer Policy, expand Computer Configuration, expand Windows Settings, expand Security Settings, expand Local Policies, and then select Security Options. Right-click Clear Virtual Memory Pagefile When System Shuts Down and then click Security (see Figure 17.5). This feature is either enabled or disabled.

Figure 17.5 Setting the Clear Virtual Memory Pagefile When System Shuts Down option

Disable CTRL+ALT+DEL Requirement For Logon

By default, Windows 2000 Professional requires users to press Ctrl+Alt+Delete to log on to the computer. By disabling this default behavior, you reduce the security on your computer. By forcing users to press Ctrl+Alt+Delete, you are using a key combination recognized only by Windows to ensure that you are giving the password only to Windows and not to a Trojan horse program waiting to capture your password. You set this option using the Group Policy snap-in. You should disable this option, forcing users to use Ctrl+Alt+Delete
(see Figure 17.6).

Figure 17.6 Setting the Disable CTRL+ALT+DEL
Requirement For Logon option

Do Not Display Last User Name In Logon Screen

By default, Windows 2000 Professional displays the last user name to log on to
the computer in the Windows Security or Log On To Windows dialog box. In
some situations, this is considered a security risk because an unauthorized user
can see a valid user account displayed on the screen, making it much easier to
break into the computer.

To enable this option and prevent the last user name from being displayed, in the
Group Policy snap-in, expand Local Computer Policy, expand Computer Configuration, expand Windows Settings, expand Security Settings, expand Local Policies
in the console tree, and then click Security Options. In the details pane, right-click
Do Not Display Last User Name In Logon Screen, click Security, and then enable
this feature. This feature is either enabled or disabled (see Figure 17.7).

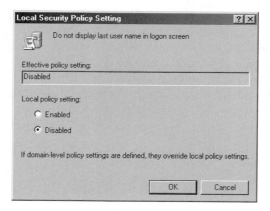

Figure 17.7 Disabling the Do Not Display Last User
Name In Logon Screen option

Practice: Configuring Security Settings

In this practice, you will configure Security Options on your computer.

▶ **To configure and test Security Options**

1. Log on to your computer as Administrator.

2. Click Start, point to Programs, point to Administrative Tools, and then click Group Policy.

3. In the Group Policy snap-in's console tree, double-click Local Computer Policy, expand Computer Configuration, expand Windows Settings, expand Security Settings, expand Local Policies, and then click Security Options.

4. Configure your computer so that the following conditions are true:

   - Users must log on to shut down the computer.

   - Users must press Ctrl+Alt+Delete to log on to the computer.

   - Windows 2000 will not display the user account last logged on the computer in the Windows Security dialog box.

5. Close the Group Policy console, save changed settings, and log off.

   Notice that you are prompted to press Ctrl+Alt+Delete to log on.

6. Press Ctrl+Alt+Delete.

   Notice that the Log On To Windows dialog box appears with the User Name box blank and the Shutdown option dimmed. (Click Options if you cannot see the Shutdown button.)

Lesson Summary

Some computers require more security than others do. In this lesson, you learned that Security Options in the Group Policy Local Security Policy snap-ins allow you to improve the effective security on any of your computers that require more security. For example, you can prevent an unauthorized user from shutting down your computer by forcing users to log on before they can shut down the computer.

You also learned that you can prevent a Trojan horse application from stealing user passwords by forcing users to press Ctrl+Alt+Delete before they can log on. Windows recognizes the Ctrl+Alt+Delete key combination, so only Windows picks up the keystrokes entered in for user name and password. You can also increase security by not displaying a valid user name, the last user account that logged on, in the Windows Security or Log On To Windows dialog box. These options and the other Security Options available help you to increase security on your network.

Review

The following questions will help you determine whether you have learned enough to move on to the next chapter. If you have difficulty answering these questions, please go back and review the material in this chapter before beginning the next chapter. See Appendix A, "Questions and Answers," for the answers to these questions.

1. Why would you want to force users to change passwords?

2. Why would you want to control the length of the passwords used on your computers?

3. Why would you want to lock out a user account?

4. Why would you want to force users to press Ctrl+Alt+Delete before they can log on to your computers?

5. How do you prevent the last user name from being displayed in the Windows Security or Log On To Windows dialog box?

C H A P T E R   1 8

Managing Data Storage

About This Chapter

This chapter introduces data storage management on NTFS-formatted volumes. You will learn about compression, which allows you to store more data on a disk, and you will learn about disk quotas, which allow you to control how much space a user can have on a disk. You will learn about how you can increase the security of files and folders on your computer by using the Encrypting File System (EFS). You will also learn about defragmenting a disk, which allows your system to access files and save files and folders more efficiently.

Before You Begin

To complete this chapter, you must have

- A computer that meets the minimum hardware requirements located in "About This Book."

- Microsoft Windows 2000 Professional installed on the computer.

Lesson 1: Managing NTFS Compression

Microsoft Windows 2000 File System (NTFS) compression enables you to compress files and folders. Compressed files and folders occupy less space on an NTFS-formatted volume, which enables you to store more data. Each file and folder on an NTFS volume has a *compression state,* which is either compressed or uncompressed.

After this lesson, you will be able to

- Manage disk compression.
- Compress and uncompress files and folders.

Estimated lesson time: 40 minutes

Using Compressed Files and Folders

Compressed files can be read and written to by any Microsoft Windows–based or MS-DOS-based application without first being uncompressed by another program. When an application, such as Microsoft Word for Windows, or an operating system command, such as Copy, requests access to a compressed file, NTFS automatically uncompresses the file before making it available. When you close or explicitly save a file, NTFS compresses it again.

NTFS allocates disk space based on the uncompressed file size. If you copy a compressed file to an NTFS volume with enough space for the compressed file but not enough space for the uncompressed file, you might get an error message stating that there is not enough disk space for the file. The file will not be copied to the volume.

Compressing Files and Folders

You can set the compression state of folders and files, and you can change the color that is used to display compressed files and folders in Windows Explorer.

If you want to set the compression state of a folder or file, right-click the folder or file in Windows Explorer, click Properties, and then click the Advanced button. In the Advanced Attributes dialog box, select the Compress Contents To Save Disk Space check box, as shown in Figure 18.1. Click OK, and then click Apply in the Properties dialog box.

Note NTFS encryption and compression are mutually exclusive. Therefore, if you select the Encrypt Contents To Secure Data check box, you can't compress the folder or file.

Figure 18.1   The Advanced Attributes dialog box

Important To change the compression state for a file or folder, you must have Write permission for that file or folder.

The compression state for a folder doesn't reflect the compression state of the files and subfolders in that folder. A folder can be compressed, yet all of the files in that folder can be uncompressed. Alternatively, an uncompressed folder can contain compressed files. When you compress a folder, Windows 2000 displays the Confirm Attribute Changes dialog box, which has the two additional options explained in Table 18.1.

Table 18.1   Confirm Attribute Changes Dialog Box Options

Option	Description
Apply Changes To This Folder Only	Compresses only the folder that you have selected
Apply Changes To This Folder, Subfolder, And Files	Compresses the folder and all subfolders and files that are contained within it and added to it subsequently

---

Note Windows 2000 doesn't support NTFS compression for cluster sizes larger than 4 KB because compression on large clusters causes performance degradation. If you select a larger cluster size when you format an NTFS volume, compression isn't available for that volume.

Selecting an Alternate Display Color for Compressed Files and Folders

Windows Explorer makes it easy for you to quickly determine whether a file or folder is compressed by allowing you to select a different display color for compressed files and folders to distinguish them from uncompressed files and folders.

You can set an alternative display color for compressed files and folders as follows:

1. In Windows Explorer, on the Tools menu, click Folder Options.
2. On the View tab, select the Display Compressed Files And Folders With Alternate Color check box.

Copying and Moving Compressed Files and Folders

Specific rules determine whether the compression state of files and folders is retained when you copy or move them within and between NTFS and FAT volumes. The following list describes how Windows 2000 treats the compression state of a file or folder when you copy or move a compressed file or folder within or between NTFS volumes or between NTFS and FAT volumes.

- Copying a file within an NTFS volume. When you copy a file within an NTFS volume (shown as A in Figure 18.2), the file inherits the compression state of the target folder. For example, if you copy a compressed file to an uncompressed folder, the file is automatically uncompressed.

- Moving a file or folder within an NTFS volume. When you move a file or folder within an NTFS volume (shown as B in Figure 18.2), the file or folder retains its original compression state. For example, if you move a compressed file to an uncompressed folder, the file remains compressed.

- Copying a file or folder between NTFS volumes. When you copy a file or folder between NTFS volumes (shown as C in Figure 18.2), the file or folder inherits the compression state of the target folder.

- Moving a file or folder between NTFS volumes. When you move a file or folder between NTFS volumes (shown as C in Figure 18.2), the file or folder inherits the compression state of the target folder. Because Windows 2000 treats a move as a copy and then a delete, the files inherit the compression state of the target folder.

- Moving or copying a file or folder to a FAT volume. Windows 2000 supports compression only for NTFS files. Because of this, when you move or copy a compressed NTFS file or folder to a FAT volume, Windows 2000 automatically uncompresses the file or folder.

- Moving or copying a compressed file or folder to a floppy disk. When you move or copy a compressed NTFS file or folder to a floppy disk, Windows 2000 automatically uncompresses the file or folder.

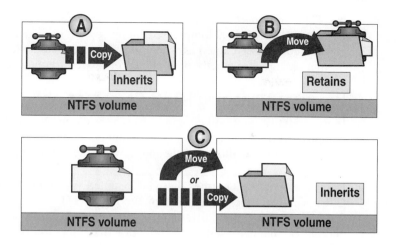

Figure 18.2   The effects of copying and moving compressed folders and files

---

Note When you copy a compressed NTFS file, Windows 2000 uncompresses the file, copies the file, and then compresses the file again as a new file. This might cause performance degradation.

Using NTFS Compression

The following list provides best practices for using compression on NTFS volumes:

- Because some file types compress more than others, select file types to compress based on the anticipated resulting file size. For example, because Windows bitmap files contain more redundant data than application executable files, this file type compresses to a smaller size. Bitmaps will often compress to less than 50 percent of the original file size, whereas application files rarely compress to less than 75 percent of the original size.

- Do not store compressed files, such as PKZIP files, in a compressed folder. Windows 2000 will attempt to compress the file, wasting system time and yielding no additional disk space.

- To make it easier to locate compressed data, use a different display color for compressed folders and files.

- Compress static data rather than data that changes frequently. Compressing and uncompressing files incurs some system overhead. By choosing to compress files that are infrequently accessed, you minimize the amount of system time that is dedicated to compression and uncompression activities.

- NTFS compression can cause performance degradation when you copy and move files. When a compressed file is copied, it is uncompressed, copied, and then compressed again as a new file. Compress static data rather than data that changes frequently or is copied or moved frequently.

Practice: Managing NTFS Compression

In this practice, you will compress files and folders. You will then display the compressed files and folders in a different color. Then you will uncompress a file and test the effects that copying and moving files have on compression.

Note This practice assumes that you installed Windows 2000 Professional on the C drive and that the C drive is formatted with NTFS. If you installed Windows 2000 Professional on a different partition and that partition is formatted with NTFS, use that drive letter when the practice refers to drive C.

Exercise 1: Compressing Files in an NTFS Partition

In this exercise, you will use Windows Explorer to compress files and folders to make more disk space available on your NTFS partition. You will also configure Windows Explorer to display the compressed files and folders in a different color. Next you will uncompress a file. Finally you will view the effects that copying and moving files has on compressed files.

▶ **To view the capacity and free space for drive C**

1. Log on as Administrator, right-click the My Computer icon on your desktop, and then click Explore.
2. Right-click drive C, and then click Properties.

   Windows 2000 displays the Local Disk (C:) Properties dialog box with the General tab active.

   What is the capacity of drive C?

   What is the free space on drive C?

3. Click Cancel to close the Local Disk (C:) Properties dialog box and return to Windows Explorer.

▶ **To compress a folder tree**

1. In Windows Explorer, expand Local Disk (C:).
2. Create a folder in drive C and name it CompTest.
3. Double-click CompTest to expand the folder.

4. Create a folder in CompTest and name it CompTest2.

5. Right-click the CompTest folder, and then click Properties.

   Windows 2000 displays the CompTest Properties dialog box with the General tab active.

6. On the General tab, click the Advanced button.

   Windows 2000 displays the Advanced Attributes dialog box.

7. Select the Compress Contents To Save Disk Space check box.

8. Select the Encrypt Contents To Secure Data check box.

   Notice that the system automatically removes the check mark from the Compress Contents To Save Disk Space check box.

9. Select the Compress Contents To Save Disk Space check box.

10. Click OK to return to the CompTest Properties dialog box.

11. Click Apply to apply your settings.

    Windows 2000 displays the Confirm Attribute Changes dialog box, prompting you to specify whether to compress only this folder or this folder, all subfolders, and all files.

12. Select the Apply Changes To This Folder, Subfolders And Files option, and then click OK.

    Windows 2000 displays the Applying Attributes message box, indicating the progress of the operation and the paths and names of folders and files as they are compressed. Because little data is on drive C, compression will complete too quickly for you to view this dialog box.

13. Click OK to close the Properties dialog box.

▶ **To display compressed files and folders with an alternate color**

1. In Windows Explorer, click Local Disk (C:) and, on the Tools menu, click Folder Options.

   The Folder Options dialog box appears with the General tab active.

2. Click the View tab.

3. In the Advanced Settings list, select the Display Compressed Files And Folders With Alternate Color check box.

4. Click OK to apply your changes.

   The names of the compressed files and folders are displayed in blue.

▶ **To uncompress a folder**

1. In Windows Explorer, expand the CompTest folder.

2. In the CompTest folder, right-click CompTest2, and then click Properties.

Windows 2000 displays the CompTest2 Properties dialog box with the General tab active.

3. On the General tab, click the Advanced button.

Windows 2000 displays the Advanced Attributes dialog box.

4. Clear the Compress Contents To Save Disk Space check box, and then click OK to apply your settings and return to the CompTest2 Properties dialog box.

5. Click OK to close the CompTest2 Properties dialog box.

Since the CompTest2 folder is empty, Windows 2000 doesn't display the Confirm Attributes Changes dialog box asking you to specify whether to uncompress only this folder or this folder and all subfolders.

What indication do you have that the CompTest2 folder is no longer compressed?

Exercise 2: Copying and Moving Files

In this exercise, you will see the effects that copying and moving files has on compressed files.

▶ **To create a compressed file**

1. In Windows Explorer, click the CompTest folder.

2. On the File menu, click New, and then click Text Document.

3. Type **Text1** and then press Enter.

How can you verify that Text1 is compressed?

▶ **To copy a compressed file to an uncompressed folder**

1. Copy Text1 to the CompTest\CompTest2 folder.

Make sure that you copy (hold down the Ctrl key while you drag the file) and do not move the file.

2. Examine the properties for Text1 in the CompTest2 folder.

Is the Text1.txt file in the CompTest\CompTest2 folder compressed or uncompressed? Why?

▶   **To move a compressed file to an uncompressed folder**

1. Examine the properties of the Text1.txt file in the CompTest folder.

   Is Text1.txt compressed or uncompressed?

2. Move Text1.txt to the CompTest\CompTest2 folder. When the Confirm File Replace dialog box appears prompting whether you want to replace the file, click Yes.

3. Examine the properties of Text1.txt in the CompTest2 folder.

   Is Text1.txt compressed or uncompressed? Why?

▶   **To uncompress the NTFS folder**

1. In Windows Explorer, right-click the CompTest folder, and then click Properties.

   Windows 2000 displays the CompTest Properties dialog box with the General tab active.

2. On the General tab, click the Advanced button.

   Windows 2000 displays the Advanced Attributes dialog box.

3. Clear the Compress Contents To Save Disk Space check box, and then click OK to return to the CompTest Properties dialog box.

4. Click Apply.

   Windows 2000 displays the Confirm Attribute Changes dialog box, prompting you to specify whether to uncompress only this folder or this folder and all subfolders.

5. Click Apply Changes To This Folder, Subfolders And All Files, and then click OK.

   Windows 2000 briefly displays the Applying Attributes message box. This might happen so fast that you don't see it.

6. Click OK to close the Properties dialog box, and then close Windows Explorer.

Lesson Summary

In this lesson, you learned how to compress and uncompress files and folders on an NTFS volume. You learned that compressed files can be read and written to by any Microsoft Windows–based or MS-DOS-based application without first being uncompressed by another program. The Windows NTFS file system automatically uncompresses the file before making it available, and when you close or explicitly save a file, NTFS compresses it again.

You also learned how to change the color that is used to display compressed files and folders in Windows Explorer to distinguish them from uncompressed files and folders. And you learned that NTFS encryption and compression are mutually exclusive.

Finally, you learned about copying and moving compressed files. When you copy a file within an NTFS volume, the file inherits the compression state of the target folder. When you move a file or folder within an NTFS volume, the file or folder retains its original compression state. When you copy or move a file or folder between NTFS volumes, the file or folder inherits the compression state of the target folder. Finally, when you move or copy a compressed NTFS file or folder to a FAT volume or a floppy disk, Windows 2000 automatically uncompresses the file or folder.

Lesson 2: Managing Disk Quotas

You use disk quotas to manage storage growth in distributed environments. *Disk quotas* allow you to allocate disk space usage based on the files and folders that users own. You can set disk quotas, quota thresholds, and quota limits for all users and for individual users. You can also monitor the amount of hard disk space that users have and the amount that they have left against their quota.

After this lesson, you will be able to
- Configure and manage disk quotas.

Estimated lesson time: 20 minutes

Understanding Windows 2000 Disk Quota Management

Windows 2000 disk quotas track and control disk usage on a per-user, per-volume basis. Windows 2000 tracks disk quotas for each volume, even if the volumes are on the same hard disk. Because quotas are tracked on a per-user basis, every user's disk space is tracked regardless of the folder in which the user stores files. Table 18.2 describes the characteristics of Windows 2000 disk quotas.

Table 18.2 Disk Quota Characteristics and Descriptions

Characteristic	Description
Disk usage is based on file and folder ownership.	Windows 2000 calculates disk space usage based on the files and folders that users own. When a user copies or saves a new file to an NTFS volume or takes ownership of a file on an NTFS volume, Windows 2000 charges the disk space for the file against the user's quota limit.
Disk quotas do not use compression.	Windows 2000 ignores compression when it calculates hard disk space usage. Users are charged for each uncompressed byte, regardless of how much hard disk space is actually used. This is done partially because file compression produces different degrees of compression for different types of files. Different uncompressed file types that are the same size might end up to be different sizes when they are compressed.
Free space for applications is based on quota limit.	When you enable disk quotas, the free space that Windows 2000 reports to applications for the volume is the amount of space remaining within the user's disk quota limit.

Note Disk quotas can be applied only to Windows 2000 NTFS volumes.

You use disk quotas to monitor and control hard disk space usage. System administrators can do the following:

- Set a disk quota limit to specify the amount of disk space for each user.

- Set a disk quota warning to specify when Windows 2000 should log an event, indicating that the user is nearing his or her limit.

- Enforce disk quota limits and deny users access if they exceed their limit, or allow them continued access.

- Log an event when a user exceeds a specified disk space threshold. The threshold could be when users exceed their quota limit, or when they exceed their warning level.

After you enable disk quotas for a volume, Windows 2000 collects disk usage data for all users who own files and folders on the volume. This allows you to monitor volume usage on a per-user basis. By default, only members of the Administrators group can view and change quota settings. However, you can allow users to view quota settings.

Setting Disk Quotas

You can enable disk quotas and enforce disk quota warnings and limits for all users or for individual users.

If you want to enable disk quotas, open the Properties dialog box for a disk, click the Quota tab, and configure the options that are described in Table 18.3 and displayed in Figure 18.3.

Table 18.3   Quota Tab Options

Option	Description
Enable Quota Management	Select this check box to enable disk quota management.
Deny Disk Space To Users Exceeding Quota Limit	Select this check box so that when users exceed their hard disk space allocation, they receive an "out of disk space" message and cannot write to the volume.
Do Not Limit Disk Usage	Click this option when you don't want to limit the amount of hard disk space for users.
Limit Disk Space To	Configure the amount of disk space that users can have.
Set Warning Level To	Configure the amount of disk space that users can fill before Windows 2000 logs an event, indicating that a user is nearing his or her limit.
Quota Entries	Click this button to open the Quota Entries For dialog box, where you can add a new entry, delete an entry, and view the per-user quota information.

Figure 18.3   The Quota tab of the Properties dialog box for a disk

You can enforce identical quota limits for all users as follows:

1. In the Limit Disk Space To box and the Set Warning Level To box, enter the values for the limit and warning level that you want to set.

2. Select the Deny Disk Space To Users Exceeding Quota Limit check box.

Windows 2000 will monitor usage and will not allow users to create files or folders on the volume when they exceed the limit.

Determining the Status of Disk Quotas

You can determine the status of disk quotas in the Properties dialog box for a disk by checking the traffic light icon and by reading the status message to its right (see Figure 18.3):

- A red traffic light indicates that disk quotas are disabled.

- A yellow traffic light indicates that Windows 2000 is rebuilding disk quota information.

- A green traffic light indicates that the disk quota system is active.

You can enforce different quota limits for one or more specific users, as follows:

1. Open the Properties dialog box for a disk, click the Quota tab, and then click the Quota Entries button.

2. In the Quota Entries For window, shown in Figure 18.4, double-click the user account for which you want to set a disk quota limit, or create an entry by clicking New Quota Entry on the Quota menu.

3. Configure the disk space limit and the warning level for each individual user.

Figure 18.4 The Quota Entries For window

Monitoring Disk Quotas

You use the Quota Entries For window to monitor usage for all users who have copied, saved, or taken ownership of files and folders on the volume. Windows 2000 will scan the volume and monitor the amount of disk space that each user occupies. Use the Quota Entries For window to view the following:

- The amount of hard disk space that each user occupies.

- Users who are over their quota-warning threshold, which is signified by a yellow triangle.

- Users who are over their quota limit, which is signified by a red circle.

- The warning threshold and the disk quota limit for each user.

Determining Best Uses of Disk Quotas

The following list provides guidelines for using disk quotas:

- If you enable disk quota settings on the volume where Windows 2000 is installed and your user account has a disk quota limit, log on as Administrator to install additional Windows 2000 components and applications. By doing so, Windows 2000 won't charge the disk space that you use to install applications against the disk quota allowance for your user account.

- You can monitor hard disk usage and generate hard disk usage information without preventing users from saving data. To do so, clear the Deny Disk Space To Users Exceeding Quota Limit check box when you enable disk quotas.

- Set more restrictive default limits for all user accounts, and then modify the limits to allow more disk space to users who work with large files.

- If computers running Windows 2000 Professional are shared by more than one user, set disk quota limits on computer volumes so that disk space is shared by all users who share the computer.

- Generally, you should set disk quotas on shared volumes to limit storage for users. Set disk quotas on public folders and network servers to ensure that users share hard disk space appropriately. When storage resources are scarce, you might want to set disk quotas on all shared hard disk space.

- Delete disk quota entries for a user who no longer stores files on a volume. You can delete quota entries for a user account only after all files that the user owns have been removed from the volume or another user has taken ownership of the files.

- Before you can delete a quota entry for a user account, you or the user must remove all files that the user owns from the volume or another user must take ownership of the files.

Practice: Enabling and Disabling Disk Quotas

In this practice, you will configure default quota management settings to limit the amount of data users can store on drive C (their hard disk drive). Next you will configure a custom quota setting for a user account. You will increase the amount of data the user can store on drive C to 20 MB with a warning level set to 16. Finally you will turn off quota management for drive C.

Note If you didn't install Windows 2000 Professional on drive C, substitute the NTFS partition on which you did install Windows 2000 Professional whenever drive C is referred to in the practice.

Exercise 1: Configuring Quota Management Settings

In this exercise, you will configure the quota management settings for drive C to limit the data that users can store on the volume. You can then configure custom quota settings for a user account.

▶ **To configure default quota management settings**

1. Log on as Administrator and create a user account, User5. Assign it the password of *password,* and clear the User Must Change Password At Next Logon check box.

2. In Windows Explorer, right-click drive C, and then click Properties.

   Windows 2000 displays the Local Disk (C:) Properties dialog box with the General tab active.

3. Click the Quota tab.

Notice that disk quotas are disabled by default.

4. On the Quota tab, click the Enable Quota Management check box.

What is the default disk space limit for new users?

5. Select Deny Disk Space To Users Exceeding Quota Limit.

6. Click Limit Disk Space To.

7. Type 10 in the Limit Disk Space To box and then type 6 in the Set Warning Level To box.

Notice the default unit size is KB.

8. Change the unit sizes to MB and then click Apply.

Windows 2000 displays the Disk Quota message box, warning you that the volume will be rescanned to update disk usage statistics if you enable quotas.

9. Click OK to enable disk quotas.

▶ **To configure quota management settings for a user**

1. On the Quota tab of the Local Disk (C:) Properties dialog box, click the Quota Entries button.

Windows 2000 displays the Quota Entries For Local Disk (C:) window.

Are any user accounts listed? Why or why not?

2. On the Quota menu, click New Quota Entry.

Windows 2000 displays the Select Users dialog box.

3. In the Look In box, select PRO1.

Note If you didn't name your computer PRO1 or if your computer is part of a domain, select the appropriate computer or domain name.

---

4. At the top of the dialog box, under Name, select User5, and then click Add.

The user name appears in the Name list at the bottom of the dialog box.

5. Click OK.

Windows 2000 displays the Add New Quota Entry dialog box.

What are the default settings for the user you just set a quota limit for?

6. Increase the amount of data that User5 can store on drive C by changing the Limit Disk Space To option to 20 MB and the Set Warning Level To option to 16 MB.

7. Click OK to return to the Quota Entries window.

8. Close the Quota Entries window.

9. Click OK to close the Local Disk (C:) Properties dialog box.

10. Log off.

▶ **To test quota management settings**

1. Log on as User5 with a password of *password*.

2. Start Windows Explorer and create a User5 folder on drive C.

3. Insert the CD-ROM you used to install Windows 2000 Professional in your CD-ROM drive.

4. If a dialog box appears as a result of inserting the CD-ROM, close it.

5. Copy the i386 folder from your CD-ROM to the User5 folder.

   Windows 2000 Professional begins copying files from the i386 folder on the CD-ROM to a new i386 folder in the User5 folder on drive C. After copying several files, however, Windows 2000 displays the Error Copying File Or Folder dialog box, indicating that there isn't enough room on the disk.

   Why did you get this error message?

6. Click OK to close the dialog box.

7. Right-click the User5 folder and then click Properties.

   Notice that the Size On Disk value is at or near your quota limit of 20 MB.

8. Close all open windows and log off.

Exercise 2: Disabling Quota Management

In this exercise, you will disable quota management settings for drive C.

▶ **To disable quota management settings for drive C**

1. Log on as Administrator and start Windows Explorer.

2. Delete the User5 folder.

3. Right-click drive C, and then click Properties.

   Windows 2000 displays the Local Disk (C:) Properties dialog box with the General tab active.

4. Click the Quota tab.

5. On the Quota tab, clear the Enable Quota Management check box.

   Notice that all quota settings for drive C are no longer available.

6. Click Apply.

   Windows 2000 displays the Disk Quota message box, warning you that if you disable quotas, the volume will be rescanned if you enable them later.

7. Click OK to close the Disk Quota message box.

8. Click OK to close the Local Disk (C:) Properties dialog box.

9. Close all applications.

Lesson Summary

In this lesson, you learned that you use disk quotas to allocate disk space usage. You can set disk quotas, quota thresholds, and quota limits for all users and for individual users. You can also monitor the amount of hard disk space that users have and the amount that they have left against their quota. You also learned that Windows 2000 ignores compression when it calculates hard disk space usage and that you can apply disk quotas only to Windows 2000 NTFS volumes.

Windows 2000 disk quotas track and control disk usage on a per-user, per-volume basis. Windows 2000 tracks disk quotas for each volume, even if the volumes are on the same hard disk. Because quotas are tracked on a per-user basis, every user's disk space is tracked regardless of the folder in which the user stores files.

Lesson 3: Increasing Security with EFS

The Microsoft Encrypting File System (EFS) provides encryption for data in NTFS files stored on disk. EFS encryption is public key-based and runs as an integrated-system service, making it easy to manage, difficult to attack, and transparent to the file owner. If a user who attempts to access an encrypted NTFS file has the private key to that file, the file can be decrypted so that the user can open the file and work with it transparently as a normal document. A user without the private key is denied access.

Windows 2000 also includes the Cipher command-line utility, which enables you to encrypt and decrypt files and folders from a command prompt. And Windows 2000 provides a recovery agent so that if the owner loses the private key, the recovery agent can still recover the encrypted file.

After this lesson, you will be able to
- Encrypt folders and files.
- Decrypt folders and files.

Estimated lesson time: 30 minutes

Understanding EFS

EFS allows users to encrypt NTFS files by using a strong public key-based cryptographic scheme that encrypts all files in a folder. Users with *roaming profiles* can use the same key with trusted remote systems. No administrative effort is needed to begin, and most operations are transparent. Backups and copies of encrypted files are also encrypted if they are in NTFS volumes. Files remain encrypted if you move or rename them, and encryption isn't defeated by temporary files created during editing and left unencrypted in the paging file or in a temporary file.

You can set policies to recover EFS-encrypted data when necessary. The recovery policy is integrated with overall Windows 2000 security policy. Control of this policy can be delegated to individuals with recovery authority, and different recovery policies can be configured for different parts of the enterprise. Data recovery discloses only the recovered data, not the key that was used to encrypt the file. Several protections are in place to ensure that data recovery is possible and that no data is lost in the event of total system failure.

EFS is implemented either from Windows Explorer or from the command line. It can be enabled or disabled for a computer, domain, or OU by resetting recovery policy in the Group Policy console in the MMC.

Note To set group policy for the domain or for an OU, your computer must be part of a Windows 2000 domain.

You can use EFS to encrypt and decrypt files on remote file servers but not to encrypt data that is transferred over the network. Windows 2000 provides network protocols, such as Secure Sockets Layer (SSL) authentication, to encrypt data over the network.

Table 18.4 lists the key features provided by Windows 2000 EFS.

Table 18.4   EFS Features

Feature	Description
Transparent encryption	In EFS, file encryption doesn't require the file owner to decrypt and re-encrypt the file on each use. Decryption and encryption happen transparently on file reads and writes to disk.
Strong protection of encryption keys	Public-key encryption resists all but the most sophisticated methods of attack. Therefore, in EFS, the file encryption keys that are used to encrypt the file are encrypted by using a public key from the user's certificate. (Note: Windows 2000 uses X.509 v3 certificates.) The list of encrypted file-encryption keys is stored with the encrypted file and is unique to it. To decrypt the file-encryption keys, the file owner supplies a private key, which only the file owner has.
Integral data recovery	If the owner's private key is unavailable, the recovery system agent can open the file using his or her own private key. There can be more than one recovery agent, each with a different public key, but at least one public recovery key must be present on the system to encrypt a file.
Secure temporary and paging files	Many applications create temporary files while you edit a document, and these temporary files can be left unencrypted on the disk. On computers running Windows 2000, EFS is implemented at the folder level, so any temporary copies of an encrypted file are also encrypted, provided that all files are on NTFS volumes. EFS resides in the Windows operating system kernel and uses the nonpaged pool to store file encryption keys, ensuring that they are never copied to the paging file.

Encrypting

The recommended method to encrypt files is to create an NTFS folder and then "encrypt" the folder. To encrypt a folder, in the Properties dialog box for the folder, click the General tab. On the General tab, click the Advanced button, and then select the Encrypt Contents To Secure Data check box. All files placed in the folder will be encrypted. The folder is now marked for encryption. Folders that are marked for encryption aren't actually encrypted; only the files within the folder are encrypted.

Note Compressed files can't be encrypted, and encrypted files can't be compressed.

After you encrypt the folder, when you save a file in that folder, the file is encrypted by using *file encryption keys,* which are fast symmetric keys designed for bulk encryption. The file is encrypted in blocks, with a different file encryption key for each block. All of the file encryption keys are stored and encrypted in the Data Decryption Field (DDF) and the Data Recovery Field (DRF) in the file header.

Note By default, encryption provided by EFS is standard 56-bit encryption. For additional security, North American users can obtain 128-bit encryption by ordering the Enhanced CryptoPAK from Microsoft. Files encrypted by the CryptoPAK cannot be decrypted, accessed, or recovered on a system that supports only 56-bit encryption.

You use a file that you encrypted just like you would use any other file. Encryption is transparent. You don't need to decrypt a file you encrypted before you can use it. When you open an encrypted file, your private key is applied to the DDF to unlock the list of file-encryption keys, allowing the file contents to appear in plain text. EFS automatically detects an encrypted file and locates a user certificate and associated private key. You open the file, make changes to it, and save it like you would any other file. However, if someone else tries to open your encrypted file, he or she will be unable to access the file and will receive an "access denied" message.

Note Encrypted files can't be shared.

Decrypting

Decrypting a folder or file refers to clearing the Encrypt Contents To Secure Data check box in a folder's or file's Advanced Attributes dialog box, which you access from the Properties dialog box for the folder or file. Once decrypted, the file remains decrypted until you select the Encrypt Contents To Secure Data check box. The only reason you might want to decrypt a file would be if other people needed access to the folder or file; for example, if you want to share the folder or make the file available across the network.

Using the Cipher Command

Windows 2000 also includes command-line utilities for the richer functionality that is required for some administrative operations. The Cipher command-line utility provides the ability to encrypt and decrypt files and folders from a command prompt.

The following example shows the available options for the Cipher command. Table 18.5 describes these options.

```
cipher [/e | /d] [/s:folder_name] [/a] [/i] [/f] [/q] [/h] [/k]
[file_name [...]]
```

Table 18.5   Cipher Command Options and Descriptions

Option	Description
/e	Encrypts the specified folders. Folders are marked so that files that are added later will be encrypted.
/d	Decrypts the specified folders. Folders are marked so that files that are added later will not be encrypted.
/s	Performs the specified operation on folders in the given folder and all subfolders.
/a	Performs the specified operation on files as well as folders. Encrypted files could be decrypted when modified, if the parent folder is not encrypted. To avoid this, encrypt the file and the parent folder.
/i	Continues performing the specified operation even after errors have occurred. By default, Cipher stops when an error is encountered.
/f	Forces the encryption operation on all specified files, even those that are already encrypted. Files that are already encrypted are skipped by default.
/q	Reports only the most essential information.
/h	Displays files with the hidden or system attributes, which are not shown by default.
/k	Creates a new file encryption key for the user running the Cipher command. Using this option causes the Cipher command to ignore all other options.
file_name	Specifies a pattern, file, or folder.

If you run the Cipher command without parameters, it displays the encryption state of the current folder and any files that it contains. You can specify multiple filenames and use wildcards. You must put spaces between multiple parameters.

Using the Recovery Agent

If the owner's private key is unavailable, a person designated as the recovery agent can open the file using his or her own private key, which is applied to the DRF to unlock the list of file-encryption keys. If the recovery agent is on another computer in the network, send the file to the recovery agent. The recovery agent can bring his or her private key to the owner's computer, but it is never a good security practice to copy a private key onto another computer.

Note The default recovery agent is the administrator of the local computer unless the computer is part of a domain. In a domain, the domain administrator is the default recovery agent.

It is a good security practice to rotate recovery agents. However, if the agent designation changes, access to the file is denied. Therefore, Microsoft recommends that you keep recovery certificates and private keys until you have updated all files that are encrypted with them.

The person designated as the recovery agent has a special certificate and associated private key that allow data recovery. To recover an encrypted file, the recovery agent would do the following:

1. Use Backup or another backup tool to restore a user's backup version of the encrypted file or folder to the computer where his or her file recovery certificate is located.

2. In Windows Explorer, open the Properties dialog box for the file or folder, and on the General tab, click the Advanced button.

3. Clear the Encrypt Contents To Secure Data check box.

4. Make a backup version of the decrypted file or folder and return the backup version to the user.

Practice: Encrypting and Decrypting Files

In this practice, you will encrypt a folder and its files.

Exercise 1: Encrypting Files

▶ **To encrypt a file**

1. Ensure you are logged on as Administrator and in Windows Explorer, on the root of drive C, create the folder Secret and in the folder Secret, create the file File1.txt. Then right-click File1 and click Properties.

   Windows 2000 displays the Properties dialog box with the General tab active.

2. Click Advanced.

   The Advance Attributes dialog box appears.

3. Click the Encrypt Contents To Secure Data check box and then click OK.

4. Click OK to close the File1 Properties dialog box.

   An Encryption Warning dialog box informs you that you are about to encrypt a file that isn't in an encrypted folder. The default is to encrypt the folder and file, but you can also choose to encrypt only the file.

5. Click Cancel, and then click Cancel again to close the Owner Properties dialog box.

6. In Windows Explorer, right-click the Secret folder and then click Properties.

7. Click Advanced.

   The Advanced Attributes dialog box appears.

8. Click the Encrypt Contents To Secure Data check box and then click OK.

9. Click OK to close the Secret Properties dialog box.

   The Confirm Attribute Changes dialog box informs you that you are about to encrypt a folder. You have two choices: you can encrypt only this folder, or you can encrypt the folder and all subfolders and files in the folder.

10. Select the Apply Changes To This Folder, Subfolders And Files option, and then click OK.

▶ **To verify that the folder's content is encrypted**

1. In the Secret folder, right-click File1 and then click Properties.

   The File1 Properties dialog box appears.

2. Click Advanced.

   The Advanced Attributes dialog box appears. Notice that the Encrypt Contents To Secure Data check box is selected.

3. Close the Advanced Attributes dialog box.

4. Close the Properties dialog box.

5. Close all windows and log off.

Exercise 2: Testing the Encrypted Files

In this exercise, you will log on using the User Five account and then attempt to open an encrypted file. You will then try to disable encryption on the encrypted files.

▶ **To test an encrypted file**

1. Log on as User5 with a password of *password*.

2. Start Windows Explorer and open the file File1.txt in the Secret folder.

   What happens?

3. Close Notepad.

▶ **To attempt to disable the encryption**

1. Right-click File1.txt and then click Properties.

2. Click Advanced.

3. Clear the Encrypt Contents To Secure Data check box and then click OK.

4. Click OK to close the File1 Properties dialog box.

The Error Applying Attributes dialog box appears and informs you that access to the file is denied.

5. Click Cancel.

6. Close all open windows and dialog boxes.

7. Log off as User5 and log on as Administrator.

Exercise 3: Decrypting Folders and Files

In this exercise, you will decrypt the folder and file that you previously encrypted.

▶ **To decrypt a file**

1. Start Windows Explorer.

2. Right-click File1.txt, and then click Properties.

3. Click Advanced.

4. Clear the Encrypt Contents To Secure Data check box and then click OK.

5. Click OK to close the File1 Properties dialog box.

6. Close Windows Explorer and log off.

Lesson Summary

In this lesson, you learned that EFS provides the core file-encryption technology for storage of NTFS files on disk. EFS allows users to encrypt NTFS files by using a strong public key-based cryptographic scheme that encrypts all files in a folder. Users with roaming profiles can use the same key with trusted remote systems. Backups and copies of encrypted files are also encrypted if they are in NTFS volumes. Files remain encrypted if you move or rename them, and encryption is not defeated by leakage to paging files. Windows 2000 also provides a recovery agent. If an owner loses the private key, the recovery agent can still recover the encrypted file.

You also learned that EFS is implemented either from Windows Explorer or from the command line, using commands such as Cipher. EFS can be enabled or disabled for a computer, domain, or OU by resetting recovery policy in the Group Policy console in the MMC.

Finally, you learned that you can use EFS to encrypt and decrypt files on remote computers, but you can't use it to encrypt data that is transferred over the network. Windows 2000 provides network protocols, such as SSL, to encrypt data over the network.

Lesson 4: Using Disk Defragmenter

Windows 2000 saves files and folders in the first available space on a hard disk and not necessarily in an area of contiguous space. This leads to file and folder fragmentation. When your hard disk contains a lot of fragmented files and folders, your computer takes longer to gain access to them because it requires several additional reads to collect the various pieces. Creating new files and folders also takes longer because the available free space on the hard disk is scattered. Your computer must save a new file or folder in various locations on the hard disk. This lesson introduces you to the Windows 2000 system tool, Disk Defragmenter, which helps you organize your hard disks.

After this lesson, you will be able to

- Describe defragmentation.
- Use Disk Defragmenter to organize your hard disks.

Estimated lesson time: 15 minutes

Defragmenting Disks

The process of finding and consolidating fragmented files and folders is called *defragmenting*. Disk Defragmenter locates fragmented files and folders and defragments them. It does this by moving the pieces of each file or folder to one location so that each file or folder occupies a single, contiguous space on the hard disk. Consequently, your system can gain access to and save files and folders more efficiently. By consolidating files and folders, Disk Defragmenter also consolidates free space, making it less likely that new files will be fragmented. Disk Defragmenter can defragment FAT, FAT32, and NTFS volumes.

You access Disk Defragmenter by selecting Start; pointing to Programs, Accessories, and System Tools; and clicking Disk Defragmenter. The Disk Defragmenter window is split into three areas, as shown in Figure 18.5.

The upper portion of the window lists the volumes that you can analyze and defragment. The middle portion provides a graphic representation of how fragmented the selected volume is. The lower portion provides a dynamic representation of the volume that continuously updates during defragmentation. The display colors indicate the condition of the volume, as follows:

- Red indicates fragmented files.
- Dark blue indicates contiguous (nonfragmented) files.
- White indicates free space on the volume.
- Green indicates system files, which Disk Defragmenter can't move.

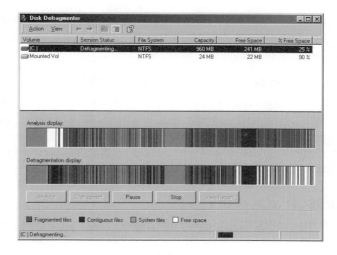

Figure 18.5   The Disk Defragmenter window

By comparing the Analysis Display band to the Defragmentation Display band during and at the conclusion of defragmentation, you can quickly see the improvement in the volume.

If you want to analyze and defragment a volume, open Disk Defragmenter by selecting a drive you want to defragment in Windows Explorer or My Computer. Click the File menu, click Properties, select the Tools tab, and click the Defragment Now button. Then click one of the buttons that are described in Table 18.6.

Table 18.6   Disk Defragmenter Options

Option	Description
Analyze	Click this button to analyze the disk for fragmentation. After the analysis, the Analysis Display band provides a graphic representation of how fragmented the volume is.
Defragment	Click this button to defragment the disk. After defragmentation, the Defragmentation Display band provides a graphic representation of the defragmented volume.

Using Disk Defragmenter Effectively

The following list provides some guidelines for using Disk Defragmenter:

- Run Disk Defragmenter when the computer will receive the least use. During defragmentation, data is moved around on the hard disk and the defragmentation process is microprocessor-intensive. The defragmentation process will adversely affect access time to other disk-based resources.

- Educate users to defragment their local hard disks at least once a month to prevent accumulation of fragmented files.

- Analyze the target volume before you install large applications, and then defragment the volume if necessary. Installations complete more quickly when the target media has adequate contiguous free space. Additionally, gaining access to the application after it is installed is faster.

- When you delete a large number of files or folders, your hard disk might become excessively fragmented, so be sure that you analyze it afterwards. Generally, you should defragment hard disks on busy file servers more often than those on single-user client computers.

Lesson Summary

In this lesson, you learned that Windows 2000 saves files and folders in the first available space on a hard disk and not necessarily in an area of contiguous space. This leads to file and folder fragmentation. You learned that when your hard disk contains a lot of fragmented files and folders, your computer takes longer to gain access to these files and folders and to create new files and folders.

You also learned about the Windows 2000 system tool, Disk Defragmenter, which locates fragmented files and folders and defragments them. Consequently, your system can gain access to and save files and folders more efficiently. By consolidating files and folders, Disk Defragmenter also consolidates free space, making it less likely that new files will be fragmented. Disk Defragmenter can defragment FAT, FAT32, and NTFS volumes.

Review

The following questions will help you determine whether you have learned enough to move on to the next chapter. If you have difficulty answering these questions, please go back and review the material in this chapter before beginning the next chapter. See Appendix A, "Questions and Answers," for the answers to these questions.

1. You are the administrator for a computer running Windows 2000 Professional. You want to restrict users to 25 MB of available storage space. How do you configure the volumes on the computer?

2. The Sales department archives legacy sales data on a network computer running Windows 2000 Professional. Several other departments share the server. You have begun to receive complaints from users in other departments that the computer has little remaining disk space. What can you do to alleviate the problem?

3. Your department has recently archived several gigabytes of data from a computer running Windows 2000 Professional to CD-ROMs. As users have been adding files to the computer, you have noticed that the computer has been taking longer than usual to gain access to the hard disk. How can you increase disk access time for the computer?

CHAPTER 19

Backing Up and Restoring Data

About This Chapter

Now that you have learned to install Microsoft Windows 2000 Professional and set up a network, it is important that you are able to ensure that your data is not lost. Luckily, Windows 2000 Professional provides the Backup Wizard to allow you to back up data. This chapter introduces you to backing up and restoring data.

Before You Begin

To complete this chapter, you must have

- A computer that meets the minimum hardware requirements located in "About This Book."
- Microsoft Windows 2000 Professional installed on the computer.

Lesson 1: Understanding How to Back Up and Restore Data

The efficient recovery of lost data is the goal of all backup jobs. A *backup job* is a single process of backing up data. Regularly backing up the data on server hard disks and client computer hard disks prevents data loss due to disk drive failures, power outages, virus infections, and other such incidents. If data loss occurs, and you have carefully planned and performed regular backup jobs, you can restore the lost data, whether the lost data is a single file or an entire hard disk.

After this lesson, you will be able to

- Identify the purpose of backing up and restoring data.
- Identify the user rights and permissions that are necessary to back up and restore data.
- Identify planning issues for backing up data.
- Identify the different backup types.

Estimated lesson time: 20 minutes

Introducing Windows Backup

Windows 2000 provides the Windows 2000 Backup And Recovery Tools, shown in Figure 19.1, which includes the Backup Wizard, a tool that allows you to easily back up and restore data. To launch Backup, on the Start menu, point to Programs, point to Accessories, point to System Tools, and then click Backup; or, on the Start menu, click Run, type **ntbackup** and then click OK. You can use Backup to back up data manually or to schedule unattended backup jobs regularly. You can back up data to a file or to a tape. Files can be stored on hard disks, removable disks (such as Iomega Zip and Jaz drives), and recordable compact discs and optical drives.

To successfully back up and restore data on a computer running Windows 2000 Professional, you must have the appropriate permissions and user rights, as described in the following list:

- All users can back up their own files and folders. They can also back up files for which they have the Read, Read & Execute, Modify, or Full Control permission.
- All users can restore files and folders for which they have the Write, Modify, or Full Control permission.
- Members of the Administrators and Backup Operators groups can back up and restore all files (regardless of the assigned permissions). By default, members of these groups have the Backup Files and Directories, and the Restore Files and Directories user rights.

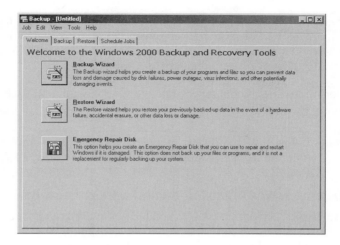

Figure 19.1   The Windows 2000 Backup And Recovery Tools

Planning Issues for Windows Backup

You should plan your backup jobs to fit your company's needs. The primary goal for backing up data is to be able to restore that data if necessary, so any backup plan that you develop should incorporate how you restore data. You should be able to quickly and successfully restore critical lost data. No single correct backup plan exists for all networks.

Consider the following issues in formulating your backup plan.

Determine Which Files and Folders to Back Up

Always back up critical files and folders that your company needs to operate, such as sales and financial records, the registry for each server, and, if you are in a domain, the directory service files based on Active Directory technology.

Determine How Often to Back Up

If data is critical for company operations, back it up daily. If users create or modify reports once a week, backing up the reports weekly is sufficient. You need to back up data only as often as it changes. For example, you don't need to do daily backups on files that rarely change, such as monthly reports.

Determine Which Target Media to Use for Storing Backup Data

With Backup Wizard, you can back up to the following removable media:

- **Files.** You can store the files on a removable media device, such as an Iomega Zip drive, or on a network location, such as a file server. The file that is created contains the files and folders that you have selected to back up. The file has a .BKF extension. Users can back up their personal data to a network server. Use this only for temporary backup jobs.

- **Tape.** A less expensive medium than other removable media, a tape is more convenient for large backup jobs because of its high storage capacity. However, tapes have a limited life and can deteriorate. Be sure that you check the manufacturer's recommendations for usage.

For information about tape rotation and archiving tapes, see Appendix D, "Managing Backup Tapes."

Note If you use a removable media device to back up and restore data, be sure to verify that the device is supported on the Windows 2000 HCL.

Determine Whether to Perform Network or Local Backup Jobs

A network backup can contain data from multiple network computers. This allows you to consolidate backup data from multiple computers to a single removable backup medium. A network backup also allows one administrator to back up the entire network. Whether you perform a network or local backup job depends on the data that must be backed up. For example, you can back up the registry and Active Directory directory services only at the computer where you are performing the backup.

If you decide to perform local backups, you must perform a local backup at each computer, including servers and client computers. You must consider several issues for performing local backups. First of all, you must move from computer to computer so that you can perform a backup at each computer, or you must rely on users to back up their own computers. Typically, most users fail to back up their data regularly. A second consideration with local backups is the number of removable storage media devices. If you use removable storage media devices, such as tape drives, you must have one for each computer, or you must move the tape drive from computer to computer so that you can perform a local backup on each computer.

You can also choose to use a combination of network and local backup jobs. Do this when critical data resides on client computers and servers and you don't have a removable storage media device for each computer. In this situation, users perform a local backup and store their backup files on a server. You then back up the server.

Examining Backup Types

Backup Wizard provides five types of backup that define which data is backed up, such as only files that have changed since the last backup. (See Figure 19.2.)

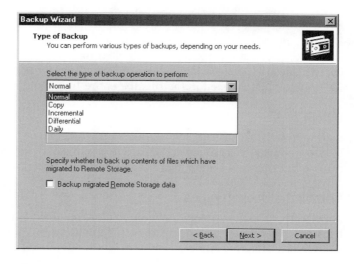

Figure 19.2   Selecting the type of backup

Some backup types use backup *markers,* also known as archive attributes, which mark a file as having changed. When a file changes, an attribute is set on the file that indicates that the file has changed since the last backup. When you back up the file, this clears or resets the attribute.

Normal

During a *normal* backup, all selected files and folders are backed up. A normal backup doesn't rely on markers to determine which files to back up. During a normal backup, any existing marks are cleared and each file is marked as having been backed up. Normal backups speed up the restore process because the backup files are the most current and you don't need to restore multiple backup jobs.

Copy

During a *copy* backup, all selected files and folders are backed up. It neither looks for nor clears markers. If you don't want to clear markers and affect other backup types, use copy. For example, use a copy backup between a normal and an incremental backup to create an archival snapshot of network data.

Incremental

During an *incremental* backup, only selected files and folders that have a marker are backed up, and then the backup clears markers. Because an incremental backup clears markers, if you did two incremental backups in a row on a file and nothing changed in the file, the file would not be backed up the second time.

Differential

During a *differential* backup, only selected files and folders that have a marker are backed up, but the backup doesn't clear markers. Because a differential backup doesn't clear markers, if you did two differential backups in a row on a file and nothing changed in the file, the entire file would be backed up each time.

Daily

During a *daily* backup, all selected files and folders that have changed during the day are backed up. Backup Wizard does not clear markers. If you want to back up all files and folders that change during the day, use a daily backup.

Combining Backup Types

An effective backup strategy is likely to combine different backup types. Some backup types require more time to back up data but less time to restore data. Conversely, other backup types require less time to back up data but more time to restore data. If you combine backup types, markers are critical. Incremental and differential backup types check for and rely on the markers.

The following are some examples of combining different backup types:

- **Normal and differential backups.** On Monday a normal backup is performed, and on Tuesday through Friday, differential backups are performed. Differential backups don't clear markers, which means that each backup includes all changes since Monday. If data becomes corrupt on Friday, you need to restore only the normal backup from Monday and the differential backup from Thursday. This strategy takes more time to back up but less time to restore.

- **Normal and incremental backups.** On Monday a normal backup is performed, and on Tuesday through Friday, incremental backups are performed. Incremental backups clear markers, which means that each backup includes only the files that changed since the previous backup. If data becomes corrupt on Friday, you need to restore the normal backup from Monday and all incremental backups, from Tuesday through Friday. This strategy takes less time to back up but more time to restore.

- **Normal, differential, and copy backups.** This strategy is the same as the first example that used normal and incremental backups, except that on Wednesday, you perform a copy backup. Copy backups include all selected files and do not clear markers or interrupt the usual backup schedule. Therefore, each differential backup includes all changes since Monday. The copy backup type done on Wednesday is not part of the Friday restore. Copy backups are helpful when you need to create a snapshot of your data.

Lesson Summary

The efficient recovery of lost data is the goal of all backup jobs. If data loss does occur, and you have carefully planned and performed regular backup jobs, you can restore the lost data. In this lesson, you learned that Windows 2000 Professional provides the Backup Wizard that allows you to easily back up and restore data. You can use it to back up data manually or to schedule unattended backup jobs regularly. Backup Wizard provides five types of backup: normal, copy, differential, incremental, and daily. You can use one of these backup types or a combination of backup types to back up your data.

Lesson 2: Backing Up Data

After you have planned your backup, including planning the type of backup to use and when to perform backup jobs, the next step is to prepare to back up your data. You must complete certain preliminary tasks before you can back up your data. Then you can perform the backup. Afterward, you can schedule and run unattended backups.

After this lesson, you will be able to

- Back up data at a computer and over the network.
- Schedule a backup job.
- Set backup options for Backup Wizard.

Estimated lesson time: 45 minutes

Performing Preliminary Tasks

An important part of each backup job is performing the preliminary tasks. One task that you must do is ensure that the files that you want to back up are closed. You should notify users to close files before you begin backing up data. Backup Wizard doesn't back up files that are locked open by applications. You can use e-mail or the Send Console Message dialog box in the Computer Management snap-in to send administrative messages to users.

You can send a console message, as follows:

1. On the Start menu, point to Programs, point to Administrative tools, and click Computer Management.
2. On the Action menu, click All Tasks, and then click Send Console Message.

   The Send Console Message dialog box appears. See Figure 19.3.
3. Type the desired message in the Message box. Note the recipients in the Recipients box. You can add or remove recipients.
4. Click Send to send the message to the listed recipients.

For more information on sending a console message, see Chapter 20, "Monitoring Access to Network Resources."

If you use a removable media device, make sure that the following preliminary tasks occur:

- The backup device is attached to a computer on the network and is turned on. If you are backing up to tape, you must attach the tape device to the computer on which you run Backup Wizard.

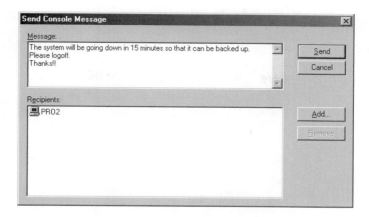

Figure 19.3   The Send Console Message dialog box

- The media device is listed on the Windows 2000 HCL.

- The media is loaded in the media device. For example, if you are using a tape drive, ensure that a tape is loaded in the tape drive.

Selecting Files and Folders to Back Up

After you have completed the preliminary tasks, you can perform the backup. You can use the Backup Wizard button shown in Figure 19.4 to start Backup Wizard. To start Backup Wizard, click Start, point to Accessories, point to System Tools, click Backup, and then click Backup Wizard; or you can use the Run command on the Start menu to run Ntbackup, and then click Backup Wizard. Click Next to close the Welcome tab and display the What To Back Up page.

The first phase is to specify what to back up by choosing one of the following options:

- **Back Up Everything On My Computer.** Backs up all files on the computer on which you are running Backup Wizard, except those files that Backup Wizard excludes by default, such as certain power management files.

- **Back Up Selected Files, Drives, Or Network Data.** Backs up selected files and folders. This includes files and folders on the computer where you run Backup Wizard and any shared file or folder on the network. When you click this option, the Backup Wizard provides a hierarchical view of the computer and the network (through My Network Places).

- **Only Back Up The System State Data.** Backs up important system components, such as the Registry and the boot files for the computer on which you are running Backup Wizard.

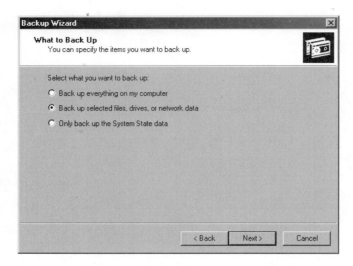

Figure 19.4   The What To Back Up page of the Backup Wizard

Specifying Backup Destination and Media Settings

After you select what you want to back up, you need to provide information about backup media. Table 19.1 describes the information that you must provide on the Where To Store The Backup page.

Table 19.1   Where To Store The Backup Page Options

Option	Description
Backup Media Type	The target medium to use, such as a tape or file. A file can be located on any disk-based media, including a hard disk, a shared network folder, or a removable disk, such as an Iomega Zip drive.
Backup Media Or File Name	The location where Windows Backup will store the data. For a tape, enter the tape name. For a file, enter the path for the backup file.

After you provide the media information, Backup Wizard displays the Completing The Backup Wizard page and you have the opportunity to do either of the following:

- Start the backup. If you click Finish, during the backup process, Backup Wizard displays status information about the backup job in the Backup Progress dialog box.

- Specify advanced backup options. If you click Advanced, the Backup wizard allows you to select the advanced backup settings listed in Table 19.2.

Table 19.2   Advanced Backup Settings

Advanced option	Description
Select The Type Of Backup Operation To Perform	Allows you to choose the backup type that is used for this backup job. Select one of the following types: normal, copy, incremental, differential, or daily.
Backup Migrated Remote	Backs up the contents of files that have been migrated to remote storage. Windows 2000 Server automatically moves files that are rarely used to remote storage.
Verify Data After Backup	Confirms that files are correctly backed up. Backup Wizard compares the backup data and the source data to verify that they are the same. *Microsoft recommends that you select this option.*
Use Hardware Compression, If Available	Enables hardware compression for tape devices that support it. If your tape device doesn't support hardware compression, this option is unavailable.
If The Archive Media Already Contains Backups:	
Append This Backup To The Media	Choose Append This Backup To The Media to store multiple backup jobs on a storage device.
Or	
Replace The Data On The Media With This Backup	Choose Replace The Data On The Media With This Backup if you don't need to save previous backup jobs and you want to save only the most recent backup data.
Allow Only The Owner And The Administrator Access To The Backup Data And To Any Backups Appended To This Media	Allows you to restrict who can gain access to the completed backup file or tape. This option is available only if you choose to replace an existing backup on a backup medium, rather than appending to the backup medium. If you back up the registry or Active Directory directory services, click this option to prevent others from getting copies of the backup job.
Backup Label	Allows you to specify a name and description for the backup job. The name and description appear in the backup log. The default is Set Created *date* At *time*. You can change the name and description to a more intuitive name (for example, Sales-normal backup September 14, 2000).
Media Label	Allows you to specify the name of the backup media (for example, the tape name). The default name is Media Created *date* At *time,* where *date* is the current date and *time* is the current time. The first time that you back up to a new medium or overwrite an existing backup job, you can specify the name, such as Active Directory backup.
When To Back Up	Allows you to specify Now or Later. If you choose Later, you specify the job name and the start date. You can also set the schedule.

Note When the backup process is complete, you can choose to review the backup report, which is the backup log. A *backup log* is a text file that records backup operations and is stored on the hard disk of the computer on which you are running Backup Wizard.

Specifying Advanced Backup Settings

When you specify advanced backup settings, you are changing the default backup settings for only the current backup job. The advanced settings cover the backup media and characteristics of the backup job.

Depending on whether you chose to back up now or later, Backup Wizard provides you with the opportunity to do either of the following:

- If you chose to finish the backup process, Backup Wizard displays the Completing The Backup Wizard settings and then presents the option to finish and immediately start the backup. During the backup, the wizard displays status information about the backup job.

- If you chose to back up later, you are shown additional dialog boxes to schedule the backup process to occur later, as described in the next section.

Scheduling Backup Jobs

Scheduling a backup job means that you can have an unattended backup job occur later when users aren't at work and files are closed. You can also schedule backup jobs to occur at regular intervals. To enable this, Windows 2000 integrates Backup Wizard with the Task Scheduler service.

You can schedule a backup, as follows:

1. Click Later on the When To Back Up page of Backup Wizard.

   Task Scheduler presents the Set Account Information dialog box, prompting you for your password. The user account must have the appropriate user rights and permissions to perform backup jobs.

   Note If the Task Scheduler service isn't running or isn't set to start automatically, Windows 2000 displays a dialog box prompting you to start the service. Click OK, and the Set Account Information dialog box appears.

2. Enter your password in the Password box and Confirm Password box, and then click OK.

   The When To Back Up page appears. You must provide a name for the backup job, and by default, the wizard displays the present date and time for the start date.

3. Type the appropriate name in the Job Name box.

4. Click Set Schedule to set a different start date and time. This selection causes Task Scheduler to display the Schedule Job dialog box.

In the Schedule Job dialog box, you can set the date, time, and number of occurrences for the backup job to repeat, such as every Friday at 10:00 P.M. You can also display all of the scheduled tasks for the computer by selecting the Show Multiple Schedules check box. This helps to prevent you from scheduling multiple tasks on the same computer at the same time.

You can click the Advanced button to also schedule how long the backup can last and for how many days, weeks, months, or years you want this schedule to continue.

After you schedule the backup job and complete Backup Wizard, Windows Backup places the backup job on the calendar on the Schedule Jobs tab in Windows Backup. The backup job automatically starts at the time that you specified.

Practice: Backing Up Files

In this practice, you will use Backup Wizard to back up some files to your hard disk. You will then create a backup job to perform a backup operation later by using Task Scheduler.

Exercise 1: Starting a Backup Job

In this exercise, you will start Backup Wizard and use it to back up files to your hard disk.

▶ **To back up files by using Backup Wizard**

1. Log on as Administrator.

2. Click Start, point to Programs, point to Accessories, point to System Tools, and then click Backup.

3. On the Welcome tab, click Backup Wizard.

   Backup Wizard starts and displays the Welcome To The Windows 2000 Backup And Recovery Tools page.

4. Click Next to continue creating the backup job.

   Backup Wizard displays the What To Back Up page, prompting you to choose the scope of the backup job.

5. Click Back Up Selected Files, Drives, Or Network Data, and then click Next to continue.

   Backup Wizard displays the Items To Back Up page, prompting you to select the local and network drives, folders, and files to be backed up.

6. Expand My Computer, expand drive C, and then click C.

Do *not* select drive C. There should not be a check mark in the check box in front of drive C.

7. In the details pane, select Boot.ini.

   You should see a check mark in the check box in front of the filename Boot.ini.

   Note Boot.ini is one of the boot files for Windows 2000 Professional. You will learn more about the Boot.ini file in Chapter 22, "The Windows 2000 Boot Process."
   ---

8. Click Next to continue.

   Backup Wizard displays the Where To Store The Backup page.

   Note If no tape drive is connected to your computer, File will be the only backup media type that is available.
   ---

9. In the Backup Media Or File Name box, type **c:\backup1.bkf** and then click Next.

   Note You wouldn't normally back up files from a drive to a file on that same drive, as you are doing in this exercise. You would normally back up data to a tape or to a file stored on another hard disk, removable disks (such as Iomega Zip and Jaz drives), or recordable compact discs or optical drives.

   Backup Wizard displays the Completing The Backup Wizard page, prompting you to finish the wizard and begin the backup job or to specify advanced options.

10. Click Advanced to specify additional backup options.

    Backup Wizard displays the Type Of Backup page, prompting you to select a backup type for this backup job.

11. Make sure that Normal is selected in the Select The Type Of Backup Operation To Perform list.

12. Make sure that the Backup Migrated Remote Storage Data check box is cleared, and then click Next.

    Backup Wizard displays the How To Back Up page, prompting you to specify whether to verify the backed up data after the backup job.

13. Select the Verify Data After Backup check box, and then click Next.

    Backup Wizard displays the Media Options page, prompting you to specify whether to append this backup job to existing media or overwrite existing backup data on the destination media.

14. Click Replace The Data On The Media With This Backup.

When is it appropriate to select the check box labeled Allow Only The Owner And The Administrator Access To The Backup Data And Any Backups Appended To This Media?

15. Make sure that the Allow Only The Owner And The Administrator Access To The Backup Data And To Any Backups Appended To This Media check box is cleared, and then click Next.

    Backup Wizard displays the Backup Label page, prompting you to supply a label for the backup job and a label for the backup media.

    Notice that Backup Wizard generates a backup label and media label by using the current date and time.

16. Press Tab to accept the default Backup Label and to move to the Media Label box.

17. In the Media Label box, type **Boot.ini file for Pro1** and then click Next.

    Backup Wizard displays the When To Backup page, prompting you to choose whether to run the backup job now or schedule this backup job.

18. Make sure that Now is selected, and then click Next.

    Backup Wizard displays the Completing The Backup Wizard page, which lists the options and settings that you selected for this backup job.

19. Click Finish to start the backup job.

    Backup Wizard briefly displays the Selection Information dialog box, indicating the estimated amount of data for, and the time to complete, the backup job.

    Then Windows Backup displays the Backup Progress dialog box, providing the status of the backup operation, statistics on the estimated and the actual amount of data being processed, the time that has elapsed, and the estimated time that remains for the backup operation.

▶ **To view the backup report**

1. When the Backup Progress dialog box indicates that the backup is complete, click Report.

   Notepad starts, displaying the backup report.

   The backup report contains key details about the backup operation, such as the time that it started and how many files were backed up.

2. Examine the report, and when you are finished, quit Notepad.

3. In the Backup Progress dialog box, click Close.

   The Backup window remains open with the Welcome tab active.

Exercise 2: Creating and Running an Unattended Backup Job

In this exercise, you will create a backup job to perform a backup operation at a later time by using Task Scheduler.

▶   **To create a scheduled backup job**

1. On the Welcome tab, click Backup Wizard.

    The Backup wizard starts and displays the Welcome To The Windows 2000 Backup And Recovery Tools page.

2. Click Next to continue creating the backup job.

    Backup Wizard displays the What To Back Up page, prompting you to choose the scope of the backup job.

3. Click Back Up Selected Files, Drives, Or Network Data, and then click Next to continue.

    Backup Wizard displays the Items To Back Up page, prompting you to select the local and network drives, folders, and files to be backed up.

4. Expand My Computer, expand drive C, and then select the System Volume Information check box.

5. Click Next to continue.

    Backup Wizard displays the Where To Store The Backup page, prompting you to select the destination for your backup data.

6. In the Backup Media Or File Name box, type **C:\backup2.bkf** and then click Next.

    Backup Wizard displays the Completing The Backup Wizard page.

7. Click Advanced to specify additional backup options.

    Backup Wizard displays the Type Of Backup page, prompting you to select a backup type for this backup job.

8. Make sure that in the Select The Type Of Backup Operation To Perform box, Normal is selected, and then click Next.

    Backup Wizard displays the How To Back Up page, prompting you to specify whether to verify the backed up data after the backup job.

9. Select the Verify Data After Backup check box, and then click Next.

    Backup Wizard displays the Media Options page, prompting you to specify whether to append this backup job to existing media or overwrite existing backup data on the destination media.

10. Click Replace The Data On The Media With This Backup option.

11. Make sure the check box labeled Allow Only The Owner And The Administrator Access To The Backup Data And To Any Backups Appended To This Media is not selected, and then click Next.

Backup Wizard displays the Backup Label page, prompting you to supply a label for the backup job and a label for the backup media.

12. In the Media Label box, type **Backup file 2 for PRO1** and then click Next.

Backup Wizard displays the When To Back Up page, prompting you to choose whether to run the backup job now or schedule this backup job.

13. Click Later.

The Set Account Information dialog box appears, prompting you for the password for the Administrator account. (If the Task Scheduler service isn't set to start automatically, first you might see a dialog box asking whether you want to start Task Scheduler. Click OK, and then the Set Account Information dialog box appears.)

Because the Task Scheduler service automatically runs applications within the security context of a valid user for the computer or domain, you are prompted for the name and password with which the scheduled backup job will run. For scheduled backup jobs, you should supply a user account that is a member of the Backup Operators group with permission to gain access to all of the folders and files to be backed up.

For purposes of this lab, you will use the Administrator account to run the scheduled backup job.

14. Make sure that PRO1\Administrator appears in the Run As box (or the name of your computer, if it isn't PRO1), and then type **password** in the Password box and the Confirm Password box.

15. Click OK.

16. In the Job Name box, type **PRO1 Backup** and then click Set Schedule.

Windows Backup displays the Schedule Job dialog box, prompting you to select the start time and schedule options for the backup job.

17. In the Schedule Task box, select Once, and in the Start Time box, enter a time two minutes from the present time, and then click OK.

The When To Back Up page remains displayed along with the scheduled backup job information.

18. Click Next to continue.

Backup Wizard displays the Completing The Backup Wizard page, displaying the options and settings that you selected for this backup job.

19. Click Finish to start the backup job.

The Backup window remains displayed with the Welcome tab active.

20. Close the Backup window.

When the time for the backup job is reached, Windows Backup starts and performs the requested backup operation.

▶   **To verify that the backup job was performed**

1. Start Microsoft Windows Explorer and click drive C.

   Does the Backup2.bkf file exist?

2. Log off Windows 2000.

Lesson Summary

In this lesson, you learned that after you have planned your backup, the next step is to prepare to back up your data. An important part of each backup job is performing the preliminary tasks. One task that you must do is ensure that the files that you want to back up are closed, because Windows Backup doesn't back up files that are locked open by applications. Next you perform the backup.

Then you learned that in Backup Wizard, the first phase is to specify what to back up. You can choose from three options: back up everything on the computer; back up selected files, drives, or network data; or back up only the system state data. After you select what you want to back up, you need to provide the target destination and the backup media or filename. Then you can finish the backup or you can specify any advanced backup options.

In the practice exercises, you backed up a portion of your files. Then you created and ran an unattended backup job.

Lesson 3: Restoring Data

In this lesson, you will learn about restoring data. The ability to restore corrupt or lost data is critical to all corporations and is the goal of all backup jobs. To ensure that you can successfully restore data, you should follow certain guidelines, such as keeping thorough documentation on all of your backup jobs.

After this lesson, you will be able to
- Restore data, whether an entire volume or a single file.

Estimated lesson time: 30 minutes

Preparing to Restore Data

To restore data, you must select the backup sets, files, and folders to restore. You can also specify additional settings based on your restore requirements. Backup provides Restore Wizard to help you restore data, or you can restore data without using the wizard.

When critical data is lost, you need to restore the data quickly. Use the following guidelines to help you prepare for restoring data:

- Base your restore strategy on the backup type that you used for the backup. If time is critical when you are restoring data, your restore strategy must ensure that the backup types that you choose for backups expedite the restore process. For example, use normal and differential backups so that you need to restore only the last normal backup and the last differential backup.

- Perform a trial restore periodically to verify that Backup Wizard is backing up your files correctly. A trial restore can uncover hardware problems that don't show up with software verifications. Restore the data to an alternate location, and then compare the restored data to the data on the original hard disk.

- Keep documentation for each backup job. Create and print a detailed backup log for each backup job. A detailed backup log contains a record of all files and folders that were backed up. By using the backup log, you can quickly locate which piece of media contains the files that you need to restore without having to load the catalogs. A *catalog* is an index of the files and folders from a backup job that Windows 2000 automatically creates and stores with the backup job and on the computer running Backup Wizard.

- Keep a record of multiple backup jobs in a calendar format that shows the days on which you perform the backup jobs. For each job, note the backup type and identify the storage that is used, such as a tape number or the name of the Iomega Zip drive. Then, if you need to restore data, you can easily review several weeks' worth of backup jobs to select which tape to use.

Selecting Backup Sets, Files, and Folders to Restore

The first step in restoring data is to select the data to restore. You can select individual files and folders, an entire backup job, or a backup set. A *backup set* is a collection of files or folders from one volume that you back up during a backup job. If you back up two volumes on a hard disk during a backup job, the job has two backup sets. You select the data to restore in the catalog.

To restore data, use Restore Wizard, as follows:

1. In Restore Wizard, expand the media type that contains the data that you want to restore. This can be either tape or file media.

2. Expand the appropriate media set until the data that you want to restore is visible. You can restore a backup set or specific files and folders.

3. Select the data that you want to restore, and then click Next.

   Restore Wizard displays the settings for the restore.

4. Do one of the following:

   - Finish the restore process. If you choose to finish the restore job, during the restore, Restore Wizard requests verification for the source of the restore media and then performs the restore. During the restore, Restore Wizard displays status information about the restore.

   - Specify advanced restore options.

Specifying Advanced Restore Settings

The advanced settings in Restore Wizard vary, depending on the type of backup media from which you are restoring, such as a tape device or an Iomega Zip drive. Table 19.3 describes the advanced restore options.

Table 19.3   Advanced Restore Settings

Option	Description
Restore Files To	The target location for the data that you are restoring. The choices are
	Original Location. Replaces corrupted or lost data.
	Alternate Location. Restores an older version of a file or does a practice restore.
	Single Folder. Consolidates the files from a tree structure into a single folder. For example, use this option if you want copies of specific files but don't want to restore the hierarchical structure of the files.
	If you select either an alternate location or a single directory, you must provide the path.

Option	Description
When Restoring Files That Already Exist (Click Options on the Tools menu to access these options.)	Whether you want to overwrite existing files. The choices are **Do Not Replace The File On My Disk (Recommended).** Prevents accidental overwriting of existing data. (This is the default.) **Replace The File On Disk Only If It Is Older Than The Backup Copy.** Verifies that the most recent copy exists on the computer. **Always Replace The File On Disk.** Restore Wizard doesn't provide a confirmation message if it encounters a duplicate filename during the restore operation.
Select The Special Restore Options You Want To Use (Click the Start Restore button to access these options.)	Whether you want to restore security or special system files. The choices are **Restore Security.** Applies the original permissions to files that you are restoring to a Microsoft Windows 2000 File System (NTFS) volume. Security settings include access permissions, audit entries, and ownership. This option is available only if you have backed up data from an NTFS volume and are restoring to an NTFS volume. **Restore Removable Storage Database.** Restores the configuration database for removable storage devices and the media pool settings. The database is located in *systemroot*\system32\ remotestorage. **Restore Junction Points, Not The Folders And File Data They Reference.** Restores junction points on your hard disk as well as the data that the junction points refer to. If you have any mounted drives, and you want to restore the data that mounted drives point to, select this check box. If you don't select this check box, the junction point will be restored but the data your junction point refers to might not be accessible. **When Restoring Replicated Data Sets, Make The Restored Data As The Primary Data For All Replicas.** Restores the data for all replicated data sets.

After you have finished using Restore Wizard, Windows Backup does the following:

- Prompts you to verify your selection of the source media to use to restore data. After the verification, Windows Backup starts the restore process.

- Displays status information about the restore process. As with a backup process, you can choose to view the report (restore log) of the restore. It contains information about the restore, such as the number of files that have been restored and the duration of the restore process.

Practice: Restoring Files

In this practice, you will restore a file that you backed up in Exercise 1 in Lesson 2 of this chapter.

Important To complete this practice, you must have completed the practice in the previous lesson, or you must have some files that you have backed up using Ntbackup that you can restore.

▶ **To restore files from a previous backup job**

1. In Windows Backup, on the Welcome tab, click Restore Wizard.

   Restore Wizard starts and displays the Welcome To The Restore Wizard page.

2. Click Next to continue creating the restore job.

   Restore Wizard displays the What To Restore page, prompting you to select the backup media from which you want to restore files.

3. In the What To Restore box, expand the File node that you created.

   Notice that the Boot.ini file for PRO1 and Backup File 2 For PRO1 are listed.

4. Expand the Boot.ini file for PRO1.

   Notice that drive C appears under the Boot.ini file for PRO1.

5. Expand drive C.

   The Backup File Name dialog box appears.

6. In the Catalog Backup File box, make sure it says C:\Backup1.bkf and then click OK.

   The Operation Status dialog box appears and then closes.

7. Select drive C and then click Next.

   Restore Wizard displays the Completing The Restore Wizard page.

8. Click Advanced.

   Restore Wizard displays the Where To Restore page.

9. In the Restore Files To list, select Alternate Location.

   Restore Wizard displays the Alternate Location box.

10. In the Alternate Location box, type **C:\Restored data** and then click Next.

    Restore Wizard displays the How To Restore page, prompting you to specify how to process duplicate files during the restore job.

11. Make sure that Do Not Replace The File On My Disk (Recommended) is selected, and then click Next.

    Restore Wizard displays the Advanced Restore Options page, prompting you to select security options for the restore job.

12. Make sure that all check boxes are cleared and then click Next.

    Restore Wizard displays the Completing The Restore Wizard page, displaying a summary of the restore options that you selected.

13. Click Finish to begin the restore process.

    Windows Backup displays the Enter Backup File Name dialog box, prompting you to supply or verify the name of the backup file that contains the folders and files to be restored.

14. Make sure that the file Backup1.bkf is entered in the Restore From Backup File box, and then click OK.

    Windows Backup displays the Selection Information dialog box, indicating the estimated amount of data for, and the time to complete, the restore job. (This dialog box might appear briefly, since you are restoring a single file.)

    Then Windows Backup displays the Restore Progress dialog box, providing the status of the restore operation, statistics on estimated and actual amount of data that is being processed, the time that has elapsed, and the estimated time that remains for the restore operation.

▶ **To view the restore report**

1. When the Restore Progress dialog box indicates that the restore is complete, click Report.

   Notepad starts, displaying the report. Notice that the details about the restore operation are appended to the previous backup log. This provides a centralized location to view all status information for backup and restore operations.

2. Examine the report, and then exit Notepad.

3. In the Restore Progress dialog box, click Close.

   The Backup window remains displayed with the Welcome tab active.

▶ **To verify that the data was restored**

1. Start Windows Explorer and expand drive C.

   Does the Restored Data folder exist?

   What are the contents of the Restored Data folder?

Note If the Restored Data folder appears to be blank, ensure that the Restored Data folder is selected, and on the Tools menu click Folder Options. On the View tab of the Folder Options dialog box, select the Show Hidden Files And Folders option and remove the check mark in front of Hide Protected Operating System Files (Recommended), and when you are prompted to confirm this action, click Yes. Click Apply and then verify that Boot (or Boot.ini) appears in the Restored Folder.

2. Close Windows Explorer, and close the Backup window.

Lesson Summary

In this lesson, you learned that Backup provides Restore Wizard to help you restore data, or you can restore data without using the wizard. The first step in restoring data is to select the data to restore. You can select individual files and folders, an entire backup job, or a backup set. The advanced settings in Restore Wizard vary, depending on the type of backup media from which you are restoring. In the practice section, you restored the data that you backed up in Exercise 1 of Lesson 2 in this chapter.

Lesson 4: Changing Windows Default Backup Options

Windows Backup allows you to change the default settings for all backup and restore jobs. These default settings are on the tabs in the Options dialog box. To access the Options dialog box, in Windows Backup, on the Tools menu, you click Options.

After this lesson, you will be able to

- Explain how to change the default options for Windows Backup.

Estimated lesson time: 5 minutes

This list provides an overview of the default options for Windows Backup:

- **General tab.** These settings affect data verification, the status information for backup and restore jobs, alert messages, and what is backed up. (See Figure 19.5.) You should select the Verify Data After The Backup Completes check box because it is critical that your backup data is not corrupt.

- **Restore tab.** These settings affect what happens when the file to restore is identical to an existing file.

- **Backup Type tab.** These settings affect the default backup type when you perform a backup job. The options you select depend on how often you back up, how quickly you want to restore, and how much storage space you have.

- **Backup Log tab.** These settings affect the amount of information that is included in the backup log.

- **Exclude Files tab.** These settings affect which files are excluded from backup jobs.

You can modify some default settings in Backup Wizard for a specific backup job. For example, the default backup type is normal, but you can change it to another backup type in Backup Wizard. However, the next time that you run Backup Wizard, the default backup type (normal) is selected.

Figure 19.5   The General tab of the Options dialog box for Windows Backup

Lesson Summary

In this lesson, you learned about the default Windows Backup options and how to change them using the tabs in the Options dialog box for Windows Backup. You also learned that you can change the default settings for individual jobs.

Review

The following questions will help you determine whether you have learned enough to move on to the next chapter. If you have difficulty answering these questions, please go back and review the material in this chapter before beginning the next chapter. See Appendix A, "Questions and Answers," for the answers to these questions.

1. If you want a user to perform backups, what do you need to do?

2. You performed a normal backup on Monday. For the remaining days of the week, you want to back up only files and folders that have changed since the previous day. What backup type do you select?

3. What are the considerations for using tapes as your backup media?

4. You are restoring a file that has the same name as a file on the volume to which you are restoring. You aren't sure which is the most current version. What do you do?

C H A P T E R   2 0

Monitoring Access to Network Resources

About This Chapter

This chapter prepares you to monitor network resources. You will learn about the Computer Management and the Shared Folders snap-ins and how to use them to view and create shares. You will also learn how to use them to view sessions and open files and how to use it to disconnect users from your shared folders.

Before You Begin

To complete this chapter, you must have

- A computer that meets or exceeds the minimum hardware requirements located in "About This Book."
- Microsoft Windows 2000 Professional installed on the computer.

Lesson 1: Monitoring Network Resources

Windows 2000 includes the Computer Management and Shared Folders snap-ins so that you can easily monitor access to network resources and send administrative messages to users. You monitor access to network resources to assess and manage current use on network servers.

After this lesson, you will be able to

- Identify three reasons for monitoring access to network resources.
- Identify the tools included with Windows 2000 to monitor access to network resources and to send administrative messages.
- Identify who can monitor access to network resources.

Estimated lesson time: 5 minutes

Understanding the Purposes for Monitoring Network Resources

The three primary reasons why it is important to assess and manage network resources are included in the following list:

- **Maintenance.** When you must perform maintenance tasks on network resources, you will need to periodically make certain resources unavailable to users. To do this you must determine which users are currently using a resource so that you can notify them before making the resource temporarily or permanently unavailable.

- **Security.** To maintain a network's security you need to monitor user access to resources that are confidential or need to be secure to verify that only authorized users are accessing them.

- **Planning.** Meeting the expanding needs of the network's users requires that you determine which resources are being used and how much they are being used so that you can plan for future system growth.

Windows 2000 includes the Computer Management and Shared Folders snap-ins so that you can easily monitor access to network resources and send administrative messages to users. When you add the Computer Management and Shared Folders snap-ins to a custom console with MMC, you specify whether you want to monitor the resources on the local computer or a remote computer.

Understanding the Requirements to Monitor Network Resources

Not all users can monitor access to network resources. Table 20.1 lists the group membership requirements for monitoring access to network resources.

Table 20.1   Groups That Can Access Network Resources

A member of these groups	Can monitor
Administrators or Server Operators for the domain	All computers in the domain.
Administrators or Power Users for a member server	Local or remote computers in the workgroup.

Lesson Summary

In this lesson, you learned that monitoring network resources helps you to determine whether the network resource is still needed and whether it is secure. Monitoring resources also helps you to plan for future growth. Windows 2000 includes the Computer Management and Shared Folders snap-ins so that you can easily monitor access to network resources. You can monitor resources on the local computer or on a remote computer. To monitor resources on a remote computer, you specify the computer on which you want to monitor resources when you add either the Computer Management or Shared Folders snap-in to a custom console.

You also learned that in a workgroup, only members of the Administrators group or the Power Users group can monitor resources for the local computer or for a remote computer in the workgroup. In a domain, only members of the Administrators group or the Server Operators group for the domain can monitor resources on all the computers in the domain.

Lesson 2: Monitoring Access to Shared Folders

You monitor access to shared folders to determine how many users currently have a connection to each folder. You can also monitor open files to determine which users are gaining access to the files, and you can disconnect users from one open file or from all open files.

After this lesson, you will be able to

- Determine the shared folders on a computer.
- Monitor shared folders.
- View and modify the properties of a shared folder.
- Monitor open files.
- Disconnect users from one or all open files.

Estimated lesson time: 15 minutes

Monitoring Shared Folders

You use the Shares folder in either the Computer Management snap-in or the Shared Folders snap-in to view a list of all shared folders on the computer and to determine how many users have a connection to each folder. In Figure 20.1, the Shares folder has been selected in the Computer Management console tree, and all the shared folders on that computer are shown in the details pane.

Figure 20.1   The Shares folder in the Computer Management window

Table 20.2 explains the information provided in the details pane shown in Figure 20.1.

Table 20.2   Information Available in the Shares Folder

Column name	Description
Shared Folder	The shared folders on the computer. This is the name that was given to the folder when it was shared.
Shared Path	The path to the shared folder.
Type	The operating system that must be running on a computer so that it can be used to gain access to the shared folder.
# Client Redirections	The number of clients who have made a remote connection to the shared folder.
Comment	Descriptive text about the folder. This comment was provided when the folder was shared.

Note Microsoft Windows 2000 doesn't update the list of shared folders, open files, and user sessions automatically. To update these lists, on the Action menu, click Refresh.

Determining How Many Users Can Access a Shared Folder Concurrently

You can use the Computer Management snap-in or Shared Folders snap-in to determine the maximum number of users that are permitted to gain access to a folder. In the Shared Folders details pane, click the shared folder for which you want to determine the maximum number of concurrent users that can access the folder. On the Action menu, click Properties, and the Properties dialog box for the shared folder appears. The General tab shows you the user limit. In Windows 2000 Professional, the maximum is 10. However, you can set this to a lower value.

You can also use the Computer Management snap-in or Shared Folders snap-in to determine whether the maximum number of users that are permitted to gain access to a folder has been reached. This is one quick and easy way to trouble-shoot connectivity problems. If a user can't connect to a share, determine the number of connections to the share and the maximum connections allowed. If the maximum number of connections have already been made, the user can't connect to the shared resource.

Modifying Shared Folder Properties

You can modify existing shared folders, including shared folder permissions, from the Shares folder. To change a shared folder's properties, click the shared folder, and then on the Action menu, click Properties. The General tab of the Properties dialog box shows you the share name, the path to the shared folder, and any comment that has been entered. The General tab also allows you to view and set a user limit for accessing the shared folder. The Security tab allows you to view and change the shared folders permissions.

Monitoring Open Files

Use the Open Files folder in either the Computer Management snap-in or Shared Folders snap-in to view a list of open files that are located in shared folders and the users who have a current connection to each file (see Figure 20.2). You can use this information when you need to contact users to notify them that you are shutting down the system. Additionally, you can determine which users have a current connection and should be contacted when another user is trying to gain access to a file that is in use.

Figure 20.2   The Open Files folder in the Computer Management window

Table 20.3 describes the information that is available in the Open Files folder.

Table 20.3   Information Available in the Open Files Folder

Column name	Description
Open File	The name of the open file on the computer.
Accessed By	The logon name of the user who has the file open.
Type	The operating system running on the computer where the user is logged on.
# Locks	The number of locks on the file. Programs can request the operating system to lock a file to gain exclusive access and prevent other programs from making changes to the file.
Open Mode	The type of access that the user's application requested when it opened the file, such as Read or Write.

Disconnecting Users from Open Files

You can disconnect users from one open file or from all open files. If you make changes to the Microsoft Windows 2000 File System (NTFS) permissions for a file that is currently opened by a user, the new permissions won't affect the user until he or she closes and then attempts to reopen the file.

You can force these changes to take place immediately by doing either of the following:

- Disconnecting all users from all open files. To disconnect all users from all open files, in the Shared Folders snap-in console tree, click Open Files, and then on the Action menu, click Disconnect All Open Files.

- Disconnecting all users from one open file. To disconnect users from one open file, in the Shared Folders snap-in console tree, click Open Files. In the details pane, select the open file, and then on the Action menu, click Close Open File.

Caution Disconnecting users from open files can result in data loss.

Practice: Managing Shared Folders

In this practice, you will use the Computer Management window to view the shared folders and open files on your computer. You will disconnect all users from all open files.

▶ **To view the shared folders on your computer**

1. Click the Start button, point to Programs, point to Administrative Tools, and then click Computer Management.

2. In the console tree of Computer Management, expand System Tools, and then expand Shared Folders.

3. In the console tree, click Shares under Shared Folders.

   Notice that the details pane shows a list of the existing Shared Folders on your computer.

▶ **To view the open files on your computer**

- In the console tree, click Open Files under Shared Folders.

   If you are working on a computer that isn't connected to a network, there won't be any open files because the open files show only connections from a remote computer to a share on your computer.

▶ **To disconnect all users from open files on your computer**

1. In the console tree, select Open Files under Shared Folders, and then click Disconnect All Open Files on the Action menu.

   If you aren't on a network, there won't be any open files to disconnect. If you are on a network, a Microsoft Management Console message box appears and prompts for whether you're sure you wish to close all resources.

2. Click OK.

3. Leave Computer Management open. You'll use it in the next practice.

Lesson Summary

In this lesson, you learned that you use the Shares folder in either the Computer Management snap-in or the Shared Folders snap-in to view a list of all shared folders on the computer and to determine how many users have a connection to each folder. The General tab of the Properties dialog box for a shared folder shows you the user limit, or maximum number of users that can concurrently connect to that share.

You also learned that you can modify existing shared folders, including shared folder permissions. To change a shared folder's properties, click the shared folder, and then on the Action menu, click Properties. The General tab of the Properties dialog box lets you view and change the user limit for accessing the shared folder. The Security tab allows you to view and change the shared folders permissions.

Lesson 3: Sharing a Folder Using the Shared Folders Snap-In

You can use either the Computer Management snap-in or the Shared Folders snap-in to share an existing folder or to create a new folder and share it on the local computer or on a remote computer. You can also modify the shared folder and NTFS permissions when you share the folder.

After this lesson, you will be able to

- Share a folder by using the Shared Folders snap-in.
- Stop sharing a folder by using the Shared Folders snap-in.

Estimated lesson time: 15 minutes

From either the Computer Management snap-in or the Shared Folders snap-in, you can run the Create Shared Folder wizard to create a new folder and share it. When you use the Shared Folders snap-in to share an existing folder or to create a new shared folder, Windows 2000 assigns the Full Control shared folder permission to the Everyone group by default. You can also assign NTFS permissions when you share the folder. Table 20.4 describes the basic share permissions you can assign to a newly created shared folder when you use the Create Shared Folder wizard.

Table 20.4 Basic Share Permissions

Option	Description
All Users Have Full Control	The Create Shared Folder wizard assigns the Full Control share permission to the Everyone group and the Full Control NTFS permission for the folder to the Everyone group. This is the default.
Administrators Have Full Control, Other Users Have Read-Only Access	The Create Shared Folder wizard assigns the Full Control Share permission to the Administrators group, and the Read share permission to the Everyone group. The wizard also assigns the Full Control NTFS permission for the folder to the Everyone group.
Administrators Have Full Control, Other Users Have No Access	The Create Shared Folder wizard assigns the Full Control share permission and the Full Control NTFS permission to the Administrators group for the folder.
Customize Share And Folder Permissions	Select this option to create your own custom permissions.

Note Using either the Computer Management snap-in or the Shared Folders snap-in is the only way to create a shared folder on a remote computer. Otherwise, you need to be physically located at the computer where the folder resides to share it.

Practice: Creating a Shared Folder

In this practice, you will use the Shared Folders snap-in to create a new shared folder on your computer.

▶ **To create a new shared folder on your computer**

1. In the console tree, under Shared Folders, click Shares.
2. On the Action menu, click New File Share.

   The Create Shared Folder wizard starts.
3. In the Create Shared Folder wizard, type **C:\Library** in the Folder To Share box.
4. Type **Library** in the Share Name box.
5. Click Next.

   A message box appears asking you whether you want to create C:\Library.
6. Click Yes.

   The Create Shared Folder wizard displays a final page of four basic share permission options. These options are described in Table 20.4 earlier. You can use one of the basic share permissions or you can create custom permissions.
7. Click Finish to accept the default permissions.

   A Create Shared Folders dialog box appears, telling you that the share has been successfully created and asking whether you want to create another shared folder.
8. Click No.

   You can also use the Shared Folders snap-in to stop sharing a shared folder.

▶ **To stop sharing a folder**

1. In the console tree, under Shared Folders, click Shares.
2. Select the Library folder in the details pane.
3. On the Action menu, click Stop Sharing.

   A message box appears asking whether you are sure you want to stop sharing the folder.
4. Click OK.

   The Library share disappears from the list of shared folders.
5. Close the Computer Management window.

Caution If you stop sharing a folder while a user has a file open, the user might lose data.

Sharing a Folder on a Remote Computer

If you want to share a folder on a remote computer, you run the MMC and add the Shared Folders snap-in to it. When you add the Shared Folders snap-in, point it to the remote computer on which you want to create and manage shared folders.

You can create a Shared Folder console to use on a remote computer, as follows:

1. On the Start menu, click Run, type **MMC** and then click OK.

   A custom console appears.

2. On the Console menu, click Add/Remove Snap-In.

   The Add/Remove Snap-In dialog box appears.

3. In the Add/Remove Snap-In dialog box, click Add.

4. In the Add Standalone Snap-In dialog box, click Shared Folders and then click Add.

   The Shared Folders dialog box appears. See Figure 20.3.

Figure 20.3   The Shared Folders dialog box, which allows you to specify a remote computer

5. In the Shared Folders dialog box, select Another Computer and then type in the name of the remote computer.

Note If you select the Allow The Selected Computer To Be Changed When Launching From The Command Line check box, you can choose which remote computer on which you want to create and manage shares. If you don't select this check box, the console is always directed to the same remote computer.

---

6. Click Finish.

7. Close the Add/Remove Snap-In and Add Standalone Snap-In dialog boxes.

Note If you want to create and manage shared folders on remote computers and you aren't in a domain, you must create the same user account with the same password on each computer. In workgroups, you don't have a central database that contains all user accounts; instead, each computer in the workgroup has its own local security database. For more information on local security databases, see Chapter 10, "Setting Up and Managing User Accounts."

Lesson Summary

In this lesson, you learned that you use the Computer Management snap-in or the Shared Folders snap-in to share an existing folder or to create a new folder and share it on the local computer or on a remote computer. You can set the shared folder and NTFS permissions when you share the folder. The Computer Management snap-in or the Shared Folders snap-in is the only tool available in Windows 2000 that allows you to create a shared folder on a remote computer.

You also learned that to create and manage shared folders on a remote computer, you create a custom console using the MMC and add the Computer Management snap-in or the Shared Folders snap-in. When creating a custom console for creating and managing shares on remote computers, you can specify one remote computer or you can allow the remote computer to be specified when the custom console is launched.

Lesson 4: Monitoring Network Users

You can also use the Computer Management snap-in or the Shared Folders snap-in to monitor which users are currently gaining access to shared folder resources on a server from a remote computer, and you can view the resources to which the users have connections. You can disconnect users and send administrative messages to computers and users, including computers and users who aren't currently gaining access to network resources.

After this lesson, you will be able to

- Disconnect a specific user from his or her network connection.
- Send administrative messages to users.

Estimated lesson time: 20 minutes

Monitoring User Sessions

You can use the Computer Management snap-in or the Shared Folders snap-in to view users who have a connection to open files on a server and the files to which they have a connection. This information enables you to determine which users you should contact when you need to stop sharing a folder or shut down the server on which the shared folder resides. You can disconnect one or more users to free idle connections to the shared folder, to prepare for a backup or restore operation, to shut down a server, and to change group membership and permissions for the shared folder.

You use the Sessions folder in the Computer Management snap-in or the Shared Folders snap-in to view a list of the users with a current network connection to the computer that you are monitoring (see Figure 20.4).

Figure 20.4 The Sessions folder in the Computer Management window

Table 20.5 describes the information that is available in the Sessions folder.

Table 20.5   Information Available in the Sessions Folder

Column name	Description
User	The users with a current network connection to this computer
Computer	The name of the user's computer
Type	The operating system running on the user's computer
Open Files	The number of files that the user has open on this computer
Connected Time	The time that has elapsed since the user established the current session
Idle Time	The time that has elapsed since the user last gained access to a resource on this computer
Guest	Whether this computer authenticated the user as a member of the built-in Guest account

Disconnecting Users

You can disconnect one or all users with a network connection to a computer. You disconnect users so that you can do any of the following:

- Have changes to shared folder and NTFS permissions take effect immediately. A user retains all permissions for a shared resource that Windows 2000 assigned when the user connected to it. Windows 2000 evaluates the permissions again the next time that a connection is made.

- Free idle connections on a computer so that other users can make a connection when you reach the maximum number of connections. User connections to resources might remain active for several minutes after a user finishes gaining access to a resource.

- Shut down a server.

Note After you disconnect a user, he or she can immediately make a new connection. If the user gains access to a shared folder from a Windows-based client computer, the client computer will automatically reestablish the connection with the shared folder. This connection will be established without user intervention unless you change the permissions to prevent the user from gaining access to the shared folder or you stop sharing the folder to prevent all users from gaining access to the shared folder.

You can disconnect a specific user, as follows:

1. In the console tree, under Shared Folders, click Sessions.

2. In the list of users in the details pane, select the user that you want to disconnect, and then click Close Session on the Action menu.

Note If you want to disconnect all users, click Sessions in the console tree, and then click Disconnect All Sessions on the Action menu.

To prevent data loss, always notify users who are accessing shared folders or files that you are ready to stop sharing a folder or shut down the computer.

Sending Administrative Messages to Users

You can send administrative messages to one or more users or computers. Send administrative messages to users who have a current connection to a computer on which network resources are shared when there will be a disruption to the computer or resource availability. Some common reasons for sending administrative messages are to notify users when you intend to do any of the following:

- Perform a backup or restore operation
- Disconnect users from a resource
- Upgrade software or hardware
- Shut down the computer

Use the Computer Management snap-in or the Shared Folders snap-in to send administrative messages to users. By default, all currently connected computers to which you can send a message appear in the list of recipients. You can add other users or computers to this list even if they don't have a current connection to resources on the computer.

Practice: Sending Console Messages

In this practice, you will use the Shared Folders snap-in to send a console message.

▶ **To send a console message**

1. Either start the Computer Management console, or use Microsoft Management Console to create a custom Shared Folders console.

2. In the console tree, under Shared Folders, click Shares.

3. On the Action menu, point to All Tasks, and then click Send Console Message.

4. In the Message box, type **Log Off Now. PRO1 is shutting down in 5 minutes.**

   If your computer isn't connected to a network, the Send button won't be available and the Recipients box will be empty.

5. Click Add.

   The Add Recipients dialog box appears.

6. Type **PRO1** in the Recipients box.

PRO1 should be the name of your computer. If you didn't name your computer PRO1, type the name of your computer in the Recipients box.

7. Click OK.

   Notice that the Send button is now available.

8. Click Send.

   A message box briefly appears showing that the message is being sent, and then the Messenger Service dialog box appears, as shown in Figure 20.5. It confirms that a message was sent from PRO1 to PRO1, indicating the date and time the message was sent, and displaying the message that was sent.

9. Click OK to close the message box.

10. Close all windows and log off.

Figure 20.5   The Messenger Service dialog box

Lesson Summary

In this lesson, you learned that you can use the Computer Management snap-in or the Shared Folders snap-in to view users who have a connection to open files on a computer and the files to which they have a connection. The Sessions folder allows you to view connections to open files on a server, and it allows you to disconnect a specific user or all users with a network connection to a computer.

You also learned that the Computer Management snap-in or the Shared Folders snap-in allows you to send administrative messages to one or more users or computers, and that by default, all currently connected computers appear in the list of recipients to which you can send a message. Finally, you learned how to add other users or computers to the list of recipients for administrative messages, even if they don't have a current connection to any resources on the computer.

Review

The following questions will help you determine whether you have learned enough to move on to the next chapter. If you have difficulty answering these questions, please go back and review the material in this chapter before beginning the next chapter. See Appendix A, "Questions and Answers," for the answers to these questions.

1. Why would you want to monitor access to network resources?

2. What can you monitor on a network with the Computer Management snap-in or the Shared Folders snap-in?

3. Why would you send an administrative message to users with current connections?

4. What can you do to prevent a user from reconnecting to a shared folder after you have disconnected the user from the shared folder?

5. How can you create and manage shares on a remote computer?

C H A P T E R   2 1

Configuring Remote Access

About This Chapter

Microsoft Windows 2000 incorporates several new protocols for use with remote access, in addition to new wizards and interfaces for configuring all types of network connections. The Network Connection wizard, for example, provides a simple interface for creating and configuring basic inbound and outbound connections. This chapter gives you an understanding of the new options and interfaces in Windows 2000 so that you can connect computers and configure protocols correctly to meet your organization's remote access requirements.

Before You Begin

To complete this chapter, you must have

- A computer that meets or exceeds the minimum hardware requirements located in "About This Book."
- Windows 2000 Professional installed on a computer meeting the specifications referred to in the preceding bullet. The computer should be installed in a workgroup, and TCP/IP should be the only installed protocol.
- A computer using a static IP address.
- A Windows 2000 Professional CD-ROM.

Lesson 1: Understanding the New Authentication Protocols in Windows 2000

Windows NT version 4 included support for several authentication protocols used to verify the credentials of users connecting to the network. These protocols included the following:

- Password Authentication Protocol (PAP)
- Challenge Handshake Authentication Protocol (CHAP)
- Microsoft Challenge Handshake Authentication Protocol (MS-CHAP)
- Shiva Password Authentication Protocol (SPAP)
- Point-to-Point Tunneling Protocol (PPTP), which provides tunneling capabilities

Windows 2000 includes support for these and several additional protocols that drastically increase your authentication, encryption, and multilinking options. The new protocols supported by Windows 2000 include Extensible Authentication Protocol (EAP), Remote Authentication Dial-in User Service (RADIUS), Internet Protocol Security (IPSec), Layer-Two Tunneling Protocol (L2TP), and Bandwidth Allocation Protocol (BAP).

After this lesson, you will be able to

- Describe the new protocols supported by Windows 2000.

Estimated lesson time: 15 minutes

The Extensible Authentication Protocol

The Extensible Authentication Protocol (EAP) is an extension to the Point-to-Point protocol (PPP) that works with dial-up, PPTP, and L2TP clients. EAP allows for an arbitrary authentication mechanism to validate a dial-in connection. The exact authentication method to be used is negotiated by the dial-in client and the remote access server. EAP supports authentication by using the following:

- **Generic token cards.** A physical card used to provide passwords. Token cards can handle several authentication methods, such as codes that change with each use.
- **MD5-CHAP.** The Message Digest 5 Challenge Handshake Authentication Protocol. This protocol encrypts user names and passwords with an MD5 algorithm.
- **Transport Level Security (TLS).** TLS is used for smart card support or other certificates. Smart cards require a card and reader. The smart card electronically stores the user's certificate and private key.

By using the EAP application programming interfaces, independent software vendors can supply new client and server authentication modules for technologies such as token cards, smart cards, biometric hardware such as retina scanners, or one-time password systems. EAP allows for the support of authentication technologies that are not yet developed. You can add EAP authentication methods on the Security tab of the remote access server's Properties dialog box.

Note For more information on EAP, see RFC 2284.

The Remote Authentication Dial-in User Service

The diversity of hardware and operating systems in today's enterprise networks requires remote user authentication to be vendor-independent and scaleable. Remote Authentication Dial-in User Service (RADIUS) support in Windows 2000 facilitates this kind of user authentication, while providing highly scaleable authentication designs for performance and fault-tolerant designs for reliability.

RADIUS provides authentication and accounting services for distributed dial-up networking. Windows 2000 can act as a RADIUS client, a RADIUS server, or both.

A RADIUS client, typically an ISP dial-up server, is a remote access server receiving authentication requests and forwarding requests to a RADIUS server. As a RADIUS client, Windows 2000 can also forward accounting information to a RADIUS accounting server. You configure RADIUS clients on the Securities tab in the remote access server's Properties dialog box.

A RADIUS server validates the RADIUS client request. Windows 2000 Internet Authentication Services (IAS) performs authentication. As a RADIUS server, IAS stores RADIUS accounting information from RADIUS clients in log files. IAS is one of the optional components that you can add during Windows 2000 installation or at a later time through Add/Remove Programs in Control Panel. You can find IAS in Administrative Tools on the Start menu.

Note For additional information on RADIUS, see RFC 2138/2139.

The Internet Protocol Security

Internet Protocol Security (IPSec) is a set of security protocols and cryptographic protection services for ensuring secure private communications over IP networks. IPSec provides aggressive protection against private network and Internet attacks while retaining ease of use. Clients negotiate a security association (SA) that acts as a private key to encrypt the data flow.

You can use IPSec policies, rather than applications or operations systems, to configure IPSec security services. The policies provide variable levels of protection for most traffic types in most existing networks. Your network security administrator can configure IPSec policies to meet the security requirements of a user, group, application, domain, site, or global enterprise.

Windows 2000 provides an administrative interface, IP Security Policy Management, to create and manage IPSec policies (centrally at the group policy level for domain members, or locally on a nondomain computer). IP Security Policy Management is a snap-in that you can add to any custom console created with the MMC. Configuring IPSec policies is beyond the scope of this course.

Note Security mechanisms for IP are defined in RFC 1825.

The Layer Two Tunneling Protocol

The Layer Two Tunneling Protocol (L2TP) is similar to PPTP in that its primary purpose is to create an encrypted tunnel through an untrusted network. L2TP differs from PPTP in that it provides tunneling but not encryption. L2TP provides a secure tunnel by cooperating with other encryption technologies such as IPSec. IPSec doesn't require L2TP, but its encryption functions complement L2TP to create a secure VPN solution.

Both PPTP and L2TP use PPP to provide an initial envelope for the data and then append additional headers for transport through the transit internetwork. Some of the key differences between PPTP and L2TP are as follows:

- PPTP requires an IP-based transit internetwork. L2TP requires only that the tunnel media provide packet-oriented, point-to-point connectivity. L2TP can use User Datagram Protocol (UDP), Frame Relay permanent virtual circuits (PVCs), X.25 VCs, or asynchronous transfer mode (ATM) VCs to operate over an IP network.

- L2TP supports header compression; PPTP does not. When header compression is enabled, L2TP operates with 4 bytes of overhead, as compared with 6 bytes for PPTP.

- L2TP supports tunnel authentication, while PPTP does not. However, when either PPTP or L2TP is used in conjunction with IPSec, IPSec provides tunnel authentication so that layer two tunnel authentication isn't necessary.

- PPTP uses PPP encryption. L2TP requires IPSec for encryption.

The Bandwidth Allocation Protocol

In Windows NT 4, Remote Access Service (RAS) supports basic Multilink capabilities. It allows the combining of multiple physical links into one logical link. Typically, two or more Integrated Services Digital Network (ISDN) lines or modem links are bundled together for greater bandwidth.

In Windows 2000, Bandwidth Allocation Protocol (BAP) and Bandwidth Allocation Control Protocol (BACP) enhance multilinked devices by dynamically adding or dropping links on demand. BAP is especially valuable to operations that have carrier charges based on bandwidth use. BAP and BACP are sometimes used interchangeably to refer to bandwidth-on-demand functionality. Both protocols are PPP control protocols and work together to provide bandwidth on demand. BAP provides an efficient mechanism for controlling connection costs while dynamically providing optimum bandwidth.

You can enable multilink and BAP protocols on a serverwide basis from the PPP tab of each remote access server's Properties dialog box. You configure BAP settings through remote access policies. Using these policies, you can specify that an extra line is dropped if link use drops below 75 percent for one group and below 25 percent for another group. Remote access policies are described later in this chapter.

Note For more information on PPP Multilink, see RFC 1990. For more information on BAP/BACP, see RFC 2125.

Lesson Summary

In this lesson, you learned that Windows NT version 4 included support for several authentication protocols used to verify the credentials of users connecting to the network. These protocols included the following: PAP, CHAP, MS-CHAP, SPAP, and PPTP, which provides tunneling capabilities.

You also learned that Windows 2000 includes support for these and several additional protocols that drastically increase your authentication, encryption, and multilinking options. These include EAP, an extension to PPP that works with dial-up, PPTP, and L2TP clients; RADIUS, which allows user authentication to be vendor-independent and provides highly scaleable authentication designs for performance and fault-tolerant designs for reliability; IPSec, a framework of open standards for ensuring secure private communications over IP networks by using cryptographic security services; L2TP, which is similar to PPTP in that its primary purpose is to create an encrypted tunnel through an untrusted network, but different from PPTP in that it provides tunneling but not encryption; and BAP and BACP, which enhance multilinked devices by dynamically adding or dropping links on demand.

Lesson 2: Configuring Inbound Connections

In Windows 2000 Professional, all of the processes for creating network connections are consolidated in the Network Connection wizard. Inbound connections are one of the types of network connections that you can create by using the Network Connection wizard.

After this lesson, you will be able to

- Configure inbound connections in Windows 2000.
- Configure remote access to allow incoming VPN connections.

Estimated lesson time: 20 minutes

Allowing Inbound Dial-up Connections

To configure and administer inbound connections on a computer running Windows 2000 Professional, you use the Network Connection wizard. To access the Network Connection wizard, click Start, point to Settings, click Network And Dial-Up Connections, and then double-click Make New Connection. The Welcome to the Network Connection wizard will appear. Click Next to continue, and the Network Connection Type page appears. Select Accept Incoming Connections (see Figure 21.1).

Figure 21.1   The Network Connection Type page

Configuring Devices for Incoming Connections

Once you have selected Accept Incoming Connections, click Next. The Devices For Incoming Connections page appears, so you can choose one of the available devices on your computer to accept incoming calls. If the device you select is configurable, click the Properties button to configure it. For example, if you have selected a modem, possible options to configure include port speed, compression, and the type of flow control. (See Figure 21.2.) The Advanced tab contains additional configurable options that might include the number of data bits, the parity, and the number of stop bits.

Figure 21.2   Configuring a device for inbound connections

Allowing Virtual Private Connections

When you are through configuring the device, click OK to close the Properties dialog box and then click Next on the Devices For Incoming Connection page. The Incoming Virtual Private Connection page appears. Select either to allow or not allow virtual private connections, and then click Next.

Specifying Users and Callback Options

You must specify the users who can access this inbound connection on the Allowed Users page shown in Figure 21.3.

Figure 21.3   Specifying the users who can access this inbound connection

After you select a user, click Properties and click the Callback tab to set the callback options. You can select Do Not Allow Callback, Allow The Caller To Set The Callback Number, or Always Use The Following Callback Number. Enabling callback causes the remote server, in this case your computer, to disconnect from the client calling in, and then to call the client computer back.

By using callback, you can have the bill for the phone call charged to your phone number rather than to the phone number of the user who called in. You can also use callback to increase security. If you specify the callback number, you don't have to worry about someone trying to break in. Even if an unauthorized user calls in, the system calls back at the number you specified, not the number of the unauthorized user.

Selecting Networking Components

After you specify the callback options, click Next, and the Networking Components page appears. You can choose the networking components you want to enable for incoming connections. You can also install additional networking components by clicking Install. For example, to install NWLink IPX/SPX/NetBIOS Compatible Transport Protocol, click Install, select Protocol, and then click Add. On the Select Network Protocol page, select NWLink IPX/SPX/NetBIOS Compatible Transport Protocol, insert the Windows 2000 Professional CD-ROM in the CD-ROM drive, and then click OK. Windows 2000 installs the protocol.

After the protocol is installed, you are returned to the Networking Components page. When you click Next, you will be prompted to type a name for the connection, and then you should click Finish. If you would like a shortcut to appear on your desktop, select the Add A Shortcut To My Desktop check box. Click Finish to create the connection.

Practice: Configuring an Inbound Connection

In this practice, you will configure an inbound connection.

▶ **To configure an inbound connection**

1. Log on as Administrator with a password of *password*.

2. On the Start menu, point to Settings, and click Network And Dial-Up Connections.

    The Network And Dial-Up Connections window appears.

3. Double-click Make New Connection.

    The Network Connection wizard appears.

4. Click Next.

    The Network Connection Type page appears.

5. Select Accept Incoming Connections, and then click Next.

    The Devices For Incoming Connections page appears.

6. Select the modem device option for your computer in the Connection Devices list, and then click Next.

    The Incoming Virtual Private Connection page appears.

7. Select Allow Virtual Private Connections, and then click Next.

    The Allowed Users page appears.

8. Select Administrator, and then click Properties.

    The Administrator Properties dialog box appears.

9. Click the Callback tab.

10. Review the Callback tab's options, leave the default Do Not Allow Callback option selected, and then click OK.

11. Click Next.

    The Networking Components page appears.

12. Review the available networking components, click Internet Protocol TCP/IP, and then click Properties.

The Incoming TCP/IP Properties dialog box appears.

13. Select Specify TCP/IP addresses.

14. In the From box, type **192.168.1.201** and in the To box, type **192.168.1.205** and then click OK.

Note If your computer is on a network and there is a valid address that you can use to test your inbound connection, use a range that includes that address.

---

15. Click Next.

16. Click Finish to accept the default Incoming Connections in The Connection Will Be Named box.

17. Close the Network And Dial-up Connections window.

Lesson Summary

In this lesson, you learned that you configure inbound connections in Windows 2000 Professional by using the Network Connection wizard. You can choose which of the available devices on your computer you will allow to accept incoming calls, and if these devices are configurable, you can click the Properties button to configure them. You must also specify which user accounts can use the inbound connections. For each user account, you can specify whether to allow callback, and if allowed, whether the caller should be able to specify the callback number or whether you want to set it.

Lesson 3: Configuring Outbound Connections

You can configure all outbound connections in Windows 2000 with the Network Connection wizard. Much of the work of configuring protocols and services is automated when you use this process. Understanding the options available in the wizard will help you to configure connections efficiently.

Three basic types of outbound connections exist:

- Dial-up connections
- Connections to a VPN
- Direct connections to another computer through a cable

After this lesson, you will be able to
- Configure outbound connections in Windows 2000.

Estimated lesson time: 25 minutes

Dial-up Connections

Dial-up connections include outbound dial-up connection to either a private network or to an ISP. To create and configure an outbound dial-up connection, use the Network Connection wizard. On the Network Connection Type page, select Dial-Up To Private Network to create a connection to a private network, or select Dial-Up To The Internet to create a connection to an ISP.

The Dial-Up To A Private Network Option

If you select the Dial-Up To Private Network option and click Next, you will be prompted to enter the phone number of the computer or network to which you want to connect; this can be an ISP for an Internet connection or the modems for your private network. Enter the phone number, click Next, and you will be prompted to specify who can use this connection. If you want this connection to be made available to all users of this computer, click For All Users, and then click Next. If you want to reserve the connection for yourself, click Only For Myself. When you click Next, you will be prompted to type a name for the connection. If you would like a shortcut to appear on your desktop, select the Add A Shortcut To My Desktop check box. Click Finish to create the connection.

The Dial-Up To The Internet Option

If you have selected the Dial-Up To The Internet option and then you click Next, the Welcome To The Internet Connection Wizard starts (see Figure 21.4). The wizard presents the following three options:

- **I Want To Sign Up For A New Internet Account.** If you select this option, the wizard will present a three-step procedure for choosing an ISP, specifying your address and billing information, and setting up your e-mail account.

- **I Want To Transfer My Existing Internet Account To This Computer.** If you already have an account with an ISP and have obtained all the necessary connection information, you can select this option to connect to your account using your phone line. If you select this option and click Next, you will be prompted to enter the telephone number you dial to connect to your ISP or the modem for your private network. To complete the wizard, you will be prompted for the user name and password that you use to log on to your ISP, and you will be prompted to type a name for the dial-up connection.

- **I Want To Set Up My Internet Account Manually, Or I Want To Connect Through A Local Area Network (LAN).** If you select this option, you have a choice of specifying that you connect to the Internet through a phone line and modem or through a LAN. You will be prompted for a proxy server and other settings.

Figure 21.4   The Welcome To The Internet Connection Wizard page

Note To configure Internet connection sharing, ensure that Enable Internet Connection Sharing For This Connection is selected on the Sharing tab of the connection's properties dialog box.

Connections to a Virtual Private Network

A VPN is a network that is created by using tunneling protocols such as PPTP or L2TP to create secure connections across an untrusted network. To create a new

VPN connection, you also use the Network Connection wizard. On the Network Connection Type page, click Connect To A Private Network Through The Internet, click Next, and then do one of the following:

- If you need to establish a connection with your ISP or some other network before connecting to the VPN, click Automatically Dial This Initial Connection, select a connection on the list, and then click Next.

- If you don't want to automatically establish an initial connection, click Do Not Dial The Initial Connection, and then click Next.

You will be prompted to type the host name or IP address of the computer or network to which you are connecting, and then click Next. If you want this connection to be made available to all users of this computer, click For All Users, and then click Next. If you want to reserve the connection for yourself, click Only For Myself. When you click Next, you will be prompted to type a name for the connection, and then click Finish. If you would like a shortcut to appear on your desktop, select the Add A Shortcut To My Desktop check box. Click Finish to create the connection.

Direct Connections to Another Computer Through a Cable

You can also use the Network Connection wizard to create a direct cable connection to another computer. On the Network Connection Type page, click Connect Directly To Another Computer, click Next, and then do one of the following:

- If your computer will be the host for the connection, click Host, and then click Next.

- If your computer will be the guest for the connection, click Guest, and then click Next.

After specifying Host or Guest, you select the port that is connected to the other computer and then click Next. You must specify the users who can access this connection and then click Next. You will be prompted to type a name for the connection. If you would like a shortcut to appear on your desktop, select the Add A Shortcut To My Desktop check box. Click Finish to create the connection.

Practice: Configuring an Outbound Connection

In this practice, you will configure an outbound connection.

▶ **To configure an outbound connection**

1. Log on as Administrator with a password of *password*.

2. On the Start menu, point to Settings, and click Network And Dial-Up Connections.

   The Network And Dial-Up Connections window appears.

3. Double-click Make New Connection.

   The Network Connection wizard appears.

4. Click Next.

5. On the Network Connection Type page, select Connect To A Private Network Through The Internet, and then click Next.

6. On the Destination Address page, type **192.168.1.202** and then click Next.

   Note If your computer is on a network and there is a valid address that you can use to test your outbound connection, use that address instead of 192.168.1.202.

   ---

7. On the Connection Availability page, select Only For Myself, and click Next.

8. Click Finish.

   The Connect Virtual Private Connection dialog box appears.

9. Ensure that the user name is set to Administrator, and type **password** for the password.

   Note If your computer is on a network and you entered a valid address in step 7, enter a valid user name and password in step 10.

   ---

10. Click Connect.

    Note If your computer is a stand-alone computer, this operation will fail. If your computer is on a network and you entered a valid address in step 7 and a valid user name and password in step 10, a message will be displayed stating that Virtual Private Connection is now connected.

    ---

11. If your connection failed, click Cancel. If you connected successfully to another computer, double-click the connection icon in the system tray, click Disconnect, and then click Yes.

    The Network And Dial-Up Connections window is again visible. Notice the Virtual Private Connection icon for the outbound connection you just created.

12. Close all windows and log off.

Lesson Summary

In this lesson, you learned that you can configure all outbound connections in Windows 2000 with the Network Connection wizard. Using the Network Connection wizard automates much of the work of configuring protocols and services. Understanding the options found in the wizard will help you to configure the three basic types of outbound connections efficiently. The three types of outbound connections are dial-up connections, connections to a VPN, and direct connections to another computer through a cable.

Review

The following questions will help you determine whether you have learned enough to move on to the next chapter. If you have difficulty answering these questions, please go back and review the material in this chapter before beginning the next chapter. See Appendix A, "Questions and Answers," for the answers to these questions.

1. What are the advantages of using L2TP over using PPTP?

2. While you're using the Network Connection wizard, you must configure two new settings regarding sharing the connection. Describe the difference between these two settings.

3. What is callback and when might you want to enable it?

C H A P T E R   2 2

The Windows 2000 Boot Process

About This Chapter

This chapter introduces you to the Microsoft Windows 2000 boot process. You will learn about the Intel-based boot process, using the Boot.ini file, and creating a Windows 2000 boot disk.

Before You Begin

To complete this chapter, you must have

- A computer that meets the minimum hardware requirements located in "About This Book."
- A blank, high-density floppy disk, which you will use to create a Windows 2000 boot disk.
- Windows 2000 Professional installed on the computer.

Lesson 1: The Boot Process

In this lesson, you will learn that the Windows 2000 boot process occurs in five stages: the preboot sequence, boot sequence, kernel load, kernel initialization, and logon. You will be able to troubleshoot more effectively by learning about the phases in the Windows 2000 boot process and the files used in each phase.

After this lesson, you will be able to

- Explain the boot process for Intel-based computers.

Estimated lesson time: 25 minutes

Files Used in the Boot Process

An Intel-based boot sequence requires certain files. Table 22.1 lists the files used in the Windows 2000 Intel-based boot process, the appropriate location of each file, and the stages of the boot process associated with each file. *Systemroot* represents the path to your Windows 2000 installation folder, which will be C:\Winnt if you've followed the installation instructions in Chapter 2, "Installing Windows 2000 Professional."

Note To view the files listed in Table 22.1, open Windows Explorer and click Folder Options on the Tools menu. On the View tab of the Folder Options dialog box, click Show Hidden Files And Folders, and clear (remove the check mark from) the Hide Protected Operating System Files (Recommended) check box. A Warning box appears indicating that it is not a good idea to display the protected operating system files. Click Yes to display them.

Table 22.1   Files Used in the Windows 2000 Boot Process

File	Location	Boot stage
Ntldr	System partition root (C:\ )	Preboot and boot
Boot.ini	System partition root	Boot
Bootsect.dos	System partition root	Boot (optional)
Ntdetect.com	System partition root	Boot
Ntbootdd.sys	System partition root	Boot (optional)
Ntoskrnl.exe	*systemroot*\System32	Kernel load
Hal.dll	*systemroot*\System32	Kernel load
System	*systemroot*\System32\Config	Kernel initialization
Device drivers (*.sys)	*systemroot*\System32\Drivers	Kernel initialization

---

Note The string *systemroot* (typed as %systemroot%) is a placeholder for the folder in the boot partition that contains the Windows 2000 system files.

Preboot Sequence

During startup, a Windows 2000–based computer initializes and then locates the boot portion of the hard disk.

The following four steps occur during the preboot sequence:

1. The computer runs power-on self test (POST) routines to determine the amount of physical memory, whether the hardware components are present, and so on. If the computer has a Plug and Play basic input/output system (BIOS), enumeration and configuration of hardware devices occurs at this stage.

2. The computer BIOS locates the boot device and loads and runs the master boot record (MBR).

3. The MBR scans the partition table to locate the active partition, loads the boot sector on the active partition into memory, and then executes it.

4. The computer loads and initializes the Ntldr file, which is the operating system loader.

Note Windows 2000 modifies the boot sector during installation so that Ntldr loads during system startup.

Boot Sequence

After the computer loads Ntldr into memory, the boot sequence gathers information about hardware and drivers in preparation for the Windows 2000 load phases. The boot sequence uses the following files: Ntldr, Boot.ini, Bootsect.dos (optional), Ntdetect.com, and Ntoskrnl.exe.

The boot sequence has four phases: initial boot loader, operating system selection, hardware detection, and configuration selection.

Initial Boot Loader

During the initial boot loader phase, Ntldr switches the microprocessor from real mode to 32-bit flat memory mode, which Ntldr requires to carry out any additional functions. Next, Ntldr starts the appropriate minifile system drivers. The minifile system drivers are built into Ntldr so that Ntldr can find and load Windows 2000 from partitions formatted with either FAT or Microsoft Windows 2000 File System (NTFS).

Operating System Selection

During the boot sequence, Ntldr reads the Boot.ini file. If more than one operating system selection is available in the Boot.ini file, then the Please Select The Operating System To Start screen appears, listing the operating systems specified in the Boot.ini file. If you don't select an entry before the timer reaches zero, Ntldr loads the operating system specified by the default parameter in the Boot.ini file. Windows 2000 Setup sets the default parameter to the most recent

Windows 2000 installation. If only one entry is in the Boot.ini file, the Please Select The Operating System To Load screen doesn't appear, and the default operating system is automatically loaded.

Note If the Boot.ini file isn't present, Ntldr attempts to load Windows 2000 from the Winnt folder on the first partition of the first disk, typically C:\Winnt.

Hardware Detection

On Intel-based computers, Ntdetect.com and Ntoskrnl.exe perform hardware detection. Ntdetect.com executes after you select Windows 2000 on the Please Select The Operating System To Start screen (or after the timer times out).

Note If you select an operating system other than Windows 2000, such as Microsoft Windows 98, Ntldr loads and executes Bootsect.dos. Bootsect.dos is a copy of the boot sector that was on the system partition at the time that Windows 2000 was installed. Passing execution to Bootsect.dos starts the boot process for the selected operating system.

Ntdetect.com collects a list of currently installed hardware components and returns this list to Ntldr for later inclusion in the registry under the HKEY_LOCAL_ MACHINE\HARDWARE key.

Ntdetect.com detects the following components:

- Bus/adapter type
- Communication ports
- Floating-point coprocessor
- Floppy disks
- Keyboard
- Mouse/pointing device
- Parallel ports
- SCSI adapters
- Video adapters

Configuration Selection

After Ntldr starts loading Windows 2000 and collects hardware information, the operating system loader process presents you with the Hardware Profile/Configuration Recovery Menu screen. The Hardware Profile/Configuration Recovery Menu screen contains a list of the hardware profiles that are set up on the computer. The first hardware profile is highlighted. You can press the Down arrow key to select another profile. You can also press L to invoke the Last Known Good Configuration option.

If there is only a single hardware profile, Ntldr doesn't display the Hardware Profile/Configuration Recovery Menu screen and loads Windows 2000 using the default hardware profile configuration.

Kernel Load

After configuration selection, the Windows 2000 kernel (Ntoskrnl.exe) loads and initializes. Ntoskrnl.exe also loads and initializes device drivers and loads services. If you press Enter when the Hardware Profile/Configuration Recovery Menu screen displays, or if Ntldr makes the selection automatically, the computer enters the kernel load phase. The screen clears and a series of white rectangles appears across the bottom of the screen.

During the kernel load phase, Ntldr does the following:

- Loads Ntoskrnl.exe but doesn't initialize it.
- Loads the hardware abstraction layer file (Hal.dll).
- Loads the HKEY_LOCAL_MACHINE\SYSTEM registry key from *systemroot*\System32\Config\System.
- Selects the control set it will use to initialize the computer. A *control set* contains configuration data used to control the system, such as a list of the device drivers and services to load and start.
- Loads device drivers with a value of 0x0 for the Start entry. These are typically low-level hardware device drivers, such as those for a hard disk. The value for the List entry, specified in the HKEY_LOCAL_MACHINE\SYSTEM\ CurrentControlSet\Control\ServiceGroupOrder subkey of the registry, defines the order in which Ntldr loads these device drivers.

Kernel Initialization

When the kernel load phase is complete, the kernel initializes, and then Ntldr passes control to the kernel. At this point, the system displays a graphical screen with a status bar indicating load status. Four tasks are accomplished during the kernel initialization stage:

1. **The Hardware key is created.** Upon successful initialization, the kernel uses the data collected during hardware detection to create the registry key HKEY_LOCAL_MACHINE\HARDWARE. This key contains information about hardware components on the system board and the interrupts used by specific hardware devices.

2. **The Clone control set is created.** The kernel creates the Clone control set by copying the control set referenced by the value of the Current entry in the HKEY_LOCAL_MACHINE\SYSTEM\Select subkey of the registry. The

Clone control set is never modified, as it is intended to be an identical copy of the data used to configure the computer and should not reflect changes made during the startup process.

3. **Device drivers are loaded and initialized.** After creating the Clone control set, the kernel initializes the low-level device drivers that were loaded during the kernel load phase. The kernel then scans the HKEY_LOCAL_MACHINE\ SYSTEM\CurrentControlSet\Services subkey of the registry for device drivers with a value of 0x1 for the Start entry. As in the kernel load phase, a device driver's value for the Group entry specifies the order in which it loads. Device drivers initialize as soon as they load.

   If an error occurs while loading and initializing a device driver, the boot process proceeds based on the value specified in the ErrorControl entry for the driver.

   Table 22.2 describes the possible ErrorControl values and the resulting boot sequence actions.

   ErrorControl values appear in the registry under the subkey HKEY_LOCAL_ MACHINE\SYSTEM\CurrentControlSet\Services*name_of_service_or_driver*\ ErrorControl.

4. **Services are started.** After the kernel loads and initializes device drivers, Session Manager (Smss.exe) starts the higher-order subsystems and services for Windows 2000. Session Manager executes the instructions in the BootExecute data item, and in the Memory Management, DOS Devices, and SubSystems keys.

   Table 22.3 describes the function of each instruction set and the resulting Session Manager action.

Table 22.2   ErrorControl Values and Resulting Action

ErrorControl value	Action
0x0 (Ignore)	The boot sequence ignores the error and proceeds without displaying an error message.
0x1 (Normal)	The boot sequence displays an error message but ignores the error and proceeds.
0x2 (Severe)	The boot sequence fails and then restarts using the LastKnownGood control set. If the boot sequence is currently using the LastKnownGood control set, the boot sequence ignores the error and proceeds.
0x3 (Critical)	The boot sequence fails and then restarts using the LastKnownGood control set. However, if the Last-KnownGood control set is causing the critical error, the boot sequence stops and displays an error message.

Table 22.3 Instruction Sets Read and Executed by Session Manager

Data item or key	Action
BootExecute data item	Session Manager executes the commands specified in this data item before it loads any services.
Memory Management key	Session Manager creates the paging file information required by Virtual Memory Manager.
DOS Devices key	Session Manager creates symbolic links that direct certain classes of commands to the correct component in the file system.
SubSystems key	Session Manager starts the Win32 subsystem, which controls all I/O and access to the video screen and starts the WinLogon process.

Logon

The logon process begins at the conclusion of the kernel initialization phase. The Win32 subsystem automatically starts Winlogon.exe, which starts Local Security Authority (Lsass.exe) and displays the Logon dialog box. You can log on at this time, even though Windows 2000 might still be initializing network device drivers.

Next, the Service Controller executes and makes a final scan of the HKEY_ LOCAL_MACHINE\SYSTEM\CurrentControlSet\Services subkey, looking for services with a value of 0x2 for the Start entry. Services with a value of 0x2 for the Start entry are marked to load automatically. These include the Workstation service and the Server service.

The services that load during this phase do so based on their values for the DependOnGroup or DependOnService entries in the registry subkey HKEY_LOCAL_MACHINE\SYSTEM\CurrentControlSet\Services.

Windows 2000 startup is not considered good until a user successfully logs on to the system. After a successful logon, the system copies the Clone control set to the LastKnownGood control set.

Lesson Summary

In this lesson, you learned that the Windows 2000 Intel-based boot process occurs in five stages: preboot sequence, boot sequence, kernel load, kernel initialization, and logon. You also learned about the files that are used in the boot process, where these files are stored, and which stage of the boot process uses them.

Lesson 2: Control Sets in the Registry

This lesson discusses the Windows 2000 control sets. A *control set* contains configuration data used to control the system, such as a list of which device drivers and services to load and start.

After this lesson, you will be able to

- Explain Windows 2000 control sets.

Estimated lesson time: 15 minutes

Windows 2000 Control Sets

A typical Windows 2000 installation contains the following control set subkeys: Clone, ControlSet001, ControlSet002, and CurrentControlSet. Control sets are stored as subkeys of the registry key HKEY_LOCAL_MACHINE\SYSTEM. The registry might contain several control sets depending on how often you change or have problems with system settings.

The CurrentControlSet subkey is a pointer to one of the ControlSet00x keys. The Clone control set is a clone of the control set used to initialize the computer (either Default or LastKnownGood), and is created by the kernel initialization process each time that you start your computer. The Clone control set isn't available after you log on.

To better understand control sets, you should know about the registry subkey HKEY_LOCAL_MACHINE\ SYSTEM\Select. The entries contained in this subkey include Current, Default, Failed, and LastKnownGood.

- **Current.** Identifies which control set is the CurrentControlSet. When you use Control Panel options or Registry Editor to change the registry, you modify information in the CurrentControlSet.

- **Default.** Identifies the control set to use the next time that Windows 2000 starts, unless you select the LastKnownGood control set. Default and Current typically contain the same control set number.

- **Failed.** Identifies the control set that was designated as failed the last time that the computer was started using the LastKnownGood control set.

- **LastKnownGood.** Identifies a copy of the control set that was used the last time that the computer started Windows 2000 successfully. After a successful logon, the Clone control set is copied to the LastKnownGood control set.

Each of these entries in HKEY_LOCAL_MACHINE\SYSTEM\Select takes a REG_DWORD data type, and the value for each entry refers to a specific control set. For example, if the value for the Current entry is set to 0x1, the CurrentControlSet points to ControlSet001. Similarly, if the value for the LastKnownGood entry is set to 0x2, the LastKnownGood control set points to ControlSet002.

The Last Known Good Process

If you change the Windows 2000 configuration to load a driver and have problems rebooting, you can use the last known good process to recover your working configuration. The last known good process uses the LastKnownGood control set, stored in the registry, to boot Windows 2000.

Windows 2000 provides two configurations for starting a computer, Default and LastKnownGood. The upper portion of Figure 22.1 shows the events that occur when you make configuration changes to your system. Any configuration changes (for example, adding or removing drivers) are saved in the Current control set.

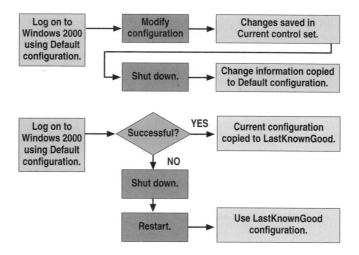

Figure 22.1   Using the Default and LastKnownGood configurations

After you reboot the computer, the kernel copies the information in the Current control set to the Clone control set during the kernel initialization phase. When you successfully log on to Windows 2000, the information in the Clone control set is copied to the LastKnownGood control set, as shown in the lower part of Figure 22.1.

If you experience startup problems that you think might relate to Windows 2000 configuration changes, shut down the computer *without* logging on, and then restart it. When you are prompted to select the operating system to start from a list of the operating systems specified in the Boot.ini file, press F8 to open the Windows 2000 Advanced Options Menu screen. Then select the Last Known Good Configuration option, or after you select Windows 2000 on the Please Select The Operating System To Start screen, you can press Spacebar to open the Hardware Profile/Configuration Recovery Menu screen, and then press L to select Last Known Good Configuration.

The next time you log on, the Current configuration is copied to the Default configuration. If your configuration changes work correctly, the next time you log on, the Current configuration is copied to the Default configuration. If your configuration changes don't work, you can restart and use the Last Known Good Configuration option to log on.

Table 22.4 summarizes the purposes of the Default and LastKnownGood configuration control sets.

Table 22.4   Default and LastKnownGood Configurations

Configuration	Description
Default	Contains information that the system saves when a computer shuts down. To start a computer using the default configuration, select Windows 2000 on the Please Select The Operating System To Start menu that the Boot.ini file presents.
LastKnownGood	Contains information that the system saves after a successful logon. The LastKnownGood control set loads only if the system is recovering from a severe or critical device driver loading error or if it is selected during the boot process.

Table 22.5 lists situations in which you can use the Last Known Good Configuration option and its related solutions.

Table 22.5   Situations for Using the Last Known Good Configuration Option

Situation	Solution
After a new device driver is installed, Windows 2000 restarts, but the system stops responding.	Use the Last Known Good Configuration option to start Windows 2000 because the LastKnownGood control set doesn't contain any reference to the new, and possibly faulty, driver.
You accidentally disable a critical device driver (such as the ScsiPort driver).	Some critical drivers are written to keep users from making the mistake of disabling them. With these drivers, the system automatically reverts to the LastKnownGood control set if a user disables the driver. If the driver doesn't automatically cause the system to revert to the LastKnownGood control set, you must manually select the Last Known Good Configuration option.

Using the LastKnownGood control set does *not* help in the following situations:

- When the problem isn't related to Windows 2000 configuration changes. Such a problem might arise from incorrectly configured user profiles or incorrect file permissions.

- After you log on. The system updates the LastKnownGood control set with Windows 2000 configuration changes after a successful logon.

- When startup failures relate to hardware failures or missing or corrupted files.

Important Starting Windows 2000 using the LastKnownGood control set overwrites any changes made since the last successful boot of Windows 2000.

Lesson Summary

In this lesson, you learned that a control set contains configuration data used to control the system, such as a list of which device drivers and services to load and which to start. Control sets are stored as subkeys of the registry key HKEY_LOCAL_MACHINE\SYSTEM, and a typical Windows 2000 installation contains the following control sets: Clone, ControlSet001, ControlSet002, and CurrentControlSet. The registry might contain several other control sets, depending on how often you have changed or had problems with system settings.

You also learned that if you make incorrect changes to a computer's configuration, you might have problems restarting your computer. If you can't restart your computer because of a configuration change, Windows 2000 provides the last known good process so that you don't have to reinstall your Windows 2000 software to restart your computer. You can boot your computer using the LastKnownGood control set. The LastKnownGood control set contains the configuration settings from the last successful restart and logon to your computer. After restarting your computer using the LastKnownGood control set, you can reconfigure the computer. The last known good process uses the LastKnownGood control set, stored in the registry, to restart Windows 2000.

Lesson 3: Advanced Boot Options

In this lesson, you will learn about the Windows 2000 advanced boot options. These options include Safe Mode, Enable Boot Logging, Enable VGA Mode, Last Known Good Configuration, Directory Services Restore Mode, and Debugging Mode.

After this lesson, you will be able to

- Explain advanced boot options.

Estimated lesson time: 5 minutes

Safe Mode

If your computer won't start, you might be able to start it by using the Safe Mode advanced boot option. Pressing F8 during the operating system selection phase displays a screen with advanced options for booting Windows 2000. If you select Safe Mode, Windows 2000 loads and uses only basic files and drivers, including the mouse, VGA monitor, keyboard, mass storage, default system services, and no network connections. If you choose to start your computer in safe mode, the background will be black, and Safe Mode will appear in all four corners of the screen (see Figure 22.2). If your computer doesn't start using safe mode, you can try Windows 2000 Automatic System Recovery.

Figure 22.2   Running Windows 2000 in Safe Mode

Safe mode has a couple of variations. You can select Safe Mode With Networking, which is identical to Safe Mode except that it adds the drivers and services necessary to enable networking to function when you restart your computer. A second variation of Safe Mode is Safe Mode With Command Prompt, which is the same as Safe Mode except when the computer restarts, it displays a command prompt.

Other Advanced Boot Options

The other advanced boot options provide additional troubleshooting avenues that you can use to circumvent a normal boot and allow you to attempt to determine the cause of a booting problem. These options are summarized as follows:

- **Enable Boot Logging.** This advanced boot option logs the loading and initialization of drivers and services for troubleshooting boot problems. All drivers and services that are loaded and initialized or that are not loaded in a file are logged. The log file, ntbtlog.txt, is located in the *windir* folder. All three versions of Safe Mode automatically create this boot log file.

- **Enable VGA Mode.** This advanced boot option starts Windows 2000 with a basic VGA driver.

- **Last Known Good Configuration.** This advanced boot option starts Windows 2000 using the registry information that Windows 2000 saved at the last logon.

- **Directory Services Restore Mode.** This advanced boot option allows the restoration of directory services based on Active Directory technology on domain controllers. This option applies only to Windows 2000 Server and not to Windows 2000 Professional.

- **Debugging Mode.** Selecting this option turns on debugging, an advanced feature that administrators can use to attempt to track down problems in programming code. This advanced boot option applies only to Windows 2000 Server and not to Windows 2000 Professional.

- **Boot Normally.** This option, although it is listed with the other advanced boot options, allows you to abort the screen of advanced boot options and proceed with a normal boot.

Note When using the advanced boot options in Windows 2000, logging is enabled with every option except Last Known Good Configuration. The system writes the log file (Ntbtlog.txt) to the *systemroot* folder. In addition, each option except Last Known Good Configuration loads the default VGA driver.

Using an advanced boot option to boot the system sets the environment variable *SAFEBOOT_OPTION* to indicate the mode used to boot the system.

Lesson Summary

In this lesson, you learned that the advanced boot options available in Windows 2000 include Safe Mode, Safe Mode With Networking, and Safe Mode With Command Prompt; Enable Boot Logging; Enable VGA Mode; Last Known Good Configuration; Directory Services Restore Mode; and Debugging Mode. These options allow you to attempt to restart your computer when a problem occurs with a normal boot. The Directory Services Restore Mode and Debugging Mode options aren't available for Windows 2000 Professional. The Boot Normally advanced boot option allows you to bypass these options and proceed with a normal boot.

Lesson 4: The Boot.ini File

In this lesson, you will learn about the Boot.ini file. When you install Windows 2000 on an Intel-based computer, Windows 2000 Setup saves the Boot.ini file in the active partition. Ntldr uses information in the Boot.ini file to display the Please Select The Operating System To Start menu, from which you select the operating system to start. In this lesson, you will learn how to modify the Boot.ini file, including modifying ARC paths and using the optional Boot.ini switches.

After this lesson, you will be able to

- Explain the purpose and function of the Boot.ini file.

Estimated lesson time: 15 minutes

Components of the Boot.ini File

The Boot.ini file includes two sections, [boot loader] and [operating systems], which contain information that Ntldr uses to create the Please Select The Operating System To Start menu. A typical Boot.ini file might contain the following lines:

```
[boot loader]

timeout=30

default=multi(0)disk(0)rdisk(1)partition(2)\ WINNT


[operating systems]

multi(0)disk(0)rdisk(1)partition(2)\ WINNT="Microsoft Windows 2000
Professional" /fastdetect

multi(0)disk(0)rdisk(1)partition(1)\ WINNT="Windows NT Workstation
Version 4.00""

multi(0)disk(0)rdisk(1)partition(1)\ WINNT="Windows NT Server
Workstation 4.00 [VGA mode]" /basevideo /sos

C:\ ="Previous Operating System on C:""
```

The [operating systems] section of a Boot.ini file that is created during a default installation of Windows 2000 Professional contains a single entry for Windows 2000. If your computer is a Windows 2000 and Windows 95- or 98-based dual-boot system, the [operating systems] section also contains an entry for starting the system using the other operating system, for example, `C:\ ="Previous Operating System on C"`. If you installed Windows 2000 on a computer and kept an installation of NT 4 on another partition of the same computer, the [operating systems] section also contains an entry for starting the system using this version of Windows NT, for example, `C:\ ="Windows NT Workstation Version 4.00"`.

ARC Paths

During installation, Windows 2000 generates the Boot.ini file, which contains Advanced RISC Computing (ARC) paths pointing to the computer's boot partition. (*RISC* stands for reduced instruction set computing, a microprocessor design that uses a small set of simple instructions for fast execution.) The following is an example of an ARC path:

```
multi(0)disk(0)rdisk(1)partition(2)
```

Table 22.6 describes the naming conventions for ARC paths.

Table 22.6   ARC Path Naming Conventions

Convention	Description
Multi(x) | scsi(x)	The adapter/disk controller. Use scsi to indicate a SCSI controller on which SCSI BIOS is *not* enabled. For all other adapter/disk controllers, use multi, including SCSI disk controllers *with* the BIOS enabled. The x represents a number that indicates the load order of the hardware adapter. For example, if you have two SCSI adapters in a computer, the first to load and initialize receives number 0, and the next SCSI adapter receives number 1.
Disk(y)	The SCSI ID. For multi, this value (y) is always 0.
Rdisk(z)	A number (z) that identifies the disk (ignored for SCSI controllers).
Partition(a)	A number (a) that identifies the partition.

In both multi and scsi conventions, multi, scsi, disk, and rdisk numbers are assigned starting with (0). Partition numbers start with (1). All nonextended partitions are assigned numbers first, followed by logical drives in extended partitions.

See Figure 22.3 for some examples of how to determine the ARC pathname.

The scsi ARC naming convention varies the disk(y) parameter for successive disks on one controller, while the multi format varies the rdisk(z) parameter.

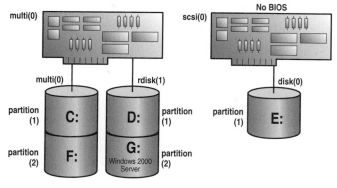

Figure 22.3   ARC paths

Boot.ini Switches

You can add a variety of switches to the entries in the [operating systems] section of the Boot.ini file to provide additional functionality. Table 22.7 describes some of the optional switches that you can use for entries in the Boot.ini file.

Table 22.7   Boot.ini Optional Switches

Switch	Description
/basevideo	Boots the computer using the standard VGA video driver. If a new video driver isn't working correctly, use this switch to start Windows 2000, and then change to a different driver.
/fastdetect=[com$x$ | com$x,y,z.$]	Disables serial mouse detection. Without a port specification, this switch disables peripheral detection on all COM ports. This switch is included in every entry in the Boot.ini file by default.
/maxmem:n	Specifies the amount of RAM that Windows 2000 uses. Use this switch if you suspect that a memory chip is bad.
/noguiboot	Boots the computer without displaying the graphical boot status screen.
/sos	Displays the device driver names as they are loading. Use this switch when startup fails while loading drivers to determine which driver is triggering the failure.

Modifications to Boot.ini

You can modify the timeout and default parameter values in the Boot.ini file by using System Properties in Control Panel. In addition, you can manually edit these and other parameter values in the Boot.ini file. For example, you might modify the Boot.ini file to add more descriptive entries for the Please Select The Operating System To Start menu or to include various switches to aid in trouble-shooting the boot process.

During Windows 2000 installation, Windows 2000 Setup sets the read-only and system attributes for the Boot.ini file. Before editing the Boot.ini file with a text editor, you must make the file visible and turn off the read-only attribute. You can change file attributes by using My Computer, Windows Explorer, or the command prompt. You use My Computer or Windows Explorer to change file attributes, as follows:

1. Double-click the icon for the drive containing the Boot.ini file.
2. On the Tools menu, click Folder Options.
3. In the Folder Options dialog box, click the View tab.
4. Under Hidden Files And Folders, click Show Hidden Files And Folders, and then click OK.
5. In the My Computer or Windows Explorer window, on the View menu, click Refresh.
6. Right-click Boot.ini, and then click Properties.
7. On the General tab, under Attributes, clear the Read-Only check box, and then click OK.

To change file attributes by using the command prompt, change to the folder containing the Boot.ini file, if necessary, and then type

```
attrib -s -r -h boot.ini
```

Once you have changed the attributes of the Boot.ini file, you can open and modify the file using a text editor.

Lesson Summary

In this lesson, you learned that when you install Windows 2000 on an Intel-based computer, Windows 2000 Setup saves the Boot.ini file in the active partition. Ntldr uses information in the Boot.ini file to display the Please Select The Operating System To Start menu, from which you select the operating system to start. You can edit the Boot.ini file, including modifying ARC paths and using the optional Boot.ini switches.

Lesson 5: Using the Recovery Console

The Windows 2000 Recovery Console is a command-line interface that you can use to perform a variety of troubleshooting and recovery tasks, including

- Starting and stopping services.
- Reading and writing data on a local drive (including drives that are formatted with the NTFS file system).
- Formatting hard disks.

After this lesson, you will be able to

- Install and use the Recovery Console.

Estimated lesson time: 20 minutes

Installing and Starting the Recovery Console

To install the Recovery Console, insert the Microsoft Windows 2000 Professional CD into your CD-ROM drive, and close the Microsoft Windows 2000 CD dialog box, if it opens. Open the Run dialog box or a Command Prompt window in Windows 2000, change to the i386 folder on the Windows 2000 CD-ROM, and then run the winnt32 command with the /cmdcons switch. After you install the Recovery Console, you can access it from the Please Select Operating System To Start menu. You can also use the Windows 2000 Setup disks or the Windows 2000 Professional CD to start your computer and then select the Recovery Console option, when you are prompted to choose repair options, to access the Recovery Console.

After you start the Recovery Console, you must specify which installation of Windows 2000 you want to log on to (if you have a dual boot or multiple boot configuration), and then you must log on as the Administrator user.

Using the Windows 2000 Recovery Console

You can also run the Recovery Console from the Windows 2000 CD-ROM. The Recovery Console provides you with a limited set of administrative commands that you can use to repair your Windows 2000 installation. You can use the following steps to start the Recovery Console from a Windows 2000 Professional CD-ROM.

1. Insert the Windows 2000 Professional CD-ROM into the CD-ROM drive and restart the computer. If your computer or the workstation you want to repair does not have a bootable CD-ROM drive, you will need to insert your Windows 2000 Setup Boot disk into your floppy disk drive, and then insert the additional Windows 2000 Setup disks when you are prompted to do so.

2. When Setup displays the Setup Notification message, read it, and then press Enter to continue.

   Setup displays the Welcome To Setup screen. Notice that, in addition to the initial installation of Windows 2000, you can use Windows 2000 Setup to repair or recover a damaged Windows 2000 installation.

3. Press R to repair a Windows 2000 installation.

   The Windows 2000 Repair Options screen appears. Notice that you can repair a Windows 2000 installation using the Recovery Console or the Emergency Repair Process.

4. Press C to start the Recovery Console.

   If you have more than one installation of Windows 2000 on the computer, you will be prompted to select which installation you want to repair.

5. Type **1** and then press Enter.

   You are prompted to enter the Administrator's password.

6. Type the Administrator password and then press Enter.

   A command prompt appears.

7. Type **Help** and press Enter for a list of the commands available.

8. When you have completed the repair process, type **exit** and press Enter.

   The computer will restart.

Understanding the Recovery Console Commands

There are a number of commands available in the Recovery Console. Table 22.8 describes some of these commands.

Table 22.8   Recovery Console commands

Command	Description
Chdir (cd)	Displays the name of the current folder or changes the current folder
Chkdsk	Checks a disk and displays a status report
Cls	Clears the screen
Copy	Copies a single file to another location
Delete (del)	Deletes one or more files
Dir	Displays a list of files and subfolders in a folder
Disable	Disables a system service or a device driver
Enable	Starts or enables a system service or a device driver
Exit	Exits the Recovery Console and restarts your computer
Fdisk	Manages partitions on your hard disks
Fixboot	Writes a new partition boot sector onto the system partition

Command	Description
Fixmbr	Repairs the master boot record of the partition boot sector
Format	Formats a disk
Help	Lists the commands that you can use in the Recovery Console
Logon	Logs on to a Windows 2000 installation
Map	Displays the drive letter mappings
Mkdir (md)	Creates a folder
More	Displays a text file
Rmdir (rd)	Deletes a folder
Rename (ren)	Renames a single file
Systemroot	Sets the current folder to the systemroot folder of the system that you are currently logged on to
Type	Displays a text file

Practice: Using the Windows 2000 Recovery Console

In this practice you will use the Windows 2000 Recovery Console to troubleshoot a Windows 2000 installation that will not boot. You will also install and start the Recovery Console, and you will look at Help to determine the commands available in the Recovery Console. You will also use the Listsvc command to view the services and then use the Disable command to disable the Alerter service.

Exercise 1: Troubleshooting a Windows 2000 Installation

In this exercise you troubleshoot a Windows 2000 installation and repair it by using the Recovery Console.

▶ **To create a system boot failure**

1. Rename the file Ntldr to Oldntldr.
2. Restart the computer.

   What error do you receive when attempting to restart the computer?

▶ **To use the Recovery Console to repair the installation**

1. Insert the Windows 2000 installation CD into the CD-ROM drive and restart the computer.

Note If your computer is not equipped with a CD-ROM drive that is capable of booting from a CD-ROM, then also insert your Windows 2000 Setup Boot disk into your floppy disk drive for step 3. Insert the other three Windows 2000 Setup disks when you are prompted to do so. (To create the Setup disks, see Appendix B, "Creating Setup Boot Disks.")

---

2. When Setup displays the Setup Notification message, read it, and then press Enter to continue.

   Setup displays the Welcome To Setup screen.

3. Press R to repair a Windows 2000 installation.

   The Windows 2000 Repair Options screen appears.

4. Press C to start the Recovery Console.

5. Type **1** and then press Enter.

   You are prompted to enter the Administrator's password.

6. Type **password** and then press Enter.

   A C:\Winnt command prompt appears.

7. Type **cd ..** and press Enter to change to the root folder (C:\). Be sure to include a space between the "cd" and the ".." characters in the command.

8. Type **copy oldntldr ntldr** and press Enter.

9. If there is a disk in your floppy drive, remove it. If your computer is capable of booting from the CD-ROM drive, remove the Windows 2000 Professional CD from your CD-ROM drive.

10. Type **exit** and press Enter.

    The computer reboots and should start normally.

Exercise 2: Installing the Windows 2000 Recovery Console

In this exercise, you will install the Recovery Console.

▶ **To install the Recovery Console**

1. Log on as Administrator.

2. Insert the Windows 2000 Professional CD into the CD-ROM drive.

3. When the Microsoft Windows 2000 CD window appears, close it.

4. In the Run dialog box, type ***<cd_drive>*:\i386\winnt32 /cmdcons** (where *<cd_drive>* represents the letter assigned to your CD-ROM drive), and then click OK.

   The Windows 2000 Setup message box appears.

5. Click Yes to install the Windows 2000 Recovery Console.

   Windows 2000 Setup installs the Windows 2000 Recovery Console to your hard disk.

6. Click OK to close the Microsoft Windows 2000 Professional Setup dialog box.

Exercise 3: Using the Windows 2000 Recovery Console

In this exercise you will use the Help command to view the available commands. You will then use the available Listsvc and Disable commands.

1. Restart your computer.

2. Select Microsoft Windows 2000 Recovery Console from the boot loader menu.

The Windows 2000 Recovery Console starts up and prompts you to select which Windows 2000 installation you would like to log on to. If you had more than one Windows 2000 installation on this computer, they would be listed here.

1. Type **1** and then press Enter.

2. Type **password** when prompted for the Administrator password, and then press Enter.

3. Type **help** and then press Enter to see the list of available commands.

    Notice the Listsvc command. You can use this command to view all available services.

4. Scroll through the list of commands, type **listsvc** and press Enter, and then scroll through the list of available services.

5. Press Esc to stop.

6. Type **disable /?** and then press Enter.

    The Disable command allows you to disable a Windows system service or driver.

7. Type **disable alerter** and then press Enter.

    Recovery Console displays several lines of text describing how the registry entry for the Alerter service has been modified. The Alerter service is now disabled.

8. Type **exit** and then press Enter to restart your computer.

Exercise 4: Restarting the Alerter service

In this exercise you will confirm that the Alerter service is disabled and then restart it.

1. Log on as Administrator.

2. Open the Computer Management window, expand Services And Applications, and then click Services.

    Notice that the Startup Type value for the Alerter service is Disabled.

3. Double-click Alerter, change the Startup Type option to Automatic, and then click OK.

4. Right-click Alerter, and then click Start.

5. Close the Computer Management window.

Lesson Summary

The Windows 2000 Recovery Console is a command-line interface that you can use to perform a variety of troubleshooting and recovery tasks, including starting and stopping services, reading and writing data on a local drive, and formatting hard disks.

You install the Recovery Console by starting a command prompt, changing to the i386 folder on the Windows 2000 CD-ROM, and running the winnt32 command with the /cmdcons switch. After you install the Recovery Console, you can access it from the Startup menu or by using the Windows 2000 Setup disks or the Windows 2000 CD to start your computer, and then selecting the Recovery Console option when you are prompted to choose repair options.

Review

The following questions will help you determine whether you have learned enough to move on to the next chapter. If you have difficulty answering these questions, please go back and review the material in this chapter before beginning the next chapter. See Appendix A, "Questions and Answers," for the answers to these questions.

1. What are the five major phases of the boot process for Intel-based computers?

2. What are the various Safe Mode advanced boot options for booting Windows 2000, and how do they differ?

3. What are the two sections of the Boot.ini file, and what information does each section contain?

4. You install a new device driver for a SCSI adapter in your computer. When you restart the computer, however, Windows 2000 stops responding after the kernel load phase. How can you get Windows 2000 to restart successfully?

CHAPTER 23

Deploying Windows 2000

About This Chapter

This chapter prepares you to automate installing Microsoft Windows 2000
Professional. It introduces the Windows 2000 System Preparation tool and
Remote Installation Services. It also addresses the issues involved with upgrad-
ing previous versions of Windows to Windows 2000 and installing service packs.

Before You Begin

To complete this chapter, you must have

- A computer that meets or exceeds the minimum hardware requirements located in "About This Book."

- The Microsoft Windows 2000 Professional CD-ROM or access to a distribution server containing the Windows 2000 Professional installation files, if
  your computer is connected to a network.

Lesson 1: Automating Installations

This lesson presents methods that will help you to automate Windows 2000 installations. When you must install Windows 2000 on computers with varying configurations, scripting provides automation with increased flexibility. You will learn how the improved Setup Manager makes it easy to create the Unattend.txt files that are necessary for scripted installations.

After this lesson, you will be able to

- Automate installations of Windows 2000 by using the Windows 2000 Setup Manager Wizard.
- Apply application update packs while upgrading previous versions of Windows.

Estimated lesson time: 45 minutes

Automating Installations by Using the Windows 2000 Setup Manager

The computers in most networks are not identical but still have many similarities. You can use installation scripts to specify the variations in the hardware configurations of the computers that are to receive installations.

One of the most significant improvements in Windows 2000 is the ease and flexibility of scripting installations. The new Windows 2000 Setup Manager Wizard allows you to quickly create a script for a customized installation of Windows 2000 without concern for cryptic text file syntax. Knowing how to use Setup Manager enables you to perform customized installations on workstations and servers that meet the specific hardware and network requirements of your organization.

You can create or modify an answer file by using Setup Manager (see Figure 23.1). Although you can still use Unattend.txt files created with a simple text editor, such as Notepad, you use Setup Manager to reduce errors in syntax. You can copy Setup Manager to your hard disk by extracting the files in the Deploy.cab file located on your Windows 2000 Professional CD-ROM in the Support\Tools folder. To extract the files, double-click the .CAB file to display the files, select the files you want to extract, right-click the files, and then click Extract on the menu that appears.

Note For detailed steps on how to install Setup Manager, see the next Practice, "Installing the Windows 2000 Installation Deployment Tools," in this chapter.

Figure 23.1   Windows Setup Manager

Setup Manager does the following:

- Provides a new, easy-to-use graphical interface with which you can create and modify answer files and UDFs
- Makes it easy to specify computer-specific or user-specific information
- Simplifies the inclusion of application setup scripts in the answer file
- Creates the distribution folder that you use for the installation files

When you start Setup Manager, you will be presented with the following three options:

- Create A New Answer File
- Create An Answer File That Duplicates This Computer's Configuration
- Modify An Existing Answer File

If you select the Create A New Answer File option, you will then need to choose the type of answer file you want to create. Setup Manager can create the following types of answer files:

- Windows 2000 unattended installation
- Sysprep Install
- Remote Installation Services (RIS)

Note Remote Installation Services will be discussed later in this chapter in Lesson 3, "Performing Remote Installations."

The remainder of the Setup Manager Wizard allows you to specify the level of user interaction with the Setup program and to enter all the information required to complete Setup.

Note The Sysdiff.exe utility is often used in conjunction with Setup Manager to install Windows using difference files. The use of Sysdiff.exe has not changed from Windows NT 4.

Practice: Installing the Windows 2000 Installation Deployment Tools

In this practice, you will extract the Windows 2000 installation deployment tools from the Windows 2000 Professional CD-ROM you used to install Windows 2000 Professional, and then you will use System Manager to create an unattended setup script.

Exercise 1: Extracting the Windows 2000 Installation Deployment Tools

In this exercise, you will extract the Windows 2000 installation deployment tools from the CD-ROM you used to install Windows 2000 Professional and copy them to your hard disk.

▶ **To install the installation deployment tools**

1. Log on as Administrator and insert the Windows 2000 Professional CD-ROM in the CD-ROM drive.

2. Start Windows Explorer and create the folder Deploy in the root folder of drive C (or in the root folder of your system drive).

    The Deploy folder will be used to contain the files extracted from the Deploy.cab file on the Windows 2000 Professional CD-ROM.

3. Double-click the Deploy file in the Support\Tools folder on drive D.

    Note If D isn't the correct drive letter for your CD-ROM drive, replace the D with the letter representing your CD-ROM drive.

    Windows 2000 displays the contents of the Deploy.cab file.

4. Select all of the files listed in the Deploy.cab file.

> **Note** To select all the files in the Deploy.cab file, hold down the Ctrl key, and then click each of the files listed. If your file icons are listed in one column, you can also select the files by clicking the first file in the list, holding down the Shift key, and then clicking the last file in the list.

5. Right-click any of the selected files and click Extract on the menu that appears.

   The Browse For Folder dialog box appears.

6. Select the Deploy folder on drive C (or your system drive, if it is a drive other than C), and then click OK.

   The Copying dialog box appears briefly as the files are extracted and copied to the Deploy folder.

7. In Windows Explorer, click the Deploy folder to view its contents.

   You should see the seven files from the Deploy.cab file listed. These files have been extracted from the .CAB file and are now ready to use.

8. Double-click Readme.txt.

9. Take a moment to view the topics covered in the Readme.txt file and then close Notepad.

Exercise 2: Using Setup Manager to Create an Unattended Setup Script

In this exercise, you will use the Windows 2000 Setup Manager to create an unattended setup script. At the same time, the Setup Manager Wizard creates a distribution folder and a .UDF file.

▶ **To create an unattended setup script using the Setup Manager Wizard**

1. In Windows Explorer, double-click the Setupmgr.exe file.

   The Windows 2000 Setup Manager Wizard appears.

2. Click Next.

   The New Or Existing Answer File page appears.

3. Ensure that the Create A New Answer File option is selected, and then click Next.

   The Product To Install page appears. Notice that you have three choices: Windows 2000 Unattended Installation, Sysprep Install, and Remote Installation Services.

4. Ensure that Windows 2000 Unattended Installation is selected, and then Click Next.

The Platform page appears. Notice you have two choices: Windows 2000 Professional or Windows 2000 Server.

5. Ensure that Windows 2000 Professional is selected, and then click Next.

   The User Interaction Level page appears. Notice that you have five choices:

   - **Provide Defaults.** The answers you provide in the answer file are the default answers that the user sees. The user can accept the default answers or change any of the answers supplied by the script.

   - **Fully Automated.** The installation is fully automated. The user doesn't have the chance to review or change the answers supplied by the script.

   - **Hide Pages.** The answers provided by the script are supplied during the installation. Any page for which the script supplies all answers is hidden from the user so that the user can't review or change the answers supplied by the script.

   - **Read Only.** The script provides the answers, and the user can view the answers on any page that is not hidden, but the user can't change the answers.

   - **GUI Attended.** The text-mode portion of the installation is automated, but the user must supply the answers for the GUI-mode portion of the installation.

6. Select Fully Automated, and then click Next.

   The License Agreement page appears.

   Note If you had chosen any option other than Fully Automated, this page would not have displayed.

   ---

7. Click I Accept The Terms Of The License Agreement, and then click Next.

   The Customize The Software page appears.

8. Enter your name in the Names box, your organization in the Organization box, and then Click Next.

   The Computer Names page appears. Notice that you have three choices:

   - Enter a series of names to be used during the various iterations of the script.

   - Provide the name of a text file to import that has one computer name per line listed. Setup imports and uses these names as the computer names in the various iterations of the script.

   - Select Automatically Generate Computer Names Based On Organization Name to allow the system to automatically generate the computer names to be used.

9. Type **PRO2** and then click Add. Repeat this step to add PRO3 and PRO4 to the list of names.

Notice that the names PRO2, PRO3, and PRO4 appear in the Computers To Be Installed box.

10. Click Next.

The Administrator Password page appears. Notice that you have two choices: Prompt The User For An Administrator Password and Use The Following Administrator Password (127 Characters Maximum).

Note On the User Interaction Level page, you selected Fully Automated, so the Prompt The User For An Administrator Password option is not available.

Notice that you can also have the administrator log on automatically, and you can set the number of times you want the administrator to log on automatically when the computer is restarted.

11. Ensure that Use The Following Administrator Password (127 Characters Maximum) is selected, and type **password** in the Password box and the Confirm Password box. Then click Next.

The Display Settings page appears. Notice that you can adjust the Colors, Screen Area, and Refresh Frequency settings for the display. You can also choose Custom to create your own settings rather than picking from the selections listed under each of the three fields.

12. Click Next to accept the default settings.

The Network Settings page appears. Notice that you can choose Typical Settings—which installs TCP/IP, enables DHCP, and installs the Client for Microsoft Networks protocol for each destination computer—or you can choose Custom Settings.

13. Select Custom Settings, and then click Next.

The Number Of Network Adapters page appears.

14. Ensure that the default option, One Network Adapter, is selected and then click Next.

The Networking Components page appears. Notice that the Client For Microsoft Networks, File And Printer Sharing For Microsoft Networks, and Internet Protocol (TCP/IP) components are installed by default.

15. Select Internet Protocol (TCP/IP), and then click Properties.

The General tab of the Internet Protocol (TCP/IP) Properties dialog box appears. Notice that it is identical to configuring TCP/IP through Network Neighborhood.

16. Click Cancel, and then click Next to accept the default settings for networking components.

The Workgroup Or Domain page appears.

17. Click Next to accept the default option, Workgroup, and the workgroup name WORKGROUP.

    The Time Zone page appears.

18. Select the appropriate time zone, and then click Next.

    The Additional Settings page appears.

19. Ensure that the default option, Yes, Edit The Additional Settings is selected, and then click Next.

    The Telephony page appears.

20. Select the appropriate setting for What Country/Region Are You In?

21. Type the appropriate numbers for What Area (Or City) Code Are You In?

22. Type the appropriate number(s) for If You Dial A Number To Access An Outside Line, What Is It?

23. Select the appropriate setting for The Phone System At This Location Uses, and then click Next.

    The Regional Settings page appears. The default selection is Use The Default Regional Settings For The Windows Version You Are Installing.

24. Click Next to accept the default.

    The Languages page appears; it allows you to add support for additional languages.

25. Click Next to accept the default.

    The Browser And Shell Settings page appears. Notice that you can choose from the following three settings: Use Default Internet Explorer Settings, Use An Autoconfiguration Script Created By The Internet Explorer Administration Kit To Configure Your Browser, and Individually Specify Proxy And Default Home Page Settings.

26. Click Next to accept the default option, Use Default Internet Explorer Settings.

    The Installation Folder page appears. Notice that you can select from three choices: A Folder Named Winnt, A Uniquely Named Folder Generated By Setup, and This Folder.

27. Select This Folder, and in the This Folder box, type **W2000Pro** and then click Next.

    The Install Printers page appears.

28. Click Next to continue without having the script install any network printers.

    The Run Once page appears. This page allows you to configure Windows to run one or more commands the first time a user logs on.

29. Click Next to continue without having the script run any additional commands.

The Distribution Folder page appears. This page allows you to have the Setup Manager Wizard create a distribution folder on your computer or network with the required installation files. You can add additional files to this distribution folder.

Note If you were upgrading systems to Windows 2000 Professional, you could add any application update packs to the distribution folder and enter the commands to apply the update packs to the application as part of the upgrade.

30. Ensure that the default option, Yes, Create Or Modify A Distribution Folder, is selected, and then click Next.

Note The other selection is No, This Answer File Will Be Used To Install From A CD. If you are going to be doing a large number of installs, you don't want to try to simultaneously install multiple computers off of a CD-ROM. Create one or more distribution folders.

The Distribution Folder Name page appears.

31. Click Next to accept the default option, Create A New Distribution Folder.

    The Additional Mass Storage Drivers page appears.

32. Click Next to continue without adding any additional drivers.

    The Hardware Abstraction Layer page appears. This page allows you to replace the default HAL.

33. Click Next to use the default Hardware Abstraction Layer.

    The Additional Commands page appears. This page allows you to specify additional commands to be run at the end of the unattended setup.

34. Click Next to continue without running any additional commands.

    The OEM Branding page appears. This page allows you to customize Windows Setup by adding your customer OEM branding. You can specify both a logo bitmap and a background bitmap.

35. Click Next to continue without specifying any OEM branding.

    The Additional Files Or Folders page appears. This page allows you to specify additional files or folders to be copied to the destination computers.

36. Click Next to continue without specifying any additional files or folders to copy.

    The Answer File Name page appears.

37. Type the path **C:\Deploy\Unattend.txt** in the Location And File Name box, and then click Next.

    The Location Of Setup Files page appears. The files can be copied from the CD-ROM or you can specify a network location.

38. Click Next to accept the default option, Copy The Files From CD.

     The Copying Files page appears while the Setup Manager Wizard copies the distribution files. This will take a few minutes. An indicator shows you the progress of the copy operation.

     The Completing The Windows 2000 Setup Manager Wizard appears.

39. Click Finish.

     Notice that three new files were created in C:\Deploy: Unattend.bat, Unattend.txt, and Unattend.udf. Notice also that a C:\Win2000dist folder was also created and shared.

▶ **To verify the existence of the distribution files**

1. Click C:\Win2000dist to view the distribution files.

2. Close Windows Explorer.

Lesson Summary

In this lesson, you learned that the Windows 2000 Setup Manager Wizard makes it easy to create the Unattend.txt files that are necessary for scripted installations. Setup Manager provides an easy-to-use graphical interface with which you can create and modify answer files and UDFs.

You also learned that before you can use the Setup Manager Wizard, you must copy the Windows 2000 deployment tools, including Setup Manager, by extracting the files located in the Deploy.cab file on the Windows 2000 Professional CD-ROM. The Setup Manager Wizard makes it easy to specify computer-specific or user-specific information, and to include application setup scripts in the answer file. The Setup Manager Wizard also creates the distribution folder that you use for the installation files.

Lesson 2: Using Disk Duplication to Deploy Windows 2000

When you install Windows 2000 on several computers with identical hardware configurations, the most efficient installation method to use is disk duplication. By creating a disk image of a Windows 2000 installation and copying that image to multiple destination computers, you save time in the rollout of Windows 2000. This method also creates a convenient baseline that you can easily copy again to a computer that is experiencing significant problems.

Disk imaging and duplication technologies are improved in Windows 2000. One of the tools that you will use for disk duplication is the improved System Preparation tool (Sysprep.exe) that now ships with Windows 2000. Knowing how to use this tool can help support professionals prepare master disk images for efficient mass installations. You can use a number of third-party disk-imaging tools to copy the image to other computers. This lesson explains how to use the System Preparation tool to prepare the master image.

After this lesson, you will be able to

- Install and use the Windows 2000 System Preparation tool to deploy Windows 2000 Professional.

Estimated lesson time: 25 minutes

Examining the Disk Duplication Process

To install Windows 2000 by using disk duplication, you first need to install and configure Windows 2000 on a test computer. After you have done this, you need to install and configure any applications and application update packs on the test computer. Then you run Sysprep.exe on the test computer to prepare the computer for duplication.

Extracting the Windows 2000 System Preparation Tool

Before you can use the Windows 2000 System Preparation tool, you must copy the necessary files onto the computer you are using to create the master image. To copy the System Preparation tool, you must extract the files from the Deploy.cab file in the Support\Tools folder on the Windows 2000 Professional CD-ROM. For the steps to do this, see Exercise 1, "Extracting the Windows 2000 Deployment Tools," in Lesson 1 of this chapter.

Using the System Preparation Tool to Prepare the Master Image

The System Preparation tool was developed to eliminate several problems you might encounter when copying disks. First of all, every computer must have a unique security ID (SID). If you copied an existing disk image to other computers, every computer on which the image was copied would have the same SID. To prevent this problem, the System Preparation tool adds a system service to the master image that will create a unique local domain SID the first time the computer to which the master image is copied is started.

The System Preparation tool also adds a Mini-Setup wizard to the master copy. The Mini-Setup wizard runs the first time the computer to which the master image is copied is started. The Mini-Setup wizard guides the user through entering such user-specific information as the following:

- End-user license agreement
- Product ID
- Regional settings
- User name
- Company name
- Network configuration
- Whether the computer is joining a workgroup or domain
- Time zone selection

Note The Mini-Setup wizard can be scripted so that this user-specific information can be entered automatically.

The System Preparation tool causes the master image to force the computer on which the master image is copied to run a full Plug and Play device detection. The hard disk controller device driver and the hardware abstraction layer (HAL) on the computer on which the disk image was generated and on the computer to which the disk image was copied must be identical. The other peripherals, such as the network adapter, the video adapter, and sound cards on the computer on which the disk image was copied, need not be identical to the ones on the computer on which the image was generated.

The System Preparation tool can also be customized; Table 23.1 describes the switches that you can use to customize Sysprep.exe.

Table 23.1   Available Switches for Sysprep.exe

Switch	Description
/quiet	Runs with no user interaction
/pnp	Forces Setup to detect Plug and Play devices on the destination computers
/reboot	Restarts the source computer
/nosidgen	Doesn't regenerate SIDs on the destination computers

Practice: Using the System Preparation Tool to Create a Master Disk Image

In this practice, you will use the Windows 2000 System Preparation tool to prepare a master image for disk duplication.

Note If you haven't completed Exercise 1 of Lesson 1 in this chapter, you must complete that exercise and extract the System Preparation tool from the Windows 2000 CD-ROM before you can complete the following exercise.

Caution If you complete the following exercise, you will have to reinstall Windows 2000 Professional on your computer.

► **To use the System Preparation tool**

1. Log on as Administrator.
2. In Windows Explorer, double-click the Sysprep.exe file in the Deploy folder.

   Note If you didn't extract the deployment tools to the Deploy folder on your system drive (C), use the correct path to Sysprep.

   A Windows 2000 System Preparation Tool message box appears, warning you that running Sysprep might modify some of the security parameters of this system.

   Note If you run Sysprep on your computer, you will lose some of the security parameters on your computer.

3. If you are certain that you don't mind having to reinstall Windows 2000 Professional, click OK to continue.
4. Your computer shuts down and prompts you to turn it off.
5. Turn your computer off.

Note You can run the Setup Manager Wizard to create a Sysprep.inf file. Sysprep.inf provides answers to the Mini-Setup wizard on the destination computers. You can also use this file to specify customized drivers. The Setup Manager Wizard creates a Sysprep folder at the root of the drive image and places Sysprep.inf in this folder. The Mini-Setup wizard checks for Sysprep.inf in the Sysprep folder at the root of the drive in which Windows 2000 is being installed.

Installing Windows 2000 from a Master Disk Image

After running Sysprep on your test computer, you are ready to run a third-party disk image copying tool to create a master disk image. Save the new disk image on a shared folder or CD-ROM. Copy this image to the multiple destination computers.

End users can then start the destination computers. The Mini-Setup wizard will prompt the user for computer-specific variables, such as the administrator password for the computer and the computer name. If a Sysprep.inf file was provided, the Mini-Setup wizard will be bypassed and the system will load Windows 2000 without user intervention. You can also automate the completion of the Mini-Setup wizard further by creating a Sysprep.inf file.

Note When you use disk duplication, the mass storage controllers and HALs for the test computer and all destination computers must be identical.

Practice: Using the System Preparation Tool to Install Windows 2000 Professional

In this practice, you will use a master disk image to install Windows 2000 Professional. You have just created a master disk image. Normally you would use a third-party tool to copy this disk image to another computer. For the purposes of this practice, you will reinstall using the master disk image as if it were a computer that had the disk image copied to it.

▶ **To install Windows 2000 from a master disk image**

1. Power on your computer.

   After a few minutes, the Welcome To The Windows 2000 Professional Setup Wizard appears.

2. Click Next.

   The License Agreement page appears.

3. Read through the license agreement, click I Accept This Agreement, and then click Next.

   The Regional Settings page appears.

4. Ensure that the System Locale, the User Locale, and the Keyboard Layout are correct, and then click Next.

   The Personalize Your Software page appears.

5. In the Name box, type your name; in the Organization box, type your organization name, and then click Next.

   The Your Product Key Page appears.

6. Enter your product key, and then click Next.

The Computer Name And Administrator Password page appears.

7. In the Computer Name box, type **PRO1** (or type the name of your computer, if you are using another valid name for your network).

8. In the Password and Confirm Password boxes, type **password** and then click Next.

   If your computer has a modem, the Modem Dialing Information page appears. If your computer doesn't have a modem, go to step 14; otherwise, continue with step 9.

9. Select the appropriate setting for the What Country/Region Are You In Now? option.

10. Type the appropriate code for the What Area Code (Or City Code) Are You In Now? setting.

11. Type the appropriate number for the If You Dial A Number To Get An Outside Line, What Is It? setting.

12. Select the appropriate option for The Phone System At This Location Uses, and then click Next.

    The Date And Time Settings page appears.

13. Ensure that the Date, Time, and Time Zone settings are correct and that the Automatically Adjust Clock For Daylight Saving Changes check box is selected, if you want Windows 2000 to adjust the clock. Then click Next.

    The Networking Settings page appears. This might take a few minutes.

14. Ensure that the default option, Typical Settings, is selected, and then click Next.

    The Workgroup Or Computer Domain page appears.

15. Ensure that the No, This Computer Is Not On A Network Or Is On A Network Without A Domain option is selected.

16. Ensure that WORKGROUP appears in the Workgroup Or Computer Domain box, and then click Next.

    The Performing Final Tasks page appears briefly, and then the Completing The Windows 2000 Setup Wizard page appears. This might take a few minutes while Setup completes.

17. Click Finish.

    The computer restarts, and the Welcome To The Network Identification Wizard appears.

18. Click Next.

    The Users Of This Computer Page appears.

19. Click Users Must Enter A User Name And Password To Use This Computer, and then click Next.

    The Completing The Network Identification Wizard appears.

20. Click Finish.

21. Log on as Administrator with a password of *password.*

Lesson Summary

The System Preparation tool (Sysprep.exe) described in this lesson prepares the master computer to be duplicated. One of the primary functions of the System Preparation tool is to delete SIDs and all other user-specific or computer-specific information. You can use four switches to customize Sysprep.exe.

This lesson also showed you that after you run Sysprep.exe on the master computer, you can use a third-party tool to capture the image and copy it to the destination computers. When the user restarts the destination computer, the Mini-Setup wizard appears but requires little input to complete. You can also automate the completion of the Mini-Setup wizard further by creating a Sysprep.inf file.

Lesson 3: Performing Remote Installations

The most efficient method of deploying Windows 2000 Professional is to use remote installation. You can perform remote installations of Windows 2000 Professional if you have a Windows 2000 Server infrastructure in place and the computers in your network support remote boot.

After this lesson, you will be able to

- Describe how to deploy Windows 2000 using Remote Installation Services.
- Install Remote Installation Services.
- Create a boot floppy.

Estimated lesson time: 40 minutes

Note To be able to install Remote Installation Services and to create a boot floppy for network interface cards that are not equipped with a Pre-Boot Execution Environment (PXE) boot ROM, or for systems with BIOSs that don't support starting from the PXE boot ROM, you must have a computer running one of the Windows 2000 Server family of products. You must also have either the CD-ROM or access to a network source of files used to install the Server product. For more information, see the section "Examining the Prerequisites," on page 544.

Understanding Remote Installation

Remote installation is the process of connecting to a server running Remote Installation Services, called the RIS server, and then starting an automated installation of Windows 2000 Professional on a local computer. Remote installation enables administrators to install Windows 2000 Professional on client computers throughout a network from a central location. This reduces the time administrators spend visiting all the computers in a network, thereby reducing the cost of deploying Windows 2000 Professional.

RIS provides the following benefits:

- Enables remote installation of Windows 2000 Professional.
- Simplifies server image management by eliminating hardware-specific images and by detecting Plug and Play hardware during setup.
- Supports recovery of the operating system and computer in the event of computer failure.
- Retains security settings after restarting the destination computer.
- Reduces TCO by allowing either users or technical staff to install the operating system on individual computers.

Installing and Configuring Remote Installation Services

Before beginning a rollout of Windows 2000 Professional using RIS, become familiar with the prerequisites for the service and install the service using the Remote Installation Services Setup wizard.

Examining the Prerequisites

RIS is available only on computers running one of the Windows 2000 Server family of products. The RIS server can be a domain controller or a member server. Table 23.2 lists the network services required for RIS and their RIS function. These network services don't have to be installed on the same computer as RIS, but they must be available somewhere on the network.

Table 23.2   Network Services Required for RIS

Network service	RIS function
DNS Service	RIS relies on the DNS server for locating both the directory service and client computer accounts.
DHCP Service	Client computers that can perform a network boot receive an IP address from the DHCP server.
Active Directory directory services	RIS relies on the directory services based on Active Directory technology in Windows 2000 for locating existing client computers as well as existing RIS servers.

Remote installation requires that RIS (included on the Windows 2000 Server CD-ROM) be installed on a volume that is shared over the network. This shared volume must meet the following criteria:

- The shared volume can't be on the same drive that is running Windows 2000 Server.
- The shared volume must be large enough to hold the RIS software and the various Windows 2000 Professional images.
- The shared volume must be formatted with the Microsoft Windows 2000 File System (NTFS).

Using the Remote Installation Services Setup Wizard

When your network meets the prerequisites for RIS, you can run the Remote Installation Services Setup wizard, which does the following:

- Installs the RIS software
- Creates the remote installation folder and copies the Windows 2000 Professional installation files to the server
- Adds .SIF files, which are a variation of an Unattend.txt file
- Configures the Client Installation wizard screens that will appear during a remote installation

- Updates the registry
- Starts the required Remote Installation Services

When installation of RIS is complete, you can configure it using the server's computer object in the Active Directory Users and Computers snap-in. For more information on the management of Active Directory objects, see Chapter 9, "Introducing Active Directory Directory Services."

The RIS server stores the RIS images used to automatically install Windows 2000 Professional on client computers that are enabled for remote boot. The RIS server can be a domain controller or a stand-alone server that is a member of a domain containing Active Directory directory services.

Practice: Installing RIS

In this practice, you will install Windows 2000 Remote Installation Services from a Windows 2000 Server CD-ROM.

Note To complete this exercise, you need to have a Windows 2000 Professional CD-ROM or access to a shared folder that contains the Windows 2000 Professional installation files. You must also have a drive on the computer running one of the Windows 2000 Server family of products on which you installed RIS that is formatted with NTFS version 5 or later and that contains enough room to hold the Windows 2000 Professional installation files. You must have available on your network a DHCP server, a DNS server, and a domain.

Exercise 1: Installing Remote Installation Services

In this exercise, you will install Remote Installation Services on a computer running Windows 2000 Server.

▶ **To install Remote Installation Services on a computer running Windows 2000 Server**

1. Log on as Administrator, and insert the Windows 2000 Server CD-ROM into your CD-ROM drive.

2. Open Control Panel, and double-click Add/Remove Programs.

   The Add/Remove Programs window appears.

3. Click Add/Remove Windows Components.

   The Windows Components page of the Windows Components Wizard appears.

4. Select the Remote Installation Services check box in the Components box, and then click Next.

   Setup installs and configures Remote Installation Services.

   The Completing The Windows Components Wizard page appears.

5. Click Finish.

   The System Settings Change dialog box appears, indicating that you must reboot before the new settings will take effect.

6. Remove the Windows 2000 Server CD-ROM from your CD-ROM drive and click Yes.

Exercise 2: Configuring Remote Installation Services

In this exercise, you will configure Remote Installation Services.

▶ **To configure Remote Installation Services**

1. Log on as Administrator.

   The Microsoft Windows 2000 Configure Your Server screen appears, indicating that you have selected components that require additional configuration.

   Note If the Microsoft Windows 2000 Configure Your Server screen doesn't appear after you restart and log on as Administrator, open Control Panel, double-click Add/Remove Programs, and click Add/Remove Windows Components. Under Set Up Services, you should see the Configure Remote Installation Services item with an associated Configure button. Skip step 2 that follows and proceed with step 3.

   ---

2. Click Finish Setup.

   The Add/Remove Programs window appears, indicating that you now need to configure Remote Installation Services.

3. Click Configure.

   The Remote Installation Services Setup Wizard appears.

4. Insert the Windows 2000 Professional CD-ROM in the CD-ROM drive of the server. If the Microsoft Windows 2000 CD dialog box appears, click Exit.

5. Read the information on the welcome screen and then click Next.

   The Remote Installation Folder Location page appears.

   Notice that the drive on which you create the Remote Installation folder can't be the system drive and must be formatted with NTFS version 5 or later.

6. Type **E:\RemoteInst** in the Path box, and click Next.

   Note Enter a path that is appropriate for your system. The folder should not exist; it will be created as part of the configuration process. Remember that the drive must be on the computer on which you installed RIS, must be formatted with NTFS version 5 or later, and must have about 300 MB of space available to hold the Windows 2000 Professional installation files.

The Initial Settings page appears.

> **Note** By default, the RIS server doesn't support client computers until you configure it to do so.

7. Select the Respond To Client Computers Requesting Service check box and then click Next.

   The Installation Source Files Location page appears.

8. Enter the path to the installation source files and then click Next.

> **Note** If you were using a Windows 2000 Professional CD-ROM in the CD-ROM drive of the server on which you were configuring RIS, you would enter *X*:\i386, where *X* is the drive letter for the CD-ROM drive.

   The Windows Installation Image Folder Name page appears.

9. Click Next to accept the default name of Win2000.pro.

   The Friendly Description And Help Text page appears.

10. Click Next to accept the default friendly description and help text.

    The Review Settings page appears.

> **Note** The default description is "Microsoft Windows 2000 Professional." The help text is "Automatically installs Windows Professional without prompting the user for input."

11. Review the information and then click Finish.

    It will take several minutes for the following steps to complete:

    - The remote installation folder is created.
    - The files needed by the services are copied.
    - The Windows installation files are copied.
    - The Client Installation Wizard screen files are updated.
    - A new unattended Setup answer file is created.
    - Remote Installation Services is created.
    - The registry is updated.
    - The required remote installation services are started.

12. When all the tasks are completed, click Done, and close any open windows.

Understanding Client Requirements for Remote Installation

Client computers that support remote installation must have one of the following configurations:

- A configuration meeting the Net PC specification
- A network interface card with a PXE boot ROM and BIOS support for starting from the PXE boot ROM
- A supported network interface card and a remote installation boot disk

Net PCs

The Net PC is a highly manageable platform with the ability to perform a network boot, manage upgrades, and prevent users from changing the hardware or operating system configuration. Additional requirements for the Net PC are the following:

- The network adapter must be set as the primary boot device within the system BIOS.
- The user account that will be used to perform the installation must be assigned the user right "Log on as a batch job."

Note The Administrator group doesn't have the right to log on to a batch job by default and thus will need to be assigned this right prior to attempting a remote installation.

- Users must be assigned permission to create computer accounts in the domain that they are joining. The domain is specified in the advanced settings on the RIS server.

Computers Not Meeting the Net PC Specification

Computers that don't directly meet the Net PC specification can still interact with the RIS server. You can enable remote installation on a computer that doesn't meet the Net PC specification by doing the following:

1. Install a network interface card with a PXE boot ROM.
2. Set the BIOS to start from the PXE boot ROM.
3. Assign the user right "Log on as a batch job" to the user account that will be used to perform the installation.
4. Assign users permission to create computer accounts in the domain that they are joining. You specify the domain in the advanced settings on the RIS server.

Creating Boot Floppies

If the network interface card in a client isn't equipped with a PXE boot ROM or the BIOS doesn't allow starting from the network interface card, create a remote installation boot disk. The boot disk simulates the PXE boot process. Windows 2000 ships with the Windows 2000 Remote Boot Disk Generator that allows you to easily create a boot disk (see Figure 23.2).

Figure 23.2   The Windows 2000 Remote Boot Disk Generator dialog box

You start the Windows 2000 Remote Boot Disk Generator by running Rbfg.exe. The Rbfg.exe file is located in the RemoteInstall\admin\i386 folder on the Remote Installation Server. These boot floppies support only the PCI-based network adapters listed in the Adapters List. To see the list of the supported network adapters, click the Adapter List button shown in Figure 23.2. A partial listing of the supported network adapter cards is shown in Figure 23.3.

Figure 23.3   Network adapters supported by boot floppies

You will also need to set the user rights and permissions. The user account that will be used to perform the installation must be assigned the user right "Log on as a batch job." The users must be assigned permission to create computer accounts in the domain that they are joining. The domain is specified in the advanced settings on the RIS server.

Practice: Creating a Remote Boot Disk

In this practice, you will create a remote boot disk.

1. Log on as Administrator.
2. Click Start and then click Run.

   The Run dialog box appears.
3. Type **E:\RemoteInstall\Admin\i386\rbfg** in the Open box.

   Note Your path to Rbfg.exe might vary. See step 6 in Exercise 2, "Configuring Remote Installation Services," in the previous practice.

4. Click OK.

   The Windows 2000 Remote Boot Disk Generator dialog box appears.
5. Read the information in the Windows 2000 Remote Boot Disk Generator dialog box and then click Adapter List.
6. Scroll through the list of supported adapters, and then click OK to return to the Windows 2000 Remote Boot Disk Generator dialog box.
7. Insert a formatted 3.5-inch floppy into your floppy disk drive.

   Note If your computer has more than one floppy disk drive, make sure you select the appropriate floppy disk drive in the Windows 2000 Remote Boot Disk Generator dialog box.

8. Click Create Disk.

   A Windows 2000 Remote Boot Disk Generator dialog box appears, prompting you to create another boot floppy.
9. Click No.
10. Click Close to close the Windows 2000 Remote Boot Disk Generator dialog box.

Lesson Summary

In this lesson, you learned that if you have a Windows 2000 Server infrastructure in place, and the computers in your network support remote boot, the most efficient method of deploying Windows 2000 Professional is to use remote installation. Remote installation is the process of connecting to an RIS server and then starting an automated installation of Windows 2000 Professional on a local computer. Remote installation enables administrators to install Windows 2000 Professional on client computers throughout a network from a central location. This reduces the time that administrators spend visiting all the computers in a network, thereby reducing the cost of deploying Windows 2000 Professional.

You also learned that client computers that support remote installation must have one of the three following configurations: a configuration meeting the Net PC specification, and the network interface card must be set as the primary boot device within the system BIOS; a network interface card with a PXE boot ROM and BIOS support for starting from the PXE boot ROM; or a supported network interface card and a remote installation boot disk.

Finally, you saw that the user account that will be used to perform the installation must be assigned the user right "Log on as a batch job," and users must be assigned permission to create computer accounts in the domain that they are joining. The domain is specified in the advanced settings on the RIS server.

Lesson 4: Upgrading Previous Versions of Windows to Windows 2000

You can upgrade most previous versions of Windows operating systems directly to Windows 2000 to take advantage of the new features offered in the Windows 2000 Professional operating system. However, before upgrading to Windows 2000, ensure that the computer hardware meets the minimum Windows 2000 hardware requirements. You must also check the Hardware Compatibility List or test the computers for hardware compatibility using the Windows 2000 Compatibility tool. You want to ensure that the hardware is compatible with Windows 2000 to avoid surprises when you start the upgrade on a large number of client computers.

For computers running previous versions of Windows that use compatible hardware, you upgrade them directly to Windows 2000. If Windows 95 and Windows 98 client systems are using incompatible or insufficient hardware, you can still take advantage of the functionality of Active Directory directory services provided by a Windows 2000 domain. To do this, you can install the Windows 2000 Directory Service Client on these systems.

After this lesson, you will be able to

- Explain how to upgrade older Windows client operating systems to Windows 2000.

Estimated lesson time: 25 minutes

Identifying Client Upgrade Paths

You can upgrade most client computers running older versions of Windows directly to Windows 2000. However, computers running Windows NT 3.1 or 3.5 require an additional step. Table 23.3 lists the Windows 2000 Professional upgrade paths for client operating systems.

Table 23.3   Windows 2000 Professional Upgrade Paths for Client OSs

Upgrade from	Upgrade to
Windows 95 and Windows 98	Windows 2000 Professional
Windows NT Workstation 3.51 and 4	Windows 2000 Professional
Windows NT 3.1 or 3.5	Windows NT 3.51 or 4 first, then upgrade to Windows 2000 Professional

Note Windows 2000 Professional also upgrades all released service packs for Windows NT Workstation 3.51 and 4.

Identifying Hardware Requirements and Compatibility

Before you upgrade a client computer to Windows 2000 Professional, make sure that it meets the minimum hardware requirements. Table 23.4 describes these hardware requirements.

Table 23.4   Windows 2000 Professional Minimum Hardware Requirements

Hardware	Minimum requirements
Processor	133 MHz or higher Pentium-compatible CPU
Memory	64 MB
Hard disk	At least 650 MB of free space on the boot partition
Video	VGA or higher video card and monitor
Other components	CD-ROM installation: CD-ROM or DVD-ROM drive
Networking	Network interface card and related cables
Accessories	Keyboard and mouse or other pointing device

Most hardware devices that functioned properly in Windows NT Workstation 4 will also function properly in Windows 2000 Professional. However, you might have to replace some third-party drivers with new drivers designed for Windows 2000. You can obtain these new drivers from the manufacturer of the specific device.

Generating a Hardware Compatibility Report

You generate a hardware and software compatibility report using the Windows 2000 Compatibility tool. This tool runs automatically during system upgrades, but Microsoft recommends that you run it before beginning the upgrade to identify any hardware and software problems. This is especially true when upgrading many computers with similar hardware, so compatibility problems can be fixed before the upgrade begins.

Generating the Report

You can generate a compatibility report using the Windows 2000 Compatibility tool in two ways:

- Run Winnt32/checkupgradeonly

  Using the /checkupgradeonly switch with the Winn32 command launches the first part of the Windows 2000 Setup program. Instead of running the entire setup process, it checks only for compatible hardware and software. This generates a report that you can analyze to determine which system components are Windows 2000 compatible.

- Run the Chkupgrd.exe utility

  This immediately generates the compatibility report. You can download this utility from http://www.microsoft.com/windows2000/upgrade/compat/RAread.asp

Reviewing the Report

Both Winnt32/checkupgradeonly and the Chkupgrd.exe utility generate the same report. This report appears as a text document; you can view it in the utility's window or save it as a text file.

The report documents the system hardware and software that is incompatible with Windows 2000. It also identifies whether you need to obtain an upgrade pack for software installed on the system, and any additional changes or modifications you must make to the system to maintain functionality in Windows 2000.

Identifying Software Compatibility

Most applications that run in either Windows NT Workstation 4 or Windows NT Workstation 3.51 will run in Windows 2000 Professional. However, some applications will be incompatible. You should remove the following software applications before you upgrade to Windows 2000 Professional:

- Any third-party networking protocols and any third-party client software that doesn't have an update in the i386\Winntupg folder on the Windows 2000 CD-ROM

- All antivirus applications and disk quota software because of the changes in the NTFS file system from version 4, which was used in Windows NT 4, and version 5, which is used in Windows 2000 Professional

- Any custom power management software or tools because Windows 2000's support of Advanced Configuration and Power Interface (ACPI) and Advanced Power Management (APM) replace these

Upgrading Compatible Windows 95 and Windows 98 Computers

For client systems that test as compatible with Windows 2000, you run the Windows 2000 Setup program (winnt32.exe) to complete the upgrade process by completing the following steps:

1. Run the winnt32.exe command.

2. Accept the license agreement.

3. If the computer you are upgrading is already a member of a domain, you must create a computer account in that domain. Windows 95 and Windows 98 clients don't require a computer account, but Windows 2000 Professional clients do.

4. You are asked to provide upgrade packs for any applications that might need them. Upgrade packs update software so it works with Windows 2000. Upgrade packs are available from the software vendor.

5. You are prompted to upgrade to NTFS. Select the upgrade if you don't plan to set up the client computer to dual boot operating systems.

6. The Windows 2000 Compatibility tool runs, generating a report. If the report shows the computer as Windows 2000 compatible, continue with the upgrade. If the report shows the computer to be incompatible with Windows 2000, terminate the upgrade process.

7. The upgrade finishes without further user intervention. After the upgrade is complete, you must enter the password for the local computer's Administrator account.

If your computer is Windows 2000 compatible, it is now upgraded and is a member of your domain. If your computer isn't Windows 2000 compatible, you must upgrade your hardware, if possible, or you can install the Windows 2000 Directory Service Client.

Installing the Directory Service Client

Windows 95 or Windows 98 computers that don't meet the hardware compatibility requirements can still take advantage of Active Directory directory services by using Directory Service Client. Directory Service Client upgrades Windows 95 and Windows 98 systems so that they support Active Directory features, including the ability to:

- Use fault-tolerant Dfs
- Search Active Directory directory services
- Change your password on any domain controller

Note Before installing Directory Service Client on a computer running Windows 95, you must install Internet Explorer 4.01 or later and enable the Active Desktop component. Otherwise, the Directory Service Client Setup wizard won't run.

You can complete the following steps to install Directory Service Client on a non-Windows 2000–compatible computer:

1. In the Clients\Win9x folder on the Windows 2000 Server or Advanced Server CD-ROM, run the Dsclient.exe command.

   The Directory Service Client Setup wizard starts.

2. Click Next.

   The Ready To Install page appears.

3. Click Next.

The Setup wizard copies files and displays a progress indicator. When copying is complete, the Installation Completed page appears.

4. Click Finish to complete the installation.

   A Systems Settings Change message box appears, advising you that your computer must restart before the new settings will take effect.

5. Click Yes to restart the computer.

Upgrading Windows NT 3.51 and 4 Clients

The upgrade process for computers running Windows NT 3.51 and 4 is similar to the upgrade process for computers running Windows 95 and Windows 98.

Verifying Compatibility

Before you perform the upgrade, you must verify that the systems are compatible with Windows 2000. Use the Windows 2000 Compatibility tool to identify any potential problems before you start the upgrade.

Upgrading Compatible Systems

Windows NT 3.51 and 4 computers that meet the hardware compatibility requirements can upgrade directly to Windows 2000. You can start the upgrade process by completing the following procedure:

1. Insert the Windows 2000 CD-ROM in the CD-ROM drive.

2. Click Start, and then click Run.

3. In the Run box, type *d*:\i386\winnt32 (where *d* is the drive letter for your CD-ROM), and then press Enter.

   The Welcome To The Windows 2000 Setup Wizard appears.

4. Select Upgrade To Windows 2000 (Recommended), and then click Next.

   The License Agreement page appears.

5. Read the license agreement and then click I Accept This Agreement.

6. Click Next.

   The Upgrading To The Windows 2000 NTFS File System page appears.

7. Click Yes, Upgrade My Drive, and then click Next.

   The Copying Installation Files page appears.

   The Restarting The Computer page appears and the computer will now restart.

The upgrade finishes without further user intervention.

Using Incompatible Systems

Computers running Windows NT 3.51 or Windows NT 4 that don't meet the hardware compatibility requirements can still log on to a Windows 2000 network, but they won't be able to take advantage of many of the Windows 2000 features. No Directory Service Client is available for computers running Windows NT 3.51.

Lesson Summary

In this lesson, you learned that you can upgrade most client computers running older versions of Windows directly to Windows 2000. However, you must first upgrade computers running Windows NT 3.1 or Windows NT 3.5 to Windows NT 3.51 or Windows NT 4, and then you can upgrade them to Windows 2000 Professional.

You also learned that before you upgrade a client computer to Windows 2000 Professional, you must make sure that it meets the minimum hardware requirements. You can generate a hardware and software compatibility report using the Windows 2000 Compatibility tool. This tool runs automatically during system upgrades, but Microsoft recommends that you run this tool before beginning the upgrade to identify any hardware and software problems. This is especially true when upgrading many computers with similar hardware, so compatibility problems can be fixed before the upgrade begins.

Finally, you learned that for client systems that test as compatible with Windows 2000, you run the Windows 2000 Setup program (Winnt32.exe) to complete the upgrade process. If your computer isn't Windows 2000 compatible, you must upgrade your hardware, if possible, or you can install Directory Service Client. Windows 95 or Windows 98 computers that don't meet the hardware compatibility requirements can still take advantage of Active Directory directory services by using Directory Service Client. Directory Service Client upgrades Windows 95 and 98 systems so that they support Active Directory features, including the ability to use fault-tolerant Dfs, search Active Directory directory services, and change your password on any domain controller.

Lesson 5: Installing Service Packs

With previous versions of Windows, you installed the Windows operating system and then applied each required service pack separately. Also, in the earlier versions of Windows, when service packs were applied to existing systems, many previously installed components had to be reinstalled. For example, applying a service pack to a computer running Windows NT Workstation 4 would cause services such as IPX or RAS to have to be reinstalled. Windows 2000 Professional eliminates the need to reinstall components after applying a service pack and allows you to apply a service pack at the same time that you install Windows 2000. This is one of the many ways that Windows 2000 reduces your TCO.

After this lesson, you will be able to

- Deploy service packs.

Estimated lesson time: 5 minutes

Slipstreaming Service Packs

Windows 2000 Professional supports service-pack slipstreaming, so service packs can be integrated with the Windows 2000 Professional installation files. This allows you to keep one master image of the operating system. When Windows 2000 Professional is installed from this master source, the appropriate files from the service pack are also installed. This saves you the time of having to manually apply service packs after each Windows 2000 installation.

To apply a new service pack, run Update.exe with the -:*distribution_folder* switch, where *distribution_folder* is the name of the folder that contains the Windows 2000 installation files. This will replace the existing Windows 2000 files with the appropriate files from the service pack. Some of the key Windows 2000 files that are replaced when you apply a service pack include the following: Layout.inf, Dosnet.inf, Txtsetup.sif, and if any drivers have changed, a new Driver.cab file.

Deploying Service Packs After Installing Windows 2000

To apply a service pack to a computer running Windows 2000, run Update.exe. Running Update.exe replaces the existing Windows 2000 files with the appropriate new files from the service pack.

In earlier versions of Windows, if you applied a service pack to your computer, each time you changed the system state by adding or removing services, you had to reapply any service packs. Windows 2000 automatically recognizes that a service pack has been applied to the system and which files have been replaced or updated. Whenever you add or remove services from a computer running Windows 2000, the system copies the required files from either the Windows 2000 installation files or from the service pack install location, so you don't have to reapply the service pack.

Lesson Summary

As you learned in this lesson, Windows 2000 Professional simplifies the installation and maintenance of service packs and supports service-pack slipstreaming, so service packs can be integrated with the Windows 2000 installation files. As you install Windows 2000, the appropriate files from the service pack(s) are automatically applied during the installation.

This lesson also explained that when you apply a service pack to a computer running Windows 2000, and you later decide to add or remove services, you don't need to reapply the service pack. Windows 2000 automatically recognizes that a service pack has been applied to the system and copies the required files from either the Windows 2000 installation files or from the service pack install location. This frees you from having to reapply the service pack every time services are added or removed from a computer.

Review

The following questions will help you determine whether you have learned enough to move on to the next chapter. If you have difficulty answering these questions, please go back and review the material in this chapter before beginning the next chapter. See Appendix A, "Questions and Answers," for the answers to these questions.

1. How do you install the Windows 2000 deployment tools, such as the Setup Manager Wizard and the System Preparation tool?

2. Which five resources are required to use Remote Installation Services to install Windows 2000 Professional?

3. Which utility is provided to create boot floppies and how do you access it?

4. You are planning on installing 45 computers with Windows 2000 Professional. You have determined that these 45 computers have seven different network adapter cards. How can you determine whether these seven different types of network adapter cards are supported by the boot floppies you created?

5. You have a laptop running Windows 95 and you want to upgrade it to Windows 2000. The computer has 16 MB of RAM, and this can be upgraded to 24 MB. Can you upgrade this computer to Windows 2000? If not, how would you make it so this computer was able to access Active Directory directory services?

6. Name at least two problems the System Preparation tool resolves that makes creating and copying a master disk image to other computers much simpler to do.

C H A P T E R   2 4

Configuring Windows 2000 for Mobile Computers

About This Chapter

This chapter prepares you to configure and administer Microsoft Windows 2000 for mobile computers. This includes configuring offline folders and files, power schemes, Hibernate mode, and Advanced Power Management (APM).

Before You Begin

To complete this chapter, you must have

- A computer that meets or exceeds the minimum hardware requirements located in "About This Book."
- Windows 2000 Professional installed on the computer.

Lesson 1: Using Offline Folders and Files

When the network is down, or when you are on the road and your laptop is undocked, offline folders and files allow you to continue working on files that are stored on shared folders on the network. These network files are cached on your local disk so they are available even if the network is not. When the network is back up or when you dock your laptop, your connection to the network is re-established. Offline files synchronize the cached files and folders on your local disk with those stored on the network.

After this lesson, you will be able to

- Configure and use offline folders and files.

Estimated lesson time: 30 minutes

Configuring Your Computer to Use Offline Folders and Files

Before you can use offline folders and files, you must configure the server or network share and your laptop. You configure offline folders and files on the Offline Files tab in the Folder Options dialog box, which you can access through the Tools menu in the My Computer window or the Windows Explorer window. You must select the Enable Offline Files and the Synchronize All Offline Files Before Logging Off check boxes to use offline files (see Figure 24.1).

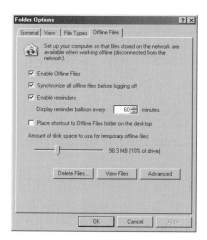

Figure 24.1 The Offline Files tab in the Folder Options dialog box

On the Offline Files tab, you can use the Delete Files button to delete the locally cached copy of a network file. The View Files button shows you the files stored in the Offline Files folder; these are the locally cached files that you have stored on your system. The Advanced button allows you to configure how your computer responds when a network connection is lost. For example, when a network connection is lost, you can configure your computer to notify you and allow you to begin working offline.

Practice: Configuring Offline Folders

In this practice, you will configure your computer running Windows 2000 Professional just as you would if it were a laptop running Windows 2000 Professional so that you can use offline folders and files. This allows you to work offline.

▶ **To configure offline folders and files on a laptop**

1. Log on as Administrator.
2. Right-click My Computer and then click Open.
3. On the Tools menu, click Folder Options.

   The Folder Options dialog box appears.

4. Click the Offline Files tab.
5. Ensure that the Enable Offline Files and the Synchronize All Offline Files Before Logging Off check boxes are selected, and then click OK.

Note By default, the Enable Offline Files check box and the Synchronize All Offline Files Before Logging Off check box are selected in Windows 2000 Professional, but they aren't selected in Windows 2000 Server.

---

6. Close the My Computer window.

Configuring Your Computer to Provide Offline Folders and Files

Before other users on the network can use offline folders and files on your computer, you must configure the resource to allow caching for offline use. You configure offline folders and files through the Windows Explorer, My Computer, or Internet Explorer window. Figure 24.2 shows the Allow Caching Of Files In This Shared Folder check box in the Caching Settings dialog box.

Figure 24.2   The Allow Caching Of Files In This Shared Folder check box

Practice: Configuring a Network Share

In this practice, you will configure a network share on a computer running Windows 2000 Professional so that users can access the files in the share and use them offline.

▶   **To enable a network share to provide files to be used offline**

1. Ensure that you are still logged on as Administrator, and start Windows Explorer.

2. Create a folder named C:\Offline.

3. Right-click Offline and then click Sharing.

    The Offline Properties dialog box appears with the Sharing tab active.

4. Click Share This Folder, and then click Caching.

    The Caching Settings dialog box appears.

5. Click the Setting drop-down list arrow.

    Notice that caching has the following three settings:

    ■ **Manual Caching For Documents.** This is the default setting. Users must manually specify any documents that they want available when they are working offline.

    ■ **Automatic Caching For Documents.** Every file a user opens is automatically downloaded and cached on the user's hard disk so that it will be available offline. If an older version of a file is already loaded on the user's hard disk, it is automatically replaced with a newer version.

    ■ **Automatic Caching For Programs.** Opened files are automatically downloaded and cached on the user's hard disk so that they will be available offline. If an older version of a file is already loaded on the user's hard disk, it is automatically replaced with a newer version.

6. Ensure that Manual Caching For Documents is selected and then click OK.

7. Click OK to close the Offline Properties dialog box.

   Leave the Windows Explorer window open.

Synchronizing Files

File synchronization is straightforward if the copy of the file on the network doesn't change while you are editing a cached version of the file. Your edits are incorporated into the copy on the network. However, it is possible that another user could edit the network version of the file while you are working offline. If both of your cached offline copies of the file and the network copy of the file are edited, you are given a choice of retaining your edited version and not updating the network copy with your edits, of overwriting your cached version with the version on the network, or of keeping a copy of both versions of the file. In the last case, you must rename your version of the file, and both copies will exist on your hard disk and on the network.

Configuring Synchronization Manager

To configure Synchronization Manager, open Windows Explorer, click the Tools menu, and then click Synchronize. Notice that you can manually synchronize your offline files with those on the network by clicking the Synchronize button. You can also configure Synchronization Manager by clicking the Setup button.

In configuring Synchronization Manager, you have three sets of options for configuring synchronization. The first set of options is accessed through the Logon/Logoff tab (see Figure 24.3). You can configure synchronization to occur when you log on, when you log off, or at both times. You can also specify that you want to be asked before synchronization occurs. You can specify the items to be synchronized at logon, at logoff, or at both times, and you can specify which network connection.

The second set of options you can use to configure Synchronization Manager is available on the On Idle tab. The configurable items are similar to those that are configurable on the Logon/Logoff tab. The following configurable settings are available on the On Idle tab:

- **When I Am Using This Network Connection.** This option allows you to specify which network connection.

- **Synchronize The Following Checked Items.** This option allows you to specify which items you want to synchronize.

- **Synchronize The Selected Items While My Computer Is Idle.** This option allows you to turn synchronization off or on during idle time.

Figure 24.3 The Logon/Logoff tab in the Synchronization Settings dialog box

The Advanced button on the On Idle tab lets you configure the following options: Automatically Synchronize The Specified Items After My Computer Has Been Idle For *X* minutes, While My Computer Remains Idle, Repeat Synchronization Every *X* minutes, and Prevent Synchronization When My Computer Is Running On Battery Power.

You access the third set of options for scheduling synchronization on the Scheduled tab. You can click Add to start the Scheduled Synchronization Wizard to do the following: specify the connection; specify the items; decide whether you want the computer to automatically connect; determine whether you are not connected when the scheduled time for synchronization arrives; specify the starting time for the synchronization; specify the frequency of the synchronization, which you can set for every day, every weekday, or every *X* days; and specify the starting date for the synchronization to begin.

Practice: Configuring Synchronization Manager

In this practice, you will configure Synchronization Manager.

▶ **To configure Synchronization Manager**

1. Ensure that you are still logged on as Administrator.

    Windows Explorer should be open from the last practice.

2. Click Tools and then click Synchronize.

The Items To Synchronize dialog box appears. This allows you to specify which folders you want to synchronize.

3. If nothing is selected, click My Current Home Page, and then click Setup.

The Synchronization Settings dialog box appears with the Logon/Logoff tab selected.

4. Review the options on the Logon/Logoff tab, and then review the options on the On Idle tab and the Scheduled tab.

5. On the Logon/Logoff tab, select My Current Home Page.

6. Ensure that the check boxes When I Log On To My Computer and When I Log Off My Computer are both selected.

7. Select the Ask Me Before Synchronizing The Items check box, and then click OK.

8. Click Close to close the Items To Synchronize dialog box, and then close the Windows Explorer window.

Lesson Summary

Windows 2000 makes it easy to work offline, as you learned in this lesson. Working with offline folders and using Synchronization Manager make maintaining the versions of files cached on local computers and network servers or shares easy to keep synchronized. Before you can use offline folders and files, you must configure the server or network share and your laptop. This lesson also explained how to configure Synchronization Manager and the various sets of options available for synchronizing files.

Lesson 2: Configuring Power Options

The Power Options program in Control Panel in Windows 2000 Professional is important to mobile computer users. This utility allows you to configure power schemes, Hibernation mode, and the APM specification. This lesson introduces each of these topics and how each is configured.

After this lesson, you will be able to

- Configure power schemes.
- Enable Hibernate mode.
- Enable Advanced Power Management.

Estimated lesson time: 15 minutes

Configuring Power Schemes

Power schemes allow you to configure Windows 2000 to turn off the power to your monitor and your hard disk, which conserves energy when you aren't using your computer temporarily. To configure power schemes, you use the Power Options program in Control Panel. Your hardware must support powering off the monitor and hard disk for you to be able to configure power schemes.

Using Hibernate Mode

When your computer hibernates, it saves the current system state to your hard disk, and then your computer shuts down. When you restart the computer after it has been hibernating, it will return to its previous state. Restarting to the previous state includes automatically restarting any programs that were running when it went into Hibernate mode, and it will even restore any network connections that were active at the time. To configure your computer to use Hibernate mode, you use the Power Options program in Control Panel. Select the Hibernate tab in the Power Options Properties dialog box, and then select the Enable Hibernate Support check box.

Caution Many commercial airlines require you to turn off portable computers during certain portions of your flight. Standby mode might make your computer appear to be turned off, but it is not. You must shut down your computer to comply with these airline requirements.

Configuring Advanced Power Management

Windows 2000 supports the APM 1.2 specification. Using APM helps reduce the power consumption of your system. To configure your computer to use APM, you use the Power Options program in Control Panel. Select the APM tab in the Power Options Properties dialog box, and then select the Enable Advanced Power Management Support check box. You must be logged on as a member of the Administrators group to configure APM.

Note APM is available only in Windows 2000 Professional. It is not available in Windows 2000 Server, Windows 2000 Advanced Server, or Windows 2000 Datacenter.

If your computer doesn't have an APM-BIOS installed, then Windows 2000 will not install APM, and the Power Options Properties dialog box will not have an APM tab. However, your computer can still function as an ACPI computer if it has an ACPI-based BIOS. The ACPI-based BIOS takes over system configuration and power management from the Plug and Play BIOS.

If your laptop has an ACPI-based BIOS, you can insert and remove PC cards on the fly and Windows 2000 will automatically detect and configure them without requiring you to restart your machine. This is known as *dynamic configuration of PC cards.* Two other similar features rely on dynamic Plug and Play and are important to mobile computers: Hot and Warm Docking/Undocking and Hot Swapping of IDE and floppy devices.

Hot and Warm Docking/Undocking means you can dock and undock from the Windows 2000 Start button without turning off your computer. Windows 2000 automatically creates two hardware profiles for laptop computers, one for the docked state and one for the undocked state. (For more information on hardware profiles, see Chapter 4, "Using Windows Control Panel.")

Hot Swapping of IDE and floppy devices means that you can remove devices such as floppy drives, DVD/CD drives, and hard disks, you can swap devices, or you can do both, without shutting down your system or restarting it. Windows 2000 automatically detects and configures these devices.

Practice: Configuring Power Options

In this practice, you will use Control Panel to configure power options.

▶ **To configure power options**

1. Ensure that you are logged on as Administrator.
2. Click Start, point to Settings, and then click Control Panel.

   Control Panel appears.
3. Double-click Power Options.

The Power Options Properties dialog box appears with the Power Schemes tab active. In the Power Schemes box, you can select one of the preconfigured power schemes or you can create your own.

4. In the Power Schemes box, select Portable/Laptop.

5. In the Turn Off Monitor drop-down list, select After 10 Minutes.

6. In the Turn Off Hard Disks drop-down list, select After 20 Minutes.

7. Click Save As, and then in the Save Scheme box, type **Airplane** and then click OK.

8. Click Apply.

9. Click the Power Scheme drop-down list arrow to verify that you just created your own power scheme. You should see Airplane listed.

   From now on, whenever you want to use this power scheme, you would select it here and then click Apply.

10. Select the Hibernate tab.

11. Select the Enable Hibernate Support check box, and then click Apply.

    By selecting the Enable Hibernate Support check box and clicking Apply, you enable Hibernate mode on your computer.

12. Select the APM tab.

Note If you don't have an APM tab because your system doesn't have an APM-BIOS installed, skip this step and go to step 14.

---

13. Select the Enable Advanced Power Management Support check box, and then click Apply.

    By selecting the Enable Advanced Power Management Support check box and clicking Apply, you enable APM support on your computer.

14. Click OK to close the Power Options Properties dialog box.

Lesson Summary

In this lesson, you learned that the Power Options program in Control Panel allows you to configure power schemes, Hibernation mode, and the APM specification. This lesson introduced each of these topics and how each is configured. Power schemes allow you to configure Windows 2000 to turn off the power to your monitor and your hard disk, which conserves energy when you aren't using your computer temporarily.

When your computer hibernates, it saves the current system state to your hard disk before shutting down, and then when you restart the computer after it has been hibernating, it will return to its previous state. Restarting to the previous state includes automatically restarting any programs that were running when it went into Hibernate mode, and it will even restore any network connections that were active at the time.

Finally, you learned that Windows 2000 supports the APM 1.2 specification. Using APM helps reduce the power consumption of your system. You must be logged on as a member of the Administrators group to configure APM. If your computer doesn't have an APM-BIOS installed, then Windows 2000 won't install APM, and the Power Options Properties dialog box won't have an APM tab. However, your computer can still function as an ACPI computer if it has an ACPI-based BIOS.

Review

The following questions will help you determine whether you have learned enough to move on to the next chapter. If you have difficulty answering these questions, please go back and review the material in this chapter before beginning the next chapter. See Appendix A, "Questions and Answers," for the answers to these questions.

1. A friend of yours just installed Windows 2000 Professional on his home computer. He called you to help him configure APM, and when you told him to double-click Power Options in Control Panel and click on the APM tab, he told you he did not have an APM tab. What is the most likely reason there is no APM tab?

2. A user calls the help desk in a panic. She spent 15 hours editing a proposal as an offline file at her house. Over the weekend, her boss came in and spent about four hours editing the same proposal. She needs to synchronize the files, but she doesn't want to lose her edits or those made by her boss. What can she do?

3. Many commercial airlines require you to turn off portable computers during certain portions of a flight. Does placing your computer in Hibernate mode comply with these airline requirements? Why or why not?

CHAPTER 25

Implementing, Managing, and Troubleshooting Hardware Devices and Drivers

About This Chapter

One of the primary tools for implementing, managing, and troubleshooting hardware devices and drivers is Device Manager, a snap-in you'll find in Computer Management. This chapter introduces Device Manager and explains how you use it to manage and troubleshoot devices.

It also introduces the System Information snap-in and explains how it helps you manage your system. You learn how to use Device Manager, the System File Checker utility, and the File Signature Verification utility to configure, monitor, and troubleshoot driver signing. You also learn how to use Device Manager to upgrade your computer from a single processor to a multiprocessor system, and you learn how to use Performance Console as a tool to monitor system performance. Finally, you learn how to install, configure, and troubleshoot various devices, including fax support, scanners, cameras, mouse devices, modems, USB, Infrared Data Association (IrDA), wireless devices, and keyboards.

Before You Begin

To complete this chapter, you must have

- A computer that meets the minimum hardware requirements located in "About This Book."
- Microsoft Windows 2000 Professional software installed on the computer.

Lesson 1: Using Device Manager and System Information

This lesson introduces Device Manager and explains how you use it to manage and troubleshoot devices. This lesson also introduces the System Information snap-in, how to use it, and how it helps you manage your system.

After this lesson, you will be able to

- Use Device Manager to configure and troubleshoot devices.
- Use System Information to manage devices.

Estimated lesson time: 30 minutes

Introducing Device Manager

Device Manager is one of the snap-ins located under System Tools in Computer Management. Device Manager provides you with a graphical view of the hardware installed on your computer (see Figure 25.1) and helps you manage and troubleshoot it. You use Device Manager to disable, uninstall, and update device drivers.

Figure 25.1   The Device Manager snap-in

Note Device Manager works with Plug and Play devices and legacy devices supported in Windows NT 4.

Device Manager helps you to determine whether the hardware on your computer is working properly. It lists devices with problems, and each device that is flagged is displayed with the corresponding status information. Windows 2000 also provides the Hardware troubleshooter in online Help to troubleshoot hardware problems.

Installing Devices

Windows 2000 Professional supports Plug and Play hardware. For most devices that are Plug and Play compliant, as long as the appropriate driver is available and the BIOS on the computer is a Plug and Play BIOS or an ACPI BIOS, Windows 2000 automatically detects, installs, and configures the device.

For the occasional Plug and Play device that is not automatically detected, installed, and configured by Windows 2000, and for non–Plug and Play hardware that Windows 2000 doesn't identify, install, and configure, you initiate the installation of the hardware with the Add/Remove Hardware wizard. For a discussion on automatic hardware installation for Plug and Play devices and on using the Add/Remove Hardware wizard for manual hardware installation, see Chapter 4, "Using Windows Control Panel."

Configuring and Troubleshooting Devices

When you manually change device configurations, Device Manager can help you to avoid problems. Device Manager allows you to identify free resources and assign a device to that resource, disable devices to free resources, and reallocate resources used by devices to free a required resource. You must be logged on as a member of the Administrators group to change resource settings. Even if you are logged on as Administrator, if your computer is connected to a network, policy settings on the network might prevent you from changing resources.

Caution Improperly changing resource settings on devices can disable your hardware and cause your computer to no longer work.

Windows 2000 automatically identifies Plug and Play devices and arbitrates their resource requests. However, the resource allocation among Plug and Play devices isn't permanent. If another Plug and Play device requests a resource that has already been allocated, Windows 2000 again arbitrates the requests to satisfy all resource requests.

You should not manually change resource settings for a Plug and Play device because Windows 2000 won't be able to arbitrate the assigned resources if requested by another Plug and Play device. In Device Manager, Plug and Play devices have a Resources tab on their Properties dialog box. To free the resource settings you manually assigned and allow Windows 2000 to again arbitrate the resources, select the Use Automatic Settings check box on the Resources tab.

Note Devices that Windows NT 4 support have fixed resource settings. These resource settings are usually defined during an upgrade from Windows NT 4 to Windows 2000 Professional, but you can also define them by using the Add New Hardware wizard in Control Panel.

You can use Device Manager to configure or troubleshoot a device as follows:

1. Right-click My Computer, and then click Manage.

   The Computer Management window opens.

2. Under System Tools, click Device Manager.

3. In the Details pane, double-click the device type, and then double-click the device you want to configure.

   The *Device* Properties dialog box appears (where *Device* is a specific device).

   The tabs available on the Properties page for the device will vary depending on the device selected but might include some of those listed in Table 25.1.

4. To configure a device, choose the appropriate tab. To troubleshoot, on the General tab, click Troubleshooter.

Table 25.1   Properties Dialog Box Tabs for Selected Devices

Tab	Function
Advanced or Advanced Properties	The properties listed will vary depending on the device selected.
General	Displays the device type, manufacturer, and location. It also displays the device status and provides a troubleshooter to help you solve any problems you are having with the device. The troubleshooter steps you through a series of questions to determine the problem and provide a solution.
Device Properties	The properties listed will vary depending on the device selected.
Driver	Displays the driver provider, driver date, driver version, and digital signer. This tab also provides the following three additional buttons: Driver Details, Uninstall, and Driver Update. These buttons allow you to get additional information on the driver, uninstall the driver, or update the driver with a newer version.
Port Settings	In a communications port (COM1) Properties dialog box, displays and allows you to configure bits per second, data bits, parity, stop bits, and flow control.
Properties	Displays options that determine the way Windows uses the device. For example, on the CD-ROM, the properties could include Volume and Digital CD Playback, which allows you to enable digital instead of analog playback. These settings determine how Windows uses the CD-ROM for playing CD music.
Resources	Displays the resource type and setting, whether there are any resource conflicts, and whether you can change the resource settings.

Using the System Information Snap-In

System Information is a snap-in that you can add to a custom console (by using the MMC) so that you can manage devices by collecting and viewing configuration information about your system. To use System Information, use the MMC to create a custom console and add the System Information snap-in to it (see Figure 25.2). When you add the snap-in to a custom console, you can focus it on the local machine or on a remote machine. The System Information snap-in also helps you to troubleshoot problems. For more information on creating custom consoles, see Chapter 3, "Using Microsoft Management Console and Task Scheduler."

Figure 25.2   The System Information snap-in

Table 25.2 lists the nodes of the System Information snap-in.

Table 25.2   System Information Nodes

Node	Description
System Summary	Displays information such as the OS, the version number of the OS, and the manufacturer of the OS. It displays the NetBIOS computer name, the computer manufacturer, model number, and type, as well as information about the processor and the BIOS. It also lists the installation folder, locale, and time zone information. Finally, it lists the total and available physical memory, the total and available virtual memory, and the page file size.
Hardware Resources	Displays hardware resource settings such as any conflicts or resource sharing, DMA, IRQs, I/O addresses, and memory addresses.

Node	Description
Components	Displays information about the configuration and status of devices including the following categories: multimedia, display, infrared, input, modems, network, ports, storage, printing, problem devices, and USB.
Software Environment	Displays what is loaded into memory at a particular instant. The display includes the drivers, environment variables, network connections, tasks, and services loaded into memory.
Internet Explorer 5	Displays configuration settings for Microsoft Internet Explorer. The summary displays the version, build, product ID, install location, language, and cipher strength. It also displays a list of associated files and version numbers, settings for connectivity, file caching, and security.

Practice: Using Device Manager and System Information

In this practice, you will use Device Manager and System Information to monitor and review your system configuration. You will also use the troubleshooter to simulate solving a problem with a disk drive.

Exercise 1: Using Device Manager to Review Devices and to Troubleshoot a Device

In this exercise, you will practice using Device Manager to review the devices on your system and to review their status. You will also use Device Manager to simulate troubleshooting an unterminated SCSI chain.

▶   **To use Device Manager**

1. Right-click My Computer, and then click Manage.

   The Computer Management window opens.

2. Under System Tools, click Device Manager.

3. In the Details pane, double-click Disk Drives, and then double-click one of the drives listed.

   The Properties page appears and the General tab shows a Device Status that indicates if any problems exist with the drive.

4. Click Troubleshooter. (Normally you would do this only if a problem was indicated with this device.)

   Notice that online Help starts with the Drives Troubleshooter displayed. Troubleshooter steps you through a series of questions to help you resolve your problem.

5. Click I'm Having A Problem With My Hard Drive Or Floppy Disk Drive, and then click Next.

6. Click Yes, I'm Having A Problem With A SCSI Device, and then click Next.

   You are asked, "Does Your Device Work When You Terminate The SCSI Chain?"

7. Click Yes, My Device Works, and then click Next.

   If an unterminated SCSI chain was the problem you were trying to solve, you would have just fixed the problem.

8. Close online Help, close the Properties dialog box for the selected disk drive, and close the Computer Management window.

Exercise 2: Using System Information

In this exercise, you will practice using System Information to view configuration information about your computer.

▶ **To use System Information**

1. Use the MMC to create a custom console and add the System Information snap-in to it, with the focus directed on the local computer.

2. Double-click System Information in the console tree.

   Notice that a Refreshing System Information message appears in the details pane while System Information takes a snapshot of the current system configuration.

3. Review the information displayed in the details pane.

4. In the details pane, double-click Hardware Resources, and then double-click IRQs.

   Are there any IRQs being shared?

5. In the console pane, double-click Software Environment, and then double-click Services.

6. Review which services are running and which services are stopped.

7. Save the custom console containing the System Information snap-in as System Information, and then close System Information.

Lesson Summary

In this lesson, you learned about two of the Windows 2000 snap-ins: Device Manager and System Information. You learned how to use Device Manager to configure and troubleshoot devices. You also learned how to use System Information quickly to gather and display your system configuration and to help you manage and troubleshoot your computer.

Lesson 2: Configuring, Monitoring, and Troubleshooting Driver Signing

Windows 2000 drivers and operating system files have been digitally signed by Microsoft to ensure their quality. In Device Manager, you can look at the Driver tab to verify that the digital signer of the installed driver is correct. Some applications overwrite existing operating files as part of their installation process. These files can cause system errors that are difficult to troubleshoot. Microsoft has greatly simplified the tracking and troubleshooting of altered files by signing the original operating system files and allowing you to easily verify these signatures.

After this lesson, you will be able to

- Configure driver signing.
- Describe the System File Checker (SFC) utility and how to use it to verify and troubleshoot driver signing.
- Use the Windows Signature Verification utility to monitor and troubleshoot driver signing.

Estimated lesson time: 20 minutes

Configuring Driver Signing

You can configure how the system responds to unsigned files by opening System in Control Panel and clicking the Hardware tab. On the Hardware tab, in the Device Manager box, click Driver Signing to display the Driver Signing Options dialog box (see Figure 25.3).

Figure 25.3   Configuring Driver Signing

The following three settings are available to configure driver signing:

- **Ignore**. This option allows any files to be installed regardless of their digital signature or the lack thereof.

- **Warn**. This option displays a warning message before allowing the installation of an unsigned file. This is the default option.

- **Block**. This option prevents the installation of unsigned files.

If you are logged on as Administrator or as a member of the Administrators group, you can select Apply Setting As System Default to apply the driver signing configuration you set up to all users who log on to this computer.

Monitoring and Troubleshooting Driver Signing

As you saw in Lesson 1, "Using Device Manager and System Information," you can use Device Manager to track the digital signature of files. Windows 2000 also provides SFC, a command-line utility that you can use to check the digital signature of files. The syntax of the System File Checker utility is as follows:

```
Sfc [/scannow] [/scanonce] [/scanboot] [/cancel] [/quiet] [/enable]
[/purgecache] [/cachesize=x]
```

Table 25.3 explains System File Checker's optional parameters.

Table 25.3   System File Checker's Parameters

Parameter	Description
/scannow	Causes the SFC utility to scan all protected system files immediately
/scanonce	Causes the SFC utility to scan all protected system files at the next system restart
/scanboot	Causes the SFC utility to scan all protected system files every time the system restarts
/cancel	Cancels all pending scans of protected system files
/quiet	Replaces all incorrect system file versions without prompting the user
/enable	Returns Windows File Protection to default operation, prompting the user to restore protected system files when files with incorrect versions are detected
/purgecache	Purges the file cache and scans all protected system files immediately
/cachesize=x	Sets the file cache size

Using the File Signature Verification Utility

Windows 2000 also provides a File Signature Verification utility. To use this utility, click Start, point to Run, type **sigverif** and press Enter. Once the File Signature Verification utility starts, you can click the Advanced button to configure it.

The File Signature Verification utility allows you to view the file's name, its location, its modification date, its type, and its version number.

Practice: Using the Windows Signature Verification Utility

In this practice, you will use the File Signature Verification utility (sigverif) to monitor and troubleshoot driver signing on your system.

▶ **To use sigverif**

1. Click Start, point to Run, type **sigverif** and then press Enter.

   The File Signature Verification dialog box appears.

2. Click Advanced.

   The Advanced File Signature Verification Settings dialog box appears with the Search tab active. Notice that by default, you are notified if any system files are not signed. Notice also that you can select Look For Other Files That Are Not Digitally Signed. This setting has the File Signature Verification utility verify nonsystem files to see whether they are digitally signed. If you select this option, you can specify the search parameters for the files you want checked.

3. Leave the default setting, Notify Me If Any System Files Are Not Signed, selected and then click the Logging tab.

   Notice that by default, the File Signature Verification utility saves the file signature verification to a log file, named Sigverif.txt.

4. Leave the default settings and click OK to close the Advanced File Signature Verification Settings dialog box.

5. Click Start.

   When the File Signature Verification utility completes its check, a Signature Verification Results window will appear if there are files that are not signed. Otherwise you will see a message box telling you that your files have been scanned and verified as being digitally signed.

6. If you get a Signature Verification Results window, review the results and then click Close to close the Signature Verification Results window. Otherwise, click OK to close the message box.

7. Click Close to exit the File Signature Verification utility.

Lesson Summary

In this lesson, you learned about the two utilities that verify the digital signatures of system files. One is a command-line utility: System File Checker. It has a number of optional parameters that let you control how and when it will run. The second utility is a Windows utility, File Signature Verification. You practiced monitoring and troubleshooting digital signatures using the File Signature Verification utility.

Lesson 3: Configuring Computers with Multiple Processors and Monitoring System Performance

This lesson explains how to use Device Manager to upgrade your computer from a single processor to a multiprocessor system. It also introduces Performance Console and explains how to use it to monitor system performance.

After this lesson, you will be able to

- Use Device Manager to update drivers.
- Use Device Manager to upgrade your computer from a single processor to a multiprocessor computer.
- Use Performance Console to monitor your system.

Estimated lesson time: 20 minutes

Scaling

Adding processors to your system to improve performance is called *scaling*. This is really more of a Windows 2000 Server family of products issue than it is a Windows 2000 Professional issue because multiprocessor configurations are typically used for processor-intensive applications, such as those found on database servers or Web servers. However, any computer that runs applications that perform heavy computation such as scientific or financial applications, and complex graphics rendering, such as computer aided design (CAD) programs, also benefit from multiprocessor systems.

Updating Drivers

You use Device Manager to upgrade drivers. You upgrade a driver whenever a newer version of the driver is released. You also update drivers to convert your computer from a single processor system to one that supports multiple processors, for example.

Use the following steps to upgrade the drivers loaded on a computer so that it can function as a multiple processor computer.

Caution This procedure upgrades only the driver on your computer. If your computer has only a single processor, upgrading the driver isn't going to make it a multiple processor computer. In fact, a computer with only one processor can no longer function if you upgrade the driver to one that supports multiple processors.

---

1. Open Device Manager, and double-click Computer.
2. Right-click the appropriate model, and then click Properties.
3. On the Driver tab, click Update Driver.

The Welcome To The Upgrade Device Driver Wizard page appears.

4. Click Next.

The Install Hardware Device Drivers page appears.

5. Click Display A List Of The Known Drivers For This Device So That I Can Choose A Specific Driver, and then click Next.

The Select A Device Driver page appears.

6. Click Show All Hardware Of This Device Class.

7. Under Manufacturers, click the appropriate manufacturer.

8. Under Models, click the appropriate computer model, and then click Next.

An Update Driver Warning might appear indicating that Windows cannot verify that the driver you want to install is compatible with your hardware, and installing it might cause your computer to become unstable or stop working. If you are sure you want to continue, click Yes. Otherwise, click No.

9. Click Next, and then click Finish.

Using Performance Console to Monitor System Performance

You can monitor the activity of your symmetric multiprocessing (SMP) system by using Performance Console and its counters. Performance Console helps you to gauge a computer's efficiency and locate and resolve current or potential problems. In Performance Console, a set of counters exists for each object. Table 25.4 describes a few of the available objects.

Table 25.4   Performance Console Objects

Object	Description
Cache	Monitors the file system cache that is used to buffer physical device data
Memory	Monitors the physical and virtual memory on the computer
PhysicalDisk	Monitors a hard disk as a whole
Processor	Monitors CPUs

Adding Counters

Adding counters to an object, such as the ones described in Table 25.4, allows you to track certain aspects of the objects. You can use the following steps to add counters to an object in Performance Console.

1. Click Start, point to Programs, point to Administrative Tools, and then click Performance.

Performance Console starts.

2. At the bottom of the console, right-click Counters and click Add Counters.

   The Add Counters dialog box appears.

3. In the Performance Object box, select the object for which you want to add counters.

4. Ensure that Select Counters From List is selected.

   You can add all counters, but that usually provides more information than you need or can interpret.

5. Select a counter from the list and click Add.

   For an explanation of a counter, select it and then click Explain.

Note If you want to add several counters at the same time, you can hold the Ctrl key down to allow you to select individual counters from the list. You can hold down the Shift key if you want to select several counters in a row, and click the first in the list that you want and then click the last in the list that you want to select. All counters listed between the first and last you clicked will automatically be selected.

---

6. When you have completed your selection of objects and counters, click Close to return to Performance Console.

Table 25.5 explains a few of the counters you might find useful in evaluating your system's performance.

Table 25.5   Performance Counters

Counter	Description
Under Processor, choose % Processor Time	The percentage of time that the processor spends executing a non-idle thread; this counter is an indicator of percentage of time that the processor is active. During some operations, this can reach 100 percent. These periods of 100 percent activity should occur only occasionally and should not reflect the normal amount of activity for the processor.
Under Processor, choose % DPC Time	Determines how much time the processor is spending processing deferred procedure calls (DPCs). *DPCs* are software interrupts or tasks that require immediate processing, causing other tasks to be handled at a lower priority. DPCs represent further processing of client requests.
Under Processor, choose Interrupts/Sec	The average number of hardware interrupts the processor is receiving and servicing in each second. It doesn't include DPCs. This counter value is an indicator of the activity of devices that generate interrupts, such as the system clock, mouse, network adapter cards, and other peripheral devices. If the processor time value is more than 90 percent and the Interrupts/Sec value is greater than 15 percent, this processor probably needs assistance to handle the interrupt load.

Counter	Description
Under System, choose Processor Queue Length	The number of threads in the processor queue. There is a single queue for processor time, even on computers with multiple processors. A sustained processor queue of greater than two threads usually indicates that the processor is causing a problem to the overall system performance.

Note Upgrading to multiple processors can increase the load on other system resources. You might need to increase other resources such as disks, memory, and network components to get the maximum benefit out of scaling.

Lesson Summary

In this lesson you learned about *scaling,* which means adding processors to your system to improve performance. Scaling tends to be more of an issue for the Windows 2000 Server family of products than it is for Windows 2000 Professional because multiprocessor configurations are typically used for processor-intensive applications, such as those on database servers or Web servers.

You also learned to use Device Manager to upgrade drivers whenever a newer version of the driver is released. You can also update drivers to convert your computer from a single processor system to one that supports multiple processors.

You learned as well that you can use Performance Console and its counters to monitor the activity of your symmetric multiprocessing (SMP) system. Performance Console helps you to gauge a computer's efficiency and locate and resolve current or potential problems. Adding counters to an object allows you to track certain aspects of the objects.

Lesson 4: Installing, Managing, and Troubleshooting Devices

This lesson explains how to install, configure, and troubleshoot miscellaneous devices, including fax and mouse support.

After this lesson, you will be able to

- Configure and troubleshoot a fax device.
- Manage and troubleshoot I/O devices.

Estimated lesson time: 15 minutes

Configuring and Troubleshooting Fax Support

If you have a fax device, such as a fax modem installed, then Control Panel will have a Fax icon. You can use the Fax icon to add, monitor, and troubleshoot fax devices, including fax modems and fax printers. Double-click the Fax icon, and then select the Advanced Options tab.

Note The Advanced Options tab appears only if you are logged on as Administrator or have administrator privileges.

The following three selections are available on the Advanced Options page:

- **Open Fax Service Management Console.** This option allows you to view any fax devices you have installed and to change any properties for any of these devices.
- **Open Fax Services Management Help.** This option allows you to start a Help session for the Open Fax Services Management Console.
- **Add A Fax Printer.** This option allows you to install a fax printer.

Using the Fax Service Management Console

Using the Fax Service Management window, you can administer fax support on your local computer or on other computers on your network. By default, you are set up to send a fax, not to receive a fax. The functionality of the Fax Service Management console includes the following:

- Setting up your fax devices to receive faxes
- Changing security permissions for users
- Changing the number of rings before a fax device answers a fax receive
- Configuring the number of retries before a fax terminates a fax send
- Configuring where to store sent and received faxes

The Open Fax Services Management Help option provides online Help for the Fax Service Management console. You can use the third option, Add A Fax Printer, to install a fax printer. The newly installed fax printer is added to the Printers folder.

Faxing a Document

You can use any Windows-based application that contains a Print command to fax a document. Click File and then click Print to open the Print dialog box. Select the fax printer, and then click Print to open the Send Fax wizard. The wizard will guide you through any configuration and help you send the fax.

Monitoring a Fax

Open Fax in Control Panel and select the Status Monitor tab. Ensure that Display The Status Monitor is selected and click OK. This option displays the Fax Monitor dialog box automatically when a fax is sent or a call is received. The Fax Monitor dialog box allows you to view details of the fax being sent— for example, whether the fax is actually being sent or whether the system is still dialing and trying to establish a connection. The Fax dialog box also allows you to easily end a fax call.

Managing and Troubleshooting I/O Devices

The list of devices that you can install is too long to include in this book. However, this section includes some of the more common devices you can install as well as how they are installed, configured, and managed.

Scanners and Cameras

Most scanners and cameras are Plug and Play devices, and Windows 2000 will install them automatically when you connect them to your computer. If they aren't installed automatically when you connect your computer, or if they aren't Plug and Play compatible, use the Scanner And Camera Installation wizard. To open this wizard, double-click Scanners And Cameras in Control Panel, and then click Add.

To configure a scanner or a camera, double-click Scanners And Cameras in Control Panel to open the Scanners And Cameras Properties dialog box, select the appropriate device, and then click Properties. To give you a configuration example, the standard color profile for Integrated Color Management (ICM 2) is RGB, but you can add, remove, or select an alternate color profile for a device. To change the color profile, click the Color Management tab. If you are having problems with your scanner or camera, click Troubleshoot in the Scanners And Cameras Properties dialog box.

Mouse Devices

Double-click the Mouse icon in Control Panel to open the Mouse Properties dialog box, which you can use to configure and troubleshoot your mouse. The Buttons tab allows you to configure your Mouse for a lefthanded or righthanded user. It also allows you to configure your mouse so that a single mouse click either selects an item or opens an item. You can also use this tab to control the double-click speed of your mouse.

The Pointers tab allows you to select or create a custom scheme for your pointer. The Motion tab allows you to adjust the speed and acceleration of your pointer and to set Snap To Default, which moves the pointer automatically to the default button in dialog boxes. The Hardware tab allows you to access the troubleshooter and advanced configuration for your mouse's port. Advanced configuration also includes uninstalling or updating your driver, viewing or changing the resources allocated to your mouse, and increasing or decreasing the sensitivity of your mouse by varying the sample rate, which changes how often Windows 2000 determines the position of your mouse.

Modems

To install or configure a modem, double-click Phone And Modem Options in Control Panel, and select the Modems tab. To configure an installed modem, select the modem from the list of installed modems and click Properties. Select the appropriate tab for the configuration changes you want to make. For example, select the General tab to set the maximum port speed, and select the Wait For Dial Tone Before Dialing check box if you want the modem to wait for a dial tone before dialing in to another computer. The Diagnostics tab helps you to troubleshoot the modem. If you want to add a modem, click Add to start the Add/Remove Hardware wizard, which will step you through the process of installing a modem. For additional information on the Add/Remove Hardware wizard, see Chapter 4, "Using Windows Control Panel."

Universal Serial Bus Devices

To install a USB device, for example, a USB game controller, attach the USB game controller to a USB port. If a USB device doesn't install properly, in Device Manager, look under Human Interface Devices. If the controller isn't listed, then check to make sure that USB is enabled in BIOS. When prompted during system startup, enter BIOS setup and enable USB. If USB is enabled in BIOS, contact the maker or vendor for your computer and obtain the current version of BIOS.

To configure the controller, select it in Device Manager and then right-click it and select Properties. In Device Status, a message will describe any problems and suggest what action you can take. You might also need to check the USB port entry in Device Manager. Click Universal Serial Bus controllers, right-click USB Hub, and then click Properties.

IrDA Devices and Wireless Devices

Most Internal IrDA devices should be installed by Windows 2000 Setup, or once you start Windows 2000 after adding one of these devices. If you attach an IrDA transceiver to a serial port, you must install it using the Add/Remove Hardware wizard. For additional information on the Add/Remove Hardware wizard, see Chapter 4, "Using Windows Control Panel."

To configure an IrDA device, in Control Panel, click Wireless Link. On the Hardware tab, click the device you want to configure and then click Properties.

Keyboards

To configure your keyboard, double-click Keyboards in Control Panel. On the Input Locales tab, you can add and remove locales and control the hot keys to switch between locales.

Note The icons you see in Control Panel will depend on the devices you have installed.

Lesson Summary

In this lesson you learned that you can use the Fax program in Control Panel, if you have a fax device installed, to add, monitor, and troubleshoot fax devices, including fax modems and fax printers. By default, you are set up to send a fax, but not to receive a fax. You also learned that you can use the Fax Service Management window to administer fax support on your local computer or on other computers on your network, including setting up fax devices to receive faxes, changing security permissions for users, configuring where to store sent and received faxes, and other settings. You also learned that you can use any Windows-based application that contains a Print command to fax a document. Generally, this involves using a Send Fax wizard that guides you through any configuration settings and helps you send the fax.

You also learned how to install, configure, and manage some of the more common devices that may be connected to your system, including: scanners and cameras, mouse devices, modems, USB devices, IrDA devices, wireless devices, and keyboards.

Review

The following questions will help you determine whether you have learned the material presented in this chapter. If you have difficulty answering these questions, please go back and review the chapter. See Appendix A, "Questions and Answers," for the answers to these questions.

1. Your boss has started to manually assign resource settings to all devices, including Plug and Play devices, and wants you to finish the job. What should you do?

2. What benefits do you gain by Microsoft digitally signing all system files?

3. What are three ways Microsoft has provided to help you make sure the files on your system have the correct digital signature?

4. You receive a call at the Help desk from a user who is trying to configure her fax settings, and she tells you that she doesn't have an Advanced Options tab. What could the problem be?

Preparation for MCP Exam 70-210

Installing Windows 2000 Professional

Installing Microsoft Windows 2000 Professional is a complex task with many decision points along the way. The Installing Windows 2000 Professional Objective Domain encapsulates this complexity by categorizing installation into preparing for and performing two types: attended (manual) installation and unattended (automated) installation. A variety of automated installation methods exist using technologies such as the Remote Installation Service (RIS), the System Preparation (SYSPREP.EXE) utility, and WINNT.EXE or WINNT32.EXE with unattended answer files. An important factor in deciding on an appropriate installation method is determining whether installed operating systems and applications will be upgraded or removed and replaced with new installations. This Objective Domain includes questions about upgrading to Windows 2000 Professional, applying updates to installed applications, and deploying service packs. A task as complex as installation requires expertise with troubleshooting installation failures, the last objective in the Installing Windows 2000 Professional Objective Domain.

The Installing Windows 2000 Professional Objective Domain measures your ability to install Windows 2000 Professional on computers containing other operating systems, to install the operating system on computers in a variety of network environments, such as Novell NetWare and UNIX, and to troubleshoot installation failures. Expect a number of case studies on the exam that test your aptitude for choosing the ideal installation method when given detailed and often complex information on various computing environments.

Tested Skills and Suggested Practices

The skills you need to successfully master the Installing Windows 2000 Professional Objective Domain on Exam 70-210: Installing, Configuring, and Administering Microsoft Windows 2000 Professional include the following:

- **Verify that a computer meets all requirements for a new installation or upgrade to Windows 2000 Professional.**

  - Practice 1: Review the minimum hardware requirements for installing Windows 2000 Professional. (See the introduction to Objective 1.1.)

  - Practice 2: Check compatibility of computers by running the Microsoft Windows 2000 Readiness Analyzer. This tool is named CHKUPGRD.EXE and can be downloaded from *http://www.microsoft.com* by first searching for the title, Windows 2000 Readiness Analyzer. Additionally, run WINNT32 with the /checkupgradeonly switch. On a computer running Microsoft Windows 95 or Microsoft Windows 98, review *%windir%*\UPGRADE.TXT; on a computer running Microsoft Windows NT, review *%windir%*\WINNT32.LOG.

  - Practice 3: Check the system BIOS to verify that it is compatible with Windows 2000. If it isn't compatible, reconfigure the BIOS, update it, or complete both procedures.

- **Manually install Windows 2000 Professional.**

  - Practice 1: Observe the phases of installation by running several Windows 2000 Professional attended installation procedures on computers with no operating system and computers with existing Windows 32-bit operating systems.

  - Practice 2: Observe the phases of installation on a computer running MS-DOS by loading SMARTDRV.EXE and then running a 16-bit (WINNT.EXE) installation of Windows 2000 Professional.

- **Create and run automated installations of Windows 2000 Professional.**

  - Practice 1: Type **winnt32 /?** and study the installation switches.

  - Practice 2: Run Setup Manager to create an unattended installation file for a single computer. Run Setup Manager again, but this time, use a UDB for multi-computer automated computer setup. Run a Windows 2000 Professional installation using the answer file and UDB file that Setup Manager created.

▪ Practice 3: Build and run a RIS-based deployment structure by doing the following: install and configure RIS on a computer running Windows 2000 Server; install and configure Windows 2000 Professional; use the RIS image preparation tool, RIPrep (RIPREP.EXE), to prepare and upload the image to a Microsoft Windows 2000 Server RIS server; and create a Remote Boot Disk or use a PXE-capable computer to boot to the network and run a RIS-based installation.

▪ Practice 4: Prepare a computer running Windows 2000 Professional for cloning by running the System Preparation (SYSPREP.EXE) utility. Use the image prepared with the System Preparation utility (often called "SysPrep") to run a semiautomated installation.

▪ Practice 5: Use Setup Manager to further automate an image installation prepared with SysPrep. Use the answer file and the SysPrep supporting files to run a fully automated installation.

▪ Practice 6: Type **sysprep /?** and review the command parameters.

- **Upgrade to Windows 2000 Professional and deploy service packs.**

  ▪ Practice 1: Run installation procedures to upgrade Windows 95, Windows 98, and Windows NT Workstation to Windows 2000 Professional.

  ▪ Practice 2: Upgrade Windows 9*x* applications that use the migration DLL facility in the Windows 2000 Professional setup routine.

  ▪ Practice 3: Run UPDATE.EXE to apply the latest Windows 2000 service pack and review the UPDATE.EXE switches.

- **Troubleshoot the Windows 2000 installation.**

  ▪ Practice 1: Open and review the contents of log files contained in the boot partition's operating system folder (*%systemroot%*) so that you are familiar with their purpose.

  ▪ Practice 2: Use the HCL to determine any hardware incompatibilities and to obtain any information on updates needed to meet compatibility requirements.

  ▪ Practice 3: Visit computer hardware manufacturer Web sites to learn about BIOS update procedures to support an installation of Windows 2000 Professional.

Further Reading

This "Further Reading" section provides lists of important readings to supplement your current understanding of the skills tested within this Objective Domain. The lists are delineated into pertinent readings for each objective within this Objective Domain. If you feel that you need additional preparation prior to taking the exam, study these sources thoroughly.

Objective 1.1

Microsoft Corporation. *Windows 2000 Professional Upgrade Guide*. Redmond, Washington: Microsoft Press, 2000. This guide explains how to prepare for a Windows 2000 Professional operating system upgrade in a simple network environment. You can locate this document at *http://www.microsoft.com* by searching for the title.

Microsoft Corporation. *MCSE Training Kit—Microsoft Windows 2000 Professional*. Redmond, Washington: Microsoft Press, 2000. Read and complete the lessons and practices in Chapter 2, "Installing Windows 2000 Professional."

Microsoft Corporation. *Microsoft Windows 2000 Professional Resource Kit*. Redmond, Washington: Microsoft Press, 2000. Read Chapter 4, "Installing Windows 2000 Professional." Review Appendix C, "Hardware Support."

Objective 1.2

Microsoft Corporation. *MCSE Training Kit—Microsoft Windows 2000 Professional*. Redmond, Washington: Microsoft Press, 2000. Read the lessons and complete the practices in Lessons 1, 2, and 3 in Chapter 23, "Deploying Windows 2000."

Microsoft Corporation. *Microsoft Windows 2000 Professional Resource Kit*. Redmond, Washington: Microsoft Press, 2000. Read Chapter 5, "Customizing and Automating Installations," and review Appendix B, "Sample Answer Files for Windows 2000 Professional Setup."

Microsoft Corporation. *Microsoft Windows 2000 Server Resource Kit Deployment and Planning Guide*. Redmond, Washington: Microsoft Press, 2000. Read Chapter 6, "Windows 2000 Professional/Client Deployment."

Microsoft Corporation. Microsoft Windows 2000 Resource Kit Deployment Tools Help (DEPTOOL.CHM). Available on the Windows 2000 Professional CD-ROM in the \Support\Tools\DEPLOY.CAB file. This online help file explains how to use Setup Manager and SysPrep.

Objective 1.3

Microsoft Corporation. *MCSE Training Kit—Microsoft Windows 2000 Professional*. Redmond, Washington: Microsoft Press, 2000. Read Lesson 4, Chapter 23, "Deploying Windows 2000."

Microsoft Corporation. "Upgrading from Previous Versions of Windows." This Web page contains a number of documents detailing upgrade paths from other operating systems. You can find this resource by searching on the title at *http://www.microsoft.com/windows2000*.

Objective 1.4

Microsoft Corporation. *MCSE Training Kit—Microsoft Windows 2000 Professional*. Redmond, Washington: Microsoft Press, 2000. Read Lesson 5, Chapter 23, "Deploying Windows 2000."

Objective 1.5

Microsoft Corporation. *Microsoft Windows 2000 Professional Resource Kit*. Redmond, Washington: Microsoft Press, 2000. Read Chapter 6, "Setup and Startup," and Chapter 31, "Troubleshooting Tools and Strategies."

OBJECTIVE   1.1

Perform an attended installation of Windows 2000 Professional.

Before installing Windows 2000 Professional, you must assess the computer's compatibility with the operating system. Compatibility falls into two categories: hardware and software. The hardware must meet the minimum requirements for running the operating system and while not mandatory, all hardware components should appear on the Windows 2000 Hardware Compatibility List (HCL).

You can find the latest edition of the HCL at *http://www.microsoft.com* by searching on the keywords, Windows 2000 HCL. You can find a local copy of the HCL in the HCL.TXT file contained in the \Support folder on the Windows 2000 Professional CD-ROM. Another important Internet location for assessing your computer's readiness for Windows 2000 Professional is the Windows 2000 home page at *http://www.microsoft.com/windows2000/*. From the Windows 2000 home page, locate the Hardware and Software Compatibility page. The Hardware and Software Compatibility page contains the Windows 2000 Readiness Analyzer program, links to information on basic input/output system (BIOS) compatibility, and summary information on upgrading from previous versions of Windows. Running the Windows 2000 Readiness Analyzer and typing **winnt32 /checkupgradeonly** at the command line verifies hardware and software compatibility.

Note Hardware compatibility does not guarantee that the Windows 2000 Professional installation CD-ROM contains all of the Windows 2000 drivers for your hardware. If the Windows 2000 Professional installation CD-ROM does not contain a required driver, contact the hardware manufacturer for a driver update.

The minimum resource requirements for a computer running Windows 2000 Professional are as follows:

- Pentium class 133-MHz processor

- 64 MB RAM

- 650 MB free space for the boot partition

- Disk space for the boot and system partitions that have not been compressed using technologies such as Windows 9*x* DriveSpace or DoubleSpace

---

Caution If an existing partition will be used for the system and boot partitions, the partition must be running a compatible file system.

After you have established hardware and software compatibility and properly configured the BIOS, you must plan how to install Windows 2000 Professional. Checking for viruses on the local computer and assessing whether existing files on the computer need to be backed up are the next critical steps you must perform prior to installation. After you back up any critical files, installation begins. Factors influencing how Windows 2000 Professional should be installed include but are not limited to the following:

- The presence or absence of an existing operating system

  If an operating system is running on the computer, assess whether it will be preserved, upgraded, or removed.

- The level of required security

- Any networks to which the computer will be connected

  The network and network service interactions will significantly affect operating system installation and configuration.

- The purpose of the installation

  You must understand how the computer running Windows 2000 Professional will be used.

To answer the questions in this objective, you must be proficient with manually installing Windows 2000 Professional on a variety of hardware platforms in various configuration states. For example, if the computer is connected to a network running Microsoft Windows NT Server or Windows 2000 Server and the computer will be joined to the domain, you must create a computer account in the domain.

Objective 1.1 Questions

70-210.01.01.001

You have acquired a new Pentium III computer with two blank hard disks, a 40x CD-ROM drive, an AGP display adapter, and a Fast Ethernet network adapter. All hardware is on the HCL. You want to achieve these results:

- Install Windows 2000 Professional on the computer.

- Minimize the time required to install Windows 2000 Professional.

- Choose a file system to enable maximum security of data on the computer.

- Have the computer join your domain.

Your proposed solution is to start the computer, access its BIOS, set the computer to boot from the CD-ROM drive, save the changes, and restart the computer. When Setup runs, complete the necessary tasks and specify the NTFS partition type. After restarting the computer again, restore the original boot disk configuration in the BIOS. When prompted, specify the appropriate domain name.

Which results does the proposed solution provide? (Choose three.)

A. Windows 2000 Professional is installed on the computer.

B. The time required to install Windows 2000 Professional is minimized.

C. The specified file system enables maximum security of data on the computer.

D. The computer joins your domain.

70-210.01.01.002

You have acquired a new Pentium III computer with two blank hard disks, a 40x CD-ROM drive, an AGP display adapter, and a Fast Ethernet network adapter. All hardware is on the HCL. You want to achieve these results:

- Install Windows 2000 Professional on the computer.

- Minimize the time required to install Windows 2000 Professional.

- Choose a file system to enable maximum security of data on the computer.

- Have the computer join your Windows 2000 domain.

Your proposed solution is to insert the Windows 2000 Professional installation CD-ROM into the CD-ROM drive and start the computer from the Setup Boot Disk. When installation runs, complete the necessary tasks, insert the other Setup Disks when prompted, and specify the NTFS partition type. When prompted, specify the appropriate domain name. Which results does the proposed solution provide? (Choose two.)

A. Windows 2000 Professional is installed on the computer.

B. The time required to install Windows 2000 Professional is minimized.

C. The specified file system enables maximum security of data on the computer.

D. The computer joins your domain.

70-210.01.01.003

You have acquired a new Pentium III computer with two blank hard disks, a 40x CD-ROM drive, an AGP display adapter, and a Fast Ethernet network adapter. All hardware is on the HCL. You want to achieve these results:

- Install Windows 2000 Professional on the computer.

- Minimize the time required to install Windows 2000 Professional.

- Choose a file system to enable maximum security of data on the computer.

- Have the computer join your domain.

Your proposed solution is to insert the Windows 2000 Professional installation CD-ROM and start the computer from the Setup Boot Disk. When Setup runs, complete the necessary tasks, insert the other Setup Disks when prompted, and specify the FAT32 partition type. When prompted, specify the appropriate domain name.

Which results does the proposed solution provide? (Choose one.)

A. Windows 2000 Professional is installed on the computer.

B. The time required to install Windows 2000 Professional is minimized.

C. The specified file system enables maximum security of data on the computer.

D. The computer joins your domain.

Objective 1.1 Answers

70-210.01.01.001

▶ **Correct Answers: A, B, and C**

A. **Correct:** The installation of Windows 2000 Professional is likely to succeed because it is being run on HCL-certified computer hardware. Installation is possible by starting the setup routine from the Windows 2000 installation CD-ROM on a computer with a bootable CD-ROM BIOS that supports the El Torito specification. After the BIOS is configured to boot from the CD-ROM drive, insert the Windows 2000 Professional installation CD-ROM into the drive bay, restart the computer, and Windows 2000 Professional installation proceeds. On computers that do not include bootable CD-ROM support, you can use the other Windows 2000 Professional installation methods: Setup Boot Disk, over-the-network, and automated installation.

B. **Correct:** By configuring the BIOS to boot from the CD-ROM drive, the four Setup Disks are unnecessary. Starting Windows 2000 Professional installation from the CD-ROM drive instead of the floppy drive reduces the installation time. Immediately after the first restart during setup, the boot from CD-ROM feature in the BIOS starts Windows 2000 Professional Setup again. The setup routine then pauses and prompts you to either continue the installation process by booting from the system partition on the fixed disk or starting the setup routine again from the CD-ROM. If no answer is provided in 30 seconds, the setup process continues from the fixed disk.

C. **Correct:** NTFS provides for local permissions at the folder and file levels. Local permissions secure the file system from both local and over-the-network access. The version of NTFS shipped with Windows 2000 Professional also supports the Encrypting File System (EFS). EFS is a security feature that enables a user to encrypt files so that others cannot read the data within them.

D. **Incorrect:** Before a computer can join a domain, you must create a computer object (previously known as a computer account in Windows NT 4 domains) in a container of the Windows 2000 domain. You can accomplish this step during the installation process if you have access to a user account with the Add Workstation To Domain privilege in the domain or the privilege to create computer objects in a container of the domain. Alternatively, an administrator or a user in a Windows 2000 domain who has been granted the necessary privilege can add the computer object to the domain prior to running the Windows 2000 Professional installation. Nothing in the proposed solution suggests that one of these procedures was completed.

70-210.01.01.002

▶ **Correct Answers: A and C**

A. **Correct:** The installation of Windows 2000 Professional is likely to succeed because it is being run on HCL-certified computer hardware. Installation is possible by booting from the Setup Boot Disk and inserting the other Setup Disks when prompted. You can create the four Setup Disks by using the MAKEBOOT.EXE or MAKEBT32.EXE utilities located in the \Bootdisk folder on the Windows 2000 Professional installation CD-ROM. MAKEBOOT.EXE creates the Setup Disks (3.5" high-density floppy disks) on computers running 16-bit operating systems and Windows 9x. MAKEBT32.EXE creates Setup Disks on computers running Windows NT or Windows 2000.

B. **Incorrect:** Installing Windows 2000 Professional using the Setup Boot Disk method is the most common manual installation method, but it's also the most tedious. Therefore, using this method does not minimize the time required to install the operating system.

C. **Correct:** NTFS provides for local permissions at the folder and file levels. Local permissions secure the file system from both local and over-the-network access. The version of NTFS shipped with Windows 2000 Professional also supports the Encrypting File System (EFS). EFS protects file data so that users without the proper decryption key cannot read it.

D. **Incorrect:** Before a computer can join a domain, you must create a computer object (previously known as a computer account in Windows NT 4 domains) in a container of the Windows 2000 domain. You can accomplish this step during the installation process if you have access to a user account with the Add Workstation To Domain privilege in the domain or the privilege to create computer objects in a container of the domain. Alternatively, an administrator or a user in a Windows 2000 domain who has been granted the necessary privilege can add the computer object to the domain prior to running the Windows 2000 Professional installation. Nothing in the proposed solution suggests that one of these procedures was completed.

70-210.01.01.003

▶ **Correct Answers: A**

A. **Correct:** The installation of Windows 2000 Professional is likely to succeed because it is being run on HCL-certified computer hardware. Installation is possible by booting from the Setup Boot Disk and inserting the other Setup Disks when prompted.

B. **Incorrect:** Installing Windows 2000 Professional using the Setup Boot Disk method is the most common manual installation method but it's also the most tedious. Therefore, using this method does not minimize the time required to install the operating system.

C. **Incorrect:** The FAT32 file system does not support local permissions at the folder and file levels. Like all file systems in Windows 2000, FAT32 supports Share permissions. Share permissions provide for over-the-network secure access at the folder level. Configuring permissions at the file level is not available, and local computer access is not affected by Share-level security. In addition, only NTFS supports EFS.

D. **Incorrect:** Before a computer can join a domain, you must create a computer object (previously known as a computer account in Windows NT 4 domains) in a container of the Windows 2000 domain. You can accomplish this step during the installation process if you have access to a user account with the Add Workstation To Domain privilege in the domain or the privilege to create computer objects in a container of the domain. Alternatively, an administrator or a user in a Windows 2000 domain who has been granted the necessary privilege can add the computer object to the domain prior to running the Windows 2000 Professional installation. Nothing in the proposed solution suggests that one of these procedures was completed.

OBJECTIVE 1.2

Perform an unattended installation of Windows 2000 Professional.

Unattended installation, also known as **automated installation**, brings efficiencies to the installation process, making it possible to rapidly deploy Windows 2000 Professional and other applications in a large network environment.

This objective requires that you know how to *plan* for an automated installation, *prepare* the automated installation environment, *customize* the answer files, and *deploy* the operating system and applications to the network.

Note Operating system deployment techniques require that you are familiar with Windows 2000 Server technologies such as Remote Installation Service (RIS). You are more likely to succeed on Exam 70-210 if you understand how to use Windows 2000 Server technology to enhance deployment of Windows 2000 Professional.

Unattended installation has evolved with the operating system. As a result, a number of preparation methods are available for creating automated installation routines, and a number of distribution methods exist to deploy these packages to the network.

The preparation methods are the following:

- Install scripts to create a partially or fully automated setup.

  These scripts consist of an answer file named UNATTEND.TXT by default, a Uniqueness Database File (UDB) to support a multicomputer automated setup routine, and a CMDLINES.TXT file for running commands during the setup routine, such as a command that runs an automated application installation.

- Use the /syspart switch to complete the setup loader and text-mode phases of installation on a fixed disk.

- Use SysPrep to prepare an installation for imaging.

  To use SysPrep, configure a reference computer exactly as the operating system should be configured for the target computers. Run SysPrep to prepare the operating system for imaging. Fully automate the installation routine with an answer file named SYSPREP.INF. You can create SYSPREP.INF by using Setup Manager. Then use an imaging utility to copy the image to a central location or removable media. From the central location, the image is distributed using a distribution method. This process demonstrates that deployment utilities can be combined to create an automated installation routine.

Note Know the purpose of the Sysprep switches: -quiet, -nosidgen, -pnp, and snf -reboot.

- Use images created with a third-party imaging tool or the RIS RIPrep utility.

Some common distribution methods are the following:

- A batch file with a distribution folder

- RIS

  RIS supports CD-based and image-based installation preparation methods. Installation is automated using answer files, image download to Preboot Execution Environment (PXE)-compliant computers, or networked computers that support the RIS remote boot disk procedure.

- Microsoft Systems Management Server (SMS)

  You use SMS for operating system upgrades prepared using answer files.

Objective 1.2 Questions

70-210.01.02.001

You want to use Setup Manager to automate the installation of Windows 2000 Professional. Which tasks must you perform to run the Windows 2000 Setup Manager? (Choose two.)

A. Copy the Windows 2000 deployment tools by extracting the files in the DEPLOY.CAB file on the Windows 2000 Professional installation CD-ROM.

B. Copy the Windows 2000 deployment tools by extracting the files in the WINSYS32.CAB file on the Windows 2000 Professional CD-ROM.

C. Run the SETUPCL.EXE application in the directory to which you extracted the .cab file.

D. Run the SETUPMGR.EXE application in the directory to which you extracted the .cab file.

70-210.01.02.002

You want to install Windows 2000 Professional on 25 computers with similar hardware configurations.

To use the System Preparation utility as part of the disk duplication process, which parts of the master (reference) and destination (target) computers must be identical or, at the very least, compatible? (Choose two.)

A. A sound card

B. A video adapter

C. A network adapter

D. A hard disk controller device driver

E. The hardware abstraction layer (HAL)

70-210.01.02.003

You are an administrator for a corporate network supporting 50 users running Windows NT Workstation 4. You want to perform RIS-based remote installations of Windows 2000 Professional on your network clients without using the remote installation boot floppy. Which conditions allow you to perform remote installations? (Choose two.)

A. The computers on your network are PXE compliant.

B. The computers on your network support operating system–level remote control.

C. You have a Windows 2000 Server infrastructure in place.

D. You have either a Windows NT Server 4 or Windows 2000 Server infrastructure in place.

Objective 1.2 Answers

70-210.01.02.001

▶ **Correct Answers: A and D**

A. **Correct:** To automate an installation by using Setup Manager, you must first copy the Windows 2000 deployment tools from the Windows 2000 Professional installation CD-ROM. Extract the files in the \Support\Tools folder named DEPLOY.CAB to a disk location. The DEPLOY.CAB file contains Setup Manager, a deployment help file, a sample answer file, and other useful deployment utilities.

B. **Incorrect:** The WINSYS32.CAB file is located in the \i386 folder on the Windows 2000 Professional installation CD-ROM. This .cab file contains two files, MWWAVE.SYS and MWWDM.SYS. These files are used to support IBM modem hardware. If you weren't sure whether A or B was correct, consider the filenames listed in these multiple-choice answers to select the most likely correct answer.

C. **Incorrect:** SETUPCL.EXE supports System Preparation utility (SysPrep) functions. SETUPCL.EXE generates a new security ID (SID) and starts the Mini Setup Wizard. The combination of SYSPREP.EXE and SETUPCL.EXE replaces the ROLLBACK.EXE utility used in automating deployment of Windows NT 4. SysPrep and Setup Manager are two different methods for preparing an automated installation. You can use Setup Manager to fully automate a SysPrep installation by generating a SYSPREP.INF file. SYSPREP.INF is called in the final stage of installation.

D. **Correct:** After Setup Manager is extracted to a folder on a disk, you start it by running SETUP-MGR.EXE. Setup Manager guides you through the process of generating an answer file to script an installation of Windows 2000 Professional. The generated script files are used for partially automated or fully automated installation.

70-210.01.02.002

▶ **Correct Answers: D and E**

A. **Incorrect:** Peripheral devices such as modems, sound cards, and network adapters can differ or be absent in the master computer and the destination computer. However, device driver installation files for all devices in the destination computer must be available in the SysPrep image. If the destination computer contains Plug and Play versions of these devices, they will be detected and installed automatically.

B. **Incorrect:** Video adapters can differ in the master computer and the destination computer. However, device driver installation files for all video adapter types in the destination computers must be available in the SysPrep image. If the destination computer contains Plug and Play versions of these devices, they will be detected and installed automatically.

C. **Incorrect:** Network adapters can differ or be absent in the master computer and the destination computer. However, device driver installation files for all network adapters in the destination computer must be in the SysPrep image. If the destination computer contains Plug and Play versions of these devices, they will be detected and installed automatically.

D. **Correct:** The disk controller device drivers in the master and destination computer must be identical. If they are not identical, you should not use SysPrep to automate the installation process. Instead, you can complete an unattended installation with an answer file. The answer file is passed to WINNT32.EXE using the /unattend:num answer_file switch. The num parameter specifies the number of seconds between finishing the setup routine and restarting the computer; the answer_file parameter specifies the name of the answer file. The /unattend switch without any parameters is used to perform an unattended operating system upgrade from Windows 9x, Windows NT 3.51, or Windows NT 4. WINNT.EXE uses the /u:answer_file /s:source_path switches for unattended installation from a 16-bit operating system such as MS-DOS or Windows 3.1. You can also use Windows 2000 Setup (WINNT32.EXE only) with the /syspart switch to complete the text phase of installation on a target disk.

E. **Correct:** The HAL on the computer where the disk image is generated must be compatible with the HAL on the target computer. (The HALs do not have to be identical.)

70-210.01.02.003

▶ **Correct Answers: A and C**

A. **Correct:** Remote installation refers to the process of automatically booting to the network, connecting to a RIS server, and starting a clean installation of Windows 2000 Professional. To automatically connect to RIS, the computer must support or emulate PXE. PXE-compliant computers automatically boot to the network when an operating system isn't installed locally and the computer is configured to boot from the network. PXE support is provided in a number of ways. The PXE ROM is embedded on the network interface card (NIC), or the system BIOS contains the PXE-complaint, remote boot ROM code. A PXE-based remote boot ROM network adapter is included on computers that are Net PC-compliant or PC98-compliant systems.

RIS can provide operating system installation services to non-PXE-complaint systems by emulating PXE using the remote installation boot floppy. The remote installation boot floppy is mentioned in the question. The remote installation boot floppy disk starts the process of remote operating system installation. The remote installation boot floppy is a PXE emulator that connects to the RIS server through a supported Peripheral Component Interconnect (PCI) network adapter. You use the RBFG.EXE utility to generate a remote installation boot floppy disk. The boot floppy disk contains many common PCI-based network adapters so that a separate network boot disk is not required. Non-PCI network adapters are not supported.

B. **Incorrect:** Remote control is a feature that allows a computer called a viewer to control the keyboard, mouse, and monitor of a computer called a host. The host must be running a remote control agent and the viewer must be running remote viewer software. Other common features of a remote control package are remote chat, remote file transfer, and remote reboot. SMS and a number of third-party products include a remote control agent and a viewer. Terminal Services also includes a version of remote control that is configured and works differently than typical remote control software. Remote control is not required for RIS and does not play a role in a RIS-based installation.

C. **Correct:** RIS is a feature included with Windows 2000 Server and Windows 2000 Advanced Server. It is used to deploy new installations of Windows 2000 Professional. Therefore, a Windows 2000 Server infrastructure is integral to using RIS. Additionally, the PXE client uses Dynamic Host Configuration Protocol (DHCP) to initiate the process of remotely installing Windows 2000 Professional on a client.

When a PXE client performs a remote boot for the first time, the computer requests an Internet Protocol (IP) address and the IP address of an active RIS server through the DHCP protocol and its PXE extensions. As part of the initial request, the client sends out its globally unique identifier (GUID), which is used to identify the client in Active Directory directory services. The client receives an IP address from the DHCP server and the IP address of the RIS server that services the client. In the RIS server's response, the client is given the name of an installation command line or boot image that it must request when contacting the RIS server for initial service.

D. **Incorrect:** A Windows NT Server 4 infrastructure cannot support RIS because RIS is a new feature in Windows 2000. RIS is designed to run as a service on Windows 2000 Server and Windows 2000 Advanced Server to deploy scripted installations or images of Windows 2000 Professional to client computers.

OBJECTIVE 1.3

Upgrade from a previous version of Windows to Windows 2000 Professional.

The next step after assessing Windows 2000 hardware compatibility is performing a clean installation of Windows 2000 Professional, upgrading an existing operating system installation, or preserving the other operating system by installing Windows 2000 Professional in a separate folder.

When Windows 2000 Professional is installed to coexist with another operating system, the computer runs in a multiboot configuration (sometimes referred to as dual-boot.) In a multiboot configuration, it is important to consider Windows 2000 file system compatibility with the previous operating system. For example, the version of NTFS in Windows 2000 (version 5) isn't fully backward compatible with Windows NT, and Windows 9x cannot read NTFS partitions without the installation of a third-party utility. A local installation of Windows NT 4 requires Service Pack 4 (SP4) or later to read partitions formatted with NTFS version 5. If Windows NT 4 contains no service pack or a service pack prior to SP4, the Windows 2000 setup routine will warn you not to continue the installation. If the installation is continued, you will not be able to boot Windows NT 4 after Windows 2000 is installed.

You can upgrade an existing operating system to Windows 2000 Professional if the computer is running Windows 95, Windows 98, Windows NT Workstation 3.51, or Windows NT Workstation 4. In all cases, you run WINNT32.EXE to initiate the upgrade to these operating systems. Consequently, you can't use WINNT.EXE, the 16-bit version of the setup routine for computers running MS-DOS and Windows 3.x, to upgrade the operating system to Windows 2000 Professional. Although no other operating system can be upgraded to Windows 2000 Professional, a multiboot configuration is an option. Make sure to disable virus-scanning software before starting a Windows 2000 Professional installation upgrade.

You might need to upgrade Windows 9x-compatible applications to run in Windows 2000. To determine compatibility, check with the application vendor and review the Microsoft software compatibility list. The Microsoft software compatibility list is located by searching for the keywords "software compatibility" at *http://www.microsoft.com/ windows2000/*. Windows 16-bit applications that use virtual device driver (VxD) files will not run properly in Windows 2000. To aid in detecting known compatibility issues, run the Windows 2000 Readiness Analyzer (CHKUPGRD.EXE) or the /checkupgrade-only installation switch. On a computer running Windows 9x, the upgrade report generated with the /checkupgradeonly switch is automatically logged locally to *%windir%* as UPGRADE.TXT. Upgrade reports can also be logged to a central location using an automated answer file. For more information on compatibility logging, read the *Windows 2000 Professional Upgrade Guide*. (See the "Further Reading" section.)

The Windows 2000 Professional setup routine allows you to upgrade third-party application dynamic-link libraries (DLLs) written for Windows 9x using migration DLLs that the application vendor provides. Using migration DLLs and carefully testing before a widespread upgrade ensures that the upgraded applications will run on Windows 2000 Professional.

An upgrade is broken into two phases: a report phase and an installation phase. The report phase displays any known incompatibilities so that they can be addressed before upgrade proceeds, and this phase generates an installation script (answer file). The installation phase migrates registry settings, user accounts, and local profiles; installs Windows 2000 Professional in the same directory as the existing Windows installation; and runs any migration DLLs specified.

Caution If a computer running Windows 9x in a Windows NT or Windows 2000 domain will be upgraded to Windows 2000, make sure to create a computer account or a computer object in the domain prior to or during the upgrade.

Installation order is an important topic when configuring a computer for multiboot. For example, you should install Windows 2000 Professional only after you install Windows 98 on a multiboot computer. If you installed Windows 98 after Windows 2000 Professional, use the Emergency Repair Disk (ERD) to recover the system partition. For details on configuring a computer for multiboot, see the *Microsoft Windows 2000 Professional Resource Kit*, Chapter 6, "Setup and Startup," pages 259–261. (See this reference under Objective 1.5 in the "Further Reading" section.)

Objective 1.3 Questions

70-210.01.03.001

You are an administrator for a corporate network supporting 50 users. Their systems are running a variety of operating systems including Windows 95, Windows 98, Windows NT 3.1, Windows NT 3.5, Windows NT 3.51, and Windows NT 4. Which of these systems can be upgraded directly to Windows 2000 Professional? (Choose two.)

A. Windows 9*x*

B. Windows NT 3.1

C. Windows NT 3.5

D. Windows NT Workstation 3.51 or Windows NT Workstation 4

70-210.01.03.002

You are an administrator for a corporate network supporting 50 users running Windows NT Workstation 4. You are planning to deploy Windows 2000 Professional on 50 computers.

You need to ensure that the existing computer hardware is compatible with Windows 2000. Which two methods can you use to generate a hardware compatibility report? (Choose two.)

A. Download and run CHKUPGRD.EXE.

B. Run MKCOMPAT.EXE from the root of the Windows 2000 installation CD-ROM.

C. Open the Run dialog box and, including the path to the \i386 folder on the Windows 2000 installation CD-ROM, type **winnt32 /checkupgrade** in the Open text box.

D. Open the Run dialog box and, including the path to the \i386 folder on the Windows 2000 installation CD-ROM, type **winnt32 /checkupgradeonly** in the Open text box.

70-210.01.03.003

You are an administrator for a corporate network supporting 50 users running Windows NT Workstation 4. You are planning to deploy Windows 2000 Professional on 50 computers.

What is the most efficient way to determine whether any of your third-party applications require updates to operate properly in Windows 2000?

A. Connect to the Windows Update Web site.

B. Contact the vendor of each software application.

C. Generate a compatibility report using the SMS Crystal Reports snap-in.

D. Generate a compatibility report using the Windows 2000 Readiness Analyzer.

Objective 1.3 Answers

70-210.01.03.001

► **Correct Answers: A and D**

A. **Correct:** Windows 2000 Professional can upgrade Windows 95 and Windows 98 to Windows 2000 Professional. Note that it is not possible to upgrade Windows 9x to Windows 2000 Server.

B. **Incorrect:** You can't upgrade Windows NT 3.1 Workstation and Windows NT 3.1 Advanced Server to Windows 2000 Professional. You can upgrade Windows NT 3.1 Workstation to Windows NT 3.51 and then upgrade Windows NT 3.51 to Windows 2000 Professional. Server versions of Windows NT cannot be upgraded to Windows 2000 Professional.

C. **Incorrect:** You can't upgrade Windows NT 3.5 Workstation to Windows 2000 Professional. You can upgrade Windows NT 3.5 Workstation to Windows NT 3.51 Workstation or Windows NT 4 Workstation and then upgrade to Windows 2000 Professional.

D. **Correct:** You can upgrade Windows NT Workstation 3.51 or Windows NT Workstation 4 to Windows 2000 Professional.

70-210.01.03.002

► **Correct Answers: A and D**

A. **Correct:** The CHKUPGRD.EXE program is the Windows 2000 Readiness Analyzer self-extracting utility available for download from the Microsoft Web site. When run without any switches, CHK-UPGRD.EXE expands files into a temporary working folder and then runs a minimal version of WINNT32.EXE designed specifically to check upgrade compatibility of the computer. This minimal version of WINNT32.EXE uses a data repository of ASCII and .htm files extracted to the temporary working folder to report any hardware and software incompatibilities found.

B. **Incorrect:** The MKCOMPAT.EXE program is a Windows 95 utility for troubleshooting problems running Windows 3.1-based programs in Windows 95.

C. **Incorrect:** The winnt32 /checkupgrade syntax is incorrect.

D. **Correct:** Typing the 32-bit Windows 2000 setup routine with the /checkupgradeonly switch included runs the Microsoft Windows 2000 Readiness Analyzer Wizard. On all operating systems capable of running the Microsoft Windows 2000 Readiness Analyzer Wizard, the upgrade report appears on the Report System Compatibility screen of the wizard. On a computer running Windows 9x, the wizard generates a log file in %windir% named UPGRADE.TXT. On a computer running Windows NT, the wizard generates a log file in %systemroot% named WINNT32.LOG. By running the 32-bit Windows 2000 setup routine with the /checkupgradeonly switch and an answer file, upgrade reports can be logged to a central location.

70-210.01.03.003

▶ **Correct Answers: D**

A. **Incorrect:** The Windows Update Web site provides updates in the form of operating system service packs, hot fixes, and drivers, not third-party applications.

B. **Incorrect:** Contacting a vendor to determine whether Windows 2000 is supported or whether updates are available or necessary is inefficient. First determine whether an update is required, and then contact the vendor to obtain an update.

C. **Incorrect:** You use the SMS Crystal Reports snap-in to create reports on data stored in the SMS database, not to generate Windows 2000 compatibility data. Instead, the SMS database is populated with Windows 2000 compatibility data using a number of SMS utilities that augment the Windows 2000 Readiness Analyzer program. These utilities allow for the easy distribution and automation of the Windows 2000 Readiness Analyzer. The output from the Windows 2000 Readiness Analyzer is then stored in the SMS 2 database. These results can then be reported by using Crystal Info for SMS.

D. **Correct:** From the list of answers, the Windows 2000 Readiness Analyzer is the most direct way to determine whether any third-party applications require updates (also called update packs) to operate properly in Windows 2000. For greater efficiency, augment the Windows 2000 Readiness Analyzer with SMS 2 or use the 32-bit Windows 2000 setup routine's /checkupgradeonly switch with an answer file so that the log it generates for each computer is centralized for easy access and analysis.

Don't use the report provided by the Windows 2000 Readiness Analyzer or /checkupgradeonly as a guarantee of compatibility because it tests only known software and hardware incompatibilities. Thorough application testing is a critical step in determining application readiness.

Deploy service packs.

Microsoft uses service packs to distribute numerous updates and hot fixes to an operating system. You can locate service packs for Microsoft operating systems on the Windows Update Web site, a centralized, online resource for Windows updates, including service packs, hot fixes, and drivers.

A shortcut to the Windows Update Web site is located near the top of the Start menu unless Group Policy restrictions remove it. This shortcut points to the Windows Update program UPDMGR.EXE, located in *%systemroot%*\system32. Running this program starts Microsoft Internet Explorer and connects to the Windows Update Web site. This Web site uses Active Setup and Microsoft ActiveX controls to provide product enhancements. These controls are downloaded and installed on the computer the first time you establish a connection with the site. Windows Update automatically compares device drivers installed on the computer with a database of updated drivers on the server. Any drivers newer than those currently installed are offered for installation.

In a medium to large network, distributing updates locally from the intranet is more efficient than applying updates externally from the Internet. To prevent users from accessing Windows Update, configure the Windows 2000 group policy setting: disable and remove links to Windows Update to restrict access to the Windows Update site.

You apply local updates using service packs. For earlier versions of Windows 32-bit operating systems such as Windows NT, you must reapply a service pack every time you install operating system components from the operating system's installation CD-ROM or a distribution point. A **distribution point** is a network share containing the operating system source files. A distribution point is synonymous with a **distribution share**.

In Windows 2000 Professional, **slipstreaming** avoids the administrative overhead of service pack reapplication. Slipstreaming allows you to apply a service pack update to the source files in the Windows 2000 Professional distribution point. When the distribution point is the source for an installation of Windows 2000 Professional, the new installation contains the service pack. Any services or drivers added to the local installation come from the distribution point, thus avoiding the need to reapply the service pack.

You complete a manual, local installation of a service pack by running the service pack UPDATE.EXE utility. If, after applying the service pack, you add any services or drivers to the local installation, you must reapply the service pack. To avoid manual service pack reapplication, type **update -s:** *distribution_folder* (where *distribution_folder* is the location containing the operating system files) to slipstream a distribution point. Then use the distribution point rather than the Windows 2000 Professional installation CD-ROM to add services or drivers to the local installation.

Objective 1.4 Questions

70-210.01.04.001

You install Windows 2000 Professional on a new Pentium III computer that is not connected to an intranet. One week later, you want to apply a service pack. What should you do?

A. Type **update**.

B. Type **update -s:** *distribution_folder*.

C. Type **update /syspart**.

D. Type **update /cmdcons**.

70-210.01.04.002

You are an administrator for a corporate network supporting 50 users running Windows NT Workstation 4. You are planning to deploy Windows 2000 Professional on 50 computers.

You want to apply a service pack simultaneously during Windows 2000 deployment by integrating the service pack with an image of the Windows installation files. What should you do?

A. Type **update**.

B. Type **update -s:** *distribution_folder*.

C. Type **update /syspart**.

D. Type **update /cmdcons**.

70-210.01.04.003

You have a home office with a dial-up Internet connection. You install and configure all hardware and software yourself. You install Windows 2000 Professional on a new Pentium III computer. One week later, you apply a service pack. If you later add another service to the installation of Windows 2000 Professional using the Windows 2000 Professional installation CD-ROM as the file source, what other task should you perform?

A. Do nothing.

B. Type **setupcl**.

C. Run SETUPMGR.EXE.

D. Reapply the service pack.

Objective 1.4 Answers

70-210.01.04.001

▶ **Correct Answers: A**

A. **Correct:** To apply a service pack to an existing installation of Windows 2000, acquire the service pack from Microsoft via CD-ROM or by downloading from their Internet site, and then type update to run UPDATE.EXE. If new services or drivers are installed, you don't have to reapply the service pack, because the system copies the required files from either the Windows 2000 installation files or from the service pack install location automatically. Alternatively, you can visit the Windows Update site so that new updates are applied automatically.

B. **Incorrect:** When you type update -s: distribution_folder, the command updates a central distribution point of Windows 2000 source files. This distribution point is then used to update a computer running Windows 2000 Professional with the latest service pack. Because the computer described in the question is not connected to an intranet, a central distribution point is not available.

C. **Incorrect:** /syspart is a valid Windows 2000 setup switch used to complete the setup loader and text-mode phases of installation on a fixed disk. The disk is then moved to another computer to continue installation. This switch is not valid for the service pack update program, UPDATE.EXE.

D. **Incorrect:** /cmdcons is a valid switch for the 32-bit Windows 2000 setup routine, which is used to create a recovery command console startup option for Windows 2000. This switch is not valid for the service pack update program, UPDATE.EXE.

70-210.01.04.002

▶ **Correct Answers: B**

A. **Incorrect:** You use UPDATE.EXE to apply a service pack to a computer already running an installation of Windows 2000. You could include UPDATE.EXE at the end of an automated installation of Windows 2000 Professional, but this is an inefficient method of applying the service pack.

B. **Correct:** You use the -s: distribution_folder switch for service pack slipstreaming. Slipstreaming applies the service pack files to a distribution point containing the operating system source files. By adding the service pack to the operating system's distribution share, the service pack will be installed when Windows 2000 is installed.

C. **Incorrect:** /syspart is a valid Windows 2000 setup switch that you use to create a partial installation of Windows 2000 on a disk before you move the disk to another computer to continue installation. This switch is not valid for the service pack update program UPDATE.EXE.

D. **Incorrect:** /cmdcons is a valid Windows 2000 setup switch that you use to create a recovery command console startup option for Windows 2000. This switch is not valid for the service pack update program UPDATE.EXE.

70-210.01.04.003

▶ **Correct Answers: A**

A. **Correct:** In earlier versions of Windows, if you applied a service pack to your computer, each time you changed the system state by adding or removing components, you had to reapply any service packs. Windows 2000 automatically recognizes that a service pack has been applied to the system and which files have been replaced or updated. Whenever you add or remove components from a computer running Windows 2000, the system copies the required files from either the Windows 2000 installation files or from the service pack install location, so you don't have to reapply the service pack.

B. **Incorrect:** SETUPCL.EXE supports the functions of SysPrep, the System Preparation utility. SET-UPCL.EXE generates a new security ID (SID) and starts the Mini Setup Wizard. SETUPCL.EXE does not play a role in service pack updates.

C. **Incorrect:** Setup Manager is a utility for generating an answer file to script an installation of Windows 2000 Professional or to fully automate a SysPrep installation procedure.

D. **Incorrect:** See answer A's explanation.

Troubleshoot failed installations.

When you troubleshoot a failed installation, you should always start by double-checking that all hardware in the computer is listed on the Hardware Compatibility List (HCL). You should remove any hardware component not on the HCL before repeating installation. Another important preinstallation or installation troubleshooting task is verifying that the basic input/output system (BIOS) is up-to-date. Vendor-provided BIOS updates and operating-specific BIOS configuration settings can resolve a number of installation failures. For example, disabling the Plug and Play Operating System (PnP OS) BIOS setting is important before installing Windows 2000 Professional on computers that don't support the Advanced Configuration and Power Interface (ACPI) specification. Additionally, you should reserve any legacy ISA device interrupt request (IRQ) settings in the BIOS on all computers before setup commences.

The next troubleshooting step is determining in which phase the installation failure is occurring. The three installation phases are the Setup Loader phase, the Text-Mode Setup phase, and the GUI-Mode Setup phase.

In the Setup Loader phase, preliminary installation files are copied from the source to the local disk. Setup Loader starts the installation process and loads a SCSI disk controller support driver, if required, and a hardware detection program. After base hardware is detected, a minimal version of the Windows 2000 kernel and additional hardware drivers are loaded. Finally the boot sector is modified to continue Windows 2000 installation.

The Text-Mode Setup phase is characterized by white text on a blue background. In this phase, installation and configuration of hardware driver detection continues. Next partitions are created and they are formatted or converted as necessary. Minimum system requirements are verified and most installation files are copied to the local disk.

GUI-Mode Setup phase marks the conclusion of the setup process. In this phase, additional devices are detected, installed, and configured; optional components are installed; additional installation files are copied; and dynamic-link library (DLL) files are registered. If installation fails in this phase, restarting the computer may resolve the failure, thus allowing setup to continue.

Four general information log files are created during setup to record the installation process: SETUPACT.LOG, SETUPERR.LOG, SETUPAPI.LOG, and SETUP-LOG.TXT. These files provide essential information about the installation process to assist in resolving installation failures.

Device-specific or component-specific log files are also generated during the setup process or when a new Plug and Play device is added. These log files are stored in *%systemroot%* (by default, C:\WINNT). The following is a list of some of the device-specific or component-specific log files generated during setup:

- COMSETUP.LOG—Logs Component Object Model (COM) setup routines

- MMDET.LOG—Logs multimedia installation and resource allocation

- NETSETUP.LOG—Logs network computer name, workgroup, and domain validation

- IIS5.LOG—Logs the installation and configuration of Internet Information Services (IIS) 5

For this objective, you must be familiar with the activities occurring in each setup phase, the purpose of the primary files or classes of files installed in each phase of setup, and the function of the installation log files. Log files are essential to troubleshooting a failed installation.

Objective 1.5 Questions

70-210.01.05.001

You attempt to install Windows 2000 Professional on a Pentium III computer, but the process fails. You suspect that a multimedia device caused the failure. Which log file should you view to determine the port ranges used by each multimedia device?

A. COMSETUP.LOG

B. MMDET.LOG

C. NETSETUP.LOG

D. WINNT32.LOG

70-210.01.05.002

You attempt to install Windows 2000 Professional on a Pentium III computer, but the process fails. Which log file should you view to determine the severity of a setup error?

A. COMSETUP.LOG

B. MMDET.LOG

C. NETSETUP.LOG

D. SETUPERR.LOG

70-210.01.05.003

You attempt to install Windows 2000 Professional on a Pentium III computer, but the process fails. Which log file should you view for an overview of all files that are copied during setup?

A. MMDET.LOG

B. NETSETUP.LOG

C. SETUPACT.LOG

D. SETUPERR.LOG

Objective 1.5 Answers

70-210.01.05.001

▶ **Correct Answers: B**

A. **Incorrect:** Use COMSETUP.LOG to troubleshoot COM component installation. This and all log files mentioned in the answer choices are stored in %systemroot%.

B. **Correct:** Use MMDET.LOG to troubleshoot multimedia device detection and resource allocation. It contains the port ranges for each multimedia device.

C. **Incorrect:** Use NETSETUP.LOG to troubleshoot network computer name, workgroup, or domain detection errors.

D. **Incorrect:** WINNT32.LOG is the output file generated on computers running Windows NT or Windows 2000 when you run the Microsoft Windows 2000 Readiness Analyzer or you type winnt32 /checkupgradeonly.

70-210.01.05.002

▶ **Correct Answers: D**

A. **Incorrect:** Use COMSETUP.LOG to troubleshoot COM component installation.

B. **Incorrect:** Use MMDET.LOG to troubleshoot multimedia device detection and resource allocation. It contains the port ranges for each multimedia device.

C. **Incorrect:** Use NETSETUP.LOG to troubleshoot network computer name registration and workgroup or domain detection.

D. **Correct:** Use SETUPERR.LOG located in %systemroot% to troubleshoot errors encountered during the installation process.

70-210.01.05.003

▶ **Correct Answers: C**

A. **Incorrect:** Use MMDET.LOG to troubleshoot multimedia device detection and resource allocation. It contains the port ranges for each multimedia device.

B. **Incorrect:** Use NETSETUP.LOG to troubleshoot network computer name registration and workgroup or domain detection.

C. **Correct:** Use SETUPACT.LOG created in %systemroot% during the setup process; it records all files copied locally during setup.

D. **Incorrect:** Use SETUPERR.LOG located in %systemroot% to troubleshoot errors encountered during the installation process.

Implementing and Conducting Administration of Resources

The core operating system *resources* in Microsoft Windows 2000 Professional are the file system, the files and folders that the file system supports, and **shares**. The three primary share types in a Windows 2000 network are folder shares, Web shares, and printer shares.

Resource implementation tasks include preparing partitions with file systems; creating folders, shares, and Internet-accessible resources; and configuring access permissions to them. After implementation, these resources require regular administration. Administration tasks include removing unnecessary partitions, shares, folders, and files; reconfiguring permissions; and troubleshooting resource access problems.

Some implementation and administration tasks are unique to the type of resource. For example, **printer shares** require print job management and printing device configuration; **partitions or volumes** require capacity management and disk access optimization.

Windows 2000 natively supports a number of file systems. The two fixed-disk file systems it supports are **file allocation table (FAT)** and **New Technology File System (NTFS)**. The FAT file system is ideal for providing access compatibility for computers configured to multiboot operating systems. NTFS is a more robust and feature-rich file system for computers that exclusively run Microsoft Windows NT or Windows 2000.

Tested Skills and Suggested Practices

The skills you need to successfully master the Implementing and Conducting Adminis-tration of Resources Objective Domain on Exam 70-210: Installing, Configuring, and Administering Microsoft Windows 2000 Professional include the following:

- **Implement and administer Windows 2000 file system features.**

  - Practice 1: Automate an unattended installation of Windows 2000 Professional that converts a primary partition to NTFS.

  - Practice 2: Compress NTFS partitions, folders, and files using the Compact command-line utility and Microsoft Windows Explorer.

  - Practice 3: Review the various Compact switches by typing **compact /?**. Type **compact** with no switches to see the compression state of folders and files.

  - Practice 4: Use Windows Explorer and the CACLS.EXE utility to configure NTFS local permissions on partitions, folders, and files.

  - Practice 5: Type **net share** at the command line to view available shares, and then type **net share /?** to view the switches supported by this utility. Finally cre-ate and remove a share using this command-line utility.

  - Practice 6: Create a share, configure permissions for a share, and delete a share using Windows Explorer.

  - Practice 7: Install Microsoft Internet Information Services (IIS) and then create and configure security for Web sharing.

  - Practice 8: Stop the Server service and then attempt to create a share. Restart the Server service, and verify that you can successfully create a share.

  - Practice 9: Create a partition using the Disk Administrator snap-in.

  - Practice 10: Format a partition from the command line by using the Disk Administrator snap-in.

- **Implement and administer Windows 2000 printing.**

  - Practice 1: Create a printer and share it using the Add Printers Wizard.

  - Practice 2: Make sure that IIS is installed to support Internet printing.

  - Practice 3: Create a new port for printing.

  - Practice 4: Connect to a printer through a UNC name and using HTTP.

  - Practice 5: Complete all administration tasks available through the Printers win-dow. For example, create a printer pool, prioritize printers, redirect documents for printing, and configure a separator page.

Further Reading

This "Further Reading" section provides lists of important readings to supplement your current understanding of the skills tested within this Objective Domain. The lists are delineated into pertinent readings for each objective within this Objective Domain. If you feel that you need additional preparation prior to taking the exam, study these sources thoroughly.

Objective 2.1

Microsoft Corporation. *MCSE Training Kit—Microsoft Windows 2000 Professional*. Redmond, Washington: Microsoft Press, 2000. Read and complete the practices in Chapter 14, "Securing Resources with NTFS Permissions."

Microsoft Corporation. *Microsoft Windows 2000 Server Resource Kit Windows 2000 Distributed Systems Guide*. Redmond, Washington: Microsoft Press, 2000. Read Chapter 12, "Access Control."

Objective 2.2

Microsoft Corporation. *Microsoft Windows 2000 Professional Help*. Redmond, Washington: Microsoft, 2000. Using the online help file included with Windows 2000 Professional, search for and read about the following topics: "Change permissions for a shared folder," "Securing shared drives," "Shared folder permissions," "Special shared folders," and "Using shared folders."

Microsoft Corporation. *MCSE Training Kit—Microsoft Windows 2000 Professional*. Redmond, Washington: Microsoft Press, 2000. Read and complete the practices in Chapter 15, "Administering Shared Folders."

Objective 2.3

Microsoft Corporation. *MCSE Training Kit—Microsoft Windows 2000 Professional*. Redmond, Washington: Microsoft Press, 2000. Read and complete the practices in Chapter 12, "Setting Up and Configuring Network Printers," and Chapter 13, "Administering Network Printers."

Microsoft Corporation. *Microsoft Windows 2000 Server Resource Kit Windows 2000 Server Operations Guide*. Redmond, Washington: Microsoft Press, 2000. Read Chapter 4, "Network Printing."

Objective 2.4

Daily, Sean. "NTFS5 vs. FAT32," *Windows 2000 Magazine.* Denver, Colorado: Duke Communications International, 2000. Sean Daily provides a comprehensive comparison of FAT32 and NTFS in Windows 2000 and how and when to use these file systems.

Microsoft Corporation. *Microsoft Windows 2000 Professional Resource Kit.* Redmond, Washington: Microsoft Press, 2000. Read Chapter 17, "File Systems."

Microsoft Corporation. *Microsoft Windows 2000 Professional installation CD-ROM.* Redmond, Washington: Microsoft, 2000. Read the release notes contained in README.DOC. You can find this file at the root of the CD-ROM.

Monitor, manage, and troubleshoot access to files and folders.

Large file types, such as multimedia files and application files that are hundreds of megabytes in size, drive greater and greater disk capacity requirements. A number of technologies are able to slow disk capacity use. The most common of these technologies is **compression**. Windows 2000 Professional includes built-in compression. Compression functions on **NTFS** partitions formatted with 4-KB cluster sizes or smaller and operates on **partitions**, **volumes**, folders, or files.

You apply compression either through Windows Explorer or from the command line with the COMPACT.EXE utility. Through Windows Explorer, you can compress an entire partition, folder, or file. Compression applied at the partition or folder level can be inherited by subfolders and files or just applied to the parent partition or folder. The COMPACT.EXE utility is ideal for running in a batch process. If the compression fails initially because a file targeted for compression is opened by another process, this utility will ensure that the compression procedure completes in the background.

Whether a file remains compressed when it is moved or copied depends on the target file system, the target partition, the target folder compression state, the file's compression state, and whether a file is moved or copied. The table on the following page shows the behavior of compression when a file is moved or copied.

Action from Source to Target	Copy	Move
Compressed file from an NTFS-formatted partition to any other file system partition	Decompressed	Decompressed.
Uncompressed file from any partition to an NTFS-formatted and compressed partition or compressed parent folder	Compressed	Compressed.
Compressed or uncompressed file from an NTFS-formatted partition to the same partition	Inherits compression state from parent folder or partition	Remains in original compression state regardless of parent folder or partition compression state.
Uncompressed or compressed file from an NTFS-formatted partition to another NTFS partition	Inherits compression state from parent folder or partition	Inherits compression state from parent folder or partition. A moved file inherits the compression state of the target parent folder or partition because a move to another partition is actually an automatic copy to the target partition and an automatic delete operation from the source partition.

The amount a file is compressed depends on the file type. ASCII, document, and bitmap files are highly compressible, whereas binary files, such as application executables, are not. Compression can affect system performance because it adds overhead to standard file I/O operations such as opening and saving a file. NTFS compression technology is convenient because compression and decompression is managed in the background. For example, when a compressed file is opened in Microsoft Word, the operating system decompresses the file before the word processor opens it. When the file is saved, the operating system returns the file to its original compressed state.

NTFS provides file system security with **local permissions**. Local permissions are stored in the **discretionary access control list (DACL)** as **access control entries (ACEs)**. The DACL is a table containing a set of configurable privileges. Each NTFS partition, folder, and file contains a DACL. Only NTFS provides this level of file system security to Windows 2000.

Note You will see DACL shortened to ACL in much of the documentation.

You configure local permissions either using Windows Explorer or from the command line using the CACLS.EXE utility. You must be able to navigate to and view or set security on partitions, folders, or files using Windows Explorer. You must also know how to use the CACLS.EXE utility to view or configure permissions from the command line. These tools can impact permissions throughout a folder hierarchy. Know how to control permission inheritance using both Windows Explorer and CACLS.EXE.

Local permission inheritance and certain **explicit rights**, such as allowing the Take Ownership permission or denying the Full Control permission, can influence user or group effective permissions. **Effective permissions** are the actual rights a user is granted to a resource, whether they are inherited or explicitly assigned. Combinations of user and group permissions configured for an NTFS resource will influence effective permissions. For example, if a user is granted the Read permission to a folder and a group in which the user is a member is granted the Write permission, then the user's effective permissions are Read and Write.

Two types of permissions exist: general permissions, such as Full Control and Read, and permission entries, such as Change permissions and Delete. General permissions are a combination of permission entries. For example, the Full Control permission means that all permission entries are allowed. The Read permission configured for a folder means that the following permission entries are allowed:

- List Folder / Read Data
- Read Attributes
- Read Extended Attributes
- Read Permissions

Copying and moving folders and files can change their DACL. NTFS permissions are affected in much the same way that compression attributes are affected by move-and-copy operations. A Resource Kit utility that is used to preserve permissions when copying NTFS files is ROBOCOPY.EXE. This utility preserves NTFS permissions when a file is *moved* or *copied* from one NTFS partition to another or when it is *copied* from one NTFS folder to another. NTFS file permissions are not changed when a file is moved from one location on a partition to another location on the same partition. Local permissions are removed when a file is moved or copied to any other file system.

Optimizing access to file resources requires careful organization of partitions, folders, and files. For example, the following practices will help to optimize file resource access:

- Protect the operating system files from file activity, such as application installation or user data storage that could cause the boot partition to run out of available disk capacity.

- A boot partition that is filled to capacity will cause the operating system to fail. Consider placing PAGEFILE.SYS on a separate partition. Other procedures to control the use of the boot partition include the following: placing user profiles in a location other than the boot partition and moving the Offline Files cache to another partition. Moving the Offline Files cache is explained in Objective Domain 4 and user profile management is explored in Objective Domain 5.

- Place application folders and data folders on a partition separate from the boot partition.

- Separate the application folders and the data folders from each other.

- Consider placing application and user data on separate partitions.

These easy practices will optimize file resource availability, simplify backup procedures, and simplify application upgrades and permission assignment.

Objective 2.1 Questions

70-210.02.01.001

You are assigned to help desk support for your corporate network. A user reports that she is unable to compress a folder on an NTFS partition. What are the two most likely causes? (Choose two.)

A. The volume is corrupt.

B. The user has been denied access to the disk volume.

C. The Encrypting File System (EFS) attribute has been applied.

D. When the volume was formatted, a cluster size greater than 4 KB was specified.

70-210.02.01.002

You set NTFS permissions on a folder named \Download on your computer running Windows 2000 Professional. The \Download folder contains several nested subfolders. By default, which folder or folders inherit the permissions you set on the \Download folder?

A. \Download

B. \Download and first-tier subfolders

C. \Download, first-tier subfolders, and second-tier subfolders

D. All subfolders

70-210.02.01.003

You have been hired to deploy a Windows 2000 network for a small business. You must also plan and establish NTFS permissions for all users. You want to simplify administration and backup operations. What should you do? (Choose two.)

A. Place applications and shared data in each user's home folder on the server.

B. Create separate folders for applications, shared data, and individual user data (home folders) on the server.

C. Place home folders and shared data beneath public folders on the server volume where your applications and operating system reside.

D. Place home folders and shared data folders beneath public folders on a server volume separate from your applications and the operating system.

Objective 2.1 Answers

70-210.02.01.001

► **Correct Answers: C and D**

A. **Incorrect:** From the user's report, it appears that she can access the folder, so it is unlikely that the volume is corrupt. Additionally, although NTFS volume corruption is possible, it is unlikely because of the protections built into this file system, such as transaction logging and cluster remapping.

B. **Incorrect:** If local permissions to the disk volume were the problem, a message box stating that access is denied would appear to the user. Because the user did not report that this message appeared, it is unlikely that the inability to compress the folder has anything to do with permissions.

C. **Correct:** Folder and file compression and encryption are mutually exclusive attributes. Thus, a compressed file cannot be encrypted and an encrypted file cannot be compressed. This is demonstrated in Windows Explorer through the Advanced Attributes dialog box. To navigate to this dialog box, access the Properties dialog box of a folder or file and then click the Advanced button. The Advanced Attributes dialog box displays check boxes, one for compression and one for encryption. Unlike traditional check boxes, you can select only one advanced attribute at a time. Note that these check boxes operate like radio buttons.

D. **Correct:** NTFS compression is designed to support cluster sizes up to 4 KB. Larger cluster sizes do not support NTFS compression. If compression is required, back up all files on the partition and reformat the partition using a cluster size of 4 KB or smaller. After the partition is reformatted, restore the files.

70-210.02.01.002

► **Correct Answers: D**

A. **Incorrect:** The question states that you applied NTFS permissions to the \Download folder. This is an explicit assignment. Inherited assignments flow from a disk to folders, subfolders, and files beneath it and from a parent folder to subfolders and files beneath it.

B. **Incorrect:** First, an explicit assignment was made to the \Download folder so inheritance was not involved in this assignment. Second, by default, inheritance flows from the parent folder to all subfolders beneath it, not just the first-tier subfolders.

C. **Incorrect:** First, an explicit assignment was made to the \Download folder so inheritance was not involved in this assignment. Second, by default, inheritance flows from the parent folder to all sub-folders beneath it, not just the first-tier and second-tier subfolders.

D. **Correct:** By default, when local permissions for a folder on an NTFS partition are modified, all sub-folders beneath it inherit those permissions. You can disable this inheritance property in the Security tab of a disk's or folder's Properties dialog box. At the bottom of the Security tab, the Allow Inheritable Permissions From Parent To Propagate To This Object check box is enabled by default.

70-210.02.01.003

▶ **Correct Answers: B and D**

A. **Incorrect:** Placing applications in each user's home folder is an inefficient use of disk space. Most applications that are run from the server should be installed only on the server, and all users should access the application from this central location. Home folder data should not be mixed with application data. If the application must be upgraded or removed, home folder data might be lost.

B. **Correct:** To simplify administration, group files into separate folders for applications, shared data, and individual user data. This is also the most efficient way to optimize access to these folder and file resources. For example, application, home, and shared data folders require different permissions because of how they are used.

C. **Incorrect:** Placing home folders and shared data folders beneath public folders does provide a manageable structure for configuring permissions. However, placing these folders on the same drive containing your applications and operating system is dangerous because user data could fill the partition to capacity and cause the operating system to fail.

D. **Correct:** Centralizing home folders and public folders on a volume that is separate from applications and the operating system is an ideal structure for administration. For example, you could choose to compress the partition containing the user data while leaving the application and operating system partition uncompressed.

OBJECTIVE 2.2

Manage and troubleshoot access to shared folders.

In Windows 2000, you can make disk resources network-accessible in two ways: through **sharing** or **Web sharing**. Sharing opens in a Windows Explorer window and uses the following **Universal Naming Convention (UNC)** syntax: *computer-name\sharename*. Web sharing opens in a browser window and uses the following **Hypertext Transfer Protocol (HTTP)** syntax: *http://computername/alias*.

Sharing is a critical step in making a folder and its contents (files and subfolders) available over the network. Additionally, sharing provides a limited form of network security using **share permissions**. These permissions are configured similarly to **NTFS** permissions, but they are limited in two important ways: First, share permissions do not provide local security, meaning that a user can log on locally and access folders regardless of the assigned share permissions. Second, you apply shares and share permissions only at the drive or folder level. In contrast, you apply NTFS local permissions at the drive, folder, or file level and provide local and network security. Sharing functions on all file systems supported in Windows 2000.

Each fixed disk in the computer is automatically assigned a hidden share name of *drive letter*$. For example, the hidden share name of drive C is C$. A share is hidden if the last character in the share name is a dollar ($) sign. The permissions assigned to these hidden shares cannot be changed. There are additional hidden shares such as Admin$ and Print$.

You create and remove shared folders by using Windows Explorer or from the command line by using the Net Share command-line utility. You can also create shares by using the Microsoft Windows Scripting Host (WSH).

Note SHARE.VBS is a WSH sharing administration script sample. See the Windows 2000 Server Resource Kit, "Remote Administration Scripts Help" file to view the syntax for SHARE.VBS.

The Server service manages sharing and share permissions. Therefore, sharing functions only if the Server service is running. The World Wide Web Publishing Service manages Web sharing and Web share permissions. Therefore, Web sharing functions only if the World Wide Web Publishing Service component of Internet Information Services (IIS) is running.

Sharing and Web sharing permissions are different. Share permissions are Full Control, Read, and Write. When a share is created, the Everyone group is granted Full Control and the number of users allowed to connect to the share—the user access limit—is set to the maximum allowed. The maximum number of concurrent connections allowed to a computer running Windows 2000 Professional is 10. The following table shows rights granted based on assigned permission:

Right to	Full Control	Change	Read
View filenames and subfolder names	x	x	x
Navigate to subfolders	x	x	x
View data in files and running programs	x	x	x
Add files and subfolders to the shared folder	x	x	
Change data in files	x	x	
Delete subfolders and files	x	x	
Change permissions (when the share is located on an NTFS partition)	x		
Take ownership (when the share is located on an NTFS partition)	x		

Sharing permissions, user access limits, and share caching are configurable settings for sharing.

The security settings for IIS enforce access to Web shares. A Web share is also called an **alias**. The security settings for IIS are categorized by access permissions and application permissions. Access permissions are Read, Write, Script Source Access, and Directory Browsing. Application permissions are None, Scripts, and Execute (includes scripts).

The inability to configure sharing or Web sharing is commonly associated with the state of its supporting service. Sharing depends on the Server service; Web sharing depends on the World Wide Web Publishing Service. Inability to access a shared resource is usually caused by improperly configured permissions, NTFS and share permission conflicts, share names that are too long for client computers running legacy operating systems, or network access problems.

Objective 2.2 Questions

70-210.02.02.001

You recently installed Windows 2000 Professional on a Pentium III computer, and then you shared the \Download folder. By default, which share permissions does Windows 2000 assign to the Everyone group? (Choose three.)

A. Full Control

B. Change

C. Read

D. List Folder Contents

70-210.02.02.002

You create the \Reports folder on a computer running Windows 2000 Professional. You share the \Reports folder, remove the Everyone group from the share permission, assign the Read share permission to user TonyV, and assign the Change share permission to the Developers group. TonyV is a member of the Developers group. Which effective share permission does TonyV have to the \Reports folder when accessing it from a remote Windows 2000 computer?

A. Read

B. Change

C. Full Control

D. No Access

70-210.02.02.003

You create and share the \Sales folder on a computer running Windows 2000 Professional. During the next two weeks, various users save Microsoft Excel files to the \Sales folder. You later decide to move the \Sales folder to a more powerful computer. Now users are calling you because they are unable to access the \Sales folder. What is the most likely cause of this problem?

A. The disk signature on the target volume is corrupt.

B. When you move a shared folder, Windows 2000 stops sharing the folder.

C. Users must log off and log back on before being able to access a shared folder that was moved.

D. To be able to move a shared folder, you must download the Microsoft Windows 2000 High Encryption Pack and apply it from the Windows Update site.

70-210.02.02.004

You are the Windows 2000 administrator for your small business. Five Pentium III computers running Windows 2000 Professional are connected in a workgroup network configuration. Which Windows 2000 user groups have the ability to share folders on computers running Windows 2000 Professional? (Choose two.)

A. Administrators

B. Backup Operators

C. Power Users

D. Server Operators

Objective 2.2 Answers

70-210.02.02.001

► **Correct Answers: A, B, and C**

A. **Correct:** By default, the Everyone group is assigned Full Control permissions to the share. All accounts are assigned membership to this special group by the operating system. It is not possible to revoke membership to this group.

B. **Correct:** The Full Control permission is a superset of the Change permission and the Read permission. When the operating system automatically assigns Full Control permission, the Change permission Allow check box is selected.

C. **Correct:** The Full Control permission is a superset of the Change permission and the Read permission. When the operating system automatically assigns Full Control permission, the Read permission Allow check box is selected.

D. **Incorrect:** The List Folder Contents permission is an NTFS local permission, not a share permission.

70-210.02.02.002

► **Correct Answers: B**

A. **Incorrect:** The user account TonyV is directly assigned the Read share permission to the \Reports folder. Through group membership, the TonyV account inherits the Change share permission. Thus, the effective share permission of TonyV is the sum of explicitly assigned permissions and permissions inherited through group membership.

B. **Correct:** Effective rights are the sum of user permissions and group permissions. TonyV is granted Read share permission to the \Reports folder and as a member of the Developers group, Change share permission to the same folder. Therefore, his effective right is Change. The Change permission is a superset of the Read permission.

C. **Incorrect:** The Full Control permission is equivalent to the Change permission on FAT volumes. However, when the Full Control permission is a user's effective right to a share on an NTFS volume, the user is able to modify NTFS local permissions and take ownership of the share folder and its subfolders and files.

D. **Incorrect:** No Access is a user's effective right to a share only if the Full Control Deny check box is selected or if the user and any groups to which the user belongs have not been granted any rights to the share.

70-210.02.02.003

▶ **Correct Answers: B**

A. **Incorrect:** A disk signature is written to a disk when the Windows 2000 Disk Administrator snap-in is used to view a disk for the first time. A corrupted disk signature suggests potential disk problems.

B. **Correct:** When a shared folder is moved, the Windows 2000 operating system automatically stops sharing the folder. This automatic share removal by the operating system avoids error messages that the Server service generates because a share cannot be recreated on operating system startup. When a folder is moved, it must be shared from its new location.

C. **Incorrect:** Logging on and logging off will not make the share accessible after it has been moved.

D. **Incorrect:** The Windows 2000 High Encryption Pack applies 128-bit encryption for secure access. The High Encryption Pack is available only to computer users in the United States because of export restrictions. This encryption pack will not make a moved share accessible.

70-210.02.02.004

▶ **Correct Answers: A and C**

A. **Correct:** In a Windows 2000 workgroup, members of the built-in Administrators local group have complete and unrestricted access to the computers where the Administrators local group resides. Therefore, any member of the Administrators local group can share folders on the local computer.

B. **Incorrect:** Members of the Backup Operators group can override security restrictions for the sole purpose of backing up or restoring files. This does not allow members of this group to create shares.

C. **Correct:** Members of the Power Users group possess most administrative privileges with some restrictions. One of those privileges is the right to share folders on the computer where the group resides.

D. **Incorrect:** The Server Operators group is found only in a Windows NT or Windows 2000 domain.

O B J E C T I V E   2 . 3

Connect to local and network print devices.

A **printer** is the software that provides local computer access to a **printing device**. A **printer share** is the facility that provides network access to a printing device. A printer accessible over the network through a **Universal Naming Convention (UNC)** name is called a **shared printer**; a printer accessible via **Hypertext Transfer Protocol (HTTP)** is called an **Internet printer**. The Server service makes the printer available through a UNC share name: *computername\printsharename*. The World Wide Web Publishing Service component of Internet Information Services (IIS) makes the printer available through a Web browser. Unlike the Server service, IIS services are not installed if you accept the default installation options when installing Windows 2000 Professional. You must install IIS and the World Wide Web Publishing Service component on the computer to support Internet printing.

A printing device attached directly to a computer is local to the computer. Attachment is usually through an LPT or COM port. Printer connections available on the computer are called **local ports**. A computer can host a printing device on other local port types besides LPT or COM ports. For example, a printer attached through an Infrared Data Association (IrDA) port uses the IR local port, and a printer attached through a universal serial bus (USB) port uses the USB local port. These local ports appear in the local port list for printers if Windows 2000 detects a printing device attached to them. After you configure the printing device as a local printer using the **Add Printer Wizard** and sharing is configured, the local computer is a **print server**. Other computers attach to the printing device over the network by choosing the Network Printer option on the Add Printer Wizard screen.

Tip You can also configure ports in the Print Server Properties dialog box by clicking File and then choosing the Server Properties option. The Printer Server Properties dialog box provides additional configuration capabilities not available in the Add Printer Wizard.

A computer can act as a print server for network-attached printers. The local computer must support the protocol running on the network-attached printer. For example, if the network-attached printer runs TCP/IP (Transmission Control Protocol/Internet Protocol), TCP/IP must be installed on the print server. Client computers running Windows operating systems can attach to the shared printer and automatically download the printer driver if the printer driver is installed on the print server.

Windows 2000 Professional print servers provide printing support to computers running MS-DOS, Windows, and UNIX operating systems. All editions of Windows 2000 support advanced printing features such as **printer pools** and **printing priority**.

After a printer is configured, you manage it using the Printers window. Management tasks are categorized by print server, printer, and document. You complete most print server management tasks by choosing Server Properties from the File menu. You complete most printer management tasks by choosing Properties from a printer's context menu. You complete most document management tasks by opening a printer in the Printers window.

A printer's Properties dialog box includes a Security tab used for configuring printer permissions. The three general permissions are Print, Manage Printers, and Manage Documents. Like **NTFS** permissions, these primary permissions are a combination of permission entries.

For this objective, you must be familiar with print server, printer, and print job management. You must also be able to delegate printer management tasks and control access to print servers and printers using permissions. Finally, you must be able to establish connections to shared printers and Internet printers.

Objective 2.3 Questions

70-210.02.03.001

You are the administrator of your computer running Windows 2000 Professional. You want to connect to a network-interface printing device using the Add Standard TCP/IP Printer Port Wizard. What can you specify to identify the port? (Choose two.)

A. A TCP/IP host name

B. An IP address

C. A Media Access Control (MAC) address

D. A Windows Internet Naming Service (WINS) computer name

70-210.02.03.002

Assuming that Microsoft Internet Print Services has not been installed, which type of client computer can use a Web browser to connect to a network printer?

A. Microsoft Windows 95

B. Microsoft Windows 98

C. Windows NT 4

D. Windows 2000

70-210.02.03.003

You are the administrator of your Windows 2000 Professional computer. Your network environment includes a Windows 2000 Server domain. The Microsoft Windows 9x client computers are not running the Windows 2000 Directory Service client or the Microsoft Internet Print Services. Considering this environment, which methods can clients running Windows 9x use to connect to a network printer when using the Add Printer Wizard?

A. Enter a UNC name.

B. Browse the network.

C. Use the URL name.

D. Search Active Directory directory services.

70-210.02.03.004

You are the administrator of a Windows 2000 Professional computer named WIN2KPRO. An HP DeskJet 540 printing device is connected to the LPT1 port and shared as HPDJ540. The user of an MS-DOS client computer calls you to ask how she can connect to the network printer. Which syntax should you instruct her to use?

A. Net use lpt1: \\win2kpro\hpdj540

B. Net use lpt1: \\hp deskjet 540\win2kpro

C. Net print lpt1: \\win2kpro\hpdj540

D. Net print lpt1: \\hp deskjet 540\win2kpro

Objective 2.3 Answers

70-210.02.03.001

▶ **Correct Answers: A and B**

A. **Correct:** A TCP/IP-based network-interface printing device uses a network interface card (NIC) and TCP/IP to connect directly to the local area network (LAN). If the printer's host name is registered on the network, it can be used to locate and connect to the port using the Microsoft Windows 2000 Standard TCP/IP Port Monitor (SPM).

B. **Correct:** All TCP/IP-based network-interface printing devices must be assigned a valid IP address. This IP address can be used to locate and connect to the port using SPM.

C. **Incorrect:** A printer's MAC address is not used to establish a port connection to a network-interface printing device running the TCP/IP protocol. The Hewlett-Packard Network Port monitor uses the MAC address to communicate with network-interface printing devices running the Data Link Control (DLC) protocol.

D. **Incorrect:** SPM uses either an IP address or IP host name to establish a port connection to a TCP/IP-based network-interface printing device.

70-210.02.03.002

▶ **Correct Answers: D**

A. **Incorrect:** Unless Microsoft Internet Print Services is installed, Windows 95 cannot connect to a printer through the Internet printing facility. A Windows 95 client computer can use standard UNC syntax \\computername\printersharename to connect to the printer. The connection is established either from the command line using the Net Share command or by using the Add Printer Wizard.

B. **Incorrect:** Unless Microsoft Internet Print Services is installed, Windows 98 cannot connect to a printer through the Internet printing facility. A Windows 98 client computer can use standard UNC syntax \\computername\printersharename to connect to the printer. The connection is established either from the command line using the Net Share command or by using the Add Printer Wizard.

C. **Incorrect:** Windows NT cannot connect to a printer through the Internet printing facility. A Windows NT client computer can use standard UNC syntax \\computername\printersharename to connect to the printer. The connection is established either from the command line using the Net Share command or by using the Add Printer Wizard.

Service Pack 7 for Windows NT 4 might provide Internet Printing Services to Windows NT 4. However, this service pack was not released before this book was published.

D. **Correct:** Client computers running Windows 2000 can connect to a printer through the Internet printing facility. The Windows 2000 computer hosting the printer, the print server, must be running IIS. When a printer is shared on a Windows 2000 computer running IIS, a Printers virtual directory is created below the default Web site. You can connect a client computer to the printer by first accessing a list of printers using the following syntax: http://computername/printers. After selecting a printer, click the Connect link appearing in the left frame of the Web page.

70-210.02.03.003

▶ **Correct Answers: A and B**

  A. **Correct:** When a client computer running a down-level operating system such as Windows 98 or Windows NT runs the Add Printer Wizard, you can enter a UNC name. If you know the print server computer name and the printer share name, entering the UNC name saves time because the browser function is not involved in making the connection.

    To streamline the printer installation process, install Windows 9x and Windows NT printer drivers from the Windows 2000 Server installation CD-ROM onto the Windows 2000 print server so that computers running Windows 9x or Windows NT will automatically download and install the printer driver. You can install additional printer drivers by running the Add Printer Driver Wizard. You start this wizard by clicking Add in the Drivers tab in the Print Server Properties dialog box. Intel-based Windows NT 4 and Windows 2000 printer drivers are installed by default.

  B. **Correct:** If you don't know the network path or queue name of a printer on the network, clicking the Browse button displays the Browse For Printer window. Here you can select a print server and printer share.

  C. **Incorrect:** Windows 9x cannot connect to a printer through the Windows 2000 Internet printing facility unless Microsoft Internet Print Services is installed. However, a Windows 9x client is able to use the Internet printing facility to view the properties of a printer through a Web browser. Windows NT is able to view the properties of an Internet printer, but it is unable to connect to the printer through this facility.

  D. **Incorrect:** Windows 9x cannot connect to a printer by browsing the Active Directory store unless the Windows 2000 Directory Services client is installed.

70-210.02.03.004

▶ **Correct Answers: A**

  A. **Correct:** The Net Use command-line utility allows a computer running a Network Driver Interface Specification (NDIS) client to establish a connection with a folder or printer share. The correct syntax for connecting to a printer share is net use lptx: \\printservername\sharename, where x is the port number, printservername is the NetBIOS computer name of the print server, and sharename is the name of the shared printer.

  B. **Incorrect:** Running the Net Use command is correct, but the computer name always precedes the share name.

  C. **Incorrect:** Print is not a valid parameter for the NET.EXE command.

  D. **Incorrect:** Print is not a valid parameter for the NET.EXE command.

OBJECTIVE 2.4

Configure and manage file systems.

Windows 2000 supports the **CD-ROM File System (CDFS), Universal Disk Format (UDF), FAT**, and **NTFS** file systems. You use CDFS for CD-ROM access and UDF primarily for **digital video disk (DVD)** access. Use FAT and NTFS for fixed and removable disk access. The implementation of UDF in Windows 2000 does not support writing to UDF volumes. Instead, you must use proprietary methods to write to UDF volumes in Windows 2000.

Three implementations of FAT exist in Windows 2000: FAT12, **FAT16**, and **FAT32**. FAT12 is for small volume formatting, such as formatting floppy disks; FAT16 and FAT32 support larger volumes. FAT16 is ideal for small disk volumes no larger than 511 MB. A volume up to 4 GB in size is supported on FAT16 but not recommended. The minimum format size of FAT32 in Windows 2000 is 512 MB, and its maximum format size is 32 GB. However, a FAT32 volume created in Windows 98 that is larger than 32 GB can be mounted by Windows 2000. FAT32 provides a higher degree of fault tolerance than FAT16, and its cluster-sizing algorithm makes more efficient use of disk space. You should use FAT16 on volumes that a multiboot computer running MS-DOS, Windows 3.*x*, or Windows 95 must access, and it shouldn't be larger than 2 GB to maintain backward compatibility. You should use FAT32 on volumes that a multiboot computer running Windows 95 OSR2 or Windows 98 must access.

NTFS supports the following features not available to FAT running in Windows 2000: local permissions, compression, encryption, disk quotas, reparse points, directory junctions, volume mount points, sparse files, volume change journals, POSIX application compatibility, distributed link tracking, and cluster remapping. The maximum theoretical size allowed for an NTFS volume is 16 exabytes, but 2 terabytes (2048 gigabytes) is the practical limit. (One exabyte is 1024 petabytes, and 1 petabyte is 1024 terabytes.)

Tip Don't worry about memorizing exactly how much an exabyte is; just know that it's much bigger than a terabyte and that even a terabyte is an enormous amount of storage capacity!

You can use the **Disk Administrator** snap-in to create or delete a partition during or after a Windows 2000 installation. You configure FAT and NTFS partitions using the Disk Administrator snap-in or from the command line using the Format command. If you run the Windows 2000 installation routine on a computer running the Windows NT version of NTFS, any mounted NTFS volumes are converted to NTFS version 5. Windows 2000 does not support previous versions of NTFS. Therefore, any time a previous version of NTFS is mounted on the computer, Windows 2000 automatically converts it to NTFS version 5. FAT volumes are manually converted to NTFS using the CONVERT.EXE command-line utility. Type **convert /?** at the command line to see the syntax for this command. Conversion is one way: After a partition is converted from FAT to NTFS, it cannot be converted back to FAT without first deleting the partition. After a partition is converted to NTFS version 5, the only way to return the partition to the previous file system is to back up the data, delete the partition, reformat the partition to the previous file system, and restore the data.

For this objective, you must be proficient with configuring and administering the NTFS and FAT file systems. You must also understand how conversion works in Windows 2000 and how to convert FAT to NTFS.

Objective 2.4 Questions

70-210.02.04.001

You have a Pentium III computer on which you want to run Windows 2000 Professional. You want to be able to set permissions on individual files. You do not need to run any other operating system on the computer. Which file system should you use on the first hard disk?

A. FAT

B. NTFS

C. CDFS

D. FAT32

70-210.02.04.002

You have a Pentium III computer with two 6-GB fixed disks on which you want to run Windows 2000 Professional. You also want to have the ability to dual-boot Windows 98. You will create a single system volume that is the size of this first fixed disk. Which file system should you use on the first hard disk?

A. FAT

B. NTFS

C. CDFS

D. FAT32

70-210.02.04.003

You are planning to deploy Windows 2000 Professional on 12 Pentium II computers running Windows 98. You want to configure Windows 2000 Setup to convert existing FAT32 file systems automatically to NTFS. What should you do?

A. Add the FileSystem = NTFS entry to SYSPREP.INF.

B. Add the FileSystem = ConvertNTFS entry to SYSPREP.INF.

C. Add the FileSystem = NTFS entry to the [Unattended] section of your answer file.

D. Add the FileSystem = ConvertNTFS entry to the [Unattended] section of your answer file.

Objective 2.4 Answers

70-210.02.04.001

▶ **Correct Answers: B**

A. **Incorrect:** The FAT file system provides operating system compatibility to support multiboot computer configurations. This legacy file system does not include advanced file system features such as local permissions. Local permissions are necessary to implement file-level access protection. You can configure folder shares to provide limited over-the-network access to folders and their contents. Share-level permissions are possible because the Server service provides the security, not the file system.

B. **Correct:** NTFS supports local permissions. Local permissions are stored as a security descriptor with each folder and file on an NTFS partition. The security descriptor contains a discretionary access control list (DACL).

The DACL is a table of access control entries (ACEs) that define user and group access. The security subsystem checks the folder's or file's DACL for ACEs that apply to the user and group security identifiers (SIDs). Many objects in Windows 2000, including user and group objects, contain SIDs. A SID uniquely identifies the object to the operating system. By comparing the ACEs on the file object with the SID or SIDs attempting to access it, the operating system can grant or deny access to the user.

C. **Incorrect:** CDFS is an implementation of ISO 9660 for Windows 2000. This file system does not support file-level security.

D. **Incorrect:** The FAT32 file system is an improvement over the legacy FAT file system. It supports larger disk partitions, minimal fault tolerance for file system recovery, and better performance for large files. FAT16 supports volumes up to 4 GB, whereas FAT32 can manage much larger volume sizes. A Windows 2000 computer running FAT32 can be configured for multiboot with Windows 95 OSR2 or Windows 98. The FAT32 features in Windows 2000 are similar to those in Windows 95 OSR2 and Windows 98.

70-210.02.04.002

▶ **Correct Answers: D**

A. **Incorrect:** The largest FAT volume supported in Windows 2000 is 4095 MB or 4 GB. A volume formatted with FAT is allocated in clusters. The default cluster size is determined by the volume size and can be as large as 64 KB. A volume of 2048 MB to 4095 MB will contain a cluster size of 64 KB. To specify a different cluster size when formatting a volume, run the Format command with the /a:size switch, where the size is the number of clusters or allocation units for the volume.

FAT12 is supported for small volumes such as floppy disks. When FAT is written without a designated number of bits, assume the 16-bit version of FAT, FAT16.

B. **Incorrect:** Microsoft supports NTFS on Windows NT and Windows 2000, but not on Windows 98. If the system volume is formatted with NTFS, it will not be possible to start Windows 98 from this volume.

Note that to dual-boot Windows NT and Windows 2000, Windows NT must be running Service Pack 4 to mount a volume converted to NTFS version 5.

C. **Incorrect:** This file system is not designed to house a functioning operating system. CDFS is supported in both Windows 98 and Windows 2000 to provide access to CD-ROM media.

D. **Correct:** This is the ideal file system for a multiboot configuration containing both Windows 98 and Windows 2000. The FAT32 format and features in Windows 2000 are similar to those of Windows 95 OSR2 and Windows 98. FAT32 allows for much larger volumes than is possible using FAT16. However, Windows 2000 imposes minimum (512 MB) and maximum (32 GB) volume size limits on FAT32. Windows 2000 can still mount a FAT32 volume created in Windows 98 that is not within Windows 2000 formatting size limits.

Cluster sizes are more flexible using FAT32 than they are using FAT16. For example, a FAT32 volume of 512 MB to 8 GB can be created using a cluster size as small as 4 KB.

70-210.02.04.003

▶ **Correct Answers: D**

A. **Incorrect:** SYSPREP.INF is the mini-setup answer file used to further automate installation of images prepared using SysPrep. NTFS conversion occurs during text-mode setup. A SysPrep installation using the SYSPREP.INF file starts in GUI-mode.

B. **Incorrect:** ConvertNTFS does not work in SYSPREP.INF because NTFS conversion happens in text mode and SysPrep begins in GUI-mode. If an installation to be prepared using SysPrep is automated before SysPrep is used, the FileSystem = ConvertNTFS entry is used in the automated installation answer file. SYSPREP.INF supports ExtendOemPartition = 1 (or additional size in megabytes) to extend the active system partition. Only NTFS supports the ExtendOemPartition command. ExtendOemPartition allows for the creation of an image no larger than is required to accommodate the image containing the operating system and applications. The ExtendOemPartition command then increases the size of the system partition to the entire available disk space or the size in megabytes that you specify.

C. **Incorrect:** NTFS conversion is possible during an automated installation routine, but FileSystem = NTFS is not the correct syntax.

D. **Correct:** In a scripted installation of Windows 2000, the FileSystem = ConvertNTFS entry in the [Unattended] section of the answer file converts the primary partition to NTFS during the text-mode phase of installation.

Implementing, Managing, and Troubleshooting Hardware Devices and Drivers

Implementing new hardware in a computer is a two-step process. First, the hardware is connected to the computer's bus and then a device driver is installed so that the operating system can communicate with it. After the hardware is operational, it must be *managed*. Management tasks vary by hardware type. For example, a hard disk is managed by configuring **volumes** and monitoring available space; a display device is managed by configuring the display adapter resolution and color depth. A device that isn't functioning properly or a failure in the operating system requires *troubleshooting*.

Troubleshooting is the process of isolating the source of a system error and correcting it. At first glance this may sound simple, but effective troubleshooting requires tenacity, creativity, and a thorough technical understanding of the system. Troubleshooting is a critical part of administering Microsoft Windows 2000 Professional.

Tested Skills and Suggested Practices

The skills that you need to successfully master the Implementing, Managing, and Troubleshooting Hardware Devices and Drivers Objective Domain on Exam 70-210: Installing, Configuring, and Administering Microsoft Windows 2000 Professional include the following:

- **Perform hardware troubleshooting using tools provided with Windows 2000 Professional and with the tools included in the Windows 2000 Professional Resource Kit.**

    - Practice 1: Run Device Manager to view driver settings. In particular, view resource allocation of various hardware devices such as a modem, a PCMCIA controller, and a USB host controller.

- Practice 2: Using Device Manager, create an All Devices And System Summary report and review the output.

- Practice 3: Run the Add/Remove Hardware Wizard to add, remove, or troubleshoot a device.

- Practice 4: Run DRIVERS.EXE to view a list of running drivers. This utility is contained in both the *Microsoft Windows 2000 Server Resource Kit* and *Windows 2000 Professional Resource Kit*.

- Practice 5: Run DXDIAG.EXE and review the screens in this utility.

- Practice 6: Run the System Information snap-in (MSINFO32.EXE), and query the System Summary node. Run the various system tools available from the System Information snap-in. To access these tools, click Windows on the Tools menu and then click the tool you want to run.

- Practice 7: Run the Windows 2000 Display, Hardware, Modem, Multimedia And Games, Print, and Sound troubleshooters. You can find these troubleshooters on line in Windows 2000 Help under Troubleshooting And Maintenance.

- Practice 8: Navigate through all interfaces described in the answer explanations accompanying the questions.

- **Perform hardware installation, configuration, and upgrade procedures.**

  - Practice 1: Run Device Manager, access the properties of installed devices, and then run the Upgrade Device Driver Wizard available from the Update Driver button in the Driver tab of each device.

  - Practice 2: Visit the Windows Update site by clicking Windows Update on the Start menu.

  - Practice 3: Install Plug and Play hardware, and observe the detection and installation process.

  - Practice 4: Install non-Plug and Play hardware, install supporting device drivers, and allocate system resources required by the hardware.

  - Practice 5: Install a second video adapter and display, and configure the computer for multiple monitor support.

- **Install and configure network adapters, protocols, and services.**

  - Practice 1: Install TCP/IP on a network adapter, and configure it with static addressing. Switch to dynamic addressing to activate APIPA.

  - Practice 2: Install the DHCP Server service on a computer running Windows 2000 Server. Configure a client computer for dynamic addressing, and verify that a dynamic address was assigned to the client computer.

- Practice 3: Use ipconfig to release and renew a DHCP assigned address.

- Practice 4: Install NWLink and CSNW, and modify the frame_type, network number, and internal network number for the adapter bound to NWLink and CSNW.

- Practice 5: Configure a computer with an APM BIOS for APM support using the Power Options program.

- Practice 6: View the Power Options dialog box on an ACPI-compliant computer, and compare the settings to a non-ACPI-compliant computer.

- Practice 7: Install a PC Card, and then stop the card's services and eject the card.

- Practice 8: Install a second processor in an APIC-compatible computer, and use Device Manager to install a multiprocessor-compatible HAL.

- Practice 9: Run the Performance snap-in to log counters contained in the Processor, System, Job Object, Process, and Thread objects. Analyze the collected data, and read the explanations included with the counters.

Further Reading

This "Further Reading" section provides lists of important readings to supplement your current understanding of the skills tested within this Objective Domain. The lists are delineated into pertinent readings for each objective within this Objective Domain. If you feel that you need additional preparation prior to taking the exam, study these sources thoroughly.

Objective 3.1

Microsoft Corporation. *Microsoft Windows 2000 Professional Resource Kit*. Redmond, Washington: Microsoft Press, 2000. Read Chapter 30, "Examining and Tuning Disk Performance," Chapter 31, "Troubleshooting Tools and Strategies," Chapter 32, "Disk Concepts and Troubleshooting," and Appendix C, "Hardware Support."

Microsoft Corporation. *Microsoft Windows 2000 Server Manual*. Redmond, Washington: Microsoft Corporation, 2000. Read the section entitled "Storing Data."

Microsoft Corporation. *MCSE Training Kit—Microsoft Windows 2000 Professional*. Redmond, Washington: Microsoft Press, 2000. Read and complete the practices in Chapter 6, "Managing Disks."

Objective 3.2

Microsoft Corporation. *Microsoft Windows 2000 Professional Resource Kit*. Redmond, Washington: Microsoft Press, 2000. Read pp. 836–843, Chapter 19, "Device Management."

Objective 3.3

Microsoft Corporation. *Microsoft Windows 2000 Professional Resource Kit*. Redmond, Washington: Microsoft Press, 2000. Read Chapter 10, "Mobile Computing"; read pp. 830–835, Chapter 19, "Device Management"; read Chapter 20, "Power Management."

Microsoft Corporation. *MCSE Training Kit—Microsoft Windows 2000 Professional*. Redmond, Washington: Microsoft Press, 2000. Read and complete the practices in Chapter 24, "Configuring Windows 2000 for Mobile Computers."

Microsoft Corporation. *Microsoft Windows 2000 Professional installation CD-ROM*. Redmond, Washington: Microsoft, 2000. Read the "Advanced Power Management" section of the README.DOC file.

Objective 3.4

Microsoft Corporation. *Microsoft Windows 2000 Professional Resource Kit*. Redmond, Washington: Microsoft Press, 2000. Read Chapter 11, "Multimedia," Chapter 12, "Telephony and Conferencing," and Chapter 15, "Scanners and Cameras."

Microsoft Corporation. *Windows 2000 Help*. Redmond, Washington: Microsoft Corporation, 2000. Read the *Troubleshooting and Maintenance* book.

Objective 3.5

Microsoft Corporation. *Device Manager Help*. Redmond, Washington: Microsoft Corporation, 2000. This file is located on line in *%systemroot%*\Help\Devmgr.chm. Read the entire contents of this help file, and navigate to the features outlined in the help file by running Device Manager.

Microsoft Corporation. *MCSE Training Kit—Microsoft Windows 2000 Professional*. Redmond, Washington: Microsoft Press, 2000. Read and complete the practices in Chapter 25, "Implementing, Managing, and Troubleshooting Hardware Devices and Drivers."

Objective 3.6

Microsoft Corporation. *Microsoft Windows 2000 Professional Resource Kit*. Redmond, Washington: Microsoft Press, 2000. Read Chapter 29, "Analyzing Processor Activity."

Objective 3.7

Microsoft Corporation. *Microsoft Windows 2000 Professional Resource Kit*. Redmond, Washington: Microsoft Press, 2000. Read pp. 880–905, Chapter 21, "Local and Remote Network Connections."

Microsoft Corporation. *MCSE Training Kit—Microsoft Windows 2000 Professional*. Redmond, Washington: Microsoft Press, 2000. Read and complete the practices in Chapter 7, "Installing and Configuring Network Protocols."

OBJECTIVE 3.1

Implement, manage, and troubleshoot disk devices.

Windows 2000 supports a variety of storage media technologies. The most common media types are fixed disks, such as Intelligent Drive Electronics or Integrated Drive Electronics (IDE), Advanced Technology Attachment (ATA) or Advanced Technology Attachment Packet Interface (ATAPI), and Small Computer Systems Interface (SCSI) drives; and removable media, such as **digital video disc** or **digital versatile disc** (DVD), compact disc read-only memory (CD-ROM), and tape devices. Storage media is physically connected to the computer's bus by a controller. A software device driver provides the communication between the controller and the operating system. Following hardware installation, storage media is managed and configured in the operating system.

To manage and configure disks and the partitions or volumes that they contain, use the Disk Administrator snap-in. For viewing and troubleshooting devices, including storage media and controllers, use Device Manager. To troubleshoot device and media failures, view the System and Application logs created by the Event Logging service. To monitor system resources, such as fixed disk activity, run the Performance snap-in and use the System Monitor and Performance Logs and Alerts nodes.

Note Use the Diskperf command-line utility to enable and disable physical and logical disk performance counters. By default, the physical disk performance counters are enabled and the logical disk performance counters are not. Type **diskperf /?** at the command line for details on using this utility. Modifications to the performance counters take effect after you restart the operating system.

Windows 2000 supports two disk storage types: **basic disks** (also known as basic storage) and **dynamic disks** (also known as dynamic storage). Basic disks use the traditional method of dividing a physical disk into primary or extended partitions with logical drives. A partition on a basic disk is called a **basic volume**. Basic volumes support other operating systems such as Microsoft Windows NT. Therefore, you must configure a computer configured for multiboot as a basic volume for the system partition. Dynamic disks are divided into **dynamic volumes**. This storage type allows for a number of advanced disk configuration features such as unlimited volumes per dynamic disk, volume spanning, volume extending, **mirroring**, **striping**, and **striping with parity**. Only Windows 2000 supports dynamic disks.

Note Striping with parity and mirroring are not supported in Windows 2000 Professional but are supported in the other editions of Windows 2000. Windows 2000 supports advanced disk configurations created on basic disks when running Windows NT. For example, a volume set created in Windows NT can be read from and written to in Windows 2000.

Installing and configuring tape devices for operation in Windows 2000 is similar to installing and configuring other media types. Windows 2000 includes an optional backup and restore utility, Windows Backup (NTBACKUP.EXE), to make use of the tape device. Windows Backup is run interactively through a graphical interface; by using a variety of switches, it can run without any user interaction. To review the switches that Windows Backup supports, in the Open text box of the Run dialog box, type **ntbackup /?**. The Windows 2000 version of Windows Backup is not limited to tape devices as its target backup media—it supports backup to any writable media type.

You can schedule backups when creating a backup job in Windows Backup or manually by using Windows 2000 Task Scheduler. You configure Task Scheduler by opening the Scheduled Tasks program in Control Panel and then from the Scheduled Task window, opening the Add Scheduled Task icon to start the Scheduled Task Wizard. The Scheduled Task window is also available by clicking the Scheduled Task program in the System Tools program group.

Objective 3.1 Questions

70-210.03.01.001

You are planning to install Windows 2000 Professional on a new Pentium III computer with two 10-GB hard disks. You want the ability to extend a volume on the second hard disk without restarting Windows. Which characteristics define the appropriate type of disk storage for use in this scenario? (Choose two).

A. A basic disk

B. A dynamic disk

C. A simple volume

D. A striped volume

70-210.03.01.002

You have a Pentium III computer running Windows 2000 Professional. You add an Iomega parallel port Zip drive to the system using the Add/Remove Hardware program in Control Panel, but Windows 2000 does not detect the Iomega parallel port Zip drive. What should you do to enable use of your Iomega parallel port Zip drive?

A. Return the Iomega parallel port Zip drive for one with a universal serial bus (USB) interface.

B. Use Registry Editor to enable a communications port for the Zip drive.

C. Use Device Manager to detect the Iomega parallel port Zip drive.

D. Contact Iomega for an updated Zip device driver that will function in Windows 2000.

70-210.03.01.003

You are responsible for deploying Windows 2000 on several computers and want to be able to apply disk quotas to limit disk space used. Which file system is required to support disk quotas?

A. FAT

B. FAT32

C. NTFS

D. Universal Disk Format (UDF)

70-210.03.01.004

You have a computer running Windows 2000 Professional with the following hard disk drive configuration:

- Disk 0: NTFS Layout: Partition (System)

- Disk 1: FAT32 Layout: Partition

- Disk 2: NTFS Layout: Simple

- Disk 3: FAT32 Layout: Partition

Which disk can be extended?

A. Disk 0

B. Disk 1

C. Disk 2

D. Disk 3

Objective 3.1 Answers

70-210.03.01.001

▶ **Correct Answers: B and C**

   A. **Incorrect:** The default disk storage type when a disk is initialized by Windows 2000 is basic storage. This storage type is available to support disk access by Windows 2000 and legacy operating systems that coexist on a computer. A basic disk can contain up to four partitions, either four primary partitions or three primary partitions and an extended partition divided into logical drives. A partition on a basic disk cannot be part of a spanned volume and cannot be extended in Windows 2000. However, a spanned volume (known as a volume set in Windows NT) created or extended in Windows NT can be read and written to by Windows 2000.

   B. **Correct:** A spanned volume is composed of 2 to 32 regions of disk space on 2 to 32 dynamic disks. All drives in the set are configured as dynamic disks to support volume spanning. Only volumes created after upgrading a basic disk to a dynamic disk can be spanned. The result of this limitation is that the system volume and the boot volume on a dynamic disk cannot be part of a spanned volume. Because volume spanning is not fault tolerant, this spanned volume limitation increases system reliability. A spanned volume is created in the Disk Management snap-in by first selecting a region of unallocated space on a dynamic disk and then starting the Create Volume Wizard. After a spanned volume is created, it can be extended. To extend a spanned volume, the volume must be formatted to the New Technology File System (NTFS). Restarting Windows 2000 is not necessary after extending a volume.

C. **Correct:** A simple volume is spanned on multiple dynamic disks. A volume is considered spanned when it contains two or more simple volumes on two or more disks. Volume spanning supports up to 32 disks. A simple volume can be a part of a volume set only if you create it after you upgrade the disk that contains it to a dynamic disk. After you create a spanned volume, you can extend it if it contains no file system or is formatted for NTFS. File allocation table (FAT) and FAT32 volumes cannot be extended. Do not confuse extended partitions with extended volumes. An extended partition is contained on a basic disk and can contain logical drives. An extended volume is a simple or spanned volume extended into additional space.

D. **Incorrect:** Like spanned volumes, striped volumes (Level 0 Redundant Array of Inexpensive Disks or RAID 0) are not fault tolerant. However, they provide significantly improved disk I/O performance because data is accessed across the striped dynamic disks. A striped volume requires at least 2 dynamic disks and supports up to 32 dynamic disks. Striping volumes is mutually exclusive of spanning volumes or extending spanned volumes. You start creating a striped volume in the same way as you create a spanned volume, by selecting a region of unallocated space in the Disk Management snap-in and starting the Create Volume Wizard.

70-210.03.01.002

▶ **Correct Answers: C**

A. **Incorrect:** Windows 2000 supports USB devices, and although returning the Iomega parallel port Zip drive for a USB Zip drive is one solution, it is not the most cost-effective or efficient way to remedy an unrecognized device problem in Windows 2000. If you are unsure whether a device is supported in Windows 2000, check the Windows 2000 Hardware Compatibility List (HCL). Also, check the README.DOC file included on the root of the Windows 2000 Professional installation CD-ROM for any fixes found close to the time that the operating system was released for distribution.

B. **Incorrect:** The Iomega parallel port Zip drive uses a standard LPT port as its interface to the system. LPT ports are automatically detected when Windows 2000 is installed. Check Device Manager to verify that the LPT ports are recognized by the operating system.

C. **Correct:** The Iomega parallel port Zip drive is considered a legacy Plug and Play device. Windows 2000 will detect this device if you locate the parallel port it is attached to in Device Manager and then, in the Port Settings tab, select the Enable Legacy Plug And Play Detection check box. This is the type of detailed information that could appear on Exam 70-210. Thus, be sure you thoroughly review the contents of the README.DOC file on the Windows 2000 Professional installation CD-ROM.

D. **Incorrect:** According to the HCL included on the installation CD-ROM, the Iomega parallel port Zip drive is supported in Windows 2000 and a driver for this device is included. This device is listed in the HCL.TXT file under the section titled "Storage/Removable Drive."

70-210.03.01.003

▶ **Correct Answers: C**

A. **Incorrect:** The FAT file system (FAT12 and FAT16) does not support advanced features such as disk quotas. It was originally designed for relatively small disk partitions and simple folder structures. In Windows 2000, the maximum size for a FAT partition is 4096 MB (4 GB). Windows 2000 supports FAT to make upgrading from other operating systems to Windows 2000 simpler and for computers that will multiboot other operating systems such as MS-DOS or Windows 3.x and Windows 2000.

B. **Incorrect:** The FAT32 file system is an improvement over FAT for a number of reasons. First, FAT32 supports a much larger partition size. Windows 2000 can be used to create a partition up to 32 GB in size, and larger FAT32 partitions created in other operating systems such as Windows 98 can be mounted, read, and written to in Windows 2000. Second, FAT32 supports more flexible cluster sizing and a larger cluster size within the FAT. A feature not supported on FAT32 is disk quotas.

C. **Correct:** NTFS provides performance improvements, reliability enhancements, and new features not found in FAT. A number of features in Windows 2000, such as the storage management based on reparse points and disk quota management, are available only on volumes formatted with NTFS. An important part of supporting disk quotas is the ability to identify file ownership. NTFS is the only file system in Windows 2000 that supports this feature. Disk quotas are applied at the volume level. It is not possible to set per-folder quota limits when using Windows 2000 disk quota management.

D. **Incorrect:** UDF is a new file system standard supported by Windows 2000 for removable disk formats such as DVD, write once, read many (WORM), and compact disc–recordable (CD-R) media. UDF is the successor to CD-ROM File System (CDFS). Like CDFS, Windows 2000 does not support writing to UDF volumes. Third-party software is necessary to write to UDF media. UDF in Windows 2000 does not support disk quotas.

70-210.03.01.004

▶ **Correct Answers: C**

A. **Incorrect:** The system partition contains the operating system startup files. This might or might not be the same partition containing the boot partition. The boot partition contains the operating system files. A layout type of partition means that Disk 0 is a basic disk. Regardless of the disk storage type, basic or dynamic, the system partition cannot be extended.

B. **Incorrect:** Disk 1 is formatted as a FAT32 partition. FAT32 cannot be extended. Additionally, a layout type of partition means that this is a basic disk storage type containing basic volumes. Basic disks and basic volumes do not support volume spanning or volume extending.

C. **Correct:** Disk 2 is a simple volume formatted as NTFS, and it is not serving as the boot or system partition. Because the question doesn't specify whether the volume was created before or after upgrading the storage type from basic to dynamic, you should assume that the volume creation occurred after the storage type was upgraded.

These conditions must be met to extend a volume: the volume does not host the boot or system partition; the volume was created after an upgrade to a dynamic disk; the dynamic volume is not striped (RAID 1 or RAID 5) or mirrored; a simple disk must contain unallocated space for the extension; and the simple or spanned volume to be extended must be running NTFS or no file system at all. An unformatted volume to be extended will be formatted as NTFS.

By definition, a volume is extended into some or all unallocated space on the disk containing the dynamic volume or another dynamic disk. To extend the simple volume, start the Disk Management snap-in, right-click the simple or spanned volume to be extended, and click Extend Volume.

D. **Incorrect:** Like Disk 1, Disk 3 is running FAT32 on a basic disk, so it cannot support extending the volume.

O B J E C T I V E   3 . 2

Implement, manage, and troubleshoot display devices.

Like Windows 98, Windows 2000 includes **multiple monitor support**. When Windows 2000 multiple monitor support is operational, it spans a single desktop over 2 to 10 monitors, effectively expanding the workspace by the number of monitors in operation.

To support this feature, a computer must contain a **Peripheral Component Interconnect (PCI)** or **Accelerated Graphics Port (AGP)** video adapter for each monitor or a distinct output channel on a single adapter for each monitor. A single video adapter with multiple outputs is common in laptop computers, but in most cases, it does not support the multiple monitor feature because the video adapter contains two video outputs on a single channel.

A video adapter embedded on the motherboard to be used for multiple monitor support must be set to Video Graphics Adapter (VGA) in the basic input/output system (BIOS). The BIOS detects the VGA device based on slot order unless the BIOS offers an option for choosing which video adapter is to be treated as the VGA device. Typically, an embedded adapter will be the first detected video adapter device. By default, Windows 2000 recognizes the first detected device as the **primary adapter**. In the case of a motherboard adapter, after installing a second video adapter, the onboard adapter becomes a **secondary adapter**.

The primary adapter displays the Logon dialog box when starting the computer. In addition, most programs will appear on the monitor connected to the primary adapter when they are first opened. Each monitor and adapter set can have a unique configuration based on its combined capabilities. For example, one set can run 800 × 600 resolution with 16-bit color at 60 Hz, while another set can run 1024 × 768 resolution with 24-bit color at 75 Hz.

After you have installed the second video adapter or output channel and it is detected, you configure multiple monitor support using the Settings tab in the Display Properties dialog box.

Note Some video adapter manufacturers include third-party software for configuring multiple monitor support.

Installing a single video adapter is similar to but simpler than installing several adapters for multiple monitor support. It is simpler because resource conflicts are less likely when only a single video adapter is installed. Windows 2000 supports most legacy video adapters that connect to an Industry Standard Architecture (ISA) bus and more modern PCI or AGP video adapters, which are required for multiple monitor support. To configure multiple monitor support, install Windows 2000 before installing another video adapter. This step will avoid the possibility of Windows 2000 Setup disabling one of the video adapters during installation.

Non-Plug and Play video adapters may require that you determine available system resources to make them function properly in Windows 2000. Required system resources to support a video adapter vary by adapter model. Common system resources to support video adapters include memory and I/O ranges, direct memory access (DMA), and interrupt requests (IRQs).

Video adapter reset failure, or memory, I/O, DMA, IRQ, and BIOS (video and system BIOS) conflicts can cause the display to fail or be skewed after a restart. An IRQ sharing conflict is the most likely cause of this behavior. BIOS conflicts are likely if cold-booting the computer resolves the video problem. To resolve this problem, reconfigure the adapter driver to use available resources.

An unreadable display or no video output is commonly caused by a video adapter and monitor configuration mismatch. For example, the display adapter may support 1280 × 1024 resolution, but the monitor may not support this resolution. Another cause of an unreadable display or no video output is the installation of an incompatible video adapter driver. Windows 2000 does not support adapter drivers built for Windows NT.

To troubleshoot an unreadable display or no video output, restart the computer in **Safe Mode** and either select the Last Known Good Configuration option or the Enable VGA Mode option on the Windows 2000 Advanced Options boot menu. If VGA mode is enabled, use the Display program in Control Panel to reconfigure the device and then restart the computer. A restart is not necessary if you use the Last Known Good Configuration option.

For this objective topic, you should be proficient in the following skills:

- Installing multiple video adapters

- Changing the primary monitor

- Arranging multiple monitor behavior

- Moving items between monitors

- Using Device Manager and the Add/Remove Hardware Wizard to configure and troubleshoot a video adapter

- Configuring and troubleshooting legacy and Plug and Play devices for operation in Windows 2000

Objective 3.2 Questions

70-210.03.02.001

You install Windows 2000 Professional on a Pentium 166 computer with an ISA-based display adapter. Windows 2000 Setup fails to detect the ISA-based display adapter. What can you do to use the ISA-based display adapter with Windows 2000?

A. Use REGCLEAN.EXE.

B. Use Registry Editor to enable use of the ISA-based display adapter.

C. Locate and manually install the correct driver for the display adapter.

D. Because Windows 2000 does not support ISA-based display adapters, you must replace it with a compatible PCI or AGP display adapter.

70-210.03.02.002

You have assembled a new Pentium III computer with an AGP video adapter. You run Windows 2000 Professional Setup, and the adapter is automatically configured. You later want to change the refresh frequency of the display. What should you do?

A. Use the Adapter tab in the Display Adapter Advanced Options dialog box.

B. Use the Monitor tab in the Display Adapter Advanced Options dialog box.

C. Open the Computer Management console and access Device Manager.

D. Open the Computer Management console and access the Services and Applications node.

70-210.03.02.003

You are planning to purchase a new Pentium III computer to run Windows 2000 Professional. The motherboard on your new computer will have a built-in display adapter. You want to extend your desktop across two monitors. What should you do? (Choose two.)

A. Install Windows 2000 after installing the second video adapter.

B. Install Windows 2000 before installing the second video adapter.

C. Ensure that the motherboard adapter is multiple-display compatible.

D. Ensure that the motherboard adapter is configured as the primary adapter.

Objective 3.2 Answers

70-210.03.02.001

▶ **Correct Answers: C**

A. **Incorrect:** The RegClean utility is designed to remove unnecessary Windows Registry entries located in HKEY_CLASSES_ROOT. RegClean does not fix every known problem with the registry. For example, it can't fix a corrupt registry. The RegClean utility was originally supplied with Microsoft Visual Basic version 4 for Windows and has since been updated.

B. **Incorrect:** In previous versions of Windows, it was sometimes necessary to use the registry to solve software configuration issues. You can still use the registry for this purpose, but new features in Windows 2000 are specifically designed to deal with unrecognized hardware devices. Therefore, this is not the recommended approach to solving a device configuration failure.

C. **Correct:** ISA devices do not support Plug and Play features available in other bus specifications such as PCI and AGP. Windows 2000 does contain detection routines designed for legacy hardware, but sometimes the operating system will not detect a device and install a driver to support it. To manually install a device driver, run the Add/Remove Hardware Wizard in Control Panel and, on the Choose A Hardware Task screen, select Add/Troubleshoot A Device and click Next. Follow the instructions that appear to install the device driver.

D. **Incorrect:** Windows 2000 supports a wide variety of legacy device drivers. If the device driver does not appear in the list of supported devices displayed through the Add/Remove Hardware Wizard, check the Windows 2000 Hardware Compatibility List (HCL) and check with the hardware vendor.

70-210.03.02.002

▶ **Correct Answers: B**

A. **Incorrect:** Use the Adapter tab to see detailed adapter hardware information, the list of video modes supported by the adapter, and the properties of the adapter. The properties of the adapter show the status of the device, the drivers loaded to support the device, and the system resources allocated to the device. This information is also shown in Device Manager.

B. **Correct:** The question states that you want to modify the monitor's refresh frequency. You configure display settings in the Monitor tab, which provides information on the model or type of monitor detected and the monitor's properties. You also configure the refresh frequency and Mode Pruning in this tab. You enable Mode Pruning by selecting the Hide Modes That This Monitor Cannot Display check box.

Mode Pruning removes display modes that the display and video adapters in combination cannot support. Only the modes that are common to both devices are made available to the system. This feature requires that the operating system know specifically which monitor and video adapter are connected to the computer. When both devices are known because they are Plug and Play compatible or they are manually specified, Mode Pruning is available. Click the List All Modes button in the Adapter tab to see a list of all modes.

Note that this question focuses on knowing how to navigate the Windows 2000 interface to configure settings. You must be able to proficiently navigate in the graphical user interface (GUI) before taking many of the Microsoft certification exams.

C. **Incorrect:** The properties of the adapter and the monitor are accessible through Device Manager. You complete system resource configuration or modification from here but not other monitor and adapter settings.

D. **Incorrect:** The Services and Applications node shows installed software below it, such as the Windows Management Instrumentation (WMI) service and other services. This interface provides a central location to configure and manage the services.

70-210.03.02.003

▶ **Correct Answers: B and C**

A. **Incorrect:** If Windows 2000 Setup detects both a motherboard video adapter and another adapter in a PCI or AGP bus slot, it will disable the motherboard video adapter. Additionally, the BIOS on some computers will detect a video adapter in a card slot and automatically disable the motherboard video adapter. If this occurs, attempt to modify the BIOS configuration so that the motherboard adapter is not disabled. Some BIOS utilities will not allow you to change this configuration setting.

B. **Correct:** When Windows 2000 is installed on a computer with a single video adapter on the motherboard, a video adapter driver will be loaded for the onboard device. After Windows 2000 is set up, shut down Windows 2000, power off the computer, and install a second PCI or AGP video adapter. Upon Windows 2000 startup, the video adapter card will be detected and the appropriate driver will be installed to support it. As long as the BIOS does not disable the motherboard video adapter, it will be possible to configure the computer to support multiple displays.

C. **Correct:** Some onboard video adapters do not support multiple displays. This is usually indicated if the motherboard video adapter is automatically disabled when a video adapter card is installed. Laptop computers contain onboard video adapters that are often disabled when connected to a docking station containing a video adapter card.

D. **Incorrect:** In a multiple monitor configuration, the onboard video adapter becomes the secondary video source. There is always one primary video source and one or more (up to nine) additional secondary video sources. The primary adapter should not be stopped in a multiple monitor configuration.

Implement, manage, and troubleshoot mobile computer hardware.

Mobile computing often involves using battery power as an energy source. Many technological advances have been made to extend battery life. There are two ways this is accomplished: by improving battery technology and by reducing power consumption. The operating system and the computer hardware can play a significant role in the latter. Reduced power consumption technology has also crossed over into desktop computer systems.

Windows 2000 supports two power management specifications: **Advanced Power Management (APM)** and **Advanced Configuration and Power Interface (ACPI)**. ACPI-compliant computers can take full advantage of reduced power consumption by controlling power requirements for Plug and Play hardware and applications. ACPI is a more advanced form of power management supported by both the operating system and the computer system hardware.

If a computer is ACPI compliant, it is indicated in Device Manager under the Computer node. ACPI support is provided by the ACPI driver (ACPI.SYS) and the ACPI embedded controller driver (ACPIEC.SYS). These drivers are loaded upon operating system startup and are located in the *%systemroot%*\System32\Drivers folder.

In ACPI systems, the operating system—not the hardware—is tasked with managing hardware power consumption. The operating system controls power consumption of the ACPI-compliant system board and all connected Plug and Play devices. To optimize power efficiency, consider replacing any legacy hardware with Plug and Play devices.

You configure APM using the Power Options program in Control Panel. Power Options will display only power management features that match the hardware's power management specifications. For example, if a computer is ACPI compliant, the APM tab will *not* appear because power management is controlled entirely by ACPI.

For this objective topic, you must be able to use the Power Options program to do the following:

- Choose or create a new power scheme and customize the power scheme settings.

- Enable or disable **Hibernation** mode.

- Configure power alarms, **Standby** mode, and advanced settings.

- Configure APM on non-ACPI-compliant computers that support APM.

Windows 2000 supports disk and monitor power level control and hibernation on all computer hardware. APM- and ACPI-compliant hardware is not necessary for these features. Standby mode requires APM- or ACPI-compliant hardware.

Hibernation requires enough disk capacity to create a file named HIBERFIL.SYS on the root of the boot partition. The file size is equal to the amount of RAM in the computer. After you enable hibernation in Power Options, Hibernate is an available option in the Shut Down Windows dialog box. Hibernation and standby activation are usually associated with a hardware controlled key or key sequence on APM or ACPI computer hardware. You use the Power Options program to configure the operating system to react to hardware events such as pressing a standby key or closing the lid.

If you will be upgrading a computer to Windows 2000 that is running third-party power management software, consider disabling it so that Windows 2000 power management support is installed.

PC Card support, previously known as **Personal Computer Memory Card International Association (PCMCIA)**, is another important enhancement, particularly for mobile computers. On a mobile computer, PC Cards plug into a PC Card slot. Windows 2000 includes CardBus support so that the 32-bit PC Card hardware can perform high-bandwidth I/O operations such as video image playback.

Note To use a network adapter in the PC Card slot, both the PC Card socket driver and network driver must be Plug and Play compatible.

To support Plug and Play capability, a PC Card contains identifying information that Windows 2000 uses to create a unique device ID called the Card Information Structure (CIS). After creating the CIS, Windows 2000 installs a driver to support the card. The three types of drivers are the following: standard Plug and Play device drivers for PC Cards, such as Network Driver Interface Specification (NDIS) version 5.*x* drivers for network adapters and miniport drivers for Small Computer Systems Interface (SCSI) cards; generic device drivers for modems and disk drives; and vendor-supplied device drivers.

If a Plug and Play device driver is contained in the DRIVER.CAB file, it is automatically installed for the device. DRIVER.CAB is copied by the Windows 2000 setup routine into the *%systemroot%*\Driver Cache\i386 folder. If the driver is not contained in the DRIVER.CAB file, the Add/Remove Hardware Wizard starts automatically.

You should be familiar with how to navigate PC Card and PC Card controller properties in Device Manager. For example, use the PCMCIA Adapters node in Device Manager to view and troubleshoot the properties of the card bus controller. Also, from the Unplug or Eject Hardware icon on the taskbar, stop a card's operation before removal.

Objective 3.3 Questions

70-210.03.03.001

You are thinking about installing Windows 2000 on your laptop computer. Your laptop computer has an APM-based BIOS, and you want to know whether the BIOS has any known problems. What should you do?

A. Use Device Manager.

B. Run the Dxdiag support tool.

C. Run the Apmstat utility.

D. Obtain a diagnostic utility from the original equipment manufacturer (OEM).

70-210.03.03.002

You install Windows 2000 Professional on a Pentium III computer. You open the Power Options program in Control Panel, but no APM tab is displayed. Which conditions are most likely to cause the absence of the APM tab from the Power Options Properties dialog box? (Choose two.)

A. APM is disabled in the BIOS.

B. The computer does not have an APM-based BIOS.

C. The computer has an ACPI-compliant system board.

D. The computer does not have a smart uninterruptible power supply (UPS) device connected to the serial port.

70-210.03.03.003

Which condition allows Windows 2000 Professional to automatically install and configure a PC Card for your laptop computer?

A. The PC Card vendor has supporting drivers for the socket.

B. The PC Card vendor has supporting drivers for the PC Card.

C. The PC Card vendor has supporting drivers for the PC Card and socket.

D. Windows 2000 Professional includes supporting drivers for the socket.

E. Windows 2000 Professional includes supporting drivers for the PC Card.

F. Windows 2000 Professional includes supporting drivers for the PC Card and socket.

Objective 3.3 Answers

70-210.03.03.001

▶ **Correct Answers: C**

A. **Incorrect:** Device Manager might display status information on the function of APM, but known problems with an APM-based BIOS will not appear in this interface. APM may appear under Device Manager's Batteries node or System Devices node, or it might not appear at all in Device Manager.

B. **Incorrect:** You use DXDIAG.EXE, located in the %systemroot%\System32 folder, to report detailed information on all installed Microsoft DirectX multimedia components and to troubleshoot any errors occurring in them. This utility tests sound, graphics output, and DirectPlay service providers, and it disables some hardware acceleration features. It has no purpose related to the Windows 2000 power management facility.

C. **Correct:** The Advanced Power Management Status (APMSTAT.EXE) utility is specifically designed for testing a computer's APM-based BIOS for compatibility with Windows 2000 APM support. This tool is located on the Windows 2000 Professional installation CD-ROM in the \Support\Tools\Support.cab file. You can extract APMSTAT.EXE from SUPPORT.CAB or run SETUP.EXE from the \Support\Tools folder to install all support utilities.

APM is a pre-ACPI standard for power management. This utility will not diagnose an ACPI-compliant system because APM is irrelevant to this platform. If a portable computer has an APM-based BIOS, Apmstat determines whether the BIOS has any known problems. If Apmstat does not report known problems, use APM to manage power on the portable computer. To accomplish this, select APM in the APM tab. This tab is part of the Power Options program in Control Panel.

D. **Incorrect:** Windows 2000 Professional includes the Apmstat utility for this purpose. Therefore, it is not necessary to contact the hardware manufacturer for a diagnostic utility. If APM does not appear to be functioning properly, check the Windows 2000 Hardware Compatibility List (HCL) and contact the manufacturer for any recommended BIOS updates.

70-210.03.03.002

▶ **Correct Answers: B and C**

A. **Incorrect:** In an APM system, the BIOS provides power management functions unless the operating system is able to supersede this role. As a result, power management can be disabled in the BIOS and APM will continue to function in the operating system. Windows 2000 Professional provides operating system–level power management if the APM 1.2 specification is supported in the BIOS.

B. **Correct:** A computer without an APM-based BIOS, a computer containing multiple processors, or a computer that supports ACPI will not show an APM tab in the Power Options Properties dialog box. Windows 2000 Professional can still provide limited power management features, specifically disk and monitor power control and hibernation, to computers without BIOS-level power management support. You configure power to the disk and monitor on the Power Schemes tab in the Power Options dialog box; you configure hibernation in the Hibernate tab. Standby mode and advanced battery management features are available only on APM and ACPI systems.

C. **Correct:** An ACPI-based computer does not contain an APM tab in the Power Options Properties dialog box. On an APM-based system, you use the APM tab to enable and disable APM support. In contrast, ACPI functions are automatic and fully controlled by the operating system. You can change individual power management settings in the Power Options Properties dialog box, but you cannot enable and disable operating system ACPI support. In an ACPI-compliant computer system, ACPI manages power consumption of all installed Plug and Play hardware, the operating system, and application software.

D. **Incorrect:** A desktop computer running Windows 2000 Professional will display a UPS tab in the Power Options Properties dialog box. You configure a Component Object Model (COM) port, UPS manufacturer, and UPS settings appropriate to the manufacturer on the UPS tab. You also view the status of the UPS service from this location.

70-210.03.03.003

▶ **Correct Answers: F**

A. **Incorrect:** PC Card vendors do not create drivers to support the socket where their cards are installed. Socket driver creation is the responsibility of the PC Card socket vendor. Manual socket driver installation is necessary for operating systems that do not include native PC Card socket driver support, such as MS-DOS.

B. **Incorrect:** PC Card vendors create the drivers to support their hardware in various operating systems. These drivers are required for device classes that Windows 2000 Professional does not natively support and devices that are not supported by the drivers included with the operating system. If the PC Card contains configuration information, the operating system initializes the device and passes the configuration information to the driver. The PC Card driver alone does not initiate an automatic installation and configuration.

C. **Incorrect:** The PC Card vendor creates drivers for the PC Card. The PC Card socket vendor creates drivers for the PC Card socket.

D. **Incorrect:** Windows 2000 Professional ships with many supporting drivers for the socket. A PC Card socket is called a CardBus Controller in the operating system. To see a list of bundled CardBus Controller drivers, run the Add/Remove Hardware Wizard and select PCMCIA Adapters from the list of hardware types. The appropriate driver bundled with Windows 2000 Professional is automatically installed when Windows 2000 Setup runs. To see if a CardBus Controller is installed and functioning properly, run Device Manager and, from the default view, select the PCMCIA Adapters node and then open the properties of the CardBus Controller appearing under this node. The PC Card socket driver alone does not initiate automatic installation and configuration of a PC Card.

E. **Incorrect:** Windows 2000 Professional ships with a number of PC Card drivers created by the PC Card vendors. The presence of the driver on the Windows 2000 Professional installation CD-ROM does not guarantee that a driver is automatically installed and configured in the operating system. The PC Card socket driver must be installed before the PC Card driver is installed.

F. **Correct:** If Windows 2000 Professional includes supporting drivers for the PC Card and for the socket, detection, installation, and configuration are automatic. If drivers are not available on the Windows 2000 Professional installation CD-ROM, the operating system might detect the devices, but you are prompted to supply an alternate location for the necessary drivers.

O B J E C T I V E   3 . 4

Implement, manage, and troubleshoot input and output (I/O) devices.

Windows 2000 supports a variety of **input/output (I/O)** hardware devices, each requiring driver installation, configuration, management, and, in some cases, troubleshooting to achieve optimal or proper operation. The first three objectives in this Objective Domain were concerned with disk, display, and **Personal Computer Memory Card International Association (PCMCIA)** device configuration. All of these devices use I/O operations to move data from one location to another. This objective focuses on the following hardware devices, which are also involved in I/O operations:

- Multimedia hardware

- **Modems**

- Wireless hardware, primarily **Infrared Data Association (IrDA) devices**

- **Universal serial bus (USB) devices**

- **Smart Card devices** (readers and cards)

Typical multimedia hardware includes CD, **digital video disc or digital versatile disc (DVD)**, camera, **Musical Instrument Digital Interface (MIDI)**, and scanner devices. DVD media is a relatively new standard for digital storage and delivery of audio, video, and data, popularized for its enormous media capacity. DVD media can hold 8 to 40 times more data than traditional CD media. Each DVD format is intended for a specific purpose. **DVD-video** is designed for video playback of **Moving Pictures Experts Group v2 (MPEG-2)** video; DVD-audio is designed for audio playback of Dolby Digital (AC-3) or MPEG-2 audio; DVD read-only memory (DVD-ROM) and DVD-recordable (DVD-R) are replacements for CD-ROM and are designed to read data; DVD-write once (DVD-WO) is designed for data archiving; and DVD-random access media (DVD-RAM) and digital versatile disc+Read/Write (DVD+RW) formats are for rewritable storage. Windows 2000 supports DVD through the **Universal Disk Format (UDF)** 1.5 file system. UDF 1.5 in Windows 2000 does *not* support recording capabilities for those DVD formats that support write operations. Instead, third-party software is necessary to record to DVD media in Windows 2000.

Any installed devices appear in Device Manager. You use this interface to perform device troubleshooting, device driver updates, and operating system resource allocation. Administrative privileges are required to modify device settings in Device Manager. If an installed device does not appear in Device Manager, this might be caused by a missing device driver or an improperly configured basic input/output system (BIOS).

Use the Add/Remove Hardware Wizard to add any device drivers for devices that Windows 2000 doesn't automatically detect. Hardware detection is usually followed by automatic device driver installation. You also use this wizard interface to remove, unplug, or troubleshoot hardware. You use the Scanners and Cameras program in Control Panel to install a digital camera, scanner, or other still image device that was not detected by Plug and Play enumeration. If running a hardware installation wizard fails to install a device, check the BIOS to make sure the device class is enabled. For example, if an installed USB controller does not appear in Device Manager, make sure that USB support is enabled in the BIOS.

Drivers for **Personal Computer/Smart Card (PC/SC)**-compliant Plug and Play smart cards and readers are included with the operating system. Smart cards typically connect through an RS-232 cable (serial connection) or in a **PC Card** socket. You use smart cards for domain authentication, remote dial-up network access, and other applications that require secure logon. Windows 2000 does not support non-PC/SC-compliant or non-Plug and Play smart card readers. To use smart cards, the network must support a **public key infrastructure (PKI)** and an **Enterprise Certification Authority (CA)**, and each computer that will use smart card logon requires a smart card reader.

If a device controlled by the BIOS appears in Device Manager but is not functioning properly (usually indicated by a yellow warning icon or red failure icon), update the BIOS. Yellow warning and red failure icons might appear in Device Manager if resource conflicts occur between I/O devices. Resource conflicts are unlikely between Plug and Play-compatible devices but are more common when non-Plug and Play drivers are installed. Use the Resource By Type and Resources By Connection Device Manager views to see how all system resources are allocated.

Devices connected to an I/O port such as a USB controller might appear in different locations in Device Manager. For example, in the Device By Type Device Manager view, USB game controllers are listed under Human Interface Devices. If a device can't be located, go to the View menu in Device Manager and then click Show Hidden Devices. You can view, delete, or uninstall devices not currently connected to the computer (phantom devices) in Device Manager by typing the following environment variable at the command line: **set devmgr_show_nonpresent_devices=1**. Next run Device Manager at the command line by typing **devmgmt.msc**. After Device Manager is running, click the Show Hidden Devices option on the View menu so that the phantom devices appear.

Tip To be able to permanently view devices not currently connected in Device Manager, select the System program in Control Panel, click the Advanced tab, click the Environment Variables button, and add the phantom devices environment variable as a new system variable.

Other important tools for troubleshooting I/O errors are the **DirectX Diagnostic Tool** (DXDIAG.EXE) and the **System Information snap-in** (MSINFO32.EXE). You use Dxdiag to report detailed information on all installed DirectX multimedia components and to troubleshoot errors occurring in any installed DirectX components. The System Information snap-in is a Microsoft Management Console (MMC) interface to hardware, system components, and software configuration data.

Device Manager and the System Information snap-in are nodes of the Computer Management snap-in. You can also start these tools independently of the Computer Management snap-in.

After a device appears in Device Manager, you configure and troubleshoot using a variety of Control Panel programs. To configure multimedia hardware, use the Scanners and Cameras program, or the Sounds and Multimedia program depending on the multimedia hardware requiring configuration. To configure and troubleshoot modems, run the Phones and Modems program, and to configure and troubleshoot IrDA devices, run the Wireless Link program.

If a DVD device appears to be set up properly, make sure that the appropriate decoding hardware or software is installed to play back or record to the media. If a supported decoder is installed, check that the display adapter and monitor can support 800 × 600 × 16 bits per pixel (BPP) graphics or better. If the DVD Player is used to play back DVD-Video, it searches all local drives for the Video_TS folder. The file in this folder is run and video streaming begins. If the same folder name exists on another local drive, the DVD Player will fail to play the DVD.

To demonstrate your proficiency with this objective, you must be able to use Device Manager and the Add/Remove Hardware Wizard to implement, manage, and troubleshoot I/O devices, and you must be able to use the individual device configuration programs in Control Panel as well.

Objective 3.4 Questions

70-210.03.04.001

You connect a legacy scanner device to a computer running Windows 2000 Professional, but the operating system does not automatically install the scanner. What should you do to install the device under Windows 2000?

A. Use Device Manager to add the scanner.

B. Use the Computer Management console to add the scanner.

C. Use the Administrative Tools program in Control Panel to add the scanner.

D. Use the Scanners and Cameras program in Control Panel to add the scanner.

70-210.03.04.002

You acquire a Pentium III computer running Windows 2000 Professional. You connect a digital camera to one of the USB ports on the computer, but Windows does not install the device. What is the most likely cause?

A. USB support is disabled in the BIOS.

B. USB support is disabled in Windows.

C. The USB port is physically damaged.

D. The device is not supported by Windows 2000. You might be able to obtain an updated driver from the device manufacturer.

70-210.03.04.003

You want to view a list of installed multimedia devices, determine driver versions, and perform diagnostics. Which interfaces should you use?

A. The Audio tab of the Sounds and Multimedia program.

B. The Sounds tab of the Sounds and Multimedia program.

C. The Hardware tab of the Sounds and Multimedia program.

D. The Sound, Video, and Game Controllers node in Device Manager.

70-210.03.04.004

Your Pentium III computer running Windows 2000 Professional has a 40× CD-ROM drive with a head-phone jack. You insert your favorite audio CD into the drive and plug a new pair of headphones into the jack on the front of the CD-ROM drive, but there is no audible sound. What is the most likely cause?

A. Windows 2000 does not support the sound card.

B. Digital CD Playback is enabled for the CD-ROM drive.

C. The CD-ROM drive is not connected to the sound card.

D. Digital CD Playback is disabled for the CD-ROM drive.

70-210.03.04.005

Which three methods can you use to install a modem under Windows 2000 Professional? (Choose three.)

A. Use Device Manager.

B. Plug in a Plug and Play modem.

C. Use the Mail and Fax program in Control Panel.

D. Use the Add/Remove Hardware program in Control Panel.

E. Use the Add/Remove Programs program in Control Panel.

F. Use the Phone and Modem Options program in Control Panel.

70-210.03.04.006

You attach an IrDA device transceiver to a serial port on your computer running Windows 2000 Professional, but Windows does not automatically install the device. What should you do to install the IrDA device?

A. Use the Wireless Link program in Control Panel.

B. Use the Add/Remove Hardware program in Control Panel.

C. Use the Add/Remove Programs program in Control Panel.

D. This is not possible because Windows 2000 does not support an IrDA device connected to a serial port.

Objective 3.4 Answers

70-210.03.04.001

▶ **Correct Answers: D**

A. **Incorrect:** Device Manager is the proper tool to use to troubleshoot devices that are known by Windows 2000 Professional. The devices that appear in Device Manager are detected either automatically by the operating system or through the manual installation of a device driver. You can use Device Manager to scan for Plug and Play-compliant hardware, but it won't detect and install legacy devices.

B. **Incorrect:** The Computer Management console contains a number of snap-ins designed to manage the operating system and hardware. Computer Management contains utilities for managing the system, storage devices, services, and applications. There is no facility in this console for installing legacy devices.

C. **Incorrect:** Double-clicking the Administrative Tools program in Control Panel displays the same list of administrative tools that are available by clicking the Start menu, pointing to Programs, and pointing to Administrative Tools. The Administrative Tools option is not available from the Start menu by default. It is enabled by selecting the Display Administrative Tools check box on the Advanced tab in the Taskbar And Start Menu Properties dialog box. There is no facility within Administrative Tools to install legacy devices.

D. **Correct:** Running the Scanners and Cameras program displays the Scanners And Cameras Properties dialog box. Clicking Add in this dialog box runs the Scanners and Cameras Installation Wizard. After a scanner or camera device driver is installed, additional configuration of the device is completed from the Scanners And Cameras Properties dialog box.

70-210.03.04.002

▶ **Correct Answers: A**

A. **Correct:** When a USB device is plugged into a port for the first time, Windows 2000 Professional detects and installs a device driver for the device. For detection and driver installation to occur, USB must be enabled in the BIOS on computers that include a USB enable/disable BIOS feature. However, many computers containing USB ports do not contain this setting in the BIOS. If USB support is provided through a USB hub card, the BIOS is not involved in enabling or disabling USB activities.

B. **Incorrect:** It is possible to disable a USB bus controller, USB hub, or USB device in Windows 2000 through Device Manager. However, to disable any of these devices using Device Manager, the device drivers must first be installed for the devices. USB bus controller and the USB hub drivers are automatically installed when Windows 2000 is installed. You could argue that one or both of these drivers were manually disabled using Device Manager, but this is less likely than USB support being disabled in the BIOS.

C. **Incorrect:** This is possible but unlikely. If a USB port (hub) is damaged, Device Manager should indicate this with a yellow warning or red failure icon next to the device.

D. **Incorrect:** This is also possible but less likely than BIOS support being disabled in the BIOS. Through Plug and Play enumeration, Windows 2000 will detect a new device even if a corresponding device driver doesn't exist for it. If you suspect that the USB device doesn't have a Windows 2000 device driver, check with the manufacturer.

70-210.03.04.003

▶ **Correct Answers: C**

A. **Incorrect:** You use the Audio tab to select the preferred device, control the volume, and configure advanced settings for sound playback, sound recording, and MIDI message playback. You also use this tab to configure Windows 2000 Professional to use only preferred devices selected in this interface.

B. **Incorrect:** You use the Sounds tab to associate sound (.wav) files with Windows events such as receiving an e-mail message or starting Windows. You also use this interface to select or create and save a sound scheme, to adjust the volume, and to indicate whether the volume control should or shouldn't appear on the taskbar.

C. **Correct:** The Hardware tab lists all installed sound and multimedia devices, such as DVD/CD-ROM drives and sound cards. Individual device and multimedia software components are shown here as well: for example, sound card game ports, legacy audio drivers, and audio codecs. If you select the item appearing in the Devices box, summary properties of each device will appear in the Hardware tab. You access detailed properties of a device by double-clicking the item listed in the Devices box or selecting the item and clicking the Properties button. You start troubleshooting by selecting the item and clicking the Troubleshooting button.

D. **Incorrect:** Some but not all multimedia devices appear under the Sound, Video, and Game Controllers node in Device Manager. For example, DVD/CD-ROM drives do not appear under this node. Double-clicking any of the items that do appear under this node shows their properties. This is the same dialog box that appears when you select the item from the Hardware tab of the Sounds And Multimedia Properties dialog box and click the Properties button.

70-210.03.04.004

▶ **Correct Answers: B**

A. **Incorrect:** It is unlikely that the sound card is part of the audio playback facility available from the headphone jack on the front of the CD-ROM drive.

B. **Correct:** If Digital CD Playback is enabled for a CD-ROM drive, audio output from the headphone jack on the CD-ROM drive is disabled. You enable/disable this property from the Properties menu of the CD-ROM drive. To view the properties, double-click the CD-ROM device in the Hardware tab of the Sounds And Multimedia Properties dialog box. In the Properties tab of the device is the Enable Digital CD Audio For This CD-ROM Device check box. Clear this check box to disable Digital CD Playback.

C. **Incorrect:** The headphone jack on the front of a CD-ROM drive will function as long as the CD-ROM drive is connected to an internal or external power source and the play instruction can be sent to the device. You should assume that the CD-ROM is playing the audio CD because the question doesn't say that the CD isn't playing, just that nothing is heard through the headphone jack.

D. **Incorrect:** Disabling Digital CD Playback will enable the headphone jack output as explained earlier.

70-210.03.04.005

▶ **Correct Answers: B, D, and F**

A. **Incorrect:** You use Device Manager to check the properties of installed devices and to scan for hardware changes. You use the Scan For Hardware Changes option if a Plug and Play device is not automatically detected after uninstalling it.

B. **Correct:** After connecting a Plug and Play modem to the computer, the Install New Modem screen of the Add/Remove Hardware Wizard appears and automatically detects the modem or allows you to manually select a modem from the list of known devices. The detection option queries the modem to configure it. If it cannot detect the modem, it prompts you to select the appropriate manufacturer and model.

C. **Incorrect:** The Mail and Fax functions are separate programs in the Windows 2000 Professional Control Panel. You use the Mail program to create and configure e-mail and fax accounts. You use the Fax program to configure fax properties such as cover page information, to obtain fax status information, and to configure advanced fax options such as adding a fax printer to the list of installed printers.

D. **Correct:** From the Add/Remove Hardware Wizard, navigate to the Add A New Device option on the Choose A Hardware Device screen. After selecting this option and clicking Next, you can either search for new hardware or select the hardware from a list. If a new modem is detected from this wizard or you select the Modems hardware type and click Next, the Install New Modem screen appears. From this screen, detection or manual installation is the same as outlined earlier.

E. **Incorrect:** You use the Add/Remove Programs program to install, remove, or update windows components and third-party software installed on the computer. Any programs listed in the Currently Installed Programs box are listed in the registry under HKEY_LOCAL_MACHINE\SOFTWARE\Microsoft\Windows\CurrentVersion\Uninstall. Each program's key data contains display name and uninstall information used by the Add/Remove Programs program. This program is not used to install a modem.

F. **Correct:** Clicking Add in the Modems tab in the Phone And Modem Options dialog box opens the Install New Modem screen of the Add/Remove Hardware Wizard. From this screen, detection or manual installation is the same as outlined earlier.

After a modem is installed, you can configure the following settings by using the Phone and Modem Options program: modem dialing rules, modem configuration, troubleshooting (diagnostics and logging), and adding or configuring existing telephony providers.

70-210.03.04.006

▶ **Correct Answers: B**

A. **Incorrect:** You use the Wireless Link program to configure file transfer, to configure photo image transfer, to view hardware properties, and to troubleshoot installed infrared port (device transceiver) hardware. This question specifically states that a device transceiver is connected to a Component Object Model (COM) port. If the transceiver is part of the computer's system board and the Wireless Link program does not appear in Control Panel, check the BIOS to confirm that the port is enabled and that a COM port is assigned to the device.

B. **Correct:** Unlike a USB port connection, it is likely that Windows 2000 Professional will not detect a Plug and Play device connected to a COM port without first running the Add/Remove Hardware Wizard. Instruct the Add/Remove Hardware Wizard to detect the hardware. Detection using the wizard occurs in two phases. Phase 1 runs Plug and Play detection; phase 2 runs more invasive detection routines to locate legacy devices. If the hardware is not detected, select Infrared Devices from the Hardware Type screen and click Next to select and install an infrared device. If the manufacturer and model of the infrared device does not appear, choose Serial Cable Using IrDA Protocol from the list of standard infrared ports.

C. **Incorrect:** You use the Add/Remove Programs program to install, remove, or update Windows components and third-party software installed on the computer. This program is not used to install new hardware.

D. **Incorrect:** The Windows 2000 Infrared Monitor service supports data transfer over infrared connections with computers, printers (IrLPT), cameras (IrTran-P), cellular phones, organizers, and other devices that use IrDA protocols supported by the service.

OBJECTIVE 3.5

Update drivers.

Windows 2000 maintains a list of installed hardware and the device drivers that support the hardware in the HKEY_LOCAL_MACHINE registry key. When a new device driver is needed, the device driver's key is queried to determine the current version of the installed driver.

A number of procedures exist for updating installed drivers. The simplest way to update drivers is by using the Windows Update tool. This tool is located on the Start menu unless network policies restrict access to it. It is also accessible through Device Manager's Upgrade Device Driver Wizard or from the Add Printer Wizard interface. If it is available, selecting Windows Update opens *http://windowsupdate.microsoft.com/*. The first visit to this site installs the Microsoft Active Setup ActiveX components. These components customize the online product update catalog for the computer running the update.

If a driver update needs to be removed, you can connect to the Windows Update site and follow the instructions to restore the previous configuration or run the Update Wizard Uninstall tool. This is a system tool available in the System Information snap-in.

Individual updates are available through a number of interfaces in Windows 2000 Professional. You update a printer driver by accessing the properties of a printer in the Printers window, clicking the Advanced tab, and clicking New Driver to start the Add Printer Driver Wizard.

Note The Windows Update button is not available in the Add Printer Driver Wizard, but it is available in the Add Printers Wizard.

You update other device drivers by accessing the properties of the device in Device Manager, clicking the Driver tab, and clicking Update Driver to start the Upgrade Device Driver Wizard. The Driver tab also includes name, location, and version information on currently installed device drivers.

The Add Printer Driver Wizard and the Upgrade Device Driver Wizard allow you to install a driver from the Windows 2000 Professional installation CD-ROM or from an alternate location. Administrator privileges are required to manually install device drivers. Plug and Play devices that are detected and automatically installed *do not* require Administrator privileges.

Objective 3.5 Questions

70-210.03.05.001

You administer a Pentium III computer running Windows 2000 Professional. Which interface should you use to upgrade drivers?

A. Device Manager.

B. The Add/Remove Hardware Wizard.

C. Environment variables.

D. The Component Services console.

70-210.03.05.002

You administer a Pentium III computer running Windows 2000 Professional. You suspect that an outdated driver is causing intermittent problems while running an application. You want to display a list of all drivers running. What should you do?

A. Use Device Manager.

B. Use the Add/Remove Hardware Wizard.

C. Use the CIPHER.EXE command-line utility.

D. Use the DRIVERS.EXE command-line utility.

70-210.03.05.003

A hard disk on your computer running Windows 98 fails, and you decide to install Windows 2000 Professional on the computer after replacing the hard disk and checking the Windows 2000 Hardware Compatibility List (HCL). You replace the hard disk and install Windows 2000 on the computer. One driver is not automatically installed by Windows 2000. Which conditions might require manual installation of drivers? (Choose all that apply.)

A. An error occurs during installation.

B. The driver package is not digitally signed.

C. The driver installation process requires a user interface to be displayed.

D. The driver package does not contain all files required to complete the installation.

70-210.03.05.004

By default, members of which group can manually install a driver on a computer running Windows 2000 Professional?

A. Administrators

B. Backup Operators

C. Power Users

D. Users

Objective 3.5 Answers

70-210.03.05.001

▶ **Correct Answers: A**

A. **Correct:** A number of methods exist to upgrade device drivers, but Device Manager is the only valid method listed in the answer choices. The Windows Update tool is another option for upgrading device drivers. To update a specific device, access the properties of the device from Device Manager and then click the Driver tab. In the Driver tab, click Update Driver to start the Upgrade Device Driver Wizard.

B. **Incorrect:** You use the Add/Remove Hardware Wizard to install new hardware and to remove, unplug, and troubleshoot existing hardware.

C. **Incorrect:** You configure environment variables from the command line or set them globally in the Environment Variables dialog box. This dialog box opens when you click the Environment Variables button located in the Advanced tab in the System Properties dialog box.

D. **Incorrect:** You use the Component Services console to install and configure Component Object Model (COM) components and COM+ applications, to view logs created by the Event Logging service, and to view, configure, and troubleshoot installed services.

70-210.03.05.002

▶ **Correct Answers: D**

A. **Incorrect:** Device Manager does display the driver or drivers associated with each installed device, and you can use it to print reports on installed devices. However, there is no facility for displaying a list of installed drivers.

B. **Incorrect:** You use the Add/Remove Hardware Wizard to install new hardware and to remove, unplug, and troubleshoot existing hardware. There is no facility for displaying a list of installed device drivers.

C. **Incorrect:** The CIPHER.EXE command-line utility is an Encrypting File System (EFS) tool that you use to display and encrypt or decrypt files and folders and create a new encryption key.

D. **Correct:** The DRIVERS.EXE command-line utility lists all of the drivers in the %system-root%\System32\Drivers folder that are currently running. You can use this tool to identify a driver that might be causing problems because of corruption or because it is missing, not loaded, or outdated. This tool is part of both the Windows 2000 Professional and Windows 2000 Server Resource Kits.

70-210.03.05.003

▶ **Correct Answers: A, B, C, and D**

A. **Correct:** Errors occurring during installation could cause a driver installation to be skipped. After installation has completed, use the Add/Remove Hardware Wizard to run the Plug and Play process to find Plug and Play devices and the hardware detection process for other devices not recognized through Plug and Play. If hardware detection fails to find the device, manually install the supporting device driver from the Add/Remove Hardware Wizard. Manual installation of a driver requires Administrator privileges.

B. **Correct:** The Windows 2000 Setup routine will not install unsigned device drivers. A driver that is signed contains a digital signature that is recognized by Windows 2000. A driver is signed after it has passed all Windows Hardware Quality Labs (WHQL) tests. Driver signing is a feature of Windows 98 and Windows 2000. After installation is complete, it is possible to manually install an unsigned driver, but this is not recommended.

By default, the user who is installing an unsigned device driver is warned but not blocked from installing an unsigned device driver. File signature verification can be configured to block unsigned driver installations (Block mode), warn the user before installing the driver (Warn mode), or provide no warning of an impending unsigned driver installation (Ignore mode). You configure File Signature Verification mode in the Driver Signing Options dialog box. Open this dialog box by clicking the Driver Signing button in the Hardware tab of the System Properties dialog box.

C. **Correct:** Some devices use a device driver with a configuration interface that is separate from the Windows 2000 Setup routine. In this case, device driver installation is completed after Windows 2000 is installed.

D. **Correct:** If a hardware vendor does not provide a unique Plug and Play device identifier, Windows 2000 will not know that it needs a special driver, so a generic driver may be installed. This limits the special features available for the device. This is common for video adapters and monitors. After the operating system installation is complete, you can install the vendor-supplied driver in place of the generic driver.

70-210.03.05.004

▶ **Correct Answers: A**

A. **Correct:** After the operating system is installed, the Administrators group is the only group able to manually install device drivers on a computer running Windows 2000 Professional. Administrators can perform any and all functions supported by the operating system. Members of the Administrators group are able to grant themselves any rights that they do not already have by default. Administrative access is required to install, update, or configure the operating system and components, such as device drivers.

B. **Incorrect:** By default, the Backup Operators local group contains the privileges required to back up and restore files and folders. Members of this group can perform backup and restore operations regardless of folder or file ownership, access permissions, or encryption settings. Members of this group are not able to install device drivers.

C. **Incorrect:** By default, members of the Power Users local group are granted fewer system-level privileges than the Administrators group but more than the Users group. Power Users can install and uninstall applications locally that do not install system services and can customize systemwide resources such as display settings, shares, and power options. Members of the Power Users group cannot manually install device drivers.

D. **Incorrect:** By default, members of the Users group cannot manually install device drivers. The Users group has fewer privileges than the Power Users group. However, most Plug and Play devices can be automatically installed without Administrator privileges. If Plug and Play cannot fully configure a device, then Administrator privileges are necessary to complete the installation.

Monitor and configure multiple processing units.

The Windows 2000 operating system kernel is able to use multiple processors to run processes and threads. Windows 2000 Professional includes support for one or two central processing units (CPUs). Support for multiple processors is provided by the **hardware abstraction layer (HAL)**, a hardware-specific operating system component that isolates the rest of the Windows 2000 operating system from the underlying hardware. Upgrading the HAL depends on the presence or absence of **Advanced Configuration and Power Interface (ACPI)** and **Advanced Programmable Interrupt Controller (APIC)** hardware on the computer. The HAL for a computer containing both ACPI and APIC hardware is upgradable to a multiprocessor system or downgradable to a uniprocessor system. The same rule applies to the hardware-specific HAL for a non-ACPI computer containing APIC hardware. Uniprocessor computers contain the simpler programmable interrupt controller (PIC) hardware, referred to as a Standard PC in Device Manager. The HAL for a computer containing ACPI and PIC hardware is not upgradable to the HAL for a PIC computer that is not ACPI compliant.

Use the Upgrade Device Driver Wizard to upgrade the HAL. This wizard is available in Device Manager. Upgrading to an incompatible HAL is likely to cause a critical system failure.

Use the Performance snap-in to monitor system resource use. Performance monitoring starts by establishing a baseline of satisfactory performance and then continuing to monitor the system to identify bottlenecks that are impacting performance. The System Monitor node in this snap-in has a number of important objects that contain counters for monitoring processor activity. The primary processor-specific objects to monitor are the following:

- Processor—Contains counters that monitor each processor individually (as individual instances).

- System—Contains counters that monitor all processors as a unit (single instance).

- Process—Contains counters that monitor each application running on the processors.

- Thread—Contains counters that monitor each unit of application execution on the processors.

- Job Object and Job Object Details—Contains groups of processes to be managed and manipulated as a unit (single instance) by one or multiple processors. You can view Web application activity counters through the Job object to determine an application's overall CPU use.

You use the Performance Logs and Alerts node of the Performance snap-in to collect performance data over time and to configure notification of exceeded activity thresholds.

Objective 3.6 Questions

70-210.03.06.001

You administer a Pentium III computer running Windows 2000 Professional. The computer has a single processor. You later decide to upgrade the hardware configuration to include two processors. How can you configure Windows 2000 Professional to distribute processing tasks across both processors?

A. Upgrade the HAL driver from Device Manager.

B. Reinstall Windows 2000 Professional.

C. Windows 2000 Professional does not support multiple processors.

D. No action is necessary because Windows 2000 will automatically begin using both processors.

70-210.03.06.002

You install Windows 2000 Professional on a computer with two processors. After installing the appropriate applications for your business, you decide to find a baseline for monitoring processor performance. While running multiple applications causing high processor activity, what is the expected range for the processor queue length?

A. 1–4

B. 2–6

C. 3–6

D. 4–7

70-210.03.06.003

Which multiprocessor configuration does Windows 2000 Professional support?

A. None

B. Symmetric multiprocessing (SMP)

C. Asymmetric multiprocessing (ASMP)

D. Both SMP and ASMP

Objective 3.6 Answers

70-210.03.06.001

▶ **Correct Answers: A**

A. **Correct:** From the question, you can infer that the computer running Windows 2000 Professional is capable of supporting a second processor. To change the installed HAL, start Device Manager and expand the Computer node to select and access the Properties dialog box for the computer. Click the Driver tab, and then click the Update Driver button to start the Upgrade Device Driver Wizard. Follow the instructions in the wizard to install the appropriate multiprocessor device driver.

B. **Incorrect:** In most cases, the Windows 2000 Professional Setup routine will detect a multiprocessor system and install a multiprocessor HAL to support it. However, this is not the most efficient choice for performing a HAL upgrade.

C. **Incorrect:** Windows 2000 Professional is capable of supporting two CPUs in a single computer.

D. **Incorrect:** The HAL that the Windows 2000 Setup routine installs on a computer with one processor is designed specifically for a uniprocessor configuration. A multiprocessor HAL must be installed to take advantage of both CPUs.

70-210.03.06.002

▶ **Correct Answers: B**

A. **Incorrect:** The System object's Processor Queue Length counter on a uniprocessor system with little activity will maintain a queue length average between 1 and 2. Therefore, a range of 1–4 does not accurately represent the activity expected on a dual-processor system displaying heavy processor use.

B. **Correct:** You observe overall processor activity by monitoring the processor queue length and processor use. A sustained queue of several waiting processor requests, combined with consistently high CPU use rate, signals a processor bottleneck. View the System object's Processor Queue Length counter to determine overall processor use on a system. Evidence of a processor bottleneck is indicated by a sustained or recurring queue of more than two threads. Therefore, a range of 2–6 threads waiting for processing is the expected range for the system described in the question.

C. **Incorrect:** A range of 3–6 suggests that the computer is heavily overused. This range is unacceptable for sustained periods. Note that the default scale for the System object's Processor Queue Length is 10. Therefore, a Processor Queue Length of 3 will appear as 30 in the Performance snap-in unless you change the scale to 1.

D. **Incorrect:** A range of 4–7 is unacceptable for sustained periods. At this range, the processor or processors might be the bottleneck. Some other reasons for this excessive queue length could be that a device in the computer is raising too many interrupts because of a hardware malfunction, or the computer does not contain enough physical RAM to service the running applications.

70-210.03.06.003

▶ **Correct Answers: B**

A. **Incorrect:** Windows 2000 Professional ships with HALs to support up to two processors.

B. **Correct:** SMP is a multiprocessor architecture in which all processors share the same memory containing a single copy of the operating system and one copy of each running application. The Windows 2000 kernel divides the workload into tasks, called threads, that are assigned to each processor.

C. **Incorrect:** ASMP is a multiprocessor architecture in which each processor serves a specific function. The operating system running on ASMP always selects the same processor to execute its instructions, while other processors service application requests.

D. **Incorrect:** The Windows 2000 operating system supports uniprocessor and multiprocessor SMP systems. ASMP is not supported by the operating system. However, it is possible for specialized hardware to support processors serving specific functions, such as disk I/O, but Windows 2000 is not involved in providing this support.

OBJECTIVE 3.7

Install, configure, and troubleshoot network adapters.

Windows 2000 Professional supports many network adapter models as well as protocols and services that use the adapter hardware. A device driver for a Plug and Play network adapter, like many other hardware devices, is installed automatically when the operating system detects the device and the device driver is contained in the DRIVER.CAB file. Installing a device driver for a network adapter that is not Plug and Play compatible is typically completed by using the Add/Remove Hardware Wizard. After a device driver is installed for a network adapter, protocols and services are *bound* to the adapter so that it can communicate on the network.

A **protocol** allows the network adapter to establish communications with the network. Windows 2000 Professional supports the Transfer Control Protocol/Internet Protocol (TCP/IP), NWLink, NetBEUI, Data Link Control (DLC), and AppleTalk protocols. Each protocol is designed to communicate with network-accessible devices that support the same protocol. For example, a computer running NWLink, Microsoft's implementation of Internetwork Packet Exchange/Sequenced Packet Exchange (IPX/SPX), can communicate with NetWare servers running IPX/SPX. The most widely used protocol is TCP/IP.

A **protocol suite** is a combination of software services that run on top of the base protocol. For example, the TCP/IP protocol suite contains File Transfer Protocol (FTP) services to support TCP/IP file transfer. Protocols must be configured to operate properly in Windows 2000. For example, TCP/IP must be configured with IP addressing information. Configuration can be manually assigned or dynamically assigned by network services such as the DHCP Server service. For small networks, IP addressing can be dynamically assigned by Automatic Private IP Addressing (APIPA).

A critical service that must run on client computers to use file and print services is the client redirector. The client redirector for accessing a Windows 2000 server is the Microsoft Client. The client redirector for accessing a NetWare server is Client Services for NetWare (CSNW).

If a network adapter is not able to communicate on the network, check Device Manager to verify that a device driver is installed and operational. If so, check that the adapter is correctly connected to the network. Next run protocol-specific configuration utilities designed to test network connections, such as ping and ipconfig. For example, if the network adapter is running TCP/IP, type **ping** *ip_address*, where *ip_address* is a valid host address on the network. If ping is unable to resolve an IP address on the network but pinging the local loopback address of 127.0.0.1 works, type **ipconfig** to verify that an address has been assigned to the network adapter. Configuration and protocol testing varies from one protocol to the next.

Objective 3.7 Questions

70-210.03.07.001

What is the most frequent cause of TCP/IP connection problems?

A. Unsupported network adapters.

B. Incorrect network adapter driver.

C. Incorrectly entered IP address data.

D. Failure of other networking components such as the hub and cables.

70-210.03.07.002

You are the administrator for a small local area network (LAN) supporting Windows NT, Windows 98, and Windows 2000. You currently use APIPA to obtain IP addresses for clients. You are considering using the DHCP Server service instead of APIPA. How should you configure Windows 2000 Professional to obtain an IP address from a computer running the DHCP Server service?

A. At a command prompt, type **ipconfig /dhcp** and press Enter.

B. No action is required because Windows 2000 Professional will automatically detect the DHCP Server service.

C. At a command prompt, type **ipconfig /release** and press Enter. Then type **ipconfig /renew** and press Enter.

D. At a command prompt, type **ipconfig /renew** and press Enter. Then type **ipconfig /release** and press Enter.

70-210.03.07.003

You are the administrator of a corporate LAN supporting a Novell NetWare server and various clients. You are planning to deploy some new computers running Windows 2000 Professional. Which conditions require you to manually assign a unique internal network number to the network adapter when using NWLink? (Choose three.)

A. An application is using the DLC protocol.

B. An application on the client computer is using the NetWare Service Advertising Protocol (SAP).

C. CSNW is installed, and multiple frame types are used on a single adapter.

D. CSNW is installed, and NWLink is bound to multiple adapters in the computer.

E. Gateway Services for NetWare (GSNW) is installed, and multiple frame types are used on a single adapter.

F. GSNW is installed, and NWLink is bound to multiple adapters in the computer.

Objective 3.7 Answers

70-210.03.07.001

▶ **Correct Answers: C**

A. **Incorrect:** Windows 2000 Professional supports hundreds of network adapters. Windows 2000 attempts to automatically detect the network adapter during operating system installation. If the network interface card (NIC) is installed after installation, Windows 2000 attempts to detect and install a driver for the adapter. You can initiate hardware detection routines after operating system installation by using the Add/Remove Hardware Wizard.

B. **Incorrect:** In most cases, if an incorrect driver is installed, Windows 2000 will not load it.

C. **Correct:** Each computer on a network running TCP/IP must be assigned a unique IP address and a valid subnet mask for the network segment in which the computer is connected. In a routed network, a default gateway address is required to communicate with computer resources on other networks. Additional IP addressing information—such as the IP addresses of Domain Name System (DNS) hosts on the network—might be required. Addressing information can be manually configured or automatically assigned. Automatic, centralized assignment is achieved by the DHCP Server service. In a simple network not running the DHCP Server service, you can avoid manual configuration by using APIPA.

D. **Incorrect:** It is possible to experience a network failure separate from the computer. However, this is not the most frequent cause of TCP/IP connection problems.

70-210.03.07.002

▶ **Correct Answers: B**

A. **Incorrect:** Ipconfig is a command-line TCP/IP configuration utility specifically designed for configuring dynamically assigned IP addressing information and for viewing IP address settings. To see a list of switches supported by ipconfig, type ipconfig /? at the command prompt. The /DHCP switch specified in the answer is not a valid ipconfig switch.

B. **Correct:** By default, the client computer periodically checks for a computer running the DHCP Server service with a valid address scope for the network in which the client is connected. Until such a server is located, the client computer will use APIPA. Additionally, when the computer is restarted, it will broadcast a modified Bootp request to the network in search of a computer running the DHCP Server service. If a host running the DHCP Server service answers, it will dynamically assign IP addressing information to the computer making the request.

C. **Incorrect:** Typing ipconfig /release at the command line will fail with a message stating that all adapters bound to DHCP do not have DHCP addresses and that all addresses were automatically configured and cannot be released.

D. **Incorrect:** If the DHCP Server service is running and it has a valid address scope for the client computer, typing ipconfig /renew will initiate IP addressing delivery by the DHCP Server service to the client computer. However, typing ipconfig /release afterward releases the IP address assigned by the DHCP Server service.

70-210.03.07.003

▶ **Correct Answers: B, C, and D**

A. **Incorrect:** You use the DLC protocol for network-connected Hewlett-Packard printers that depend on DLC and to access Systems Network Architecture (SNA) hosts over an SNA network running DLC. This protocol is not used to access NetWare resources.

B. **Correct:** NWLink uses a nonzero eight-digit hexadecimal internal network number for routing purposes. This network number is internal because NWLink uses it inside the computer. The internal network number must not be confused with the network number (also known as the external network number) that is used to uniquely identify an IPX/SPX network segment. If the client computer is acting as an application server by running a SAP application such as Microsoft SQL Server, the internal network number uniquely identifies the computer to the network so that other clients can access the application.

C. **Correct:** CSNW is the client redirector used by Windows 2000 Professional to communicate over NWLink with network-accessible NetWare resources. A frame type defines how network packets are formatted before being sent over the network. Each frame type supported on a single adapter requires a unique internal network number to avoid internal collisions with packets using a different frame type.

D. **Correct:** NWLink is Microsoft's implementation of the IPX/SPX protocol. Each network adapter in the computer running this protocol requires a unique internal network number so that packets created by the computer are internally routed to the appropriate adapter.

E. **Incorrect:** GSNW is installed on Windows 2000 Server, not Windows 2000 Professional. GSNW enables a computer running Windows 2000 Server to connect to computers running the NetWare 3.x or 4.x network operating system. GSNW contains the client redirector software in CSNW, and you use it to create gateways to NetWare resources. Creating a gateway allows computers running the Microsoft client redirector to gain access to NetWare resources through the gateway.

F. **Incorrect:** GSNW is a service available in Windows 2000 Server, as described earlier.

Monitoring and Optimizing System Performance and Reliability

Two important goals in the design of Microsoft Windows 2000 Professional were to create an operating system with performance and reliability that rivaled that of Microsoft Windows 98 and Microsoft Windows NT.

To improve reliability, Windows 2000 and Windows NT separate user processes from system processes, which protects critical operating system functions from errant applications. For the majority of user applications, memory space is separated to decrease the possibility of one application failure affecting other running applications. The only exception to this is running Windows 16-bit applications, which share the same memory space; however, each Windows 16-bit application can run in its own memory space if configured to do so. Because of these improvements, most operating system failures in Windows NT occur because of misbehaving device drivers.

Driver signing in Windows 2000 addresses this problem by helping to ensure the quality of device drivers and other critical system files before they are installed. Microsoft places a digital signature on a device driver or other critical system file after it has met a certain level of testing in the Microsoft Windows Hardware Quality Lab (WHQL). The operating system detects and maintains signed files to block or warn the installers of critical system files that are unsigned.

A reliable system is one that makes user data and applications highly available and system configuration flexible. The former is accomplished by the **Offline Files** feature. Files and programs can be made available to the user even when the primary network storage location of the data is off line. Flexible configuration is achieved by **hardware profiles**. Hardware profiles maintain unique driver and service configurations for the computer. They are created automatically during the Windows 2000 Setup routine, and they can be created manually from the Hardware Profiles dialog box.

Recoverability is an important part of system reliability. A system characterized as reliable must contain tools and techniques for recovery in the event of system failure. Windows 2000 includes a number of important recovery tools such as the **Advanced Options menu**, the **Recovery Console**, **Emergency Repair**, and **Windows Backup**.

Windows Backup as well as any command that can run in Windows 2000 can be scheduled. You can create schedules using either the Scheduled Tasks window or the AT command-line utility.

Monitoring how the system uses resources is an important step in optimizing operating system and application performance. The **Performance console** and **Task Manager** are important tools for monitoring the system.

Tested Skills and Suggested Practices

The skills you need to successfully master the Monitoring and Optimizing System Performance and Reliability Objective Domain on Exam 70-210: Installing, Configuring, and Administering Microsoft Windows 2000 Professional include the following:

- **Troubleshoot system operations and recover from system failures.**

  - Practice 1: Run the File Signature Verification utility (SIGVERIF.EXE) to view unsigned files. Adjust the advanced settings to scan for files in other folders and to adjust log file settings. View the log file.

  - Practice 2: Run the System File Checker utility using the /scannow and /scanonce switches. Reset WFP using the /enable switch.

  - Practice 3: Run a System State backup. Restore System State files that are allowed to be redirected to an alternate location. Review the contents of *%systemroot%*\Repair\Regback after running a System State backup.

  - Practice 4: Create an ERD using Windows Backup. Compare the contents of the Emergency Repair Disk to the contents of *%systemroot%*\Repair to verify that the registry files were *not* copied to the disk.

  - Practice 5: Review the Emergency Repair options available from the Text mode of the Windows 2000 Setup routine.

  - Practice 6: Open the Advanced Options Menu by pressing F8 during system startup. Run the various Safe Mode options, and perform a normal boot logging procedure. After each startup, review the contents of *%systemroot%*\Ntbtlog.txt.

  - Practice 7: Open the Advanced Options Menu by pressing F8 when a computer in Hibernate mode is coming out of hibernation. Compare the options appearing here to the Advanced Options Menu options appearing during a system startup.

- Practice 8: Install the Recovery Console to the system partition. Start the Recovery Console from the boot menu.

- Practice 9: Start the Recovery Console from the Windows 2000 Setup routine.

- Practice 10: In the Recovery Console, type **help** to see a list of commands. Type the name of each command followed by **/?** to learn about the purpose of each command.

- Practice 11: Restore the registry from a recent backup stored in the *%system-root%*\Repair\Regback folder.

- Practice 12: Start the Local Security Settings console by clicking the Local Security Policy icon in the Administrative Tools program group. Enable the two Recovery Console policies appearing under the Security Settings-Local Policies-Security Options node. Next start the Recovery Console, use the Set command to access all files and folders, and use another Set command to allow files to be copied to removable media.

- **Schedule tasks.**

  - Practice 1: Open the Windows 2000 Command Reference from Windows 2000 Help. Locate and read about the AT command. Read the AT notes page available from the Related Topics link at the bottom of the AT command Help page.

  - Practice 2: Use the AT command to schedule a task. View the AT command and compare it to a task scheduled using the Scheduled Task Wizard.

  - Practice 3: Copy a task created on one computer to another computer in a workgroup. Review the changes to task privileges and the changed user context of the copied task. Attempt to manually run a task from the task's context menu.

- **Configure and troubleshoot Offline Files.**

  - Practice 1: Enable Offline Files and configure synchronization for a folder and its contents.

  - Practice 2: Configure a share for automatic file caching. On the client computer configured for Offline Files, select and open a file contained below the share and then check the Client Side Cache in the Offline Files Folder window to verify that the file was synchronized.

  - Practice 3: Test manual file caching on the client computer by running the Offline Files Wizard to pin files.

  - Practice 4: Open the Synchronization Settings dialog box, and for the LAN connection, schedule synchronization, configure idle synchronization, and configure logon and logoff synchronization behavior.

- **Monitor system performance.**

  - Practice 1: Run Task Manager and view the columns not appearing by default on the Processes tab. Sort the columns to determine which process has created the most page faults, which process has spawned the most threads, and which processes have a base priority of high.

  - Practice 2: View Kernel Times on Task Manager's Performance tab.

  - Practice 3: Pause and resume the Task Manager display.

  - Practice 4: In the Windows 2000 Professional Resource Kit, Chapter 27, locate the "Getting the Most from System Monitor," "Getting the Most from Performance Logs and Alerts," and "Working with Task Manager" sections. Open the corresponding tools in Microsoft Windows 2000 Professional, and navigate to all the items discussed in these three sections.

  - Practice 5: Create a Trace log and then use the TRACEDMP.EXE tool in the Windows 2000 Professional or Server Resource Kit to extract the log data. Open and review the resulting text file in Microsoft Notepad and the resulting comma-delimited file in Microsoft Excel.

  - Practice 6: Save a Counter log as an .html file and view it using Microsoft Internet Explorer. Change the System Monitor control in Internet Explorer so that it collects real-time data.

  - Practice 7: Insert the System Monitor Microsoft ActiveX control into an Excel worksheet using the Other Controls button on the Control Toolbox toolbar.

  - Practice 8: Run both System Monitor and Task Manager. Next find Table 27.6 in Chapter 27 of the Windows 2000 Professional Resource Kit. Then using the table and the two monitoring applications, compare Task Manager counters to System Monitor counters.

  - Practice 9: Create a performance baseline in the Performance console using Table 27.7 in Chapter 27 of the Windows 2000 Professional Resource Kit as your guide. Create the baseline using data collected over several weeks of normal activity. Compare the collected data to threshold data provided in Table 27.8.

  - Practice 10: Using the Alerts feature of the Performance Logs and Alerts snap-in, create an alert that sends your user account a network message when free space on any fixed disk in the computer has dropped below 15 percent.

Further Reading

This "Further Reading" section provides lists of important readings to supplement your current understanding of the skills tested within this Objective Domain. The lists are delineated into pertinent readings for each objective within this Objective Domain. If you feel that you need additional preparation prior to taking the exam, study these sources thoroughly.

Objective 4.1

Microsoft Corporation. *Microsoft Windows 2000 Professional Resource Kit*. Redmond, Washington: Microsoft Press, 2000. Read pp. 1419–1428, "Maintenance and Update Tools," pp. 1429–1437, "System File and Driver Tools," and pp. 1467–1478, "Troubleshooting Procedures" in Chapter 31, "Troubleshooting Tools and Strategies."

Microsoft Corporation. *MCSE Training Kit—Microsoft Windows 2000 Professional*. Redmond, Washington: Microsoft Press, 2000. Read and complete the practices in Lesson 2, Chapter 25, "Implementing, Managing, and Troubleshooting Hardware Devices and Drivers."

Objective 4.2

Microsoft Corporation. *MCSE Training Kit—Microsoft Windows 2000 Professional*. Redmond, Washington: Microsoft Press, 2000. Read and complete the practices in Lesson 3, Chapter 3, "Using Microsoft Management Console and Task Scheduler."

Objective 4.3

Microsoft Corporation. *Microsoft Windows 2000 Professional Resource Kit*. Redmond, Washington: Microsoft Press, 2000. Read pp. 373–383, "Using Offline Files and Folders" in Chapter 9, "Managing Files, Folders, and Search Methods," and pp. 406–417, "Configuring Offline Files for Portable Computers" in Chapter 10, "Mobile Computing."

Microsoft Corporation. *MCSE Training Kit—Microsoft Windows 2000 Professional*. Redmond, Washington: Microsoft Press, 2000. Read and complete the practices in Lesson 1, Chapter 24, "Configuring Windows 2000 for Mobile Computers."

Objective 4.4

Microsoft Corporation. *Microsoft Windows 2000 Professional Resource Kit*. Redmond, Washington: Microsoft Press, 2000. Read Chapter 27, "Overview of Performance Monitoring," Chapter 28, "Evaluating Memory and Cache Usage," Chapter 29, "Analyzing Processor Activity," and Chapter 30, "Examining and Tuning Disk Performance."

Microsoft Corporation. "Windows 2000 Performance Tuning." This article can be downloaded from *http://www.microsoft.com/windows2000* by searching on the article title.

Objective 4.5

Microsoft Corporation. *Microsoft Windows 2000 Professional Resource Kit*. Redmond, Washington: Microsoft Press, 2000. Read pp. 435-445, "Managing Hardware on Portable Computers" in Chapter 10, "Mobile Computing."

Objective 4.6

Microsoft Corporation. *Microsoft Windows 2000 Professional Resource Kit*. Redmond, Washington: Microsoft Press, 2000. Read pp. 797–813, "Overview of Backups" in Chapter 18, "Removable Storage and Backup," and pp. 1398–1419, "Startup and Recovery Tools" in Chapter 31, "Troubleshooting Tools and Strategies."

Microsoft Corporation. *MCSE Training Kit—Microsoft Windows 2000 Professional*. Redmond, Washington: Microsoft Press, 2000. Read and complete the practices in Lessons 1, 3, and 5 in Chapter 19, "Backing Up and Restoring Data," and read Chapter 22, "The Windows 2000 Boot Process."

OBJECTIVE 4.1

Manage and troubleshoot driver signing.

Thousands of system files are installed when the Windows 2000 Setup routine and application installation routines are run. The files that are installed support all aspects of operating system and application functions. Service pack updates, hot fixes, and application updates replace targeted system files. In Windows operating systems prior to Windows 2000, operating system updates and numerous application installations are much more likely to cause an operating system failure or application failure than in Windows 2000.

Windows 2000 includes a number of important features and tools to manage system files and troubleshoot failures in drivers and other critical system files. **Windows File Protection (WFP)** protects against the replacement of critical system files and reduces file version mismatches. Before a system file is replaced, the operating system notifies WFP of an impending replacement. WFP checks the file's digital signature and compares it to the signature of the installed version of the file. If the digital signature doesn't match, a notification of the file replacement event is logged to the System event log and then the original file is restored from the *%systemroot%*\System32\Dllcache folder or, if it is not contained in this folder, from the Windows 2000 Professional installation CD-ROM.

The WFP facility is automatic; the System File Checker (SFC) utility is run manually to augment WFP. The SFC utility scans protected files, checks for version mismatches, reinstalls the correct system files to the *%systemroot%*\System32\Dllcache folder, repairs this folder if it becomes corrupted or unusable, and provides scan-scheduling capability.

If you suspect that a signed driver is not functioning properly, run **Driver Verifier Manager** (VERIFIER.EXE). This utility contains both a command-line and Windows interface. Typing **verifier /?** at the command line shows the switches this utility supports. Running verifier without any switches starts the Driver Verifier Manager Windows interface. After configuring a driver for verification by Driver Verifier Manager, restart the computer and then run procedures that access the device driver. Driver problems appear during startup or in the Windows interface. After a driver is verified, use Driver Verifier Manager to disable driver verification.

The Windows 2000 **signature checking** facility verifies that a driver is signed before it is installed. Three settings exist for signature checking: Level 0 (ignore) essentially disables signature checking; Level 1 (warn) prompts the installer of an impending unsigned driver installation; and Level 2 (block) prevents the installation of unsigned drivers. The default setting is Level 1. You set signature checking in the Driver Signing Options dialog box. To open this dialog box, click the Driver Signing button on the Hardware tab in the System Properties dialog box.

Signature checking is automatic, but the **File Signature Verification** (SIGVERIF.EXE) Windows utility allows for manual signature verification. This utility provides the following information: whether files are signed, the publisher of signed files, the date the file was modified, file version information, and which catalog holds a matching signature for the file. Catalogs are stored in a folder below *%systemroot%*\System32\Catroot. The primary catalog for Windows 2000 system files is NT5.CAT.

Objective 4.1 Questions

70-210.04.01.001

You are the chief administrator for your local area network (LAN), and you configure an unattended setup of Windows 2000 Professional. You need to install unsigned drivers during the installation of Windows 2000 Professional. When you run the unattended setup routine on a test computer, a prompt is displayed warning of impending unsigned driver installation. How can you disable the prompt?

A. Add the following entry to the [Data] section of UNATTEND.TXT: DriverSigningPolicy = Ignore.

B. Add the following entry to the [Unattended] section of UNATTEND.TXT: DriverSigningPolicy = Ignore.

C. Add the following entry to the [SetupParams] section of UNATTEND.TXT: DriverSigningPolicy = Ignore.

D. Add the following entry to the [GuiUnattended] section of UNATTEND.TXT: DriverSigningPolicy = Ignore.

70-210.04.01.002

You want to troubleshoot driver signing on your computer running Windows 2000 Professional. Which command-line utility can you use to check the signature of files?

A. EFSINFO

B. MCAST

C. SFC

D. SIGVERIF

70-210.04.01.003

You want to ensure that unsigned drivers are not installed on your computer running Windows 2000 Professional. What should you do?

A. No action is required.

B. Change the File Signature Verification setting to Ignore.

C. Change the File Signature Verification setting to Warn.

D. Change the File Signature Verification setting to Block.

Objective 4.1 Answers

70-210.04.01.001

▶ **Correct Answers: B**

A. **Incorrect:** The [Data] section of an answer file is required when performing an unattended installation by booting directly from the Windows 2000 Professional installation CD-ROM. The value names it supports are AutoPartition, MsDosInitiated, UnattendedInstall, and UseBIOSTo-Boot. You can find an explanation of these values in the UNATTEND.DOC file located in the \Support\Tools\DEPLOY.CAB file on the Windows 2000 Professional installation CD-ROM.

B. **Correct:** The [Unattended] section of an answer file is a required section of an answer-file-based installation of Windows 2000. This section contains the DriverSigningPolicy setting. The value of DriverSigningPolicy determines how unsigned drivers are processed during an unattended installation of Windows 2000 Professional. A value of block instructs the installation routine not to install the unsigned driver. A value of warn instructs the installation to display a prompt before allowing the installation of an unsigned driver. Each unsigned driver will cause the prompt to reappear. A value of ignore instructs the installation to continue even if the driver is not signed. A value of ignore is inadvisable unless the unsigned drivers have been thoroughly tested on the computers where they will be installed.

C. **Incorrect:** The [SetupParams] section is added to an answer file to specify a command to run when Windows 2000 installation completes but before the system settings are saved. This section requires a single value name of UserExecute, which is set equal to a path and program name. This section is equivalent to the WINNT command-line switch of /e and the WINNT32 command-line switch of /cmd:.

D. **Incorrect:** The [GuiUnattended] section of an answer file is used to specify GUI-mode setup behavior for both an answer-file-based setup of Windows 2000 and an automated setup of Windows 2000 using SYSPREP.EXE. For a list of the value names used in this section, review the UNATTEND.DOC file, located in the \Support\Tools\DEPLOY.CAB file on the Windows 2000 Professional installation CD-ROM.

70-210.04.01.002

▶ **Correct Answers: D**

A. **Incorrect:** EFSINFO.EXE is a troubleshooting tool used to view information about encrypted files, including information about the Encrypting File System (EFS) user account and the recovery agent accounts. This tool is part of the Windows 2000 Server and Windows 2000 Professional Resource Kits.

B. **Incorrect:** MCAST.EXE is a tool used to diagnose and resolve problems with audio and video multicasting. This tool is part of the Windows 2000 Server and Windows 2000 Professional Resource Kits.

C. **Incorrect:** SFC is a command-line utility that scans protected system files and replaces any protected files that were overwritten after the installation of Windows 2000 Professional. The SFC utility checks the catalogs to determine correct file versions. A Windows Update procedure automatically updates the catalog so that SFC doesn't overwrite files that are properly updated.

D. **Correct:** SIGVERIF.EXE is a GUI-based utility that provides feedback on signed and unsigned files. After this utility runs, a list of unsigned drivers appears. A log file named SIGVERIF.TXT is created in the %systemroot% folder. This log file contains a detailed list of all signed and unsigned drivers. By default, SIGVERIF scans the system files, but you configure this setting and other settings from the Advanced File Signature Verification Settings dialog box. This dialog box opens when you click the Advanced button in the File Signature Verification dialog box. Additionally, you can view log files by clicking the View Log button in the Advanced File Signature Verification Settings dialog box.

70-210.04.01.003

▶ **Correct Answers: D**

A. **Incorrect:** You configure file signature verification in the Driver Signing Options dialog box. Level 1 (warn) is the default setting for file signature verification. As a result, a user is prompted about any impending unsigned driver installation. Therefore, it is possible to install an unsigned driver if no action is taken to reconfigure this setting.

B. **Incorrect:** This setting disables file signature verification so that any driver, whether it is signed or not, can be installed.

C. **Incorrect:** This is the default setting for file signature checking, as explained earlier. As a result, it is possible for a user to install an unsigned driver.

D. **Correct:** Changing the File Signature Verification setting to Level 2 (block) ensures that unsigned drivers cannot be installed on the computer when running Windows 2000 Professional. You configure this setting in the Driver Signing Options dialog box.

OBJECTIVE 4.2

Configure, manage, and troubleshoot Scheduled Tasks.

Windows 2000 includes the Scheduled Task Wizard and the AT command-line utility for configuring operation schedules for processes that run in Windows 2000, such as a program or script. Scheduled tasks depend on the accuracy of the computer's clock. Make sure that the system clock is accurate.

A task scheduled using the AT utility appears in the Scheduled Tasks window but is managed from the AT command-line utility. Using either interface (the wizard or command-line utility), you can schedule, reschedule, disable, or remove a task. Task configuration allows for controlling exactly how the task will operate. For example, setting the user context for the task, stopping the task if it runs too long, allowing the task to run only when the computer is idle, and not allowing the task to run if the computer is running on batteries. Task security protects against modifications to the task by unauthorized personnel.

Task management involves reviewing tasks that the Task Scheduler service has attempted to start. The Scheduled Tasks window provides summary results of task operation. Detailed results are contained in the Task log. The log is stored in %systemroot% and is named SCHEDLGU.TXT. Viewing the log file is an important troubleshooting measure to determine exactly why a task has failed to run. View the log file by clicking the View Log command on the Advanced menu in the Scheduled Tasks window. Other important management tasks completed from the Advanced menu include configuring the user context for all AT scheduled tasks, configuring notification of missed tasks, and controlling the state of the Task Scheduler service.

All tasks scheduled from the Scheduled Task Wizard can run using any valid user account. Tasks scheduled using the AT utility appear in the Scheduled Tasks window but run in the user context of the AT service account. Modifying the properties of an AT scheduled task in the Scheduled Tasks window converts the AT task to a scheduled task. Scheduling or modifying a task requires that the Task Scheduler service is either running or paused. The task will run only if the Task Scheduler service is running.

Windows Backup (NTBACKUP.EXE) uses the Task Scheduler service when backups are scheduled. Use the View Log option in Task Scheduler to verify that the backup started. For details on the backup process, view the Backup log in the Backup Reports dialog box in Windows Backup.

Objective 4.2 Questions

70-210.04.02.001

Your Pentium computer runs Windows 2000 Professional and has an internal Seagate STT8000 tape backup device. You successfully performed a full system backup using the tape device. You use Task Scheduler to create a scheduled job to run Windows Backup. The backup operation fails. What is the most likely cause of this failure?

A. The backup tape has failed.

B. The correct tape is not mounted in the tape drive.

C. The correct device driver for the tape drive is not loaded.

D. Windows 2000 does not support the tape device.

70-210.04.02.002

Which two methods can you use to create a scheduled task in Windows 2000 Professional? (Choose two.)

A. Open Control Panel and double-click the Scheduled Tasks program.

B. Open Control Panel and double-click the Administrative Tools folder.

C. On the Start menu, point to Programs, point to Administrative Tools, and click Scheduled Tasks.

D. On the Start menu, point to Programs, point to Accessories, point to System Tools, and click Scheduled Tasks.

70-210.04.02.003

You are the administrator of APM-compliant and ACPI-compliant computers running Windows 2000 Professional. Each computer has a third-party disk defragmentation utility installed that can be scheduled. Each computer is accessed by multiple users.

You want to achieve these results: schedule disk defragmentation to occur during nonworking hours; ensure that computers in Sleep mode are also defragmented; set up the same disk defragmentation maintenance task on other computers in the workgroup running Windows 2000 Professional; and prevent users from manually running a scheduled task that you create.

The proposed solution is as follows: use the Scheduled Task Wizard to create a task to defragment the disk during nonworking hours; use the Security tab in the Scheduled Task Wizard Advanced Options dialog box to set the appropriate permissions; and copy the scheduled task to all other Windows 2000 Professional computers in the workgroup.

Which result does the proposed solution provide?

A. Disk defragmentation is scheduled to occur during nonworking hours.

B. Computers in Sleep mode are also defragmented.

C. The same disk defragmentation maintenance task occurs on other Windows 2000 Professional computers in the workgroup.

D. Users are prevented from manually running the scheduled task.

70-210.04.02.004

You are the administrator of ACPI-compliant Pentium III computers running Windows 2000 Professional. Each computer has a third-party disk defragmentation utility installed that can be scheduled.

You want to achieve these results: schedule disk defragmentation to occur during nonworking hours; ensure that computers in Sleep mode are also defragmented; set up the same disk defragmentation maintenance task on other Windows 2000 Professional computers in the workgroup; and prevent users from manually running a scheduled task that you create.

The proposed solution is as follows: use the Scheduled Task Wizard to create a task to defragment the disk during nonworking hours; select the Wake The Computer To Run This Task check box; copy the scheduled task to all other Windows 2000 Professional computers in the workgroup; and use the Security tab in the Scheduled Task Wizard Advanced Options dialog box to set the appropriate permissions for the task on each computer in the workgroup.

Which results does the proposed solution provide? (Choose all that apply.)

A. Disk defragmentation is scheduled to occur during nonworking hours.

B. Computers in Sleep mode are also defragmented.

C. The same disk defragmentation maintenance task occurs on other Windows 2000 Professional computers in the workgroup.

D. Users are prevented from manually running the scheduled task.

Objective 4.2 Answers

70-210.04.02.001

▶ **Correct Answers: B**

  A. **Incorrect:** A tape failure is possible but is not the most likely cause of a failed backup job. A hardware failure might appear in the System or Application event logs. Viewing the backup report generated from backup logging in Windows Backup will show when and if the backup started and completed. The default backup summary logging level is sufficient to indicate a failed backup procedure.

  B. **Correct:** When the tape media mounted in the drive is different than the media name specified in Windows Backup and a changer containing the correct media is not in use, the backup operation fails. Review the Backup log to identify this failure.

  C. **Incorrect:** The question states that a successful backup has been performed using this hardware. Therefore, it is likely that the correct device driver is installed and running. To verify that the device driver is operational, review the properties of the device in Device Manager.

  D. **Incorrect:** The question states that a successful backup has been performed using this hardware, so it is unlikely that Windows 2000 does not support the device. If an incompatibility is suspected, check the Hardware Compatibility List (HCL).

70-210.04.02.002

▶ **Correct Answers: A and D**

  A. **Correct:** Double-clicking the Scheduled Tasks program in Control Panel opens the Scheduled Tasks window. In this window, you can schedule a new task or modify or delete an existing task.

  B. **Incorrect:** The Administrative Tools folder in Control Panel points to the \Documents and Settings\All Users\Start Menu\Programs\Administrative Tools folder. Even if the Administrative Tools program group is configured not to appear on the Programs menu, the Administrative Tools folder still appears in Control Panel. This folder does not contain a shortcut to the Scheduled Tasks window.

  C. **Incorrect:** The Administrative Tools program group points to the same set of shortcuts contained in Control Panel's Administrative Tools folder.

  D. **Correct:** The Scheduled Tasks program appears in the System Tools program group.

70-210.04.02.003

▶ **Correct Answers: A**

A. **Correct:** The first sentence in the proposed solution states that the task is scheduled to occur during nonworking hours. A task is scheduled when you create it using the Scheduled Task Wizard. You adjust an existing task's schedule by accessing the properties of the task and then clicking the Schedule tab to modify the settings on this tab.

B. **Incorrect:** Nothing in the proposed solution suggests that the task was modified to wake up a computer to run the task. The Wake The Computer To Run This Task check box appears on the Settings tab of the task's properties on computers that support this feature. ACPI-compliant computers include this feature; non-ACPI-compliant computers do not.

C. **Incorrect:** The last part of the proposed solution states that the task is copied to all other computers in the workgroup. Tasks are sent and received as files. Thus, you can send tasks in a number of ways. For example, within Windows Explorer, double-click the My Network Places icon and double-click a computer icon. Then double-click the Scheduled Tasks program for each Windows 2000 computer to view its Scheduled Tasks folder. Task files have an extension of .job and are stored in the %systemroot%\Tasks folder. For efficiency, create a batch file that copies the scheduled task to each computer on the network that should run it.

The problem with attempting to run a task copied to other computers in the workgroup is that the user account specified to run the task will be invalid. User accounts in a workgroup are computer specific. Therefore, a user logged on locally to a computer in a workgroup must configure the task with a valid user account before it will run. Moving to a domain model solves this administrative problem.

Another option is to use the AT command-line utility to create a scheduled task to run on all computers in the workgroup. The first AT parameter is the Universal Naming Convention (UNC) name of the computer. Make sure to configure the AT Service Account on each computer in the workgroup. To configure the AT Service Account, in the Scheduled Tasks window, click Advanced and then select the AT Service Account option. When the AT Service Account Configuration dialog box appears, specify an account capable of running the scheduled tasks. Next create a batch file containing the AT command targeted at each computer in the workgroup.

D. **Incorrect:** The proposed solution explains that you set security on the task before copying it to members of the workgroup. It is possible to restrict the task so only specific personnel are allowed to manually run the task. However, copying the task to other computers in the workgroup causes the permissions to be reset to the default settings of the Scheduled Task folder on the target computer. The default settings include Read & Execute, Read, and Write assigned to the Everyone special group. As a result of the Write permission, members of this group are able to manually run the task. One way to solve this problem is to create a Windows 2000 domain and move all members of the workgroup to the domain. Then follow the procedures as outlined in the proposed solution.

70-210.04.02.004

▶ **Correct Answers: A, B, and D**

A. **Correct:** The first sentence in the proposed solution states that the task is scheduled to occur during nonworking hours. A task is scheduled when it is created using the Scheduled Task Wizard. You adjust an existing task's schedule by accessing the properties of the task and then clicking the Schedule tab to modify the settings on this tab. You can also use the AT command-line utility to schedule a task for the computer. The task you schedule using the AT command appears in the Scheduled Tasks window on each computer in the workgroup.

B. **Correct:** The proposed solution explains that the task was modified to wake up a computer to run the task. The Wake The Computer To Run This Task check box appears on the Settings tab of the task's properties on computers that support this feature. As explained in the question, all computers in the workgroup are ACPI compliant, so this feature will be available.

C. **Incorrect:** As outlined in the previous question, the problem with attempting to run a task copied to other computers in the workgroup is that the user account specified to run the task will be invalid. User accounts in a workgroup are computer specific. Therefore, a user logged on locally to a computer in a workgroup must configure the task with a valid user account before it will run. Moving to a domain model solves this administrative problem.

D. **Correct:** The question states that privileges are reassigned after the task is copied to target computers in the workgroup. This approach will take significant administrative effort if more than a dozen or so computers are in the workgroup. Moving a workgroup of computers to a domain model will reduce administrative overhead by centralizing user account administration.

OBJECTIVE 4.3

Manage and troubleshoot the use and synchronization of Offline Files.

Traditionally, files accessed over a network connection were unavailable when the network connection was lost. The **Offline Files** feature in Windows 2000 Professional is a facility to **synchronize** files from a network to a local disk so if the network is disconnected, files are available off line. Offline files are made available on a network resource through folder sharing. The computer that hosts the share runs the Server service and is considered the server; the computer that accesses the share runs the client redirector and is considered the client. The Microsoft Network Server service and client redirector use the Server Message Block (SMB) protocol and a transport protocol for network communication. This is the only network software combination that supports Offline Files.

After sharing a network-accessible resource, the Offline Files feature is enabled and configured centrally using group policies, or it is configured independently on each computer on the Offline Files tab of the Folder Options dialog box. To locate the Offline Files tab, access the network share using Windows Explorer and then locate a folder below the share that will be synchronized. On the Tools pull-down menu, click Folder Options to open the Folder Options dialog box and then click the Offline Files tab. You also use this tab to access the Offline Files folder, and you can create a shortcut to this folder on the desktop from the Offline Files tab.

Enabling and configuring Offline Files initiates an update of the *%systemroot%*\Csc hidden database cache folder with offline file configuration information. The Client Side Cache (CSC) is the database for the cache.

Tip If the boot partition has limited disk space, use the Offline Files Cache Mover utility (CACHEMOV.EXE) in the Windows 2000 Professional or Server Resource Kit to move the CSC database to a partition on a fixed disk with more space.

Files are not automatically synchronized as a result of enabling and configuring Offline Files. Instead, files are made available off line through either **automatic file caching** or **manual file caching**. Automatic file caching copies any files selected or opened on the client computer to the cache. Interestingly, selecting a file without opening it stores it in the cache. Automatic file caching is configured from the server (the computer containing the shared resource) at the share level so that any files or folders below the share are configured for automatic file caching. The default caching setting on the share is Manual Caching For Documents, so this must be changed to support automatic file caching. The cache size on the client is adjustable and is set by default to 10 percent of the total disk capacity available on the partition containing the CSC folder. Files cached automatically are not guaranteed to be available in the cache. As the cache approaches the maximum configured cache size, files are deleted on a first in, first out (FIFO) basis.

Files are made permanently available off line on a client through manual file caching, which is configured on the client using the Offline Files Wizard. To start the Offline Files Wizard, open Windows Explorer and then select a share or any of its contents. On the File menu, click Make Available Offline. The share must be located on a remote computer and it must be configured for caching, or the Make Available Offline command will not appear. A folder's contents or a specific file selected and configured for manual file caching is considered *pinned* because it is always available off line.

Certain file types cannot be cached, such as .pst (Microsoft Outlook personal store files) and .mdb (Microsoft Access database files). You can modify this exclusion list through the Files Not Cached Group Policy setting.

Files are synchronized between the online and offline cache either manually or automatically based on one of the following events: logon, logoff, idle time, or a fixed schedule. To accomplish manual synchronization, click Synchronize on the Tools menu in Windows Explorer to open the Items To Synchronize dialog box. Then click the Synchronize button. To configure synchronization settings, click the Setup button in the Items To Synchronize dialog box.

Objective 4.3 Questions

70-210.04.03.001

You are an administrator for a local area network (LAN) supporting computers running Windows 2000. Every day, you store your data on a computer running Windows 2000 Server. You want to use the Offline Files feature on your laptop computer running Windows 2000 Professional while you are away from the office on business. Which computer or computers must you configure?

A. None

B. The server

C. Your laptop

D. Both the server and your laptop

70-210.04.03.002

Your company operates a LAN supporting computers running Windows 2000 Professional. Other users on the network need to edit offline documents in one folder on your computer running Windows 2000 Professional. You want opened files to be automatically downloaded and made available when working off line. After you have configured the server for automatic download, users will enable and configure Offline Files on the Offline Files tab in the Folder Options dialog box. How should you configure the share to support automatic download?

A. Share the appropriate folder on your computer.

B. Share the appropriate folder on your computer. On the Sharing tab in the *folder_name* Properties dialog box, click the Caching button and select the Automatic Caching For Documents setting.

C. Share the appropriate folder on your computer. On the Sharing tab in the *folder_name* Properties dialog box, click the Caching button and select the Automatic Caching For Programs setting.

D. Share the appropriate folder on your computer. On the Sharing tab in the *folder_name* Properties dialog box, click the Caching button and select the Manual Caching For Documents setting.

70-210.04.03.003

Your company operates a LAN supporting computers running Windows 2000 Professional. Other users on the network need to edit offline documents in one folder on your computer running Windows 2000 Professional. If users edit both the cached offline copy of a file and the network version of a file, which two choices exist when you want to save all changes without renaming one version of the file? (Choose two.)

A. Use the Indexing Service to merge the changes.

B. Use the Synchronization Merge Wizard to merge the changes.

C. Overwrite the cached version with the version on the network.

D. Retain the cached version and do not update the network copy.

70-210.04.03.004

You are an administrator for a LAN supporting computers running Windows 2000. Every day, you store your data on a computer running Windows 2000 Server. You want to use the Offline Files feature on your laptop computer running Windows 2000 Professional while you are away from the office on business. This feature is enabled on the laptop, and the Offline Files Wizard has been run previously for another share on the network. The Offline Files Wizard defaults were specified when it was run previously. The laptop is connected to the network. Before you leave, you want to accomplish these results:

- Synchronize the appropriate files.

- Automatically synchronize files after your laptop has been idle for 15 minutes.

- Automatically repeat synchronization every 60 minutes that your laptop remains idle.

- Prevent synchronization when your laptop is running on battery power.

The proposed solution is to share the folder located on the computer running Windows 2000 Server that contains the files. On the client, open Windows Explorer, select the share containing the files, and on the File menu, click Make Available Offline. In the Confirm Offline Subfolders dialog box, choose whether just the folder share content or the folder share content and all subfolders and their content should be available off line. After synchronization completes, click Synchronize on the Tools menu. In the Items To Synchronize dialog box, click the Setup button. On the Logon/Logoff tab in the Synchronization Settings dialog box, select the offline files to synchronize.

Which result or results does the proposed solution provide? (Choose all that apply.)

A. The appropriate files are automatically synchronized when you log on or log off the laptop computer.

B. Files are automatically synchronized after your laptop has been idle for 15 minutes.

C. Synchronization runs automatically every weekday at 11:45 AM.

D. Synchronization is prevented when your laptop is idle and running on battery power.

Objective 4.3 Answers

70-210.04.03.001

▶ **Correct Answers: D**

A. **Incorrect:** Offline file caching must be configured before the client computer—the laptop in this question—will store cached files.

B. **Incorrect:** The computer that hosts the share is always considered the server, whether the share is hosted on a computer running Windows 2000 Server or Windows 2000 Professional. Setting up a share is the first step in configuring the Offline Files feature. After the share is created, use the Windows interface (Windows Explorer or My Computer) to access the properties of the share. On the Sharing tab, click Caching to open the Caching Settings dialog box and configure how data will be cached. In this dialog box, you enable or disable caching and you configure how data will be cached. The default cache setting is Manual Caching For Documents. This setting supports only manual file caching. The other two settings, Automatic Caching For Programs and Automatic Caching For Documents, support both automatic and manual file caching. Use the former if the share hosts read-only data or applications that run from the network; use the latter if the share hosts data that users modified.

C. **Incorrect:** The computer that accesses the share and maintains a local cache of offline files is the client computer. The client computer maintains the caching database, whose default location is the %systemroot%\Csc folder. If a share is configured for caching, the client computer is able to pin a folder's contents or files for manual file caching using the Offline Files Wizard. When the Offline Files Wizard is run once, any additional files pinned are automatically synchronized without launching the wizard. If the share is configured for automatic file caching, the client computer will automatically cache selected or opened files. Files that are automatically cached are not guaranteed to be available. When the cache reaches its maximum size, automatically cached files are removed from the local cache on a FIFO basis. Files that are manually cached are not limited by the specified cache size. Manually cached files can occupy up to 2 GB of disk space if it's available on the client computer.

D. **Correct:** As described in answer explanation B, a share must be configured on the server. Caching is automatically enabled and set to Manual Caching For Documents. As described in answer explanation C, the client computer accesses the share and files are either manually or automatically cached. To guarantee that files are available off line, pin the files below the share using the Make Available Offline command on the File menu in the Windows interface.

70-210.04.03.002

▶ **Correct Answers: B**

A. **Incorrect:** Sharing the folder is an important first step. Simply sharing the folder enables caching with a setting of Manual Caching For Documents. When a user selects or opens a file located below a cached share configured for manual caching, the file is not automatically downloaded.

B. **Correct:** After a disk or folder is shared, caching is enabled and set only for manual caching. Clicking the Caching button opens the Caching Settings dialog box. In the Setting drop-down list box, select Automatic Caching For Documents. After a client computer is configured for offline file access to this share or its contents, selecting or opening any file or folder automatically downloads the file. The Automatic Caching For Documents setting will download programs to the cache only when the program is opened.

C. **Incorrect:** Selecting the Automatic Caching For Programs setting in the Cache Settings dialog box downloads programs and their components automatically when the program is selected or opened. This behavior is important so that any components of the program run inside the program are automatically downloaded to the cache as well. This setting is not recommended for program access on computers that are frequently disconnected from the network, such as portable computers. Instead, install programs that must be available off line directly onto the portable computer. Automatic caching for programs works best for programs that are regularly run over a network where share access is intermittent.

D. **Incorrect:** This is the default setting when a share is created. When a user selects or opens a file located below a cached share configured for manual caching, the file is not automatically downloaded.

70-210.04.03.003

▶ **Correct Answers: C and D**

A. **Incorrect:** The Indexing Service runs in the background and creates indexes of the contents and properties of documents on the local computer, on network-accessible shares, and on local Web content if Microsoft Internet Information Services (IIS) is installed. This service does not play a direct role in managing Offline Files or the synchronization process.

B. **Incorrect:** There is no such wizard included with the operating system.

C. **Correct:** If both the cached copy and the network copy of a file are changed, during synchronization, a Resolve File Conflicts dialog box opens. This dialog box contains three radio buttons. The first radio button allows you to save both files with different names. The locally cached copy of the file is renamed by appending the username and a version number to the prefix of the file, and then it is copied to the network. The cached version of the original file is replaced with the network copy of the file. The second radio button allows you to overwrite the network version with the cached version of the file. The third radio button overwrites the cached version with the network version of the file.

D. **Correct:** This is equivalent to the first radio button in the Resolve File Conflicts dialog box. The cached version is renamed and copied to the network. The network copy of the file is not updated but during the synchronization process, it will replace the locally cached version of the file. The Resolve File Conflicts dialog box also includes file version information, the ability to view both versions of the file, and a check box for configuring how all synchronization conflicts will be addressed.

70-210.04.03.004

▶ **Correct Answers: A and D**

A. **Correct:** The default setting for the Offline Files Wizard is to automatically synchronize files on logon and logoff. These settings are initially configured in the wizard. After the wizard completes, clicking Synchronize on the Tools menu opens the Items To Synchronize dialog box. Clicking the Setup button in this dialog box opens the Synchronization Settings dialog box. On the Logon/Logoff tab, both the When I Log On To My Computer and the When I Log Off Of My Computer check boxes are enabled. Automatic synchronization on logon and logoff is not the same as automatic file caching. The Offline Files Wizard specifically configures files for manual file caching. Therefore, the files are permanently available on the client computer.

B. **Incorrect:** Configuring synchronization based on how long a computer has been idle is completed in the Synchronization Settings dialog box on the On Idle tab. Select the Offline Files path from the Synchronize The Following Checked Items box, select the Synchronize The Selected Items While My Computer Is Idle check box, and then click Advanced. Clicking the Advanced button opens the Idle Settings dialog box. The default settings are to automatically synchronize the selected items after the computer is idle for 15 minutes. This synchronization is completed every 60 minutes if the computer remains idle. The proposed solution does not include enabling the Synchronize The Selected Items While My Computer Is Idle check box.

C. **Incorrect:** You schedule a synchronization task in the Synchronization Settings dialog box on the Scheduled tab. Clicking the Add button on the Scheduled tab starts the Scheduled Synchronization Wizard. This wizard provides a scheduled task interface. If the client is off line when scheduled synchronization is to occur, a computer appears on the taskbar. Double-clicking the computer shows the Offline Files Status dialog box, which informs you of a failed scheduled synchronization. The synchronization task can be canceled, or, when the computer is reconnected to the network, this synchronization task can be completed. In the proposed solution, no task was scheduled for this synchronization.

D. **Correct:** Another setting in the Idle Settings dialog box is the Prevent Synchronization When My Computer Is Running On Battery Power check box. This check box is enabled by default. However, in the proposed solution, the Synchronize The Selected Items While My Computer Is Idle check box is not selected. Therefore, synchronization will never occur when the computer is idle. The fact that the computer is running on battery power when the computer is idle is irrelevant. Synchronization will occur on logon and logoff only. The computer is not idle during these events.

Optimize and troubleshoot performance of the Windows 2000 Professional desktop.

Determining system performance is accomplished by monitoring how the operating system and applications use hardware resources. Performance is measured in terms of *system throughput*, the amount of work done in a unit of time. A user perceives performance as *response time*, the amount of time required to complete a task. As system throughput degrades in an overused system, the queue length for hardware service such as disk I/O or processor time increases. The user perceives this condition as poor response time. The feedback provided by monitoring throughput and queue length is then used to optimize response time. The system is monitored for an extended period of time when response time is satisfactory. The data collected during this period serves as the baseline for measuring future performance.

How Windows 2000 and applications are using hardware resources is best viewed using the **Performance console**. The Performance console contains the System Monitor ActiveX control (SYSMON.OCX) and the Performance Logs and Alerts snap-in. A summary view of activity is available from Windows **Task Manager**.

Task Manager displays information on applications and their processes currently running on the computer and how the processes are using a processor or processors and memory. You can start Task Manager in a number of ways. One way is to press Ctrl+Shift+Esc. Task Manager contains three tabs: Applications, Processes, and Performance. One important feature available in Task Manager but not available in the Performance console is the ability to forcibly end an application or its processes.

The Performance console (PERFMON.MSC) collects data from *instances*, unique copies of performance objects. *Performance objects* are symbolic representations of hardware resources, applications, protocols, and services. To tie the concept of objects to instances, consider the following example. If Windows 2000 is using two paging files, the Paging File object will show an instance of each paging file and a Total instance representing both paging files. Attributes of performance objects are called *counters* in the Performance console. To continue with the paging file example, the counters of the Paging File object are %Usage and %Usage Peak.

When you open the Performance console, performance counters query the registry for system resource data. Typing **perfmon /wmi** instructs the console to query the Windows Management Instrumentation (WMI) repository instead of the registry to obtain system resource data. The repository is to WMI as the registry is to the operating system.

Data is displayed immediately using the System Monitor node in the Performance console. Data is collected for later viewing by configuring the Counter logs and Trace logs in the Performance Logs and Alerts snap-in. Data is *sampled* using Counter logs and *traced* using, you guessed it, Trace logs. Sampling collects data at fixed intervals, such as every 15 seconds, whereas tracing collects data based on system events, such as processes created or deleted.

Counter logs can be configured to output binary (.blg), comma-delimited (.csv), or tab-delimited (.tsv) file data. All Counter log file types are viewable using System Monitor. Comma-delimited and tab-delimited text files are also viewable using applications that can read them, such as Excel. Two types of binary log files exist: circular and linear. Circular log files create log files until they reach a user-defined size and then a new log file is generated. Linear log files can be limited to a user-defined size or be set to grow to 1 GB or all remaining disk space, whichever comes first.

Trace logs generate binary (.etl) files. System Monitor cannot read these files. A utility such as TRACEDMP.EXE must be used to extract data from Trace logs for viewing in other applications. TRACEDMP.EXE is a utility contained in the Windows 2000 Server and Professional Resource Kits. This utility reads the .etl file and creates a SUMMARY.TXT file and a DUMPFILE.CSV file for review.

The Performance Logs and Alerts snap-in also contains an Alerts node that is used to configure thresholds for system events, such as a disk partition reaching capacity. The thresholds fire triggers. The triggers are configured to perform any function that can run in Windows 2000, such as sending a network message or running a program.

Because System Monitor is an ActiveX control, it is easily displayed in applications that support this object type. For example, System Monitor can be displayed in Internet Explorer or in a Microsoft Office application, such as Microsoft Word. The simplest way to export the OLE Custom eXtension (OCX) is to select a Counter log and on the Action menu, click Save Settings As. The file is then saved as a standard .html file and viewed in Internet Explorer. System Monitor is fully functional whether it is running as part of the Performance console or in another application.

You view data in System Monitor in one of three views: chart, histogram, or report. The chart and histogram views are typically used for analyzing real-time data. The report view is ideal for viewing a summary of data collected in counter logs. You can use all views to see real-time and logged data.

Through logging, obtain a baseline and then continue to monitor the counters that are part of your baseline settings. At minimum, track utilization and throughput counters and those counters that might indicate a resource bottleneck. For instance, to monitor utilization, collect data on Logical Disk\%Free Space, Processor\%Processor Time, Memory\Available Bytes, and Network Segment\%Net Utilization. To monitor throughput, collect data on Network Interface\Packets/sec and PhysicalDisk\Disk Bytes/sec. To monitor bottlenecks, collect data on System\Processor Queue Length, Processor\Interrupts/sec, and LogicalDisk\Avg. Disk Queue Length.

Note Logical disk counters are not enabled by default. At the command line, type **diskperf /yv** and restart the computer.

Hardware, operating system, and application troubleshooting is often necessary to solve performance problems. For example, a network adapter that is failing might overburden the processor with unnecessary interrupt request (IRQ) calls. This activity might manifest itself through unusually high processor use. Task Manager, the System Monitor node, and the Performance Logs and Alerts snap-in are important tools for monitoring and troubleshooting operating system and application performance problems.

This objective covers a lot of ground. Most of the overview provided here explores the utilities used to monitor performance. The questions included with this objective explore configuration changes that help you optimize and troubleshoot a computer running Windows 2000 Professional. The "Further Readings" section for this objective includes Chapters 27–30 in the Windows 2000 Professional Resource Kit, which you should review to supplement your studies of this objective.

Objective 4.4 Questions

70-210.04.04.001

You want to move the paging file to another hard disk on your computer running Windows 2000 Professional. What should you do?

A. In the System Properties dialog box, click the General tab and then click the Change button.

B. In the System Properties dialog box, click the Performance tab and then click the Change button.

C. In the System Properties dialog box, click the Environment tab and then click the Change button.

D. In the System Properties dialog box, click the Advanced tab and then click the Performance Options button.

E. In the System Properties dialog box, click the Advanced tab and then click the Environment Variables button.

F. In the System Properties dialog box, click the Advanced tab and then click the Startup And Recovery button.

70-210.04.04.002

You suspect that the processor is causing a performance bottleneck on your computer running Windows 2000 Professional. What should you do to validate this assumption?

A. Use System Monitor to collect data on Processor\% Processor Time and Processor\Interrupts/sec. Analyze when and for how long these values are low.

B. Use System Monitor to collect data on Processor\% Processor Time and Processor\Interrupts/sec. Analyze when and for how long these values are high.

C. Use System Monitor to collect data on Processor\% Processor Time and System\Processor Queue Length. Analyze when and for how long these values are low.

D. Use System Monitor to collect data on Processor\% Processor Time and System\Processor Queue Length. Analyze when and for how long these values are high.

70-210.04.04.003

You want to improve the performance of the New Technology File System (NTFS) fixed disks on your computer running Windows 2000 Professional. Which options might you consider to improve NTFS performance? (Choose three.)

A. Disable the last access update.

B. Disable creation of long names.

C. Disable creation of short names.

D. Reserve appropriate space for the master file table (MFT).

Objective 4.4 Answers

70-210.04.04.001

▶ **Correct Answers: D**

A. **Incorrect:** The General tab in the System Properties dialog box contains summary information about the operating system; to whom the product is registered, including the registration ID; and the processor type or types, system compatibility, and amount of installed RAM.

B. **Incorrect:** There is no Performance tab in the System Properties dialog box. The Performance tab is part of Task Manager and provides summary information on processor and memory utilization.

C. **Incorrect:** There is no Environment tab in the System Properties dialog box.

D. **Correct:** Clicking the Advanced tab's Performance Options button opens the Performance Options dialog box. You use this dialog box to optimize response time for foreground (applications) or background (service) operations.

In the Performance Options dialog box, click the Change button and the Virtual Memory dialog box opens. Select a new drive that will host the paging file, and then use the options in the Paging File Size For Selected Drive section to set the paging file's initial size and maximum size. Next select the drive that is currently hosting the paging file and set its initial size and maximum size to 0. After you restart the computer, PAGEFILE.SYS will be created in the new location. You also use the Virtual Memory dialog box to view total paging file size and to set the maximum allowable registry size.

One reason to consider moving the paging file is if monitoring the system suggests that the disk hosting the paging file is overused. Continue to monitor the original disk and the new disk to verify that moving the paging file remedied the problem. If not, excessive disk use on the drive hosting the paging file might suggest that the bottleneck is because of insufficient RAM. Consider increasing the amount of installed RAM. Additionally, check the running processes to verify that there isn't a memory leak or an application that is overusing RAM.

E. **Incorrect:** Clicking the Advanced tab's Environment Variables button opens the Environment Variables dialog box. User and system-level environment variables are added, modified, or deleted from here.

F. **Incorrect:** Clicking the Advanced tab's Startup And Recovery button opens the Startup And Recovery dialog box. You configure system startup and system failure behavior in this dialog box.

Unlike Windows NT, the system failure dump directory can be located anywhere, not just on the boot partition. However, a paging file must be available on the boot partition to initially hold the dump information. Windows 2000 provides three types of system dumps: Small Memory Dump (64 KB), Kernel Memory Dump, and Complete Memory Dump. The Small Memory Dump (64 KB) option requires a paging file on the boot partition that is only 2 MB in size. On the other end of the spectrum, the Complete Memory Dump option requires a paging file equal to the size of physical RAM to hold the entire contents of RAM if a system failure occurs.

70-210.04.04.002

▶ **Correct Answers: D**

A. **Incorrect:** The Processor\%Processor Time value measures the percentage of time that the processor was busy running nonidle threads during the specified time interval. This counter is a primary indicator of processor activity because it measures all process activity except for the System Idle Process. Measuring this counter for its lowest value will not identify a busy processor.

A processor is always running at full speed; however, on a processor that is not overused, most of the processor time is spent running the System Idle Process, which has no base priority, so all other processes run at a higher priority. On a system whose processor is not the bottleneck, open Task Manager and review the CPU and CPU Time columns for this process. You should see that this is the busiest process in the system.

The Processor\Interrupts/sec value measures the average rate at which a processor handles interrupts from attached hardware devices. This counter is an indirect indicator of interrupt-driven device activity, such as disk controllers and network adapters. A failing device might raise an excessive number of interrupts, so monitoring the system for an excessive number of Processor\Interrupts/sec values could indicate a failing device. Measuring this counter for its lowest value will not identify a busy processor.

B. **Incorrect:** Processor\% Processor Time is an important indicator of processor activity, but an excessively high value for Processor\Interrupts/sec might indicate failing hardware. See answer explanation A for details on both of these counters.

C. **Incorrect:** As outlined in answer explanation A, Processor\% Processor Time is an important indicator of processor use. However, analyzing when the value for this counter is low doesn't help to determine when the processor is overused.

System\Processor Queue Length measures the number of threads ready for processing but not running. The Processor Queue Length counter is part of the System object instead of the Processor object because there is a single queue for processor time even on multiprocessor computers. A sustained processor queue of greater than two threads might be an indication of a processor bottleneck. Measuring this counter when it's at its lowest is likely to return a result of 0 unless the processor is always running at 100 percent utilization. This counter displays only the last observed value; it is not an average.

D. **Correct:** As summarized in answer explanation A, Processor\% Processor Time is a useful indicator of an overused processor if the value sustains a high value, perhaps 80 percent or greater. This, combined with a System\Processor Queue Length greater than 2, suggests that the processor is a bottleneck.

70-210.04.04.003

▶ **Correct Answers: A, C, and D**

A. **Correct:** NTFS tags each folder with the last access date and time in an NTFS partition whenever the folder structure is traversed. Traversing large disks with large folder structures is slowed by this date-and-time stamping process. To disable the last access update on NTFS partitions, add the NtfsDisableLastAccessUpdate value name with a REG_DWORD data type and a value of 1 to the HKEY_LOCAL_MACHINE\SYSTEM\CurrentControlSet\Control\FileSystem key.

B. **Incorrect:** Creation of long filenames (LFNs) is automatic and cannot be disabled in NTFS. The file allocation table (FAT) file system can be prevented from creating LFNs by setting the value of the Win31FileSystem registry entry to 1. This entry is located in the HKEY_LOCAL_MACHINE\SYSTEM\CurrentControlSet\Control\FileSystem key. Preventing LFN creation on the FAT file system might be necessary if the computer multiboots a legacy operating system and if disk tools unaware of LFNs are used to manage the FAT partitions. Files that already have both long and short filenames are unaffected by this change. Therefore, legacy disk tools might destroy LFNs on existing files.

C. **Correct:** For compatibility with MS-DOS or Windows 3.x applications that are unaware of LFNs, FAT, FAT32, and NTFS generate short filenames in 8.3 format when a file is created. Generating short filenames contributes to file system overhead. To disable the generation of 8.3 filenames on NTFS partitions, change the value of the NtfsDisable8dot3NameCreation registry entry from 0 to 1. This entry is located in the HKEY_LOCAL_MACHINE\SYSTEM\CurrentControlSet\Control\FileSystem key. Files that already have both long and short filenames are unaffected by this change.

D. **Correct:** NTFS uses the MFT as a file index. File properties including location information and entire files, if the files are small, are stored in the MFT. The MFT stores at least one entry for every file on an NTFS partition. As files are added to a partition, the MFT grows. Because the MFT is a file itself, it is susceptible to fragmentation. Excessive fragmentation in files impacts performance. The standard disk defragmenter included with Windows 2000 does not defragment the MFT. Therefore, to avoid fragmentation in the MFT, NTFS reserves space for it. The default space reservation is adequate for relatively small partitions that will not contain many files. To increase contiguous space allocation for larger partitions that will contain many files, add the NtfsMftZoneReservation value name with a REG_DWORD data type and a value of 2, 3, or 4 to the HKEY_LOCAL_MACHINE\SYSTEM\CurrentControlSet\Control\FileSystem key. The larger the value of this registry entry, the more space that is allocated to the MFT.

OBJECTIVE 4.5

Manage hardware profiles.

A **hardware profile** contains configuration information that Windows 2000 Professional checks during the startup process to determine which drivers to load and which services to start. Hardware profiles are particularly important to support portable computers that are used in and out of a docking station.

Hardware profiles are created automatically or manually. Windows 2000 automatically creates two profiles—the Docked Profile and the Undocked Profile—when an operating system basic input/output system (BIOS) query detects a hardware manufacturer's dock ID and serial number. Through Plug and Play enumeration, the operating system automatically selects the correct hardware profile based on whether the portable computer is docked or undocked. Portable computers that are not fully Plug and Play compliant might require manual hardware profile creation.

You create hardware profiles by opening the System Properties dialog box and clicking the Hardware tab. On this tab, click the Hardware Profiles button, and in the Hardware Profiles dialog box, copy the default profile. You also configure how a hardware profile is selected on startup in this dialog box. A copied profile contains the same device and service startup configuration as the original profile. So the next step is to configure the copied profile.

You configure a hardware profile by first starting the computer and selecting the profile to be configured. After Windows 2000 has started, use Device Manager and the Services window to modify the profile's configuration. In Device Manager, access the properties of a device. On the General tab of the device's properties, select the Device Usage drop-down list box to specify whether the device is enabled for all profiles, disabled for the current profile, or disabled for all profiles. In the Services window, access the properties of a service. On the Log On tab, select the hardware profile appearing in the You Can Enable Or Disable This Service For The Hardware Profiles Listed Below check box. Then click Enable or Disable to change the state of the service for the selected profile.

Objective 4.5 Questions

70-210.04.05.001

Your laptop computer running Windows 2000 Professional is not fully Plug and Play compliant, and you want to create new hardware profiles for docked and undocked states. How do you navigate to the dialog box used to create a new profile?

A. Open the Computer Management console, expand the System Tools node, and click the Hardware Profiles node.

B. Open the Computer Management console, expand the Services and Applications node, and click the Hardware Profiles node.

C. Open the System program in Control Panel, click the Hardware tab in the System Properties dialog box, and click the Hardware Profiles button.

D. Open the System program in Control Panel, click the Advanced tab in the System Properties dialog box, and then click the Hardware Profiles button.

70-210.04.05.002

You have a laptop computer that is not fully Plug and Play compliant running Windows 2000 Professional, and you want to modify the hardware profile. What should you do before modifying the hardware profile?

A. No preparation is recommended.

B. Back up the system partition and the registry, and then restart the computer.

C. Make a copy of the default profile, restart the computer, and then select and modify the copied profile.

D. Make a copy of the default profile, restart the computer, and then select and modify the default profile.

70-210.04.05.003

You purchase a new laptop computer running Windows 2000 Professional. You plan to use it in a docking station to connect to a network at your office. All devices and device drivers support Plug and Play, and the computer is ACPI compliant. You want to use two hardware profiles corresponding to docked and undocked states. What should you do?

A. No action is required.

B. Create a new hardware profile for the docked state.

C. Create two new hardware profiles, one for the docked state and one for the undocked state.

D. In the *profile_name* Properties dialog box, select the This Is A Portable Computer option.

Objective 4.5 Answers

70-210.04.05.001

▶ **Correct Answers: C**

A. **Incorrect:** The System Tools node of the Computer Management console does not contain a Hardware Profiles node for creating hardware profiles. Hardware profiles can be modified in the Computer Management console by selecting the Device Manager snap-in located below the System Tools node and accessing the properties of devices appearing in the details pane.

B. **Incorrect:** The Services and Applications node of the Computer Management console does not contain a Hardware Profiles node. Note that Hardware Profiles is not a snap-in, a snap-in extension, or an ActiveX control.

C. **Correct:** The Hardware Profiles button is located on the Hardware tab in the System Properties dialog box. One way to open the System Properties dialog box is from Control Panel's System program. Another way to open the System Properties dialog box is by accessing the properties of the My Computer icon.

D. **Incorrect:** The Advanced tab in the System Properties dialog box contains three buttons: Performance Options, Environment Variables, and Startup And Recovery. If you are not familiar with these buttons, review the answer explanations to the first question in the previous objective.

70-210.04.05.002

▶ **Correct Answers: C**

A. **Incorrect:** Improper profile modification could cause the computer to fail when it is restarted; for example, stopping a critical service or disabling a necessary device driver. If the computer is not fully Plug and Play compliant, it might not be able to recover from this failure. One possible solution is to select Last Known Good Configuration on the Advanced Options menu when the computer is restarted.

B. **Incorrect:** Completing a backup of the system partition and the registry is a good disaster recovery measure. However, this is not an efficient way to prepare for modifying a hardware profile.

C. **Correct:** After copying the existing profile, you must restart the computer before you can modify the new (copied) profile by using Device Manager. If your goal is to modify only services that are enabled or disabled for a particular hardware profile, a restart is not necessary. If the modifications made to the new hardware profile leave the operating system in an unstable state, restart the computer and select the original hardware profile. After Windows 2000 has started using the default profile, navigate to the copied profile and delete it.

D. **Incorrect:** You should not alter the default profile created during the Windows 2000 Professional installation process.

70-210.04.05.003

▶ **Correct Answers: A**

A. **Correct:** Windows 2000 Professional creates a Docked Profile and an Undocked Profile if a portable computer is docking capable, is fully ACPI compliant, and runs only Plug and Play devices and device drivers. You should never manually alter the two hardware profiles on a computer meeting all of these conditions.

B. **Incorrect:** Copying the existing hardware profile and configuring it to load device drivers for the docked state and the devices contained in the docking station is not necessary for the computer described in the question. If the computer is not fully ACPI compliant or it runs legacy non-Plug and Play devices, then creating a separate docked hardware profile might be necessary.

C. **Incorrect:** Both hardware profiles are created on the computer described in the question. Windows 2000 Professional queries the BIOS to find a dock ID and serial number. If it finds this identifier, it automatically creates the docked and undocked hardware profiles.

D. **Incorrect:** The Hardware Profiles dialog box contains a Properties button. Clicking this button displays the profile_name Properties dialog box where profile_name is the name of the selected profile. This dialog box shows dock ID and serial number information if any is found by querying the BIOS. If the computer does not meet the hardware specifications outlined in the question, you can manually configure the hardware profile to indicate that it is used on a portable computer and to specify the computer's docking state. In addition, the profile_name Properties dialog box is used to control whether the profile appears when Windows starts. You should not alter these configuration settings for the computer described in the question.

O B J E C T I V E   4 . 6

Recover systems and user data.

Windows 2000 Professional includes a powerful set of tools and utilities that, in combination, can help you recover a failed system and the user data contained on it. The tools summarized here include **Windows Backup (NTBACKUP.EXE)**, the **Advanced Options menu** (**Safe Mode** and other advanced startup options), and the **Recovery Console**.

Windows Backup backs up data to tape or to disk. The tape can be housed in a single tape drive or be part of a media changer. The Removable Storage Service manages tape backups for Windows Backup. File backups to fixed or removable disks are managed directly by Windows Backup. The target of a compressed file backup can be a local disk or a network-accessible share. Windows Backup supports a number of backup types: Normal (full backup), Incremental, Differential, Copy, and Daily. Normal, Incremental, and Differential backup types are part of a scheduled backup routine. Copy and Daily backup types work independently of a backup schedule. Users with Administrator or Backup Operator-level privileges can back up and restore files.

Windows Backup also provides a **System State** backup option. This option appears in Windows Backup on the Backup tab. A System State backup backs up the Windows 2000 boot files, system files on the boot partition (both in the Program Files folder and the System32 folder), performance counter configuration files, the COM+ Class Registration database, and the registry. Boot files include the system files. By using backup advanced options, it is possible to include all files under Windows File Protection (WFP) control with the System State backup. System State data is typically restored locally. Except for the COM+ Class Registration database, a restore of system state can be redirected to an alternate location. A user with local administrative privileges is necessary to restore system state data.

Note Windows Backup also includes the command on the Tools menu to create an **Emergency Repair Disk (ERD)**.

When a backup runs, files locked by the operating system are backed up. Files locked by other processes and remote registry files are not backed up. Therefore, you must close all applications before a backup runs. Windows Backup also does not back up files when the proper privilege is not granted or when the file is listed on the Exclude Files tab in the Windows Backup Options dialog box. System State data on remote computers cannot be backed up. Instead, create a local backup of System State data and then use a remote backup procedure to back up the System State data located in a share on the remote computer.

The encrypted file attribute is maintained when files are backed up. Therefore, you should also back up the certificates corresponding to the encrypted files. Create a custom console, and add the Certificates snap-in to the console. Select a certificate to save to disk, and click Export on the All Tasks menu. The export procedure starts the Certificate Export Wizard. After the certificate is exported, use Windows Backup to store it on the backup media.

In the event of a system failure, you can use Windows Backup to perform restore procedures. Before deciding to run a restore procedure, you can try other, more efficient ways to recover from system failures. Use the Advanced Options menu to solve startup delays or failures. Some common failures include system instability from a recently installed device driver or application, or an incompatible video display setting.

You open the Advanced Options menu by pressing F8 during startup. Menu commands valid for Windows 2000 Professional include various Safe Modes (with and without networking, and command prompt only). Use the Safe Mode startup commands to resolve device driver, system service, or autostarting application failures. When the computer is started in any Safe Mode, boot logging is automatic. You enable boot logging for a normal startup by clicking Enable Boot Logging on the menu. The Boot log is stored in *%systemroot%* and is named NTBTLOG.TXT. If the file already exists, the next logging procedure appends to the existing file. You resolve incompatible display settings by selecting the Enable VGA Mode command. You can solve system configuration changes that cause the system to fail by selecting the Last Known Good Configuration command. Troubleshooting a system with a kernel debugger starts by choosing Debugging Mode on the menu.

If the procedures available from the Advanced Options menu do not resolve a system error, the Recovery Console might do the trick. The Recovery Console runs a Windows 2000 command interpreter to provide access to the local disk. You start the Recovery Console in one of two ways: either from the Windows 2000 Setup routine or from the local disk. To start it from the setup routine, press R when prompted by the installation routine; this displays the Repair Options screen. From the Repair Options screen, press C to start the Recovery Console.

To install the Recovery Console to the local disk, locate the \i386 folder on the Windows 2000 Professional installation CD-ROM and then type **winnt32 /cmdcons**. Installing the utility to the local disk is a convenient method of starting the Recovery

Console, but if the disk is failing, starting the Recovery Console from the Windows 2000 Setup routine might be the only viable option. When the Recovery Console is started, you are prompted to select the Windows 2000 installation you want to start and to type the administrator password of that installation. The Recovery Console provides limited access to specific folders on the system. Removing the prompt for an Administrator password and gaining unrestricted access to all drives and folders can be accomplished through two policy settings:

- Recovery Console: Allow Administrative Logon

- Recovery Console: Allow Floppy Copy and Access to All Drives and All Folders

After setting the second listed policy, type **set allowallpaths = true** in the Recovery Console to enable full access to all drives and folders, and type **set allowsremovablemedia = true** to allow copying files to removable media, such as disks. The spaces separating the equal sign from the value names and values are required.

Note You modify policy settings using the Local Security Settings console or through the Group Policy snap-in. Creating a custom console with the Group Policy snap-in configured for the local computer appears as the Local Computer Policy node in the console.

All file systems that Windows 2000 supports are accessible by using the Recovery Console. The console includes a number of disk utilities, such as Chkdsk, Diskpart, Fixboot, and Fixmbr; file system utilities like Expand, Md, Rd, and Ren; and miscellaneous utilities like Systemroot, Map, Set, and Listsvc. When at the Recovery Console command prompt, typing **Help** displays a list of all available commands. To learn more about a specific command, type the command's name followed by **/?** or **/help**.

If the *%systemroot%*\Repair\Regback folder is current, use the Recovery Console to recover the registry. After the Recovery Console is started, copy the registry files from the *%systemroot%*\Repair\Regback folder to the *%systemroot%*\System32\Config folder.

Using the Recovery Console is a better way to restore a damaged registry than running an Emergency Repair. This is because the registry files in the *%systemroot%*\Repair folder are from the original installation of Windows 2000 Professional, so any changes to the system after the original installation are lost when you run an Emergency Repair. In contrast, the registry data from the *%systemroot%*\Repair\Regback folder is current if one of two procedures are followed: if a backup of System State data is run, or if the creation of an ERD in Windows Backup included enabling the Also Backup The Registry To The Repair Directory check box. Interestingly, running the ERD creation process with this check box enabled doesn't update the *%systemroot%*\Repair folder as you might expect from its name; instead, it updates the *%systemroot%*\Repair\Regback folder.

Objective 4.6 Questions

70-210.04.06.001

You need to plan a backup strategy for your computer running Windows 2000 Professional. You need to back up data every night. Using Windows Backup, which backup plan should you choose to minimize the time needed to restore data?

A. Normal

B. Copy

C. Incremental

D. Differential

E. Normal and Differential

F. Normal and Incremental

70-210.04.06.002

You receive a new computer running Windows 2000 Professional, and you want to have the ability to use the Windows 2000 Recovery Console. What should you do to enable the Recovery Console to be started?

A. No action is required because it is installed by default.

B. Open the System program in Control Panel, click the Advanced tab, click the Startup And Recovery button, and install the Recovery Console.

C. Insert the Windows 2000 Professional installation CD-ROM, and close the Setup dialog box if it appears. At a command prompt, switch to the root folder on the CD-ROM, run SETUP /CMDCONS, and install the Recovery Console.

D. Insert the Windows 2000 Professional installation CD-ROM, and close the Setup dialog box if it appears. At a command prompt, switch to the \i386 folder on the CD-ROM, run WINNT32 /CMDCONS, and install the Recovery Console.

70-210.04.06.003

Which methods can you use to repair a Windows 2000 Professional installation? (Choose two.)

A. Use the Local System Restore mode.

B. Use the Recovery Console.

C. Use the Emergency Repair process.

D. Use the Directory Services Restore mode.

70-210.04.06.004

Your Windows 2000 Professional system fails to start, and you want to try starting in Safe Mode. After restarting the computer, what should you do to start in Safe Mode?

A. Use the Recovery Console.

B. Use the Emergency Repair process.

C. Press F8 during startup when prompted.

D. No action is required because Windows 2000 automatically initiates Safe Mode after system startup has failed.

Objective 4.6 Answers

70-210.04.06.001

▶ **Correct Answers: E**

A. **Incorrect:** A Normal backup type, typically known as a Full backup, backs up every file regardless of whether it was backed up previously. The archive attribute is cleared from the files using this backup type. It is the operating system's job to place an archive attribute on any new or modified file. A Normal backup takes the most time of any backup type that is part of a schedule and the least time to perform a restore procedure. A restore procedure using this backup type alone requires the most recent Normal backup. Because it is the most time-intensive backup type for performing nightly backups, running this backup type for all scheduled backups does not provide the most efficient backup plan.

B. **Incorrect:** A Copy backup type is used outside of a regularly scheduled backup routine and backs up all targeted files. This backup type ignores the archive attribute and does not alter it on any targeted files containing the attribute. A restore procedure requires the most recent Copy backup type. The Copy backup type is not part of a backup plan.

C. **Incorrect:** The Incremental backup type backs up all targeted files containing the archive attribute. This backup type clears the archive attribute on files it backs up. So every time it is run, only new and modified files targeted for backup are backed up. This is the fastest backup type for backing up data and the slowest to restore data. An Incremental backup type is usually combined with a Normal backup type to form a backup plan.

D. **Incorrect:** The Differential backup type backs up all targeted files containing the archive attribute. This backup type does not clear the archive attribute on files it backs up. So every time it is run, all targeted files with the archive attribute are backed up. This is a moderately fast backup type for backing up and restoring data. An Incremental backup type is usually combined with a Normal backup type to form a backup plan.

E. **Correct:** A daily backup plan that includes a weekly Normal backup type and on all other days, a Differential backup type is the most efficient backup plan for both backup and recovery. The Normal backup type clears the archive attribute when it runs, while the Differential backup type does not. Therefore, if a Normal backup runs on Monday morning, then a Differential backup runs on Tuesday morning. The Differential backup contains only the files that changed between Monday morning and Tuesday morning. The contents of a Differential backup run on Tuesday morning are identical to an Incremental backup, but the next Differential backup will be different. The Differential backup run on Wednesday morning will contain all new and modified files since the last Normal backup on Monday morning. This is because a Differential backup backs up all targeted files containing the archive attribute but does not clear the archive attribute. A full restore procedure requires the most recent Normal backup (Monday morning), followed by the most recent Differential backup (Wednesday morning).

F. **Incorrect:** A daily backup plan that includes a weekly Normal backup type and on all other days, an Incremental backup type, is the most efficient backup plan for backup but not for recovery. Both backup types clear the archive attribute when they run. Therefore, if a Normal backup runs on Monday morning, then an Incremental backup runs on Tuesday morning. The Incremental backup contains only the files that changed between Monday morning and Tuesday morning. The contents of an Incremental backup run on Tuesday morning are identical to a Differential backup, but the next Incremental backup will be different. The Incremental backup run on Wednesday morning will contain all new and modified files since the last Incremental backup on Tuesday morning. This is because each Incremental backup clears the archive attribute during the backup process. This restore process is less efficient than the Normal and Differential backup plan outlined in answer explanation E because a full restore procedure requires the most recent Normal backup (Monday morning), followed by each Incremental backup in sequence (Tuesday morning and then Wednesday morning).

70-210.04.06.002

▶ **Correct Answers: D**

A. **Incorrect:** The Recovery Console is not installed by default. If the Recovery Console is not installed locally, it can still be run from the Windows 2000 Setup routine.

B. **Incorrect:** Clicking the Advanced tab's Startup And Recovery button opens the Startup And Recovery dialog box. System startup and system failure behavior is configured in this dialog box. The Recovery Console is not installed in this dialog box.

C. **Incorrect:** SETUP.EXE located on the root of the Windows 2000 Professional installation CD-ROM opens the Windows Setup dialog box. The program does not contain any switches.

D. **Correct:** Typing Winnt32 /cmdcons starts the Setup routine and installs approximately 7 MB of files, primarily drivers. Some of these files are used to start the Windows 2000 command interpreter from the local disk. The files are installed to the system partition (usually C) into a folder named \Cmdcons. The Cmdcons folder is marked with the System, Hidden, and Read Only attributes (SHR). An option to start the Recovery Console is added to BOOT.INI. The Recovery Console path in BOOT.INI points to the BOOTSECT.DAT file contained in the Cmdcons folder.

70-210.04.06.003

▶ **Correct Answers: B and C**

    A. **Incorrect:** This is not a valid recovery option.

    B. **Correct:** The Recovery Console provides access to the local disk so that recovery commands can be run, such as Fixmbr to repair the Master Boot Record or Disable servicename, where service-name is the name of a service to disable. The Recovery Console is the preferred method of restoring a damaged registry given that the %systemroot%\Repair\Regback folder contains current registry information.

    C. **Correct:** You start Emergency Repair by entering the Repair Options console in Text mode of the Windows 2000 Setup routine and pressing R. There are two ways to run Emergency Repair: use Manual Repair or Fast Repair. A Manual Repair allows you to choose which repair procedures should occur; Fast Repair runs all repair procedures. The Emergency Repair process returns the computer to its state when Windows 2000 was first installed. All system changes and updates are lost. System files are replaced with the files on the Windows 2000 Professional installation CD-ROM, and the registry is restored from the Repair folder. In Windows 2000, the registry files are not copied to the ERD as they were in Windows NT. Therefore, the %systemroot%\Repair folder is critical to a registry restore when the Emergency Repair is run.

    D. **Incorrect:** This command does appear on the Advanced Options menu, but it is valid only for computers running Server editions of Windows 2000 and Microsoft Active Directory directory services.

70-210.04.06.004

▶ **Correct Answers: C**

    A. **Incorrect:** The Recovery Console runs the Windows 2000 command interpreter. The console does not run any installation of Windows 2000 on the local computer; it simply makes an installation accessible from the command line.

    B. **Incorrect:** You start the Emergency Repair process from the Repair Options screen of the Windows 2000 Setup routine. Safe Mode is not started from the Windows 2000 Setup routine.

    C. **Correct:** Pressing F8 when prompted during Windows 2000 startup opens the Advanced Options menu. There are three versions of Safe Mode available on the menu: Safe Mode, Safe Mode With Networking, and Safe Mode With Command Prompt. Safe Mode starts the operating system but loads only critical device drivers and services. Safe Mode With Networking starts the operating system and loads critical device drivers and network services. If network-based group policies are running, they will be applied if you select this version of Safe Mode. Safe Mode With Command Prompt is similar to Safe Mode except that a command prompt serves as the shell instead of the Windows Explorer interface. The Video Graphics Adapter (VGA) driver is loaded so graphical utilities are available from the command-line interface.

    D. **Incorrect:** Unlike Windows 95 and Windows 98, Safe Mode is not automatically started by Windows 2000 after a failed startup.

Configuring and Troubleshooting the Desktop Environment

Objective Domain 3 examined troubleshooting hardware and the Microsoft Windows 2000 device drivers that support such troubleshooting. Objective Domain 4 examined how to configure Windows 2000 for optimal performance and reliability. This objective explores how to *configure* a Microsoft Windows 2000 Professional desktop to support the user experience and how to *troubleshoot* problems with the desktop environment.

Like hardware profiles, **user profiles** are created to distinguish between different computing environments. They are specifically designed to personalize a user's desktop settings based on a user's account name. Unlike hardware profiles, user profiles can be configured to move between computers on the network. This feature is called *roaming*, and a profile configured in this way is aptly called a **roaming user profile**. You customize a profile by adjusting desktop settings, such as adding a shortcut to the desktop. If a roaming user profile should not be customized by users, it can be converted to a **mandatory user profile**. A mandatory user profile is ideal for sharing among multiple users who use the same desktop settings.

Localization is an important language feature of a personalized desktop environment. Localization includes supporting one or multiple languages in the Windows interface, configuring local settings appropriate to a user, and configuring Windows 2000 Professional to operate in multiple locations.

User-specific requirements extend beyond user profiles and localization. Another critical feature of a personalized desktop is user-specific application availability. For example, a computer user in the Accounting department will need access to accounting software, while a user in the Marketing department will need access to contact management software. Both staff members will need access to standard desktop applications such as Microsoft Office. Working together, network-based **Group Policy** and the Microsoft **Windows Installer Service** make custom application delivery possible. Objective 5.3 focuses specifically on managing applications using the Windows Installer Service and Windows Installer packages.

You personalize Windows 2000 Professional desktops by configuring desktop settings, such as enabling the **Active Desktop**, configuring a screen saver, and redirecting the My Documents folder to the network. These settings are centrally managed through Group Policy. You configure Group Policy locally by using the Local Computer Policy object of the Group Policy snap-in. This snap-in is not part of a default console in Windows 2000 Professional, but it can be made part of a custom console by typing **gpedit.msc** in the Run dialog box. The Group Policy snap-in appears as the Local Computer Policy node in the console. You accomplish central network management of Group Policy by using Active Directory services and a console containing the Group Policy snap-in. From server editions of Windows 2000 configured as domain controllers, Group Policy can be applied at the domain, domain controller, organizational unit (OU), site, or computer level.

Accessibility services are an important part of personalizing a desktop for computer users with special needs, such as high-contrast display settings for users who have difficulty seeing the display and translation of sounds into visual captions for users who have difficulty hearing computer sounds. You configure these settings and many other accessibility options locally from the Accessibility Options program in Control Panel or from the icons contained in the Accessibility program group.

Another important user-configurable service in Windows 2000 Professional is the desktop fax facility. This feature allows you to send and receive fax transmissions on the computer rather than through a fax machine.

Desktop settings, accessibility services, and fax services may require troubleshooting steps to maintain proper operation. A number of important troubleshooting tools are contained in the Windows 2000 Professional Resource Kit. Some of these tools are mentioned in the objective overviews accompanying each objective in this chapter.

Tested Skills and Suggested Practices

The skills you need to successfully master the Configuring and Troubleshooting the Desktop Environment Objective Domain on Exam 70-210: Installing, Configuring, and Administering Microsoft Windows 2000 Professional include the following:

- **Manage user profiles.**
  - Practice 1: Go to the command line, and type **set** to see a list of configured environment variables. First identify the environment variable that points to *%systemdrive%*\Documents and Settings\All Users. Next identify the path defined by the *%userprofiles%* environment variable.
  - Practice 2: Access the contents of the All Users profile and the Local User profile folders.

■ Practice 3: Delete a local user account, and then re-create a user account using the same name as the deleted user account. Log on with the new user account. Go to the command line, and determine the profile folder name assigned to the new user. Repeat this procedure at least twice.

■ Practice 4: Configure a roaming user profile on a workgroup computer. Then configure a fully functional roaming user profile on Microsoft Windows 2000 Server. Copy a local user profile to the network location designated for the roaming user profile. Configure a domain user account for the roaming user profile, and log on as the domain user.

■ Practice 5: Configure both types of mandatory user profiles (NTUSER.MAN) and *profile_folder*.MAN. Log on to domain user accounts configured for each of these mandatory user profiles. Disconnect the workstation from the network, and then attempt to log on again as the domain users configured for the two types of mandatory user profiles. Identify which mandatory user profile allows you to log on with the cached version of the profile.

■ Practice 6: Deploy and support language features in Windows 2000 Professional.

■ Practice 7: Install an additional language group to provide multilingual viewing and editing. Visit a Web site written in a language supported by the newly installed language group. Print a page of the Web site to verify that printing in the language appearing in your Web browser is possible.

■ Practice 8: Using the Microsoft Windows 2000 MultiLanguage Version CD-ROM, install menu and dialog box support for a language contained in the language group you installed in the previous practice. Configure the Menus And Dialogs drop-down list box in the Regional Options dialog box for the newly installed language.

■ Practice 9: After installing the Windows 2000 MultiLanguage Version, verify that *%systemroot %*\Muisetup.log was created. If any errors were generated during MultiLanguage Version setup, review the log.

■ Practice 10: Verify that installing and running the MultiLanguage Version of Windows 2000 do not change applications that are not part of the operating system installation.

■ Practice 11: Configure the various settings available in the Regional Options program in Control Panel, such as adding an input locale and switching between the installed input locales from the status area of the taskbar.

■ Practice 12: Create an automated installation of Windows 2000 Professional that installs several language groups. To lessen the effort of creating the answer file, use the Setup Manager Wizard.

- **Automate the process of software installation using the Windows Installer Service.**

  - Practice 1: Run a Windows Installer package (.msi) installation routine. Use the Add/Remove Programs program to modify the installation and to remove it.

  - Practice 2: Customize a Windows Installer package installation routine using a transform (.mst) file. Run the customized installation routine by calling the .mst file in the Windows Installer command line.

  - Practice 3: Use the Software Installation extension (part of the Windows 2000 Server Group Policy snap-in) to assign an .msi file under the User Configuration node, and then log on as a domain user targeted for this assignment. Open the shortcut created by the assignment to install the application. Complete the same procedure with a different .msi package, but this time, assign the .msi package to a Computer Configuration node and verify that after restarting the targeted computer, the application is installed. Finally publish a third .msi package, and verify that it appears in the Add/Remove Programs dialog box by clicking the Add New Programs icon.

  - Practice 4: Configure the Apply Group Policy permission so that the Authenticated Users group does not get an assigned package and another group that you designate does get the package.

- **Customize desktop settings.**

  - Practice 1: Enable Web content on the Active Desktop. Configure the Active Desktop to display an HTML document as a background. Visit the Microsoft Windows Technologies Active Desktop Gallery to add Active Desktop items. To access the gallery, click the Visit Gallery button in the New Active Desktop Item dialog box.

  - Practice 2: Run the Local Computer Policy object of the Group Policy snap-in to view local policy settings. Experiment with the settings contained in the Administrative Templates folder of the User Configuration node. Concentrate on the following folders: Desktop, Desktop\Active Desktop, Start Menu & Task Bar, and Control Panel\Display.

  - Practice 3: Experiment with the Start menu and taskbar configuration by modifying the settings contained in the Taskbar And Start Menu Properties dialog box.

  - Practice 4: Right-click the Start menu to open its context menu, and then click Explore All Users. Repeat this procedure, but this time, click Explore. Compare the contents of the two Windows Explorer windows that appear.

■ **Install and use the Windows 2000 Fax Service.**

■ Practice 1: On a computer containing a fax-capable device, verify that the Fax Service and a fax printer are installed.

■ Practice 2: Use the Fax Service Management console to enable both inbound and outbound fax support. Configure the fax device so that received faxes are automatically printed, saved in a folder, and sent to an e-mail profile on the computer.

■ Practice 3: Use the Fax Service Management console to enable the archiving of sent faxes.

■ Practice 4: Open the Fax program, and complete the fields on the User Information tab. Create a new cover page using the Cover Page Editor, available by clicking New on the Cover Page tab.

■ Practice 5: Delete the Fax printer appearing in the Printers window. Then, on the Advanced Options tab in the Fax Properties dialog box, click Add A Fax Printer.

■ Practice 6: After sending and receiving faxes, view the Application log to verify fax activity. Reconfigure logging levels using the Fax Service Management console, and then revisit the Application log to view the changes to fax logging activity.

■ **Configure accessibility services.**

■ Practice 1: Log on as a user with Administrative privileges, and then use the Accessibility Wizard to configure accessibility-related administrative options available to a user with Administrative privileges. Complete the same procedure, but log on as a user with User privileges to note the difference in the available settings.

■ Practice 2: Log on as a user with Administrative privileges, and then start Utility Manager to configure startup options for the accessibility tools appearing in Utility Manager.

■ Practice 3: Configure the Magnifier, Narrator, and On-Screen Keyboard.

■ Practice 4: Use the Accessibility Options program to configure the various accessibility features appearing in this interface. Use the General tab of the Accessibility Options dialog box to set administrative options. Compare the administrative options appearing on the General tab to the options you examined by running the Accessibility Wizard as a user with Administrative privileges.

Further Reading

This "Further Reading" section provides lists of important readings to supplement your current understanding of the skills tested within this Objective Domain. The lists are delineated into pertinent readings for each objective within this Objective Domain. If you feel that you need additional preparation prior to taking the exam, study these sources thoroughly.

Objective 5.1

Microsoft Corporation. *Microsoft Windows 2000 Professional Resource Kit*. Redmond, Washington: Microsoft Press, 2000. Read pp. 286–288 in Chapter 7, "Introduction to Configuration Management," and pp. 446–447 in Chapter 10, "Mobile Computing."

Microsoft Corporation. *MCSE Training Kit—Microsoft Windows 2000 Professional*. Redmond, Washington: Microsoft Press, 2000. Read and complete the practices in Lesson 4, Chapter 10, "Setting Up and Managing User Accounts."

Microsoft Corporation. *"Users and Computers"* in *Windows 2000 Server Help*. Redmond, Washington: Microsoft Corporation, 2000. Read the How To section of "User Profiles."

Microsoft Corporation. The *Windows 2000 Server Deployment Planning Guide* volume of the *Microsoft Windows 2000 Server Resource Kit*. Redmond, Washington: Microsoft Press, 2000. Read Chapter 24, "Applying Change and Configuration Management." Visit the Microsoft TechNet site at *http://www.microsoft.com/TechNet/win2000/dguide/chapt-24.asp* to read this chapter. This resource ties together the technologies involved in user configuration management.

Objective 5.2

The Global Software Development Web site. Visit this site at *http://www.microsoft.com/globaldev*. If the site has been moved, search on the Web site title. Review the FAQs and articles about globalization.

Microsoft Corporation. *Microsoft Windows 2000 Professional Resource Kit*. Redmond, Washington: Microsoft Press, 2000. Read pp. 179–181 in Chapter 5, "Customizing and Automating Installation," and pp. 316–322 in Chapter 7, "Introduction to Configuration Management."

Windows 2000 MUI SetupHelp. Review the three topics contained in this online help file. This file (MUISETUP.HLP) is at the root of the Windows 2000 MultiLanguage Version CD-ROM.

Objective 5.3

Microsoft Corporation. *Microsoft Windows 2000 Professional Resource Kit*. Redmond, Washington: Microsoft Press, 2000. Read pp. 188–189 in Chapter 5, "Customizing and Automating Installations," and pp. 446–447 in Chapter 10, "Mobile Computing."

Microsoft Corporation. *The Distributed Systems Guide* volume of the *Microsoft Windows 2000 Server Resource Kit*. Redmond, Washington: Microsoft Press, 2000. Read the "Windows Installer Technology" section.

Microsoft Corporation. "Step-by-Step Guide to Software Installation and Maintenance." You can download this article by searching on its title at *http://www.microsoft.com/windows2000*.

Microsoft Corporation. "Windows Installer." You can download this article by searching on its title at *http://www.microsoft.com/windows2000*.

Objective 5.4

Microsoft Corporation. *Microsoft Windows 2000 Professional Resource Kit*. Redmond, Washington: Microsoft Press, 2000. Read pp. 289–301 in Chapter 7, "Introduction to Configuration and Management," and Chapter 8, "Customizing the Desktop."

Microsoft Corporation. *MCSE Training Kit—Microsoft Windows 2000 Professional*. Redmond, Washington: Microsoft Press, 2000. Read and complete the practices in Lesson 2, Chapter 17, "Configuring Group Policy and Local Security Policy."

Objective 5.5

Microsoft Corporation. *MCSE Training Kit—Microsoft Windows 2000 Professional*. Redmond, Washington: Microsoft Press, 2000. Read and complete the practices in Lesson 4, Chapter 25, "Implementing, Managing, and Troubleshooting Hardware Devices and Drivers."

Microsoft Corporation. *Control Panel in Windows 2000 Help*. Redmond, Washington: Microsoft Corporation, 2000. Read the "Fax" section.

Objective 5.6

The Microsoft Accessibility Web site. Visit this site at *www.microsoft.com/enable*. If the site has been moved, search on the Web site title. Read the introductory sections on "Accessibility" and "Microsoft," and review the step-by-step guides.

Microsoft Corporation. *Microsoft Windows 2000 Professional Resource Kit*. Redmond, Washington: Microsoft Press, 2000. Read Appendix A, "Accessibility for People with Disabilities."

O B J E C T I V E   5 . 1

Configure and manage user profiles.

User profiles make it possible to personalize desktop settings based on the user's account name. Individual desktop settings, such as network connections, the location of the My Documents folder, and the contents of the Quick Launch toolbar are contained in a user profile. There are two types of user profiles: local and roaming. **Local user profiles** are generated in one of two ways: when Windows 2000 Professional is installed and when a user logs on for the first time. The two local user profiles automatically created when Windows 2000 Professional is installed are the **All Users profile** and the **Default User profile**. Each profile is stored below the *%systemdrive%*\Documents and Settings folder with these folder names: All Users and Default User, respectively.

When a user with no user profile below the Documents and Settings folder logs on, a profile folder is automatically generated for the user account by copying the contents of the Default User folder to a folder uniquely named after the user account name. Naming conflicts are resolved by appending the profile's folder name with *.computername* for a workgroup-based logon or *.domainname* for a domain-based logon. If appending the workgroup name or domain name does not resolve to a unique folder name, a three-digit number, such as .000 or .001, is appended to the *.computername* or *.domainname* extension. The environment variable pointing to the folder containing the user's profile is *%userprofile%*. The user's profile and the All Users profile remain in distinct folders, but their settings are merged in the user's desktop environment. The environment variable that points to the All Users folder is *%allusersprofile%*.

You can copy local user profiles to other users of the local computer. Copying and permitting another user to use a profile is configured on the User Profiles tab in the System Properties dialog box. Local user profiles and **roaming user profiles** stored on the local computer also appear on the User Profiles tab. Local user profiles are specific to the computer where they are created.

Roaming user profiles allow a user to move from one computer to another in a network and retain his or her unique desktop settings. To change a local user profile into a domain-based roaming user profile, copy the local user profile to a network location. Then, from the properties of a domain user account, click the Profile tab and set the

Profile Path text box to the network location containing the copied profile. Be sure you share the roaming user profile parent folder and give users the ability to read and write to it. When the user logs on to another computer using his or her domain account name, the profile is accessed from the server and a local copy of the roaming user profile is cached to the local computer. When the user logs off from the computer, any desktop updates are copied to the roaming user profile assigned to the user account. If updates to a roaming user profile are not allowed, the roaming user profile can be configured as a **mandatory user profile**. Mandatory user profiles are ideal when many users share the same profile, such as computers used in a public kiosk or computers in a highly secure environment where custom settings are not allowed.

You can make a profile mandatory in two ways: either rename the NTUSER.DAT file (located in the user's Roaming User Profile folder) to NTUSER.MAN, or rename the profile folder by appending a .man extension to it—for example, setting a user's profile path to a folder named \Restricted.man. The important difference between these two methods of creating a mandatory user profile is that the first method, renaming the file, permits the user to log on with a locally cached version of the profile if the roaming user profile folder is unavailable. In contrast, adding a .man extension to the profile folder does *not* allow the user to log on unless the roaming user profile folder is available. Users of a mandatory user profile can customize their desktops, but the changes are not saved, so the desktop environment is reset for the next time they log on to the network.

Note Contrary to much of the documentation on roaming user profiles, it *is* possible to create a roaming user profile in a workgroup. However, the other features of user configuration management, such as centralized Group Policy and, in particular, folder redirection, are not available in a workgroup-based network.

Two important profile and Group Policy troubleshooting tools contained in the Windows 2000 Professional and Server Resource Kits are the Group Policy Results (GPRESULT.EXE) utility and the Delete Profile (DELPROF.EXE) utility. Typing **gpresult** at the command line displays important information such as which group policies were applied to the computer at logon, where the roaming and local user profiles are contained, and security group membership for the currently logged on user. You use the Delete Profile command-line utility to delete unwanted or unused profiles. Removing unused profiles can be important if available disk space is at a premium.

Objective 5.1 Questions

70-210.05.01.001

You are the administrator of your company's network supporting computers running Windows 2000 Professional and Windows 2000 Server. You want users of Windows 2000 Professional on your network to be able to log on to any computer on the network and have their user settings follow them. What should you do?

A. Configure the Windows 2000 Professional computers to join the domain, and create a local user profile for each user.

B. Configure the Windows 2000 Professional computers to join the domain, and configure a roaming user profile for each user.

C. Configure the Windows 2000 Professional computers to join the workgroup, and create a local user profile for each user.

D. Configure the Windows 2000 Professional computers to join the workgroup, and create a roaming user profile for each user.

70-210.05.01.002

You are the administrator of a local area network (LAN) supporting Windows 2000 Professional computers. You are not currently supporting Certificate Services. Which items can you include in a client's roaming user profile? (Choose two.)

A. Documents

B. Network drives

C. Encrypted files

D. Encrypted folders

70-210.05.01.003

You are the administrator of your company's network supporting computers running Windows 2000 Professional and Windows 2000 Server. You want users of Windows 2000 Professional on your network to be able to log on to any computer on the network and have their user settings follow them. You also want to prevent users from saving changes to their profiles. What should you do?

A. Configure the computers running Windows 2000 Professional to join the workgroup, and create a mandatory user profile for each user.

B. Configure the computers running Windows 2000 Professional to join the workgroup, and create a roaming user profile for each user.

C. Configure the computers running Windows 2000 Professional to join the domain, and create a roaming user profile for each user.

D. Configure the computers running Windows 2000 Professional to join the domain, and configure a mandatory user profile for each user.

70-210.05.01.004

You are the administrator of a small network supporting five client computers running Windows 2000 Professional. Which type of user profile can you use if you want to keep profile administration to a minimum, you want to let users manage their own desktop settings, and you don't want to install an additional computer on the network?

A. Local

B. Mandatory

C. Roaming

D. Roving

Objective 5.1 Answers

70-210.05.01.001

▶ **Correct Answers: B**

A. **Incorrect:** Joining the domain is an important configuration step in a Windows 2000–based network to support user logon from any workstation. However, this is not enough to support the requirement that user settings follow the user from workstation to workstation. The first time a user logs on to a domain, a local user profile is created automatically by copying the contents of the default user profile to a folder named after the user account name. If the folder name isn't unique, it is appended with the domain name in which the computer is a member. If this doesn't resolve to a unique name, then a three-digit number is appended to the folder name as well. For example, the first time the Administrator account from the MICROSOFT domain is used to log on to a workstation, a profile is generated in a folder named Administrator.Microsoft because a local user profile named Administrator already exists. The operating system knows that these two user accounts are different because the security ID (SID) of the local Administrator account and the SID of the Administrator account in the domain are different. The resulting profile is a combination of the folders whose values are contained in the %userprofile% and %allusersprofile% environment variables. A local user profile applies only to the computer where it is created.

B. **Correct:** After joining the computers to the domain, you configure roaming user profiles for each user through the properties of the user account. Locate the Profile tab in the user's Properties dialog box, and in the Profile Path text box, type in the path to a network share where the user profile will be stored. The path you specify must be a network location to which the user has read and write privileges. Include the environment variable %username% at the end of the network path so that a unique folder for the user is created below the network share. For example, create a network share named \\server01\profiles. Then access the user account properties of a user account named MaxN, and in the Profile Path text box, type \\server01\profiles\%username%. A folder named MaxN will be created below the network share. The user MaxN will be granted Full Control permission to this folder, and all other user rights, including access by the Administrators group, are removed. If this is undesirable, a member of the Administrators group can take ownership of the folder and reassign privileges, or an easier method is to create the folder manually and assign local permissions to the folder before pointing the user account profile path to the folder. To retain a local user account's desktop settings, copy the local user profile to the network location for the roaming user profile. After the profile is configured, each time MaxN moves from computer to computer, the profile is cached from the server location to the local computer. At logoff, the server profile is updated.

C. **Incorrect:** The first time a user logs on to a workgroup computer, a local user profile is created automatically by copying the contents of the default user profile to a folder named after the user account name. If the folder name isn't unique, it is appended with the computer name. If this doesn't resolve to a unique name, then a three-digit number is appended to the folder name as well. This naming conflict might occur if a local account is deleted and then an account of the same name is re-created. Even though the account names are identical, the SID of each account is different. The resulting profile is a combination of the folders whose values are contained in the %userprofile% and %allusersprofile% environment variables. A local user profile applies only to the computer where it is created. Furthermore, a user account on a workgroup computer is stored locally and applies only to the computer that contains it.

D. **Incorrect:** A workgroup computer does support roaming user profiles. Accessing the properties of a local user account shows the Profile tab and the Profile Path text box for configuring a roaming user profile. The profile path can be a local folder or a network share. A local user profile configured using the Profile Path text box appears as a roaming user profile in the System Properties dialog box on the User Profiles tab. The profile is cached locally in a folder assigned to the %userprofile% environment variable. When the user logs off the computer, the locally cached profile is copied to the location designated in the Profile Path text box. A roaming user profile configured on a workgroup computer is not as functional as a domain-based user account and roaming user profile combination because the user account is local to the workgroup computer where it is created. It is possible to set up a user account with the same name and password on another computer in the workgroup and designate the same network share profile path. However, this is not the ideal method of supporting roaming user profiles because of the administrative overhead associated with implementing this solution.

70-210.05.01.002

▶ **Correct Answers: A and B**

A. **Correct:** The contents of the My Documents folder are stored locally in a user's cached profile unless the target path of My Documents is changed to an alternate location. Applications such as Microsoft Word will use the target path designated by My Documents as the location to open and store files. When the user logs off a computer, the contents of My Documents in the local cache update the contents of My Documents in the network share containing the roaming user profile. The Folder Redirection Group Policy setting for domain user accounts allows for the separation of user data from the roaming user profile.

B. **Correct:** Any network connections made by a user of a computer configured for a roaming user profile are saved to the network share containing the roaming user profile unless the user is configured to use a mandatory user profile.

C. **Incorrect:** By default, encrypted files and folders cannot be included in a roaming user profile. To store encrypted files in a roaming user profile, you must use Certificate Services to store the keys necessary to decrypt the files or directories in the profile. After the keys are available in the profile, it is possible to store the encrypted files and folders. Alternatively, you can redirect encrypted files using Group Policy.

D. **Incorrect:** Like encrypted files, encrypted folders cannot be included in a roaming user profile without additional configuration. To store encrypted files in a roaming user profile, you must use Certificate Services to store the keys necessary to decrypt the files or directories in the profile. After the keys are available in the profile, it is possible to store the encrypted files and folders. Alternatively, you can redirect encrypted files using Group Policy.

70-210.05.01.003

▶ **Correct Answers: D**

A. **Incorrect:** The user accounts on a computer in a workgroup are local to the computer. Therefore, roaming user profiles, mandatory or otherwise, are difficult to support because an account on each computer in the workgroup that a user can log on to would need to be created to support the profile. In addition, each user account would need to be able to access the network share containing the mandatory roaming profile.

B. **Incorrect:** The user accounts on a computer in a workgroup are local to the computer. Local computer accounts are an administrative burden for profile management because an account on each computer in the workgroup that a user can log on to would need to be created to support the profile. In addition, each user account would need to be able to access the network share containing the roaming profile. Additionally, using roaming user profiles that are not mandatory does not prevent users from saving desktop settings to their profile when they log off.

C. **Incorrect:** Domain user accounts are required to ease administration of roaming user profiles. In the properties of the domain user account, specify a profile path using the following syntax: \\computer_name\share_name\%username%, where computer_name\share_name specifies the Universal Naming Convention (UNC) path to the parent folder for user profiles. The %username% variable resolves to the user's logon name. If a subfolder named after the user does not exist below the profile parent folder, the folder is created and the user account is assigned the Full Control permission to the folder. Using roaming user profiles that are not mandatory does not prevent users from saving desktop settings to their profiles when they log off.

D. **Correct:** After following the steps just outlined, there are two methods to configure a profile to be mandatory. The first method is to rename the NTUSER.DAT file to NTUSER.MAN. NTUSER.DAT is automatically created in the parent profile folder. For example, if you create a profile folder named Restricted, rename the NTUSER.DAT in that folder to NTUSER.MAN. The next time a user whose profile path points to this folder logs off, his or her locally cached version of the profile will be labeled Mandatory. You can confirm this by opening the My Computer Properties dialog box and then clicking the User Profiles tab. The locally cached profile will display Mandatory in the Type column.

70-210.05.01.004

▶ **Correct Answers: A**

A. **Correct:** When a user logs on for the first time, the default user profile is copied to a profile folder named after the user. Folder naming conflicts are resolved as explained in the objective overview. The desktop settings that appear are a combination of the Local User profile and the All Users profile. This is ideal for a small network where roaming user profiles are not necessary. This keeps profile administration to a minimum because profiles are created automatically.

B. **Incorrect:** A mandatory user profile is a roaming user profile set to mandatory by renaming NTUSER.DAT to NTUSER.MAN or by appending a roaming user profile folder below a profile share with a .man extension. Pointing the user's profile path to a mandatory user profile on one of the computers in the workgroup will work, but as a result, the users will not be able to customize their desktops.

C. **Incorrect:** It is possible to configure roaming user profiles in a workgroup, but this does not reduce administrative overhead. In addition, the question states that you do not want to install an additional computer on the network. Therefore, setting up domain-based roaming user profiles is not an option.

D. **Incorrect:** The word roving is sometimes used to describe a user's movement from computer to computer in a routed network. Roving is not used to describe profiles.

OBJECTIVE 5.2

Configure support for multiple languages or multiple locations.

Three different versions of Windows 2000 Professional exist: the **English Version**, the **Translated Version**, and the **MultiLanguage Version**. Each version provides varying levels of **multilanguage support**. The English Version allows the user to edit, view, and print information in more than 60 languages. This feature is called **Multilingual Editing and Viewing**. The Translated Version provides the same support as the English Version, and it includes a language-specific user interface for menus, help files, dialog boxes, and file system components. The MultiLanguage Version provides the same language support as the other two versions, and it allows the user to switch the user interface language, hence the name *multilanguage*. Selecting the appropriate version depends on the level of required language support. The English Version is sufficient for infrequent electronic communication in a non-English language. The Translated Version is appropriate when full language support is needed for a small number of languages throughout an organization. Each edition of the Translated Version user interface is language specific. The MultiLanguage Version is ideal when full language support is needed for many languages throughout an organization. Using the MultiLanguage Version eases administration because a single version of Windows 2000 Professional is deployed throughout the network using the Multilanguage Pack, and users or administrators are able to switch the user interface language as necessary.

Multilingual editing, viewing, and printing settings for all versions of Windows 2000 are configured in the Regional Options dialog box, which you open by double-clicking the Regional Options program in Control Panel. In this dialog box, you can do the following:

- Configure locale information using predefined language schemes, such as English (United States) or Dutch (Belgium). You can also define custom settings for the defined language schemes.

  This applies to the current user and affects date, time, and currency formatting.

- Set up system language settings to support viewing and editing documents in other languages.

This applies to the computer. Any check box enabled in the Language Settings For The System box requires the corresponding language groups to be installed. For example, if the computer will read documents in Korean, Spanish, and English, the Korean check box and the Western Europe And United States check box must be enabled. The Western Europe And United States language group includes support for Spanish, English, and other languages, such as German.

- Modify input locales to change keyboard layouts, such as Dvorak right-handed or left-handed keyboard layouts.

If the MultiLanguage Version of Windows 2000 is installed, a Menus And Dialogs drop-down list box appears on the General tab in the Regional Options dialog box. Use this drop-down list box to select any installed language. The language can apply to all users logging on to the computer or just to the user installing the language version files. After restarting the computer, the majority of Windows 2000 menu, dialog box, and help file text appears in the selected language. This does not change the language appearing in applications and help files not bundled with the operating system, some icons on the desktop, and folder names. For example, the English Version Windows 2000 Resource Kit help files appear in English.

Objective 5.2 Questions

70-210.05.02.001

Users in your company need multiple-language support. A user wants to create documents in Windows Notepad: some in English and some in Greek. What should you do at the user's computer running Windows 2000 Professional?

A. In Notepad, select the Greek version.

B. Install the Greek localized version of Windows 2000 Professional.

C. Close Notepad. Use the Regional Options program in Control Panel to enable support for Greek language system settings. After the language support files are installed, restart Notepad.

D. Use the Regional Options program in Control Panel to enable support for Greek language system settings. After the language support files are installed, restart the computer and then restart Notepad.

70-210.05.02.002

You want to perform an unattended upgrade of Microsoft Windows NT 4 Workstation to the English Version of Windows 2000 Professional. You use the Windows 2000 Setup Manager Wizard to create an answer file named UNATTEND.TXT at the root of the C drive. You also use the wizard to configure the [RegionalSettings] section of your answer file to specify the locale settings as English and include the Korean language group and the Japanese language group. In the [Unattended] section of the answer file, you specify NTUpgrade=yes and set UnattendMode=Fullunattended. In the [UserData] section, you have included the ProductID if one was supplied with your copy of the Windows 2000 Professional installation CD-ROM. All other installation settings necessary to automate the installation, such as OemSkipEula=Yes, are specified in the appropriate sections of the answer file. When you run the Windows 2000 setup routine, you include the /unattend switch and the path to the answer file. Which other command-line settings must be specified to make sure that the proper files are copied and that the installation does not pause for user input? (Choose two.)

A. Specify /rx:lang\kor in your WINNT32.EXE command.

B. Specify /copysource:lang\kor /copysource:lang\jpn in your WINNT32.EXE command.

C. Set OEMSkipRegional = 1 in the [GuiUnattended] section of the answer file.

D. Specify /s:*install_source*, where *install_source* is the location of the Windows 2000 Professional distribution files.

70-210.05.02.003

You are preparing to install the Windows 2000 Professional MultiLanguage Version on a new Pentium III computer. You want to specify the language applied to all new user accounts created on the computer. Which tool should you use?

A. CACHEMOV.EXE

B. GPRESULT.EXE

C. MUISETUP.EXE

D. SECEDIT.EXE

Objective 5.2 Answers

70-210.05.02.001

▶ **Correct Answers: D**

A. **Incorrect:** You use Windows applications, including Notepad, to view, edit, and print documents in multiple languages provided the proper language groups are installed on the system. Toggling between languages is not an available setting in Notepad.

B. **Incorrect:** Localized versions of the operating system are available, but this is an inefficient and expensive way to gain multilanguage support for viewing, editing, and printing documents in other languages. The localized version provides multilingual editing, viewing, and printing capability and additional support for interface-specific language changes.

If your goal is to provide a fully localized version of Windows 2000, you should use the localized version of Windows 2000 rather then the MultiLanguage Version. When the MultiLanguage Version is configured for a language, it will look and behave similarly to the localized version, with some exceptions. All 16-bit code, bitmaps, registry keys, values, folders, and filenames are not localized.

C. **Incorrect:** All versions of Windows 2000 provide multilingual editing, viewing, and printing capability, but the proper language group must be installed to support this capability. The Western Europe and United States language group, installed by default in the English language version of Windows 2000, supports English and other languages, such as Spanish. The Greek language group must be installed to support Greek language system settings. The language group installation requires files from the Windows 2000 Professional installation CD-ROM unless you installed the distribution files elsewhere. After the installation of a new language group, you are prompted to restart the computer.

D. **Correct:** After the installation of a new language group, you are prompted to restart the computer. After the language group is installed, you can view, edit, and print the document in its native language.

70-210.05.02.002

▶ **Correct Answers: B and D**

A. **Incorrect:** The /rx switch is valid for 16-bit Windows 2000 Professional Setup (WINNT.EXE). Typing winnt /rx:lang\kor from the Windows 2000 Professional installation CD-ROM on a computer running a 16-bit operating system will copy the Korean language group files that are located in the \I386\Lang\Kor folder. This is not a valid 32-bit Windows 2000 Professional Setup switch.

B. **Correct:** The /copysource switch is valid for 32-bit Windows 2000 Professional Setup (WINNT32.EXE). The Korean language group files will be copied from the \Lang\Kor folder, and the Japanese language group files will be copied from the \Lang\Jpn folder.

C. **Incorrect:** This answer file setting allows unattended Setup to skip the Regional Settings page in GUI mode Setup and Mini-Setup. The question states that regional settings were specified using the Setup Manager Wizard and that all settings necessary to fully automate the installation were included in the answer file.

D. **Correct:** The /s:install_source source switch and parameter is required so that the Windows 2000 Professional setup routine does not prompt you for the location of the installation files. If the installation is run from the Windows 2000 Professional installation CD-ROM and the drive containing the CD-ROM appears as D in Windows NT Workstation, the switch is /s:d:\i386.

Combined with the information provided in the question, in this answer explanation, and in the previous answer explanation, the command you would type to fully automate the installation is d:\i386\winnt32 /s:d:\i386 /unattend:c:\unattend.txt /copysource:lang\jpn /copysource:lang\kor.

70-210.05.02.003

▶ **Correct Answers: C**

A. **Incorrect:** The Cache Move utility (CACHEMOV.EXE) allows for the relocation of the Offline Files cache to a different volume. By default, the cache is created on the boot partition (%systemdrive%). If disk capacity is at a premium on the boot partition, use Cache Move to relocate the cache to a different volume, thus providing additional capacity for the Offline Files cache.

B. **Incorrect:** The application of Group Policy and other settings, such as group membership, are displayed by the Group Policy Results tool (GPRESULT.EXE). This tool is included in the Windows 2000 Professional and Server Resource Kits. Typing gpresult at the command line displays information relevant to troubleshooting the application of Group Policy, such as which group policies were applied to the computer at logon, where the roaming and local user profiles are contained, and security group membership for the currently logged on user. This tool is not used to specify language settings.

C. **Correct:** The Windows 2000 MultiLanguage Version Setup utility (MUISETUP.EXE) installs language setting files onto versions of Windows 2000 supporting a MultiLanguage Version upgrade. The MultiLanguage Version Setup utility runs in the user interface or at the command line. Running the utility in the user interface displays the Multilanguage File Installation dialog box. In the main area of this dialog box, you enable or disable language settings for menus and dialogs. From the drop-down list box also appearing in this dialog box, you select the default language settings for menus and dialogs to be used for all existing users and any new users added to the system. If the language group necessary to support a language setting is not installed, MultiLanguage Version Setup will attempt to install the required language group. If Windows 2000 Professional was installed from CD-ROM, MUISETUP.EXE will prompt you to insert the Windows 2000 Professional installation CD-ROM to install the language group. After the language group is installed, MultiLanguage Version Setup continues to install the files necessary to support language settings. If a required language group was not installed prior to running MUISETUP.EXE, a reboot will be necessary to complete the language group installation.

MultiLanguage Version Setup runs from the command line to support automated installation. For example, assuming that MUISETUP.EXE is located at the root of the D drive, typing the following command, d:\muisetup.exe /i 040c 0413 /d 0413 /r /s, will install two language settings, set a default language, and complete the command without user involvement. The /i switch installs the languages corresponding to the specified language IDs, /d sets the default language, /r suppresses the reboot message, and /s suppresses the installation complete message. In the example, 040c corresponds to French and 0413 corresponds to Dutch. The languages and their corresponding language IDs are listed in the help file accompanying MUISETUP.EXE. The installation process and any errors encountered during MultiLanguage Version Setup are recorded in %systemroot%\Muisetup.log.

D. **Incorrect:** The SECEDIT.EXE command-line utility creates and applies security templates and analyzes system security. It is typically used on a network where security must be analyzed, applied automatically, or both. It is useful for deploying a consistent security policy to all computers on a network.

OBJECTIVE 5.3

Manage applications by using Windows Installer packages.

To improve the reliability and availability of applications and their installation routines, Windows 2000 Professional includes the **Windows Installer Service**. This service provides a framework within the operating system for installing and maintaining applications. Features and components of an application managed by the Windows Installer Service can be installed when the installation routine is run or when a feature or component not installed is called by the user. Windows Installer features and components can also be configured to run from the CD-ROM or to never be installed with the application. Damaged applications are automatically repaired by the Windows Installer Service, and application removal is standardized through the Add/Remove Programs dialog box. To use the Windows Installer Service, an application installation must be *packaged* into an .msi file.

Note Windows Installer packages are created by software manufacturers such as Microsoft. Custom applications are packaged using third-party installation packaging tools. The Windows 2000 Server and Professional installation CD-ROMs include the .msi packaging console by Veritas Software, WinInstall LE. The installation routine for this console is contained in the \Valueadd\3rdparty\Mgmt\Winstle folder.

Each Windows Installer .msi file is a self-contained database called a *package* that is read by the Windows Installer Service to install entire applications, application features, and application components. A *feature* is part of an application; for example, Microsoft Excel for Windows is part of the Microsoft Office suite. A *component* is part of a feature; for example, EXCEL.EXE is a component of Microsoft Excel for Windows. The application's product files are compressed into cabinet (.cab) files and stored in the same folder with the .msi or in subfolders below the package. Instructions in a Windows Installer package include the features or components to install or remove. Installation includes everything required for proper operation, such as adding registry entries, configuring shortcuts, adding program groups, and installing .dll and .exe files. Some Windows Installer packages, such as Microsoft Office 2000, can be customized using transform (.mst) files and Setup settings (.ini) files. There might be a number of additional command-line parameters included with the package. Read the documentation accompanying an .msi package to determine which command-line parameters the package supports.

Objective 5.3 Questions

70-210.05.03.001

You want to use Windows Installer to deploy software applications on computers running Windows 2000. The software should appear as though it has been installed, but it should not actually be installed until users attempt to run the application. You also want to ensure that only authorized users can run the application. How should you configure the package? (Choose two.)

A. Assign the application to the users.

B. Publish the application to the users.

C. Set the Deny check box on the Apply Group Policy permission for the Authenticated Users group. Next add a group containing members and grant the group Allow for the Apply Group Policy permission.

D. Clear the Allow check box on the Assign Group Policy permission for the Authenticated Users group. Next add a group containing members, and grant the group Allow for the Apply Group Policy permission.

70-210.05.03.002

You are the administrator for a network supporting Windows 2000 Active Directory services. You want to use Windows Installer to deploy a software application on computers running Windows 2000 Professional while achieving these desired results:

- The software should appear as though it has been installed, but it should not actually be installed until users attempt to run the application.

- The application should always be available to roaming users who log on to several different computers in a typical workday.

- If the software is deleted for any reason, it should be reinstalled at logon.

- Only authorized users should be allowed to run the application.

Your proposed solution is to assign the software package to the users in the appropriate OU.

Which results does the proposed solution provide? (Choose three.)

A. The software appears to be installed, but it is not actually installed until users attempt to run the application.

B. The application is always available to roaming users who log on to several different computers in a typical workday.

C. If the software is deleted on a user's computer, it will be reinstalled at logon.

D. Only authorized users can run the application.

70-210.05.03.003

You are the administrator for a network supporting Windows 2000 Active Directory services. You want to use the Windows Installer Service to deploy software applications on computers running Windows 2000 Professional. You do not want the applications to be advertised. What should you do?

A. Assign applications to users.

B. Assign applications to computers.

C. Publish applications to users.

D. Publish applications to computers.

Objective 5.3 Answers

70-210.05.03.001

▶ **Correct Answers: A and D**

A. **Correct:** Using the Software Installation extension (part of the Windows 2000 Server Group Policy snap-in), Windows Installer (.msi) files are assigned or published to a user or assigned to a computer. Assigning an application using the extension under the User Configuration Group Policy node advertises the application to all applicable users at their next logon to a computer running Windows 2000. The assignment is available from any Windows 2000 Professional computer where the users can log on. The assigned application is installed the first time the user attempts to run it by either selecting the application on the Start menu or activating a document associated with the application.

Alternatively, assigning an application using the Software Installation extension under the Computer Configuration Group Policy node causes the installation to be performed automatically, and it usually occurs soon after the computer finishes its startup process. If installation begins after startup, the logon process is delayed until the installation completes.

B. **Incorrect:** Publishing an application using the Software Installation extension under the User Configuration Group Policy node makes the application available for installation. To install a published application, targeted users can click the published application in the Add/Remove Programs program or attempt to open a file associated with the application. Published applications appear in the Add/Remove Programs dialog box by clicking the Add New Programs icon. Publishing an application to users does not install the application or create a desktop shortcut on computers where the targeted users log on.

C. **Incorrect:** The Apply Group Policy permission is an access control entry (ACE) placed on the Group Policy object (GPO). For example, a GPO created for an organizational unit (OU) contains the Apply Group Policy permission. By default, the Authenticated Users special group is assigned Allow for the Apply Group Policy permission. The result of this setting is that all group policies set on a container, such as an OU, pertain to all user objects within the container. User objects are made members of the Authenticated Users group when they successfully log on to the Microsoft Active Directory domain. Setting Deny on the Apply Group Policy permission explicitly disables the application of the container's Group Policy settings. Group members or individual users authorized to run the assigned application won't be able to run the application because of the explicit denial.

D. **Correct:** Clearing the Allow check box does not explicitly grant or deny members of the Authenticated Users group the ability to apply Group Policy settings; therefore, membership in the Authenticated Users group will have no effect on allowing or denying Group Policy settings. Group members or individual users assigned Allow for the Apply Group Policy permission will be authorized to run the assigned application.

70-210.05.03.002

▶ **Correct Answers: A, B, and C**

A. **Correct:** Assigning an application package (.msi) file using the Software Installation extension under the User Configuration Group Policy node advertises the application to all applicable users at their next logon to a computer running Windows 2000. The assigned application is installed the first time the user attempts to run it either by selecting the application on the Start menu or by activating a document associated with the application.

B. **Correct:** The assignment is available from any Windows 2000 Professional computer where the users can log on. By default, a GPO created or linked to an OU applies to all applicable objects within the OU.

C. **Correct:** This is a feature of the Windows Installer Service. This service automatically repairs a damaged or deleted application in much the same way that an assigned application is installed. When an assigned application that is not installed calls the Windows Installer Service to resolve a path, the service installs the package's components. A component is a collection of files, registry keys, and other resources that are all installed or uninstalled together. If the component was previously installed, the Windows Installer Service determines whether it is damaged by verifying the existence of the component's keypath. A keypath is a resource within a component, such as a program file or registry value. If a keypath is missing, a repair is performed automatically. Therefore, if a user deletes an application that is assigned, it will be automatically reinstalled at logon.

D. **Incorrect:** Because the Apply Group Policy permission is granted to all authenticated users, the assigned application is available to all users within the OU. To restrict the application to authorized users, clear the Allow check box on the Assign Group Policy permission for the Authenticated Users group. Next add a group containing members who are authorized to run the application, and grant the group Allow for the Apply Group Policy permission. Group members must also be assigned the Read permission to the distribution point containing the package files.

70-210.05.03.003

▶ **Correct Answers: C**

A. **Incorrect:** Assigning an application to users advertises the Windows Installer package to them at their next logon to a computer running Windows 2000.

B. **Incorrect:** Assigning an application to a computer causes the installation to be performed automatically and usually soon after the computer finishes its startup process. If installation begins after startup, the logon process is delayed until the installation completes.

C. **Correct:** Publishing an application to users makes the Windows Installer package available for installation. To install a published application, targeted users can click the published application in the Add/Remove Programs program or attempt to open a file associated with the application. Published applications appear in the Add/Remove Programs dialog box by clicking the Add New Programs icon. Publishing an application to users does not advertise the Windows Installer package because the application is not installed and a shortcut is not created on computers where the targeted users log on.

D. **Incorrect:** Applications cannot be published to computers, only assigned. Assigning an application to a computer causes the installation to be performed automatically.

Configure and troubleshoot desktop settings.

Configuring desktop settings allows you to customize most user interface elements, such as the Start menu, taskbar, toolbars, desktop shortcuts, the desktop background, and Active Desktop items. Earlier objectives explored some desktop and feature customizations, such as adding printers to the Printers window, creating scheduled tasks, configuring Offline Files, and adjusting display settings. This objective focuses on less essential desktop customizations that help increase productivity.

Two common methods exist for configuring desktop settings: through the various user interface components supporting the desktop or through Group Policy. For example, the Active Desktop is enabled or disabled in the General tab in the Folder Options dialog box or in the Group Policy snap-in from the \User Configuration\Administrative Templates\Desktop\Active Desktop container. Group Policy serves largely to enforce desktop settings. The Group Policy snap-in categorizes configuration options on a per-user or per-computer basis. All desktop settings specific to a user are written below the HKEY_CURRENT_USER registry key; all desktop settings specific to a computer are written below the HKEY_LOCAL_MACHINE key. In the Group Policy snap-in, the majority of desktop policy settings are located under the \User Configuration\Administrative Templates folder, specifically the Start Menu & Taskbar, Desktop, Desktop\Active Desktop, and Control Panel\Display Group Policy folders. For example, use the Control Panel\Display Group Policy folder to disable the Display program in Control Panel or set password protection on the screen saver.

Tip To use a custom shell instead of EXPLORER.EXE, copy the new shell to an accessible location. Then, from the \User Configuration\Administrative Templates\System Group Policy folder, specify the shell filename in the Custom User Interface Group Policy setting.

The desktop settings of a computer *not* on a Windows 2000 network running Active Directory services are enforced using the Local Computer Policy node of the Group Policy snap-in, or using the System Policy Editor (POLEDIT.EXE). The System Policy Editor is included with Windows 2000 Server, primarily for Windows NT 4, Windows 95, and Windows 98–style policy configuration. Desktop settings of Windows 2000 computers on a Windows 2000 network running Active Directory services are centrally controlled by network-based Group Policy. To avoid policy conflicts, it is best *not* to enable Windows NT 4 System Policy and use only Windows 2000 Group Policy specifically for computers running Windows 2000.

The Windows 2000 Active Desktop is an important part of desktop customization. This feature displays Web components, such as Web pages or Microsoft ActiveX controls, on the desktop. Active Desktop is enabled in a number of ways. One way is to open the Folder Options dialog box and select the Enable Web Content On My Desktop option button. Standard Hypertext Markup Language (HTML) is displayed as the Active Desktop *background* from the Display Properties dialog box in the Background tab. Active Desktop *items*, such as a .jpeg image file or a Uniform Resource Locator (URL), are added to the desktop in the Display Properties dialog box in the Web tab. When a local file is added as a desktop item, such as a Web page or a .gif file, it is static content. When a URL is added as an item to the Active Desktop, the Offline Files feature is used to provide dynamic content from the URL. Offline File synchronization settings allow for offline content update on demand or on a schedule. Web content is made available off line, updated, browsed, and locked down in the Display Properties dialog box in the Web tab or directly from the Active Desktop context menu. Active Desktop settings are enforced using the settings contained in the Desktop\Active Desktop Group Policy container.

The \User Configuration\Administrative Templates\Desktop Group Policy folder contains settings to remove, hide, or show some of the default icons that appear on the desktop and on the Start menu, such as My Computer, My Network Places, and Microsoft Internet Explorer. Prohibiting modifications to some critical desktop settings are configured from the Desktop Group Policy folder, such as prohibiting users from changing the My Documents path. This is an especially important setting if the target folder location for My Documents is redirected to a network share. Another important setting available from this Group Policy folder is the ability to prevent saving taskbar and window repositioning when a user logs off. This is useful in maintaining a consistent desktop for multiple users who share the same logon ID.

The Start and Programs menus are important launching points for modifying system and desktop settings and running applications. Properties of the menu are configured from the Taskbar And Start Menu Properties dialog box. This dialog box is available from the Taskbar And Menu item on the Settings menu. Some of the Start menu properties configured from here include enabling or disabling the Personalized Menus feature, adding or removing shortcuts from the Start menu, viewing the contents of the Start menu from Windows Explorer, re-sorting the menu's contents, and choosing menu settings, such as displaying the Administrative Tools group under the Start menu's Programs group. Some taskbar-specific settings include enabling and disabling the appearance of the clock in the status area and autohiding the taskbar.

The Programs menu, which you access from the Start menu, contains menu groups and icons created from two user profiles, the All Users profile and the currently logged on user's profile. Either profile's menu is conveniently opened for editing from the context menu of the Programs group.

The taskbar consists of toolbars, running tasks, and the status area. Windows 2000 Professional includes the Quick Launch, Address, Desktop, and Links toolbars. These default toolbars are selected for viewing from the Toolbars option located on the taskbar's context menu. You can also create new toolbars from the New Toolbar option. A new toolbar consists of a folder's contents or a URL. A toolbar can float on the desktop or be part of the taskbar. Start menu and taskbar settings are enforced using policy settings in the Start Menu & Taskbar Group Policy container.

When you *troubleshoot* desktop settings, start by checking which Group Policy objects (GPOs) are being applied to the user's desktop. Group Policy registry application and other settings, such as group membership, are displayed by the Group Policy Results tool (GPRESULT.EXE). This tool is included in the Windows 2000 Professional and Server Resource Kits. Both Resource Kits include the Group Policy reference. This reference and the explanations of each Group Policy included in the Group Policy snap-in will help you understand the implications of specific Group Policy settings. Common desktop errors are often related to new features, such as personalized menus and Active Desktop settings. Enable or disable these features as necessary to resolve errors associated with them.

Objective 5.4 Questions

70-210.05.04.001

You are the administrator of a local area network (LAN) supporting computers running Windows 2000. A user calls and reports that he selected a .bmp file for the background wallpaper on his Windows 2000 Professional computer before choosing to use Active Desktop wallpaper. The Active Desktop runs in the foreground, covering up the system wallpaper. When he presses Ctrl+Alt+Delete, Active Desktop is disabled and his .bmp file appears.

What is the most likely cause of this behavior?

A. The registry is corrupt.

B. This behavior is normal.

C. A conflicting user profile exists.

D. A conflicting GPO exists.

70-210.05.04.002

You are the administrator of a LAN supporting computers running Windows 2000 Professional. You want to configure the network so users retain their desktop settings when they log on to other Windows 2000 computers on the network, and you want them to access their documents from a network location. This must be accomplished without compromising mobile user network and data access over a slow-bandwidth connection. What should you do? (Choose two.)

A. Configure local user profiles.

B. Configure roaming user profiles.

C. Use Group Policy to redirect personal folders to a network server.

D. Use the Indexing Service to redirect personal folders to a network server.

70-210.05.04.003

You are the administrator for a LAN supporting new computers running Windows 2000 Professional. You want to prevent users from seeing local drives in My Computer. What should you do?

A. Disable the local drives in the basic input/output system (BIOS).

B. In CONFIG.SYS, specify LASTDRIVE=A.

C. Use Windows Explorer to hide all local drives.

D. Configure the appropriate Group Policy settings.

70-210.05.04.004

You are the administrator of a LAN supporting computers running Windows 2000 Professional. You have almost completed your Group Policy settings, and all users have access to Windows Help. You want to achieve these results:

- Prevent common users from using the Administrative Tools folder in Control Panel.

- Prevent common users from using the Display program in Control Panel.

- Prevent common users from using the Internet Options program in Control Panel.

- Prevent common users from using the Network And Dial-Up Connections program in Control Panel.

Your proposed solution is to configure the Hide Specified Control Panel Applets Group Policy setting to hide the icons for Administrative Tools, Display, Internet Options, and Network And Dial-Up Connections.

Which result does the proposed solution provide?

A. Users are prevented from using the Administrative Tools folder in Control Panel.

B. Users are prevented from using the Display program in Control Panel.

C. Users are prevented from using the Internet Options program in Control Panel.

D. Users are not prevented from accessing any of the specified Control Panel programs or folders.

E. Users are prevented from using the Network And Dial-Up Connections program in Control Panel.

Objective 5.4 Answers

70-210.05.04.001

▶ **Correct Answers: B**

A. **Incorrect:** Active Desktop configuration information is stored in the registry under the HKEY_CURRENT_USER\Software\Microsoft\InternetExplorer\Desktop registry key. Below this registry key, the Components key contains information on all added Active Desktop items. There are other important subkeys, such as the Safe Mode key, which is loaded when starting the computer in Safe Mode. If the Desktop area of the registry were corrupted, Active Desktop would fail to load on startup.

B. **Correct:** Active Desktop is part of Internet Explorer and is overlaid on the Windows Explorer shell. If you choose a .bmp file for the desktop wallpaper and then use an Active Desktop element for the desktop wallpaper, the Active Desktop element is displayed on top of the .bmp. When you log off or when you are logged in and you press Ctrl+Alt+Delete, Active Desktop is not running, so the .bmp file appears.

C. **Incorrect:** User profiles are connected to the user logging on to the system. A single user profile is merged with the All Users profile when a user logs on to the system.

D. **Incorrect:** Local Group Policy settings are stored on each computer running Windows 2000. This GPO contains a subset of the settings available in Windows 2000 Server–based GPOs. Any Local Group Policy settings in conflict with Windows 2000 Server–based Group Policy settings are over-written by default when the equivalent server-based Group Policy settings are enabled. Group Policy conflicts are handled in a predictable way. The question describes configuration procedures undertaken by the user, so the behavior exhibited by the computer is unlikely to be related to Group Policy settings.

70-210.05.04.002

▶ **Correct Answers: B and C**

A. **Incorrect:** A local user profile does not move from computer to computer. For users to retain their desktop settings from computer to computer, configure roaming user profiles.

B. **Correct:** After a user account is configured to use a roaming user profile and the user logs on to the network, the user's profile located on the network is cached to the local computer. Updates to desktop settings are written to the cached profile. When the user logs off the network, the cached profile updates the network profile. As long as the roaming user profile is not mandatory, when a user logs on to a computer that is disconnected from the network, the locally cached profile is loaded transparently.

C. **Correct:** By default, a roaming user profile contains a number of personal folders, including the My Documents and My Pictures folders. By redirecting these folders to an alternate network location, users work on the data contained in these folders as if the folders were local to the computer. Additionally, when a user logs off the network, My Documents and My Pictures are not synchronized with the roaming user profile. To complete the process of decoupling My Documents and My Pictures, configure Offline Files for these folders. In combining folder redirection with Offline Files, mobile users transparently synchronize the network-based My Documents folder contents with a locally cached copy of the files. If My Pictures is not specifically redirected through Group Policy, it will be redirected with My Documents because it is contained within My Documents. When users are no longer connected to the network, they can continue to work on the locally cached copy of their data files.

D. **Incorrect:** The Indexing Service runs in the background and creates indexes of the contents and properties of documents on the local computer, on network-accessible shares, and on local Web content if Microsoft Internet Information Services (IIS) is installed. This service does not play a direct role in managing roaming user profiles or folder redirection.

70-210.05.04.003

▶ **Correct Answers: D**

A. **Incorrect:** Drives are not disabled in the BIOS. It is possible to disable a disk device in the BIOS, but either this will cause a system startup failure if the disk containing the active partition is disabled, or the disabled disk will not be detected by the operating system. If the operating system successfully starts, disabled disks will be unavailable to both the computer user and the operating system.

B. **Incorrect:** Windows 2000 does not read the legacy startup file CONFIG.SYS. If a shortcut is created for an MS-DOS application, you can specify the startup files for the Windows 2000 command interpreter for MS-DOS. The default startup files for the command interpreter are CONFIG.NT and AUTOEXEC.NT, and they are contained in the %systemroot%\System32 folder.

The LASTDRIVE command is used by operating systems other than Windows NT or Windows 2000, such as MS-DOS and Windows 98, to make driver letters accessible to the operating system.

C. **Incorrect:** Windows Explorer does not contain a setting for hiding local drives.

D. **Correct:** The Hide These Specified Drives In My Computer Group Policy setting allows you to hide all drives or a combination of drives from A through D. This Group Policy setting is applied through local computer policy or in a network running Windows 2000 Server, through network Group Policy. The specified drives are hidden in My Computer, My Network Places, and Windows Explorer. This policy is located under Administrative Templates in the Windows Components\Windows Explorer container.

The Prevent Access To Drives From My Computer Group Policy setting, also in the Windows Explorer container, prevents access to viewing content on drives appearing in My Computer, Windows Explorer, and in My Network Places. If this policy is configured, the drives will appear in the interface (unless Hide These Specified Drives In My Computer is enabled), but double-clicking them will open a Group Policy restriction message box. This setting also disables the Run command, the Map Network Drive dialog box, and running a directory command (DIR) at the command line.

70-210.05.04.004

▶ **Correct Answers: D**

A. **Incorrect:** The Hide Specified Control Panel Applets Group Policy setting allows you to disallow Control Panel programs (.cpl) files or folders from appearing in Control Panel. This does not restrict the program from being started by other means. Control Panel programs are associated with CONTROL.EXE so that when a .cpl file such as ACCESS.CPL is run, CONTROL.EXE opens the Accessibility Options dialog box. Control Panel folders, such as the Administrative Tools folder, are opened by EXPLORER.EXE. Therefore, just hiding the program or folder does not restrict the user from accessing the feature in some other way. Many of these programs are also available from Windows 2000 Help.

The Hide Specified Control Panel Applets Group Policy setting is applied through local computer policy or, in a network running Windows 2000 Server, through network Group Policy. The specified .cpl or folder name added to this policy setting will not appear in Control Panel. This policy is located under the User Configuration node in the Administrative Templates\Control Panel container.

To limit access to the Administrative Tools folder, verify that the Display Administrative Tools check box is cleared in the Advanced tab of the Taskbar And Start Menu Properties dialog box. Then enable the Disable Changes To Taskbar And Start Menu Settings Group Policy setting. This setting is located under the User Configuration node in the Administrative Templates\Start Menu & Taskbar container.

B. **Incorrect:** As described already, the program or folder can be accessed in other ways even if it does not appear in Control Panel. You can open the Display Properties dialog box by opening DESK.CPL. Opening this .cpl file is equivalent to accessing the Display program in Control Panel.

   To disable access to the Display Properties dialog box, enable the Disable Display In Control Panel Group Policy setting. Configure this setting under the User Configuration node in the Administrative Templates\Control Panel\Display container.

C. **Incorrect:** As described already, the program or folder can be accessed in other ways, even if it does not appear in Control Panel. You can open the Internet Properties dialog box by opening INETCPL.CPL. Opening this .cpl file is equivalent to accessing the Internet Options program in Control Panel.

   To disable access to the Internet Properties dialog box, enable the Group Policy settings located under the User Configuration node in the Administrative Templates\Windows Components\Internet Explorer\Internet Control Panel container.

D. **Correct:** As described already, a number of other ways exist to start programs or open folders that are typically available in Control Panel. To disable a user from accessing all .cpl files, enable the Disable Control Panel Group Policy setting. This setting is located under the User Configuration node in the Administrative Templates\Control Panel container.

E. **Incorrect:** As described already, the program or folder can be accessed in other ways even if it does not appear in Control Panel. You can open the Network And Dial-Up Connections dialog box by opening NCPA.CPL. Opening this .cpl file is equivalent to accessing the Network And Dial-Up Connections program in Control Panel.

   To disable access to the Network And Dial-Up Connections dialog box, configure the Group Policy settings located under the User Configuration node in the Administrative Templates\Network\Network And Dial-Up Connections container.

O B J E C T I V E   5 . 5

Configure and troubleshoot fax support.

Windows 2000 Professional includes the necessary software to send and receive faxes through a fax-capable device, such as a fax modem. If Windows 2000 detects the presence of a fax device, it installs the Fax Service and the Windows NT Fax Driver. The Fax Service appears in the Services window, and the Windows NT Fax Driver appears in the Printers window as a printer named Fax. Faxes are sent from an application as a print job whose destination is the Fax printer. Sending a print job to the Fax printer starts the Send Fax Wizard to gather information about how, when, and where the fax is to be sent. The Fax printer driver receives the job details and sends it to the Fax Service. The Fax Service queues the fax job for sending through the fax-capable device. The fax-capable device uses the instructions provided by the Fax Service to transmit the fax. The Fax printer cannot be shared. Thus, other users on the network are unable to send faxes through a fax printer on another computer.

Faxes are received through the fax device. The Windows 2000 Fax Monitor watches for incoming faxes and receives the fax as a .tif image file. When the image file is received, it can be saved to a folder, sent via e-mail to a configured e-mail profile, or sent to a printing device. Any combination of these three options is available, but routing the image file to the Received Faxes folder is the default setting. The image files are viewed through the Imaging For Windows Preview utility or any installed image viewer capable of reading .tif files. To route faxes to a network printer or to an e-mail profile, the Fax Service *must* be configured with a logon account with the necessary rights to read the user's e-mail profile or profiles, to access a network printer, or both. By default, the Fax Service is configured to use the Local System account, which does not support network printing or local e-mail profile access.

Two common paths exist to configure fax support: from the Fax program in Control Panel and from icons in the Fax program group. To access the Fax program group, go to the Start menu, point to Programs, point to Accessories, and then click Communications.

You complete the following tasks from the Fax program:

- Configuring user information that will be inserted on a cover page

- Creating, opening for editing, and deleting cover pages and adding them to the list of available cover pages

You create and edit cover pages by using the Cover Page Editor. This editor starts automatically when a new cover page is created or when an existing cover page is opened for editing. This utility reads and saves files with a .cov extension.

- Configuring Status Monitor options, such as displaying the status monitor on the status bar portion of the taskbar and enabling Manual Answer for the first fax-capable device in the computer

  Selecting Manual Answer for the first fax-capable device sets to 99 the number of rings necessary to answer an incoming fax request. When the Fax Service detects an incoming call, a message box appears asking you whether the fax device should answer the call.

- Running the Fax Service Management console to configure incoming and outgoing fax service using a fax-capable device and to configure fax logging

  Logging information is stored in the Windows 2000 Application log and viewed using Event Viewer. Fax logging events are categorized as Inbound, Outbound, Initialization/Termination, and Unknown.

- Opening Fax Service Management help

- Adding a fax printer to the Printers window

  Use this feature if a user has deleted the Fax printer from the Printers window.

The following tasks are completed from the Fax program group:

- Viewing and managing the outgoing fax queue

- Starting the Fax Service Management console

- Sending a cover page as a fax

- Viewing the fax Help file

  This is not the same help file that is started from the Fax program.

- Opening and managing the contents of the My Faxes folder

  This folder can contain subfolders for both incoming and outgoing faxes, depending on how incoming and outgoing faxes are configured.

To fax a document through Microsoft Outlook, you must install the Fax Mail Transport service to an e-mail profile. Create a new profile containing your personal store, your address book, and the Fax Mail Transport service. Any address book entries containing a fax number as a transport option will be able to receive e-mails as a faxed document sent through the Fax Mail Transport service. Incoming faxes can also be received as e-mail, but this feature does *not* require the Fax Mail Transport service. Instead, incoming faxes are routed to an e-mail profile by the Fax Service.

Objective 5.5 Questions

70-210.05.05.001

TonyV, a user on the network, attempts to configure his computer running Windows 2000 Professional to use the Fax Service. TonyV is able to send outgoing faxes using Windows 2000 Professional but is unable to receive incoming faxes. What should you do to allow Windows 2000 Professional to receive incoming fax documents?

A. Open the Fax program in Device Manager, open the Advanced Options tab, and open the Fax Service Management console to configure the Fax Service on the local computer.

B. Open the Fax program in Control Panel, open the Advanced Options tab, and open the Fax Service Management console to configure the Fax Service on the local computer.

C. Open the Fax program in Control Panel, access the Advanced Options tab, and open Fax Service Management Help to configure the Fax Service on the local computer.

D. Open the Fax program in Control Panel, access the Advanced Options tab, and add and configure a Fax printer on the local computer.

70-210.05.05.002

A new user on your network calls you to ask for help with using the Windows 2000 Professional Fax Service. The user reports that no Fax program appears in Control Panel. You know that the user's computer is new, and all hardware is on the Windows 2000 Hardware Compatibility List (HCL). What is the most likely cause of this behavior?

A. The computer has a defective fax device installed.

B. The computer has no fax device logically installed.

C. The computer has no fax device physically installed.

D. The Windows 2000 Professional registry files are corrupt.

70-210.05.05.003

A new user on your network calls you to ask for help with using the Windows 2000 Professional Fax Service. The user needs to set up the Fax Service to store sent faxes on a network drive. How should you advise the user?

A. Open the Fax program in Control Panel, open the User Information tab, and open the Fax Service Management console to configure the Fax Service on the local computer.

B. Open the Fax program in Control Panel, open the Advanced Options tab, and open the Fax Service Management console to configure the Fax Service on the local computer.

C. Open the Fax program in Control Panel, open the Advanced Options tab, and open Fax Service Management Help to configure the Fax Service on the local computer.

D. Open the Fax program in Control Panel, open the Advanced Options tab, and add and configure a Fax printer on the local computer.

Objective 5.5 Answers

70-210.05.05.001

▶ **Correct Answers: B**

A. **Incorrect:** Fax hardware and the device driver installed to support the hardware appear in Device Manager. The Fax Service Management console is not available from Device Manager.

B. **Correct:** In the Fax Service Management console, select the Devices node in the console tree. Next, in the details pane, click the fax device to be used for receiving faxes and then, on the Action menu, click Properties. In the device name Properties dialog box, select the Enable Receive check box.

The Fax Service Management console is also accessible by clicking the Fax Service Management program located on the Start menu in the Programs\Accessories\Communications\Fax program group.

C. **Incorrect:** The Open Fax Service Management Help icon in the Advanced Options tab provides an overview of Fax Service Management and instructions on using and configuring Fax Service Management options. This help file is also available by clicking the Help toolbar button in the Fax Service Management console. Another important help file for using fax services is available by clicking Help in the Fax program group.

D. **Incorrect:** The Add A Fax Printer button in the Advanced Options tab is used to add a Fax printer to the Printers window. If Windows 2000 Professional detects the presence of a fax-capable device, it automatically creates a Fax printer in the Printers folder. Applications can then print to the Fax printer. When the job is spooled to the Fax printer, the Fax Service intercepts the job and launches the fax-sending interface so that you can specify additional fax information and send the fax to a fax destination. If the Fax printer is accidentally deleted from the Printers folder, Add A Fax Printer is an important feature for reinstalling the Fax printer.

70-210.05.05.002

▶ **Correct Answers: C**

A. **Incorrect:** If the Windows 2000 installation routine detects a fax-capable device, it installs the Fax Service, the Fax program in Control Panel, the Fax program group, and the Fax printer to the Printers window. It is unlikely that a defective fax device will cause Windows 2000 to fail fax device detection.

B. **Incorrect:** When the Windows 2000 installation routine detects a fax-capable device, it installs the necessary driver and interface software to show a logical fax device in Control Panel, a Fax program group, and a Fax printer. It is unlikely that the user deleted the FAX.CPL file from the %systemroot%\System32 folder. It is possible that a Group Policy setting restricts the Fax program from appearing in Control Panel, but nothing in the question suggests that Group Policy settings have been customized.

C. **Correct:** If the Windows 2000 installation routine does not detect a fax-capable device, it will not install the Windows 2000 fax components. Therefore, this is the most likely reason for the absence of the Fax program in Control Panel.

D. **Incorrect:** It is unlikely that a registry corruption would cause the disappearance of the Fax program in Control Panel.

70-210.05.05.003

▶ **Correct Answers: B**

A. **Incorrect:** The User Information tab contains data that is used by the Fax Service to complete fields in a fax cover page. The Fax Service Management console is not opened from this tab.

B. **Correct:** In the Fax Service Management console, select Fax Service On Local Computer, the root of the console tree. On the Action menu, click Properties. In the Fax Service On Local Computer Properties dialog box, select the Archive Outgoing Faxes In check box. In the text box that appears, specify the network location where sent faxes should be stored.

   The Fax Service Management console is also accessible by clicking Fax Service Management, located on the Start menu in the Programs\Accessories\Communications\Fax program group.

C. **Incorrect:** The Open Fax Service Management Help icon in the Advanced Options tab provides an overview of Fax Service Management and instructions on using and configuring Fax Service Management options. This help file is also available by clicking the Help toolbar button in the Fax Service Management console. Another important help file for using fax features is available by clicking Help in the Fax program group.

D. **Incorrect:** The Add A Fax Printer button in the Advanced Options tab is used to add a Fax printer to the Printers window. If Windows 2000 Professional detects the presence of a fax-capable device, it automatically creates a Fax printer in the Printers folder. Applications can then print to the Fax printer. When the job is spooled to the Fax printer, the Fax Service intercepts the job and launches the fax-sending interface so that you can specify additional fax information and send the fax to a fax destination. If the Fax printer is accidentally deleted from the Printers folder, clicking the Add A Fax Printer button is a simple way to reinstall the Fax printer.

Configure and troubleshoot accessibility services.

Accessibility services in Windows 2000 Professional provide a set of features to make the computer more manageable to people with various disabilities. Three tools are available for *configuring* accessibility services: the **Accessibility Options program** in Control Panel and two tools in the **Accessibility program group**, **Utility Manager** and the **Accessibility Wizard**. To show the contents of the Accessibility program group, go to the Start menu, point to Programs, point to Accessories, and then point to Accessibility.

Use the Accessibility Options program to configure keyboard, sound, display, and mouse settings to assist people with special mobility, visual, or hearing needs. Use the General tab in the Accessibility Options dialog box to control how the computer's accessibility options react to idle time and to control how notifications are delivered when an accessibility feature is enabled or disabled. Additionally, use this tab to configure **SerialKey** devices, to determine whether accessibility options apply to only the logged on user or all users, and to determine whether new users will receive the accessibility service configuration. A **SerialKey device** is alternative keyboard and mouse input hardware that connects to a computer's serial port.

The Accessibility Wizard aggregates accessibility features that are related. For example, you can use this wizard to select the text size that is most appropriate to the user. This setting can range from the default text size to text enlarged using the Magnifier utility. Other wizard options allow you to choose statements that describe the disability. Based on your selection or selections, wizard screens appear to configure the computer for the disability. Accessibility-related administrative options are also available from the wizard.

Running Utility Manager shows a screen that consolidates three important accessibility utilities: the Magnifier, the Narrator, and the On-Screen Keyboard. Any of these utilities can be configured by a user with Administrative privileges to start automatically when Utility Manager starts or when Windows starts. The Narrator utility starts automatically to aid a visually impaired user in configuring Utility Manager settings.

The Narrator is a text-to-speech utility that reads text displayed on the desktop, including the contents of an active window and text you select or type. The Narrator is not guaranteed to work with all applications. It has been tested with utilities such as Notepad, Microsoft Wordpad, the Windows Explorer shell, and the Windows 2000 setup routine. The Magnifier utility makes anything appearing on the desktop more readable by creating a separate window that displays a magnified view of the desktop, a high-contrast view of the desktop, or both. The Narrator and Magnifier are designed to assist users with visual disabilities. The On-Screen Keyboard utility displays a keyboard on the desktop to enable users with mobility impairments to type data using a pointing device or a joystick.

The Magnifier, Narrator, and On-Screen Keyboard can be started independently of Utility Manager by clicking their corresponding icons in the Accessibility program group. These three utilities provide minimum levels of functionality. Most computer users with visual or mobility impairments will need utilities with greater capability. The Microsoft Accessibility Web site at *http://www.microsoft.com/enable* contains a comprehensive list of hardware and software designed to assist computer users with visual, auditory, or mobility impairments.

Note The SoundSentry and ShowSounds features for the hearing impaired are part of the Accessibility Options program and do not appear as icons in the Accessibility program group.

Objective 5.6 Questions

70-210.05.06.001

Kathy has difficulty using a standard PC keyboard and mouse. You log on to her computer as Administrator and enable the StickyKeys and FilterKeys options. When Kathy logs on to her computer, the accessibility options you set are not loaded. What should you do?

A. Log on as Kathy, and use Utility Manager to configure the settings.

B. Log on as Administrator, and use Utility Manager to configure the settings.

C. Log on as Kathy, and use the Accessibility Wizard or the Accessibility Options program to enable the appropriate options.

D. Log on as Administrator, and use the Accessibility Options program in Control Panel to enable the Apply All Settings To Defaults For New Users option.

70-210.05.06.002

David has difficulty seeing a computer monitor. You want to configure David's computer to run the Magnifier each time he logs on to his computer, but you don't want the Magnifier to start when other users log on to the computer. What should you do?

A. Log on as David, and use Utility Manager to enable the appropriate option.

B. Log on as Administrator, and use Utility Manager to enable the appropriate option.

C. Log on as David, and use the Accessibility Wizard to enable the appropriate option.

D. Log on as Administrator, and use the Accessibility Options program in Control Panel to enable the High Contrast setting.

70-210.05.06.003

Randy has difficulty hearing computer sounds, and you want to configure his Windows 2000 Professional computer to generate visual warnings when the computer makes a sound. Which accessibility option should you enable?

A. FilterKeys

B. ShowSounds

C. SoundSentry

D. StickyKeys

Objective 5.6 Answers

70-210.05.06.001

▶ **Correct Answers: C**

A. **Incorrect:** Utility Manager consolidates three important accessibility utilities: the Magnifier, the Narrator, and the On-Screen Keyboard. All of these utilities are configured to start automatically when Utility Manager starts or when Windows starts. The Narrator utility starts automatically to aid a visually impaired user in configuring the Utility Manager settings. Regardless of how you log on to the computer, Utility Manager is not used to configure a computer to use the StickyKeys and Filter-Keys options.

B. **Incorrect:** As described already, Utility Manager is not used to configure a computer to use the StickyKeys and FilterKeys options.

C. **Correct:** The Accessibility Wizard is located on the Start menu in the Programs\Accessories\Accessibility program group. After starting this wizard, navigate to the Set Wizard Options screen and then select the I Have Difficulty Using The Keyboard Or Mouse check box. After clicking Next, the StickyKeys screen appears where you can enable the StickyKeys feature. Clicking Next again displays the BounceKeys screen. Enabling this feature is equivalent to enabling FilterKeys in the Accessibility Options program. Advanced configuration settings for FilterKeys are available from the Accessibility Options program, not through the wizard.

If you were logged on with Administrative privileges and you selected the I Want To Set Administrative Options check box, the third to last screen in the Accessibility Wizard would be the Default Accessibility Settings screen. From this screen, you can make the accessibility settings apply to the currently logged on user and all new user accounts or just the currently logged on user. Because you are logged on as Kathy, accessibility settings apply only to her user profile.

The second to last screen in the wizard allows you to save the settings to an Accessibility Wizard Settings (.acw) file so that the settings can be imported to another computer. To import the settings to another computer, simply open the .acw file on the new computer.

Using the Accessibility Options program, you enable StickyKeys and FilterKeys in the Keyboard tab in the Accessibility Options dialog box. After you enable and configure these features, click the General tab and select the Apply All Settings To Logon Desktop check box so that the settings apply only when the Kathy user account is used to log on to the computer.

D. **Incorrect:** This setting is available in the General tab in the Accessibility Options dialog box. Setting this Administrative option means that all new users will receive whatever accessibility settings were enabled in the Accessibility Options program or through the Accessibility Wizard.

70-210.05.06.002

▶ **Correct Answers: C**

   A. **Incorrect:** Unless David is granted Administrative privileges to the computer, he will not be able to configure Utility Manager so that the Magnifier starts automatically when Windows starts.

   B. **Incorrect:** A user account with Administrative privileges to the computer is able to configure Utility Manager. To start the Magnifier when Windows starts, click the Magnifier in the top box and then select the Start Automatically When Windows Starts check box. This sets the Start With Windows registry entry to 1 in the HKEY_LOCAL_MACHINE\SOFTWARE\Microsoft\Windows NT\Current-Version\Accessibility\Utility Manager\Magnifier registry key. Then, when Windows 2000 is started, the Magnifier will start automatically. The Magnifier will appear each time any user logs on to the system, not just David.

   C. **Correct:** After logging on as David and starting the Accessibility Wizard, navigate to the Display Settings screen and then select the Use Microsoft Magnifier check box. The Microsoft Magnifier dialog box appears, and a portion of the screen is magnified. After you click OK, the Magnifier Settings dialog box appears. After configuring the Magnifier, continue to move through the Accessibility Wizard to complete additional accessibility options. Because you are logged on as David, this accessibility configuration applies only to his user profile.

   D. **Incorrect:** The Use High Contrast setting is enabled in the Display tab in the Accessibility Options dialog box or using the Accessibility Wizard. This setting may help David see the computer, but it does not enable the Magnifier.

70-210.05.06.003

▶ **Correct Answers: C**

   A. **Incorrect:** The FilterKeys feature is designed to assist users with mobility impairments by configuring the keyboard to ignore brief or repeated keystrokes and to adjust the keyboard repeat rate.

   B. **Incorrect:** The ShowSounds feature is designed to assist users with auditory impairments by configuring programs that usually convey information only by sound to provide all information visually, such as by displaying text captions or informative icons.

   C. **Correct:** The SoundSentry feature is designed to assist users with auditory impairments by flashing part of the desktop screen every time the system's built-in speaker plays a sound. You can specify which part of the screen flashes by clicking Settings. The settings include flashing the active caption bar, the active window, or the entire desktop.

   D. **Incorrect:** The StickyKeys feature is designed to assist users who have difficulty pressing two keys simultaneously by configuring the keyboard so that when the Ctrl, Alt, Shift, or Windows logo keys are pressed, they remain active until the next time the user presses a key other than one of these four keys.

Implementing, Managing, and Troubleshooting Network Protocols and Services

The **Transmission Control Protocol/Internet Protocol (TCP/IP)** is a mature and feature-rich transport protocol used for Internet and most intranet data communications throughout the world. The services provided by TCP/IP have evolved with the explosive growth of computer networks. Understanding how to install, configure, and troubleshoot the protocol and the services it provides is critical to uninterrupted data communications, and it is an important part of most Microsoft Windows 2000 networks. Specifically, you must be proficient with installing, maintaining, and troubleshooting TCP/IP and its related services in Windows 2000.

Network protocols and services extend beyond local area network (LAN) communication. An important extension to the LAN is the wide area network (WAN). Many types of WAN technologies provide varying levels of services to expand the reach of the network. This Objective Domain is primarily concerned with **dial-up** and **virtual private network (VPN)** WAN connections. Windows 2000 provides these connection services through the remote access client. You must be proficient with installing, configuring, and troubleshooting the remote access client features.

The physical LAN or WAN medium and the transport protocol are only part of establishing a connection with a Microsoft network. A common task after connecting to a Microsoft network is accessing shared network resources. The two types of shared resources common to Microsoft networks are folders and printers. You must be able to create and configure these shared resources and troubleshoot them if resource sharing is not operating properly.

Note This Objective Domain specifically focuses on folder shares. See Objective Domain 2, "Implementing and Conducting Administration of Resources," for information on printer shares.

Tested Skills and Suggested Practices

The skills you need to successfully master the Implementing, Managing, and Troubleshooting Network Protocols and Services Objective Domain on Exam 70-210: Installing, Configuring, and Administering Microsoft Windows 2000 Professional include the following:

- **Install, configure, and maintain the proper operation of TCP/IP and core services of this protocol suite.**

    - Practice 1: Install TCP/IP on two computers and configure them for static IP addressing. Then verify that the two computers can communicate using TCP/IP.

    - Practice 2: Configure TCP/IP to use APIPA. Verify that two computers configured for APIPA are able to communicate with each other.

    - Practice 3: Install the DHCP Server service on a computer running Microsoft Windows 2000 Server. Activate a scope so that an IP address and a subnet mask are dynamically allocated to DHCP clients. Verify that the two computers previously configured for APIPA now receive their dynamic addressing from the DHCP Server service.

    - Practice 4: Install the DNS server and the WINS server on a computer running Windows 2000 Server.

    - Practice 5: Configure the DHCP Server service to supply DHCP clients with DNS, WINS, node type, and default gateway information.

■ Practice 6: Configure advanced TCP/IP settings in the properties of a LAN. For example, add a connection-specific DNS suffix, create and import an LMHOSTS file, and add a WINS server address.

■ Practice 7: Manually configure routes using the Route command. Next, if there is a router on the network that uses RIP to send route updates, install the RIP Listener networking service.

■ **Install, configure, and maintain the proper operation of remote access client connections: dial-up, VPN, and incoming connection types.**

■ Practice 1: Using the Network Connection Wizard, create and configure a dial-up, VPN, and incoming connection. Use the dial-up and VPN connections to connect to remote resources. Use the dial-up connection again to connect to the incoming connection.

■ Practice 2: After connecting to a remote resource, review the authentication protocol data encryption and other settings from the status details of an active connection. Disconnect from the external resource, and then reconfigure the security settings of the connections. Attempt to reconnect to an external resource, and review the status details of the connection again.

■ Practice 3: Share a connection and review the IP addressing settings allocated to the ICS computer and computers on the network that will connect to external resources through this connection. Use the ICS connection by configuring and running a Web browser on another computer on the same network. Verify that demand dialing is enabled, and review the advanced settings of an ICS connection.

■ Practice 4: Create and configure a Multilink connection. Use the connection to access external resources. Use the status details of an active Multilink connection to suspend or resume a physical connection.

■ Practice 5: Use the Netsh dial-up scripting utility to enable PPP logging. Also, run the utility to review some of the advanced remote access scripting capabilities it provides. After logging a PPP session, review the log and disable PPP logging using Netsh.

■ **Create and configure shared resources in a Windows 2000 network so that Windows clients can use the shares.**

   ■ Practice 1: At the command line, type **net use /?** and **net share /?** to review the switches available for connecting to a share and for sharing a local resource.

   ■ Practice 2: Configure share permissions and access shared resources using accounts that are granted different share permissions.

   ■ Practice 3: Configure local permissions for a share on an NTFS partition. Test access to the contents of the share, and resolve any conflicts between share permissions and local permissions.

   ■ Practice 4: Create user accounts and assign each user account to one of the following groups: Administrators, Backup Operators, Power Users, and Users. Log on as each user, and test the privileges granted to each user through the group membership.

   ■ Practice 5: Use the Shared Folders snap-in to perform share management tasks on the local computer and on a remote computer running either Windows 2000 or Microsoft Windows NT 4.

Further Reading

This "Further Reading" section provides lists of important readings to supplement your current understanding of the skills tested within this Objective Domain. The lists are delineated into pertinent readings for each objective within this Objective Domain. If you feel that you need additional preparation prior to taking the exam, study these sources thoroughly.

Objective 6.1

Daily, Sean. "Navigating Name Resolution," Part 1, June 2000 and Part 2, July 2000, *Windows 2000 Magazine*. Duke Communications International, Denver, Colorado. Sean Daily discusses name resolution and how to troubleshoot problems with the name resolution mechanism in Windows 2000.

Microsoft Corporation. *Microsoft TechNet*. Redmond, Washington: Microsoft Corporation, 2000. Read "MS Windows 2000 TCP/IP Implementation Details" located under Microsoft Windows 2000 Server—Technical Notes.

Microsoft Corporation. *Microsoft Windows 2000 Professional Resource Kit*. Redmond, Washington: Microsoft Press, 2000. Read about and run the troubleshooting tools listed on pp. 1452–1465, Chapter 31, "Troubleshooting Tools and Strategies"; read pp. 900–905, Chapter 21, "Local and Remote Network Connections"; and read Chapter 22, "TCP/IP in Windows 2000 Professional."

Microsoft Corporation. *Microsoft Windows 2000 Server Resource Kit—Windows 2000 Server TCP/IP Core Networking Guide*. Redmond, Washington: Microsoft Press, 2000. For an excellent introduction to TCP/IP and troubleshooting TCP/IP in Windows 2000, read Chapter 1, "Introduction to TCP/IP," Chapter 2, "Windows 2000 TCP/IP," and Chapter 3, "TCP/IP Troubleshooting."

Microsoft Corporation. *MCSE Training Kit—Microsoft Windows 2000 Professional*. Redmond, Washington: Microsoft Press, 2000. Read and complete the practices in Lesson 1, Chapter 7, "Installing and Configuring Network Protocols," and Chapter 8, "Using the DNS Service"; Read Appendix C, "Understanding the DHCP Service."

Objective 6.2

Microsoft Corporation. *Microsoft Windows 2000 Server Resource Kit Internetworking Guide*. Redmond, Washington: Microsoft Press, 2000. Read Chapter 2, "Routing and Remote Access."

Microsoft Corporation. *Microsoft Windows 2000 Professional Resource Kit*. Redmond, Washington: Microsoft Press, 2000. Read pp. 575–587, Chapter 13, "Security," and Chapter 21, "Local and Remote Network Connections."

Microsoft Corporation. *Windows 2000 Professional Help—Networking and Dial-up Connections*. Read this entire online help file.

Microsoft Corporation. *MCSE Training Kit—Microsoft Windows 2000 Professional*. Redmond, Washington: Microsoft Press, 2000. Read and complete the practices in Chapter 21, "Configuring Remote Access."

Microsoft Corporation. "Privacy Protected Network Access: Virtual Private Networking and Intranet Security." You can download this article from *http://www.microsoft.com/windows2000* by searching on the article title.

Microsoft Corporation. "Windows 2000-Based Virtual Private Networking: Supporting VPN Operability." You can download this article from *http://www.microsoft.com/windows2000* by searching on the article title.

Microsoft Corporation. "Virtual Private Networking: An Overview." You can download this article from *http://www.microsoft.com/windows2000* by searching on the article title.

Objective 6.3

Microsoft Corporation. *MCSE Training Kit—Microsoft Windows 2000 Professional.* Redmond, Washington: Microsoft Press, 2000. Read and complete the practices in Chapter 15, "Administering Shared Folders."

Microsoft Corporation. *Microsoft Windows 2000 Professional Resource Kit.* Redmond, Washington: Microsoft Press, 2000. Read pp. 545–559, Chapter 13, "Security."

OBJECTIVE 6.1

Configure and troubleshoot the TCP/IP protocol.

After you install and *bind* Transmission Control Protocol/Internet Protocol (TCP/IP) to a local area network (LAN) or a wide area network (WAN) adapter, including **IP over ATM** in Windows 2000, the core tasks for configuring TCP/IP on a network include the following: configuring **dynamic** or **static** IP addressing, configuring **name resolution**, and configuring **TCP/IP security**. Addressing information, such as IP address, subnet mask, and default gateway, is either manually assigned (static) or automatically assigned (dynamic). Dynamic Host Configuration Protocol (DHCP) is used to automatically assign such addressing information. You can also dynamically assign a default gateway using **Internet Control Message Protocol (ICMP) Router Discovery** and discover network routes through **Routing Information Protocol (RIP) listening**. RIP listening is especially useful for automatic route configuration on computers with multiple LAN adapters, called **multihomed** computers. On small networks, you can use **Automatic Private IP Addressing (APIPA)** to dynamically assign an IP address and a subnet mask to client computers. APIPA is disabled if the DHCP Server service is detected and operational for the subnet containing the client computer.

Note Like APIPA, **Internet Connection Sharing (ICS)** dynamically assigns IP addressing information. ICS is explored in Objective 6.2.

You accomplish **name resolution**, the method used to translate friendly names into IP addresses, by using files—HOSTS and LMHOSTS; or you use services—Domain Name System (DNS) and Microsoft Windows Internet Naming Service (WINS) servers. The primary function of the HOSTS file and DNS service is to translate IP host names into IP addresses. The primary function of the LMHOSTS file and WINS is to translate NetBIOS names into IP addresses. You accomplish TCP/IP security in Windows 2000 by configuring filtering, authentication, and encryption services. **TCP/IP filters**, **IP Security (IPSec)**, and **virtual private networks (VPN)** are some of the resources available in Windows 2000 used to secure data transmission.

Protocol performance is an important consideration, particularly in larger networks and networks requiring specific services. The Windows 2000 implementation of TCP/IP supports a number of performance enhancements, including a larger default **TCP receive window** size than previous implementations of TCP/IP for Windows. This feature allows TCP/IP hosts to send more data at once before requiring an acknowledgment from the receiver. The Windows 2000 TCP/IP protocol is capable of negotiating an even larger window size with the sending host. This ability to increase window size is provided by the **Window Scale** option. This feature is especially important for maintaining performance levels in high-bandwidth, high-latency networks. A number of other performance enhancements exist such as TCP/IP **Selective Acknowledgement (SACK)** and **Quality of Service (QoS)** support.

TCP/IP is a complex and mature protocol suite. With this complexity and maturity comes a robust toolset for troubleshooting TCP/IP-based networks. To diagnose whether the TCP/IP stack is loaded and configured properly, use tools such as Ipconfig, Ping, Pathping, Tracert, and Route. Also, check that the DHCP Server service is available and that the DHCP Client service is running. The DHCP Client service is important for dynamic address allocation from DHCP or from the APIPA DHCP allocator component and for dynamic DNS (DDNS) registration.

To troubleshoot name resolution problems, determine whether the problem is related to NetBIOS name resolution or host name resolution. If it is a NetBIOS name resolution issue, review the LMHOSTS file, check that WINS is functioning properly, and run Nbtstat to display NetBIOS over TCP/IP activity. If it is a host resolution problem, review the HOSTS file and verify proper DNS operation using utilities such as Nslookup. To get a summary status report of network activity, run the Network Diagnostics (NETDIAG.EXE) utility.

A useful troubleshooting utility used for capturing and analyzing network traffic is Network Monitor. Network Monitor is one of the Management and Monitoring Tool installation options in Windows 2000 Server. The Windows 2000 Server version of Network Monitor is not available for installation in Windows 2000 Professional. A Windows 2000 Professional computer can install the Network Monitor driver from the Windows 2000 Professional installation CD-ROM to capture network packets on behalf of Network Monitor. The Network Monitor driver is remotely configured and controlled from a computer running the version of Network Monitor included with Systems Management Server (SMS) 2.0. The version of Network Monitor included with SMS 2.0 can be installed on any version of Windows 2000.

Objective 6.1 Questions

70-210.06.01.001

You are the administrator of a LAN supporting computers running Windows 2000 Professional. Because of the small size of the network, a DHCP server has not yet been installed and you and an assistant assign IP addresses manually.

A TCP/IP error is detected on a computer running Windows 2000 Professional. You investigate by running the Ipconfig command-line utility, which reports an IP address and subnet mask of 0.0.0.0. What is the most likely cause of this problem?

A. The network adapter card has failed.

B. A duplicate IP address exists on the network.

C. A duplicate default gateway exists on the network.

70-210.06.01.002

You are the administrator of a LAN supporting computers running Windows 2000 Professional. One DHCP server is used to configure TCP/IP on client computers. APIPA is disabled.

A TCP/IP error is detected on a computer running Windows 2000 Professional. The computer is configured to obtain an IP address automatically. You investigate by running the Ipconfig command-line utility, which reports an IP address of 0.0.0.0. What is the most likely cause of this problem?

A. A duplicate IP address exists on the network.

B. A duplicate subnet mask exists on the network.

C. A duplicate default gateway exists on the network.

D. The client was unable to obtain an IP address from a DHCP server.

70-210.06.01.003

The user of computer Student1 is unable to connect to resources on server FilePrint1 using the computer name, but a connection is possible using an IP address.

Review the diagram below to see the TCP/IP configuration of Student1.

Which parameter is most likely preventing a connection using the computer name?

A. The IP address

B. The subnet mask

C. The default gateway

D. The primary WINS server

70-210.06.01.004

The user of Student2 is unable to connect to a shared resource on FilePrint1.

Review the diagram of the TCP/IP configuration of Student2 below.

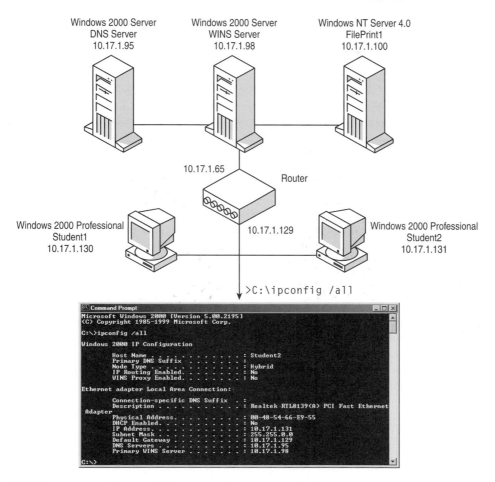

Which parameter is most likely preventing a connection?

A. The IP address

B. The subnet mask

C. The default gateway

D. The primary WINS server

Objective 6.1 Answers

70-210.06.01.001

▶ **Correct Answers: B**

A. **Incorrect:** If the network adapter card fails, the local area connection information shown by running Ipconfig would not appear for the failed adapter.

B. **Correct:** Two hosts on the same network cannot use the same IP address. In some types of client operating systems, it is possible to configure an identical IP address on two computers located on the same network. However, network communications for the two computers sharing the same IP address are unreliable and will ultimately fail. The Windows 2000 TCP/IP protocol stack checks the network to verify that the same IP address isn't already running. If it is and both computers are connected to the network and running Windows 2000, a Microsoft TCP/IP message box appears on the computer where the identical address is configured (computer B). This message box explains that the IP address is already in use. On the computer already using this address (computer A), a Windows – System Error message box appears. This message box explains that an IP address conflict has been detected and directs the user to consult the System log for details. The System log on computer A shows the Media Access Control (MAC) address of computer B. Typing ipconfig shows IP addressing information so that you can extract the subnet ID from the portion of an IP address that is the host ID.

   If a host with an IP address of 10.17.1.130 has a subnet mask of 255.255.255.192, the network ID is 10.17.1.128, the subnet ID is 0.0.0.128, and the host ID is 0.0.0.2.

C. **Incorrect:** The default gateway is the IP address of a network interface in a router. Routers contain two or more network interfaces so that packets from one network can be sent to another network through the router. Each client computer needing to send packets through the router is configured with one or more default gateways. Each default gateway is located on the same network as the client computer. When a router receives a packet that is destined for another network, it is the router's job to direct the traffic to the correct network or forward the packet to another router.

70-210.06.01.002

▶ **Correct Answers: D**

A. **Incorrect:** Because the computer is configured to obtain an IP address automatically, it is unlikely that an address running on the network is also assigned (leased) to the client computer. It is possible for an IP address to be manually assigned to a device on the network that is within an address scope activated in the DHCP server. However, the DHCP Client service running on a Microsoft Windows 98 or Windows 2000 client will recognize the conflict and decline the lease offer from the server. The DHCP Server service then tags the address with a BAD_ADDRESS attribute so that it will no longer be offered to clients. To avoid the client's involvement in this conflict detection, you can configure the DHCP Server service to detect IP address conflicts before an address is assigned to a client. By default, conflict detection is disabled on the DHCP Server service because server-based conflict detection will slow the assignment of IP addresses; therefore, you should enable this feature only for troubleshooting purposes.

B. **Incorrect:** All computers located on the same network segment share the same subnet mask. The subnet mask is a 32-bit value that distinguishes the portion of an IP address that is the network ID and subnet ID from the portion of an IP address that is the host ID.

C. **Incorrect:** The default gateway is the IP address of a network interface in a router. Routers contain two or more network interfaces so that packets from one network can be sent to another network through the router. Each client computer needing to send packets through the router is configured with one or more default gateways. Each default gateway is located on the same network as the client computer. When a router receives a packet that is destined for another network, it is the router's job to direct the traffic to the correct network or forward the packet to another router.

D. **Correct:** If the DHCP server is unavailable or if there is a problem with the client computer's network adapter configuration, the client will not be able to obtain an IP address lease from the DHCP Server service. If other client computers on the same network are able to lease an address from the DHCP Server service, check the client's network configuration. If client computers on the network are unable to lease an address from the DHCP Server service, check the server's configuration.

70-210.06.01.003

▶ **Correct Answers: D**

A. **Incorrect:** The question states that Student1 is able to connect to FilePrint1 using the IP address of 10.17.1.100. If a connection is possible with an IP address but a connection is not possible using a host name, then the problem is likely related to an improper entry in a name resolution file, such as the HOSTS file, or an improperly configured name resolution service, such as the DNS service.

B. **Incorrect:** Because Student1 is able to connect to FilePrint1 using the IP address of FilePrint1, it appears that network addressing is configured correctly.

   You can verify a legal network configuration using the information provided in the diagram. The subnet mask for the network containing Student1 is 255.255.255.192. The range of IP addresses for this network is 10.17.1.129–10.17.1.190. The IP address of 10.17.1.130 assigned to Student1 falls within this range. Assuming that the subnet mask for FilePrint1 is also 255.255.255.192, the address range for computers on this network is 10.17.1.64–10.17.1.127. The IP address of 10.17.1.100 assigned to FilePrint1 falls within this range.

C. **Incorrect:** Because the Student1 computer is able to connect to FilePrint1 using the IP address of FilePrint1, it is able to send and receive packets through the router shown in the diagram or Exhibit.

   According to the diagram, Student1 should use the router interface of 10.17.1.129 as its default gateway. The default gateway always specifies the IP address of a router interface on the same network segment as the client. The diagram verifies that Student1 is configured for the 10.17.1.129 default gateway address.

D. **Correct:** The only WINS server appearing in the diagram is located on the network containing FilePrint1. Student1 is capable of using this WINS server to resolve NetBIOS names to IP addresses. However, notice that in the diagram, the WINS server address is 10.17.1.98, but in the diagram, the client is configured for a primary WINS server address of 10.17.2.98. According to the diagram, there is no WINS server with this IP address on the network.

70-210.06.01.004

▶ **Correct Answers: B**

A. **Incorrect:** Nothing in the diagram suggests that the IP address assigned to Student2 of 10.17.1.131 is incorrect. The other client, Student1, uses an address of 10.17.1.130, which is only 1 bit different in the fourth octet and thus appears to be a legal address for this network.

B. **Correct:** Three classes of addresses are used for typical TCP/IP communications: class A, class B, and class C. Each class allows a specific number of networks and hosts per subnet, as defined by the subnet mask. The subnet mask for a class A address is 255.0.0.0, for a class B address is 255.255.0.0, and for a class C address is 255.255.255.0. The class specification also defines the value of the first octet in the IP address. The first octet decimal value for a class A address ranges from 1–126, for a class B address from 128–191, and for a class C address from 192–223. Therefore, an IP address with a value of 10 in the first octet suggests a class A address type. A class A address supports up to 16,777,214 hosts per network.

Notice that in the diagram, Student2 is using a subnet mask of 255.255.0.0, which is typically used for class B addressing. Windows 2000 doesn't prevent this configuration even though it doesn't comply with the class A addressing specification. Most routers will comply with the class addressing specification so the router will not forward the packets from Student2 to FilePrint1. Therefore, Student2 will not be able to connect to shared resources on FilePrint1 using TCP/IP.

It is worth pointing out that if Student1 is configured with a subnet mask such as 255.255.255.192 and Student 2 is configured with a subnet mask of 255.255.0.0, the two computers will be able to communicate with each other using their IP addresses. Ideally, though, they should both be configured with the subnet mask of 255.255.255.192.

C. **Incorrect:** According to the diagram, Student2 should use the router interface of 10.17.1.129 as its default gateway. The default gateway always specifies the IP address of a router interface on the same network segment as the client. The diagram verifies that Student2 is configured for the 10.17.1.129 default gateway address.

D. **Incorrect:** The only WINS server appearing in the diagram is located on the network containing FilePrint1. Student2 is capable of using this WINS server to resolve NetBIOS names to IP addresses. Notice that in the diagram, the WINS server address is 10.17.1.98 and in the diagram, the client is configured for a primary WINS server address of 10.17.1.98.

OBJECTIVE 6.2

Connect to computers by using dial-up networking.

The purpose of dial-up networking is to allow you to connect to and access remote network resources, such as an Internet service provider (ISP) or a corporate intranet. You accomplish this in Windows 2000 Professional by creating a **connection** in the Network And Dial-Up Connections window. Each connection appearing in this window contains settings that are unique to the connection. All network adapters detected by Windows 2000 are automatically displayed in this window. Any other connection types, such as **dial-up**, **virtual private network (VPN)**, or **incoming**, are created by running the Network Connection Wizard. You start this wizard by opening the Make New Connection icon in the Network And Dial-Up Connections window.

Dial-up interface hardware specified using the Network Connection Wizard includes modems, Integrated Services Digital Network (ISDN) and Asymmetric Digital Subscriber Line (ADSL) adapters, or an X.25 device. Dial-up connections (incoming) can be accepted through a modem, the Internet, an LPT port, or a COM port. Direct connections, also listed as an incoming connection, are made through an LPT, COM, or infrared port.

A Windows 2000 dial-up client can use the Serial Line Internet Protocol (SLIP) to connect to legacy dial-up servers, the Microsoft RAS Protocol (AsyBEUI) to connect to legacy Windows NT dial-up servers, or the Point-to-Point Protocol (PPP). You should *always* use connections based on PPP if the dial-up server supports PPP because it is the only protocol that allows for advanced security features and performance features. The Windows 2000 *dial-up* facility supports both AsyBEUI and PPP dial-up clients.

PPP connections in Windows 2000 include a number of important security features such as secure user authentication, mutual authentication, data encryption, and callback. You control the configuration of these features either through the properties of a connection or using Local Group Policy settings. You can secure an inbound connection by setting remote access permissions. Additional features available in Windows 2000 Server Routing and Remote Access service (RRAS) include caller-ID verification, Network Group Policy settings, and Remote Access Policy settings.

The **Internet Connection Sharing (ICS)** feature makes a dial-up client connection available to other computers on the network. This feature works similarly to APIPA by assigning an IP address and default mask to clients on the same network. Unlike APIPA, ICS sets a default gateway on client computers so that packets destined for another network are sent to the computer configured for ICS. The computer with the ICS dial-up or VPN connection acts as a router for incoming and outgoing packets.

Demand dialing automatically dials a connection when required. Combining demand dialing with ICS makes the connection configured for ICS available when users send packets to their default gateway. The default gateway in this case is the network adapter of the computer configured for ICS.

A feature designed to improve dial-up performance is dynamic multiple device dialing (Multilink). When a connection is configured for Multilink, additional bandwidth is available to the connection by establishing additional physical connections to the dial-up server. All connections are combined and load balanced to improve performance. When bandwidth requirements decrease, you can configure Multilink to drop the number of operational links to save on connection costs. This feature relies on the Bandwidth Allocation Protocol (BAP), and both the dial-up server and the client must be configured to support Multilink.

A remote access client supports two types of VPN connections: Point-to-Point Tunneling Protocol (PPTP) and Layer Two Tunneling Protocol (L2TP) with **IP Security (IPSec)**. A VPN connection allows you to securely tunnel packets of data through a public network such as the Internet. The packet tunnel uses TCP/IP, but the protocol inside the tunnel can be TCP/IP, IPX/SPX, or NetBEUI.

Note AppleTalk remote access for incoming connections to a computer running Windows 2000 Professional is supported by the AppleTalk Control Protocol (ATCP). The Windows 2000 Server operating system running RRAS includes the added benefit of acting as an AppleTalk router for incoming connections.

Dial-up and VPN connections support a variety of advanced user authentication methods, such as Extensible Authentication Protocol-Transport Level Security (EAP-TLS), which provides certificate-based encrypted authentication. Other authentication protocols from unencrypted Password Authentication Protocol (PAP) to Microsoft CHAP version 2 (MS-CHAP v2) are supported. EAP and MS-CHAP v2 are the only two authentication protocols that support mutual authentication. Mutual authentication verifies the identity of both the client and the server involved in the remote connection. You must choose an authentication protocol that meets or exceeds your security requirements and that is supported by the client and the remote access server.

Data encryption is supported between the remote access client and the remote access server using either Microsoft Point-to-Point Encryption (MPPE) or IPSec. MPPE requires either EAP-TLS or any of the MS-CHAP authentication protocols. You can use MPPE for either dial-up PPP or PPTP-based VPN connections. IPSec can apply to any connection, including the local area network (LAN) connection. IPSec provides L2TP with encryption services so that data is transmitted securely from the remote access client to its final destination on the remote network. Because IPSec is providing encryption services to L2TP, any authentication protocol including PAP and Shiva Password Authentication Protocol (SPAP) is allowed. L2TP is only a tunneling protocol; with IPSec, L2TP operates as a VPN.

Several important troubleshooting tools aid in solving configuration problems with the dial-up facility. For example, you can use PPP logging for troubleshooting PPP connections. You will establish most dial-up connections you make using PPP. PPP logging is available on a Windows 2000 dial-up server and on the client. To enable PPP logging on a client, use the Netsh dial-up scripting utility. Type **netsh ?** at the command line for information on using this utility. If you suspect that the problem is related to modem communications, review the Modem log contained in *%systemroot%*\Modemlog_*model*.txt. The log is automatically overwritten unless you adjust the logging settings using the Phone and Modem Options program in Control Panel.

If you are able to establish a connection with the remote network but you are unable to communicate with remote resources, run Netdiag to review a summary report of network communications. If a dial-up device is unavailable for configuration in the Network And Dial-Up Connections window, check the dial-up hardware in Device Manager and use the Add/Remove Hardware Wizard to install the device.

Objective 6.2 Questions

70-210.06.02.001

You want to use your Windows 2000 Professional computer with two external modems to dial in to your ISP. You configure a dial-up connection using the two modems, but when the connection is completed, only one of the modems is being used. What should you do in Windows 2000 Professional to dial both modems?

A. Use the Modems tab of the Phone And Modem Options dialog box.

B. Use the Advanced tab of the Phone And Modem Options dialog box.

C. Use the Options tab of the *connection_name* Properties dialog box to enable Multilink connections.

D. Use the Networking tab of the *connection_name* Connection Properties dialog box to enable Multilink connections.

70-210.06.02.002

You are the administrator of your company's network supporting computers running Windows 2000 Professional. Management wants you to enable every computer on the network to browse Internet resources. Your only available Internet connection is a dial-up connection to an ISP using a 56 Kbps analog modem. You install the modem in one of the computers running Windows 2000 Professional, and make a new connection for it in the Network And Dial-Up Connections window. What else must you do? (Choose two.)

A. Enable ICS on the computer where the modem resides.

B. Enable ICS on all computers running Windows 2000 Professional.

C. Manually assign IP addresses to all computers without modems that are running Windows 2000 Professional.

D. Configure all Windows 2000 Professional computers without a modem to obtain an IP address automatically.

70-210.06.02.003

You want to connect to a remote Windows 2000 computer using a VPN connection from your computer running Windows 2000 Professional. The dial-up server to be used for the VPN connection does not support encrypted authentication. In this case, which two protocols can you use together to provide tunneling and encryption services for a secure VPN connection? (Choose two.)

A. IPSec

B. L2TP

C. MPPE

D. PPTP

70-210.06.02.004

You attempt to dial in to a remote access server, and you monitor the progress of the connection. The status indicates connecting, authorizing, and disconnecting. You specify the option to bring up a terminal window after dialing, but this causes an unintelligible combination of characters to be displayed before disconnecting.

Review the diagram below to view the Security tab in the Dial-Up Connection To Internet Properties dialog box.

What should you do to allow the connection to be completed?

A. Specify the option to allow an unsecured password, and clear the Show Terminal Window check box.

B. Specify the option to require a secured password, select the Run Script check box, and then select *%systemroot%*\System32\Ras\Pppmenu.scp from the drop-down list box to establish a connection with the PPP host.

C. Select the Automatically Use My Windows Logon Name And Password check box, and clear the Show Terminal Window check box.

D. Select the Advanced (Custom Settings) radio button, and then click the Settings button. In the Advanced Security Settings dialog box, select the Use Extensible Authentication Protocol (EAP) radio button and click OK.

Objective 6.2 Answers

70-210.06.02.001

▶ **Correct Answers: C**

A. **Incorrect:** In the Modems tab of the Phone And Modem Options dialog box, you install any modems that were not automatically detected through Plug and Play enumeration. Clicking the Add button in the Phone And Modem Options dialog box starts the Add/Remove Hardware Wizard and shows the Install New Modem screen. The Modems tab is also an important place to begin troubleshooting modem problems. To troubleshoot an installed modem, select the modem and then click Properties. In the modem Properties dialog box, you can adjust the modem's configuration, perform modem diagnostics, and adjust the modem logging function so that the Modem log contained in %systemroot%\Modemlog_model.txt is appended to rather than overwritten.

B. **Incorrect:** In the Advanced tab of the Phone And Modem Options dialog box, you install and configure telephony providers. Telephony Service Providers (TSPs) resolve the protocol-independent call model of the Telephony API (TAPI) into protocol-specific call-control mechanisms.

C. **Correct:** All dial-up hardware devices installed in Windows 2000, including infrared ports, appear in the Connect Using box in the General tab of the connection_name Properties dialog box. After you select the devices that should be used to establish a Multilink connection, click the Options tab to enable Multilink. If you select multiple devices for the connection, then the Multiple Devices drop-down list box will be available near the bottom of the Options tab. This drop-down list box contains three settings: Dial Only First Available Device, Dial All Devices, and Dial Devices Only As Needed. The second and third options enable Multilink dialing. The third option, Dial Devices Only As Needed, allows you to set additional configuration options to control the bandwidth thresholds that cause additional devices to be connected or disconnected.

D. **Incorrect:** You use the Networking tab of the connection_name Properties dialog box to specify the type of dial-up server to use—either PPP or SLIP—to configure advanced PPP settings, and to configure the installed networking components. The advanced setting Negotiate Multi-Link For Single Link Connections allows PPP to throttle bandwidth over a single line if the server supports this feature. This might slightly improve download performance from the dial-up server.

70-210.06.02.002

▶ **Correct Answers: A and D**

   A. **Correct:** After the modem is installed and a connection is created for it, you must access the properties of the connection, click the Sharing tab, and then select the Enable Internet Connection Sharing For This Connection check box. When you enable this check box, the On-Demand Dialing check box is enabled. This setting instructs ICS to automatically dial the connection when users on the network attempt to send data whose destination is the external network.

     After ICS is configured, the computer containing the connection will be assigned the IP address of 192.168.0.1 and a class C subnet mask of 255.255.255.0. On-demand dialing, the DHCP allocator, and the DNS proxy are enabled, and the ICS service is started. The DNS proxy allows the ICS computer to resolve host names to IP addresses on behalf of the clients using the connection.

     Advanced settings for the ICS connection are available by clicking the Settings button. These settings allow you to configure network applications that should be available to computers sharing the connection and services to provide to users on remote networks. If your goal is to simply provide Web site access (port 80) through the ICS connection, it is not necessary to configure advanced settings.

   B. **Incorrect:** Only one computer on the network should be configured for ICS. All computers on the network will then use the computer configured for ICS to reach external resources available from the connection.

   C. **Incorrect:** When the ICS service is started, the DHCP allocator is enabled. Like a DHCP server, the DHCP allocator automatically assigns an IP address, subnet mask, and default gateway to client computers. The allocator is configured with a default scope of 192.168.0.1 to 192.168.0.254 and a subnet mask of 255.255.255.0. 192.168.0.1 is assigned to the ICS computer's LAN connection, and all other computers receive an address from the scope. All computers that will use the ICS computer to reach external resources are assigned the default gateway address of 192.168.0.1.

   D. **Correct:** The DHCP allocator in the ICS computer assigns each computer on the network IP addressing information so that packets destined for a remote network will be sent to the ICS computer. The DHCP allocator can assign the IP address, subnet mask, and default gateway only if the computers that will use the ICS computer are configured to obtain an IP address automatically.

     If the DHCP Server service is running on the network, you should not use ICS. In this case, the DHCP Server service will allocate addressing information to the client computers and the ICS service will not be available to the clients. ICS is designed for small office or home networks.

70-210.06.02.003

▶ **Correct Answers: A and B**

    A. **Correct:** Forming a tunnel does not guarantee the creation of a VPN. A VPN requires that the tunneled data travels securely. IPSec provides encryption to make an L2TP tunnel a VPN. IPSec provides end-to-end encryption services without regard to the authentication protocol. Therefore, even if a dial-up server supports only PAP, the data can travel securely over the transit internetwork using IPSec. A transit internetwork is the shared or public network used by encapsulated data. A typical transit internetwork is the Internet or a private intranet.

    B. **Correct:** L2TP encapsulates PPP frames and sends the frames over the transit internetwork. Unlike PPTP, L2TP does not encrypt the data; instead, IPSec provides this service to L2TP. L2TP can be used as a tunneling protocol over the Internet or over private intranets.

    C. **Incorrect:** PPTP uses MPPE. MPPE is available only when either EAP-TLS (smart card or other certificate-based services) or one of the MS-CHAP security protocols is used between the dial-up client and the dial-up server. This is required because MPPE uses EAP or MS-CHAP to generate the encryption key pairs.

    D. **Incorrect:** PPTP uses MPPE for data encryption services. Because MPPE requires either EAP-TLS (smart card or other certificate-based services) or MS-CHAP to generate the encryption key, the dial-up server cannot use PAP for encrypted PPTP traffic.

70-210.06.02.004

▶ **Correct Answers: A**

    A. **Correct:** Based on the Required Secure Password setting appearing in the diagram, this dial-up connection requires that the dial-up server use either CHAP, MS-CHAP, or MS-CHAP v2 to authenticate the dial-up client's identity. The client begins the connection process, and then when the client enters the authentication phase, the connection attempts to send identity information securely, but the dial-up server isn't accommodating that request. Therefore, the client disconnects the call. To verify that this is what is happening, at the command prompt, type netsh ras set tracing ppp enabled and then attempt the connection again. After the call is disconnected, type netsh ras set tracing ppp disabled to stop the PPP logging process. Then review the contents of the PPP.LOG file created in the %systemroot%\Tracing folder. To resolve this problem, select the Allow Unsecured Password option.

The terminal window appears because the Show Terminal Window check box is selected. The terminal window contains unintelligible characters probably because the dial-up server or security host does not require manual or scripted input or because nothing was entered into the window within a specified time. A security host is an authentication device located between the client and the server that verifies whether a connection is authorized to connect to a dial-up server. If you are connecting directly to a Windows 2000 Server RRAS server, then the terminal window is not necessary. To stop the terminal window from appearing, clear the Show Terminal Window check box.

B. **Incorrect:** The Require A Secured Password option means that the client's identity must be transmitted securely using CHAP, MS-CHAP, or MS-CHAP v2 authentication protocols. If the server is unable to accommodate this request, the connection is dropped.

A terminal window is appearing with unreadable text probably because it doesn't need to be displayed to gain access. Assigning the PPPMENU.SCP script file to the connection's attributes will cause the client to send scripted data back to the dial-up server or intermediate host. The question does not indicate that this data is required to establish a connection with the server.

C. **Incorrect:** Nothing in the question indicates that the dial-up server expects user identity information that matches your Windows 2000 logon name, password, and optionally, domain name.

A connection configured to automatically use the Windows logon name, password, and optionally, domain name is useful for mobile client computers that are operated by different corporate users. The connection's user ID will match the identity of the user logging on to the computer. The option to automatically use the Windows logon name, password, and optionally, domain name is available only if you select the Require A Secured Password option.

As described in the previous answer explanations for this question, the terminal window is not necessary, so clearing the Show Terminal Window check box is correct.

D. **Incorrect:** If the connection is failing, setting the EAP option isn't likely to solve the problem. To use this option, the client and server must be configured to use one of two EAP types: either EAP-TLS or EAP-MD5. EAP-TLS requires a user certificate on the client and a machine certificate on the server. A client certificate is typically stored locally on a device such as the fixed disk or smart card. The client and server exchange and verify each other's certificates. If the client is configured for MD5-Challenge (EAP-MD5), authentication is performed during the connection authentication phase rather than during the link negotiation phase, but a certificate is not used for authentication.

OBJECTIVE 6.3

Connect to shared resources on a Microsoft network.

In the first two objectives of this chapter, you explored the physical connections and most common protocols used to transport packets, authenticate users, and encrypt both user identity and data being transmitted across a network. This objective investigates accessing file system resources in a Microsoft network after you establish a connection to the network.

File system resources (folders and files) are made available to network users by creating shares. A share points to either a disk or a folder. The Server service and the Computer Browser service make shares available to the network. The Computer Browser service publishes computer name and share information; the Server service allows users to connect to these resources. These services are part of the File and Printer Sharing for Microsoft Networks component.

You can create a share in a number of ways. For example, at the command line, you can type **net share home=e:\homefolders /unlimited /remark:"shared home folder"** to share a folder named Homefolders with a share name of home. The /unlimited switch grants an unlimited number of users access to it, and the /remark switch adds a comment to describe the share's purpose. You can create a folder share in the user interface in the Sharing tab in the *foldername* Properties dialog box. You can open this dialog box in Windows Explorer by selecting a folder and on the context menu, clicking Sharing. You can follow this same procedure to share a drive by first selecting a drive.

You can connect to a share or a folder below a share in a number of ways. For example, at the command line, you can type **net use * \\server01.domain01.local\home\user1** to connect the first available drive letter to a Windows 2000 Server named server01.domain01.local with a share named home and a folder named User1. If drive J were the next available drive on the computer, then opening the J drive would show the contents of the User1 folder. You can connect to a share in the user interface in the Map Network Drive dialog box. This dialog box is available by opening Windows Explorer and clicking the Map Network Drive command on the Tools menu.

File system resources are protected by the Server service using **share permissions**, and they are protected on an NTFS partition by using **local permissions**. All file systems can be protected over the network using share permissions, but only partitions formatted with NTFS can be protected locally and over the network using local permissions.

The three share permissions are Read, Change, and Full Control. The Read share permission allows a user to view and open all folders and files in the share and access the properties of these file system objects. The Read share permission provides adequate privileges for running most applications. The Change share permission grants the user the privilege to modify the attributes, edit the contents, and delete folders and files below the share. You should grant the Read share permission along with the Change share permission, or users will not be able to access the share. The Change share permission provides adequate privileges for data that users need to modify. The Full Control permission grants the user all Read and Change permissions plus the privilege to edit the discretionary access control list (DACL) and take ownership. These privileges apply to the share and the folders and files below the share if the share is located on a partition formatted for NTFS. Shares, folders, and files located on a FAT partition do not contain DACLs or ownership information.

Note DACL and ownership features are NTFS local permissions.

A user's effective rights for all shares are the combination of the share permissions assigned to the user and any groups in which the user is a member. The Deny assignment overrides any other permissions granted to the share. For example, if a group in which a user is a member is granted the Read share permission but the user is explicitly denied the Read share permission, the user's effective right is Deny on Read. For shares located on NTFS partitions, local permissions and share permissions can conflict. The rule in this case is that the most restrictive permissions apply. For example, if a user is granted the Full Control share permission to a folder named User1 but the local permission granted to the user for this folder is Read, then the user's effective right is Read.

All permissions (share and local) are inherited unless inheritance is specifically blocked. By default, the Everyone group is granted the Full Control share permission when a share is created. If a folder or file is created on an NTFS partition, the object inherits the local permission of its parent folder. If local permissions are not modified on an NTFS partition or parent folder, the default local permission is Full Control granted to the Everyone group.

Objective 6.3 Questions

70-210.06.03.001

You are the administrator of a workgroup supporting computers running Windows 2000 Professional. The Reports shared folder resides on an NTFS partition in a computer running Windows 2000 Professional. Some users report that they can open files but not make changes. You want to enable users to edit files without granting more rights and permissions than necessary. Which additional permissions should you grant? (Choose two.)

A. The Read share permission

B. The Change share permission

C. The Write local permission

D. The Modify local permission

70-210.06.03.002

You are the network administrator of a workgroup supporting computers running Windows 2000 Professional. You hire LisaC to share folders, install and configure software, and install Plug and Play hardware. To which local group should you add her user account?

A. The Administrators group

B. The Backup Operators group

C. The Power Users group

D. The Users group

70-210.06.03.003

You are the administrator of a LAN supporting computers running Windows 2000 Professional. You want to connect to the Sales shared folder on a computer named Corp1. Which syntax should you use in the Run dialog box?

A. \Corp1\Sales\

B. \\Sales\Corp1

C. \\Corp1\Sales

D. \Sales\Corp1\\

Objective 6.3 Answers

70-210.06.03.001

▶ **Correct Answers: B and C**

A. **Incorrect:** The users are able to open files, but they are not able to make changes. The Read share permission provides this privilege level. With the Read permission alone, users are not able to modify the attributes of folders and files or edit their contents.

B. **Correct:** The Change share permission grants the users the ability to modify the attributes of folders and files below the share. Share permissions apply only when users access the contents of a share over the network. The Read share permission already assigned to the share must remain for users to access the share.

C. **Correct:** A local permission is a combination of a specific set of privileges called special permissions. The Write local permission provides the Create Files/Write Data, Create Folders/Append Data, Write Attributes, and Write Extended Attributes special permissions. The Write local permission does not grant the Change Permissions special permission. This special permission is different than the Change share permission—it grants the right to change the DACL on files and folders.

Because the users are able to open files contained in the Reports folder, the Read local permission must already be assigned to the folders and files below this share. The Read local permission provides the List Folder/Read Data, Read Attributes, Read Extended Attributes, and the Read Permissions special permissions.

In summary, the users are granted the Read and Change share permissions and the Read and Write local permissions. This combination of rights meets the requirements of this question: Users are able to edit the contents of files below the share. Users are also able to modify the attributes on files. However, this combination of permissions does not allow the users to move, rename, or delete folders or files below the share.

To ease administration and avoid share permission and local permission conflicts on NTFS partitions, consider modifying local permissions and leaving the share permission on a folder set to Full Control for the Everyone group.

D. **Incorrect:** The Modify local permission grants the users a different set of privileges than they require. This permission grants the user some of the privileges provided by the Write permission plus the Traverse Folder/Execute File, List Folder/Read Data, Read Extended Attributes, and Delete special permissions.

70-210.06.03.002

▶ **Correct Answers: C**

A. **Incorrect:** The Administrators group will allow LisaC to complete the tasks listed in the question, but it also gives her additional privileges that are unnecessary to meet the requirements. Members of the Administrators group are unlimited in their power to perform system administration tasks.

B. **Incorrect:** The Backup Operators group will allow LisaC to restore files on the computer, regardless of any permissions that protect those files. Members of the Backup Operators group can log on to the computer and shut it down, but they cannot share folders, install and configure software, or install hardware, Plug and Play or otherwise.

C. **Correct:** The Power Users group will allow LisaC to share folders and configure applications. She will also be able to install applications that do not modify operating system files or install system services. She will not be able to add or remove any Windows components. The question doesn't specifically outline which applications need to be installed, but limiting it to applications that are not Windows components and that do not modify operating system files or install system services is prudent. She will also be able to install Plug and Play hardware as long as the operating system detects the hardware. The operating system must detect the hardware because members of the Power Users group are not allowed to run the Add/Remove Hardware Wizard.

D. **Incorrect:** The Users group is too limited in its privileges for LisaC to complete any of the tasks outlined in the question. Users group membership provides a secure environment in which to run programs. Members of the Users group cannot modify systemwide registry settings, operating system files, or program files. They can shut down computers running Windows 2000 Professional, install Plug and Play hardware, run certified Windows 2000 programs that have been installed by administrators, create local groups, and manage the local groups that they create.

If a legacy application will not run, you may have to adjust the user's privileges or make the user a member of the Power Users group. Members of the Users group have full control of data files they create, their local profile, and the part of the registry represented by the HKEY_CURRENT_USER key.

70-210.06.03.003

▶ **Correct Answers: C**

A. **Incorrect:** Connecting to a share on another computer by typing a command in the Run dialog box opens a window to the share. The computer name always precedes the share name. However, the syntax shown in this answer is incorrect because a Universal Naming Convention (UNC) name always begins with two backslashes.

B. **Incorrect:** The computer name always precedes the share name when specifying UNC syntax. This answer shows the share name preceding the computer name.

C. **Correct:** The correct syntax using the UNC is \\computername\sharename. The syntax shown in the question is correct to connect to a computer with a NetBIOS name of Corp1 hosting a share named sales.

   If Corp1 had a fully qualified domain name (FQDN) of corp1.microsoft.com, you could access the share by typing \\corp1.microsoft.com\sales. A UNC name can also use an IP address instead of a NetBIOS computer name or a FQDN. For example, if the IP address of corp1.microsoft.com is 10.1.1.100, you can connect to the share by typing \\10.1.1.100\sales.

   If Corp1 is running Microsoft Internet Information Services (IIS), specifically the World Wide Web Publishing Service of IIS, then you can share the folder using the Web Sharing tab in the foldername Properties dialog box. If the folder is Web shared with Read and Directory Browsing access permissions enabled, then the same folder can be opened through a Web browser using any of the following addresses: http://corp1/sales, http://corp1.microsoft.com/sales, or http://10.1.1.100/sales.

D. **Incorrect:** The computer name always precedes the share name when specifying UNC syntax. The answer shows the share name preceding the computer name. Also, the UNC name always begins with two backslashes.

O B J E C T I V E D O M A I N 7

Implementing, Monitoring, and Troubleshooting Security

Configuring and managing security is a critical and often overlooked task when installing standalone or networked computers. Physical security is an important first step in securing computing resources and data from unauthorized access. Because mobility and network data access are critical to today's network operations, physical isolation of all computing resources is unrealistic. Computers that are networked or mobile make data more accessible and are at an even greater risk than computers that are physically secure and not connected to a network. Therefore, the next important security measure is protecting the computer's data through **user authentication**.

On most networks, user authentication is achieved by entering a username/password combination. Microsoft Windows 2000 enhances the user authentication process through a number of important technologies, including **Group Policy** and **smart cards**. The authentication process is further protected through sophisticated **authentication algorithms** and **encryption services**. The data that traverses the network is protected using virtual private networks (VPNs), which were explored in Objective Domain 6, and **IP Security (IPSec)**. You can use New Technology File System (NTFS) permissions and the **Encrypting File System (EFS)** to protect file system data from unauthorized access. You can also use shares to provide some additional protection for over-the-network resource access. However, NTFS and EFS provide a significantly more robust security infrastructure than shares do. If you suspect unauthorized data or computing resource access, Windows 2000 **auditing** allows you to track access to objects such as printers, folders, and files.

Configuring security is a complex task. To ease the configuration and deployment of a consistent security policy, Windows 2000 allows you to import security policy from one computer to another or to import predefined **security templates**. The **Security Configuration and Analysis snap-in** allows you to simplify the process of configuring and deploying security. This tool provides for the configuration and deployment of consistent security settings, including Group Policy application, event-log access, restricted group membership, system-service configuration, registry access, and file system access.

Tested Skills and Suggested Practices

The skills you need to successfully master the Implementing, Monitoring, and Troubleshooting Security Objective Domain on Exam 70-210: Installing, Configuring, and Administering Microsoft Windows 2000 Professional include the following:

- **Use EFS and recover encrypted data.**

  - Practice 1: Encrypt and decrypt folders and files.

  - Practice 2: Recover encrypted files from a computer running Windows 2000 in a workgroup and in a domain.

  - Practice 3: At the command prompt, type **cipher /?** to view the Cipher command-line switches. Run the switch used to encrypt a folder and its contents, run the switch that displays hidden and system files that are not encrypted by default, and run the switch that creates a new encryption key.

  - Practice 4: At the command prompt, type **efsinfo /?** to view the Efsinfo command-line switches.

  - Practice 5: Create a recovery agent using Microsoft Windows 2000 Server Certificate Services, and then add it to a standalone or workgroup computer using the Local Security Settings console.

- **Configure and troubleshoot local Group Policy security settings.**

  - Practice 1: Open the Local Security Settings console on a workgroup or standalone computer, and configure the two types of account policies: password policy and account lockout policy.

  - Practice 2: In the Local Security Settings console, open each of the IP Security policies appearing in the details pane. Review the various settings, and verify that default Kerberos authentication applies to all preconfigured rules. Review the General tab appearing in the Properties dialog box of each IP Security policy.

■ Practice 3: Create a custom console containing the IP Security Policy Management snap-in. Set the focus of the snap-in to the local computer. Then create a new IPSec policy using the IP Security Policy Wizard. Configure the policy with a default response setting and Kerberos authentication. Notice that if the computer is not a member of a Windows 2000 domain, Kerberos authentication is not used. Do not assign this policy to the computer.

■ Practice 4: Review the contents of and features available in the Manage IP Filter Lists And Filter Actions dialog box.

- **Configure, administer, and troubleshoot user accounts in a workgroup.**

  ■ Practice 1: Create users and groups using the Local Users and Groups snap-in in the Computer Management console.

  ■ Practice 2: Open the Local Security Settings console, and select the User Rights Assignment folder below the Local Policies node. Click the Action menu, and then click Export List. Save the exported list as a comma-delimited file (.csv). Open the .csv file in Microsoft Excel, and review the local groups appearing in the Local Setting column to determine each group's user rights assignments.

  ■ Practice 3: Experiment with the policies appearing in the User Rights Assignment and Audit Policy folders.

- **Configure and troubleshoot Windows 2000 workgroup and domain authentication.**

  ■ Practice 1: Create a local user account, log on interactively with this account, and then attempt to access network resources.

  ■ Practice 2: Create two identically named local user accounts on two computers running Windows 2000 Professional. Assign both user accounts the same password. Attempt to access resources on one computer from the other computer.

  ■ Practice 3: Create a user account in a Windows 2000 domain. Join the domain, and log on with this user account. Be sure you log on to the domain at least twice: the first time with the user account name and the second time with the UPN.

- **Configure and apply a consistent security configuration to multiple computers.**

  ■ Practice 1: Configure the policy settings appearing in the Security Options node in a local GPO.

  ■ Practice 2: Import a security template to multiple computers using the Local Security Settings console.

- Practice 3: Use the Security Configuration and Analysis snap-in to analyze a computer's security configuration. Configure the computer's security using the snap-in. Save the database as a new template, and import the template to other computers in a workgroup.

- Practice 4: View the log file created by the Security Configuration and Analysis snap-in after you run the Configure Computer Now command.

- Practice 5: Import a security template to a domain-based GPO.

Further Reading

This "Further Reading" section provides lists of important readings to supplement your current understanding of the skills tested within this Objective Domain. The lists are delineated into pertinent readings for each objective within this Objective Domain. If you feel that you need additional preparation prior to taking the exam, study these sources thoroughly.

Objective 7.1

Microsoft Corporation. "Encrypting File System for Windows 2000." You can download this article by searching on its title at *http://www.microsoft.com/windows2000*.

Microsoft Corporation. *MCSE Training Kit—Microsoft Windows 2000 Professional*. Redmond, Washington: Microsoft Press, 2000. Read and complete the practices in Lesson 3, Chapter 18, "Managing Data Storage."

Microsoft Corporation. *Microsoft Windows 2000 Professional Resource Kit*. Redmond, Washington: Microsoft Press, 2000. Read about EFS and PKI on pp. 587–620, Chapter 13, "Security"; read pp. 735–737, Chapter 17, "File Systems."

Microsoft Corporation. *MCSE Training Kit—Microsoft Windows 2000 Server*. Redmond, Washington: Microsoft Press, 2000. Read Lesson 2, Chapter 11, "Public Key Technologies."

Objective 7.2

Microsoft Corporation. *Microsoft Windows 2000 Professional Resource Kit*. Redmond, Washington: Microsoft Press, 2000. Read pp. 560–572, Chapter 13, "Security," and pp. 289–302, Chapter 7, "Introduction to Configuration and Management."

Microsoft Corporation. "Step-by-Step Guide to Configuring Enterprise Security Policies." You can download this article by searching on its title at *http://www.microsoft.com/windows2000*.

Microsoft Corporation. "Step-by-Step Guide to Understanding the Group Policy Feature Set." You can download this article by searching on its title at *http://www.microsoft.com/windows2000*.

Microsoft Corporation. *MCSE Training Kit—Microsoft Windows 2000 Professional.* Redmond, Washington: Microsoft Press, 2000. Read and complete the practices in Chapter 17, "Configuring Group Policy and Local Security Policy."

Objective 7.3

Microsoft Corporation. "Default Access Control Settings." You can download this article by searching on its title at *http://www.microsoft.com/windows2000*.

Microsoft Corporation. *Microsoft Windows 2000 Professional Resource Kit Group Policy Reference* online help file. Redmond, Washington: Microsoft Press, 2000. Read explanations of the Group Policy settings for audit policy and user rights assignments.

Microsoft Corporation. *Microsoft Windows 2000 Professional Resource Kit.* Redmond, Washington: Microsoft Press, 2000. Read pp. 545–559, Chapter 13, "Security."

Microsoft Corporation. *MCSE Training Kit—Microsoft Windows 2000 Professional.* Redmond, Washington: Microsoft Press, 2000. Read and complete the practices in Lesson 3, Chapter 16, "Auditing Resources and Events."

Objective 7.4

Microsoft Corporation. *Microsoft Windows 2000 Professional Resource Kit.* Redmond, Washington: Microsoft Press, 2000. Read pp. 540–545, Chapter 13, "Security."

Microsoft Corporation. *MCSE Training Kit—Microsoft Windows 2000 Professional.* Redmond, Washington: Microsoft Press, 2000. Read and complete the practices in Chapter 10, "Setting Up and Managing User Accounts"; and read Lesson 1, Chapter 21, "Configuring Remote Access."

Microsoft Corporation. "Smart Card Logon." You can download this article by searching on its title at *http://www.microsoft.com/windows2000*.

Microsoft Corporation. "Windows 2000 Kerberos Interoperability." You can download this article by searching on its title at *http://www.microsoft.com/windows2000*.

Objective 7.5

Microsoft Corporation. "Step-by-Step Guide to Using the Security Configuration Tool Set." You can download this article by searching on its title at *http://www.microsoft.com/windows2000*.

Microsoft Corporation. *Microsoft Windows 2000 Professional Resource Kit*. Redmond, Washington: Microsoft Press, 2000. Read pp. 572–575 and pp. 583–587, Chapter 13, "Security."

O B J E C T I V E   7 . 1

Encrypt data on a hard disk by using Encrypting File System (EFS).

All versions of New Technology File System (NTFS) use local permissions to restrict access to files. However, local permissions won't protect data if the partition is accessed locally using an operating system other than Microsoft Windows NT or Windows 2000. When NTFS was released with Windows NT 3.1, Windows NT was the only operating system able to locally access files on NTFS partitions protected with local permissions. Since then, third-party utilities have been released that bypass local permissions to allow partial or full access to NTFS partitions even when running other operating systems, such as MS-DOS or Microsoft Windows 98.

Microsoft includes **Encrypting File System (EFS)** support with Windows 2000 to counter the vulnerability of protected data located on an NTFS partition. EFS provides file encryption services by using a **symmetric encryption algorithm** and a **file encryption key**. A partition *must* be running NTFS version 5 to support encryption. Encryption is applied as a folder or file attribute. You can use one of two common methods to set the encryption attribute: either from Windows Explorer or from the command line using CIPHER.EXE.

To enable encryption from Windows Explorer, access the properties of a folder or file and, in the General tab, click the Advanced button to open the Advanced Properties dialog box. The last option in this dialog box is the Encrypt Contents To Secure Data check box. This check box is mutually exclusive of the Compress Contents To Save Disk Space check box. This is because an encrypted file cannot be compressed, and a compressed file cannot be encrypted. The Cipher command-line utility allows you to view encryption settings on folders and files as well as encrypt and decrypt them. Additional management functions provided with Cipher include the ability to force encryption and create a new file encryption key.

A command-line utility for displaying details of file encryption settings is EFS-INFO.EXE. This utility displays the following file encryption information: the user allowed to decrypt a file, the recovery agent or agents, and the certificate thumbnail (identifier). Running Efsinfo is an easy way to find out the recovery agents for an encrypted folder or file. Efsinfo is included with the Windows 2000 Professional and Server Resource Kits.

When you set the encryption attribute on a folder, you have the option of encrypting just the folder or all of its contents (including subfolders). Any new files created in an encrypted folder are automatically encrypted, including files copied to the folder. An encrypted file remains encrypted if it is copied or moved to one of the following:

- The same partition

- A different NTFS partition on the same computer

- An NTFS partition on another computer running Windows 2000

Note If an encrypted file is copied to another computer running Windows 2000, the other computer must support an equal or greater level of encryption to preserve the encryption attribute.

An encrypted file is decrypted if it is moved to a **file allocation table (FAT)** partition or another computer running a version of NTFS earlier than version 5. You must be allowed to decrypt the file; otherwise, a copy or move operation to a partition that does not support encryption will fail. If you open an encrypted file in a program and that program creates temporary files in an encrypted folder, the temporary files are encrypted. If the program creates temporary files in an unencrypted folder, the temporary files are not encrypted. Therefore, encrypt the temporary folder to maximize file security.

Because EFS is tightly integrated with NTFS, encryption and **decryption** are completed in the background with little user intervention. The process of generating a **public-key pair** and getting the public key certified is completed silently and in the background. Even though encryption and decryption are background processes, the EFS infrastructure provides a high level of security. To decrypt a file, a user must have access to a valid **certificate** and associated **private key**. You can store the certificate and private key locally or on a device such as a **smart card** or floppy disk.

To tighten security further, use the Microsoft Windows 2000 System Key (SysKey) utility to configure security for the private startup key. After encryption is enabled, either by using this tool or by encrypting a folder or file, encryption cannot be disabled. Using SysKey, you can specify the password key that must be entered on startup to unlock the system, or you can use the system-generated password key. If you use the system-generated password key, you can store the key on a floppy disk that must be inserted to start the system or store the key locally. Local storage of a system-generated password key is the default setting.

The danger of such a high level of security is that the loss of a private key used to encrypt the file could mean that the file cannot be decrypted. Windows 2000 protects against this by requiring that at least one user account be configured with a recovery agent certificate and a private key. On a standalone or workgroup computer, the user account created at the first logon following operating system installation is designated as the recovery agent. This is typically the local Administrator account, but it will be a different account if one is created during operating system installation.

You can add alternate recovery agents to a standalone or workgroup computer from the Add Recovery Agent Wizard. To start this wizard, open the Local Security Settings console, select the Encrypted Data Recovery Agents folder located below the Public Key Policies folder, click the Action menu, and then click Add. The Add Recovery Agent Wizard will request a certificate (.cer) file created for recovery. You must use Certificate Services running on Windows 2000 Server to create alternate recovery agent certificates.

If a computer running Windows 2000 Professional is made a member of a Windows 2000 domain, the domain Administrator account becomes the recovery agent. The domain Administrator account is designated as the data recovery agent in the Default Domain Policy Group Policy object (GPO). Additional recovery agents are added to any domain-based GPO, such as an organizational unit (OU) GPO.

Objective 7.1 Questions

70-210.07.01.001

You administer a Pentium III computer running Windows 2000 Professional. You want to encrypt a folder using a command prompt. Which command-line utility should you use?

A. Cipher

B. Efsinfo

C. Drivers

D. Nfsadmin

70-210.07.01.002

You are the administrator of a workgroup supporting computers running Windows 2000 Professional. Sandra stores her files on an encrypted NTFS partition. She is out of town on a business trip, and you need to access some of her encrypted files for an important meeting. You do not know Sandra's password, but you know that the default recovery agent is the Administrator account. Which procedure is recommended for accessing Sandra's encrypted files?

A. Log on to Sandra's computer as Administrator, and decrypt the files.

B. Log on to Sandra's computer as a member of the Backup Operators group, and decrypt the files.

C. Log on to Sandra's computer as a member of the Backup Operators group, and take ownership of the files.

D. Log on to another computer as Administrator, restore a backup version of the files, and decrypt the files.

70-210.07.01.003

You are the administrator of a domain supporting 80 computers running Windows 2000 and 4 computers running Windows 2000 Server. Users save work to home folders on a server. The NTFS partition containing the home folders uses EFS. Ingo leaves the company, and you move his files from the home folder to his manager's folder. The manager attempts to open the files, but an Access Denied error message appears. The default recovery agent is in use. How can you access the encrypted files?

A. Grant the manager NTFS Full Control permission.

B. Grant the manager NTFS Take Ownership permission.

C. Log on as the local Administrator, and recover the files.

D. Log on as the domain Administrator, and recover the files.

70-210.07.01.004

You are the administrator of a workgroup supporting computers running Windows 2000 Professional. A remote computer running Windows 2000 Professional named Win2000rem is used for remote encryption. You want to achieve these results:

- Use EFS to encrypt files on Win2000rem.

- Use EFS to encrypt data transferred over the network.

- Use EFS to encrypt the \Docs folder on your computer running Windows 2000 Professional.

- Set an OU Group Policy for recovery of EFS-encrypted data.

Your proposed solution is to log on to your computer as Administrator, use Windows Explorer to encrypt the \Docs folder, and use the Cipher command-line utility to encrypt the appropriate folders and files on Win2000rem.

Which results does the proposed solution provide? (Choose two.)

A. Files in the \Docs folder on Win2000rem are encrypted using EFS.

B. Data transferred over the network is encrypted using EFS.

C. The \Docs folder on your computer is encrypted using EFS.

D. An OU Group Policy is defined for recovery of EFS-encrypted data.

Objective 7.1 Answers

70-210.07.01.001

▶ **Correct Answers: A**

A. **Correct:** The Cipher command-line utility (CIPHER.EXE) allows you to create new file encryption keys and view, encrypt, and decrypt folders and files. To encrypt a folder using this utility, type cipher /e path_name\ folder_name, where path_name is the folder path and folder_name is the name of the folder you want to encrypt. To encrypt a folder and all of its subfolders, type cipher /e /s: path_name\ folder_name. To encrypt a folder, all of its subfolders, and all files in the folder hierarchy, type cipher /e /s: path_name\ folder_name /a.

B. **Incorrect:** The Efsinfo command-line utility (EFSINFO.EXE) provides detailed information on encrypted files and folders. Suppose you use the Cipher command-line utility to create a new encryption key for the current user by typing cipher /k. If you later wanted to view the encryption key thumbnail you created, you would type efsinfo /y. You can't use Efsinfo to encrypt or decrypt folders or files.

C. **Incorrect:** The Drivers command-line utility (DRIVERS.EXE) lists all of the drivers in the %systemroot%\System32\Drivers folder that are currently running. You can use this utility to identify a driver that might be causing problems because of corruption or because it is missing, not loaded, or outdated. This utility is part of both the Windows 2000 Professional and Windows 2000 Server Resource Kits; you can't use it to manage EFS.

D. **Incorrect:** The Nfsadmin command-line utility (NFSADMIN.EXE) allows you to configure and administer a Windows 2000 client running the NFS Client to access a Network File System (NFS) resource. You can't use this utility to manage EFS.

70-210.07.01.002

▶ **Correct Answers: A**

A. **Correct:** In a workgroup, the Administrator local user account is set as the default recovery agent when the operating system is installed, and a new user account is not created during setup. To decrypt the files, log on as Administrator and decrypt the files using either Windows Explorer or the Cipher command-line utility.

To verify that the local administrator is the default recovery agent, log on with the Administrator account and open the Local Security Settings console. To open this console, click the Start menu, point to Programs, point to Administrative Tools, and then click Local Security Policy. In the Local Security Settings console, expand the Public Key Policies container and then select the Encrypted Data Recovery Agent folder. Notice that the Administrator certificate appears in the details pane. From here, you can add recovery agents and export certificates and keys (if available) using the Certificate Export Wizard. Use Efsinfo to check the recovery agent or agents assigned to a folder or file. For example, to check the recovery agent for a file named DOCUMENT.DOC in the D:\Home\Sandra folder on a computer named Computer1, type efsinfo /r d:\home\sandra\document.doc on Computer1. Efsinfo will return something like this:

```
document.doc: Encrypted
Recovery Agents: COMPUTER1\Administrator (OU=EFS File Encryption Certificate, L=EFS,
CN=Administrator)
```

B. **Incorrect:** The members of the Backup Operators group are not assigned as recovery agents. A user is assigned as an alternate recovery agent on a standalone or workgroup computer by adding the user's .cer certificate file. You add the .cer file by using the Add Recovery Agent Wizard available from the Local Security Settings console on a computer containing the user's certificate. You must create certificate files for recovery in Certificate Services and then import them using the Add Recovery Agent Wizard. Certificate Services is available in Windows 2000 Server. To manage certificates stored locally, you can use the Certificates snap-in. This snap-in is not part of a console installed by default, so you must create a custom console containing this snap-in.

C. **Incorrect:** Members of the Backup Operators group are not granted the right to take ownership. Even if they were granted the Take Ownership right, taking ownership does not grant the right to decrypt files.

D. **Incorrect:** The Windows 2000 version of Microsoft Windows Backup (NTBACKUP.EXE) retains the encryption attributes of folders and files. If a recovery procedure cannot be completed on Sandra's computer and a backup file contains the encrypted folders and files, the backup can be sent to a computer containing a valid recovery agent. Before you can restore the backup file and decrypt the data, import a recovery agent certificate and private key that is valid on Sandra's computer to the computer used for data recovery.

This procedure is unnecessary because you can log on to Sandra's computer using the local Administrator account and decrypt the encrypted files.

70-210.07.01.003

▶ **Correct Answers: D**

A. **Incorrect:** The encryption attribute is separate from NTFS local permissions. You will be able to change the discretionary access control list (DACL) on Ingo's files if you have the appropriate permissions to do so. However, the manager will not be able to decrypt Ingo's files because he is not designated as the recovery agent.

B. **Incorrect:** The encryption attribute is separate from the NTFS Take Ownership permission. You will be able to assign the Take Ownership permission to Ingo's former manager if you have the appropriate permissions to do so. However, the manager will not be able to decrypt Ingo's files because he is not designated as the recovery agent.

C. **Incorrect:** After a computer is joined to a Windows 2000 domain, the default recovery agent becomes domain_name\Administrator, where domain_name is the name of the domain to which the computer is joined. You can verify the recovery agent for a folder or file by running Efsinfo with the /r switch.

D. **Correct:** When a Windows 2000 Professional computer becomes a member of a Windows 2000 domain, the domain Administrator account becomes the recovery agent. The domain Administrator account is designated as the encryption recovery agent in the Default Domain Policy GPO.

70-210.07.01.004

▶ **Correct Answers: A and C**

A. **Correct:** Encryption is available by default and is activated by setting the encryption attribute on a file or folder. By encrypting the \Docs folder on the remote computer, any files created in this folder are encrypted. You should apply this encryption when the folder is empty. If files are in the folder and you choose to apply encryption to the folders, subfolders, and files, other users who are not recovery agents on the computer will not be able to decrypt the files.

B. **Incorrect:** Data encryption is integrated with NTFS version 5 and functions locally. Data is not encrypted by EFS as it traverses the network. You can use IP Security (IPSec) to encrypt data as it travels over the network. Data can be encrypted over a dial-up line by implementing a virtual private network (VPN), such as Point-to-Point Tunneling Protocol (PPTP) or Layer Two Tunneling Protocol (L2TP) over IPSec.

C. **Correct:** As with the remote computer (Win2000rem), encryption is available by default. On both the remote computer and the local computer, the first user created during the Windows 2000 setup routine or the local Administrator account is designated as the recovery agent.

D. **Incorrect:** An OU is a construct of a Windows 2000 domain. If the computers are members of a Windows 2000 domain, you can assign a GPO to the OU containing the computers and then configure a recovery agent Group Policy setting in this GPO. By default, the domain Administrator account is designated as the recovery agent in the Default Domain Policy GPO.

OBJECTIVE 7.2

Implement, configure, manage, and troubleshoot local security policy.

You apply workgroup and standalone computer security to a computer running Windows 2000 Professional through **local security policy**. You configure and view local security policy from the **Local Security Settings console**, which you open from the Local Security Policy icon in Administrative Tools.

Four categories of local security policies exist: **account policies**, **local policies**, **public key policies**, and **IP Security policies**. In Objective 7.1, you examined the **Encrypting File System (EFS)** recovery policy, which is a public key policy setting. This policy setting appears in the Public Key Policies\Encrypted Data Recovery folder of the Local Security Settings console. This objective explores the other three policy categories. Account policies are categorized by password policy and account lockout policy. Local policies are categorized by audit policy, user rights assignment, and security options. IP Security policies are categorized by three types of IP Security (IPSec) rules, from Unsecured to Require Secured Communication Between Two Endpoints.

To configure most policy settings, select a node or folder object in the console tree appearing in the Local Security Settings console. Then double-click the security setting appearing in the details pane to set the properties of the setting. For example, to deny the local Guest account from logging on locally, expand the Local Policies node and then select the User Rights Assignment folder. In the details pane, double-click the Log On Locally setting to open the Local Security Policy Setting dialog box. To the right of *computer_name*\Guest, clear the Local Policy Setting check box.

When a computer becomes a member of a Windows 2000 domain, domain-based security policy overrides local security policy. The Default Domain Policy Group Policy object (GPO) is applied to the computer unless Group Policy settings are changed. The security applied to a computer in the domain appears in the Domain Security Policy console and is part of the Default Domain Policy GPO.

The greater the number of GPOs and settings within each GPO configured for a computer, the longer it takes for the computer to start up and complete the logon process. Therefore, minimize the number of GPOs applied to a computer in a domain and minimize the settings applied to a computer in a domain, in a workgroup, or on a standalone computer.

Objective 7.2 Questions

70-210.07.02.001

You are the administrator of a workgroup supporting computers running Windows 2000 Professional. You want to use Group Policy to configure a user account password policy that enforces a minimum password length on all workgroup computers. How can you accomplish this task?

A. Open the Users and Passwords program in Control Panel, select the Password Policy check box, and click the Advanced Password Settings button. In the Advanced Password Settings dialog box, configure minimum password length.

B. Open the Local Security Policy icon in the Administrative Tools folder. In the Local Security Settings console, use the Account Policies node to configure password settings.

C. Open the Computer Management icon from the Administrative Tools folder. In the Computer Management console, click the Security Settings node, and in the details pane, configure password settings.

D. Create a custom Microsoft Management Console (MMC), add the Group Policy snap-in, save it with the name GPO, and select the check box called Allow The Focus Of The Group Policy Snap-In To Be Changed When Launching From The Command Line. This Only Applies If You Save The Console. Using the custom Group Policy console, connect to each computer in the workgroup and configure minimum password length.

70-210.07.02.002

You want to prevent users from using passwords that contain user account names. Which GPO should you configure?

A. Enforce Password History

B. Minimum Password Age

C. Minimum Password Length

D. Passwords Must Meet Complexity Requirements

70-210.07.02.003

You are the administrator of a workgroup supporting Windows 2000 Professional computers. You want to configure an Account Lockout Policy that locks users out after four invalid logon attempts. You have configured the Account Lockout Threshold policy setting value to 4. You also want users to be locked out indefinitely until the Administrator unlocks the user account. What should you do?

A. Set Account Lockout Duration to 0.

B. Set Account Lockout Threshold to 0.

C. Set Account Lockout Duration to 99,999.

D. Take no action because this is the default setting.

Objective 7.2 Answers

70-210.07.02.001

▶ **Correct Answers: B**

A. **Incorrect:** The Users and Passwords program contains many of the features available through the Local Users and Groups snap-in. In the Users tab in this program, you can add, remove, and modify the properties of local user accounts and set passwords. In the Advanced tab, you can manage certificates, start the Local Users and Groups snap-in, and configure whether users are required to press Ctrl+Alt+Delete before logon. You can't use this program to configure Group Policy settings.

B. **Correct:** The Local Security Settings console contains the Security Settings extension of the Group Policy snap-in. You configure security settings for a standalone or workgroup computer from this extension. Configuring policy in this way applies to the computer where the Local Security Settings console is run. Therefore, you must run this console on each computer in the workgroup to set minimum password length.

To configure minimum password length on a computer, open the Local Security Settings console from the Local Security Policy icon. In the Local Security Settings console, expand the Account Policies node and then click the Password Policy folder. In the details pane, double-click the Minimum Password Length policy setting. In the Local Security Policy Setting dialog box, set the password length. The default is 0, which means no password is required.

C. **Incorrect:** The Security Settings node is not part of the Computer Management console.

D. **Incorrect:** Security Settings is an extension of the Group Policy snap-in. The extension containing security settings for a workgroup computer appears in the Windows Settings folder located below the Computer Configuration node. After you have navigated to this location, you can follow the procedure previously to configure minimum password length. This procedure works only on the local computer.

As outlined in the question, you can view Group Policy settings on other computers in the workgroup using a saved console. You can also use the default Group Policy console (GPEDIT.MSC) to complete this task. Before configuring Group Policy settings on another computer, you must be able to connect to it with local administrator privileges. To open Group Policy on another computer in the workgroup named Computer0 with a saved Group Policy named GPO, first open a command prompt and locate the folder containing the custom console. From the folder, type gpo.msc /gpcomputer:"computer01". Using the default Group Policy console, you can type gpedit.msc /gpcomputer:"computer01" to open Group Policy on another computer.

This answer is incorrect because in the release version of Windows 2000 Professional, the only computer configuration security settings available remotely in a workgroup are IP Security Policies. The Account Policies, Local Policies, and Public Key Policies nodes do not appear. As outlined previously, you configure minimum password length from the Password Policy folder below the Account Policies node. You can run the Group Policy snap-in locally to configure this policy.

70-210.07.02.002

▶ **Correct Answers: D**

A. **Incorrect:** This policy setting does not enforce the content of a password. The Enforce Password History policy setting dictates the number of unique new passwords that a user logging on to a computer must use before an old password can be reused. The password history value ranges between 0 and 24 passwords. This setting enhances security by ensuring that the password change policy isn't negated by a user changing a password to an old password.

By default, this policy setting is defined in the Default Domain Policy GPO with a value of 1. On standalone or workgroup computers running Windows 2000 Professional, the local security policy for this value is set to 0.

B. **Incorrect:** This policy setting does not enforce the content of a password. The Minimum Password Age policy setting dictates the period of time (in days) that a password must be used before the user can change it. You can allow immediate password change with a policy setting value of 0, or you can configure values between 1 and 999 days.

By default, this policy setting is defined in the Default Domain Policy GPO. It is also defined in the local security policy of standalone and workgroup computers running Windows 2000 Professional with a value of 0. This means that the user can change his or her password immediately.

For the Enforce Password History policy setting to be effective, configure the Minimum Password Age policy setting to a value other than 0. Even if this policy setting is configured with a value of 1 or more, an administrator can change the user's password at any time.

C. **Incorrect:** The Minimum Password Length policy setting does enforce the content of a password by requiring a minimum number of characters in the password. In most cases, this policy setting does allow the password to contain the user account name. The only exception to this rule is if the user account name does not meet the Minimum Password Length policy setting value. For example, if the Minimum Password Length policy setting is set to 5, the MaxN user account cannot be the password because it doesn't contain enough characters.

By default, this policy setting is defined in the Default Domain Policy GPO and in the local security policy of standalone and workgroup computers running Windows 2000 Professional with a value of 0.

D. **Correct:** The Passwords Must Meet Complexity Requirements policy setting does enforce the content of a password by verifying that the password meets a specific set of complexity requirements. The requirements are that the password cannot contain all or part of the user's account name, is at least six characters long, and contains characters from three of the following items: English uppercase characters (A...Z), English lowercase characters (a...z), base 10 digits (0...9), and nonalphanumeric characters (for example, !,$#,%). This policy is enforced only when a user account is created or a password is changed.

By default, this policy setting is disabled in the Default Domain Policy GPO and in the local security policy of standalone and workgroup computers running Windows 2000 Professional.

70-210.07.02.003

▶ **Correct Answers: A**

A. **Correct:** The Account Lockout Duration policy setting dictates the number of minutes a locked-out account remains locked out before automatically becoming unlocked. The range is 1 to 99,999 minutes. By setting the lockout duration to 0, the account will be locked out until an administrator explicitly unlocks it.

   By default, this policy setting is not defined because it has meaning only when you specify an account lockout threshold.

B. **Incorrect:** The question states that this policy setting value was configured to four invalid logon attempts. Setting this value to 0 means that the account will never be locked out. The Account Lockout Threshold policy setting dictates the number of failed logon attempts that will cause a user account to be locked out. A locked-out account cannot be used until an administrator resets it or the Account Lockout Duration expires. You can set values between 1 and 999 failed logon attempts, or you can specify that the account will never be locked out by setting the value to 0.

   When you assign the Account Lockout Threshold policy setting a value other than 0, a Suggested Value Changes dialog box appears recommending that the Account Lockout Duration and Reset Account Lockout Counter After policy setting values be changed from Not Defined to 30 Minutes. Therefore, if you set the Account Lockout Threshold policy setting value to four invalid logon attempts and a user attempts four logons with incorrect passwords, the account will be locked for 30 minutes. If a user attempts fewer than four invalid logons in a 30-minute period, the invalid logon attempts counter will be reset to 0. Because you are configuring the Account Lockout Duration policy setting value to 0, the Reset Account Lockout Counter After policy setting has no effect.

   Failed password attempts against standalone or workgroup computers that have been locked using either Ctrl+Alt+Delete or password-protected screen savers do not count as failed logon attempts.

C. **Incorrect:** An Account Lockout Duration of 99,999 means that an account will be disabled for 99,999 minutes, or approximately 69 days. After 69 days, the account will be automatically enabled. This is the maximum lockout duration that the computer automatically resets. This does not satisfy the requirement described in the question that the users be locked out indefinitely until the Administrator unlocks the user account.

D. **Incorrect:** The Account Lockout Threshold policy setting value is 0, and the Account Lockout Duration and Reset Account Lockout Counter After policy settings are not defined. These are the default setting values in the Default Domain Policy GPO and in the local security policy of standalone and workgroup computers running Windows 2000 Professional.

Implement, configure, manage, and troubleshoot local user accounts.

A critical security measure in all networks is controlling initial access through user account configuration. In Windows 2000 Professional and Windows 2000 Server running as a standalone or member server, user accounts and groups are stored locally in a security accounts database. Windows 2000 domain user accounts and other domain objects, such as security groups and **Group Policy**, exist in the Microsoft Active Directory store. The Active Directory store is shared and managed by computers running Windows 2000 Server as domain controllers.

This objective covers **local user account** administration, including creating and modifying user accounts, account settings, group membership, and local policy configuration. Specific emphasis is placed on configuring local policies for auditing user account activity and assigning user rights.

Note Account policies (Password Policy and Account Lockout Policy) were explored in the previous objective.

You complete most local user account administration from the **Local Users and Groups snap-in** appearing in the Computer Management console. This snap-in contains the Users and Groups folders. You can also use the **User and Passwords program** in Control Panel to complete user administration tasks using wizards.

From the Users folder, you create, modify, and delete local user accounts. By default, the Users folder contains two built-in accounts: Administrator and Guest. You can rename these accounts, but you cannot delete them. The Guest account is disabled by default. In the GUI-Mode phase of a Windows 2000 Professional setup procedure, you can create an account that is initially named by extracting the value specified in the User Name text box. This account is automatically granted administrator privileges. Except for the built-in Administrator account, you can disable all accounts.

From the Groups folder, you create, modify, and delete group accounts. By default, the Groups folder contains the Administrators, Backup Operators, Guests, Power Users, Replicator, and Users built-in **local groups**. The following privileges are assigned to user accounts that are members of these groups:

- Administrators have complete and unrestricted access to the computer. The default member of this group is Administrator. If a user is created during the installation of Windows 2000 Professional, it is also made a member of this group.

- Backup Operators override security restrictions for the sole purpose of backing up or restoring files. This group contains no members by default.

- Guests are granted the same access as any member of the Everyone special group. The default member of this group is the Guest user account, which is more restricted than user accounts manually added to the Guests group.

- Power Users possess most administrative powers with some restrictions. Power Users can run legacy applications in addition to certified applications. This group contains no members by default.

- Replicator supports file replication in a domain. This group contains no members by default.

- Users are prevented from making accidental or intentional systemwide changes. Users can run certified applications but not most legacy applications. The Authenticated Users and Interactive special groups are members of the Users group. When a user account is created, it is automatically made a member of the Users group.

User rights assignments dictate what a user or group is able to do on the computer. By default, the Everyone group and the local groups (except for the Guests group) are assigned various user rights. No user account is directly assigned user rights by default, but you can assign user rights to user accounts or other groups. For example, the Users group is granted the rights to shut down the computer, remove the computer from a docking station, log on locally, access the computer from the network, and bypass traverse checking. The Bypass Traverse Checking user right determines whether you can move through a folder hierarchy on the computer even though you might not have the permissions to view a folder or folders in the hierarchy. You configure user rights from the **User Rights Assignment folder** under the Local Policies node in the Security Settings console.

Note Any policies configured in a domain-based Group Policy object (GPO) override local policy settings, including user rights assignment.

Audit policy settings dictate which security-related activity the Event Log service should log in the Security log. By default, nothing is audited. Audit policy tracks success and failure attempts. You configure whether one or both types of attempts should be tracked. For example, when you enable the Audit Logon Events audit policy, you configure whether to log successful attempts, failed attempts, or both types of attempts in the Security log. You configure audit policy from the **Audit Policy folder** under the Local Policies node in the Security Settings console.

Note Objective 7.5 explores the Security Options folder under the Local Policies node.

Objective 7.3 Questions

70-210.07.03.001

You are the administrator of a computer running Windows 2000 Professional that multiple users share. An unauthorized user is suspected of deleting your documents. You want to audit the activity of the user to detect unauthorized actions. What should you do? (Choose two.)

A. Enable success auditing of the Audit Object Access policy setting.

B. Add the suspected user account to the SACL of the folder containing your documents.

C. Enable failure auditing of the Process Tracking policy setting.

D. Enable success auditing of the Process Tracking policy setting.

70-210.07.03.002

You are the administrator of a computer running Windows 2000 Professional that multiple users share. A user is suspected of changing the system time. You want to establish an audit policy to detect whether a user changes the system time. What should you do?

A. Enable auditing of the Audit Logon Events policy setting.

B. Enable auditing of the Audit Object Access policy setting.

C. Enable auditing of the Audit Privilege Use policy setting.

D. Enable auditing of the Audit System Events policy setting.

70-210.07.03.003

You are the administrator of a network supporting computers running Windows 2000 Professional. Geof, a user, is leaving the company and is being replaced by Alix. You want to deny access to the Geof user account and assign the Alix user account the same level of access that the Geof user account had. How can you accomplish these goals with minimum administration?

A. Copy the Geof user profile to the Alix user account.

B. Rename Geof's user account to Alix, and change the password.

C. Delete the Geof user account, create a new user account for Alix, and assign it the same permissions that Geof's account was assigned.

D. Disable the Geof user account, create a new user account for Alix, and assign it the same permissions that the Geof user account was assigned.

70-210.07.03.004

Jolie is a member of the local Administrators group on your computer running Windows 2000 Professional, which is shared among multiple users. A few users report that Jolie has accidentally deleted some of their Microsoft Word documents. Their documents are stored in individual folders assigned to each user who logs on to the computer, and each user is granted full control of his or her documents folder. You restore the missing documents from backup. You want to limit Jolie's access by allowing her only to back up data and reinstall applications. What should you do?

A. Remove the Jolie user account from the local Administrators group, and add the account to the Users group.

B. Remove the Jolie user account from the local Administrators group, and add it to the Power Users group. Add the Administrator local group to the parent folder containing all user documents and remove the Everyone group from the same folder.

C. Remove the Jolie user account from the local Administrators group, and add it to the Backup Operators and Power Users groups. Add the Administrators local group to the parent folder containing all user documents, and remove the Everyone group from the same folder.

D. Allow Jolie's user account to remain in the local Administrators group, and configure NTFS permissions to restrict her access to Read permissions on user documents.

70-210.07.03.005

You are the administrator of a workgroup supporting computers running Windows 2000 Professional. Which user rights assignment policies should you restrict to prevent unauthorized access to network resources and denial-of-service attacks? (Choose two.)

A. Bypass Traverse Checking

B. Enable Computer And User Accounts To Be Trusted For Delegation

C. Increase Quotas

D. Deny Access To This Computer From The Network

Objective 7.3 Answers

70-210.07.03.001

▶ **Correct Answers: A and B**

    A. **Correct:** Configuring the Audit Object Access policy setting to monitor access attempts allows you to enable object auditing of objects such as folders and files on a New Technology File System (NTFS) partition, registry keys, and printers. Each of these objects contains an empty system access control list (SACL). Success audits generate an audit entry in the Security log when a user successfully accesses an object that has a configured SACL. Failure audits generate an audit entry in the Security log when a user unsuccessfully attempts to access an object. Defining the Audit Object Access policy setting to monitor failure audits isn't necessary because your goal is to track a user's success in deleting your documents.

    B. **Correct:** Configuring the Audit Object Access policy setting is necessary to enable object auditing, but it does not begin object access security logging. After you define this policy setting, you must configure an object's SACL. An object containing an SACL is configured for auditing in the Security tab in the object's Properties dialog box. In the Security tab, click the Advanced button to open the Access Control Settings dialog box for the object. Click the Auditing tab in the Access Control Settings dialog box, add users or groups who should be audited, and then select the types of events you want to audit.

    To track a specific user who you suspect is deleting your files, add the user to the audit list for the SACL on the folder containing your documents. Apply the audit entry to the folder, subfolders, and files, and configure the Delete and Delete Subfolders And Files access events. You might want to configure auditing for other successful access events such as List Folder/Read Data and Create Files/Write Data. After the suspected user has used the computer, check the Security log in Event Viewer.

    C. **Incorrect:** Configuring the Audit Process Tracking policy setting to monitor access attempts allows you to audit detailed tracking information for events such as program activation, process exit, handle duplication, and indirect object access. Failure audits generate an audit entry when the process being tracked fails.

    D. **Incorrect:** Success audits generate an audit entry when the process being tracked completes the audited event successfully.

70-210.07.03.002

▶ **Correct Answers: C**

  A. **Incorrect:** Configuring the Audit Logon Events policy setting to monitor access attempts allows you to audit each instance of a user logging on or logging off a computer where the computer was used to validate the account. Success audits generate an audit entry when account logon occurs successfully. Failure audits generate an audit entry when an attempted occurrence of the account logon fails.

  B. **Incorrect:** Configuring the Audit Object Access policy setting to monitor access attempts allows you to enable object auditing of objects such as folders and files on an NTFS partition, registry keys, and printers. Success audits generate an audit entry in the Security log when a user successfully accesses an object that has a configured SACL. Failure audits generate an audit entry in the Security log when a user unsuccessfully attempts to access an object.

  C. **Correct:** Configuring the Audit Privilege Use policy setting to monitor access attempts allows you to audit each time a user exercises a user right. Success audits generate an audit entry when a user right is successfully exercised. Failure audits generate an audit entry when the exercise of a user right fails.

    The Change The System Time user rights assignment is granted to the Power Users and Administrators groups by default. If you haven't changed this user rights assignment, the user changing the time must be a Power Users or Administrators group member. After you configure the Audit Privilege Use policy setting for successful attempts and the system time is changed, review the Security log for this event. The event ID for this event is 577, and the privilege is SeSystemtimePrivilege. You can look up event IDs using the Windows 2000 Professional Resource Kit Error and Event Messages Help file.

  D. **Incorrect:** Configuring the Audit System Events policy setting to monitor access attempts allows you to audit when a user restarts or shuts down the computer or when an event has occurred that affects either the system security or the Security log. Success audits generate an audit entry when a system event is successfully executed. Failure audits generate an audit entry when a system event is unsuccessfully attempted.

70-210.07.03.003

▶ **Correct Answers: B**

  A. **Incorrect:** Assuming that the Geof user profile is accessible by the Alix user account, the Alix user profile settings will match Geof's. However, depending on how security is configured, the Alix user account will probably not have access to Geof's files on an NTFS partition or in shares accessed over the network. Also, the Geof user account remains active, so if Geof is able to connect to the internal network, he will be able to gain access to his file resources.

B. **Correct:** Each user account contains a unique security ID (SID). The SID is granted access to resources and is symbolically represented by a user account name. Therefore, renaming the Geof user account to Alix will maintain the Geof user account security settings with a new name of Alix. Changing the password helps ensure that Geof will not be able to access resources previously available to him. This implicitly denies Geof access because the Geof user account no longer exists with the same username and password combination.

C. **Incorrect:** This will achieve the final objective of granting the Alix user account access to resources previously available to Geof, and it removes the Geof user account so that Geof can no longer access the network. However, this might require a significant amount of administrative effort, depending on the number of resources accessible by the Geof user account and the complexity of the security configuration.

D. **Incorrect:** Disabling the Geof user account achieves the objective of denying Geof access to resources. However, creating a new Alix user account and assigning the same permissions that the Geof user account had requires the same amount of administrative effort outlined previously.

70-210.07.03.004

▶ **Correct Answers: C**

A. **Incorrect:** Members of the Users local group are not able to back up data and install applications. Therefore, making the Jolie user account a member of only the Users local group will not allow Jolie to complete the administrative tasks that are her responsibility.

B. **Incorrect:** Members of the Power Users local group are able to install applications but are unable to back up and restore data. You can verify this by viewing the user right assignments Backup Files And Directories and Restore Files And Directories. The Administrators and Backup Operators local groups are assigned these privileges by default. No other group is assigned these user rights.

C. **Correct:** Members of the Power Users local group are able to install applications, so this membership satisfies one of Jolie's administrative responsibilities. Members of the Backup Operators local group are able to back up and restore files on the computer regardless of any permissions protecting the files. This permission satisfies her other administrative responsibility.

Removing Full Control from the Everyone group to the parent folder restricts access to the folder. By default, all folders and files in the parent folder inherit this permission. Adding the Administrators local group to the parent folder ensures easy access to members of the Administrators local group. Because the Jolie user account is no longer a member of the Administrators local group, Jolie will not be able to accidentally delete other users' documents.

D. **Incorrect:** NTFS permissions are cumulative unless a specific access denial is configured. Therefore, as a member of the Everyone group, Jolie's effective rights are Full Control. Even if her effective permissions were Read, as a member of the Administrators local group, she can take ownership of files and reassign rights to herself and then delete files.

70-210.07.03.005

▶ **Correct Answers: B and C**

A. **Incorrect:** The Bypass Traverse Checking user rights assignment grants the privilege to navigate through a folder structure even if a user does not have rights to the folders in the hierarchy. Users are not able to view the contents of folders with this user right. The Everyone, Users, Power Users, Backup Operators, and Administrators groups are granted this user rights assignment by default.

B. **Correct:** The Enable Computer And User Accounts To Be Trusted For Delegation user rights assignment grants the privilege to access resources on another computer using a client's delegated credentials. This user rights assignment is typically granted to a service account. The service account is assigned to a process that accesses other computer resources on the network. This privilege is not granted to any users or groups by default because it makes the computer vulnerable to attack by Trojan horse programs—programs that masquerade as another program in an attempt to obtain information such as username and password.

C. **Correct:** The Increase Quotas user rights assignment grants the privilege to use a process with write property access to another process to increase the processor quota assigned to the other process. This privilege is useful for system tuning, and it is required by the Cluster service account in Windows 2000 clusters. You can use this privilege to launch a denial-of-service attack, an explicit attempt to prevent legitimate users of a service from using that service. Using the Increase Quotas privilege, the attacker attempts to disrupt service to a specific system by excessively increasing the processor quota assigned to a process. The Administrators local group is granted this assignment by default.

D. **Incorrect:** The Deny Access To This Computer From The Network user rights assignment restricts users from connecting to a computer over the network. This user right is applied to users or groups. When users with this user rights assignment attempt to access the computer over the network, a message box appears stating that the user has not been granted the requested logon type. This policy is highly restrictive and is not assigned to any users or groups by default.

O B J E C T I V E   7 . 4

Implement, configure, manage, and troubleshoot local user authentication.

A user's credentials are authenticated against a database of identity information. In a workgroup or standalone computer, the database of identity information is the local security accounts store. In a Windows 2000 domain, the database of identity information is the Active Directory store. Certificate stores are important identity information stores for high security. Certificate stores are associated with users, services, and computers.

This objective covers supporting **user authentication** using the local security accounts store and the Active Directory store. Specifically, you must know how to configure and troubleshoot authentication to either store.

User authentication is the process of verifying a user's identity. You log on interactively to gain initial access to their computer or to the network. After the interactive logon process is complete, you access network resources using a network authentication method, such as Kerberos version 5. If you log on locally, you must provide network authentication credentials to access network resources. If you log on to a Windows 2000 domain (the Active Directory store), the interactive logon credentials are used to transparently authenticate you to network resources. You can obtain **logon credentials** by entering a username/password combination or by inserting a **smart card** and entering a personal identification number (PIN).

If you intend to log on interactively to a standalone or workgroup computer with a username/password combination, the Log On To text box contains the name of the computer. After a computer joins a Windows 2000 domain, the Log On To text box is populated with the logon domain and other domains in the hierarchy. A computer must be joined to the domain before a domain user can log on interactively. When you log on to a Windows 2000 domain, the Log On To text box contains the domain name. To avoid having to select the appropriate domain from the Log On To text box, you can log on with a **user principal name (UPN)**. A UPN is identical in syntax to an e-mail name: *username@ domain_name*, where *username* is the user account name and *domain_name* is the fully qualified domain name (FQDN) or custom suffix defined in the Active Directory store.

If you intend to log on interactively to a Windows 2000 domain from a Windows 2000 client using a smart card, the process begins by inserting a smart card into a smart card reader. This event causes a prompt for a PIN to appear. The PIN you enter is used to authenticate to the smart card, not to the domain. A public key certificate stored on the smart card is used to authenticate to the domain using the Kerberos version 5 protocol. Extensible Authentication Protocol-Transport Level Security (EAP-TLS) is used for Point-to-Point Protocol (PPP)-based logon with a smart card.

You use a variety of authentication protocols in a number of communication scenarios. For example, you use **Kerberos authentication** when a Windows 2000 Professional workstation logs on to a Windows 2000 domain. **IP Security (IPSec)** also uses Kerberos authentication by default. You can configure both network logon and IPSec for other authentication methods, such as certificates and shared secret keys. Remote access using PPP, which was explored in Objective 6.2, provides additional authentication protocols to secure remote access connections.

Objective 7.4 Questions

70-210.07.04.001

You are the administrator of your company's network. You add two new user accounts, FlorianV and ClausR, to a computer running Windows 2000 Professional that several users share. When FlorianV attempts to log on, an error message appears stating, "The system is unable to copy \Documents and Settings\All Users to \Documents and Settings\FlorianV. DETAIL – Access is denied." What should you do to allow FlorianV to log on?

A. Copy the All Users profile to the Default User profile.

B. Copy the Default User profile to the All Users profile.

C. Reset the permissions on the \Documents and Settings\All Users folder.

D. Reset the permissions on the \Documents and Settings\Default User folder.

70-210.07.04.002

You are the administrator of a domain supporting Windows 2000 computers. You create a local user account named AlanC on a computer running Windows 2000 Professional. You are unable to assign access permissions for domain resources to AlanC. How can you assign permissions for domain resources to this user?

A. Create a local user account on a member server.

B. Create a local user account on a domain controller.

C. Create a domain user account on a member server.

D. Create a domain user account on a domain controller.

70-210.07.04.003

You are the administrator of a domain supporting computers running Windows 2000 Professional. You want to implement a smart card logon process for your mobile clients. Which protocol should you use?

A. PAP

B. SPAP

C. CHAP

D. EAP-TLS

E. MS-CHAP

F. MS-CHAP v2

Objective 7.4 Answers

70-210.07.04.001

▶ **Correct Answers: D**

A. **Incorrect:** You generate local user profiles in one of two ways: when Windows 2000 Professional is installed and when a user logs on for the first time. The two user profiles automatically created when Windows 2000 Professional is installed are the All Users profile and the Default User profile. These two profiles serve distinct roles, so you should not copy the All Users profile to the Default User profile.

B. **Incorrect:** These two profiles serve distinct roles, so you should not copy the Default User profile to the All Users profile.

C. **Incorrect:** If the FlorianV user account is denied access to the All Users folder, when she attempts to log on, an error message appears stating that "D:\Documents and Settings\All Users\Desktop is not accessible. Access is denied." However, Florian can click OK and continue the logon process. The FlorianV user account will not have access to the contents of the All Users profile.

D. **Correct:** When a user with no user profile under the Documents and Settings folder logs on, a profile folder is automatically generated for that user by copying the contents of the Default User folder to a folder uniquely named for the user. By default, the Default User folder inherits the local permissions of Full Control assigned to the Everyone group. If this permission is removed and no alternate permission is assigned to allow the new user to access the Default User folder, a profile cannot be created for the user. If a profile cannot be created, the user is not allowed to log on. A solution to this problem is to reset the permissions on the Default User folder and then have the new user log on interactively.

70-210.07.04.002

▶ **Correct Answers: D**

A. **Incorrect:** You can create a local user account on the member server named AlanC with an identical password as the other AlanC user account. Then assign access permissions for local resources on the member server to the local user account. This will provide transparent access to resources on the member server. However, this does not provide access to other domain resources. Also, this method requires significant administrative overhead.

B. **Incorrect:** Domain controllers contain domain user accounts, not local user accounts. Therefore, it is not possible to create local user accounts on a domain controller.

C. **Incorrect:** Member servers contain local user accounts and are joined to a Windows NT or Windows 2000 domain. You cannot create domain user accounts on a member server. You can, however, create domain user accounts from a member server, but the account is located in the Active Directory store on domain controllers.

D. **Correct:** The AlanC local user account is designed to provide access to local resources on the computer. The full name of the AlanC local user account is computername\AlanC, where computername is the name of the computer where the local user account was created. This type of account is not granted access to domain resources. Instead, create a domain user account named AlanC. The full name of the AlanC user account name is AlanC@domain_name or AlanC@unique_suffix. Domain user accounts are designed to provide access to domainwide resources. After creating the account, make AlanC a member of a group or groups that are granted access permissions for domain resources. You can also directly assign permissions to the AlanC user account for domain resources.

70-210.07.04.003

▶ **Correct Answers: D**

A. **Incorrect:** Password Authentication Protocol (PAP) sends identity data unencrypted from a PPP client to the server. PAP is not used in the smart card logon process.

B. **Incorrect:** Shiva Password Authentication Protocol (SPAP) authenticates PPP clients to Shiva remote access servers and Windows 2000 remote access servers. SPAP follows a similar authentication process as PAP except that the password is encrypted before it is sent to the remote access server. SPAP is not used in the smart card logon process.

C. **Incorrect:** Challenge Handshake Authentication Protocol (CHAP) is an improvement over PAP and SPAP because the user's password is never sent over the PPP connection. Instead, the client runs the Message Digest 5 (MD5) hashing algorithm against the password entered locally, the session ID, and a challenge string sent by the dial-in server. The user name in clear text and the return string (hash) is sent to the dial-in server. The dial-in server duplicates the operation against the locally stored client password and compares the result with the response sent by the client. If there is a match, the dial-in server grants the client access. You can't use CHAP in the smart card logon process.

D. **Correct:** EAP-TLS uses transport layer security when a PPP connection is established. Mutual authentication and encryption services are provided between client and server using certificates. The client exchanges a user certificate that can be stored on a smart card or on the local disk, and the server sends a machine certificate.

E. **Incorrect:** Microsoft-CHAP (MS-CHAP) carries out a similar challenge response process as outlined for CHAP except that the password is already encrypted using the MD4 hashing algorithm. The dial-in server compares the encrypted password sent by the client with the locally stored encrypted version of the password. MS-CHAP is not used in the smart card logon process.

F. **Incorrect:** Microsoft-CHAP version 2 (MS-CHAP v2) is more secure then MS-CHAP and is also used for PPP communications. The dial-in server sends the client a session ID and a challenge string. The PPP client responds with its username, a client challenge string, and a response to the server's challenge string that is encrypted using the Secure Hash Algorithm (SHA). SHA hashes the server and client challenge string, the session ID, and the user's encrypted password. When the dial-in server receives the response from the client, it returns a success or failure response and an authenticated response using all of the data sent to it from the client. After the client verifies the return data, the connection is established. MS-CHAP v2 is not used in the smart card logon process.

OBJECTIVE 7.5

Implement, configure, manage, and troubleshoot a security configuration.

The previous objectives in this chapter examined all of the security policies except those contained in the **Security Options** folder. On a standalone or workgroup computer, the Security Options folder is located below the Local Policies node. The policies contained in the Security Options folder are applied to the computer and affect all users who use the computer. Some of the policies are extensions of other policies, such as the Audit Use Of Backup And Restore Privilege policy setting. This policy adds to the events that can be audited on a computer running Windows 2000. Other policy settings change the default behavior of Windows 2000, such as the Disable Ctrl+Alt+Delete requirement for logon.

As you might have surmised by now, the sheer number of policy settings, file system permissions, and security groups and the way these security features interact with each other make configuring security on a single computer a complex task. Even more difficult is implementing a consistent security configuration from one computer to the next. Centralized permissions, domain-based Group Policy objects (GPOs), security groups, and user accounts ease the administrative burden of applying a consistent security configuration across the network, but they don't decrease the complexity of security configuration. **Security templates** are used for this purpose.

A security template is an .inf file containing security configuration settings. You apply the policy settings to a standalone or workgroup computer by importing them into the Security Settings node of the local GPO. To import a security template, select the Security Settings node in the Local Security Settings console and, on the Action menu, click Import Policy. You can import a security template into all of the computers in a workgroup to apply consistent security policy. You can also import a security template into a domain-based GPO. Through normal GPO client processing, the policy settings in the domain-based GPO are disseminated to all computers affected by the GPO. Microsoft includes a number of security templates in the *%systemroot%*\Security\Templates folder. Each template is a profile of security settings for a variety of computing environments requiring differing levels of security.

You can also use the **Security Configuration and Analysis snap-in** to import one or more security templates. This snap-in goes beyond applying security policy settings contained in a single template. The Security Configuration and Analysis snap-in allows you to merge multiple security templates to create a composite template and apply event log, restricted group, system services, registry, and file system configurations. You also use this snap-in to analyze a computer's security configuration against an existing security template or a composite template.

Objective 7.5 Questions

70-210.07.05.001

You are the administrator of a workgroup supporting computers running Windows 2000 Professional. Users need to run legacy applications on Windows 2000 Professional, but you do not want the users to be members of the Power Users group. Which security template type should you use?

A. Basic

B. Optional Component File Security

C. Compatible

D. Secure

E. High Secure

70-210.07.05.002

You are the administrator of a domain supporting computers running Windows 2000 Professional, Windows 98, and Windows NT 4. Windows 98 and Windows NT 4 computers access resources on computers running Windows 2000. Which types of security templates might you consider applying to the computers running Windows 2000? (Choose four.)

A. Basic

B. Optional Component File security

C. Compatible

D. Secure

E. High Secure

70-210.07.05.003

You are the administrator of a workgroup supporting computers running Windows 2000 Professional in North America. You want to configure a remote IP Security (IPSec) communication policy that will help protect against known key attacks. What should you do? (Choose four.)

A. Use the Data Encryption Standard (DES) algorithm.

B. Use the 3DES algorithm.

C. Use session key lifetimes less than 50 MB.

D. Use session key lifetimes greater than 50 MB.

E. Enable Perfect Forward Secrecy (PFS) for the master key.

F. Enable PFS for the session key.

Objective 7.5 Answers

70-210.07.05.001

► **Correct Answers: C**

A. **Incorrect:** There are three Basic security templates: BASICDC.INF for Windows 2000 domain controllers, BASICSV.INF for Windows 2000 standalone servers, and BASICWK.INF for Windows 2000 Professional workstations. The Basic security templates apply Windows 2000 default access control settings. Apply this template type if you are trying to troubleshoot a computer running Windows 2000 and you suspect that the problem is related to the security configuration. Also, to update a security configuration, apply this template type to a computer upgraded from Windows NT 4 to Windows 2000.

B. **Incorrect:** There are two Optional Component File security templates: OCFILESS.INF for Windows 2000 Server domain controller and standalone servers, and OCSFILESW.INF for Windows 2000 Professional workstations. The Optional Component File security templates apply default access control settings to Windows 2000 optional components installed during or after the Windows 2000 installation process. You should apply this type of template after applying a Basic security template.

C. **Correct:** Applying the Compatible security template, COMPATWS.INF, configures security settings that allow members of the Users group to run legacy applications. After this security configuration is applied, users do not need to be members of the Power Users group to run legacy applications.

D. **Incorrect:** There are two Secure security templates: SECUREDC.INF for Windows 2000 domain controllers and SECUREWS.INF for Windows 2000 Server standalone servers and Windows 2000 Professional workstations. This template type focuses on configuring more restrictive group membership, enabling policy settings that are part of audit policy and account policy, configuring restricted event log access, and modifying registry settings for security.

E. **Incorrect:** There are two High Secure security templates: HISECDC.INF for Windows 2000 domain controllers and HISECWS.INF for Windows 2000 Server standalone servers and Windows 2000 Professional workstations. Many of the settings in the Secure security template are even more restrictive in the High Secure security template. After applying a Secure or High Secure security template type, test the configuration thoroughly before moving the computer into a production environment.

70-210.07.05.002

▶ **Correct Answers: A, B, C, and D**

A. **Correct:** The Basic security templates apply Windows 2000 default access control settings to computers running Windows 2000. These settings are more secure than the default settings found on a computer running Windows NT 4 or Windows 98. However, down-level clients should still be able to access resources running on Windows 2000 computers configured with default access control settings.

B. **Correct:** The Optional Component File security templates apply default access control settings to Windows 2000 optional components installed during or after the Windows 2000 installation process. As described in answer explanation A, the default settings found on a computer running Windows 2000 are appropriate for down-level client access.

C. **Correct:** Applying the Compatible security template configures security settings that allow members of the Users group to run legacy applications. This is less secure than the default security settings. Therefore, down-level clients will not have trouble accessing resources secured with this template.

D. **Correct:** This template type applies a security configuration that is more secure than the default settings. However, the Secure template type does not modify file system permissions. Therefore, users configured with the appropriate permissions should still be able to access resources on this computer, even when access is achieved from a down-level client.

E. **Incorrect:** This template type applies the most secure configuration of any defined template type. Applying this template to the Windows 2000 computers accessed by Windows NT 4 or Windows 98 clients might cause access problems. Careful testing should follow the application of any template that applies a security configuration greater than the default settings.

70-210.07.05.003

▶ **Correct Answers: B, C, E, and F**

A. **Incorrect:** IPSec uses Internet Key Exchange (IKE) for security negotiation and for authentication between sender and receiver. During security negotiation, the sender and receiver agree on the encryption algorithm, the hash algorithm, the authentication method, and the length of keying material to be exchanged to create the shared master and session keys. Security negotiation might be initially encrypted, but this depends on the negotiated authentication method. IKE uses an encryption protocol to secure the authentication process, and IPSec uses an encryption algorithm to protect data following successful authentication. The encryption algorithm used in all IPSec communication is either DES or Data Encryption Standard 3 (3DES). DES is less secure than 3DES because DES uses a 56-bit key.

B. **Correct:** The 3DES encryption algorithm uses a longer key than DES for greater security. Computers running Windows 2000 require the High Encryption Pack to use the 3DES encryption algorithm. If a Windows 2000 computer not running the High Encryption Pack receives a request to negotiate 3DES encryption, it might not be able to negotiate a connection. IPSec policy determines this, which might or might not allow for the less secure DES encryption algorithm to be negotiated. Because of export restrictions, it is not legal to use the High Encryption Pack in all countries.

C. **Correct:** Session key lifetimes determine when new session keys are regenerated to continue communication between two endpoints. You can use default session key lifetimes defined in IPSec rules or specify the intervals between key regeneration. The intervals between session key regeneration are based on the amount of data transferred and the number of seconds the session key has been in use. Limiting session key lifetimes to 50 MB means that a new session key will be regenerated after 50 MB of data has been transferred.

D. **Incorrect:** Session key lifetimes longer than 50 MB of data transfer give an attacker more time to initiate a key attack.

E. **Correct:** The intervals between master key regeneration are based on the number of minutes the key has been in use and the number of session keys that have been regenerated with a single master key. Configuring intervals determines when a key is regenerated, not how. PFS determines how a new key is generated to guarantee that compromising a single key permits access only to data protected by that single key. Therefore, enabling PFS for the master key ensures that no previously used master keying material or master keys will be reused for key regeneration.

F. **Correct:** Enabling session key PFS ensures that no previously used session keys or keying material will be reused for key regeneration.

APPENDIX   A

Questions and Answers

The following questions and answers are for Part 1 of this book.

Chapter 1

Review Questions

1. What is the major difference between a workgroup and a domain?

   The major difference between a workgroup and a domain is where the user account information resides for user logon authentication. For a workgroup, user account information resides in the local security database on each computer in the workgroup. For the domain, the user account information resides in the Active Directory database.

2. What are Active Directory directory services, and what do they provide?

   Active Directory directory services comprise the Windows 2000 directory service. A directory service consists of a database that stores information about network resources, such as computers and printers, and the services that make this information available to users and applications. Active Directory directory services also provide administrators with the capability to control access to resources.

3. What information must a user provide when he or she logs on to a computer?

   A user name and a password.

4. What happens when a user logs on locally to a computer?

   Windows 2000 authenticates the user during the logon process by comparing the user's logon information to the user's information in the local database and verifies the identity of the user. Only valid users can gain access to resources and data on a computer.

5. How do you use the Windows 2000 Security dialog box?

   The Windows 2000 Security dialog box provides easy access to important security options, which include the ability to lock a computer, change a password, log off of a computer, stop programs that aren't responding, and shut down the computer.

Chapter 2

Review Questions

1. Your company has decided to install Windows 2000 Professional on all new computers that are purchased for desktop users. What should you do before you purchase new computers to ensure that Windows 2000 can be installed and run without difficulty?

   Verify that the hardware components meet the minimum requirements for Windows 2000. Also, verify that all of the hardware components that are installed in the new computers are on the Windows 2000 HCL. If a component is not listed, contact the manufacturer to verify that a Windows 2000 driver is available.

2. You are attempting to install Windows 2000 Professional from a CD-ROM; however, you have discovered that your computer doesn't support booting from the CD-ROM drive. How can you install Windows 2000?

   Start the computer by using the Setup boot disks. When prompted, insert the Windows 2000 Professional CD-ROM, and then continue setup.

3. You are installing Windows 2000 Server on a computer that will be a client in an existing Windows 2000 domain. You want to add the computer to the domain during installation. What information do you need, and which computers must be available on the network before you run the Setup program?

   You need the DNS domain name of the domain that you are joining. You must also make sure that a computer account for the client exists in the domain, or you must have the user name and password of a user account in the domain with the authority to create computer accounts in the domain. A server running the DNS service and a domain controller in the domain you are joining must be available on the network.

4. You are using a CD-ROM to install Windows 2000 Professional on a computer that was previously running another operating system. How should you configure the hard disk to simplify the installation process?

   Use a disk partitioning tool to remove any existing partitions, and then create and format a new partition for the Windows 2000 installation.

5. You are installing Windows 2000 Professional over the network. Before you install to a client computer, what must you do?

   Locate the path to the shared installation files on the distribution server. Create a 650-MB FAT partition on the target computer (2 GB recommended). Create a client disk with a network client so that you can connect from the computer, without an operating system, to the distribution server.

Chapter 3

Practice Questions

Lesson 2: Using Consoles

Practice: Creating a Customized Microsoft Management Console

▶ **To remove extensions from a snap-in**

12. Click Computer Management (Local), and then click the Extensions tab.

    The MMC displays a list of available extensions for the Computer Management snap-in.

    What option determines which extensions the MMC displays in the Available Extensions list in this dialog box?

    The available extensions depend on which snap-in you select.

Review Questions

1. When and why would you use an extension?

   You use an extension when specific snap-ins need additional functionality—extensions are snap-ins that provide additional administrative functionality to another snap-in.

2. You need to create a custom console for an administrator who needs to use only the Computer Management and Active Directory Users And Computers snap-ins. The administrator

   a. Must not be able to add any additional snap-ins.

   b. Needs full access to all snap-ins.

   c. Must be able to navigate between snap-ins.

   Which console mode would you use to configure the custom console?

   User mode, Full Access.

3. What do you need to do to remotely administer a computer running Windows 2000 Server from a computer running Windows 2000 Professional?

   Windows 2000 Professional doesn't include all snap-ins that are included with Windows 2000 Server. To enable remote administration of many Windows 2000 Server components from a computer running Windows 2000 Professional, you need to add the required snap-ins on the computer running Windows 2000 Professional.

4. You need to schedule a maintenance utility to automatically run once a week on your computer, which is running Windows 2000 Professional. How do you accomplish this?

   Use Task Scheduler to schedule the necessary maintenance utilities to run at specific times.

Chapter 4

Review Questions

1. What should you do if you can't see any output on the secondary display?

   If you can't see any output on the secondary display, try the following:
   - **Activate the device in the Display Properties dialog box.**
   - **Confirm that you chose the correct video driver.**
   - **Restart the computer and check its status in Device Manager.**
   - **Switch the order of the display adapters on the motherboard.**

2. You have configured recovery options on a computer running Windows 2000 Professional to write debugging information to a file if a system failure occurs. You notice, however, that the file isn't being created. What could be causing this problem?

   The problem could be one or more of the following:
   - **The paging file size could be set to less than the amount of physical RAM in your system.**
   - **The paging file might not be located on your boot partition.**
   - **You might not have enough free space to create the Memory.dmp file.**

3. How can you optimize virtual memory performance?

   To optimize virtual memory, do the following:
   - **If you have multiple hard disks, create a separate paging file on each hard disk.**
   - **Move the paging file off of the disk that contains the Windows 2000 system files.**
   - **Set the minimum size of the paging file to be equal to or greater than the amount of disk space that is allocated by Virtual Memory Manager when your system is operating under a typical load.**

4. You installed a new network interface card (NIC) in your computer, but it doesn't seem to be working. Describe how you would troubleshoot this problem.

   You would do the following to troubleshoot the problem:
   - **Check Device Manager to determine whether Windows 2000 properly detected the network card.**
   - **If the card isn't listed in Device Manager, run the Add/Remove Hardware wizard to have Windows 2000 detect the new card. If the card is listed in Device Manager but the icon representing the new card contains either an exclamation mark or a stop sign, view the properties of the card for further details. You might need to reinstall the drivers for the card, or the card might be causing a resource conflict.**

Chapter 5

Practice Questions

Lesson 2: Using Registry Editor

Practice: Using Registry Editor

Exercise 1: Exploring the Registry

▶ **To view information in the registry**

6. Double-click the HARDWARE\DESCRIPTION\System subkey to expand it, and then answer the following questions:

   What is the basic input/output system (BIOS) version of your computer and its date?

   Answers will vary based on the contents of the SYSTEMBIOSVERSION and SYSTEMBIOSDATE entries.

   What is the computer type of your local machine according to the Identifier entry?

   Answers might vary; it will likely be AT/AT compatible.

7. Expand the SOFTWARE\Microsoft\Windows NT\CurrentVersion subkey, and then fill in the following information.

Software configuration	Value and string
Current build number	**2195 (for Evaluation Software and retail versions)**
Current version	**5**
Registered organization	**Answers will vary.**
Registered owner	**Answers will vary.**

Review Questions

1. What is the registry and what does it do?

   The registry is a hierarchical database that stores Windows 2000 hardware and software settings. The registry controls the Windows 2000 operating system by providing the appropriate initialization information to start applications and load components, such as device drivers and network protocols. The registry contains a variety of different types of data, including the hardware installed on the computer, the installed device drivers, applications, network protocols, and network adapter card settings.

2. What is a hive?

   A hive is a discrete body of keys, subkeys, and entries. Each hive has a corresponding registry file and a .LOG file located in *systemroot*

System32\Config. **Windows 2000 uses the .LOG file to record changes and to ensure the integrity of the registry.**

3. What is the recommended editor for viewing and modifying the registry?

   Regedt32.exe is the recommended editor for viewing and modifying the registry.

4. What option should you enable when you are viewing the contents of the registry? Why?

   Using Registry Editor incorrectly can cause serious, systemwide problems that could require reinstallation of Windows 2000. When using Registry Editor to view data, save a backup copy of the registry file before viewing and click Read Only Mode on the Options menu to prevent accidental updating or deleting of configuration data.

Chapter 6

Practice Questions

Lesson 2: Common Disk Management Tasks

Practice: Working with Dynamic Storage

Exercise 2: Extending a Volume

▶ **To examine the new volume**

8. Change the working directory to the root directory of drive C (if necessary) or to the root directory of the drive where you mounted your volume, type **dir** and then press Enter.

   How much free space does the Dir command report?

   Answer will vary.

   Why is there a difference between the free space reported for drive C and the free space reported for C:\Mount? (If you mounted your volume on a drive other than drive C, replace C with the appropriate drive letter.)

   The amount of free space reported for C:\Mount is the amount of free space available on the mounted volume.

Review Questions

1. You install a new 10-GB disk drive that you want to divide into five equal 2-GB sections. What are your options?

   You can leave the disk as a basic disk and then create a combination of primary partitions (up to three) and logical drives in an extended partition; or, you can upgrade the disk to a dynamic disk and create five 2-GB simple volumes.

2. You are trying to create a striped volume on your Windows NT Server to improve performance. You confirm that you have enough unallocated disk space on two disks in your computer, but when you right-click an area of unallocated space on a disk, your only option is to create a partition. What is the problem and how would you resolve it?

You can create striped volumes only on dynamic disks. The option to create a partition rather than a volume indicates that the disk you are trying to use is a basic disk. You will need to upgrade all of the disks that you want to use in your striped volume to dynamic disks before you stripe them.

3. You add a new disk to your computer and attempt to extend an existing volume to include the unallocated space on the new disk, but the option to extend the volume isn't available. What is the problem and how would you resolve it?

The existing volume is not formatted with Microsoft Windows 2000 File System (NTFS). You can extend only NTFS volumes. You should back up any data on the existing volume, convert it to NTFS, and then extend the volume.

4. You dual boot your computer with Windows 98 and Windows 2000 Professional. You upgrade a second drive—which you are using to archive files—from basic storage to dynamic storage. The next time you try to access your archived files from Windows 98, you are unable to read the files. Why?

Only Windows 2000 can read dynamic storage.

Chapter 7

Practice Questions

Lesson 1: TCP/IP

Practice: Installing and Configuring TCP/IP

Exercise 2: Configuring TCP/IP to Use a Static IP Address

▶ **To test the static TCP/IP configuration**

6. To verify that the IP address is working and configured for your adapter, type **ping 127.0.0.1** and then press Enter.

What happens?

Four Reply from 127.0.0.l messages should appear.

7. If you have a computer that you are using to test connectivity, type **ping ip_address** (where *ip_address* is the IP address of the computer you are using to test connectivity), and then press Enter. If you don't have a computer to test connectivity, skip to step 8.

What happens?

Four Reply from *ip_address* messages should appear.

Exercise 3: Configuring TCP/IP to Automatically Obtain an IP Address

▶ **To configure TCP/IP to automatically obtain an IP address**

4. Click Obtain An IP Address Automatically.

   Which IP address settings will the DHCP Service configure for your computer?

   IP address and subnet mask.

Exercise 4: Obtaining an IP Address by Using Automatic Private IP Addressing

▶ **To obtain an IP address by using Automatic Private IP Addressing**

2. At the command prompt, type **ipconfig /renew** and then press Enter.

   There will be a pause while Windows 2000 attempts to locate a DHCP server on the network.

   What message appears, and what does it indicate?

   DHCP Server Unreachable.

   Your computer was not assigned an address from a DHCP server because there wasn't one available.

▶ **To test the TCP/IP configuration**

1. At the command prompt, type **ipconfig | more** and then press Enter.

2. Pressing Spacebar as necessary, record the current TCP/IP settings for your local area connection in the following table.

Setting	Value
IP address	**Answer will vary.**
Subnet mask	**Answer will vary.**
Default gateway	**Answer will vary.**

   Is this the same IP address assigned to your computer in Exercise 3? Why or why not?

   No, the IP address isn't the same as the one assigned in Exercise 3. In this exercise, the Automatic Private IP Addressing feature of Windows 2000 assigned the IP address because a DHCP server wasn't available. In Exercise 3, the DHCP Service assigned an IP address.

5. If you have a computer to test TCP/IP connectivity with your computer, type **ping *ip_address*** (where *ip_address* is the IP address of the computer that you are using to test connectivity), and then press Enter. If you don't have a computer to test connectivity, skip this step and proceed to Exercise 5.

   Were you successful? Why or why not?

Answers will vary. If you don't have a computer that you can use to test your computer's connectivity, you can't do this exercise.

- No, because the computer you are using to test your computer's connectivity is configured with a static IP address in another network and no default gateway is configured on your computer.

- Yes, because the computer you are using to test your computer's connectivity is also configured with an IP address assigned by Automatic Private IP Addressing and it is on the same subnet so that a default gateway is unnecessary.

Lesson 2: NWLink

Practice: Installing and Configuring NWLink

▶ **To install and configure NWLink**

4. Click Protocol, and then click Add.

   The Select Network Protocol dialog box appears.

   Which protocols can you install?

   AppleTalk, DLC, NetBEUI, Network Monitor Driver, and NWLink IPX/SPX/NetBIOS Compatible Transport Protocol.

6. Select NWLink IPX/SPX/NetBIOS Compatible Transport Protocol, and then click Properties.

   Which type of frame detection is selected by default?

   Auto frame type detection.

Lesson 4: Network Bindings

Practice: Working with Network Bindings

Exercise 1: Changing the Binding Order of a Protocol

▶ **To change the protocol binding order**

2. Maximize the Network And Dial-Up Connections window, and on the Advanced menu, click Advanced Settings.

   The Advanced Settings dialog box appears.

   What is the order of the protocols listed under Client For Microsoft Networks in the Bindings For Local Area Connection list?

   The first protocol listed under Client For Microsoft Networks is NWLink IPX/SPX/NetBIOS Compatible Transport Protocol, and the second one is Internet Protocol (TCP/IP).

Review Questions

1. Your computer running Windows 2000 Client for Microsoft Networks was configured manually for TCP/IP. You can connect to any host on your own subnet, but you can't connect to or even ping any host on a remote subnet. What is the likely cause of the problem and how would you fix it?

   The default gateway might be missing or incorrect. You specify the default gateway in the Internet Protocol (TCP/IP) Properties dialog box (under Network And Dial-Up Connections in My Network Places). Other possibilities are that the default gateway is offline or that the subnet mask is incorrect.

2. Your computer running Windows 2000 Professional can communicate with some, but not all, of the NetWare servers on your network. Some of the NetWare servers are running frame type 802.2 and some are running 802.3. What is the likely cause of the problem?

   Although the NWLink implementation in Windows 2000 can automatically detect a frame type for IPX/SPX-compatible protocols, it can automatically detect only one frame type. This network uses two frame types; you must manually configure the additional frame type (802.3).

3. What are the limitations of the NetBEUI protocol?

   NetBEUI can't be routed and therefore is not suitable for WANs. Since NetBEUI isn't routable, you must connect computers running Windows 2000 and NetBEUI by using bridges instead of routers.

   The NetBEUI protocol relies on broadcasts for many of its functions, such as name registration and discovery, so it creates more broadcast traffic than other protocols.

4. What is the primary function of the DLC protocol?

   DLC provides connectivity to IBM mainframes and to LAN print devices that are directly attached to the network.

5. What is the significance of the binding order of network protocols?

   You specify the binding order to optimize network performance. For example, a computer running Windows 2000 Workstation has NetBEUI, NWLink IPX/SPX, and TCP/IP installed. However, most of the servers to which this computer connects are running only TCP/IP. You would adjust the binding order so that the workstation binding to TCP/IP is listed before the workstation bindings for the other protocols. In this way, when a user attempts to connect to a server, Client for Microsoft Networks first attempts to use TCP/IP to establish the connection.

Chapter 8

Review Questions

1. What is the function of the following DNS components?

   Domain name space

   The domain name space provides the hierarchical structure for the DNS distributed database.

   Zones

   Zones are used to divide the domain name space into administrative units.

   Name servers

   Name servers store the zone information and perform name resolution for their authoritative domain name spaces.

2. Why would you want to have multiple name servers?

   Installing multiple name servers provides redundancy, reduces the load on the server that stores the primary zone database file, and allows for faster access speed for remote locations.

3. What's the difference between a forward lookup query and a reverse lookup query?

   A forward lookup query resolves a name to an IP address. A reverse lookup query resolves an IP address to a name.

4. When would you configure your connection to obtain a DNS server address automatically?

   Configure your connection to obtain a DNS server address automatically only if you have a functioning DHCP server on the network that can provide the IP address of functioning DNS servers on the network.

Chapter 9

Review Questions

1. What are four major features of Active Directory directory services?

   Active Directory directory services offer simplified administration, scaleability, open standards support, and support for standard name formats.

2. What are sites and domains, and how are they different?

   A site is a combination of one or more IP subnets that should be connected by a high-speed link.

   A domain is a logical grouping of servers and other network resources organized under a single name.

A site is a component of Active Directory directory services' physical structure, while a domain is a component of the logical structure.

3. What is the schema, and how can you extend it?

The schema contains a formal definition of the contents and structure of Active Directory directory services, including all attributes, classes, and class properties. You can extend the schema by using the Schema Manager snap-in or the Active Directory Services Interface (ADSI).

4. Which Windows 2000 products provide Active Directory directory services?

Only the Windows 2000 Server products, which include Windows 2000 Server, Windows 2000 Advanced Server, and Windows 2000 Datacenter, provide Active Directory directory services. Windows 2000 Professional doesn't provide Active Directory directory services, but clients running Windows 2000 Professional that are members of a domain can use Active Directory directory services.

Chapter 10

Review Questions

1. Where does Windows 2000 create local user accounts?

When you create a local user account, Windows 2000 creates the account only in that computer's security database.

2. What different capabilities do domain user accounts and local user accounts provide to users?

A domain user account allows a user to log on to the domain from any computer in the network and to gain access to resources anywhere in the domain, provided the user has permission to access these resources. A local user account allows the user to log on at and gain access to resources on only the computer where you create the local user account.

3. What should you consider when you plan new user accounts?

- A naming convention that ensures unique but consistent user account names.
- Whether you or the user will determine the user account password.
- Whether the user account should be disabled.

4. What information is required to create a local user account?

A user name.

5. What are built-in user accounts and what are they used for?

Windows 2000 automatically creates accounts called built-in accounts. Two commonly used built-in accounts are Administrator and Guest. You use the built-in Administrator account to manage the overall computer (for example, creating and modifying user accounts and groups, and setting account properties on user accounts). You use the built-in Guest account to give occasional users the ability to log on and gain access to resources.

Chapter 11

Review Questions

1. Why should you use groups?

   Use groups to simplify administration by granting rights and assigning permissions once to the group rather than multiple times to each individual member.

2. How do you create a local group?

   Start the Computer Management snap-in and expand Local Users And Groups. Right-click Groups, and then click New Group. Fill in the appropriate fields and then click Create.

3. Are there any consequences to deleting a group?

   When you delete a group, the unique identifier that the system uses to represent the group is lost. Even if you create a second group with the same name, the group will not have the same identifier, so you must grant the group any permissions or rights that it once had, and you must add back the users who need to be a member of that group.

4. What's the difference between built-in local groups and local groups?

   You create local groups and assign the appropriate permissions to them.

   Windows 2000 Professional comes with precreated built-in local groups. You can't create built-in local groups. Built-in local groups give rights to perform system tasks on a single computer, such as backing up and restoring files, changing the system time, and administering system resources.

Chapter 12

Review Questions

1. What's the difference between a printer and a print device?

   A printer is the software interface between the operating system and the print device. The print device is the hardware device that produces printed documents.

2. A print server can connect to two different types of print devices. What are these two types of print devices, and what are the differences?

   The two types are local and network-interface print devices. A local print device is connected directly to a physical port of the print server.

A network-interface print device is connected to the print server through the network. Also, a network-interface print device requires a network interface card.

3. You have added and shared a printer. What must you do to set up client computers running Windows 2000 so that users can print, and why?

You (or the user) must make a connection to the printer from the client computer. When you make a connection to the printer from the client computer, Windows 2000 automatically copies the printer driver to the client computer.

4. What advantages does connecting to a printer by using http://*server_name*/printers provide for users?

It allows a user to make a connection to a printer without having to use the Add Printer wizard. It makes a connection to a Web site, which displays all of the printers for which the user has permission. The Web site also provides information on the printers to help the user make the correct selection. Also, a Web designer can customize this Web page, such as by displaying a floor plan that shows the location of print devices, which makes it easier for users to choose a print device.

5. Why would you connect multiple printers to one print device?

To set priorities between the printers so that users can send critical documents to the printer with the highest priority. These documents will always print before documents that are sent from printers with lower priorities.

6. Why would you create a printer pool?

To speed up printing. Users can print to one printer that has several print devices so that documents do not wait in the print queue. It also simplifies administration; it's easier to manage one printer for several print devices than it is to manage one printer for each print device.

Chapter 13

Practice Questions

Lesson 2: Managing Printers
Practice: Performing Printer Management
Exercise 3: Taking Ownership of a Printer

▶ **To take ownership of a printer**

2. On the Security tab, click Advanced, and then click the Owner tab.

Who currently owns the printer?

The Administrators group.

Lesson 3: Managing Documents

Practice: Managing Documents

▶ **To set a notification**

3. In the printer's window, select README.txt, and then click Properties on the Document menu.

   Windows 2000 displays the README.txt Document Properties dialog box with the General tab active.

   Which user is specified in the Notify box? Why?

   The Notify box currently displays the user Administrator because Administrator printed the document.

▶ **To increase the priority of a document**

1. In the README.txt Document Properties dialog box, on the General tab, notice the default priority.

   What is the current priority? Is it the lowest or highest priority?

   The current priority is the default of 1, which is the lowest priority.

Review Questions

1. For which printer permission does a user need to change the priority on another user's document?

   The Manage Documents permission.

2. In an environment where many users print to the same print device, how can you help reduce the likelihood of users picking up the wrong documents?

   Create a separator page that identifies and separates printed documents.

3. Can you redirect a single document?

   No. You can change the configuration of the print server only to send documents to another printer or print device, which redirects all documents on that printer.

4. A user needs to print a large document. How can the user print the job after hours, without being present while the document prints?

   You can control print jobs by setting the printing time. You set the printing time for a document on the General tab of the Properties dialog box for the document. To open the Properties dialog box for a document, select the document in the printer's window, click the Document menu, and then click Properties. Click Only From in the Schedule section of the Properties dialog box, and then set the Only From hour to the earliest time you want the document to begin printing after regular business hours. Set the To time to a couple of hours before normal business hours start. To set the printing time for a document, you must be the owner of

the document or have the Manage Documents permission for the appropriate printer.

5. What are the advantages of using a Web browser to administer printing?

You can administer any printer on a Windows 2000 print server on the intranet by using any computer running a Web browser, regardless of whether the computer is running Windows 2000 or has the correct printer driver installed. Additionally, a Web browser provides a summary page and reports real-time print device status, and you can customize the interface.

Chapter 14

Practice Questions

Lesson 3: Assigning NTFS Permissions

Practice: Planning and Assigning NTFS Permissions

Exercise 1: Planning NTFS Permissions

When you apply custom permissions to a folder or file, which default permission entry should you remove?

The Full Control permission for the Everyone group.

Complete the following table to plan and record your permissions:

Path	User account or group	NTFS permissions	Block inheritance (yes/no)
Apps	Administrators group	Full Control	Yes
Apps\WordProcessing	Users group	Read & Execute	No
Apps\Spreadsheet	Accounting group Managers group Executives group	Read & Execute Read & Execute Read & Execute	No
Apps\Database	Accounting group Managers group Executives group	Read & Execute Read & Execute Read & Execute	No
Public	Administrators group Creator Owner Users group	Full Control Full Control Write	Yes
Public\Library	Administrators group Users group	Full Control Read & Execute	Yes
Public\Manuals	Administrators group Users group User81	Full Control Read & Execute Modify	Yes

Exercise 2: Assigning NTFS Permissions for the Public Folder

▶ **To remove permissions from the Everyone group**

4. Click the Security tab to display the permissions for the Public folder.

   Windows 2000 displays the Public Properties dialog box with the Security tab active.

   What are the existing folder permissions?

   The Everyone group has Full Control.

   Notice that the current allowed permissions can't be modified.

5. Under Name, select the Everyone group, and then click Remove.

   What do you see?

   Windows 2000 displays a message box indicating that you can't remove "Everyone" because the folder is inheriting the permissions for the Everyone group from its parent folder. To change permissions for Everyone, you must first block inheritance.

8. Click Remove.

   What are the existing folder permissions?

   No permissions are currently assigned.

▶ **To assign permissions to the Users group for the Public folder**

4. Click OK to return to the Public Properties dialog box.

   What are the existing allowed folder permissions?

   The Users group has the following permissions: Read & Execute, List Folder Contents, and Read. These are the default permissions that Windows 2000 assigns when you add a user account or group to the list of permissions.

▶ **To assign permissions to the CREATOR OWNER group for the Public folder**

7. Under Permission Entries, select CREATOR OWNER if necessary.

   Which permissions are assigned to CREATOR OWNER, and where do these permissions apply?

   Full Control permission is applied to subfolders and files only. Permissions that are assigned to the CREATOR OWNER group are not applied to the folder but only to new files and folders that are created within the folder.

▶ **To test the folder permissions that you assigned for the Public folder**

3. In the Public folder, attempt to create a text file named User81.

   Were you successful? Why or why not?

   Yes, because the Users group is assigned the Write permission for the Public folder.

Exercise 4: Testing NTFS Permissions

▶ **To test permissions for the Misc folder while logged on as User81**

3. Attempt to create a file in the Misc folder.

   Were you successful? Why or why not?

   No, because only User82 has NTFS permissions to create and modify files in the Misc folder.

▶ **To test permissions for the Misc folder while logged on as User82**

3. Attempt to create a file in the Misc folder.

   Were you successful? Why or why not?

   Yes, because User82 has the Modify permission for the folder.

▶ **To test permissions for the Manuals folder while logged on as Administrator**

3. Attempt to create a file in the Manuals folder.

   Were you successful? Why or why not?

   Yes, because the Administrators group has the Full Control permission for the Manuals folder.

▶ **To test permissions for the Manuals folder while logged on as User81**

3. Attempt to create a file in the Manuals folder.

   Were you successful? Why or why not?

   No, because User81 has only the Read & Execute permission for the Manuals folder.

▶ **To test permissions for the Manuals folder while logged on as User82**

3. Attempt to create a file in the Manuals folder.

   Were you successful? Why or why not?

   Yes, because User82 is a member of the Accounting group, which has been assigned the Modify permission for the Manuals folder.

Lesson 6: Solving Permissions Problems

Practice: Managing NTFS Permissions

Exercise 1: Taking Ownership of a File

► **To determine the permissions for a file**

4. Click the Security tab to display the permissions for the Owner.txt file.

What are the current allowed permissions for Owner.txt?

The Administrators group has the Full Control permission.

The Users group has the Read & Execute permission.

6. Click the Owner tab.

Who is the current owner of the Owner.txt file?

The Administrators group.

► **To take ownership of a file**

6. Click Advanced to display the Access Control Settings For Owner dialog box, and then click the Owner tab.

Who is the current owner of Owner.txt?

The Administrators group.

7. In the Change Owner To box, select User84, and then click Apply.

Who is the current owner of Owner.txt?

User84.

Exercise 2: Copying and Moving Folders

► **To create a folder while logged on as a user**

1. While you are logged on as User84, in Windows Explorer, in drive C, create a folder named Temp1.

What are the permissions that are assigned to the folder?

The Everyone group has Full Control.

Who is the owner? Why?

User84 is the owner because the person who creates a folder or file is the owner.

► **To create a folder while logged on as Administrator**

2. In drive C, create the following two folders: Temp2 and Temp3.

What are the permissions for the folders that you just created?

The Everyone group has the Full Control permission.

Who is the owner of the Temp2 and Temp3 folders? Why?

The Administrators group is the owner of the Temp2 and Temp3 folders because a member of the Administrators group created these folders.

▶ **To copy a folder to another folder within a Windows 2000 NTFS volume**

2. Select C:\Temp1\Temp2, and then compare the permissions and ownership with C:\Temp2.

Who is the owner of C:\Temp1\Temp2 and what are the permissions? Why?

The owner is still the Administrators group because you are logged on as Administrator. When a folder or file is copied within an NTFS volume, the person who copies the folder or file becomes the owner.

The Everyone group has the Full Control permission because when a folder or file is copied within an NTFS volume, the folder or file inherits the permissions of the folder into which it is copied.

▶ **To move a folder within the same NTFS volume**

2. In Windows Explorer, select C:\Temp3, and then move it to C:\Temp1.

What happens to the permissions and ownership for C:\Temp1\Temp3? Why?

The Backup Operators group has Read & Execute permission and the Users group has Full Control. The Administrators group is the owner of C:\Temp1\Temp3.

C:\Temp1\Temp3 retains the original permissions as C:\Temp3. This is because when a file or folder is moved within the same NTFS volume, the file or folder retains its original permissions. Even though User84 did the moving, the folder's creator remains the owner.

Exercise 3: Deleting a File With All Permissions Denied

▶ **To view the result of the Full Control permission for a folder**

1. In Windows Explorer, double-click Noaccess.txt in the Fullaccess folder to open the file.

Were you successful? Why or why not?

No. The Everyone group has been denied the Full Control permission for C:\ FullControl\Noaccess.txt. The Administrator user account is a member of the Everyone group.

4. Delete Noaccess.txt.

Were you successful? Why or why not?

Yes, because Full Control includes the Delete Subfolders and Files special permission for POSIX compliance. This special permission allows a user to delete files in the root of a folder to which the user has been assigned the Full Control permission. This permission overrides the file permissions.

How would you prevent users with Full Control permission for a folder from deleting a file in that folder for which they have been denied the Full Control permission?

Allow users all of the individual permissions, and then deny users the Delete Subfolders and Files special permission.

Review Questions

1. What is the default permission when a volume is formatted with NTFS? Who has access to the volume?

   The default permission is Full Control. The Everyone group has access to the volume.

2. If a user has Write permission for a folder and is also a member of a group with Read permission for the folder, what are the user's effective permissions for the folder?

   The user has both Read permission and Write permission for the folder because NTFS permissions are cumulative.

3. If you assign the Modify permission to a user account for a folder and the Read permission for a file, and then you copy the file to that folder, which permission does the user have for the file?

   The user can modify the file because the file inherits the Modify permission from the folder.

4. What happens to permissions that are assigned to a file when the file is moved from one folder to another folder on the same NTFS volume? What happens when the file is moved to a folder on another NTFS volume?

   When the file is moved from one folder to another folder on the same NTFS volume, the file retains its permissions. When the file is moved to a folder on a different NTFS volume, the file inherits the permissions of the destination folder.

5. If an employee leaves the company, what must you do to transfer ownership of his or her files and folders to another employee?

   You must be logged on as Administrator to take ownership of the employee's folders and files. Assign the Take Ownership special access permission to another employee to allow that employee to take ownership of the folders and files. Notify the employee to whom you assigned Take Ownership to take ownership of the folders and files.

6. What three details should you check when a user can't gain access to a resource?

Check the permissions that are assigned to the user account and to groups in which the user is a member.

Check whether the user account, or a group of which the user is a member, has been denied permission for the file or folder.

Check whether the folder or file has been copied to any other file or folder or moved to another volume. If it has, the permissions will have changed.

Chapter 15

Practice Questions

Lesson 1: Understanding Shared Folders

Practice: Applied Permissions

1. User101 is a member of Group1, Group2, and Group3. Group1 has Read permission and Group3 has Full Control permission for FolderA. Group2 has no permissions assigned for FolderA. What are User101's effective permissions for FolderA?

Since User101 gets the permissions of all groups, User101's effective permission for FolderA is Full Control, which also includes all capabilities of the Read permission.

2. User101 is also a member of the Sales group, which has the Read permission for FolderB. User101 has been denied the shared folder permission Full Control for FolderB as an individual user. What are User101's effective permissions for FolderB?

User101 has no access to FolderB. Even though User101 is a member of the Sales group, which has Read permission for FolderB, User101 has been denied Full Control access to FolderB. Denied permissions override all other permissions.

Lesson 4: Combining Shared Folder Permissions and NTFS Permissions

Practice: Managing Shared Folders

Exercise 1: Combining Permissions

1. In the first example, the Data folder is shared. The Sales group has the shared folder Read permission for the Data folder and the NTFS Full Control permission for the Sales subfolder.

What are the Sales group's effective permissions for the Sales subfolder when they gain access to the Sales subfolder by making a connection to the Data shared folder?

The Sales group has the Read permission for the Sales subfolder because when shared folder permissions are combined with NTFS permissions, the more restrictive permission applies.

2. In the second example, the Users folder contains user home folders. Each user home folder contains data that is accessible only to the user for whom the folder is named. The Users folder has been shared, and the Users group has the shared folder Full Control permission for the Users folder. User1 and User2 have the NTFS Full Control permission for *only* their home folder and no NTFS permissions for other folders. These users are all members of the Users group.

What permissions does User1 have when he or she accesses the User1 subfolder by making a connection to the Users shared folder? What are User1's permissions for the User2 subfolder?

User1 has the Full Control permission for the User1 subfolder because both the shared folder permission and the NTFS permission allow Full Control. User1 can't access the User2 subfolder because she or he has no NTFS permissions to gain access to it.

Exercise 2: Planning Shared Folders

Record your answers in the table.

You have two choices for permissions. You can rely entirely on NTFS permissions and assign Full Control for all shared folders to the Everyone group, or you can use shared folder permissions according to resource needs. The following suggested shared folders include required permissions if you decide to assign shared folder permissions.

-   **Share Management Guidelines as MgmtGd. Assign the Full Control permission to the Managers group.**

-   **Share Data as Data. Assign the Full Control permission to the Administrators built-in group.**

-   **Share Data\Customer Service as CustServ. Assign the Change permission to the Customer Service group.**

-   **Share Data\Public as Public. Assign the Change permission to the Users built-in group.**

-   **Share Applications as Apps. Assign the Read permission to the Users built-in group and the Full Control permission to the Administrators built-in group.**

-   **Share Project Management as ProjMan. Assign the Change permission to the Managers group and the Full Control permission to the Administrators built-in group.**

- Share Database\Customers as CustDB. Assign the Change permission to the CustomerDBFull group, the Read permission to the CustomerDBRead group, and the Full Control permission to the Administrators built-in group.

- Share Users as Users. Create a folder for every employee below this folder. Assign the Full Control permission to each employee for his or her own folder. Preferably, have Windows 2000 create the folder and assign permissions automatically when you create each user account.

Exercise 4: Assigning Shared Folder Permissions

▶ **To assign Full Control to the Administrators group**

3. Click OK.

   Windows 2000 adds Administrators to the list of names with permissions.

   Which type of access does Windows 2000 assign to Administrators by default?

   The Read permission.

4. In the Permissions box, under Allow, click the Full Control check box.

   Why did Windows Explorer also select the Change permission for you?

   Full Control includes both the Change permission and the Read permission.

Exercise 5 (Optional): Connecting to a Shared Folder

▶ **To connect a network drive to a shared folder by using the Map Network Drive command**

5. To complete the connection, click Finish.

   Windows 2000 displays the MktApps On 'PRO1' (P:) window.

   How does Windows Explorer indicate that this drive points to a remote shared folder?

   Windows Explorer uses an icon that shows a network cable attached to the drive. The network cable icon indicates a mapped network drive.

Exercise 8 (Optional): Testing NTFS and Shared Folder Permissions

▶ **To test permissions for the Manuals folder when a user logs on locally**

3. In the Manuals folder, attempt to create a file.

   Were you successful? Why or why not?

   No. Only Administrators have the NTFS permission to create and modify files in the Manuals folder.

▶ **To test permissions for the Manuals folder when a user makes a connection over the network**

7. In the Manuals window, attempt to create a file.

Were you successful? Why or why not?

No. Although the Users group has the Full Control shared folder permission for \\PRO1\MktApps, only Administrators have the NTFS permission to create and modify files in the Manuals folder.

▶ **To test permissions for the Manuals folder when a user logs on over the network as Administrator**

4. In the Manuals window, attempt to create a file.

Were you successful? Why or why not?

Yes. Administrator has the Full Control NTFS permission for the folder and Full Control Shared folder permissions for \\PRO1\MktApps\Manuals.

▶ **To test permissions for the Public folder when a user makes a connection over the network**

5. In the Public window, attempt to create a file.

Were you successful? Why or why not?

Yes. User1 has the Full Control NTFS permission for the folder and Full Control Shared folder permissions for \\PRO1\MktApps\Public.

Review Questions

1. When a folder is shared on a FAT volume, what does a user with the Full Control shared folder permissions for the folder have access to?

   All folders and files in the shared folder.

2. What are the shared folder permissions?

   Full Control, Change, and Read.

3. By default, what are the permissions that are assigned to a shared folder?

   The Everyone group is assigned the Full Control permission.

4. When a folder is shared on an NTFS volume, what does a user with the Full Control shared folder permissions for the folder have access to?

   Only the folder, but not necessarily any of the folder's contents. The user would also need NTFS permissions for each file and subfolder in the shared folder to gain access to those files and subfolders.

5. When you share a public folder, why should you use centralized data folders?

   Centralized data folders enable data to be backed up easily.

6. What is the best way to secure files and folders that you share on NTFS partitions?

Put the files that you want to share in a shared folder and keep the default shared folder permission (the Everyone group with the Full Control permission for the shared folder). Assign NTFS permissions to users and groups to control access to all contents in the shared folder or to individual files.

Chapter 16

Review Questions

1. What two tasks must you perform to audit access to a file?

Set the audit policy for object access and configure the file for the type of access to audit.

2. Who can set up auditing for a computer?

By default, only members of the Administrators group can set up and administer auditing. You can also give other users the Manage Auditing and Security log user right, which is required to configure an audit policy and review audit logs.

3. When you view a security log, how do you determine whether an event failed or succeeded?

Successful events appear with a key icon; unsuccessful events appear with a lock icon.

4. If you click the Do Not Overwrite Events option in the Properties dialog box for an audit log, what happens when the log file becomes full?

Windows 2000 will stop. You must clear the log manually.

Chapter 17

Practice Questions

Lesson 1: Configuring Account Policies

Practice: Configuring Account Policies

Exercise 2: Configuring and Testing Additional Account Policies Settings

▶ **To configure Account Policies settings**

1. Use the Group Policy snap-in to configure the following Account Policies settings:

   - A user should have at least five different passwords before he or she accesses a previously used password.

- After changing a password, a user must wait 24 hours before changing it again.
- A user should change his or her password every three weeks.

Which settings did you use for each of the three listed items?

Set Enforce Password History to 5 so that a user must have at least five different passwords before he or she can access a previously used password.

Set Minimum Password Age to one day so that a user must wait 24 hours before he or she can change it again.

Set Maximum Password Age to 21 days so that a user must change his/her password every three weeks.

▶ **To test Account Policies settings**

2. Change your password to *waters*.

   Were you successful? Why or why not?

   You were successful because the minimum password length is set to 6, and the password *waters* contains six characters.

3. Change your password to *papers*.

   Were you successful? Why or why not?

   You weren't successful because you must wait 24 hours (one day) before you can change your password a second time. A Change Password dialog box appeared indicating that you can't change the password at this time.

Exercise 3: Configuring Account Lockout Policy

▶ **To configure the Account Lockout Policy settings**

5. Use Account Lockout Policy settings to do the following:

   - Lock out a user account after four failed logon attempts.
   - Lock out user accounts until the administrator unlocks the user account.

   Which Account Lockout Policy settings did you use for each of the two conditions?

   Set Account Lockout Threshold to 4 to lock out a user account after four failed logon attempts. When you set one of the three Account Lockout Policy options and the other two options have not been set, a dialog box appears indicating that the other two options will be set to default values.

   Set Account Lockout Duration to 0 to have locked accounts remain locked until the administrator unlocks them.

Review Questions

1. Why would you want to force users to change passwords?

   Forcing users to change passwords regularly will decrease the chances of an unauthorized person breaking into your computer. If a user account and password combination for your computer falls into unauthorized hands, forcing users to change their passwords regularly will cause the user account and password combination to fail and secure the computer.

2. Why would you want to control the length of the passwords used on your computers?

   Longer passwords are more difficult to figure out because there are more characters to discover. In general, you want to do what you can to make it difficult to get unauthorized access to your computers.

3. Why would you want to lock out a user account?

   If a user forgets his or her password, he or she can ask the administrator to reset the password. If someone repeatedly enters an incorrect password, the person is probably trying to gain unauthorized access to your computer. Setting a limit on the number of failed logon attempts and locking out any user account that exceeds this number makes it more difficult for someone to gain unauthorized access to your computers.

4. Why would you want to force users to press Ctrl+Alt+Delete before they can log on to your computers?

   To increase security on your computers, you can force users to press Ctrl+Alt+Delete before they can log on. This key combination is recognized only by Windows and ensures that only Windows is receiving the password and not a Trojan horse program waiting to capture your password.

5. How do you prevent the last user name from being displayed in the Windows Security or Log On To Windows dialog box?

   To prevent the last user name from being displayed in the Windows Security or Log On To Windows dialog box, click the Local Policies node in the console tree of the Local Security Settings window, and then click Security Options. In the details pane, right-click Do Not Display Last User Name In Logon Screen, click Security, and then disable this feature.

Chapter 18

Practice Questions

Lesson 1: Managing NTFS Compression

Practice: Managing NTFS Compression

Exercise 1: Compressing Files in an NTFS Partition

▶ **To view the capacity and free space for drive C**

2. Right-click drive C, and then click Properties.

   Windows 2000 displays the Local Disk (C:) Properties dialog box with the General tab active.

   What is the capacity of drive C?

   Answers will vary.

   What is the free space on drive C?

   Answers will vary.

▶ **To uncompress a folder**

5. Click OK to close the CompTest2 Properties dialog box.

   Since the CompTest2 folder is empty, Windows 2000 doesn't display the Confirm Attributes Changes dialog box asking you to specify whether to uncompress only this folder or this folder and all subfolders.

   What indication do you have that the CompTest2 folder is no longer compressed?

   The CompTest2 folder name is displayed in black.

Exercise 2: Copying and Moving Files

▶ **To create a compressed file**

3. Type **Text1** and then press Enter.

   How can you verify that Text1 is compressed?

   The name of the file is displayed in blue. You could also check the properties for the file.

▶ **To copy a compressed file to an uncompressed folder**

2. Examine the properties for Text1 in the CompTest2 folder.

   Is the Text1.txt file in the CompTest\CompTest2 folder compressed or uncompressed? Why?

   Uncompressed. A new file inherits the compression attribute of the folder in which it is created.

▶ **To move a compressed file to an uncompressed folder**

1. Examine the properties of the Text1.txt file in the CompTest folder.

   Is Text1.txt compressed or uncompressed?

   Compressed.

3. Examine the properties of Text1.txt in the CompTest2 folder.

   Is Text1.txt compressed or uncompressed? Why?

   Compressed. When a file is moved to a new folder on the same partition, its compression attribute doesn't change.

Lesson 2: Managing Disk Quotas

Practice: Enabling and Disabling Disk Quotas

Exercise 1: Configuring Quota Management Settings

▶ **To configure default quota management settings**

4. On the Quota tab, click the Enable Quota Management check box.

   What is the default disk space limit for new users?

   1 KB.

▶ **To configure quota management settings for a user**

1. On the Quota tab of the Local Disk (C:) Properties dialog box, click the Quota Entries button.

   Windows 2000 displays the Quota Entries For Local Disk (C:) window.

   Are any user accounts listed? Why or why not?

   Yes. The accounts listed are those that have logged on and gained access to drive C.

5. Click OK.

   Windows 2000 displays the Add New Quota Entry dialog box.

   What are the default settings for the user you just set a quota limit for?

   Limit disk space to 10 MB and Set the warning level to 6 MB. These are the default settings that are selected for drive C.

▶ **To test quota management settings**

5. Copy the i386 folder from your CD-ROM to the User5 folder.

Windows 2000 Professional begins copying files from the i386 folder on the CD-ROM to a new i386 folder in the User5 folder on drive C. After copying several files, however, Windows 2000 displays the Error Copying File Or Folder dialog box indicating that there isn't enough room on the disk.

Why did you get this error message?

You have exceeded your quota limit and since the Deny Disk Space To Users Exceeding Quota Limit check box is selected, once you exceed your quota limit, you can't use more disk space.

Lesson 3: Increasing Security with EFS

Practice: Encrypting and Decrypting Files

Exercise 2: Testing the Encrypted Files

▶ **To test an encrypted file**

2. Start Windows Explorer and open the file File1.txt in the Secret folder.

What happens?

A Notepad dialog box appears indicating that Access Is Denied.

Review Questions

1. You are the administrator for a computer running Windows 2000 Professional. You want to restrict users to 25 MB of available storage space. How do you configure the volumes on the computer?

Format all volumes with NTFS and enable disk quotas for all of the volumes. Specify a limit of 25 MB and select the Deny Disk Space To Users Exceeding Quota Limit check box.

2. The Sales department archives legacy sales data on a network computer running Windows 2000 Professional. Several other departments share the server. You have begun to receive complaints from users in other departments that the computer has little remaining disk space. What can you do to alleviate the problem?

Compress the folders that the Sales department uses to store archive data.

3. Your department has recently archived several gigabytes of data from a computer running Windows 2000 Professional to CD-ROMs. As users have been adding files to the computer, you have noticed that the computer has been taking longer than usual to gain access to the hard disk. How can you increase disk access time for the computer?

Use Disk Defragmenter to defragment files on the computer's hard disk.

Chapter 19

Practice Questions

Lesson 2: Backing Up Data

Practice: Backing Up Files

Exercise 1: Starting a Backup Job

▶ **To back up files by using Backup wizard**

14. Click Replace The Data On The Media With This Backup.

    When is it appropriate to select the check box labeled Allow Only The Owner And The Administrator Access To The Backup Data And To Any Backups Appended To This Media?

    Unless the data that is being backed up will be restored by anyone other than the person doing the backing up or an administrator, you should consider selecting this check box if you want to minimize the risk of unauthorized access to your data.

Exercise 2: Creating and Running an Unattended Backup Job

▶ **To verify that the backup job was performed**

1. Start Microsoft Windows Explorer and click drive C.

   Does the Backup2.bkf file exist?

   Yes.

Lesson 3: Restoring Data

Practice: Restoring Files

▶ **To verify that the data was restored**

1. Start Windows Explorer and expand drive C.

   Does the Restored Data folder exist?

   Yes.

   What are the contents of the Restored Data folder?

   The file Boot.ini.

Review Questions

1. If you want a user to perform backups, what do you need to do?

   Make sure that the user is a member of the Administrators or Backup Operators groups.

2. You performed a normal backup on Monday. For the remaining days of the week, you want to back up only files and folders that have changed since the previous day. What backup type do you select?

   Incremental. The incremental backup type backs up changes since the last markers were set and then clears the markers. Thus, for Tuesday through Friday, you back up only changes since the previous day.

3. What are the considerations for using tapes as your backup media?

   Tapes are a less expensive medium and are more convenient for large backups because of their higher storage capacity. However, the medium deteriorates with time and thus has a limited lifespan.

4. You are restoring a file that has the same name as a file on the volume to which you are restoring. You aren't sure which is the most current version. What do you do?

   Do not replace the file. Restore the file to another location, and then compare the two files.

Chapter 20

Review Questions

1. Why would you want to monitor access to network resources?

   For performing maintenance tasks that require making resources unavailable, you want to notify users before making the resource unavailable. To maintain a network's security, you need to monitor which users are gaining access to which resources. For planning purposes, you want to determine which resources are being used and how often they are being used.

2. What can you monitor on a network with the Computer Management snap-in or the Shared Folders snap-in?

   You can monitor the number of users who have a current connection to the computer that you are monitoring, the files to which users are currently gaining access and which users are currently gaining access to each file, the shared folders to which users are currently gaining access on the network, and how many users have a connection to each folder. You can monitor all this information on the computer where you are physically located or on a remote computer.

3. Why would you send an administrative message to users with current connections?

   To inform the users that you are about to disconnect them from the resource so that you can perform a backup or restore operation, upgrade software or hardware, or shut down the computer.

4. What can you do to prevent a user from reconnecting to a shared folder after you have disconnected the user from the shared folder?

   To prevent all users from reconnecting, stop sharing the folder. To prevent only one user from reconnecting, change the permissions for the folder so that the user no longer has access, and then disconnect the user from the shared folder.

5. How can you create and manage shares on a remote computer?

   To create and manage shares on a remote folder, use the MMC to create a custom console and add the Shared Folders snap-in to it. When you add the Shared Folders snap-in, you specify the remote computer on which you want to create and manage shares. When adding the Shared Folders snap-in to the console, you can also select the Allow The Selected Computer To Be Changed When Launching From The Command Line check box so that you can choose the remote computer on which you want to create and manage shares.

Chapter 21

Review Questions

1. What are the advantages of using L2TP over using PPTP?

   L2TP supports more types of internetworks, it supports header compression, and it cooperates with IPSec for encryption.

2. While you're using the Network Connection wizard, you must configure two new settings regarding sharing the connection. Describe the difference between these two settings.

   The settings are whether you want to allow others that use the computer to use the connection (access to the connection) and whether you want to allow other computers to access resources through this port (sharing the connection once it is established).

3. What is callback and when might you want to enable it?

   The callback feature causes the remote server to disconnect and call back the client attempting to access the remote server. By using callback, you can have the bill for the phone call charged to your phone number rather than to the phone number of the user who called in. You can also use callback to increase security by specifying the callback number. Even if an unauthorized user calls in, the system calls back at the number you specified, not the number of the unauthorized user.

Chapter 22

Practice Questions

Lesson 5: Using the Recovery Console

Practice: Using the Windows 2000 Recovery Console

Exercise 1: Troubleshooting a Windows 2000 Installation

▶ **To create a system boot failure**

2. Restart the computer.

   What error do you receive when attempting to restart the computer?

   NTLDR is missing.
   Press Ctrl+Alt+Del to restart.

Review Questions

1. What are the five major phases of the boot process for Intel-based computers?

   The boot process for Intel-based computers includes the preboot sequence, boot sequence, kernel load, kernel initialization, and logon phases.

2. What are the various Safe Mode advanced boot options for booting Windows 2000, and how do they differ?

   The Safe Mode option loads only the basic devices and drivers required to start the system, including the mouse, keyboard, mass storage devices, base video, and the standard/default set of system services.

   The Safe Mode With Networking option loads the devices and drivers loaded with the Safe Mode option, but it also loads the services and drivers required for networking.

   The Safe Mode With Command Prompt option is identical to the Safe Mode option, but it launches a command prompt instead of Windows Explorer.

3. What are the two sections of the Boot.ini file, and what information does each section contain?

   The two sections of the Boot.ini file are [boot loader] and [operating systems]. The [boot loader] section of Boot.ini specifies the default operating system and provides a timeout value.

The [operating systems] section of Boot.ini contains the list of operating systems that appear in the Boot Loader Operating System Selection menu. Each entry includes the path to the operating system and the name that appears in the Boot Loader Operating System Selection menu (the text between the quotation marks). Each entry can also contain optional parameters.

4. You install a new device driver for a SCSI adapter in your computer. When you restart the computer, however, Windows 2000 stops responding after the kernel load phase. How can you get Windows 2000 to restart successfully?

Select the Last Known Good Configuration option to use the LastKnownGood configuration control to start Windows 2000 because it doesn't contain any reference to the new, and possibly faulty, driver.

Chapter 23

Review Questions

1. How do you install the Windows 2000 deployment tools, such as the Setup Manager Wizard and the System Preparation tool?

To install the Windows 2000 Setup Tools, display the contents of the Deploy.cab file, which is located in the Support\Tools folder on the Windows 2000 CD-ROM. Select all the files you want to extract, right-click a selected file, and then select Extract from the menu. You will be prompted for a destination, the location and name of a folder, for the extracted files.

2. Which five resources are required to use Remote Installation Services to install Windows 2000 Professional?

A Windows 2000 Server with RIS installed, a DNS server available on the network, a DHCP server available on the network, a Windows 2000 domain to provide Active Directory directory services, and client computers that meet the Net PC specification or have a boot floppy to connect to the RIS server.

3. Which utility is provided to create boot floppies and how do you access it?

Windows 2000 ships with the Windows 2000 Remote Boot Disk Generator, rbfg.exe, which is used to create boot disks. It is found on the RIS Server in the folder where the Windows 2000 Professional installation files are stored. The path is RemoteInst\Admin\i386\rbfg.exe.

4. You are planning on installing 45 computers with Windows 2000 Professional. You have determined that these 45 computers have seven different network adapter cards. How can you determine whether these seven different types of network adapter cards are supported by the boot floppies you created?

The boot floppies created using Rbfg only support the PCI-based network adapters listed in the Adapters List. Start Rbfg.exe and then click the Adapter List button to see the list of supported adapters.

5. You have a laptop running Windows 95 and you want to upgrade it to Windows 2000. The computer has 16 MB of RAM, and this can be upgraded to 24 MB. Can you upgrade this computer to Windows 2000? If not, how would you make it so this computer was able to access Active Directory directory services?

No, Windows 2000 Professional requires at least 32 MB of memory. You can install the Directory Service Client for Windows 95 or 98. The laptop would then be able to access Active Directory directory services.

6. Name at least two problems the System Preparation tool resolves that makes creating and copying a master disk image to other computers much simpler to do.

The System Preparation tool adds a system service to the master image that will create a unique local domain security ID (SID) the first time the computer to which the master image is copied is started.

The System Preparation tool adds a Mini-Setup wizard to the master disk image that runs the first time the computer to which the master image is copied is started. It guides the user through entering the user-specific information such as the end-user license agreement, the Product ID, user name, company name, and time zone selection.

The System Preparation tool causes the master image to force the computer on which the master image is copied to run a full Plug and Play device detection, so that peripherals, such as the network adapter, the video adapter, and sound cards on the computer on which the disk image was copied need not be identical to the ones on the computer on which the image was generated.

Chapter 24

Review Questions

1. A friend of yours just installed Windows 2000 Professional on his home computer. He called you to help him configure APM, and when you told him to double-click Power Options in Control Panel and click on the APM tab, he told you he did not have an APM tab. What is the most likely reason there is no APM tab?

The most likely reason there is no APM is that his computer does not have an APM-based BIOS installed. When Windows 2000 does not detect an APM-based BIOS, Setup does not install APM and there is no APM tab in the Power Options Properties dialog box.

2. A user calls the help desk in a panic. She spent 15 hours editing a proposal as an offline file at her house. Over the weekend, her boss came in and spent about four hours editing the same proposal. She needs to synchronize the files, but she doesn't want to lose her edits or those made by her boss. What can she do?

If both her cached offline copy of the file and the network copy of the file are edited, she should rename her version of the file so that both copies will exist on her hard disk and on the network. She could then compare the two and edit her version, adding any edits made by her boss.

3. Many commercial airlines require you to turn off portable computers during certain portions of a flight. Does placing your computer in Hibernate mode comply with these airline requirements? Why or why not?

No. Hibernate mode makes your computer appear to be turned off, but it is not. You must shut down your computer to comply with these airline requirements.

Chapter 25

Practice Questions

Lesson 1: Using Device Manager and System Information

Practice: Using Device Manager and System Information

Exercise 2: Using System Information

▶ **To use System Information**

4. In the details pane, double-click Hardware Resources, and then double-click IRQs.

Are there any IRQs being shared?

Answer will vary.

Review Questions

1. Your boss has started to manually assign resource settings to all devices, including Plug and Play devices, and wants you to finish the job. What should you do?

Explain to your boss that it is not a good idea to manually change or assign resource settings for Plug and Play devices. Windows 2000 arbitrates resources, but if you manually assign them, then Windows 2000 will not be able to arbitrate the assigned resources if requested by another Plug and Play device.

Once you have convinced your boss that this is not a good idea, start Device Manager. Plug and Play devices have a Resources tab on their Properties page. You can free the resource settings that were manually assigned and allow Windows 2000 to again arbitrate the resources by selecting the Use Automatic Settings check box on the Resources tab.

2. What benefits do you gain by Microsoft digitally signing all system files?

Windows 2000 drivers and operating system files are digitally signed by Microsoft to ensure the files have not been tampered with. Some applications overwrite existing operating files as part of their installation process. These files may cause system errors that are difficult to troubleshoot. Device Manager allows you to look at the Driver tab and verify that the digital signer of the installed driver is correct. This can save you many frustrating hours of trying to resolve problems caused by a file that replaced one or more original operating system drivers.

3. What are three ways Microsoft has provided to help you make sure the files on your system have the correct digital signature?

Windows 2000 provides Device Manager, which allows you to verify that the digital signer of the installed driver is correct. Windows 2000 also provides two utilities to verify the digital signatures. The first utility is the File Signature Verification utility, sigverif. Windows 2000 also provides System File Checker (SFC), a command-line utility that you can use to check the digital signature of files.

4. You receive a call at the Help desk from a user who is trying to configure her fax settings, and she tells you that she does not have an Advanced Options tab. What could the problem be?

For the Advanced Options tab to display, the user must be logged on as Administrator or have administrator privileges.

A P P E N D I X   B

Creating Setup Boot Disks

Unless your computer supports booting from a CD-ROM drive, you must have the four Windows 2000 Professional Setup disks to complete the installation of Microsoft Windows 2000 Professional. To create these Setup disks, complete the following procedure.

1. Label the four 1.44 MB disks with the appropriate product name, as follows:

   Windows 2000 Professional Setup Boot Disk

   Windows 2000 Professional Setup Disk #2

   Windows 2000 Professional Setup Disk #3

   Windows 2000 Professional Setup Disk #4

2. Insert the Microsoft Windows 2000 Professional CD-ROM into the CD-ROM drive.

3. If the Windows 2000 CD-ROM dialog box appears prompting you to upgrade to Windows 2000, click No.

4. Open a Command Prompt window.

5. At the command prompt, change to your CD-ROM drive. For example, if your CD-ROM drive letter is E, type **e:** and press Enter.

6. At the command prompt, change to the Bootdisk folder by typing **cd bootdisk** and pressing Enter.

7. With Bootdisk as the active folder, type **makeboot a:** (where *a:* is the floppy disk drive) and then press Enter.

   Windows 2000 displays a message indicating that this script creates the four Windows 2000 Setup disks for installing from a CD-ROM. It also indicates that four blank formatted floppy disks are required.

8. Press any key to continue.

   Windows 2000 displays a message prompting you to insert the disk labeled Disk 1. (This is the disk you labeled Windows 2000 Professional Setup Boot Disk.)

9. Insert the blank formatted disk labeled Windows 2000 Professional Setup Boot Disk into drive A, and then press any key to continue.

   After Windows 2000 creates the disk image, it displays a message prompting you to insert the disk labeled Disk 2.

10. Remove Disk 1, insert the blank formatted disk labeled Windows 2000 Professional Setup Disk #2 into drive A, and then press any key to continue.

    After Windows 2000 creates the disk image, it displays a message prompting you to insert the disk labeled Disk 3.

11. Remove Disk #2, insert the blank formatted disk labeled Windows 2000 Professional Setup Disk #3 into drive A, and then press any key to continue.

    After Windows 2000 creates the disk image, it displays a message prompting you to insert the disk labeled Disk 4.

12. Remove Disk 3, insert the blank formatted disk labeled Windows 2000 Professional Setup Disk #4 into drive A, and then press any key to continue.

    After Windows 2000 creates the disk image, it displays a message indicating that the imaging process is done.

13. At the command prompt, type **exit** and then press Enter.

14. Remove the disk from drive A and the CD-ROM from the CD-ROM drive.

APPENDIX C

Understanding the DHCP Service

The Dynamic Host Configuration Protocol (DHCP) Service in Microsoft Windows 2000 centralizes and manages the allocation of Microsoft Transmission Control Protocol/Internet Protocol (TCP/IP) configuration information by assigning Internet Protocol (IP) addresses automatically to computers that are configured as DHCP clients. Implementing the DHCP Service can eliminate many of the configuration problems associated with configuring TCP/IP manually.

To introduce you to DHCP, the following six topics are covered in this appendix:

- The Bootstrap Protocol (BOOTP)
- Manual versus automatic TCP/IP configuration
- The requirements for a server running the DHCP Service
- The requirements for DHCP clients
- The DHCP lease process
- IP lease renewal and release

The Bootstrap Protocol

The Bootstrap Protocol, based on the User Datagram Protocol/Internet Protocol (UDP/IP), enables a booting host to configure itself dynamically. DHCP is an extension of BOOTP, which enables diskless clients to start up and automatically configure TCP/IP. Each time that a DHCP client starts, it requests IP addressing information from a DHCP server, including the following:

- An IP address
- A subnet mask
- Optional values, such as the following:
    - A default gateway address
    - A Domain Name System (DNS) server address
    - A Windows Internet Name Service (WINS) server address

When a DHCP server receives a request for an IP address, it selects IP addressing information from a pool of addresses that are defined in its database and offers the IP addressing information to the DHCP client, as shown in Figure C.1. If the client accepts the offer, the DHCP server leases the IP addressing information to the client for a specified period of time.

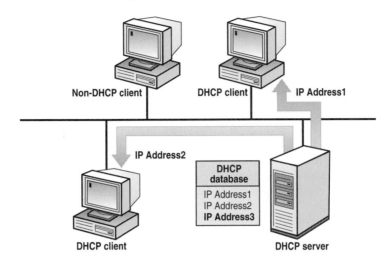

Figure C.1   A DHCP server provides IP addresses to DHCP clients

Manual Versus Automatic TCP/IP Configuration

To understand why the DHCP Service is beneficial for configuring TCP/IP on clients, it is useful to contrast the manual method of configuring TCP/IP with the automatic method using DHCP, as shown in Table C.1.

Table C.1   Configuring TCP/IP Manually Versus Using the DHCP Service

Configuring TCP/IP manually	Configuring TCP/IP using DHCP
Users can pick an IP address randomly rather than obtaining a valid IP address from the network administrator. Using incorrect addresses can lead to network problems that can be difficult to trace to the source.	Users no longer need to acquire IP addressing information from an administrator to configure TCP/IP. The DHCP Service supplies all the necessary configuration information to all the DHCP clients.
Typing the IP address, subnet mask, or default gateway can lead to problems ranging from difficulty communicating, if the default gateway or subnet mask is incorrect, to problems associated with a duplicate IP address.	Correct configuration information ensures correct configuration, which eliminates most difficult-to-trace network problems.

Configuring TCP/IP manually	Configuring TCP/IP using DHCP
There is administrative overhead for networks if you frequently move computers from one subnet to another. For example, you must change the IP address and default gateway address for a client to communicate from a new location.	Having servers running the DHCP Service on each subnet eliminates the overhead of having to manually reconfigure IP addresses, subnet masks, and default gateways when you move computers from one subnet to another.

To implement DHCP, you must install and configure the DHCP Service on at least one computer running Windows 2000 Server within the TCP/IP network. The computer can be configured as a domain controller or as a stand-alone server. In addition, for DHCP to function properly, you must configure the server and all of the clients.

Requirements for a Server Running the DHCP Service

A DHCP server requires a computer running Windows 2000 Server that is configured with the following:

- The DHCP Service.
- A static IP address (it can't be a DHCP client itself), subnet mask, default gateway (if necessary), and other TCP/IP parameters.
- A DHCP scope. A *scope* is a range of IP addresses that are available for lease or assignment to clients.

Requirements for DHCP Clients

A DHCP client requires a computer that is DHCP-enabled and running any of the following supported operating systems:

- Windows 2000, Windows NT Server version 3.51 or later, or Windows NT Workstation version 3.51 or later.
- Microsoft Windows 95 or later.
- Windows for Workgroups version 3.11 running Microsoft TCP/IP-32, which is included on the Windows 2000 Server CD-ROM.
- Microsoft Network Client version 3 for Microsoft MS-DOS with the real-mode TCP/IP driver, which is included on the Windows 2000 Server CD-ROM.
- LAN Manager version 2.2c, which is included on the Windows 2000 Server CD-ROM. LAN Manager 2.2c for OS/2 is not supported.

The DHCP Lease Process

To understand the DHCP lease process, you must first understand when the lease process occurs. The DHCP lease process occurs when one of the following events happens:

- TCP/IP is initialized for the first time on a DHCP client.
- A client requests a specific IP address and is denied, possibly because the DHCP server dropped the lease.
- A client previously leased an IP address but released the IP address and requires a new one.

DHCP uses a four-phase process to lease IP addressing information to a DHCP client for a specific period of time: DHCPDISCOVER, DHCPOFFER, DHCPREQUEST, and DHCPACK. (See Figure C.2.)

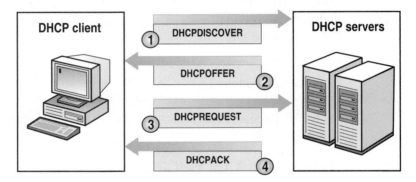

Figure C.2 The DHCP lease process

The DHCPDISCOVER Phase

The first phase in the DHCP lease process is DHCPDISCOVER. To begin the DHCP lease process, a client initializes a limited version of TCP/IP and broadcasts a DHCPDISCOVER message requesting the location of a DHCP server and IP addressing information. Because the client doesn't know the IP address of a DHCP server, the client uses 0.0.0.0 as the source address and 255.255.255.255 as the destination address.

The DHCPDISCOVER message contains the client's hardware address and computer name so that the DHCP servers can determine which client sent the request.

The DHCPOFFER Phase

The second phase in the DHCP lease process is DHCPOFFER. All DHCP servers that receive the IP lease request and have a valid client configuration broadcast a DHCPOFFER message that includes the following information:

- The client's hardware address
- An offered IP address
- A subnet mask
- The length of the lease
- A server identifier (the IP address of the offering DHCP server)

The DHCP server sends a broadcast because the client doesn't yet have an IP address. The DHCP client selects the IP address from the first offer that it receives. The DHCP server that is issuing the IP address reserves the address so that it can't be offered to another DHCP client.

The DHCPREQUEST Phase

The third phase in the DHCP lease process occurs after the client receives a DHCPOFFER from at least one DHCP server and selects an IP address. The client broadcasts a DHCPREQUEST message to all DHCP servers, indicating that it has accepted an offer. The DHCPREQUEST message includes the server identifier (IP address) of the server whose offer it accepted. All other DHCP servers then retract their offers and retain their IP addresses for the next IP lease request.

The DHCPACK Phase

The final phase in a successful DHCP lease process occurs when the DHCP server issuing the accepted offer broadcasts a successful acknowledgment to the client in the form of a DHCPACK message. This message contains a valid lease for an IP address and possibly other configuration information.

When the DHCP client receives the acknowledgment, TCP/IP is completely initialized and the client is considered a bound DHCP client. Once bound, the client can use TCP/IP to communicate on the network.

The DHCPNACK Message

If the DHCPREQUEST is not successful, the DHCP server broadcasts a negative acknowledgement (DHCPNACK). A DHCP server broadcasts a DHCPNACK if

- The client is trying to lease its previous IP address, and the IP address is no longer available.
- The IP address is invalid because the client physically has been moved to a different subnet.

When the client receives an unsuccessful acknowledgment, it resumes the DHCP lease process.

Note If a computer has multiple network adapters that are bound to TCP/IP, the DHCP process occurs separately over each adapter. The DHCP Service assigns a unique IP address to each adapter in the computer that is bound to TCP/IP.

IP Lease Renewal and Release

All DHCP clients attempt to renew their lease when 50 percent of the lease time has expired. To renew its lease, a DHCP client sends a DHCPREQUEST message directly to the DHCP server from which it obtained the lease. If the DHCP server is available, it renews the lease and sends the client a DHCPACK message with the new lease time and any updated configuration parameters, as shown in Figure C.3. The client updates its configuration when it receives the acknowledgment.

Figure C.3   Renewing an IP lease

Note Each time a DHCP client restarts, it attempts to lease the same IP address from the original DHCP server. If the lease request is unsuccessful and lease time is still available, the DHCP client continues to use the same IP address until the next attempt to renew the lease.

If a DHCP client can't renew its lease with the original DHCP server at the 50 percent interval, the client broadcasts a DHCPREQUEST to contact any available DHCP server when 87.5 percent of the lease time has expired. Any DHCP server can respond with a DHCPACK message (renewing the lease) or a DHCPNACK message (forcing the DHCP client to reinitialize and obtain a lease for a different IP address).

If the lease expires, or if a DHCPNACK message is received, the DHCP client must immediately discontinue using that IP address. The DHCP client then begins the DHCP lease process to lease a new IP address.

Using Ipconfig to Renew a Lease

Use the ipconfig command with the /renew switch to send a DHCPREQUEST message to the DHCP server to receive updated options and lease time. If the DHCP server is unavailable, the client continues using the current DHCP-supplied configuration options.

Using Ipconfig to Release a Lease

Use the ipconfig command with the /release switch to cause a DHCP client to send a DHCPRELEASE message to the DHCP server and to release its lease. This is useful when you are moving a client to a different network and the client will not need its previous lease. TCP/IP communications with the client will stop after you issue this command.

Microsoft DHCP clients don't initiate DHCPRELEASE messages when shutting down. If a client remains shut down for the length of its lease (and the lease is not renewed), the DHCP server might assign that client's IP address to a different client after the lease expires. A client has a better chance of receiving the same IP address during initialization if it doesn't send a DHCPRELEASE message.

APPENDIX D

Managing Backup Tapes

If you use tapes as your backup medium, consider the distinction between rotating tapes and archiving tapes. *Rotating tapes* means reusing them when the data stored on them is no longer viable for restoring. This common practice helps to lower the cost of backing up data. *Archiving tapes* means storing the tape to keep a record of the data rather than as prevention against data loss. When you archive a tape, you remove that tape from the tape rotation. Archived tapes are useful for maintaining a record of data for a specific date and time, such as employee records at the end of a fiscal year.

Rotating and Archiving Tapes

The following two examples provide strategies for rotating and archiving tapes.

Rotation and Archive Example 1

The following table illustrates one strategy for rotating and archiving tapes and is explained below.

	Monday	Tuesday	Wednesday	Thursday	Friday
Week 1	Tape 1	Tape 2	Tape 3	Tape 4	Tape 5 (Archive)
Week 2	Tape 1 (Replace or Append)	Tape 2 (Replace or Append)	Tape 3 (Replace or Append)	Tape 4 (Replace or Append)	Tape 6 (Archive)

- Week 1. The backup job for each day of the week is on a different tape. The backup tape for Friday is archived and removed from rotation.

- Week 2. For this week, you reuse the tapes for the same day of the week (the Monday backup job is on the previous Monday tape 1). You can either replace or append to the existing backup job. However, on Friday, use a new tape that you archive and remove from rotation.

Rotation and Archive Example 2

The following table illustrates another strategy for rotating and archiving tapes and is explained below.

	Monday	Tuesday	Wednesday	Thursday	Friday
Week 1	Tape 1	Tape 1 (Append)	Tape 1 (Append)	Tape 1 (Append)	Tape 2 (Archive)
Week 2	Tape 1	Tape 1 (Append)	Tape 1 (Append)	Tape 1 (Append)	Tape 3 (Archive)

- Week 1. The backup job for each day of the week, except Friday, is on the same tape. The backup tape for Friday is archived and removed from rotation. Use the same tape for the Monday through Thursday backup jobs and append each new backup job to the previous one. The Friday backup job is on a different tape (tape 2) that you archive and remove from rotation.

- Week 2. For this week, reuse the tape from the previous week (tape 1) for all backup jobs. The Friday backup job is on a tape (tape 3) that is different from the one that you used the previous Friday. You archive and remove this tape from rotation.

Determining the Number of Tapes Required

When determining the number of tapes you need, consider the tape rotation and archival schedule, the amount of the data that you back up, and the tape life cycle.

The life cycle of a tape depends on the tape itself and storage conditions. Follow the tape manufacturer's usage guidelines. If your company doesn't have a suitable storage facility, consider using a third-party company that specializes in offsite storage for backup media.

Glossary

access control entry (ACE) The entries on the access control list (ACL) that control user account or group access to a resource. The entry must allow the type of access that is requested (for example, Read access) for the user to gain access. If no ACE exists in the ACL, the user can't gain access to the resource or folder on an NTFS partition.

access control list (ACL) The ACL contains a list of all user accounts and groups that have been granted access for the file or folder on an NTFS partition or volume, as well as the type of access that they have been granted. When a user attempts to gain access to a resource, the ACL must contain an entry, called an access control entry (ACE), for the user account or group to which the user belongs. *See also* access control entry.

access permissions Features that control access to shared resources in Windows 2000.

Account *See* user account.

account lockout A Windows 2000 security feature that locks a user account if a number of failed logon attempts occur within a specified amount of time, based on account policy lockout settings. (Locked accounts can't log on.) Account policy controls how passwords must be used by all user accounts in an individual computer or in a domain.

ACE *See* access control entry.

ACL *See* access control list.

Active Directory directory services The directory services included in Windows 2000 Server products. These directory services identify all resources on a network and make them accessible to users and applications.

Address Resolution Protocol (ARP) A protocol that determines hardware addresses (MAC addresses) that correspond to an IP address.

ADSL *See* asymmetric digital subscriber line (ADSL).

agent A program that performs a background task for a user and reports to the user when the task is done or when some expected event has taken place.

American National Standards Institute (ANSI) An organization of American industry and business groups dedicated to the development of trade and communications standards. ANSI is the American representative to the International Organization for Standardization (ISO). *See also* International Organization for Standardization (ISO).

American Standard Code for Information Interchange (ASCII) A coding scheme that assigns numeric values to letters, numbers, punctuation marks, and certain other characters. By standardizing the values used for these characters, ASCII enables computers and computer programs to exchange information.

ANSI *See* American National Standards Institute (ANSI).

application layer The top (seventh) layer of the OSI reference model. This layer serves as the window that application processes use to access network services. It represents the services that directly support user applications, such as software for file transfers, database access, and e-mail.

application programming interface (API) A set of routines that an application program uses to request and carry out lower-level services performed by the operating system.

application protocol A protocol that works at the higher end of the OSI reference model, providing application-to-application interaction and data exchange. Popular application protocols include File Transfer Access and Management (FTAM), a file access protocol; Simple Mail Transfer Protocol (SMTP), a TCP/IP protocol for transferring e-mail; Telnet, a TCP/IP protocol for logging on to remote hosts and processing data locally; and NetWare Core Protocol (NCP), the primary protocol used to transmit information between a NetWare server and its clients.

ARP *See* Address Resolution Protocol (ARP).

asymmetric digital subscriber line (ADSL) A recent modem technology that converts existing twisted-pair telephone lines into access paths for multimedia and high-speed data communications. These new connections can transmit more than 8 Mbps to the subscriber and up to 1 Mbps from the subscriber. ADSL is recognized as a physical layer transmission protocol for unshielded twisted-pair media.

asynchronous transfer mode (ATM) An advanced implementation of packet switching that provides high-speed data transmission rates to send fixed-size cells over broadband LANs or WANs. Cells are 53 bytes—48 bytes of data with five additional bytes of address. ATM accommodates voice, data, fax, real-time video, CD-quality audio, imaging, and multimegabit data transmission. ATM uses switches as multiplexers to permit several computers to put data on a network simultaneously. Most commercial ATM boards transmit data at about 155 Mbps, but theoretically, a rate of 1.2 gigabits per second is possible.

asynchronous transmission A form of data transmission in which information is sent one character at a time, with variable time intervals between characters. Asynchronous transmission doesn't rely on a shared timer that allows the sending and receiving units to separate characters by specific time periods. Therefore, each transmitted charac-

ter consists of a number of data bits (that compose the character itself), preceded by a start bit and ending in an optional parity bit followed by a 1-, 1.5-, or 2-stop bit.

ATM *See* asynchronous transfer mode (ATM).

auditing A process that tracks network activities by user accounts and a routine element of network security. Auditing can produce records or list users who have accessed—or attempted to access—specific resources; help administrators identify unauthorized activity; and track activities such as logon attempts, connection and disconnection from designated resources, changes made to files and directories, server events and modifications, password changes, and logon parameter changes.

audit policy A policy that defines the types of security events that Windows 2000 records in the security log on each computer.

authentication A verification based on user name, passwords, and time and account restrictions.

back end In a client/server application, the part of the program that runs on the server.

backup A duplicate copy of a program, a disk, or data, made to secure valuable files from loss.

backup job A single process of backing up data.

Bandwidth Allocation Protocol (BAP) A PPP control protocol that helps provide bandwidth on demand. BAP dynamically controls the use of multilinked lines and is an efficient mechanism for controlling connection costs while dynamically providing optimum bandwidth.

BAP *See* Bandwidth Allocation Protocol (BAP).

base I/O port A port that specifies a channel through which information is transferred between a computer's hardware, such as the network interface card (NIC), and its CPU.

base memory address A setting that defines the address of the location in a computer's memory (RAM) that is used by the NIC. This setting is sometimes called the RAM start address.

baud A measure of data-transmission speed named after the French engineer and telegrapher Jean-Maurice-Emile Baudot. It is a measure of the speed of oscillation of the sound wave on which a bit of data is carried over telephone lines. Because baud was originally used to measure the transmission speed of telegraph equipment, the term sometimes refers to the data-transmission speed of a modem. However, current modems can send at a speed higher than 1-bit per oscillation, so baud is being replaced by the more accurate bps (bits per second) as a measure of modem speed.

baud rate The speed at which a modem can transmit data. Often confused with bps (the number of bits per second transmitted), baud rate actually measures the number of events, or signal changes, that occur in one second. Because one event can actually encode more than one bit in high-speed digital communication, baud rate and bps are not always synonymous, and the latter is the more accurate term to apply to modems. For example, the 9600-baud modem that encodes 4-bits per event actually operates at 2400 baud but transmits at 9600 bps (2400 events times 4-bits per event), and thus should be called a 9600-bps modem.

binary synchronous communications protocol (bisync) A communications protocol developed by IBM. Bisync transmissions are encoded in either ASCII or EBCDIC. Messages can be of any length and are sent in units called frames that are optionally preceded by a message header. Because bisync uses synchronous transmission, in which message elements are separated by a specific time interval, each frame is preceded and followed by special characters that enable the sending and receiving machines to synchronize their clocks.

bind A term used to describe the association of two pieces of information with one another.

binding A process that establishes the communication channel between network components on different levels to enable communication between those components. For example, the binding of a protocol driver (such as TCP/IP) and a network adapter.

bit A short word for binary digit: either 1 or 0 in the binary number system. In processing and storage, a bit is the smallest unit of information handled by a computer. It is represented physically by an element such as a single pulse sent through a circuit or a small spot on a magnetic disk capable of storing either a 1 or 0. Eight bits make a byte.

bits per second (bps) A measure of the speed at which a device can transfer data. *See also* baud rate.

bit time The time it takes for each station to receive and store a bit.

boot-sector virus A type of virus that resides in the first sector of a floppy disk or hard disk. When the computer is booted, the virus executes. In this common method of transmitting viruses from one floppy disk to another, the virus replicates itself onto the new disk each time a new disk is inserted and accessed.

bottleneck A device or program that significantly degrades network performance. Poor network performance results when a device uses noticeably more CPU time than it should, consumes too much of a resource, or lacks the capacity to handle the load. Potential bottlenecks can be found in the CPU, memory, NIC, and other components.

Bps *See* bits per second (bps).

broadcast A transmission sent simultaneously to more than one recipient. In communication and on networks, a broadcast message is one distributed to all stations or computers on the network.

broadcast storm An event that occurs when so many broadcast messages are on the network that they approach or surpass the capacity of the network bandwidth. This can happen when one computer on the network transmits a flood of frames saturating the network with traffic so it can no longer carry messages from any other computer. Such a broadcast storm can shut down a network.

buffer A reserved portion of RAM in which data is held temporarily, pending an opportunity to complete its transfer to or from a storage device or another location in memory.

built-in groups One type of group account used by Microsoft Windows 2000. Built-in groups, as the name implies, are included with the network operating system. Built-in groups have been granted useful collections of rights and built-in abilities. In most cases, a built-in group provides all the capabilities needed by a particular user. For example, if a user account belongs to the built-in Administrators group, logging on with that account gives the user administrative capabilities. *See also* user account.

Bus Parallel wires or cabling that connect components in a computer.

Byte A unit of information consisting of 8 bits. In computer processing or storage, a byte is equivalent to a single character, such as a letter, numeral, or punctuation mark. Because a byte represents only a small amount of information, amounts of computer memory are usually given in kilobytes (1,024 bytes, or 2 raised to the 10th power), megabytes (1,048,576 bytes, or 2 raised to the 20th power), gigabytes (1,024 megabytes), terabytes (1,024 gigabytes), petabytes (1,024 terabytes), or exabytes (1,024 petabytes).

cache A special memory subsystem or part of RAM in which frequently used data values are duplicated for quick access. A memory cache stores the contents of frequently accessed RAM locations and the addresses where these data items are stored. When the processor references an address in memory, the cache checks to *See* whether it holds that address. If it does hold the address, the data is returned to the processor; if it doesn't, regular memory access occurs. A cache is useful when RAM accesses are slow as compared to the microprocessor speed.

callback A Windows 2000 feature that you can set to cause the remote server to disconnect and call back the client attempting to access the remote server. This reduces the client's phone bill by having the call charged to the remote server's phone number. The callback feature can also improve security by calling back the phone number that you specified.

central processing unit (CPU) The computational and control unit of a computer, the device that interprets and carries out instructions. Single-chip CPUs, called microprocessors, made personal computers possible. Examples include the 80286, 80386, 80486, and Pentium processors.

client A computer that accesses shared network resources provided by another computer, called a server.

client/server A network architecture designed around the concept of distributed processing in which a task is divided between a back end (server), which stores and distributes data, and a front end (client), which requests specific data from the server.

codec (compressor/decompressor) A compression/decompression technology for digital video and stereo audio.

companion virus A virus that uses the name of a real program but has a different file extension from that of the program. The virus is activated when its companion program is opened. The companion virus uses a .COM file extension, which overrides the .EXE file extension and activates the virus.

compression state The state of each file and folder on an NTFS volume. the compression state that can be either compressed or uncompressed.

CPU *See* central processing unit (CPU).

database management system (DBMS) A layer of software between the physical database and the user. The DBMS manages all requests for database action from the user, including keeping track of the physical details of file locations and formats, indexing schemes, and so on. In addition, a DBMS permits centralized control of security and data integrity requirements.

data encryption *See* encryption.

data encryption standard (DES) A commonly used, highly sophisticated algorithm developed by the U.S. National Bureau of Standards for encrypting and decoding data. *See also* encryption.

data frames Logical, structured packages in which data can be placed. Data being transmitted is segmented into small units and combined with control information such as message-start and message-end indicators. Each package of information is transmitted as a single unit, called a frame. The data-link layer packages raw bits from the physical layer into data frames. The exact format of the frame used by the network depends on the topology. *See also* frame.

data-link layer The second layer in the OSI reference model. This layer packages raw bits from the physical layer into data frames. *See also* Open Systems Interconnection (OSI) reference model.

data stream An undifferentiated, byte-by-byte flow of data.

DBMS *See* database management system (DBMS).

defragmenting The process of finding and consolidating fragmented files and folders. Defragmenting involves moving the pieces of each file or folder to one location so that each file or folder occupies a single, contiguous space on the hard disk. The system can then gain access to files and folders and save them more efficiently.

DES *See* data encryption standard (DES).

device A generic term for a computer subsystem. Printers, serial ports, and disk drives are referred to as devices.

DHCP *See* Dynamic Host Configuration Protocol (DHCP).

digital A system that encodes information numerically, such as 0 and 1, in a binary context. Computers use digital encoding to process data. A digital signal is a discrete binary state, either on or off.

digital line A communication line that carries information only in binary-encoded (digital) form. To minimize distortion and noise interference, a digital line uses repeaters to regenerate the signal periodically during transmission.

digital video disc (DVD) Also known as a digital versatile disc, an optical storage medium with higher capacity and bandwidth than a compact disc. A DVD can hold a full-length film with up to 133 minutes of high-quality video, in MPEG-2 format, and audio.

direct memory access (DMA) Memory access that doesn't involve the microprocessor, frequently employed for data transfer directly between memory and an "intelligent" peripheral device such as a disk drive.

direct memory access (DMA) channel A channel for direct memory access that doesn't involve the microprocessor, providing data transfer directly between memory and a disk drive.

Directory A storage space for information about network resources, as well as all the services that make the information available and useful. The resources stored in the Directory, such as user data, printers, servers, databases, groups, computers, and security policies, are known as objects. The Directory is part of Active Directory directory services.

directory service A network service that identifies all resources on a network and makes them accessible to users and applications.

disk duplexing *See* disk mirroring; fault tolerance.

disk duplicating *See* disk mirroring.

diskless computers Computers that have neither a floppy disk nor a hard disk. Diskless computers depend on special ROM to provide users with an interface through which they can log on to the network.

disk mirroring A technique, also known as disk duplicating, in which all or part of a hard disk is duplicated onto one or more hard disks, each of which ideally is attached to its own controller. With disk mirroring, any change made to the original disk is simultaneously made to the other disk or disks. Disk mirroring is used in situations in which a backup copy of current data must be maintained at all times. *See also* disk striping; fault tolerance.

disk striping A technique that divides data into 64 K blocks and spreads it equally in a fixed rate and order among all disks in an array. However, disk striping doesn't provide any fault tolerance because there is no data redundancy. If any partition in the set fails, all data is lost. *See also* disk mirroring; fault tolerance.

distribution server A server that stores the distribution folder structure, which contains the files needed to install a product—for example, Windows 2000.

DMA *See* direct memory access (DMA).

DMA channel *See* direct memory access (DMA) channel.

DNS *See* Domain Name System (DNS).

domain For Microsoft networking, a collection of computers and users that share a common database and security policy that are stored on a computer running Windows 2000 Server and configured as a domain controller. Each domain has a unique name. *See also* workgroup.

domain controller For Microsoft networking, the Windows 2000 Server-based computer that authenticates domain logons and maintains the security policy and master database for a domain.

domain name space The naming scheme that provides the hierarchical structure for the DNS database.

Domain Name System (DNS) A general-purpose, distributed, replicated data-query service used primarily on the Internet for translating host names into Internet addresses.

downtime The amount of time a computer system or associated hardware remains nonfunctional. Although downtime can occur because hardware fails unexpectedly, it can also be a scheduled event, such as when a network is shut down to allow time for maintaining the system, changing hardware, or archiving files.

driver A software component that permits a computer system to communicate with a device. For example, a printer driver is a device driver that translates computer data into a form understood by the target printer. In most cases, the driver also manipulates the hardware to transmit the data to the device.

dual in-line package (DIP) switch One or more small rocker or sliding switches that can be set to one of two states—closed or open—to control options on a circuit board.

DVD *See* digital video disc (DVD).

Dynamic Host Configuration Protocol (DHCP) A protocol for automatic TCP/IP configuration that provides static and dynamic address allocation and management. *See also* Transport Control Protocol/Internet Protocol (TCP/IP).

EAP *See* Extensible Authentication Protocol (EAP).

EBCDIC *See* Extended Binary Coded Decimal Interchange Code (EBCDIC).

effective permissions The sum of the NTFS permissions assigned to the user account and to all of the groups to which the user belongs. If a user has Read permission for a folder and is a member of a group with Write permission for the same folder, then the user has both Read and Write permission for the folder.

EISA *See* Extended Industry Standard Architecture (EISA).

encryption The process of making information indecipherable to protect it from unauthorized viewing or use, especially during transmission or when the data is stored on a transportable magnetic medium. A key is required to decode the information. *See also* CCEP; data encryption standard (DES).

Enhanced Small Device Interface (ESDI) A standard that can be used with high-capacity hard disks and tape drives to enable high-speed communication with a computer. ESDI drivers typically transfer data at about 10 Mbps.

ESDI *See* Enhanced Small Device Interface (ESDI).

event An action or occurrence to which a program might respond. Examples of events are mouse clicks, key presses, and mouse movements. Also, any significant occurrence in the system or in a program that requires users to be notified or an entry to be added to a log.

exabyte *See* byte.

Extended Binary Coded Decimal Interchange Code (EBCDIC) A coding scheme developed by IBM for use with IBM mainframes and PCs as a standard method of assigning binary (numeric) values to alphabetic, numeric, punctuation, and transmission-control characters.

Extended Industry Standard Architecture (EISA) A 32-bit bus design for x86-based computers introduced in 1988. EISA was specified by an industry consortium of nine computer-industry companies (AST Research, Compaq, Epson, Hewlett-Packard, NEC, Olivetti, Tandy, Wyse, and Zenith). An EISA device uses cards that are upwardly compatible from ISA. *See also* Industry Standard Architecture (ISA).

Extensible Authentication Protocol (EAP) An extension to the Point-to-Point Protocol (PPP) that works with Dial-Up, PPTP, and L2TP clients. EAP allows for an arbitrary authentication mechanism to validate a dial-in connection. The exact authentication method to be used is negotiated by the dial-in client and the remote access server.

fault tolerance The ability of a computer or an operating system to respond to an event such as a power outage or a hardware failure in such a way that no data is lost and any work in progress is not corrupted.

Fiber Distributed Data Interface (FDDI) A standard developed by ANSI for high-speed, fiber-optic local area networks. FDDI provides specifications for transmission rates of 100 Mbps on networks based on the Token Ring standard.

file infector A type of virus that attaches itself to a file or program and activates any time the file is used. Many subcategories of file infectors exist. *See also* companion virus; macro virus; polymorphic virus; stealth virus.

File Transfer Protocol (FTP) A process that provides file transfers between local and remote computers. FTP supports several commands that allow bidirectional transfer of binary and ASCII files between computers. The FTP client is installed with the TCP/IP connectivity utilities. *See also* American Standard Code for Information Interchange (ASCII), Transport Control Protocol/Internet Protocol (TCP/IP).

firewall A security system, usually a combination of hardware and software, intended to protect a network against external threats coming from another network, including the Internet. Firewalls prevent an organization's networked computers from communicating directly with computers that are external to the network, and vice versa. Instead, all incoming and outgoing communication is routed through a proxy server outside the organization's network. Firewalls also audit network activity, recording the volume of traffic and information about unauthorized attempts to gain access. *See also* proxy server.

firmware Software routines stored in ROM. Unlike RAM, ROM stays intact even in the absence of electrical power. Startup routines and low-level I/O instructions are stored in firmware.

flow control The regulation of the flow of data through routers to ensure that no segment becomes overloaded with transmissions.

forest A grouping or hierarchical arrangement of one or more domain trees that form a disjoint namespace.

frame A package of information transmitted on a network as a single unit. Frame is a term most often used with Ethernet networks. A frame is similar to the packet used in other networks. *See also* data frames; packet.

frame preamble Header information, added to the beginning of a data frame in the physical layer of the OSI reference model.

frame relay An advanced, fast-packet, variable-length digital packet-switching technology. It is a point-to-point system that uses a private virtual circuit (PVC) to transmit variable-length frames at the data-link layer of the OSI reference model. Frame relay networks can also provide subscribers with bandwidth, as needed, that allows users to make nearly any type of transmission.

front end In a client/server application, refers to the part of the program carried out on the client computer.

FTP *See* File Transfer Protocol (FTP).

full-duplex transmission Communication that takes place simultaneously, in both directions. Also called duplex transmission. *See also* half-duplex transmission.

gateway A device used to connect networks using different protocols so that information can be passed from one system to the other. Gateways functions at the network layer of the OSI reference model.

Gb *See* gigabit.

GB *See* gigabyte.

gigabit A unit of measure that equals 1,073,741,824 bits. Also referred to as 1 billion bits.

gigabyte A unit of measure that commonly refers to 1 thousand megabytes. However, the precise meaning often varies with the context. A gigabyte is 1 billion bytes. In the context of computing, bytes are often expressed in multiples of powers of 2. Therefore, a gigabyte can also be either

1,000 megabytes or 1,024 megabytes, where a megabyte is considered to be 1,048,576 bytes (2 raised to the 20th power).

global catalog A service and a physical storage location that contains a replica of selected attributes for every object in Active Directory directory services.

global group One type of group account used by Microsoft Windows 2000. Used across an entire domain, global groups are created on domain controllers in the domain in which the user accounts reside. Global groups can contain user accounts only from the domain in which the global group is created. Members of global groups obtain resource permissions when the global group is added to a local group. *See also* group.

group In networking, an account containing other accounts that are called members. The permissions and rights granted to a group are also provided to its members; thus, groups offer a convenient way to grant common capabilities to collections of user accounts. For Windows 2000, groups are managed with the Computer Management snap-in. For Windows 2000 Server, groups are managed with the Active Directory Users and Computers snap-in.

half-duplex transmission Communication that takes place in either direction, but not both directions at the same time. *See also* full-duplex transmission.

handshaking A term applied to modem-to-modem communication. Refers to the process by which information is transmitted between the sending and receiving devices to maintain and coordinate data flow between them. Proper handshaking ensures that the receiving device will be ready to accept data before the sending device transmits.

hard disk One or more inflexible platters coated with material that allows the magnetic recording of computer data. A typical hard disk rotates at

up to 7,200 revolutions per minute (RPM), and the read/write heads ride over the surface of the disk on a cushion of air 10 to 25 millionths of an inch deep. A hard disk is sealed to prevent contaminants from interfering with the close head-to-disk tolerances. Hard disks provide faster access to data than floppy disks and are capable of storing much more information. Because platters are rigid, they can be stacked so that one hard-disk drive can access more than one platter. Most hard disks have between two and eight platters.

hardware The physical components of a computer system, including any peripheral equipment such as printers, modems, and mouse devices.

hardware compatibility list (HCL) A list of computers and peripherals that have been tested and have passed compatibility testing with the product for which the HCL is being developed. For example, the Windows 2000 HCL lists the products that have been tested and found to be compatible with Windows 2000.

hardware loopback A connector on a computer that is useful for troubleshooting hardware problems, allowing data to be transmitted to a line and then returned as received data. If the transmitted data doesn't return, the hardware loopback detects a hardware malfunction.

HCL *See* hardware compatibility list (HCL).

HDLC *See* High-Level Data Link Control (HDLC).

header In network data transmission, one of the three sections of a packet component. It includes an alert signal to indicate that the packet is being transmitted, the source address, the destination address, and clock information to synchronize transmission.

hertz (Hz) The unit of frequency measurement. Frequency measures how often a periodic event occurs, such as the manner in which a wave's amplitude changes with time. One hertz equals one cycle per second. Frequency is often measured in kilohertz (KHz, 1000 Hz), megahertz (MHz), gigahertz (GHz, 1000 MHz), or terahertz (THz, 10,000 GHz).

High-Level Data Link Control (HDLC) A widely accepted international protocol developed by the International Organization for Standardization (ISO) that governs information transfer. HDLC is a bit-oriented, synchronous protocol that applies to the data-link (message packaging) layer of the OSI reference model. Under the HDLC protocol, data is transmitted in frames, each of which can contain a variable amount of data, but which must be organized in a particular way. *See also* data frames; frame.

host *See* server.

hot fixing *See* sector sparing.

HTML *See* Hypertext Markup Language (HTML).

Hypertext Markup Language (HTML) A language developed for writing pages for the World Wide Web. HTML allows text to include codes that define fonts, layout, embedded graphics, and hypertext links. Hypertext provides a method for presenting text, images, sound, and videos that are linked together in a nonsequential web of associations.

Hypertext Transport Protocol (HTTP) The method by which World Wide Web pages are transferred over the network.

ICM *See* Image Color Management (ICM) 2.

ICMP *See* Internet Control Message Protocol (ICMP).

IDE *See* Integrated Device Electronics (IDE).

IEEE *See* Institute of Electrical and Electronics Engineers (IEEE).

IEEE Project 802 A networking model developed by the IEEE and named for the year and month it began (February 1980). Project 802 defines LAN standards for the physical and data-link layers of the OSI reference model. Project 802 divides the data-link layer into two sublayers: media access control (MAC) and logical link control (LLC).

Image Color Management (ICM) 2 An operating system API that helps ensure that the colors you see on your monitor match those on your scanner and printer.

Industry Standard Architecture (ISA) An unofficial designation for the bus design of the IBM Personal Computer (PC) PC/XT. It allows various adapters to be added to the system by inserting plug-in cards into expansion slots. Commonly, ISA refers to the expansion slots themselves; such slots are called 8-bit slots or 16-bit slots. *See also* Extended Industry Standard Architecture (EISA); Micro Channel Architecture.

infrared transmission Electromagnetic radiation with frequencies in the electromagnetic spectrum in the range just below that of visible red light. In network communications, infrared technology offers extremely high transmission rates and wide bandwidth in line-of-sight communications.

Institute of Electrical and Electronics Engineers (IEEE) An organization of engineering and electronics professionals, noted in networking for developing the IEEE 802.*x* standards for the physical and data-link layers of the OSI reference model, applied in a variety of network configurations.

Integrated Device Electronics (IDE) A type of disk-drive interface in which the controller electronics reside on the drive itself, eliminating the need for a separate network interface card. The IDE interface is compatible with the Western Digital ST-506 controller.

Integrated Services Digital Network (ISDN) A worldwide digital communication network that evolved from existing telephone services. The goal of the ISDN is to replace current telephone lines, which require digital-to-analog conversions, with completely digital switching and transmission facilities capable of carrying data ranging from voice to computer transmissions, music, and video. The ISDN is built on two main types of communications channels: B channels, that carry voice, data, or images at a rate of 64 Kbps (kilobits per second), and a D channel, that carries control information, signaling, and link-management data at 16 Kbps. Standard ISDN Basic Rate desktop service is called 2B+D. Computers and other devices connect to ISDN lines through simple standardized interfaces.

interfaces Boundaries that separate the layers from each other. For example, in the OSI reference model, each layer provides some service or action that prepares the data for delivery over the network to another computer.

International Organization for Standardization (ISO) An organization made up of standards-setting groups from various countries. For example, the United States member is the American National Standards Institute (ANSI). The ISO works to establish global standards for communications and information exchange. Primary among its accomplishments is development of the widely accepted OSI reference model. Note that the ISO is often wrongly identified as the International Standards Organization, probably because of the abbreviation ISO; however, ISO is derived from *isos*, which means equal in Greek, rather than an acronym.

Internet Control Message Protocol (ICMP) A protocol used by IP and higher-level protocols to send and receive status reports about information being transmitted.

Internet Protocol (IP) The TCP/IP protocol for packet forwarding. *See also* Transport Control Protocol/Internet Protocol (TCP/IP).

Internet Protocol Security (IPSec) A framework of open standards for ensuring secure private communications over IP networks by using cryptographic security services.

Internetworking The intercommunication in a network that is made up of smaller networks.

Internetwork Packet Exchange/Sequenced Packet Exchange (IPX/SPX) A protocol stack that is used in Novell networks. IPX is the NetWare protocol for packet forwarding and routing. It is a relatively small and fast protocol on a LAN, is a derivative of Xerox Network System (XNS), and supports routing. SPX is a connection-oriented protocol used to guarantee the delivery of the data being sent. NWLink is the Microsoft implementation of the IPX/SPX protocol.

Interoperability The ability of components in one system to work with components in other systems.

interrupt request (IRQ) An electronic signal sent to a computer's CPU to indicate that an event has taken place that requires the processor's attention.

IP *See* Internet Protocol (IP). *See also* Transport Control Protocol/Internet Protocol (TCP/IP).

ipconfig A diagnostic command that displays all current TCP/IP network configuration values. It is of particular use on systems running DHCP because it allows users to determine which TCP/IP configuration values have been configured by the DHCP server. *See also* winipcfg.

IPSec *See* Internet Protocol Security (IPSec).

IPX/SPX *See* Internetwork Packet Exchange/Sequenced Packet Exchange (IPX/SPX).

IRQ *See* interrupt request (IRQ).

ISA *See* Industry Standard Architecture (ISA).

ISDN *See* Integrated Services Digital Network (ISDN).

ISO *See* International Organization for Standardization (ISO).

jumper A small plastic-and-metal plug or wire for connecting different points in an electronic circuit. Jumpers are used to select a particular circuit or option from several possible configurations. You can use jumpers on network interface cards to select the type of connection through which the card will transmit, either DIX or BNC.

Kevlar A brand name of the DuPont Corporation for the fibers in the reinforcing layer of plastic that surrounds each glass strand of a fiber-optic connector. The name is sometimes used generically.

key In database management, an identifier for a record or group of records in a data file. Most often, the key is defined as the contents of a single field, called the key field in some database management programs and the index field in others. Keys are maintained in tables and are indexed to speed record retrieval. Keys also refer to code that deciphers encrypted data.

kilo (K) A measurement that refers to 1,000 in the metric system. In computing terminology, because computing is based on powers of 2, kilo is most often used to mean 1,024 (2 raised to the 10th power). To distinguish between the two contexts, a lowercase k is often used to indicate 1,000 and an uppercase K is used for 1,024. A kilobyte is 1,024 bytes.

kilobit (Kbit) A measurement that equals 1,024 bits. *See also* bit; kilo (K).

kilobyte (KB) A measurement that refers to 1,024 bytes. *See also* byte; kilo (K).

L2TP *See* Layer-Two Tunneling Protocol (L2TP).

LAN *See* local area network (LAN).

LAN requester *See* requester (LAN requester).

laser transmission A wireless network that uses a laser beam to carry data between devices.

LAT *See* local area transport (LAT).

layering The coordination of various protocols in a specific architecture that allows the protocols to work together to ensure that the data is prepared, transferred, received, and acted upon as intended.

Layer-Two Tunneling Protocol (L2TP) A protocol whose primary purpose is to create an encrypted tunnel through an untrusted network. L2TP is similar to PPTP in that it provides tunneling, but it doesn't provide encryption. L2TP provides a secure tunnel by cooperating with other encryption technologies such as IPSec. L2TP functions with IPSec to provide a secure virtual private network solution.

link The communication system that connects two LANs. Equipment that provides the link, including bridges, routers, and gateways.

local area network (LAN) Computers connected in a geographically confined network, such as in the same building, campus, or office park.

local area transport (LAT) A nonroutable protocol from Digital Equipment Corporation.

local group One type of group account used by Microsoft Windows 2000. Implemented in each local computer's account database, local groups contain user accounts and other global groups that need to have access, rights, and permissions assigned to a resource on a local computer. Local groups can't contain other local groups.

local user The user at the computer.

logical link control (LLC) sublayer One of two sublayers created by the IEEE Project 802 out of the data-link layer of the OSI reference model. The LLC is the upper sublayer that manages data-link communication and defines the use of logical interface points, called service access points (SAPs), used by computers to transfer information from the LLC sublayer to the upper OSI layers. *See also* media access control (MAC) sublayer; service access point (SAP).

macro virus A file-infector virus named because it is written as a macro for a specific application. Macro viruses are difficult to detect and they are becoming more common, often infecting widely used applications, such as word-processing programs. When an infected file is opened, the virus attaches itself to the application and then infects any files accessed by that application. *See also* file infector.

Mb *See* megabit (Mb).

MB *See* megabyte (MB).

Mbps *See* millions of bits per second (Mbps).

media The cable or wire that connects the vast majority of LANs today, which acts as the LAN transmission medium and carries data between computers.

media access control (MAC) driver The device driver located at the media access control sublayer of the OSI reference model. This driver is also known as the NIC driver. It provides low-level access to NICs by providing data-transmission support and some basic NIC management functions. These drivers also pass data from the physical layer to transport protocols at the network and transport layers.

media access control (MAC) sublayer One of two sublayers created by the IEEE Project 802 out of the data-link layer of the OSI reference model. The MAC sublayer communicates directly with the network interface card and is responsible for delivering error-free data between two computers on the network. *See also* logical link control (LLC) sublayer.

megabit (Mb) A measurement that is usually 1,048,576 bits; sometimes interpreted as 1 million bits. *See also* bit.

megabyte (MB) A measurement that is usually 1,048,576 bytes (2 raised to the 20th power); sometimes interpreted as 1 million bytes. *See also* byte.

Micro Channel Architecture The design of the bus in IBM PS/2 computers (except models 25 and 30). The Micro Channel is electrically and physically incompatible with the IBM PC/AT bus. Unlike the PC/AT bus, the Micro Channel functions as either a 16-bit or 32-bit bus. The Micro Channel can also be driven independently by multiple bus master processors. *See also* Extended Industry Standard Architecture (EISA); Industry Standard Architecture (ISA).

Microcom Network Protocol (MNP) The standard for asynchronous data-error control developed by Microcom Systems. The method works so well that other companies have adopted not only the initial version of the protocol, but later versions as well. Currently, several modem vendors incorporate MNP Classes 2, 3, 4, and 5.

Microsoft Technical Information Network (TechNet) A network that provides informational support for all aspects of networking, with an emphasis on Microsoft products.

millions of bits per second (Mbps) The unit of measurement of supported transmission rates on the following physical media: coaxial cable, twisted-pair cable, and fiber-optic cable. *See also* bit.

MNP *See* Microcom Network Protocol (MNP).

mobile computing A technique that incorporates wireless adapters using cellular telephone technology to connect portable computers with the cabled network.

modem A communication device that enables a computer to transmit information over a standard telephone line. Because a computer is digital, it works with discrete electrical signals representing binary 1 and binary 0. A telephone is analog and carries a signal that can have many variations. Modems are needed to convert digital signals to analog and back. When transmitting, modems impose (modulate) a computer's digital signals onto a continuous carrier frequency on the telephone line. When receiving, modems sift out (demodulate) the information from the carrier and transfer it in digital form to the computer.

multitasking A mode of operation offered by an operating system in which a computer works on more than one task at a time. The two primary types of multitasking are preemptive and nonpreemptive. In preemptive multitasking, the operating system can take control of the processor without the task's cooperation. In nonpreemptive multitasking, the processor is never taken from a task. The task itself decides when to give up the processor. A true multitasking operating system can run as many tasks as it has processors. When there are more tasks than processors, the computer must "time slice" so that the available processors devote a certain amount of time to one task and then move on to the next task, alternating between tasks until all the tasks are completed.

Name Binding Protocol (NBP) An Apple protocol responsible for keeping track of entities on the network and matching names with Internet addresses. It works at the transport layer of the OSI reference model.

namespace Any bounded area in which a name can be resolved. Name resolution is the process of translating a name into some object or information that the name represents. The Active Directory namespace is based on the DNS naming scheme, which allows for interoperability with Internet technologies.

NBP *See* Name Binding Protocol (NBP).

nbtstat A diagnostic command that displays protocol statistics and current TCP/IP connections using NetBIOS over TCP/IP (NetBT). This command is available only if the TCP/IP protocol has been installed. *See also* netstat.

NDIS *See* Network Driver Interface Specification (NDIS).

NetBIOS Enhanced User Interface (NetBEUI) A protocol supplied with all Microsoft network products. NetBEUI advantages include small stack size (important for MS-DOS-based computers), speed of data transfer on the network medium, and compatibility with all Microsoft-based networks. The major drawback of NetBEUI is that it is a LAN transport protocol and therefore does not support routing. It is also limited to Microsoft-based networks.

netstat A diagnostic command that displays protocol statistics and current TCP/IP network connections. This command is available only if the TCP/IP protocol has been installed. *See also* nbtstat.

NetWare Core Protocol (NCP) A protocol that defines the connection control and service-request encoding that make it possible for clients and servers to interact. This is the protocol that provides transport and session services. NetWare security is also provided within this protocol.

network In the context of computers, a system in which a number of independent computers are linked together to share data and peripherals, such as hard disks and printers.

network adapter card *See* network interface card (NIC).

network basic input/output system (NetBIOS) An application programming interface (API) that can be used by application programs on a LAN consisting of IBM-compatible microcomputers running MS-DOS, OS/2, or some version of UNIX. Primarily of interest to programmers, NetBIOS provides application programs with a uniform set of commands for requesting the lower-level network services required to conduct sessions between nodes on a network and transmit information between them.

Network Driver Interface Specification (NDIS) A standard that defines an interface for communication between the media access control (MAC) sublayer and protocol drivers. NDIS allows for a flexible environment of data exchange. It defines the software interface, called the NDIS interface, which is used by protocol drivers to communicate with the network interface card. The advantage of NDIS is that it offers protocol multiplexing so that multiple protocol stacks can be used at the same time. *See also* Open Data-Link Interface (ODI).

network interface card (NIC) An expansion card installed in each computer and server on the network. The NIC acts as the physical interface or connection between the computer and the network cable.

network layer The third layer in the OSI reference model. This layer is responsible for addressing messages and translating logical addresses and names into physical addresses. This layer also determines the route from the source to the destination computer. It determines which path the data should take based on network conditions, priority of service, and other factors. It also manages traffic problems such as switching, routing, and controlling the congestion of data packets on the network. *See also* Open Systems Interconnection (OSI) reference model.

network monitors Monitors that track all or a selected part of network traffic. They examine frame-level packets and gather information about packet types, errors, and packet traffic to and from each computer.

NIC *See* network interface card (NIC).

node On a LAN, a device that is connected to the network and is capable of communicating with other network devices. For example, clients, servers, and repeaters are called nodes.

nonpreemptive multitasking A form of multitasking in which the processor is never taken from a task. The task itself decides when to give up the processor. Programs written for nonpreemptive multitasking systems must include provisions for yielding control of the processor. No other program can run until the nonpreemptive program gives up control of the processor. *See also* multitasking; preemptive multitasking.

Novell NetWare One of the leading network architectures.

Object A distinct, named set of attributes that represent a network resource. Object attributes are characteristics of objects in the Directory. For example, the attributes of a user account might include the user's first and last names, department, and e-mail address.

ODI *See* Open Data-Link Interface (ODI).

ohm The unit of measurement for electrical resistance. A resistance of 1 ohm will pass 1 ampere of current when a voltage of 1 volt is applied. A 100-watt incandescent bulb has a resistance of approximately 130 ohms.

Open Data-Link Interface (ODI) A specification defined by Novell and Apple to simplify driver development and to provide support for multiple protocols on a single network interface card. Similar to NDIS in many respects, ODI allows Novell NetWare drivers to be written without concern for the protocol that will be used on top of them.

Open Shortest Path First (OSPF) A routing protocol for IP networks, such as the Internet, that allows a router to calculate the shortest path to each node for sending messages.

Open Systems Interconnection (OSI) reference model A seven-layer architecture that standardizes levels of service and types of interaction for computers exchanging information through a network. It is used to describe the flow of data between the physical connection to the network and the end-user application. This model is the best-known and most widely used model for describing networking environments. Following is the OSI seven-layer focus from highest to lowest level:

7. application layer. Program-to-program transfer of information

6. presentation layer. Text formatting and display-code conversion

5. session layer. Establishing, maintaining, and coordinating communication

4. transport layer. Accurate delivery and service quality

3. network layer. Transport routes, message handling, and transfer

2. data-link layer. Coding, addressing, and transmitting information

1. physical layer. Hardware connections

organizational unit (OU) A container that you use to organize objects within a domain into logical administrative groups. An OU can contain objects such as user accounts, groups, computers, printers, applications, file shares, and so on.

OSI *See* Open Systems Interconnection (OSI) reference model.

OSPF *See* Open Shortest Path First (OSPF).

packet A unit of information transmitted as a whole from one device to another on a network. In packet-switching networks, a packet is defined more specifically as a transmission unit of fixed maximum size that consists of binary digits representing data; a header containing an identification number, source, and destination addresses; and sometimes error-control data. *See also* frame.

packet assembler/disassembler (PAD) A device that breaks large chunks of data into packets, usually for transmissions over an X.25 network, and reassembles them at the other end. *See also* packet switching.

Packet Internet Groper (ping) A simple utility that tests whether a network connection is complete, from the server to the workstation, by sending a message to the remote computer. If the remote computer receives the message, it responds with a reply message. The reply consists of the remote workstation's IP address, the number of bytes in the message, how long it took to reply-given in milliseconds (ms)-and the length of Time to Live (TTL) in seconds. Ping works at the IP level and will often respond even when higher level TCP-based services cannot.

packet switching A message delivery technique in which small units of information (packets) are relayed through stations in a computer network along the best route available between the source and the destination. Data is broken into smaller units and then repacked in a process called packet assembler/disassembler (PAD). Although each packet can travel along a different path, and the packets composing a message can arrive at different times or out of sequence, the receiving computer reassembles the original message. Packet-switching networks are considered fast and efficient. Standards for packet switching on networks are documented in the CCITT recommendation X.25.

PAD *See* packet assembler/disassembler (PAD).

page-description language (PDL) A language that communicates to a printer how printed output should appear. The printer uses the PDL to construct text and graphics to create the page image. PDLs are like blueprints in that they set parameters and features such as type sizes and fonts, but they leave the drawing to the printer.

paging file A special file on one or more of the hard disks of a computer running Windows 2000. Windows 2000 uses virtual memory to store some of the program code and other information in RAM and to temporarily store some of the program code and other information on the computer's hard disks. This increases the amount of available memory on the computer.

parity An error-checking procedure in which the number of 1s must always be the same— either odd or even—for each group of bits transmitted without error. Parity is used for checking data transferred within a computer or between computers.

partition A portion of a physical disk that functions as if it were a physically separate unit.

password-protected share The access to a shared resource that is granted when a user enters the appropriate password.

PDA *See* personal digital assistant (PDA).

PDL *See* page-description language (PDL).

PDN *See* public data network (PDN).

peer-to-peer network A network that has no dedicated servers or hierarchy among the computers. All computers are equal and, therefore, known as peers. Generally, each computer functions as both client and server.

peripheral A term used for devices such as disk drives, printers, modems, mouse devices, and joysticks that are connected to a computer and controlled by its microprocessor.

Peripheral Component Interconnect (PCI) A 32-bit local bus used in most Pentium computers and in the Apple Power Macintosh that meets most of the requirements for providing Plug and Play functionality.

permanent virtual circuit (PVC) A permanent logical connection between two nodes on a packet-switching network; similar to leased lines that are permanent and virtual, except that with PVC, the customer pays for only the time the line is used. This type of connection service is gaining importance because both frame relay and ATM use it. *See also* packet switching; virtual circuit.

permissions *See* access permissions.

personal digital assistant (PDA) A type of hand-held computer that provides functions including personal organization features—like a calendar, note taking, database manipulation, calculator, and communications. For communication, a PDA uses cellular or wireless technology that is often built into the system but that can be supplemented or enhanced by means of a PC Card.

petabyte *See* byte.

phase change rewritable (PCR) A type of rewritable optical technology in which the optical devices come from one manufacturer (Matsushita/Panasonic) and the media comes from two (Panasonic and Plasmon).

physical layer The first (bottommost) layer of the OSI reference model. This layer addresses the transmission of the unstructured raw bit stream over a physical medium (the networking cable). The physical layer relates the electrical/optical, mechanical, and functional interfaces to the cable and also carries the signals that transmit data generated by all of the higher OSI layers. *See also* Open Systems Interconnection (OSI) reference model.

ping *See* Packet Internet Groper (ping).

Plug and Play (PnP) A capability that enables a computer system to automatically configure a device added to it. Plug and Play capability exists in Macintoshes based on the NuBus and, since Windows 95, on PC-compatible computers. Also refers to specifications developed by Intel and Microsoft that allow a PC to configure itself automatically to work with peripherals such as monitors, modems, and printers.

point-to-point configuration Dedicated circuits that are also known as private, or leased, lines. They are the most popular WAN communication circuits in use today. The carrier guarantees full-duplex bandwidth by setting up a permanent link from each endpoint, using bridges and routers to connect LANs through the circuits. *See also* Point-to-Point Protocol (PPP); Point-to-Point Tunneling Protocol (PPTP).

Point-to-Point Protocol (PPP) A data-link protocol for transmitting TCP/IP packets over dial-up telephone connections, such as between a computer and the Internet. PPP was developed by the Internet Engineering Task Force in 1991.

Point-to-Point Tunneling Protocol (PPTP) An extension of the Point-to-Point Protocol that is used for communications on the Internet. Microsoft developed PPTP to support virtual private networks (VPNs), which allow individuals and organizations to use the Internet as a secure means of communication. PPTP supports encapsulation of encrypted packets in secure wrappers that can be transmitted over a TCP/IP connection. *See also* virtual private network (VPN).

polymorphic virus A variant of a file-infector virus that is named for the fact that it changes its appearance each time it is replicated. This makes it difficult to detect because no two versions of the virus are exactly the same. *See also* file infector.

polyvinyl chloride (PVC) The material most commonly used for insulating and jacketing cable.

preemptive multitasking A form of multitasking (the ability of a computer's operating system to work on more than one task at a time). With preemptive multitasking—as opposed to nonpreemptive multitasking—the operating system can take control of the processor without the task's cooperation. *See also* nonpreemptive multitasking.

presentation layer The sixth layer of the OSI reference model. This layer determines the form used to exchange data between networked computers. At the sending computer, this layer translates data from a format sent down from the application layer into a commonly recognized, intermediary format. At the receiving end, this layer translates the intermediary format into a format useful to that computer's application layer. The presentation layer manages network security issues by providing services such as data encryption, provides rules for data transfer, and performs data compression to reduce the number of bits that need to be transmitted. *See also* Open Systems Interconnection (OSI) reference model.

print device The hardware device that produces printed documents.

print queue A buffer in which a print job is held until the printer is ready to print it.

print server The computer on which the printers that are associated with local and network-interface print devices reside. The print server receives and processes documents from client computers. You set up and share network printers on print servers.

printer The software interface between the operating system and the print device. The printer defines where a document will go to reach the print device, when it will go, and how various other aspects of the printing process will be handled.

printer driver One or more files containing information that Windows 2000 requires to convert print commands into a specific printer language, such as PostScript. A printer driver is specific to each print device model.

printer pool A printer that is connected to multiple print devices through multiple ports on a print server. The print server can be local or network-interface print devices. Print devices should be identical; however, you can use print devices that are not identical but use the same printer driver.

printer port The software interface through which a computer communicates with a print device by means of a locally attached interface. These supported interfaces include LPT, COM, USB, and network-attached devices such as the HP JetDirect and Intel NetPort.

Private Branch Exchange (PBX) or Private Automated Branch Exchange (PABX) A switching telephone network that allows callers within an organization to place intraorganizational calls without going through the public telephone system.

protocol The system of rules and procedures that govern communication between two or more devices. Many varieties of protocols exist, and not all are compatible, but as long as two devices are using the same protocol, they can exchange data. Protocols exist within protocols, as well, governing different aspects of communication. Some protocols, such as the RS-232 standard, affect hardware connections. Other standards govern data transmission, including the parameters and handshaking signals such as XON/OFF used in asynchronous (typically, modem) communications, as well as such data-coding methods as bit- and byte-oriented protocols. Still other protocols, such as the widely used Xmodem, govern file transfer, and others, such as CSMA/CD, define the methods by which messages are passed around the stations on a LAN. Protocols represent attempts to ease the complex process of enabling computers of different makes and models to communicate. Additional examples of protocols include the OSI model, IBM's SNA, and the Internet suite, including TCP/IP. *See also* Systems Network Architecture (SNA); Transport Control Protocol/Internet Protocol (TCP/IP).

protocol driver The driver responsible for offering four or five basic services to other layers in the network, while "hiding" the details of how the services are actually implemented. Services performed include session management, datagram service, data segmentation and sequencing, acknowledgment, and possibly routing across a WAN.

protocol stack A layered set of protocols that work together to provide a set of network functions.

proxy server A firewall component that manages Internet traffic to and from a local area network (LAN). The proxy server decides whether it is safe to let a particular message or file pass through to the organization's network, providing access control to the network, and filters and discards requests as specified by the owner, including requests for unauthorized access to proprietary data. *See also* firewall.

public data network (PDN) A commercial packet-switching or circuit-switching WAN service provided by local and long-distance telephone carriers.

PVC *See* permanent virtual circuit (PVC).

RADIUS *See* Remote Authentication Dial-In User Service.

RAID *See* redundant array of independent disks (RAID).

random access memory (RAM) Semiconductor-based memory that can be read and written to by the microprocessor or other hardware devices.

The storage locations can be accessed in any order. Note that the various types of ROM memory are also capable of random access. However, the term RAM is generally understood to refer to volatile memory, which can be written as well as read. *See also* read-only memory (ROM).

read-only memory (ROM) Semiconductor-based memory that contains instructions or data that can be read but not modified. *See also* random access memory (RAM).

redirector Networking software that accepts I/O requests for remote files, named pipes, or mail slots and sends (redirects) the requests to a network service on another computer.

reduced instruction set computing (RISC) A type of microprocessor design that focuses on rapid and efficient processing of a relatively small set of instructions. RISC design is based on the premise that most of the instructions that a computer decodes and executes are simple. As a result, RISC architecture limits the number of instructions that are built into the microprocessor but optimizes each so it can be carried out rapidly, usually within a single clock cycle. RISC chips execute simple instructions faster than microprocessors designed to handle a much wider array of instructions. However, they are slower than general-purpose complex instruction set computing (CISC) chips when executing complex instructions, which must be broken down into many machine instructions before they can be carried out by RISC microprocessors.

redundancy system A fault-tolerant system that protects data by duplicating it in different physical sources. Data redundancy allows access to data even if part of the data system fails. *See also* fault tolerance.

redundant An array of inexpensive disks (RAID). *See also* redundant array of independent disks (RAID).

redundant array of independent disks (RAID) A standardization of fault-tolerant options in five levels. The levels offer various combinations of performance, reliability, and cost. Formerly known as redundant array of inexpensive disks.

Remote Authentication Dial-In User Service (RADIUS) A security authentication protocol widely used by Internet Service Providers (ISPs). RADIUS provides authentication and accounting services for distributed dial-up networking.

remote-boot programmable read-only memory (PROM) A special chip in the network interface card that contains the hardwired code that starts the computer and connects the user to the network, used in computers for which there are no hard disks or floppy drives. *See also* diskless computers.

remote installation The process of connecting to a server running Remote Installation Services (RIS), called the RIS server, and then starting an automated installation of Windows 2000 Professional on a local computer.

remote user A user who dials in to the server over modems and telephone lines from a remote location.

requester (LAN requester) Software that resides in a computer and forwards requests for network services from the computer's application programs to the appropriate server. *See also* redirector.

resources Any part of a computer system. Users on a network can share computer resources, such as hard disks, printers, modems, CD-ROM drives, and even the processor.

rights The authorization with which a user is entitled to perform certain actions on a computer network. Rights apply to the system as a whole, whereas permissions apply to specific objects.

For example, a user might have the right to back up an entire computer system, including the files that the user doesn't have permission to access. *See also* access permissions.

RISC *See* reduced instruction set computing (RISC).

ROM *See* read-only memory (ROM).

routable protocols The protocols that support multipath LAN-to-LAN communications. *See also* protocol.

router A device used to connect networks of different types, such as those using different architectures and protocols. Routers work at the network layer of the OSI reference model. This means they can switch and route packets across multiple networks, which they do by exchanging protocol-specific information between separate networks. Routers determine the best path for sending data and filter broadcast traffic to the local segment.

Routing Information Protocol (RIP) A protocol that uses distance-vector algorithms to determine routes. With RIP, routers transfer information among other routers to update their internal routing tables and use that information to determine the best routes based on hop counts between routers. TCP/IP and IPX support RIP.

RS-232 standard An industry standard for serial communication connections adopted by the Electrical Industries Association (EIA). This recommended standard defines the specific lines and signal characteristics used by serial communications controllers to standardize the transmission of serial data between devices.

SAP *See* service access point (SAP); Service Advertising Protocol (SAP).

schema A database description to the database management system that contains a formal definition of the contents and structure of Active Directory directory services, including all attributes, classes, and class properties. For each object class, the schema defines which attributes an instance of the class must have, which additional attributes it can have, and which object class can be a parent of the current object class.

SCSI *See* Small Computer System Interface (SCSI).

SDLC *See* Synchronous Data Link Control (SDLC).

sector A portion of the data-storage area on a disk. A disk is divided into sides (top and bottom), tracks (rings on each surface), and sectors (sections of each ring). Sectors are the smallest physical storage units on a disk and are of fixed size—typically capable of holding 512 bytes of information apiece.

sector sparing A fault-tolerant system also called hot fixing. It automatically adds sector-recovery capabilities to the file system during operation. If bad sectors are found during disk I/O, the fault-tolerant driver will attempt to move the data to a good sector and map out the bad sector. If the mapping is successful, the file system is not alerted. It is possible for SCSI devices to perform sector sparing, but AT devices (ESDI and IDE) cannot.

security The act of making computers and data stored on them safe from harm or unauthorized access.

Security log A log that records security events. For example, valid and invalid logon attempts and events relating to creating, opening, or deleting files or other objects.

segment The length of cable on a network between two terminators. A segment can also refer to messages that have been broken up into smaller units by the protocol driver.

Sequenced Packet Exchange (SPX) Part of Novell's IPX/SPX protocol suite for sequenced data. *See also* Internetwork Packet Exchange/Sequenced Packet Exchange (IPX/SPX).

Serial Line Internet Protocol (SLIP) As defined in RFC 1055, an internet protocol that is normally used on Ethernet over a serial line—for example, an RS-232 serial port connected to a modem.

serial transmission A one-way data transfer. The data travels on a network cable with one bit following another.

server A computer that provides shared resources to network users. *See also* client.

server-based network A network in which resource security and most other network functions are provided by dedicated servers. Server-based networks have become the standard model for networks serving more than 10 users. *See also* peer-to-peer network.

server message block (SMB) The protocol developed by Microsoft, Intel, and IBM that defines a series of commands used to pass information between network computers. The redirector packages SMB requests into a network control block (NCB) structure that can be sent over the network to a remote device. The network provider listens for SMB messages destined for it and removes the data portion of the SMB request so that it can be processed by a local device.

service access point (SAP) The interface between each of the seven layers in the OSI protocol stack that has connection points, similar to addresses, used for communication between layers. Any protocol layer can have multiple SAPs active at one time.

Service Advertising Protocol (SAP) A protocol that allows service-providing nodes (including file, printer, gateway, and application servers) to advertise their services and addresses.

session A connection or link between stations on the network.

session layer The fifth layer of the OSI reference model. This layer allows two applications on different computers to establish, use, and end a connection called a session. This layer performs name recognition and functions, such as security, needed to allow two applications to communicate over the network. The session layer provides synchronization between user tasks. This layer also implements dialog control between communicating processes, regulating which side transmits, when, for how long, and so on. *See also* Open Systems Interconnection (OSI) reference model.

session management The process that establishes, maintains, and terminates connections between stations on the network.

sharing The means by which files or folders are publicly posted on a network for access by anyone on the network.

shell A piece of software, usually a separate program, that provides direct communication between the user and the operating system. This usually takes the form of a command-line interface. Examples of shells are Macintosh Finder and the MS-DOS command interface program Command.com.

Simple Mail Transfer Protocol (SMTP) A TCP/IP protocol for transferring e-mail. *See also* application protocol; Transport Control Protocol/Internet Protocol (TCP/IP).

Simple Network Management Protocol (SNMP) A TCP/IP protocol for monitoring networks. SNMP uses a request and response process. In SNMP, short utility programs, called agents, monitor the network traffic and behavior in key network components to gather statistical data, which they put into a management information base (MIB). To collect the information into a usable form, a special management console program regularly polls the agents and downloads the information in their MIBs. If any of the data falls either above or below parameters set by the manager, the management console program can present signals on the monitor locating the trouble and notify designated support staff by automatically dialing a pager number.

simultaneous peripheral operation online (spool) A process that facilitates the process of moving a print job from the network into a printer.

site A combination of one or more IP subnets, typically connected by a high-speed link.

Small Computer System Interface (SCSI) Pronounced "skuzzy," a standard, high-speed parallel interface defined by ANSI. A SCSI interface is used for connecting microcomputers to peripheral devices, such as hard disks and printers, and to other computers and LANs.

SMB *See* server message block (SMB).

SMP *See* symmetric multiprocessing (SMP).

SMTP *See* Simple Mail Transfer Protocol (SMTP).

SNMP *See* Simple Network Management Protocol (SNMP).

software Computer programs or sets of instructions that allow the hardware to work. Software can be grouped into four categories: system software, such as operating systems, which control the workings of the computer; application software, such as word-processing programs, spreadsheets, and databases, which perform the tasks for which people use computers; network software, which enables groups of computers to communicate; and language software, which provides programmers with the tools they need to write programs.

SONET *See* Synchronous Optical Network (SONET).

spanning tree algorithm (STA) An algorithm (mathematical procedure) implemented to eliminate redundant routes and to avoid situations in which multiple LANs are joined by more than one path by the IEEE 802.1 Network Management Committee. Under STA, bridges exchange certain control information in an attempt to find redundant routes. The bridges determine which would be the most efficient route and then use that one and disable the others. Any of the disabled routes can be reactivated if the primary route becomes unavailable.

SPX *See* Sequenced Packet Exchange (SPX).

SQL *See* structured query language (SQL).

STA *See* spanning tree algorithm (STA).

stand-alone computer A computer that isn't connected to any other computers and isn't part of a network.

stand-alone environment A work environment in which each user has a personal computer but works independently, unable to share files and other important information that would be readily available through server access in a networking environment.

stealth virus A variant of a file-infector virus. This virus is so named because it attempts to hide from detection. When an antivirus program attempts to find it, the stealth virus tries to intercept the probe and return false information indicating that it does not exist.

stripe set A form of fault tolerance that combines multiple areas of unformatted free space into one large logical drive, distributing data storage across all drives simultaneously. In Windows 2000, a stripe set requires at least two physical drives and can use up to 32 physical drives. Stripe sets can combine areas on different types of drives, such as Small Computer System Interface (SCSI), Enhanced Small Device Interface (ESDI), and Integrated Device Electronics (IDE) drives.

structured query language (SQL) A standard language for creating, updating, and querying relational database management systems.

Switched Multimegabit Data Services (SMDS) A high-speed, switched-packet service that can provide speeds of up to 34 Mbps.

switched virtual circuit (SVC) A logical connection between end computers that uses a specific route across the network. Network resources are dedicated to the circuit, and the route is maintained until the connection is terminated. These are also known as point-to-multipoint connections. *See also* virtual circuit.

symmetric multiprocessing (SMP) A system that uses any available processor on an as-needed basis. With this approach, the system load and application needs can be distributed evenly across all available processors.

synchronous A form of communication that relies on a timing scheme coordinated between two devices to separate groups of bits and transmit them in blocks called frames. Special characters are used to begin the synchronization and check its accuracy periodically. Because the bits are sent and received in a timed, controlled (synchronized) fashion, start and stop bits are not required. Transmission stops at the end of one transmission and starts again with a new one. It is a start/stop approach, and more efficient than asynchronous transmission. If an error occurs, the synchronous error detection and correction scheme implements a retransmission. However, because more sophisticated technology and equipment is required to transmit synchronously, it is more expensive than asynchronous transmission.

Synchronous Data Link Control (SDLC) The data link (data transmission) protocol most widely used in networks conforming to IBM's SNA. SDLC is a communications guideline that defines the format in which information is transmitted.

As its name implies, SDLC applies to synchronous transmissions. SDLC is also a bit-oriented protocol and organizes information in structured units called frames.

Synchronous Optical Network (SONET) A fiber-optic technology that can transmit data at more than one gigabit per second. Networks based on this technology are capable of delivering voice, data, and video. SONET is a standard for optical transport formulated by the Exchange Carriers Standards Association (ECSA) for ANSI.

Systems Network Architecture (SNA) An IBM-proprietary high-level networking protocol standard for IBM and IBM-compatible mainframe systems. *See also* protocol.

TCO *See* total cost of ownership (TCO).

TCP *See* Transmission Control Protocol (TCP).

TCP/IP *See* Transport Control Protocol/Internet Protocol (TCP/IP).

TDI *See* transport driver interface (TDI).

TechNet *See* Microsoft Technical Information Network (TechNet).

Telnet The command and program used to log in from one Internet site to another. The Telnet command and program brings the user to the login prompt of another host.

terabyte *See* byte.

throughput A measure of the data transfer rate through a component, connection, or system. In networking, throughput is a good indicator of the system's total performance because it defines how well the components work together to transfer data from one computer to another. In this case, the throughput would indicate how many bytes or packets the network could process per second.

topology The arrangement or layout of computers, cables, and other components on a network. Topology is the standard term that most network professionals use when referring to the network's basic design.

total cost of ownership (TCO) The total amount of money and time associated with purchasing computer hardware and software, and deploying, configuring, and maintaining the hardware and software. It includes hardware and software updates, training, maintenance and administration, and technical support. One other major factor is lost productivity due to user errors, hardware problems, software upgrades, and retraining.

tracert A Traceroute command-line utility that shows every router interface through which a TCP/IP packet passes on its way to a destination.

trailer One of the three sections of a packet component. The exact content of the trailer varies depending on the protocol, but it usually includes an error-checking component, or cyclical redundancy check (CRC).

transceiver A device that connects a computer to the network. The term is derived from transmitter/receiver; thus, a transceiver is a device that receives and transmits signals. It switches the parallel data stream used on the computer's bus into a serial data stream used in the cables connecting the computers.

Transmission Control Protocol (TCP) The TCP/IP protocol for sequenced data. *See also* Transport Control Protocol/Internet Protocol (TCP/IP).

Transport Control Protocol/Internet Protocol (TCP/IP) An industry standard suite of protocols providing communications in a heterogeneous environment. In addition, TCP/IP provides a routable enterprise networking protocol and access to the Internet and its resources. It is a transport layer protocol that actually consists of several other protocols in a stack that operates at the session layer. Most networks support TCP/IP as a protocol.

transport driver interface (TDI) An interface that works between the file-system driver and the transport protocols, allowing any protocol written to TDI to communicate with the file-system drivers.

transport layer The fourth layer of the OSI reference model. It ensures that messages are delivered error free, in sequence, and without losses or duplications. This layer repackages messages for efficient transmission over the network. At the receiving end, the transport layer unpacks the messages, reassembles the original messages, and sends an acknowledgment of receipt. *See also* Open Systems Interconnection (OSI) reference model.

transport protocols Protocols that provide for communication sessions between computers and ensure that data is able to move reliably between computers.

tree A grouping of hierarchical arrangements of one or more Windows 2000 domains that share a contiguous namespace.

Trojan horse virus A type of virus that appears to be a legitimate program that might be found on any system. The Trojan horse virus can destroy files and cause physical damage to disks.

trust relationship A link between domains that enables pass-through authentication, in which a user has only one user account in one domain, yet can access the entire network. User accounts and global groups defined in a trusted domain can be given rights and resource permissions in a trusting domain even though those accounts don't exist in the trusting domain's database. A trusting domain honors the logon authentication of a trusted domain.

UART *See* universal asynchronous receiver transmitter (UART).

UDP *See* User Datagram Protocol (UDP).

Uniform Resource Locator (URL) An address for a resource on the Internet that provides the hypertext links between documents on the World Wide Web (WWW). Every resource on the Internet has its own location identifier, or URL, that specifies the server to access as well as the access method and the location. URLs can use various protocols including FTP and HTTP.

uninterruptible power supply (UPS) A device connected between a computer or another piece of electronic equipment and a power source, such as an electrical outlet. The UPS ensures that the electrical flow to the computer is not interrupted because of a blackout and, in most cases, protects the computer against potentially damaging events such as power surges and brownouts. Different UPS models offer different levels of protection. All UPS units are equipped with a battery and loss-of-power sensor. If the sensor detects a loss of power, it immediately switches over to the battery so that users have time to save their work and shut off the computer. Most higher-end models have features such as power filtering, sophisticated surge protection, and a serial port so that an operating system capable of communicating with a UPS (such as Windows 2000) can work with the UPS to facilitate automatic system shutdown.

universal asynchronous receiver transmitter (UART) A module, usually composed of a single integrated circuit, that contains both the receiving and transmitting circuits required for asynchronous serial communication. Two computers, each equipped with a UART, can communicate over a simple wire connection. The operation of the sending and receiving units are not synchronized by a common clock signal, so the data stream itself must contain information about when packets of information (usually bytes) begin and end. This information about the beginning and ending of a packet is provided by the start and stop bits in the data stream. A UART is the most common type of circuit used in personal-computer modems.

universal serial bus (USB) A serial bus with a data transfer rate of 12 megabits per second (Mbps) for connecting peripherals to a microcomputer. USB can connect up to 127 peripheral devices to the system through a single, general-purpose port. This is accomplished by daisy chaining peripherals together. USB is designed to support the ability to automatically add and configure new devices and the ability to add such devices without having to shut down and restart the system.

UPS *See* uninterruptible power supply (UPS).

URL *See* Uniform Resource Locator (URL).

USB *See* universal serial bus (USB).

user account An account that consists of all of the information that defines a user on a network. This includes the user name and password required for the user to log on, the groups in which the user account has membership, and the rights and permissions the user has for using the system and accessing its resources.

User Datagram Protocol (UDP) A connectionless protocol, responsible for end-to-end data transmission.

user groups Groups of users who meet online or in person to discuss installation, administration, and other network challenges for the purpose of sharing and drawing on each other's expertise in developing ideas and solutions.

virtual circuit A series of logical connections between a sending computer and a receiving computer. The connection is made after both computers exchange information and agree on communication parameters that establish and maintain the connection, including maximum message size and path. Virtual circuits incorporate communication parameters such as acknowledgments, flow control, and error control to ensure reliability. They can be either temporary, lasting only as long as the conversation, or permanent, lasting as long as the users keep the communication channel open.

virtual memory The space on one or more of a computer's hard disks used by Windows 2000 as if it were RAM. This space on the hard disks is known as a paging file. The benefit of virtual memory is being able to run more applications at one time than would be possible by using just the RAM (physical memory) on the computer.

virtual private network (VPN) A set of computers on a public network such as the Internet that communicate among themselves using encryption technology. In this way, their messages are safe from being intercepted and understood by unauthorized users. VPNs operate as if the computers were connected by private lines.

virus Computer programming, or code, that hides in computer programs or on the boot sector of storage devices such as hard-disk drives and floppy-disk drives. The primary purpose of a virus is to reproduce itself as often as possible; a secondary purpose is to disrupt the operation of the computer or the program.

volume set A collection of hard-disk partitions that are treated as a single partition, thus increasing the disk space available in a single drive letter. Volume sets are created by combining between 2 and 32 areas of unformatted free space on one or more physical drives. These spaces form one large logical volume set that is treated like a single partition.

VPN *See* virtual private network (VPN).

wide area network (WAN) A computer network that uses long-range telecommunication links to connect networked computers across long distances.

winipcfg A diagnostic command specific to Microsoft Windows 95 and 98. Although this graphical user interface utility (GUI) duplicates the functionality of ipconfig, its GUI makes it easier to use. *See also* ipconfig.

workgroup A collection of computers grouped for sharing resources such as data and peripherals over a LAN. Each workgroup is identified by a unique name. *See also* domain; peer-to-peer network.

World Wide Web (the Web, or WWW) The Internet multimedia service that contains a vast storehouse of hypertext documents written in HTML. *See also* Hypertext Markup Language (HTML).

WORM *See* Write-Once Read-Many (WORM).

Write-Once Read-Many (WORM) Any type of storage medium to which data can be written only once but can be read any number of times. Typically, this is an optical disc whose surface is permanently etched using a laser to record information.

Zone A discrete portion of the domain name space. Zones provide a way to partition the domain name space into discrete manageable sections.

Index

Z

Vernier Calipers

Vernier calipers are used to measure linear distances between two exterior or interior surfaces. Machinists, engineers, and archaeologists all use calipers of various sizes, usually machined from high-precision tool steel. When closed, calipers resemble a ruler with a large bird's beak at one end and a smaller beak across from it. The jaws of the large beak are used to measure the linear distance between two exterior surfaces. The smaller jaws, known as the *nibs*, can accurately measure the linear distance between two interior surfaces. The *slide assembly* contains a Vernier scale—a series of tiny numbers and lines scaled for precise measurement—stamped on its front face, often with metric units on one side and English units on the other.

At Microsoft Press, we use tools to illustrate our books for software developers and IT professionals. Tools very simply and powerfully symbolize human inventiveness. They're a metaphor for people extending their capabilities, precision, and reach. From simple calipers and pliers to digital micrometers and lasers, these stylized illustrations give each book a visual identity, and a personality to the series. With tools and knowledge, there's no limit to creativity and innovation. Our tagline says it all: *the tools you need to put technology to work.*

Learn how to use Microsoft
.NET Enterprise Servers
and strategies to solve common e-business problems.

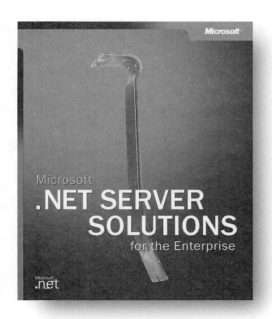

**Microsoft® .NET Server Solutions
for the Enterprise**

U.S.A. **$49.99**
Canada $72.99
ISBN: 0-7356-1569-1

Planning, developing, and deploying enterprise e-business solutions across different platforms can be challenging. MICROSOFT .NET SERVER SOLUTIONS FOR THE ENTERPRISE simplifies the process. This fact-filled guidebook combines a wealth of technical information with real-world scenarios to deliver clear, concrete details on how to solve common e-business integration problems. Each chapter presents a specific e-business problem along with a detailed discussion of the Microsoft .NET Server tools and technologies used to solve it—complete with schematic diagrams and other help. You'll learn how to make Microsoft .NET Servers work together to solve problems—and how to prepare for future Web-based services.

microsoft.com/mspress

The *practical, portable*
guide to Windows 2000!

Whether you support 50 users or 5000, this indispensable guide provides fast answers for the day-to-day administration of Windows 2000 Server and Windows 2000 Professional. This popular, pocket-sized resource has been fully updated with new information on security, interoperability with Windows XP Professional, and the latest service packs. Use it to zero in on essential system support issues and procedures—gleaning critical details through quick-reference tables, step-by-step instructions, and lists. It's the precise information you need to solve problems and get the job done—whether you're at your desk or in the field!

Microsoft® Windows® 2000 Administrator's Pocket Consultant, Second Edition
U.S.A. $29.99
Canada $43.99
ISBN: 0-7356-1792-9

microsoft.com/mspress